Implementing ISO 14000

Implementing ISO 14000

A Practical, Comprehensive Guide to the ISO 14000 Environmental Management Standards

Edited by **Tom Tibor** *and* **Ira Feldman**

IRWIN
Professional Publishing®
Chicago • London • Singapore

Library of Congress Cataloging-in-Publication Data

Implementing ISO 14000 : a practical, comprehensive guide to the ISO
  14000 environmental management standards / edited by Tom Tibor and
  Ira Feldman
        p.   cm.
   Includes index.
   ISBN 0-7863-1014-6
   1. ISO 14000 Series Standards.   2. Environmental protection–
  –Standards.   I. Tibor, Tom.   II. Feldman, Ira.
  TS155.7.I47   1997
  658.4'08—dc20   96–43763

Printed in the United States of America
1 2 3 4 5 6 7 8 9 0 DOC 3 2 1 0 9 8 7 6

BRIEF CONTENTS

CONTENTS

PART TWO

Implementing ISO 14001   35

Chapter 3   ISO 14001 Implementation—Getting Started   37
Reeva I. Schiffman, Esq., B. Tod Delaney, PhD, PE, DEE,
and Scott Fleming

Chapter 4   Employee Training and Awareness   75
W. Gary Wilson, Esq.

Chapter 5   Environmental Management System Documentation   95
W. D. Anderson

P A R T   F O U R

ISO 14001 Registration   327

PART FIVE

Regulatory and Enforcement Issues   **355**

PART SEVEN

ISO 14000 in Perspective   471

PREFACE

INTRODUCTION

The publication of this book coincides with the passage of the first international standards for environmental management—the ISO 14000 series. The ISO 14000 standards promise to play an important role in promoting better environmental management worldwide. This book is a comprehensive guide to implementing an effective environmental management system (EMS) that conforms to the requirements of the ISO 14001 EMS specification standard. It also offers a detailed description of other developing standards in the ISO 14000 series. These standards provide useful tools for environmental managers. They include standards for environmental auditing, environmental performance evaluation, eco-labeling and life-cycle assessment.

Implementing ISO 14000 serves a broad audience. It is, of course, directed at environmental managers and others with direct responsibility for environmental matters in organizations. Because the ISO 14000 model encourages the integration of environmental issues into overall business decision making, however, the book will also be useful to others in the organization including environmental attorneys, health and safety personnel, chief financial officers, marketing managers, communication directors, and top management. It will also be of interest to quality managers in companies that have implemented one of the ISO 9000 series of quality management standards or are planning to do so.

CONTENTS

The goals of this book are as follows:

- Trace the background and development of the ISO 14000 series of environmental management standards.

- Explain the requirements of the ISO 14001 EMS specification standard.
- Provide detailed implementation guidance for every aspect of ISO 14001.
- Describe the requirements of other environmental management initiatives, such as the European Union's Eco-Management and Audit Scheme (EMAS).
- Describe strategies for integrating an ISO 9000-based quality system with an ISO 14000-based EMS.
- Offer implementation case studies of ISO 14000 and perspectives on other EMS tools, including environmental auditing, environmental performance evaluation, life-cycle assessment, and environmental labeling.
- Describe the ISO 14000 registration process.
- Provide guidance on related issues, such as the legal implications of ISO 14001 implementation and regulatory issues.

HOW TO USE THE BOOK

Some terms used in this book should be explained to avoid confusion. First, the phrase "ISO 14000." In one sense, it is a shorthand phrase that actually refers to the "ISO 14000 series of environmental management standards," of which there are already over two dozen standards in development. "ISO 14000" or "the ISO 14000 series" is often used to make the text user-friendly.

Also, the phrase "ISO 14000 registration (certification)" is commonly used even though the actual standard used in the registration process is the specification standard—ISO 14001. Registration refers to the process whereby an independent third party audits the organization's environmental management system to evaluate whether it conforms to the requirements of the ISO 14001 specification standard.

Registration is one of several ways to implement ISO 14000. A company can develop an environmental management system and self-declare that it complies with ISO 14001 requirements. Or it may have its environmental management system audited by a customer as part of a contractual arrangement. Thus the phrase "ISO 14000 implementation" does not automatically imply ISO 14000 registration. Organizations can use the standards internally without planning to seek third-party registration.

To dispel confusion, this book will use the phrase "ISO 14000" only in the context of general discussions, such as "the ISO 14000 process." References to specific standards will always use the specific term (i.e., "ISO 14001"), and the same will hold true regarding the registration process (i.e., "ISO 14001 registration").

Finally, the terms *accreditation, certification,* and *registration* can cause confusion. To clarify the meanings, the Conformity Assessment Committee of the International Organization for Standardization (CASCO), in its *ISO/IEC Guide 2: General terms and their definitions concerning standardization and certification* defines the terms as follows:

Accreditation: Procedure by which an authoritative body gives formal recognition that a body or person is competent to carry out specific tasks.

Certification: Procedure by which a third party gives written assurance that a product, process, or service conforms to specific requirements.

Registration: Procedure by which a body indicates relevant characteristics of a product, process, or service, or particulars of a body or person, and then includes or registers the product, process, or service in an appropriate publicly available list.

Although certification and registration are slightly different in these definitions, they are synonymous in common usage. The United States favors the term *registration* while the international community prefers *certification.* This book generally uses *registration* but because it has been written for an international audience, occasionally, uses *certification.*

ACKNOWLEDGMENTS

We would like to thank all those who made this project possible: the many contributors who contributed their time and expertise; our colleagues in the environmental management field; and our spouses and families for their support. We'd also like to thank Carey Ann Mathews for her hard work and thorough editing of the final manuscript.

Tom Tibor
Ira Feldman

The Future of Environmental Management

Ira R. Feldman

In the United States and abroad, we are already seeing a fundamental re-shaping of thinking in the interrelated fields of environmental management, regulation, and policy. A new framework is emerging, driven by a complex mix of regulatory, and perhaps more importantly, non-regulatory trends such as ISO 14000. Call it a "sea change." Call it "downsizing" or "rightsizing." Or call it a "new paradigm." The future of environmental management is now.

Some believe that two basic pressures—one internal, one external to the corporate entity—are redefining environmental management. Inside the company, the trend is toward the integration of environment, health and safety considerations into traditional business operations. Outside the company, as the regulatory landscape changes, a wider range of stakeholders are demanding excellence in environmental performance, and global competitiveness issues are becoming more important than ever.

In response to these twin pressures, industry seeks a more flexible, consistent, and lower-cost response to the existing regulatory system. At present, however, many "reg reform" efforts in the United States are either bogged down in partisan politics or too narrowly focused on a specific element of the existing system. What these efforts have in common, though, is that they are proceeding without an adequate understanding of industry's current EH&S practices or industry's ultimate goals.

Rather than getting caught up in a short-term partisan debate, many in industry have expressed the desire for a long-term "glide path" to avoid wild swings of the pendulum away from regulation and toward laissez-faire environmental policy. Extensive discussions with corporate environmental leaders reveal the most significant goals that are driving industry's efforts to take a more proactive, innovative approach to environmental management. The most frequently cited are the following:

- Operational flexibility
- Cost savings

- Public recognition/enhanced image
- Access to capital

Achieving these goals will require a new approach to environmental management. ISO 14000 will play an important role in beginning the shift away from prescriptive regulations to a greater reliance on a management systems approach. The many emerging non-regulatory trends that emphasize regulatory flexibility and enhance global competitiveness represent building blocks for the U.S. environmental regulatory system.

Nonregulatory Trends

A number of ongoing nonregulatory trends will significantly impact the fate of environmental management. Several key trends include the following:

- The development of international environmental management standards.
- The U.S. Sentencing Guidelines for Environmental Violations.
- Increasing demands for disclosure of environmental information.
- Greater awareness of environmental justice issues.
- Growing interest in the financial community in the environmental performance of companies.
- Pressure on the bottom line.

These trends are shaping the world of corporate environmental strategy—at times more than the regulations themselves. In fact, companies of all sizes have already started to invest in or respond to these important trends.

In general, however, efforts by companies to move "beyond compliance," to establish an "environmental leadership" position, or to achieve and maintain "environmental excellence" have been ad hoc, uncoordinated, and poorly communicated to key stakeholders. Certainly, many companies have reduced and/or prevented pollution, cut operating costs, and gained favorable publicity as a result of their environmental management efforts. But in terms of obtaining flexible and consistent treatment from the regulatory system, the return on investment in environmental excellence has been close to nonexistent.

The Regulatory Driver

The regulatory driver for ISO 14000 implementation has largely been overlooked in the United States to date. It is important to state clearly that it would be inappropriate to convert ISO 14001, designed as a voluntary consensus standard, directly into a regulatory requirement. But, as an adjunct to environmental regulation, ISO 14001 could serve both as a voluntary basis for "beyond compliance" incentives for industry and as a mechanism for prioritizing increasingly scarce regulatory agency resources.

The conventional wisdom in the United States has been that the ISO 14000 series will be widely embraced only if accepted by the marketplace. Initially, it is quite likely that competitive and commercial pressures, in the form of contractual provisions, procurement guidelines and the like, will drive implementation of the ISO 14001 specification.

Many companies are rapidly realizing, however, that customer and supplier demand is only one element of the implementation equation for the ISO 14000 series. The determinative factor for many organizations may, in fact, be the internal use of ISO 14001 as a vehicle for improving environmental performance and achieving greater cost efficiencies.

Organizations also will consider the role of ISO 14001 certification (or self-declaration) in improving their communication of environmental performance to a range of stakeholders—consumers, lenders, the neighboring community to name but a few. In time, however, the strongest driver for the successful implementation of ISO 14000 may prove to be its regulatory application.

The Dual Pathway Approach

Over the past few years, there has been much creative energy devoted to thinking of alternative or parallel pathways by such groups as the Eco-Efficiency Task Force of the President's Council on Sustainable Development, several of the Common Sense Initiative sectors, and the Aspen Institute series on environmental regulation. In general, the term "greentracking" connotes an approach to environmental excellence through proactive compliance activities, or the "voluntary excellence" pathway in a dual track regulatory system, providing an "opt out" alternative to the "command and control" approach.

The Environmental Leadership Project (ELP) and Project XL pilots likely will demonstrate that a management systems approach offers an opportunity to establish a new regime—an alternate regulatory pathway that would enable companies that make a commitment to enhanced environmental management activities to "opt out" of the traditional "command and control" model.

This alternative or dual track would not replace or revamp the current system, nor would it relax any standards or performance requirements stipulated by existing regulations. Instead, it would offer regulated entities a choice: operate under command-and-control, or strive to reach the alternative track, which would be built on emerging environmental management trends and would be a more flexible, consistent and lower-cost system.

The National Environmental Policy Institute (NEPI) in its Phase One report, "Reinventing the Vehicle for Environmental Management," released in August 1995, recommended the creation of an alternative regulatory track based on "environmental excellence." The report states: "Regulated entities that commit to environmental excellence principles, implement comprehensive management systems, and strive to continuously improve their performance should be able to opt out of the command-and-control system into a more flexible, consistent regulatory scheme."

The NEPI report is careful to recognize that the proposed two-track system does not mean eliminating all mandatory aspects of environmental regulation—"command and control" mechanisms must necessarily continue to exist as one of the components of the two-track system. The guts of the NEPI two-track proposal relies on the separation, or "filtering," of the regulated community based on environmental excellence criteria, as opposed to arbitrary indicators such as compliance history, TRI releases, or the SIC code. For entities that meet the requirements for environmental excellence, the regulatory world would include a range of mechanisms (for example, faster/easier permitting, consolidated reporting, third-party verification, etc.) that would be more flexible, more consistent and cost less compared to command-and-control.

The Role of ISO 14000

While ISO 14000 is not an excellence program per se, it can form the core component of a proactive voluntary excellence track in a "dual track" regulatory scheme. And although ISO 14001 certification itself is not evidence of environmental excellence, in combination with other corporate environmental commitments such as auditing, benchmarking, mentoring, and external voluntary reporting, an excellence program begins to take shape.

The ISO 14001 approach has several key advantages:

- ISO 14001 is *multimedia* and comprehensive, so it encourages companies to take a holistic rather than media-specific approach to environmental performance.

- The documentation and communication requirements of the ISO 14001 EMS specification provide a basis for *integrated monitoring* and *recordkeeping,* and could provide the impetus for establishing a consolidated reporting mechanism.

- A commitment to ISO 14001 comes with a requirement to aim for "prevention of pollution," so increased attention will be paid to pollution prevention opportunities with less reliance on "end-of-the-pipe" solutions.

- Under ISO 14001, an EMS must include not only a commitment to compliance, but also to document conformance with voluntary obligations. Thus, ISO 14001 provides a basis for *integrating voluntary programs* such as EPA's 33/50 program or industry-specific initiatives such as the Chemical Manufacturers Association's Responsible Care® program into a single, coherent framework.

- Finally, ISO 14001 is verifiable. While self-declaration may be available, third-party verification will provide a comfort level to stakeholders and could form the basis for privatizing inspections for a subset of the regulated community. Regulators would then focus attention on bad actors or divert resources to compliance assurance activities for small- and medium-size businesses.

Under this proposal, ISO 14001 remains strictly voluntary, as intended. It is available to those organizations that want to "opt out" of command-and-control.

Toward a Unified Environmental Statute?

One of the most interesting aspects of the NEPI "greentracking" proposal is that this alternative track could lay the foundation for the development and passage of a unified environmental statute. Such a statute would address all media, establish a set of goals, establish a common metric for risk, embrace a powerful set of environmental management tools, and institute a sensible system of decision making at appropriate local, state, and national levels.

In short, it would seek to remove the inconsistencies contained in the plethora of statutes that currently fall under the EPA's purview and provide the Administrator with the clear direction and the tools to properly manage the Agency. One aspect of a unified statute that is appealing to many is that it would create oversight discipline for Congress. With seventeen separate statutes, there is too much opportunity for Congress to pursue unfocused and often conflicting objectives.

The Dual Track and the EPA

In the proposed dual track system, the EPA would have a new role and a new mandate. While there is still no consensus about what that role would be, we envision it would include setting the national standards and facilitating partnerships between the various stakeholders. It will also extend to information collection and analysis, risk identification and assessment, establishment of national standards, and enforcement.

The two-track approach protects environmental gains made over previous decades while providing a strong incentive for business to pursue alternative approaches. It will still be necessary, in the NEPI vision, for Congress and the EPA to set national minimum environmental goals and standards mandated across all states.

The dual track or greentracking approach provides an important comfort level to stakeholders. Regulators, financial and insurance institutions, environmental groups, local communities, and other interested parties will know with a high degree of certainty that entities that take the alternative track take their environmental obligations seriously, have comprehensive systems in place to deal with the range of issues they face, and, in fact, deserve more flexible, consistent treatment.

CONCLUSION

It is becoming increasingly clear that the time is ripe to shift away from command-and-control to a greater reliance on an environmental management approach. Greater reliance on less bureaucratic and more flexible systems enjoys widespread popular and political support. Many businesses, anxious both to eliminate unnecessary costs and be good environmental citizens, are ready to embrace new approaches. They believe that protecting human health and the environment can create and support a climate conducive to economic development. Many companies are initiating environmental management efforts such as publishing environmental reports, conducting audits, and benchmarking. They need clear signals from regulatory authorities, however, that proactive environmental management efforts will not be discouraged or even penalized by intractable government policies.

One of the most significant of these environmental management efforts is the development of the ISO 14000 series of environmental management standards. Will the ISO 14000 series be the key that "unlocks" the command-and-control "box?" There is good reason for both industry and regulators to be optimistic.

REFERENCES

I. Feldman. "ISO 14000: A Component of a Management Systems Alternative to 'Command and Control' Regulation," *ELI Environmental Forum,* November 1995.

I. Feldman and M. Schiavo. "A Private Road to Environmental Excellence: The Working of Green Track," *Corporate Environmental Strategy,* Summer 1995.

I. Feldman and M. Schiavo. "Developing an Environmental Excellence Program: Lessons Learned from the Environmental Leadership Program," *Total Quality Environmental Management,* Summer 1995.

I. Feldman and M. Schiavo. "Environmental Leadership: EPA's Beyond Compliance Program." In *Environmental Auditing Handbook,* Executive Enterprises Publications, 1994; reprinted in *Total Quality Environmental Management,* May 1994.

I. Feldman and M. Schiavo. "Incentives and Certainty: EPA Introduces New Audit Policy," *SONREEL News,* May-June 1995.

T. Tibor and I. Feldman. "ISO 14000 and the Eco-Management and Audit Scheme," *European Community Marketing Guide,* October 1995.

T. Tibor and I. Feldman. "The Road to Global Green Management," *American Papermaker,* November 1995.

National Environmental Policy Institute. *Reinventing the Vehicle for Environmental Management,* (Washington, D.C.) August, 1995.

PART ONE

ISO 14000 and Strategic Environmental Management

CHAPTER 1

Environmental Management for the 21st Century

Neil Drobny

INTRODUCTION

As the 20th century draws to a close, concerns about environmental issues have taken on a new light and an increased urgency. We have learned much about the impacts of humankind on planet earth, and much of what we have learned is disturbing.

Hardly a day goes by when we are not reminded of our increasingly interconnected world. Due to rapid technology transfer, technology is available worldwide shortly after it is developed. Such availability fuels global competition by opening new markets for nearly all companies regardless of size, location, or product; this trend will accelerate as the information superhighway becomes economically accessible to hundreds of millions of people around the world.

A consensus is emerging that believes better global planning for the use of the earth and its natural resources is necessary to sustain the planet's ability to support future generations. Additionally, we must monitor the impact of our plans as applied, making corrective actions and adjustments as needed.

This is the essence of environmental management. It is a task that must be undertaken by all countries and all cultures. And because the earth and its resources transcend political boundaries, environmental management efforts worldwide must be coordinated within an apolitical framework that will allow individual and local efforts to be mutually supportive and synergistic.

The Prevention Paradigm

There is a growing recognition that we can no longer treat environmental issues as an after-the-fact concern, but rather we must deal with them in a preventive mode in all aspects of everyday life and work. At the consumer level, the interest in recycling and green products is an example of the new prevention paradigm. At the corporate level, this new way of thinking translates into the notion that the management of environmental concerns exceeds the job of the designated manager and his or her staff, to include "everyone's" job in the organization. Employees and managers who make decisions concerning raw materials, processes, and packaging, for example, all have an impact on a company's environmental performance. Further, many forward-looking organizations combine the management of environmental, health, and safety issues, recognizing their interconnectedness.

Continuous Improvement

Living in a world with rapidly changing conditions and expectations means that continuous improvement must be a cornerstone of environmental management in the 21st century. This should occur in the same fashion that continuous improvement has become the cornerstone of the worldwide quality management.

Better Management = Competitive Advantage

Corporations that manage environmental issues effectively and comprehensively enjoy competitive advantages over those that do not.[1] The few companies that have kept records of the benefits of environmental expenditures as well as the costs, can clearly show that sound environmental management makes good business sense.

Additionally, many stakeholders of both large and small corporations have environmental management high on their lists of performance expectations and standards. These stakeholders include the public, investors, lenders, the media, and perhaps most importantly, customers. For example, no company can afford to enter into a business relationship with a supplier whose ability to deliver might be jeopardized by a shutdown due to poor environmental management.

The Move to Full-Cost Accounting

These changes profoundly impact how organizations view and account for environmental costs. Through the 1980s, organizations focused on minimizing the major direct costs associated with compliance—fines, penalties, treatment facilities, and site remediation; this is still the primary focus in many organizations. In the 1990s however, proactive organizations wishing to remain competitive in the global economy of the 21st century, look at the life-cycle cost of the products and processes. This approach requires new "full-cost" accounting systems and data.

For example, 3M Corporation, which has had an aggressive pollution program for many years, has documented several hundred million dollars in savings as a result of proactive environmental efforts. Among U.S. corporations that spend two percent of sales revenues on environmental management and an estimated 20 percent of corporate capital investment on environmental projects, the potential for savings is enormous.

Cost concerns in the future will be expanded even further to include the full range of external costs associated with the activities of the enterprise. Attention will also be paid to hidden opportunity costs associated with not managing in a holistic, proactive, preventive mode.

The ISO 14000 standards offer the framework within which these complex but necessary environmental management tasks can be carried out uniformly across cultures and economic systems.

A BRIEF HISTORY OF ENVIRONMENTAL MANAGEMENT

The Industrial Revolution sowed the seeds of today's major environmental problems, and 20th century developments fertilized them. Man viewed the earth's resources as virtually limitless, and vast wildernesses appeared to be bottomless pits for wastes and residues. All resources appeared free. Today, as 5.5 billion people compete for key resources, some of which are diminishing, we now know that the resources are not endless. We are learning more about the effect that two hundred years of industrial activity has had on the earth and its biosphere.

Even through the early 1970s, there was little recognition of hazardous waste and a limited focus on air and water quality. Environmental regulations were at a minimum. Consistent with the lack of government involvement, private involvement with environmental issues was also limited. Environmental costs were kept to a bare minimum, ignored whenever possible, and almost never measured.

The 1970s saw an onset of recognition that the earth's oceans, air, and land could no longer be viewed as receptacles of unlimited capacity for more and more waste. While there were many reasons for this new awareness, one cause was space exploration. In 1969, human beings traveled to the moon and saw the earth for the first time as a fragile biosphere in a harsh and foreboding universe.

As awareness of problems grew, priorities for corrective actions were set. An increased emphasis on accounting for site remediation costs evolved. Fines increased. And, unfortunately, an increased number of disasters helped to heighten awareness. Corporate actions were largely reactive, however, and only focused on compliance with minimal regulatory requirements. Corporate actions dealt primarily with matters "inside the fence" and focused on dealing with the environmental impacts of product manufacture and raw material extraction. Further, corporate organizational structures usually isolated their environmental departments from other business functions, including even health and safety.

Beyond Compliance

Corporations in the 1990s, however, are rethinking what effective environmental management means and what the actual payoffs are. Mere compliance with regulations is no longer adequate. One problem is that regulations vary from country to country, and would lead to patchwork environmental performance if used as the basis for a global environmental management paradigm. Further, most regulations evolved in prescriptive frameworks that sidestepped the issue of true environmental benefit. As the disadvantages of the command-and-control regulatory approach became more apparent, the stage was set for a more management-focused approach such as that embodied in the ISO 14000 standards. Increased interest by the public and other stakeholders in corporate environmental management decision making also fueled this evolution. From consumer choice to investor demands, the scrutiny of corporate environmental management has a greater influence now than at any time in the past.

In his remarks at the 1992 U.N. Environmental Conference in Rio De Janeiro, Frank Popoff, CEO of Dow Chemical Company (USA) made clear: The 1970s was the decade of denial, the 1980s the decade of data, and the 1990s the decade of dialogue with the public.

Enter Sustainable Development

The 1992 Rio conference introduced the world to the concept of sustainable development, a notion coined by the 1987 Brundtland Commission report, *Our Common Future*.[2] Briefly stated, sustainable development is an approach to development that utilizes the earth and its resources in a manner that does not compromise the ability of future generations to meet their needs. Partially resulting from agreements reached at the 1992 Rio conference, sustainable development emerged as the foundation upon which national (and even some local) governments and many major organizations worldwide elected to build their environmental policies for the 21st century.

The significance of the sustainable development concept to the emerging world-wide paradigm shift in environmental management is evidenced by the fact that the international business community *voluntarily* elected to adopt many codes and charters that promote sustainability in one form or another. One of the most visible examples is the *Business Charter for Sustainable Development* developed by the International Chamber of Commerce. This charter lays out 16 principles for environmental management that translate sustainability principles into operations terms. Over 1,200 corporations, including more than 25 percent of the Fortune 500, have endorsed these principles. (See Appendix C for the 16 principles of the Business Charter.)

Taking the Road Less Traveled

On a global scale, the need for sustainable development has become increasingly apparent and accepted. The ISO 14000 standards offer a framework to implement and manage according to the principles of sustainability.

An organization can choose to be a leader or a follower. By identifying the environmental costs of its operations broadly and by initiating prevention-based measures in all aspects of product manufacture, distribution, use, and disposal, organizations can handle their responsibilities proactively instead of reactively. Organizations can use integration of environmental controls throughout a business and implementation of a life-cycle approach to product and process design analysis to prevent pollution by identifying and effectively managing all activities with potential environmental impact.

Organizations choosing this path will set standards for other companies to follow and will consequently achieve a competitive advantage.

Individuals and businesses of all types must accept responsibility for the stewardship of the earth, not only as a means of pollution control and resource management, but also as a way of balancing human activity with nature's expertise in renewing itself. Future prosperity, which is essential for a healthy global economy, depends on preserving the earth's natural wealth and sustaining a healthy ecological balance.

BACKGROUND AND DEVELOPMENT OF THE ISO 14000 SERIES

The Parallels with Quality

The ISO 14000 series grew, in part, out of the ISO 9000 quality standards series. That environmental management has roots in quality management is not surprising. The late Edward Deming, one father of the modern discipline of quality management, noted that quality cannot rely on inspection at the end of the manufacturing process; it must be built into every aspect of the business, from designing through manufacturing, sales, and servicing. Likewise, environmental protection can no longer depend only on end-of-pipe controls, which are often inefficient and inadequate. Pollution prevention and other environmental issues must be addressed throughout all aspects of the design, manufacturing, and distribution processes.

During development of the ISO 9000 standards, consideration was given to incorporation of environmental management systems into the overall quality management process. Consistent with Deming's observations, many stakeholders recognized that given the complex environmental issues that organizations face, end-of-pipe systems were inadequate to protect the environment or to effectively and efficiently assure compliance with legal requirements. Environmental protection and compliance can best be achieved by integrating environmental considerations into industrial operations in a systematic way, including R&D, design, raw materials selection, production, distribution, use, and ultimate disposal of a product.

The Decision to Proceed with a Separate Standard

To consider the matter, ISO established the Strategic Advisory Committee on the Environment (SAGE) in 1991. The group studied the United Kingdom's BS 7750 and other national environmental management standards as possible starting points for an ISO environmental standard. After much debate and consideration, in 1993 SAGE recommended the establishment of an ISO technical committee to begin work on a new set of environmental management standards. SAGE believed that there were too many issues to be covered to build into the quality standard itself without diverting from the success of the ISO 9000 Series.

In 1993, SAGE disbanded, and ISO formed Technical Committee (TC) 207, with a charter to establish environmental standards in five areas: (1) management systems, (2) auditing, (3) labeling, (4) environmental performance evaluation, and (5) life-cycle assessment. ISO also organized a special work group to look at the environmental aspects of product standards. Subcommittees corresponding to each area carry out the work of negotiating and drafting specific standards. TC 207 held its first plenary meeting in Toronto in June 1993. Over 200 delegates from more than 30 countries attended.

WHY IMPLEMENT AN ENVIRONMENTAL MANAGEMENT SYSTEM (EMS)?

What Is an EMS?

The framework, or backbone, for the set of ISO 14000 standards is the environmental management system—the "EMS." The primary steps in establishing an EMS are as follows:

1. Create an environmental policy.
2. Set objectives and targets.
3. Implement a program to achieve those objectives.
4. Monitor and measure its effectiveness.
5. Review the system and correct problems to improve it and overall environmental performance.

What Does an EMS Do?

The EMS is a set of management tools, principles, and procedures that an organization can use to help protect human health and the environment from the potential impacts of the organization's activities, products, and services. As such, an EMS will also assist in maintaining and improving the quality of the environment. Organizations that adopt an EMS as part of their overall management system will be well positioned to provide internal assurance to interested stakeholders that the following conditions are true:

- A management infrastructure is in place to follow up on established environmental policies, objectives, and targets.
- Emphasis is placed on preventing problems rather than fixing them after the fact.
- Evidence of compliance can be provided.
- An effort has been made to build continual improvement into the management culture.

An organization that has implemented an EMS will enjoy competitive advantage in global markets over organizations that have not. There are two primary reasons for this. One is that managing in accord with EMS principles drives managers to seek the most economic means of performing work. Additionally, as with ISO 9000, certain global markets may eventually become closed to companies in particular industries if ISO 14000 conformance cannot be established.

BENEFITS OF EMS IMPLEMENTATION

Reduced Operating Costs

First and foremost is the economic advantage of reduced operating costs. The pollution prevention and waste management/reduction underpinnings of ISO 14000 will drive managers to continually seek lower-cost solutions. Another source of reduced costs will be lower insurance rates and more attractive borrowing opportunities that will accrue to the organization because of lower operating liabilities.

Improved Financial Performance

A study released on Earth Day 1995 concluded that of the financial performance of S&P 500 companies broken down into 85 industrial categories, "cleaner" corporations performed as well or better than "dirtier" firms in the same industry categories. For example, in a category of firms judged to be emitters of highly toxic materials, "cleaner" firms were noted to deliver a return on investment of 32.1 percent versus 23.7 percent for the "dirtier" firms.[3] Implementation of an EMS will help an organization operate in a cleaner manner and thereby enjoy benefits that will be of interest to shareholders and the investor community as a whole.

Increased Access to Markets

One of the often quoted reasons for implementing ISO 14001 is that certain markets may become closed to organizations that do not adopt ISO standards. Even if markets are open, companies that implement an ISO 14001 EMS can use ISO 14001 certification to differentiate themselves from their competitors.

Regulatory Relief

In the United States, the Environmental Protection Agency is exploring whether an organization's commitment to implementing an EMS might be "traded" for relief from certain environmental regulatory burdens. EPA is considering whether to relax permitting, reporting and inspection requirements and even possibly reduced fines when violations do occur. Several EPA programs are providing programmatic umbrellas under which such possibilities are being explored, including Project XL, The Common Sense Initiative and the Environmental Leadership Project.

Improved Environmental Performance

While not specifically a parameter of EMS effectiveness, improved environmental performance will most certainly result from implementing an EMS designed along ISO 14000 guidelines. As organizations ponder the environmental impacts of their activities, products, and services, they will make changes that benefit not only their own effectiveness but the environment as well. This will, in turn, help industry to shed its label as an antienvironmental segment of society.

Improved Community Relations

Improved community relations will also benefit from improved environmental performance. Community relations, and overall public image, will be helped by the open communications with stakeholders that is encouraged by the ISO EMS principles.

Improved Customer Relations

Improved relations with customers can be yet another benefit of implementing an EMS. EMS implementation provides customers with an additional layer of assurance that the organization will not be shut down due to environmental incidents or accidents. In the just-in-time supply and production chains that have developed throughout the world, interruptions in the supply of goods or raw materials can play havoc with a manufacturer or end producer. When suppliers take precautions against occurrences such as interruptions in the supply of goods or raw materials, the supplier scores points with manufacturers, end producers, and customers.

Employee Involvement and Education

Implementation of an EMS in an organization makes environmental performance everyone's job. This builds a broad base of awareness to best prevent or solve problems at operating levels and locations. The training components of the EMS will lead to greater organizational awareness regarding how employees can assist in the improvement of an organization's environmental performance. There is a decided morale dimension of the process as well: Employees prefer working for organizations that take environmental responsibility seriously.

Potential Impact on World Trade

ISO 14000 will hopefully have a positive impact on world trade and prevent some undesirable developments. Prior to initiation of the ISO 14000 process, many countries and industry groups began formulating their own standards for environmental management systems and related issues. Had these separate efforts continued, the plethora of standards would have resulted in gridlock in world trade and raised costs for all participants. ISO 14000, in contrast, opens the possibility of a level playing field, at least as far as environmental issues are concerned.

Uniform national standards are also endorsed by the world trade community. For example, the World Trade Organization (WTO) agreement (formerly the General Agreement on Tariffs and Trade (GATT)) favors the use of international standards in its Agreement on Technical Barriers to Trade.

As was noted earlier, conformance to the ISO 14001 standard may become a condition of doing business in many parts of the world. The European Union leads the promotion of this concept, but the notion of conditional business is picking up support in many other regions as well.

POTENTIAL CONCERNS AND CAVEATS ABOUT ISO 14000

Notwithstanding the many potential benefits of ISO 14000 and implementation of an EMS, hurdles still remain.

Third-Party Registration Issues

An organization can attain ISO 14001 status by having a third party "register" or "certify" the organization's conformance to the requirements of the standard. Another method is through "self-declaration." There are many issues to resolve, however, including the following:

- Will self-declaration be widely accepted?
- How will the registrars become accredited?
- How can organizations be assured that the auditor is competent?
- How can reciprocity in recognition of registration certificates worldwide be achieved?

Small and Medium-Size Businesses

One of the most debated issues is whether small and medium-size (SMEs) organizations will have the resources to handle the additional administrative burden. This issue is one of the questions to be answered by an ISO 14000 pilot project being conducted by NSF International in Ann Arbor, Michigan.[4] With the aid of an EPA grant, NSF has assembled a group of 18 companies to field test implementation of the ISO 14001 EMS standard. Many of the participants in the project are small and medium-size businesses. While the project is only about half complete, no strong evidence has emerged that SMEs will face an insurmountable hurdle in moving in the direction of EMS implementation. Nevertheless, there are other special concerns in an SME organization:

- First, identifying a management team sufficiently separate from day-to-day operations and production to provide truly independent audits and reviews of the EMS implementation may be difficult. Often in a small organization, management crosses into operations in the interest of efficiency and other practical considerations. In such cases, the same people might have EMS implementation duties and general management duties. There is not an easy answer to this dilemma.

- Second, it is unclear whether the management culture can accommodate the extensive documentation requirements involved with an ISO-based EMS. Documentation starts with a formal environmental policy and includes written procedures, goals, and targets and written assessments of results and corrective actions. Such formality is foreign to many small organizations.

- A third issue is the cost of registration. While the ISO 14001 standard provides the option of self-declaring conformance with the EMS requirements, there is some concern that formal registration by a third party will be the only means of conformance verification that carries weight in global markets. Should this occur, SMEs will be disadvantaged by the cost burden of the formal registration requirement, which would, in turn, create a trade barrier.

Relationship to Regulatory Structures

Environmental regulatory structures vary widely throughout the world. How various governments will interpret the ISO 14000 standards vis-á-vis their own regulations is unknown. One concern is that governments may use ISO 14000 to determine legal requirements and other aspects of enforcement programs including penalties and fines. That would clearly be a misuse of what TC 207 intended and would jeopardize widespread support for the standard. ISO 14000 is intended to be a voluntary standard, and that is one reason it has garnered so much support.

Impact on Environmental Performance

While ISO 14000 is not an environmental performance standard *per se,* the expectation is that improved management will lead to improved environmental performance. If it turns out that organizations somehow find ways to achieve ISO 14001 conformance and to obtain registration certificates but fail to genuinely improve their environmental performance, the credibility of the process will be lost. Stakeholders who gave their support to the ISO process will lose confidence in the standard. This would jeopardize survival of the usage of the ISO standards and lead to a proliferation of independent national standards. Such a result would complicate an organization's relationships and would not benefit the environment to the degree that would be possible with a uniform global standard.

CONCLUSIONS

Environmental issues have both local and global dimensions. ISO 14001 is the avenue through which the management of environmental issues has achieved global recognition and status. ISO also represents the awareness that what is good for the environment is also good business. This claim has been made altruistically by many for several decades, but not until ISO 14001 was it embraced so uniformly and unanimously by business and government leaders worldwide.

After decades of piecemeal efforts by companies and governments, ISO 14001 provides a level playing field on which the world's environmental issues can be worked out, not as a zero sum game but in a win-win framework. The standard will have a profound effect on how businesses and other organizations manage their environmental affairs in the 21st century.

ISO 14001 also brings recognition to the fact that effective environmental management must be the responsibility of nearly everyone in an organization. The commitment must start at the top and be carried through in all its details by top management. As with ISO 9000, the rule is to "do what you say and say what you do." Only top management can ensure that an organization's culture embodies this principle.

BIOGRAPHY

Neil Drobny, PE, PhD

Neil Drobny joined Commodore Applied Technologies, Inc., an environmental technology company, in 1994, and serves as executive vice president. His primary responsibilities include developing joint ventures and other business opportunities for commercializing Commodore technology in the industrial and commercial marketplace.

Before his work at Commodore, Dr. Drobny was president and principal stockholder of ERM–Midwest, Inc., an environmental consulting firm that was part of the international ERM Group. He also cofounded and served as the first president of ERM/EnviroClean–Midwest, Inc., an affiliated remediation company.

Dr. Drobny received his Ph.D. in civil engineering from Ohio State University after completing his undergraduate work in engineering at Dartmouth College. He is a Diplomat of the American Academy of Environmental Engineers, and a member of the American Society of Civil Engineers, the National Society of Professional Engineers, the Water Environmental Federation, and the Air and Waste Management Association.

NOTES

1. "Are Regs Bleeding the Economy?" *Business Week*, July 17, 1995, pp. 75–76.
2. Brundtland, Gro Harlem. *Our Common Future.* Oxford University Press, New York. 1987.
3. Cohen, Mark A., Scott A. Fenn and Johnathan S. Naimon. *"Environmental and Financial Performance: Are They Related?"* Investor Responsibility Research Center, Inc. Washington D.C. April 1995. 27 pp.
4. Diamond, Craig P. "Voluntary Environmental Management System Standards: Case Studies in Implementation." *Total Quality Environmental Management,* Winter 1995–96, pp. 9–23.

CHAPTER 2

Development of ISO 14000

Tom Tibor and Ira Feldman

INTRODUCTION

The ISO 14000 environmental management standards are one series among thousands of international standards. What are international standards and why do we need them? The International Organization for Standardization (ISO) refers to a standard as a documented agreement containing technical specifications or other precise criteria to be used consistently as a rule, guideline, or definition of characteristics to ensure that materials, products, processes, and services are fit for their purpose. Ideally, standards are designed to facilitate international trade by increasing the reliability and effectiveness of goods and services.

What is ISO?

Based in Geneva, Switzerland, ISO is a specialized international agency whose members are the national standards bodies of 111 countries. ISO was founded in 1946 to develop manufacturing, trade, and communication standards. Participation in standards development varies by country. Some countries are represented by governmental or quasi-governmental bodies. The American National Standards Institute (ANSI) is the United States member body to ISO. The goal of ISO standards is to facilitate the efficient exchange of goods and services. All standards developed by ISO are voluntary; however, countries often adopt ISO standards and make them mandatory.

ISO is structured into approximately 180 technical committees (TCs) each of which specializes in drafting standards in a particular area. ISO develops standards in all industries except those related to electrical and electronic engineering, which are developed by the Geneva-based International Electrotechnical Commission (IEC).

Member nations to ISO form technical advisory groups (TAGs) that provide input to the TCs as part of the standards development process. ISO receives input from government, industry, and other interested parties before promulgating a standard. After a draft standard is voted on by all member countries, it is published as an international standard. Each nation can then adopt a version of the standard as its national standard.

DEVELOPMENT OF ISO 14000

From Products to Processes

For most of its history, ISO focused on product technical standards. ISO has developed industrial standards in a wide variety of areas. ISO standards for film speeds, standardized freight containers, the size and shape of screw threads, and paper sizes are just a few of the thousands of ISO technical standards. In 1979, however, it took a sharp turn into the area of management standards. In 1979, ISO formed Technical

---

B O X 2–1

THE ISO STANDARDS PROCESS

ISO follows a few key principles in its standards development process. These include the following:

- Consensus. The views of all interests are taken into account: manufacturers, vendors and users, consumer groups, testing laboratories, governments, engineering professions, and research organizations.
- Industry-wide standards. The goal is to draft standards that satisfy industries and customers worldwide.
- Voluntary standards. International standardization is market driven and therefore based on voluntary involvement of all interests in the marketplace.

DEVELOPING A STANDARD

ISO technical committees (TC) develop international standards through a five-step process:

1. Proposal stage
2. Preparatory stage
3. Committee stage
4. Approval stage
5. Publication stage

Committee 176 (TC 176) to develop global standards for quality management and quality assurance systems. ISO intended to harmonize different and conflicting requirements for quality systems. The work of TC 176 culminated in 1987 with the publication of the ISO 9000 quality standards. Since ISO 9000 is largely the forerunner of ISO 14000, it is instructive to describe the basic content and rationale of the ISO 9000 series.

ISO 9000

The ISO 9000 series are generic standards for quality management and quality assurance. The basic rationale of ISO 9000 is that consistently meeting specifications for quality products and services depends partly on implementing and maintaining a systematic quality system. An effective system helps to ensure consistent results and provide confidence to customers.

Although the ultimate purpose of the ISO 9000 standards is to improve products or services, the standards do not specifically apply to products or services themselves but to the processes and systems that produce the products or services.

The proposal stage confirms the need for a new standard. Members of the relevant TC or subcommittee (SC) then submit a new work item proposal (NWI) for vote. The proposal is accepted if a majority of the participating (P) members of the TC/SC vote in favor and at least five P members declare their commitment to participate actively in the project.

During the preparatory stage, working groups of experts develop working drafts (WD) of the proposed standard. When the working groups are satisfied that the WD is ready to become a standard, it is forwarded to the SC and advanced to the committee draft (CD) stage.

The CD is registered by ISO's central secretariat and is distributed by the P members of the TC/SC for comments and voting. Successive committee drafts may be considered until consensus is reached on the content of the CD. It then advances to the Draft International Standard (DIS) stage.

During the approval stage, the DIS is circulated for voting and comment within a period of five months. It is approved if a two-thirds majority of the P members of the TC/SC are in favor *and* not more than one-quarter of the total number of votes cast are negative. If the voting is negative, the DIS is returned to the TC for revision. If the standard is approved with editorial comments, a final DIS (FDIS) is prepared, incorporating those comments and the FDIS is sent out for a two-month, "yes-or-no" vote, with no further comments permitted.

If approved, the final stage is publication. The text is sent to the ISO Central Secretariat, which publishes the International Standard.

The ISO 9000 series standards describe the basic elements of a quality-management system and provide guidance for implementing the quality system. The standards focus on basic management elements, such as developing policies for quality, putting a system in place to achieve its objectives, measuring and monitoring progress, reviewing the system, and making improvements. The ISO 9000 standards are used to determine whether these important elements are in place; the standards do not tell a company how it must run its business.

The ISO 9000 series covers a broad scope of quality system elements—they are flexible and relatively uncomplicated. Basically, the standards require a company to document what it does, do what it documents, review the process, and change it when necessary.

A company that has achieved ISO 9000 registration can attest that it has a documented quality system that is fully deployed and consistently followed. The standards in the series that are used for registration purposes include ISO 9001, ISO 9002, and ISO 9003. ISO 9001 is the most comprehensive and covers all elements, from design/development through production, installation, and service. Other standards, such as ISO 9000 and ISO 9004, provide guidance for using the standards and for implementing their elements internally.

The ISO 9000 standards apply to all types of companies, large and small, in both manufacturing and services. Over 90 countries have adopted the series. More than 100,000 company facilities worldwide have achieved registration to one of the three conformance standards in the series: ISO 9001, ISO 9002, or ISO 9003.

Reasons for Registration

For some companies, registration to ISO 9000 is a legal requirement to enter regulated markets. This is the case for industry sectors that produce medical devices in the European Union. In other cases, registration is a precondition to placing a contractual purchase order.

Governments are implementing ISO 9000, incorporating its requirements into their regulatory structure, or evaluating its potential to help meet regulatory goals. Agencies involved in ISO 9000 activities in the United States include the Food and Drug Administration, Department of Defense, Federal Aviation Administration, and others.

The primary driver for ISO 9000 adoption, however, is marketplace pressure. Compliance with ISO 9000 standards, via a third-party registration process, is a de facto condition for doing business in several industry sectors. Companies implement ISO 9000 to maintain market share and to keep up with or get ahead of their competition.

In addition, ISO 9000-registered companies have realized internal benefits: better operating efficiency, higher quality, reduced costs, and greater productivity. The basic requirements of ISO 9000 are described in Table 2–1.

T A B L E   2–1

ISO 9001 Requirements

The basic requirements of ISO 9001 are contained in 20 clauses. The following are the clauses contained in *ANSI/ASQC Q9001 - 1994, Quality Systems-Model for Quality Assurance in Design, Development, Production, Installation and Servicing.*

1	Scope	4.10	Inspection and testing
2	Normative reference	4.11	Control of inspection, measuring, and test equipment
3	Definitions		
4	Quality-system requirements	4.12	Inspection and test status
4.1	Management responsibility	4.13	Control of nonconforming product
4.2	Quality system	4.14	Corrective and preventive action
4.3	Contract review	4.15	Handling, storage, packaging, preservation, and delivery
4.4	Design control		
4.5	Document and data control	4.16	Control of quality records
4.6	Purchasing	4.17	Internal quality audits
4.7	Control of customer-supplied product	4.18	Training
4.8	Product identification and traceability	4.19	Servicing
4.9	Process control	4.20	Statistical techniques

THE ISO 14000 SERIES

Scope of TC 207

Partly in response to the acceptance of the ISO 9000 quality management and quality assurance standards and partly in response to the proliferation of various environmental standards worldwide, ISO began to look at the environmental management field. As described in Chapter One, ISO eventually formed TC 207 to develop standards in the environmental management area.

The specific scope of TC 207's work is standardization in the field of environmental management tools and systems. ISO 14000 deals with management systems and methods, not product or technical standards. The final result of TC 207's work will be a comprehensive set of standards for every aspect of environmental management. Excluded from TC 207's scope are the following:

- Test methods for pollutants. These are the responsibility of other ISO technical committees: ISO/TC 146 (air quality), ISO/TC 147 (water quality), ISO/TC 190 (soil quality), and ISO/TC 43 (acoustics).
- Setting caps regarding pollutants or effluents.
- Setting environmental performance levels.
- Standardization of products.

B O X   2–2

MAKEUP AND STRUCTURE OF TC 207

TC 207 is divided into six international subcommittees and one working group. Subcommittee members include representatives from industry, standards organizations, government, environmental organizations, and other interested groups. Each nation sets up a technical advisory group (TAG) to the international subcommittee. Thus, in the United States, the American National Standards Institute (ANSI), which is the U.S. representative to TC 207, set up a U.S. TAG to TC 207. Each international subcommittee has a corresponding national subcommittee known as a SubTAG. Thus, there are SubTAGs for EMS, auditing, EPE, and so on.

The primary purpose of the TAG in each nation is to develop and transmit to ISO its national position on a particular standard, in the form of comments and voting ballots. The American Society for Testing and Materials (ASTM), along with the American Society for Quality Control (ASQC) administers the U.S. TAG to ISO, on behalf of the American National Standards Institute (ANSI), the U.S. member body to ISO.

System, Not Performance

TC 207's scope of work excludes anything that relates to actual environmental performance. The ISO 14000 standards are process, not performance, standards. They focus on setting up a system to achieve internally set policies, objectives, and targets. The standards require that such policies include elements such as compliance with laws and regulations and the prevention of pollution. But the standards do not dictate how the organization will achieve these goals, nor do they prescribe the type or level of performance required.

Regulations often prescribe not only performance goals but the technology with which to achieve them. In the United States, EPA regulations sometimes call for maximum achievable control technology (MACT) or best available control technology (BACT). There is rarely agreement, however, over what constitutes BACT and MACT. And industry usually resists being told what technology to use to achieve regulatory mandates. Under the European Union's EMAS regulation, companies are to include Economically Viable and Achievable Best Available Technology (EVABAT) wherever possible. Thus, EMAS has performance aspects.

In short, the ISO 14000 series, like ISO 9000, focus on the processes necessary to achieve results, not the results themselves. The ISO 14000 series are flexible standards that recognize the differences in approaches to environmental management worldwide. The overall goal of ISO 14000 implementation and certification is to increase confidence among all stakeholders that an organization has a system in place that is likely to lead to better environmental performance.

Management Systems and Tools

The work of TC 207 is divided into six Subcommittees and a special Working Group. Canada is the Secretariat of TC 207, and six other countries head the committee's six subcommittees. As shown in Figure 2–1, several of the Subcommittees are further broken down into work groups, depending upon the number of standards planned by each Subcommittee's scope of work.

The work on the EMS standards focuses on the basic elements needed to set up an effective environmental management system. Subcommittee 1 has developed the ISO 14001 specification for an environmental management system. This is the standard

FIGURE 2–1

ISO/TC 207 Subcommittees and Working Groups

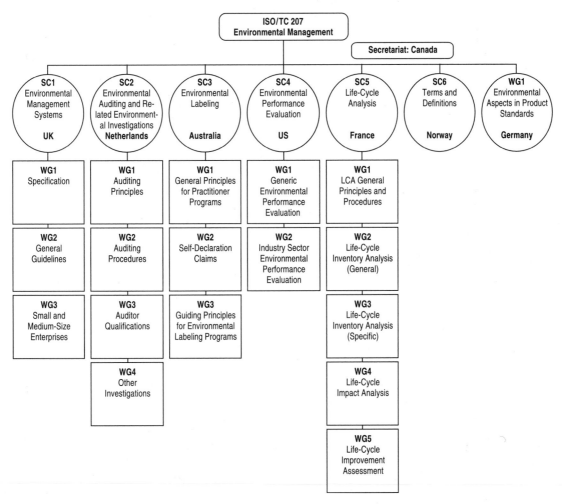

that will be used for third-party registration purposes. (Registration, also known as certification, refers to an independent third-party audit of the EMS and the consequent awarding of a certificate confirming that the organization's EMS conforms to ISO 14001 requirements.) Subcommittee 1 has also developed a guidance standard, ISO 14004, that offers detailed guidance about environmental management principles and methods.

Subcommittee 2 (SC2) has developed a set of guidance standards for environmental auditing. These focus on the general principles of environmental auditing, auditing an environmental management system, and necessary qualifications for environmental auditors. Future work by SC2 may include standards for other types of environmental audits, such as environmental site assessments.

Subcommittee 3 (SC3) is developing standards that address the full range of environmental claims and declarations made by companies. Standards are in development to harmonize the practices of over two dozen national eco-labeling programs and to harmonize the claims made by manufacturers.

Subcommittee 4 (SC4) is focusing on ways to measure environmental performance: how to develop useful indicators to track environmental performance, how to set up an environmental performance evaluation process, and how to report performance information, both internally and externally.

The work on life-cycle assessment (LCA) by Subcommittee 5 (SC5) is geared to providing environmental managers and LCA practitioners with an introduction to life-cycle assessment concepts and life-cycle assessment methods.

Subcommittee 6 (SC6) on terms and definitions is helping to harmonize the definitions used in the other standards and to develop a definitions standard, ISO CD 14050. A high priority of TC 207 is to create a common, international language for environmental management.

Finally, a special Working Group 1 committee has developed an ISO Guide (ISO Guide 64) regarding environmental aspects in product standards. This guide is designed for standards writers. It will acquaint them with how environmental issues arise when writing product technical standards.

The main purpose of the ISO 14000 standards is to promote more uniform, efficient, and effective environmental management by organizations worldwide. A list of the developing standards in the ISO 14000 family is shown in Table 2–2. A helpful way to classify the standards is shown in Figure 2–2. The EMS, auditing, and environmental performance evaluation standards focus on organizational evaluation. The life-cycle assessment and labeling standards and the guide for standards writers focus on product and process evaluation.

Conformance versus Guidance

A key point to remember is that of the many standards in the developing ISO 14000 family, only ISO 14001—the specification for an EMS system—is designed for third-party registration purposes. Specification standards contain requirements that may be objectively audited for certification/registration purposes and/or self-declaration purposes.

TABLE 2-2

TC 207 Subcommittees and Standards

The following is a list of TC 207 Subcommittee work. It includes standards in various stages of development, from working documents to published international standards. As of the publication of this book, only the ISO 14001 and ISO 14004 EMS standards, and the ISO 14010–14012 auditing standards have been issued as international standards.

SC1—Environmental Management Systems (EMS)

ISO 14001 Environmental management systems—Specification with guidance for use.

ISO 14004 Environmental management systems—General guidelines on principles, systems, and supporting techniques.

SC2—Environmental Auditing

ISO 14010 Guidelines for environmental auditing—General principles of environmental auditing.

ISO 14011/1 Guidelines for environmental auditing—Audit procedures—Auditing of environmental management systems.

ISO 14012 Guidelines for environmental auditing—Qualification criteria for environmental auditors.

ISO 14014 Initial reviews (New Work Item Proposal).

ISO 14015 Environmental Site Assessments.

SC3—Environmental Labeling

ISO 14020 Goals and principles of all environmental labeling.

ISO 14021 Environmental labels and declarations—Self-declaration environmental claims—Terms and definitions.

ISO 14022 Environmental labels and declarations—Symbols.

ISO 14023 Environmental labels and declarations—Testing and Verification.

ISO 14024 Environmental labels and declarations—Environmental labeling Type I—Guiding principles and procedures.

ISO 1402X Type III labeling.

SC4—Environmental Performance Evaluation

ISO 14031 Evaluation of the environmental performance of the management system and its relationship to the environment.

SC5—Life-Cycle Assessment

ISO 14040 Environmental management—life-cycle assessment—General principles and guidelines.

ISO 14041 Environmental management—life-cycle assessment—Inventory analysis.

ISO 14042 Environmental management—life-cycle assessment—Impact assessment.

ISO 14043 Environmental management—life-cycle assessment—Interpretation.

SC6—Terms and Definitions

ISO 14050 Terms and Definitions Guide on the Principles for ISO/TC SC6 Terminology Work.

WG1—Environmental Aspects in Product Standards

ISO Guide 64 Guide for the inclusion of environmental aspects in product standards.

FIGURE 2–2

The ISO 14000 Series of Environmental Management Standards

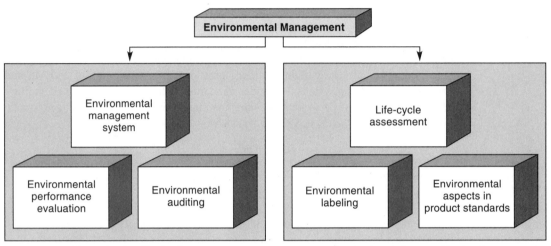

All other standards in the ISO 14000 series are designed for guidance purposes only. Guidance standards provide useful information to organizations but are not designed for third-party verification. Of course, an organization can use the ISO 14001 specification standard for internal guidance only or for self-declaration purposes. It may choose not to seek third-party verification of its EMS system. If the organization chooses to seek registration, however, the registration audit will focus on conformity only to ISO 14001 requirements.

Of the other guidance standards, there is a possibility that one of the labeling standards could form the basis for some type of third-party verification. This is the standard that focuses on harmonizing criteria and procedures for the over two dozen national labeling programs worldwide. The global marketplace may see value in having these programs demonstrate, via a third-party verification process, that their procedures conform to the labeling guidelines. For now, however, this is speculative.

Stand-Alone Standards

Another central concept is that standards in the ISO 14000 family are designed for use as stand-alone documents and also as a related set of system tools. The ISO 14001 EMS specification standard describes the basic elements of an effective EMS program. An organization can use only ISO 14001 as the basis for its EMS, if that is sufficient for its needs. Or it can implement the guidance from one or more of the other standards. For example, it can develop an environmental performance evaluation (EPE) process using guidance from the work of SC4. At the same time, the EPE process can be helpful to an organization that does not have an EMS in existence or to an organization that doesn't even plan to implement ISO 14001.

Guidance Standards Do Not Become Requirements

The fact that an organization uses the guidance standards as part of their EMS development does not imply that the elements in those guidance standards become requirements during a third-party audit. If an organization seeks registration of its EMS and has implemented the guidance from other standards, such as the environmental auditing or the environmental performance evaluation standard, the auditor should not make the elements from those standards mandatory in the audit.

OVERVIEW OF ISO 14001

Subcommittee 1 is developing the specification standard for environmental management systems, ISO 14001, and a guidance standard for environmental management, ISO 14004. The ISO 14001 standard describes the basic requirements of an environmental management system. It is the standard that companies will implement and the standard to which they will either self-declare conformance or to which they will seek third-party registration. ISO 14004 is a guidance standard that provides companies with valuable information about implementing an EMS. This section introduces ISO 14001. The detailed requirements of ISO 14001 are discussed in the next chapter.

ISO 14004 versus ISO 14001

It is critical to understand the difference between ISO 14004 and ISO 14001. ISO 14001 is the specification standard. It includes the basic elements necessary for an effective environmental management system. Although it can be used internally, for self-declaration purposes, and in contractual situations, the principal use of ISO 14001 is anticipated to be third-party registration. Thus, ISO 14001 contains only those requirements that may be objectively audited for registration purposes or for self-declaration purposes.

In contrast, ISO 14004 is a guidance standard. It offers useful guidance in the form of examples, and descriptions related to the development and implementation of environmental management systems. The standard also addresses how to coordinate an EMS with other management systems. Although ISO 14001 and ISO 14004 share key concepts and definitions, ISO 14004 is intended for use as a voluntary, internal management tool and is not intended for use by EMS certification/registration bodies as a specification standard.[1] Guidance from ISO 14004 is incorporated in the discussion of ISO 14001 implementation in the next section of this book.

The ISO 14001 Model

The ISO 14001 standard is organized according to a five-step systems model, as shown in Figure 2–3:

FIGURE 2–3

Environmental Management System Model

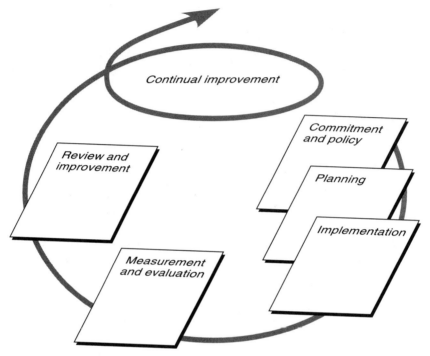

Adapted from ISO 14001

1. Environmental Policy. The organization defines an environmental policy and ensures commitment to an EMS.

2. Planning. The organization designs a plan to fulfill its policy.

3. Implementation and operation. The organization develops the human, financial, technological, and other capabilities to achieve its policy, objectives, and targets.

4. Checking and corrective action. The organization measures, monitors, and evaluates its environmental performance.

5. Management review. Finally, the organization reviews and continually improves its environmental management system, with the overall objective of improving its environmental performance.

These steps make up a cycle of continual improvement, using the plan-do-check-review concept used often in total quality management circles. The ISO 14004 guidance standard emphasizes that an organization's EMS is viewed as "an organizing framework" that helps the organization achieve its goals and objectives.

ISO 14001 Requirements

The basic requirements of ISO 14001 are contained in Section 4 of the standard. They are shown in Table 2–3. The standard also contains three informative Annexes. Annex A provides additional information on the requirements. According to the Annex, it "is intended to avoid misinterpretation of the specification." Actually, the existence of Annex A was the subject of extensive debate among the standards developers. Several delegations, primarily those from Europe, wanted to include additional requirements in the specification.

T A B L E   2–3

ISO 14001 Environmental Management Systems—Specification with Guidance for Use

0	Introduction
1	Scope
2	Normative References
3	Definitions
4	Environmental Management System
4.1	General Requirements
4.2	Environmental Policy
4.3	Planning
	4.3.1 Environmental aspects
	4.3.2 Legal and other requirements
	4.3.3 Objectives and targets
	4.3.4 Environmental management program(s)
4.4	Implementation and Operation
	4.4.1 Structure and responsibility
	4.4.2 Training, awareness, and competence
	4.4.3 Communication
	4.4.4 Environmental management system documentation
	4.4.5 Document control
	4.4.6 Operational control
	4.4.7 Emergency preparedness and response
4.5	Checking and Corrective Action
	4.5.1 Monitoring and measurement
	4.5.2 Nonconformance and corrective and preventive action
	4.5.3 Records
	4.5.4 Environmental management system audit
4.6	Management Review
Annex A (Informative) Guidance on the use of the specification	
Annex B (Informative) Links between ISO 14001 and ISO 9001	
Annex C (Informative) Bibliography	

For example, several delegations lobbied for the inclusion of a requirement that an organization conduct an initial review of its environmental aspects. This requirement was rejected and language suggesting an initial review was moved into the informative Annex A. It is important to remember that Annex A is not part of the specification and nothing suggested in Annex A constitutes a requirement of the standard for either internal use or external registration. Annex B is a table that displays links between ISO 14001 and ISO 9001 and Annex C is a bibliography.

Applicability

The ISO 14001 standard is applicable to all types and sizes of organizations. It is meant to accommodate diverse geographical, cultural, and social conditions and to be successfully applied everywhere.[2]

ISO 14001 states that organizations can use ISO 14001 for five purposes:

1. Implement, maintain and improve an EMS.
2. Assure that its EMS conforms with its environmental policy.
3. Demonstrate this conformance to others.
4. Seek ISO 14001 certification/registration.
5. Make a self-declaration of conformity.

Although it is expected that many, if not most, organizations will implement ISO 14001 to seek third-party registration, the standard is designed for internal use as well.

No Performance Criteria

A critical point is that the standard "does not establish absolute requirements for environmental performance beyond commitment, in the policy, to compliance with applicable legislation and regulations and to continual improvement." The EMS described in ISO 14001 applies to "those environmental aspects which the organization can control and over which it can be expected to have an influence. It does not itself state specific environmental performance criteria."

The implication is that two organizations that do similar things and achieve different environmental performance can both conform to ISO 14001. It also implies that the role of ISO 14001 is not to create performance levels or other performance requirements. Those are the responsibility of regulatory authorities in the country where the site or facility is located.

ISO 14001 Certification Complements but Is Not a Substitute for Regulatory Compliance

ISO 14001 registration does not guarantee that a particular facility has achieved the best possible environmental performance, only that it has the basis elements of an EMS in place. The continual improvement mentioned in the standard refers to continual improvement of the management system, not of environmental performance directly.

ISO 14001 describes a management framework. It is not a method for compliance with regulatory requirements, although better compliance may well be a result of effective implementation of an ISO 14001-type EMS. Annex A to ISO 14001, which is informative and does not contain requirements, emphasizes that the basic purpose of an EMS is to provide an organization with a process and a framework to achieve and systematically control the level of environmental performance it sets for itself. The level of performance depends on economic, regulatory, and other circumstances.

An effective EMS, the annex notes, "will not, in itself, necessarily result in an immediate reduction of adverse environmental impacts." Of course, the basic theme is that, over time, organizations with an effective EMS will improve their performance.

Best Available Technology

The ISO 14001 standard does not require that an organization use the best available technology (BAT) in creating its EMS. The introduction to the standard notes that the EMS "should encourage organizations to consider implementation of best available technology where appropriate and where economically viable." It also encourages organizations to consider the cost-effectiveness of such technology. This viewpoint is echoed in Clause 4.3.3 on objectives and targets, where the standard says that organizations must consider, among other factors, "its technological options" when setting objectives and targets. Annex A echoes the language of Clause 4.3.3 by stating that "an organization may consider the use of best available technology where economically viable, cost effective and judged appropriate."

The standards developers avoided any prescriptive requirement that would reduce the flexibility of the standard, especially for small and medium-size companies. A technological requirement would also raise the implementation costs for many companies in developing countries and elsewhere. Also, there is the view that BAT does not necessarily result in improved environmental performance.

Does Not Include Health and Safety

The ISO 14000 standard does not address requirements for occupational health and safety management, and such requirements will not be audited. However, the standard does not prevent organizations from incorporating health and safety issues into their EMS programs. Again, many organizations may adapt an EMS from existing environmental, health, and safety programs. The standard emphasizes, however, that the certification process will only address the EMS aspects required by ISO 14001. (See Chapter 18 for information about occupational health and safety.)

No Need to Reinvent the Wheel

The Introduction to ISO 14001 also points out that ISO 14001 shares many common management principles with ISO 9000. Thus, organizations can adapt an existing ISO 9000 system to form a basis for an EMS. A company need not reinvent the wheel by establishing ISO 14001 elements that are independent of existing management systems.

Environmental management is an integral part of an organization's overall management system and its elements should be coordinated with existing efforts in other areas. (Part 3 of this book discusses ISO 9000/ISO 14000 integration issues.)

Level and Complexity of the EMS

When an organization registers to ISO 14001 or self-declares compliance, it declares that a specific EMS complies with the standard. The EMS can cover the entire organization, a specific facility or operating unit, or several facilities. The organization must decide the level of detail and complexity of the EMS and decide whether the EMS applies to specific activities, processes, and products.

ISO 14001—Basic Terms and Definitions

A key goal of the entire ISO 14000 process is to create a common international language for environmental management. To that end, definitions are critical and have been the subject of lengthy debate in the ISO 14000 development process.

Organization

Organization is referred to in Clause 3.12 of ISO 14001 as "a company, corporation, firm, authority or institution, or part or combination thereof, whether incorporated or not, public or private, that has its own functions and administration." This is a broad definition that can encompass almost any type of organization that produces products and/or services. A note to the definition emphasizes that "for organizations with more than one operating unit, a single operating unit may be defined as an organization." If a company is registering to ISO 14001, the actual scope of the registration may apply to a site, a plant, an operation that is part of a site, or several sites that share the same environmental management system. It is up to the organization, working with the registrar, to define the precise scope of the EMS and the products, processes, or services to which it applies. (See Chapter 20 for more details on defining the scope of the EMS for ISO 14001 registration purposes.)

Environment

The *environment* is defined in Clause 3.2 of ISO 14001 as the "surroundings in which an organization operates, including air, water, land, natural resources, flora, fauna, humans and their interrelation." A note to the definition states that the "surroundings in this context extend from within the organization to the global system." Like the definition of *organization,* this is also a broad definition. It encourages organizations to consider a wide variety of environmental impacts. From a practical point of view, however, the environment that concerns a company most directly would be the surroundings in which an organization's activities, products, and service have a significant environmental impact and over which the organization can exercise some reasonable control or influence. This influence and control can extend from local through regional and even global conditions, depending on the nature of the organization.

Environmental Aspect

An *environmental aspect* is defined in Clause 3.3 of ISO 14001 as an "element of an organization's activities, products or services that can interact with the environment." A note defines a significant environmental aspect as "an environmental aspect that has or can have a significant environmental impact."

As will be discussed in the next chapter, it is up to the organization to first identify the environmental aspects of its products, processes, and services when setting up an EMS. Then it explores the impacts of those products, processes, and services and identifies those that are significant.

Environmental Impact

An *environmental impact* is "any change to the environment, whether adverse or beneficial, wholly or partially resulting from an organization's activities, products or services." The environmental aspects of an organization's activities result in environmental impacts.

Environmental Management System

An *environmental management system* is "the part of the overall management system that includes organizational structure, planning activities, responsibilities, practices, procedures, processes and resources for developing, implementing, achieving, reviewing and maintaining the environmental policy."

Environmental Management System Audit

An *Environmental Management System audit* is a "systematic and documented verification process of objectively obtaining and evaluating evidence to determine whether an organization's environmental management system conforms to the environmental management system audit criteria set by the organization, and for communication of the results of this process to management." The EMS audit is not the same as an audit for regulatory compliance; an EMS audit evaluates the management system whereas an audit for regulatory compliance focuses on environmental performance. (Chapter 9 discusses these distinctions in greater detail.)

Environmental Performance

Environmental performance refers to "measurable results of the environmental management system, related to an organization's control of its environmental aspects, based on its environmental policy, objectives and targets."[3] This is also a broad definition.

The scope and extent of the environmental performance of concern to the EMS is defined by the way the organization defines its environmental aspects.

Continual Improvement

Continual improvement refers to the "process of enhancing the environmental management system to achieve improvements in overall environmental performance in line with the organization's environmental policy." A note to the definition emphasizes that "the process need not take place in all areas of activity simultaneously." This definition, the subject of vigorous debate during the standards development process, refers to continual improvement of the system, not necessarily continual improvement of environmental performance itself. Thus, an organization can work toward an increasingly more efficient EMS, one that ensures that environmental performance complies with government regulations but does not go beyond the baseline performance set by regulations. The expectation, however, is that system improvement will lead inevitably to performance improvement.

CONCLUSION

The details of the ISO 14001 standard are discussed in the next chapter of this book. The standard is relatively short. The primary clauses are no more than nine pages long. The requirements are straightforward and deceptively simple. As the familiar saying goes, "The devil is in the details." Companies that have well-developed management systems in place, such as ISO 9000, are well situated to comply with ISO 14001 requirements. Companies with no systems or less-developed systems face a greater challenge. The next part of this book offers a detailed road map to meet that challenge.

BIOGRAPHIES

Tom Tibor and Ira Feldman, Esq.

Tom Tibor is president of Gateway Communications, a company specializing in developing print publications and video programs for business, training, and education. Mr. Tibor has written and edited several regulatory and standards publications, including *The ISO 9000 Handbook, The ISO 9000 Registered Company Directory* and reports on European Community medical device and product liability directives. He has also written and produced a variety of video programs for government, industry and associations. Mr. Tibor is a member of the U.S. Technical Advisory Group to ISO Technical Committee 207 on environmental management.

Ira Feldman is president of gt strategies + solutions, an interdisciplinary environmental management consulting firm in Washington, D.C. He co-chairs the ISO 14000 Legal Issues Forum and was recently elected Vice Chair of the U.S. Sub-TAG on environmental performance evaluation. He has served as a U.S. "expert" (i.e., international delegate) to the ISO 14000 process for SC4 (environmental performance evaluation) and SC6 (terms and definitions). Formerly, Mr. Feldman was special counsel in the Office of Compliance at U.S. EPA Headquarters, where he directed the Environmental Leadership program and chaired the taskforce that revised the Agency's policies on environmental auditing and self-disclosure. Before joining the EPA, he practiced environmental law in the private sector, with particular emphasis on the environmental aspects of large-scale merger, acquisition, and real estate transactions.

Tibor and Feldman coauthored *ISO 14000: A Guide to the New Environmental Management Standards* (Irwin, 1996).

NOTES

1. There is some difference of opinion regarding the role of ISO 14004, even among the standards developers. The standard is not designed to give the impression that implementing ISO 14004 results in a system that is superior to, or exceeds, ISO 14001. According to this view, ISO 14004 is not "better" than ISO 14001 nor does it necessarily describe an "environmental excellence program" that goes beyond the basics of ISO 14001. The ISO 14001 standard contains all the necessary elements of an effective EMS program.

2. Although the generic standard is designed to apply to all types and sizes of businesses, it remains to be seen whether small to medium-size enterprises (SMEs) will find the standard appealing or useful.

3. As explained in Chapter 8 on environmental performance evaluation, it is possible to have environmental performance without an environmental management system or to measure performance without developing an EMS.

PART TWO

Implementing ISO 14001

CHAPTER 3

ISO 14001 Implementation—
Getting Started

Reeva I. Schiffman, B. Tod Delaney, and Scott Fleming

INTRODUCTION AND OVERVIEW

The underlying premise of ISO 14000 is improvement of environmental performance through self-regulation and market-driven pressure. An environment management system (EMS) provides organizations with order and consistency, which enables them to address environmental concerns through the allocation of resources, assignment of responsibilities, and ongoing evaluation of practices, procedures, and processes.

An EMS is essential to an organization's ability to anticipate and meet its environmental objectives and to ensure continuous compliance with national and/or international requirements. An EMS provides a framework to balance and integrate economic and environmental interests. Designing an EMS is an ongoing and interactive process. The structure, responsibilities, practices, procedures, processes, and resources for implementing environmental policies, objectives, and targets must be coordinated with existing efforts in other areas, including operations, finance, quality, and occupational health and safety.

ISO 14001 requires that an organization develop an environmental management program to address all of its environmental objectives and targets and describe how each will be achieved. The program must include a specific plan that describes the actions required to meet each objective and target, the person(s) responsible for meeting each objective, and a timescale detailing when each target will be attained. Objectives and targets can be prioritized within the program, but all objectives must be included.

The management program can also be subdivided into multiple action plans that apply to a specific project, process, or product, or a single program can be developed to achieve the environmental objectives and targets of the organization. The project management of an EMS should be approached in the same manner as any other project.

The project management approach will encourage the optimum use of resources to complete the EMS on time, within budget constraints, and pursuant to specification. A Gantt chart, that displays time and schedule information, is a useful management tool for highlighting the critical action steps, timings, and milestones throughout the development of the EMS program.

Implementing an EMS will likely be easier in small-to-medium-size companies because decision makers and responsible managers are closer to the workings of the operations and product design. Small companies may be able to avoid getting bogged down in a sea of paper in their documentation efforts. Stakeholders and interested parties are not as broad and diverse for a smaller company. Less sophisticated training and communications systems will likely suffice, and decisions to change current practices and implement system enhancements will likely be easier to execute.

In addition, if an organization is already ISO 9000–certified, many of the materials already prepared for that certification can be used for ISO 14000, with only minor revisions. For example, organization and personnel procedures, records and control of documents, and audit and review procedures can be used for both ISO 9000 and ISO 14000.

Finally, the level of effort required to implement ISO 14000 depends to a large extent on the state of a company's existing EMS. If a company has systems in place to achieve environmental compliance and foster quality management, initial investments will be minimal. If these elements are not in place, however, this effort can be extensive, requiring significant resources.

FIVE BASIC EMS STEPS

The EMS requirements are contained in Section 4 of ISO 14001. The most basic requirement, in Clause 4.1, is to establish and maintain an EMS that includes all requirements described in the standard. The model for an EMS is based on five basic steps. These are discussed in general terms below and in more detail in the remainder of this chapter.

1. **Commitment and policy.** An organization defines its environmental policy and ensures commitment to it. Top management must commit to continual improvement of the EMS, prevention of pollution, and compliance with applicable law. The environmental policy must be relevant to the nature, scale, and environmental impacts of activities, products, and services. The policy must be documented, available to the public, and communicated to employees.

2. **Planning.** An organization formulates a plan to fulfill its environmental policy. During this planning phase, the organization develops a cross-functional team and identifies significant environmental impacts of activities, products, and services, along with legal and other standards to which the organization subscribes. It then sets objectives and quantifies them wherever practicable.

3. **Implementation.** The third step is to put the plan into action by providing resources and support mechanisms necessary to achieve the environmental policy and the objectives and targets. In this step, the organization defines the roles and responsibilities of all involved in the process, including senior management representatives. It identifies and provides necessary resources. The organization identifies activities and processes with significant environmental impacts and implements procedures to manage those activities and processes. It establishes training procedures and carries them out. It establishes and implements internal and external communications procedures.

4. **Measurement and Evaluation.** The organization measures, monitors, and evaluates its environmental performance against its objectives and targets. It generates specific procedures for conducting performance evaluations. (Chapter 8 discusses environmental performance evaluation in detail.) It monitors and measures processes on a regular basis and tracks performance and conformance with objectives and targets. The organization conducts audits of the EMS to identify areas that require improvement and nonconformances that must be corrected.

5. **Review and Improvement.** The final major step is to develop procedures to review and continually improve the environmental management system, with the objective of improving its overall environmental performance. The organization compares actual performance with its objectives and targets, then identifies and corrects the root causes of deficiencies. It also identifies further opportunities for improvement.

Now comes the big question: Where does an organization begin?

Recognize that it is not as important where in the ISO 14001 EMS process an organization starts; the value is in the fact that it begins the implementation process. Implementation strategies will differ from organization to organization depending on factors such as the size of the company, familiarity with total quality management (ISO 9000) principles, and the status of existing environmental management systems. Figure 3–1 illustrates one potential scenario, using a flow chart, for implementing the ISO 14000 EMS process.

COMMITMENT AND POLICY

Environmental Policy—Clause 4.2

Clause 4.2 requires the organization to define an environmental policy. ISO 14001 defines an *environmental policy* in Clause 3.9 as a "statement by the organization of its intentions and principles in relation to its overall environmental performance which provides a framework for action and for the setting of its environmental objectives and targets."

FIGURE 3–1

ISO 14001 Implementation Process

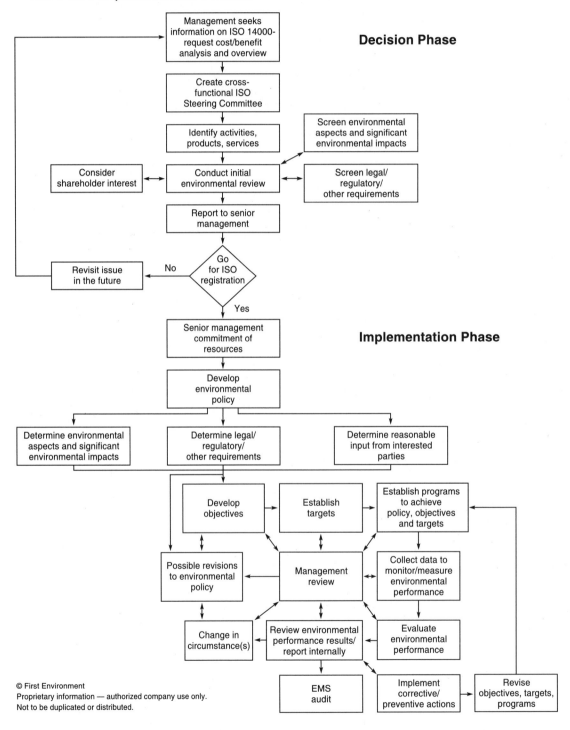

Clause 4.2 requires that the environmental policy, whatever its specific contents, meets the following criteria:

- Is appropriate to the nature, scale, and environmental impacts of the organization's activities, products, and services.
- Includes a commitment to continual improvement.
- Includes a commitment to prevention of pollution.
- Includes a commitment to comply with relevant environmental legislation and regulations, and with other requirements to which the organization subscribes.
- Provides the framework for setting and reviewing environmental objectives and targets.
- Is documented, implemented, maintained, and communicated to all employees.
- Is available to the public.

The environmental policy gives an overall sense of the organization's direction and commitment to the environment. Familiar policy statements include phrases such as these:

- "Company X is committed to protecting the environment and the health and safety of all its employees and customers."
- "All of Company X's plants and products comply with all applicable governmental standards as well as Company X's internal standards and policies."
- "Company X is dedicated to implementing methods and strategies for preventing pollution, reducing waste, and conserving resources."

Includes Internal Policies and Standards

The requirements to which the organization can declare compliance can also include internal policies, including those for health and safety, existing audit program standards, corporate emergency response policies, and other such requirements.

Commitment to Compliance

The policy must reflect the organization's commitment to comply with all applicable laws and regulations. ISO 14001 registration is not a substitute for compliance; it complements compliance with national laws and regulations.

Prevention of Pollution

Prevention of pollution in the context of ISO 14001 is a broad concept and is defined in Clause 3.13 of ISO 14001 as the "use of processes, practices, materials or products that avoid, reduce or control pollution, which may include recycling, treatment, process changes, control mechanisms, efficient use of resources and material substitution." This broad definition offers companies and nations around the world flexibility in interpreting the kinds of pollution prevention methods they can use to fulfill these requirements. Note that the definition does not include waste since waste need not be pollution.

Continual Improvement

Continual improvement refers to continual improvement of the EMS. It is defined in Clause 3.1 as the "process of enhancing the environmental management system to achieve improvements in overall environmental performance in line with the organization's environmental policy." A note to the definition adds that the process need not take place in all areas of activity simultaneously. There is general agreement among the standards developers that the basic purpose of improving the system is to improve environmental performance, but the standard focuses on improving the system, not on the results achieved by the system.

Set Up a Task Force/Steering Committee

An organization can begin the process of developing an EMS and defining its environmental policy by setting up a task force or a steering committee comprised of members involved in all facets of the organization. Team members should be selected from appropriate management levels to ensure peer review. Collectively, the team should be multidisciplinary, representing all facets of the organization, from management systems, finance, and quality to direct experience with the type of operations at hand.

Team members should have appropriate expertise, knowledge of operations, and proficiency in auditing techniques. They should be educated with regard to the ISO 14000 requirements and should be impartial.

By assembling consensus groups of employees from all business units within the company, employees will respect the program and will appreciate what is being implemented. As will be seen in later discussions, employee motivation is essential to the successful development of an EMS.

Once assembled, this team should critically review the products and services produced by the organization. Before an organization can develop a meaningful, plausible, and realistic environmental policy, it has to identify and thoroughly understand the components of its products and services.

Top Management Commitment

EMS implementation is driven from the top. If one element is to be singled out as the most important ingredient in the successful implementation of an environmental management system, it is strong, dedicated commitment and total involvement from senior management.

Simply stated, *without top management commitment, the environmental management system will fail.*

For the EMS to be successful, the organization's top-level management and its facility managers must champion their environmental responsibilities, strongly support the EMS, and take full responsibility for its implementation. Recent experience with ISO 9000 has shown that one of the most significant pitfalls in implementation of total quality management principles has been uncommitted top management, standing on the sidelines, neither understanding nor believing in the requirements of the ISO 9000 standard.

Senior management commitment may originate from a variety of sources, including direct and indirect marketplace pressures, regulatory requirements, growth ambitions, and/or personal beliefs in the need to balance business goals with environmental responsibilities. Regardless of the source, true commitment towards improving the environmental management of an organization is essential.

Commitment cannot be delegated and then ignored and does not involve the blind approval of procedures. Senior management must go beyond simply introducing the EMS framework because the implementation process will not build momentum on its own.

Top management must play an active, visible, daily role in the implementation process. Upper management must make its purpose clear to its employees and foster employee awareness and motivation while making certain that all employees are environmentally accountable. Employees must know top management is genuinely behind the drive for ISO 14001 implementation.

Management can demonstrate its commitment in a wide variety of ways: actively participating in the project, defining and implementing key policies, providing funding and allocating the appropriate resources, reviewing and approving essential processes, applying pressure and support when and where needed, and maintaining the overall environmental effort as a high priority for the organization. This effort on the part of upper management cannot end once the EMS is established and implemented; rather, top management must remain focused and committed to continual improvement of the EMS.

Initial Environmental Review

With an EMS team and senior commitment in place, the next step is to define the current status of the organization. The organization must ask and answer the question: Where are we now? The current position of an organization with regard to the environment can be evaluated by means of an initial environmental review.

Remember: An initial environmental review is *not required* by ISO 14001. Annex A to ISO 14001, however, in Clause A.3.1 *recommends* that an organization, especially one with no existing environmental management system, should "establish its current position with regard to the environment by means of a review."

What the Review Should Address

The review should address the full range of operating conditions, normal as well as abnormal operations, including potential emergencies. Clause 4.1.3 of the ISO 14004 guidance standard suggests these areas of inquiry for an initial environmental review:

1. Identification of legislative and regulatory requirements.
2. Identification of environmental aspects of its activities, products, or services to determine those that have or can have significant environmental impacts and liabilities.
3. Evaluation of performance compared with relevant internal criteria, external standards, regulations, codes of practice, and sets of principles and guidelines.
4. Existing environmental management practices and procedures.
5. Identification of the existing policies and procedures dealing with procurement and contracting activities.
6. Feedback from the investigation of previous incidents of noncompliance.
7. Opportunities for competitive advantage.
8. The views of interested parties.
9. Functions or activities of other organizational systems that can enable or impede environmental performance.

Independence and Objectivity A consultant or in-house personnel can conduct the initial review; however, this assessment of the organization's work and environmental effects must derive from an entirely neutral or independent viewpoint. The future of the EMS may actually depend upon the thoroughness, accuracy, and integrity of the initial review. The results of this initial review will dictate the direction that the organization needs to proceed to achieve ISO 14001 registration.

Brainstorming An organization can begin the review by conducting a brainstorming session involving the EMS team. At least one to three full days should be set aside to begin the initial review process by walking through each activity, process, or service and conducting an assessment of each as it relates, where applicable, to the areas of inquiry described in Clause 4.1.3 of ISO 14004.

The team can collect additional information by using one or more of the following techniques: questionnaires, interviews, checklists, direct inspection and measurement, and records review. Outside sources often provide valuable information. Such organizations include government agencies involved in environmental laws and permits, local or regional libraries or databases, industry associations, business relationships, and professional consultants.

Gap Analysis

During the implementation process, an organization will have to conduct some type of gap analysis to determine gaps between existing processes and procedures and those required by the ISO 14001 standard. This procedure will help identify the improvements required to achieve conformity with the standard. The initial review-related provisions can assist organizations that wish to define the framework, criteria, and requirements of their current EMS.

The gap analysis is not the same as the initial review. The initial review is a tool that can be used to screen and identify the current position of the organization with regard to the environment. Information obtained from the initial environmental review will be evaluated and used to develop the organization's environmental policy. The environmental policy sets the framework for where you want to go. Thus, the initial review tells you where you are now. The gap analysis measures the distance between where you are and where you need to go.

Every EMS will include such basic elements as policy, planning and goal-setting, programs (i.e., training), measurement, auditing, reporting and communications, documentation and recordkeeping, and management review. These components will vary from organization to organization and may include requirements of environmental laws and regulations, industry commitments, and other applicable criteria, such as internal requirements.

A word of caution. If your company is not in the practice of performing routine environmental compliance or system audits, it is possible that an initial review might reveal previously unknown noncompliance situations. Therefore, an organization should consult with its attorneys regarding the feasibility of conducting the review under the cloak of attorney/client privilege. (See Chapters 10 and 11 for a discussion of legal issues.)

Develop the Environmental Policy

Now that the initial review has evaluated the organization's activities, products, and services; the associated environmental aspects and impacts; legal and other requirements; and existing management practices, procedures, and policies, the organization can begin to formulate and develop its *environmental policy.*

The environmental policy should recognize that all aspects of an organization's operations may have an impact on the environment. The policy statement should be relevant and straightforward. It is a declaration that environmental protection is a priority and that the organization is committed to continued improvement of environmental performance and compliance with laws and regulations. In essence, the policy statement establishes an overall sense of direction and sets the parameters of action for an organization.

The environmental policy should be built upon the organization's mission, its objectives, and its integral business focus. The policy should incorporate the organization's vision, core values, and beliefs. It should take into account the cultural and ethical position of the organization, in addition to the image to which the organization aspires.

The policy should consider the views of interested parties, including the expectations of shareholders, customers, lenders, regulators, employees, consumers, and community and environmental groups. The policy should incorporate guiding principles

B O X   3–1

DEFINING THE SCOPE OF THE EMS

A key aspect of the initial planning process is to define the scope of the EMS, either for internal implementation purposes or for registration purposes. The registration audit focuses on an EMS whose scope should be clearly defined in terms of products, services, and processes. Of course, many organizations already have an EMS of some type, and thus the scope of the EMS is already defined, either explicitly or implicitly.

The requirements of ISO 14001 allow the organization flexibility in defining the scope of its EMS. An EMS can be designed at the site or facility level, across several facilities or to encompass the entire enterprise. The decision how to define the scope depends on many factors, including the type, size, and structure of the organization and its products and services. It is also important to note that an organization need not introduce an EMS everywhere at the same time. It can take an incremental approach to EMS implementation.

The following are some factors to keep in mind when defining the scope of the EMS:

- What is the scope of the existing environmental management system, if any?
- How well established are existing environmental management systems? The organization may choose to begin an ISO 14001 pilot project at a site with a relatively advanced EMS to achieve early success. Alternatively, it may be advantageous to begin where nothing exists.
- What products and services does the organization provide? The scope of the EMS may be confined to facilities that provide the same product or service or to all facilities.
- Are there facilities or sites with a higher priority need for an EMS? This may be due to critical environmental problems at certain facilities or sites. Or the need may be driven by the location of the site in another country, such as in Europe where there may be a demand to register the EMS to the Eco-Management and Audit Scheme (EMAS).
- What is the structure of the organization? For example, if it is highly centralized, an enterprise-wide EMS may be more appropriate. If de-centralized, however, ISO 14001 implementation may be planned at the site level, with the decision left to each plant.
- Are some sites registered to an ISO 9000 standard? If so, the scope of the EMS can be defined similarly to the ISO 9000 quality management system.

Finally, there are resource factors that inevitably will come into play. The organization may not have the resources to implement the EMS across the entire enterprise. Sometimes, the scope decision can only come after a thorough initial review that provides additional information about the existing EMS and its level of development.

The Editors

that focus the actions of the organization and provide an ethical position in areas of importance to the organization and its stakeholders.

In addition, the policy must include a commitment to continual improvement, prevention of pollution, coordination with other organizational policies, specific local or regional conditions, and compliance with relevant environmental regulations, laws, and other criteria to which the organization subscribes.

Management must draft a policy that is appropriate to its organization. Specific examples of issues that can be addressed in the policy include commitments to do the following:

- Minimize any significant adverse environmental impacts of new developments through the use of the integrated environmental management procedures and planning.
- Develop environmental performance evaluation procedures and associated indicators.
- Make use of life-cycle thinking.
- Design products in such a way as to minimize their environmental impacts in production, use, and disposal.
- Prevent pollution, reduce waste and the consumption of resources (materials, fuel, and energy), and commit to recovery and recycling, as opposed to disposal, where feasible.
- Provide education and training.
- Share environmental experiences.
- Involve and communicate with interested parties.
- Work towards sustainable development.
- Encourage the use of EMS by suppliers and contractors.

PLANNING

During the planning stage, the areas identified during the initial review warrant a more detailed evaluation. Clause 4.3 of ISO 14001 includes four basic steps in planning the EMS:

1. Identify environmental aspects of the organization's activities that it can control and influence to determine which are associated with significant environmental impacts.
2. Identify and maintain access to legal and all other requirements that apply to the environmental aspects of the activities, products, and services.
3. Set, establish, and review objectives and targets.
4. Establish the EMS by designating responsibility for meeting targets within a specified means and timeframe.

Environmental Aspects (4.3.1)

An organization's policy, objective, and targets should be based on knowledge about the environmental aspects and significant environmental impacts associated with its activities, products, and services. An *environmental aspect* is defined in Clause 3.3 as an "element of an organization's activities, products or services that can interact with the environment." A note to the definition adds that "a significant environmental aspect is an environmental aspect that has or can have a significant environmental impact."

Clause 4.3.1 requires that the organization establish and maintain an up-to-date procedure to "identify the environmental aspects of its activities, products or services that it can control and over which it can be expected to have an influence, in order to determine those which have or can have significant impacts on the environment."

The organization must then make sure that the aspects "related to these significant impacts are considered in setting its environmental objectives." An environmental aspect could involve a discharge, an emission, or reuse of a material, among other things. An *environmental impact* is defined in Clause 3.4 as "any change to the environment, whether adverse or beneficial, wholly or partially resulting from an organization's activities, products or services." Identification of the environmental aspects is an ongoing process that determines current and potential impacts of an organization's activities on the environment.

Types of Environmental Aspects and Impacts

Various types of aspects/impacts should be analyzed, including the following:

- Operational aspects.
- Aspects associated with the product or service provided.
- Aspects associated with contractors.

The methods used to identify these aspects/impacts include audits, monitoring data, input from others, and outside audits. The process used to identify aspects should be clearly spelled out because it is a requirement of the certification process. The aspects/impacts can be analyzed via a variety of methods including these:

- Risk assessment.
- Immediate employee/environmental impact.
- Regulatory compliance.
- Impact in terms of compliance with organization standards.
- Consistency with best business/industry practice, also known as benchmarking.

Determining Significant Environmental Aspects

The next step is to prioritize the environmental aspects and impacts. The ISO 14001 standard focuses attention on *those impacts that the organization can control and over which it can be expected to have an influence.*

It can be an imposing task to develop, evaluate, and maintain the list of aspects and determine which aspects are significant. An organization can tackle this complex assignment by breaking down its operations into a series of activities or processes. Flowcharts can be used to map out each process. Normal, start-up, and emergency operating conditions must be considered.

The organization should identify as many environmental aspects as possible associated with each activity or process. At the conclusion of this step, the organization will have an extensive list of environmental aspects. It should review the list of aspects and identify as many actual and potential positive and negative impacts associated with each aspect.

The organization then screens these aspects and develops a list of significant aspects; the significance of each differ from one organization to another. Material Safety Data Sheets may be a useful source of information during the screening process. The degree of detail required to evaluate the environmental aspects depends on the likely environmental significance of the aspect, the extent of concern of other interested parties, and existing knowledge as to the type of effect.

Any aspects that are subject to environmental regulations must be considered significant. Remaining aspects must be evaluated individually. The following criteria should assist in further screening the remaining aspects from an environmental standpoint:

- The scale and severity of the impact.
- The likelihood of its occurrence.
- The duration of the impact.

Because an EMS is designed to provide a framework to balance and integrate economic and environmental interests, business and environmental concerns should be evaluated at this stage of the process. The organization should evaluate the impacts in terms of potential regulatory and legal exposure, the difficulty of changing the impact, the cost of changing the impact, the effect of the change on other activities and processes, the concerns of interested parties, and the effect on the public image of the organization. In addition, an organization must consider environmental aspects when developing future projects or processes. Aspects should be considered at the earliest stages of product/project planning.

Ideally, aspect evaluation should include every phase of the operation. A manufacturing facility for example, should evaluate aspects for all phases of the overall operation, from product conception to fabrication, storage, distribution, use, and eventually ultimate disposal.

B O X   3–2

NORTHERN TELECOM'S ENVIRONMENTAL IMPACTS

According to its Internet site on the World Wide Web, Northern Telecom, in its implementation of ISO 14001, focuses on the environmental aspects of its activities. For example, Northern Telecom classifies effects as "controllable," "influenceable," and "unclassified." It defines *controllable* effects as all significant effects that NT could directly control if it so chose. Areas that should be examined include the following:

- Emissions to atmosphere.
- Discharges to water.
- Solid waste generation.
- Land or ground water contamination.
- Consumption of energy and natural resources.
- Noise and odor.

Influenceable effects are those significant effects from goods and services acquired or used by NT that are beyond direct control but can be influenced by NT. Examples include the following:

- Mercury in OEM components.
- Toxics in products and packing materials.

Unclassified effects are those that are currently considered neither controllable nor influenceable but that can be said to have an undesirable effect on the environment.

Since most organizations must work within budget constraints, not all impacts can be addressed at once. Those impacts that are causing obvious damage to the environment or human health should be a priority, as should impacts that are costing the organization a considerable amount of money.

Legal and Regulatory Requirements (4.3.2)

After identification of the significant environmental impacts, the organization must examine the legal and regulatory requirements associated with these aspects and develop methods to track legal and other requirements of its activities, products, and services.

Clause 4.3.2 of ISO 14001 requires the organization to "establish and maintain a procedure to identify and have access to legal and other requirements to which the organization subscribes." These are the requirements directly "applicable to the environmental aspects of its activities, products or services."

The environmental policy requires that an organization be committed to compliance with all relevant legislation and regulations. This is a daunting task. Environmental management is one of the most heavily regulated disciplines, and industry must deal with numerous regulations that often overlap and conflict. Requirements to be identified in an EMS include international, federal, state, regional, and local regulations; legislative acts; laws; certification standards; corporate policies; customer agreements; court decisions; permits; and proposed legislation.

Other requirements might include an organization's internal priorities and criteria that developed because there were no external standards or because the standards failed to meet the organization's needs. An organization might have internal performance criteria in areas including management systems; employee responsibilities; suppliers; contractors; acquisition, property management and divestiture; process risk reduction; process change; energy management; and transportation.

Note that the standard requires that organizations establish and maintain a procedure for identifying and accessing within the organization updated regulatory information directly attributable to the environmental aspects of its activities. It does not require an organization to document the actual requirements, only the procedure used to identify and access the appropriate regulations.

According to ISO 14004, the regulations can exist in several forms:

- Those specific to the activity.
- General environmental laws, licenses, and permits.
- Agreements with public authorities (POTWs).
- Industry-specific regulations.
- Those specific to the organization's products or services.

Many sources are available to help identify environmental regulations and ongoing changes. An organization should contact all levels of government; describe its processes, aspects, and potential impacts; and ask a lot of questions. The organization does not need to divulge its identity while gathering this information. Government representatives can provide valuable information when prodded sufficiently. Industry associations or groups, commercial databases, on-line services, and specialty publications, as well as professional consulting services also provide valuable information.

Although ISO 14001 does not require preparation of a manual of regulations, it is advisable to compile at least one complete set of applicable regulations. This will facilitate accessing current regulations and other legal requirements as well as tracking proposed and amended regulations and other legal requirements. The system should be designed not only to ensure that an organization is in compliance with all current legislation but also to keep the organization abreast of changing and future regulatory requirements.

Ideally, the organization will incorporate the identification procedure with other business practices so that the appropriate regulations are available whenever an organization is evaluating new processes, products, or services. In this way, environmental regulations and concerns can be integrated into the initial decision-making process instead of simply applying end-of-pipe environmental solutions once the process has been implemented.

Objectives and Targets (4.3.3)

The next step in planning the EMS is to establish objectives and targets that support and are consistent with an organization's environmental policy. Clause 4.3.3 of ISO 14001 requires the organization to "establish and maintain documented environmental objectives and targets at each relevant function and level within the organization." Clause 3.7 defines an *environmental objective* as an "overall environmental goal, arising from the environmental policy, that an organization sets itself to achieve, and which is quantified where practicable."

Where the environmental policy outlines the environmental principles and overall environmental goals of the organization, the objectives and targets translate these principles into specific and measurable terms.

Establishing objectives and targets for the EMS links the established policy with the system implementation. The environmental policy document guides an organization in establishing objectives. Targets should be in line with objectives, time constrained, measurable, and clear in their accountability for action.

It is important to note the distinction between policy, objective, and target. A policy is a general, higher-level commitment. An objective is a broad plan to help achieve the policy. A target is the goal (i.e., numerical) that measures the success of the objectives. For example:

Policy: The organization is committed to finding substitutes for toxic chemicals.

Objective: Reduce use of chemical solvents and substitute biodegradable cleaners.

Target: Reduce use of chemical solvents 80 percent by 1998.

Objectives and targets must be consistent and should be incorporated into the organization's strategic plan. They must support legislative compliance and impact mitigation, business requirements, and reasonable views of interested parties.

The following are some possible objectives:

- Reduce waste and the depletion of resources.
- Reduce or eliminate the release of pollutants into the environment.
- Promote environmental awareness among employees and the community.

Environmental targets can then be set to achieve these objectives within a specified time frame. The targets should be specific and measurable. Measurement can usually be in the form of environmental performance indicators such as quantity of raw material or energy used, quantity of a specific compound emitted, waste produced per quantity of finished product, percent waste recycled, or number of environmental incidents/accidents.

Achievable Objectives and Targets

Objectives and targets should not be "wish lists" for environmental performance. An organization's EMS will be evaluated based on its ability to achieve its objectives and targets, so it is imperative that they are realistic. Objectives and targets should be linked to environmental performance indicators so that continual improvement can be monitored. (See Chapter 8 for a detailed discussion of environmental performance evaluation and environmental performance indicators.)

Where practical, objectives and targets must be applied to each department function or process that has an environmental impact. Those personnel responsible for achieving objectives and targets should be involved in establishing them. This will ensure that the targets are practical and will give the personnel more of a stake in meeting them.

Objectives and targets must address regulatory compliance, significant environmental aspects, technology options, and pollution prevention along with the financial, business, and operational requirements.[1] Other considerations can include continuous improvement, stakeholder expectations, and synergy with the organization's overall objectives and business requirements. Although ISO 14001 encourages an organization to consider use of the best available technology, the standard does not address specific technology use requirements.

Environmental Management Program (4.3.4)

The final planning step requires establishing and maintaining an environmental management system that can achieve the company's objectives and targets. According to Clause 4.3.4, the organization must do the following:

- Designate responsibility for achieving objectives and targets at each relevant function and level.
- Provide the means for fulfilling the objectives and targets.
- Determine a time frame for achieving them.

Basically, the EMS details what must be done, by whom, how, and by when. The standard points out that the EMS should be amended to ensure that it applies to "new developments and new or modified activities, products, or services."

IMPLEMENTATION

Once an organization establishes the planning elements, it should prepare and implement the actual environmental management programs and operational controls. Section 4.4 of ISO 14001, includes seven clauses that describe the implementation phase:

1. Structure and responsibility.
2. Training, awareness, and competence.

3. Communication.

4. Environmental management system documentation.

5. Document control.

6. Operational control.

7. Emergency preparedness and response.

These requirements are described in general in this section. Other chapters in this book go into more detail regarding implementation areas.

The programs, controls, and procedures must address the objectives and targets. They are the systems that realize an organization's objectives and targets. Environmental management planning will be most effective if it is integrated into the organization's strategic plan. Environmental management programs should address schedules, resources, and responsibilities for achieving the organization's objectives and targets at every relevant level of the organization.

The success of an environmental management program depends to a great extent on how well it measures environmental performance. Measurement is important because if an organization cannot measure performance, it cannot be improved. Continuous improvement should not be viewed as a last step but rather as an integral part of every aspect of the environmental management system. As such, setting goals and using performance measures are crucial to maintaining continuous improvement.

All too often, corporate mission statements are not readily translated into the concrete objectives that are necessary to guide company operations. The environmental vision must be tied to specific goals that can be integrated into an organization's business strategy. The goals should be challenging, yet achievable and measurable so that employees will remain motivated and the process can be managed. Corporate policies can be translated into manageable goals by starting with the broad statements and breaking them down into increasingly specific elements until measurable performance parameters are developed.

Performance measures link goals, strategy, and effective implementation. Studies have shown that the five key success factors for environmental programs are support from senior management; an involved operating company; clear goals; effective performance measures; and results linked to reward and recognition.

Structure and Responsibility (4.4.1)

To achieve its environmental objectives, an organization should focus and align its people, systems, strategy, resources, and structure. Clause 4.4.1 of ISO 14001 requires the organization to do the following:

- Define, document, and communicate roles, responsibility, and authority to "facilitate effective environmental management."

- "Provide resources essential to the implementation and control of the environmental management system," including human, technological and financial.

- Appoint a management representative who ensures that the EMS requirements are "established, implemented and maintained" and reports on the performance of the EMS to top management as part of the review and improvement cycle.

The organization must define and make available the appropriate human, physical, and financial resources essential to implementing its policies and objectives. Management must define and document the organizational structure, clearly defining job descriptions and responsibilities for all employees whose work functions impact or potentially impact the environment.

The organization accomplishes this requirement by preparing schematic organizational charts outlining technical and functional interfaces along with job descriptions. The level of detail is based on necessity, but the job function must be clear, as well as the boundaries of authority and responsibility. Additionally, lines of communication within the organization must also be understood. Organizations have different structures and need to understand and define environmental responsibilities based on their own processes.

Employees at all levels should be accountable for environmental performance in support of the EMS. Adequate authority should be delegated to individuals to allow them to carry out their designated job functions. They should have a clear understanding of their responsibility and be able to take appropriate action. Everyone should be made aware of and feel responsible for completing the requirements of the EMS.

The Management Representative

Senior management must provide the resources required to implement and maintain the EMS. Senior management must take opportunities to demonstrate its commitment to the policy for it to receive respect from customers, suppliers, and employees. In addition, top management should assign responsibility for the implementation, maintenance, and improvement of the EMS to a management representative.

The management representative should report directly to the CEO. Larger organizations may form a team to fulfill these responsibilities. The following attributes/talents should be sought in an EMS management representative, or "champion":

- Project-management skills.
- Interpersonal or facilitation skills.
- Information systems skills.
- Communication skills.
- Analytical skills.
- Legal and technical research capabilities.
- Systems auditing skills.

In smaller companies, one person will likely be the champion and must have the ability to wear many hats.

The champion must ensure that the EMS complies with the requirements of ISO 14001. This position requires extensive knowledge of the environmental issues concerning the organization and a clear understanding of the organization's purpose, structure, and flow. The champion should have the authority to establish, implement, and maintain the EMS and to enforce the requirements of the standard. There must be a direct link or traceability to senior management. The standard does not require a full-time champion. Implementation of an EMS in accordance with ISO 14001 will require establishing several project implementation teams. The champion should be responsible for defining, establishing, and directing the overall activities of the teams. The teams should consist of employees who understand their part of the business and know how to document it.

Additional duties of the champion can include defining, documenting, and scheduling a plan for ISO 14001 implementation, developing and instituting a training program, working with senior management to develop continual improvement programs, and ensuring the organization's readiness for third-party audits. The champion should try to involve everyone within the organization in order to create companywide involvement.

Employee Training, Awareness, and Competence (4.4.2)

Implementing an environmental management system to comply with ISO 14001 will require change. People tend to resist change because they do not understand the reasons for it or the consequences of it. This lack of understanding can be a significant barrier to ISO 14001 implementation. People will not become involved in a process they know very little about. It is therefore essential that, before an organization begins the process of implementing ISO 14001, it informs its employees about the standard and the specifics of the EMS.

No amount of management can motivate an uninformed employee. Tasks cannot simply be delegated without first explaining their purpose and the consequences of not completing them. If employees perceive the efforts required to implement and maintain ISO 14001 as temporary or do not fully understand the ramifications of noncompliance with the EMS, they will resist implementation efforts.

It is therefore essential that everyone in the organization understands the requirements of ISO 14001 and comprehends why achieving and maintaining registration is important to the company. ISO 14001 implementation requires full participation of all employees. Management therefore needs to provide environmental awareness training and be committed to a trained and effective workforce. Through education and training, employees will begin to understand the implementation process and how ISO 14001 affects them. Motivation of personnel begins with their understanding of the tasks they are expected to perform and how these tasks fall into the overall EMS.

The specific requirements of Clause 4.4.2, on training, include the following:

- Identify training needs.

- Provide appropriate training to "all personnel whose work may create a significant impact upon the environment."

- Ensure that personnel who perform tasks that cause significant environmental impacts are competent on the basis of appropriate education training and/or experience.
- Establish and maintain procedures for awareness training of employees at each relevant function and level to ensure awareness of the following:
  - Importance of conforming with the environmental policy, procedures, and requirements of the EMS.
  - Significant environmental impacts, actual or potential, of their work activities and the environmental benefits of improved personal performance.
  - Their roles and responsibilities in the EMS.
  - Potential consequences of departure from specified operating procedures.

Developing a Training Program

The standard focuses training requirements on all employees whose work has or potentially has an environmental impact. These employees must be trained with regard to the environmental consequences of their work.

To accomplish this task, the organization must first have a clear and thorough understanding of the significant environmental impacts associated with its full range of activities, products, and services. Once the organization recognizes the impacts, individual personnel can then be identified and targeted for specific training.

Personnel from all levels within the organization should be considered, from top management, through middle management to line management, down to operations. Anyone who is involved in maintaining the EMS and meeting the environmental objectives and goals should be included. Therefore, the training should also involve financial, public affairs, research and development, engineering, and marketing personnel. Marketing, for example, serves as the link to the customer. Marketing personnel know the customer's needs and can help the organization understand the customer's priorities and expectations in terms of the organization's environmental commitment and performance.

After identifying those personnel who require detailed training, the next step is to determine what type of training is necessary to implement the EMS. The type and extent of training will depend on both the specific job function and potential environmental impact of the position along with the employee's knowledge base and educational background. Employees must be qualified to perform their assigned tasks.

Employee training programs should include compliance with the environmental policy and objectives, procedures, customer and stakeholder concerns, the environmental effects of work activities, the individual role and responsibility of employees in achieving compliance with the requirements, and the potential consequences of departure from the stated procedures.

Training can consist of formal education, past work experience, courses, seminars, or even supervised on-the-job training. Consideration should be given to both experience and demonstrated skills. The need to require formal qualification of personnel performing operations that can have a direct and significant impact on the environment should be evaluated and implemented where necessary. Similar qualifications are expected of any outside personnel or contractors who work at the site.

Documenting Training

Documentation of training is essential. ISO 14001, in Clause 4.5.3 Records, requires that individual training records be kept for all employees. An authorized individual must maintain and approve a formal training record. The formal training record reflects the current work assignment and documents the employee's education, experience, and training.

The organization must establish and maintain documented procedures for determining the qualifications of employees, assigning qualified individuals to the appropriate tasks, identifying required training needs for personnel, and initiating and maintaining records.

The management of training issues should include a list of employees by department, specifying the type of training required, general educational background of the employee, and specific coursework completed along with any other significant information.

For example, if an employee is trained in a new or modified procedure, a sign-off sheet can be used as evidence that the employee has learned the procedure. This sign-off sheet is a record and may be kept in the training file as evidence that the training was performed. External auditors will rely heavily upon training records to verify that the training program meets ISO 14001 requirements. Therefore, complete, understandable training documentation is essential for ISO 14001 certification registration. (See Chapter 4 for a detailed discussion of employee training and awareness.)

Communication and Reporting (4.4.3)

Effective communication and reporting is essential for the successful implementation of an EMS. Communication and reporting refers to the dissemination of information both internally and externally, where desired.

In Clause 4.4.3, ISO 14001 requires the organization to establish and maintain procedures for internal and external communication regarding "its environmental aspects and environmental management system." Procedures for internal communication are required between the various levels and functions of the organization.

Procedures for external communication must cover "receiving, documenting and responding to relevant communication from external interested parties." The organization must also consider "processes for external communication on its significant environmental aspects and record its decision."

The organization should establish procedures to provide information that demonstrates management's commitment to the environment. The material should consider environmental issues associated with the organization's activities, products, or services and should foster increased awareness of the organization's policies, objectives, targets, and programs.

The EMS should include a process for communicating the organization's environmental policy to both employees and the public as well as for receiving and responding to employee concerns and the concerns of other interested parties.

The organization should implement a procedure to ensure that results from monitoring and system verification, including audit and management review, are communicated to appropriate people within the organization. These communications should be adequate to support continuous improvement and should in fact recognize employees (or interested parties) for their suggestions and/or successes.

BOX 3-3

WHO ARE INTERESTED PARTIES?

Interested parties are defined in ISO 14001 as individuals or groups "concerned with or affected by the performance of an organization." This is a broad definition and includes groups that vary widely in the level of their stake in the organization and how affected they may be by its operations. Interested parties can include local, national or international groups and organizations, including the following:

- Environmental groups and other non-governmental organizations.
- Customers and suppliers.
- Local community groups.
- Insurance companies.
- Government regulators and legislative bodies.
- The media.
- Company employees.
- Management representatives.
- Shareholders and other investors.
- Academic and research institutions.

These groups may have a wide variety of information needs, based on their interests. These needs can include financial, EH&S, legal, statistical and other types of information. Thus, the organization may need to use several methods to identify the views of interested parties. Some of these methods include the following:

- Surveys and questionnaires.
- Scheduled meetings and workshops.
- Market research studies.
- Reviews of public statements or reports by interested parties.
- Regular participation in activities of interested parties, such as local community groups.

With regard to both internal and external communication, two-way communication should be encouraged. Insufficient and untimely two-way communication can be a significant barrier to change. Without effective communication, employees will not understand the full nature of the EMS nor the reasons behind its use. There will then be little acceptance of the EMS, let alone genuine commitment.

Internal Communication Methods

Internal communication can be accomplished in a variety of ways. Management can schedule informal meetings for communicating information with all employees affected by ISO 14001 implementation. Early in the process, these meetings can include an overview of ISO 14001 and its importance to the organization, the environmental policy, training plans, and employee responsibilities, along with the status of the implementation process.

As the EMS is implemented, the meetings will include results from internal monitoring, corrective action, environmental incidents, noncompliance issues, and improvement opportunities. Newsletters can be another effective tool for internal communication. They can be distributed monthly and should include updates on the progress of the EMS implementation, recognition of employee contributions to the project, and information on what is expected to be completed next.

Continuous improvement is a key element of the environmental policy. Line personnel who are closest to the operation can be a valuable source of information concerning process improvement and pollution-prevention opportunities. There should be a system in place to effectively communicate their input and ideas concerning continuous improvement. The organization can maintain an environmental hotline or even a suggestion box for this purpose.

External Communication Methods

External communication can be accomplished through a company's annual report, industry publications, government records, or even paid advertising. It is important to remember that communications with external parties must be documented. Regardless of the method used for communication, the information should be understandable and adequately explained, verifiable, accurate, and presented in a consistent form to be comparable over time.

Environmental Management System Documentation (4.4.4)

In Clause 4.4.4, ISO 14001 requires the preparation and maintenance of documentation, in paper or electronic form that does the following:

- Describes the core elements of the management system and their interaction.
- Provides direction to related documentation.

BOX 3–4

GREEN REPORTING

Many companies are issuing periodic, publicly available reports on their environmental performance. Early reports did not adhere to any standards. But groups such as the Public Environmental Reporting Initiative (PERI) and the Coalition for Environmentally Responsible Economies (CERES) have adopted public reporting/ disclosure standards that include a variety of metrics for air and water emissions, wastewater discharge, and solid/hazardous waste generation. Companies are including such data in these "green annual reports." The PERI guidelines, developed by several companies in the United States, provide a flexible framework for public environmental reporting—a framework that can be adapted and used by companies of any size and within any national jurisdiction. (See the appendices in the back of this book for the contents of the PERI guidelines.)

Creating, using, and maintaining documentation is central to the effectiveness of EMS implementation. Written documentation allows an evaluation of current conditions and procedures and measurement of current performance. With this baseline information, the organization can establish reliable measurements of improvements.

Written documentation is evidence that thought has been given to procedures, policies, and goals. It is also an irreplaceable reference resource for outside assessors. An organization should collect and retain documents that are meaningful in terms of environmental management. Many regulations require that documents be retained for specific periods of time. Also, the threat of potential lawsuits compels accurate and reliable record and document control.

Implementing Documentation Procedures

The organization must implement procedures to identify, document, communicate, and revise environmental management procedures and to develop and maintain EMS documentation. These procedures should describe how EMS documentation is integrated with existing documentation, where appropriate, and describe how employees access relevant EMS documentation.

The ISO 14001 requirements for documentation are stated in a few words, but their implementation is extensive. Necessary documentation should cover the following areas:

- The environmental policy, objectives, and goals.
- Roles and responsibilities of employees.
- Communication from external interested parties.
- Operational control procedures.

- Monitoring equipment maintenance records.
- Training records.
- Audit results and reviews.
- Management reviews.

(Documentation is discussed in more detail in Chapter 5.)

Documentation Must Add Value

EMS documentation should not be viewed as simply an exercise to comply with ISO 14001 without adding company value or meaning. It is harmful to institute more requirements without considering their added value to the organization. Organizations are challenged to develop sufficient documentation so that the requirements of ISO 14001 are met, while assisting, not interfering, with the operation. Documentation should be useful and usable. When setting up an EMS documentation system, it is important to first consider what will enable the organization to manage its environmental concerns, then later worry about ISO compliance.

Keep It Simple

Two basic rules of ISO documentation are "document what you do" and "do what you document." When creating EMS documentation, simplicity is critical. Procedures that are too complex will not be used. In addition, clear, concise documentation will make it easier to audit an organization's system. Every detail need not be meticulously documented. Extensive and excessive detail will result in greater implementation and compliance difficulties.

When documenting policies and procedures, avoid using the words *always* and *never* unless they are absolutely necessary. These words can result in serious stumbling blocks during both implementation and external auditing.

Document Format

The structure of a document is as important as its content. A well-structured document will allow the reader to easily find information and to access only what is of interest. A flowchart can be a very useful tool for developing documentation. It is one of the easiest and most clear methods for documenting a process or procedure. A key guideline in writing EMS documentation is to keep all processes and procedures short and simple.

Wherever practical, include a flowchart followed by text. The goal is for each document to be as concise as possible, ideally two to four pages. Flowcharts provide several advantages. In addition to providing a clear visual display of a process or procedure, flowcharts also encourage the people who are defining a process or procedure to think through all of the steps. Flowcharts can also be used to highlight responsibilities, policies, objectives, and targets.

Organizations should design documents in a standard company format so that all documents will appear as part of an organized document system. Throughout the documentation process, it is important to remember the purpose of the document and the intended audience. The owner of a document is the person responsible for creating it, arranging for authorization, and making any future revisions. In the event that an individual's job assignments change over time, it is best to assign a job title to the document, not to an individual. Any documentation that needs to be revised must go through the same authority that approved the original document. All revisions must be dated and easily identified.

Document Control (4.4.5)

Once the necessary EMS documentation has been generated, the organization must create a document control system. Clause 4.4.5 requires document-control procedures that ensure the following:

- Documents can be located.
- Documents are legible, dated (with dates of revision), readily identifiable, maintained in an orderly manner, and retained for a specific period.
- Documents are periodically reviewed, revised as necessary, and approved for adequacy by authorized personnel.
- Current versions of relevant documents are available at all locations where they are needed.
- Obsolete documents are promptly removed or otherwise assured against unintended use.
- Obsolete documents that are retained for legal and/or knowledge-preservation purposes are suitably identified.

The clause also requires the organization to establish procedures for creating and modifying various types of documents.

A Master List of Documents

Document control focuses on assuring that the correct version of a document is available to those employees who need it to fulfill their responsibilities. This can be accomplished by maintaining a master list of documents that identifies who has what information and its location, the level of approval, and revision status. A central person should be responsible for the complete master document. In this way, the changes or revised copies of changed documents can be sent to the appropriate person in a reasonable time, and the obsolete document can be removed and documented.

Electronic or Paper?

Obviously, the nature of the documentation can vary depending on the size and complexity of the organization. Depending on the volume of documentation that needs to be monitored and maintained, a database may be necessary. The decision to produce documentation in electronic or paper form should be made early in the process.

Electronic methods will make documentation easier to manage as the EMS expands. It will also offer better management and control of information, less reliance on personnel for handling the documentation, and ease of updating and retrieving information. Paper documentation, while easier to read, can be more costly, require additional circulation time, and require storage of paper files. (Chapter 6 discusses the use of information technology in more detail.)

Operational Control (4.4.6)

Another key step in implementing the EMS is operational control of those operations and activities associated with significant environmental aspects. The organization must implement operational procedures and controls to ensure that the organization's policy, objectives, and targets can be met.

Clause 4.4.6 of ISO 14001 requires the organization to plan these operations and activities, including maintenance, to ensure they are carried out under specified conditions. The organization does this by doing the following:

- "Establishing and maintaining documented procedures to cover situations where the absence of the procedures could lead to deviations from the environmental policy and the objectives and targets.
- Stipulating operating criteria in the procedures.
- Establishing procedures related to the identifiable significant environmental aspects of goods and services used by the organization.
- Communicating relevant procedures and requirements to suppliers and contractors."

The control systems should specify the purpose and relationships to objectives and targets, responsibilities, time frames, and resources. When the operational control systems are cross-referenced or related to the objectives and targets, they will be more meaningful, and responsible individuals will be encouraged to improve the system with an eye towards achieving the targets and objectives.

What to Control

As the standard implies, when developing or modifying operational controls, an organization should consider those operations and activities contributing to significant environmental impacts. The ISO 14004 guidance document suggests consideration of the following:

- R&D design and engineering.
- Purchasing.
- Contractors.

- Raw materials handling and storage.
- Production and maintenance processes.
- Laboratories.
- Storage of products.
- Transport.
- Marketing, advertising.
- Customer service.
- Acquisition or construction of property and facilities.

Operational control is a very demanding requirement. Satisfying this element of ISO 14001 will require extensive effort and documentation. The organization must exercise adequate and continuous control over all activities involving identified significant environmental aspects when setting up the EMS. While this task may not seem too involved when applied strictly to a production process, it can become quite extensive when applied to every operation and activity that can contribute to environmental impacts. These activities include purchasing, design and engineering, storage of raw materials and products, transportation, advertising and so on.

Operational Control Procedures to Document

Documented procedures are required when their absence could lead to deviations from the environmental policy and the organization's objectives and targets. Depending on its interpretation, this statement could require formal documentation for every procedure that could potentially impact the environment.

It is the responsibility of management to decide which activities to document. Management's decision to require formal documentation may be affected by the operator's training and qualifications and the significance of the activity. Documented procedures should be stated simply, unambiguously, and understandably and should indicate methods to be used and the criteria to be satisfied.

Equipment Maintenance

An organization should regularly maintain any production and servicing equipment that is used in activities involving environmental impacts. A maintenance plan should be used to verify equipment performance and accuracy. Records should be maintained of all equipment that requires calibration. Operating and maintenance manuals must be readily available to all personnel using the equipment.

Suppliers and Contractors

The organization is also responsible for establishing and maintaining procedures to identify the significant aspects of goods and services used by the organization. Any specific product or service requirements shall be communicated to suppliers and contractors. The ISO 14004 guidance document suggests that it may be useful to divide activities into three categories:

1. Pollution prevention and resource conservation activities in new capital projects, process changes and resource management, property acquisitions, divestitures and property management, and new products and packaging.

2. Daily management activities to assure conformance to internal and external organizational requirements, and to ensure their efficiency and effectiveness.

3. Strategic management activities to anticipate and respond to changing environmental requirements.

Emergency Preparedness and Response (4.4.7)

Clause 4.4.7 requires that the organization develop procedures to do the following:

- Identify the potential for accidents and emergency situations.
- Respond to accidents and emergency situations.
- Prevent and mitigate the environmental impacts that may be associated with them.

The organization must review and revise its procedures as needed, especially after accidents or emergencies. It must test its procedures periodically where practicable.

A Proactive Approach

In many instances, organizations develop emergency procedures in response to an environmental incident to prevent its recurrence. While ISO 14001 requires organizations to review and revise their emergency response procedures after an environmental incident, the standard goes a step further. It takes a more proactive approach in its requirement to plan for unexpected or accidental incidents and to establish procedures to identify and respond to these emergency situations.

When developing operating procedures and controls, the organization should consider accidental emissions to the air, discharges to the land or water, and specific effects on the environment and ecosystem resulting from accidental releases.

The plan is designed to give companies an opportunity to foresee and prevent an accident. An organization should review its processes and associated environmental aspects under abnormal and emergency operating situations and evaluate the potential environmental aspects associated with these conditions. It should establish and test plans to prevent or minimize the environmental impacts wherever practical.

An organization can use if–then flowcharts to determine action steps for a wide variety of emergency scenarios. Emergency plans can include a list of key personnel to contact, their responsibilities, communication plans, access to hazardous materials information, and emergency services contacts.

Emergency Response Training

Training will play a key role in emergency response preparedness. It is impossible to anticipate and plan for every possible emergency situation. The most important emergency response tool is a well-trained workforce that understands the environmental impacts of their job. An educated workforce will be better prepared to think and logically react to any emergency situation.

MEASUREMENT AND EVALUATION

After an organization implements an EMS, the next key question to ask is: How is the organization doing? Section 4.5, Checking and Corrective Action, calls on the organization to establish procedures to measure, monitor, and evaluate its environmental performance, discover problems, and correct them. There are four clauses corresponding to four general aspects of the process:

1. Monitoring and measurement (4.5.1).
2. Nonconformance and corrective and preventive action (4.5.2).
3. Records (4.5.3).
4. Environmental management system audit (4.5.4).

Monitoring and Measurement (4.5.1)

The success of an environmental management program depends to a great extent on how well it measures environmental performance. Clause 4.5.1 requires "documented procedures to monitor and measure on a regular basis the key characteristics of its operations and activities" that have significant environmental impacts.

This involves procedures to perform the following tasks:

- Record information to track performance, relevant operational controls, and conformance with objectives and targets.
- Calibrate and maintain monitoring equipment and retain records of the process.
- Periodically evaluate compliance with relevant environmental legislation and regulations.

Setting goals and using performance measures are crucial to maintaining continuous improvement. The measurement system should monitor actual performance versus the organization's environmental objectives and targets, including an evaluation of compliance with relevant environmental legislation and regulations.

The organization should analyze the results to determine areas of success and to identify those areas requiring corrective action and/or improvement. The organization should develop procedures to ensure the reliability of data, such as sampling protocols, calibration of instruments, and test equipment.

Environmental Performance Indicators

The task of evaluating performance and identifying appropriate environmental performance indicators is an ongoing process. Experience in implementing total quality management has shown that there are several principles to guide an organization when developing performance measures. These include the following:

- To assess improvements, measure the result directly (i.e., percent reduction in toxic chemical emissions per unit of production).
- Set specific numeric goals.
- Encourage teamwork between multiple departments within the organizations through joint measures.

Often, the cause of the problem and the resolution of the problem fall within two different departments. Simple, action-oriented measures that concentrate on one result are best.

Although currently there are no standards for measuring environmental performance, SC4 of TC 207 is developing standards for environmental performance evaluation (EPE). (See Chapter 8.) EPE is a process to "measure, analyze, assess and describe an organization's environmental performance against agreed criteria for appropriate management purposes." The goal of EPE is to give management a tool for generating the accurate information it needs to measure and track environmental performance to help meet its objectives and targets. Not only will EPE provide input to the monitoring and measuring stages of the EMS process, it will also provide input to the planning and implementation phases and will help companies prioritize environmental aspects and significant impacts.

Corrective and Preventive Action (4.5.2)

Based on the findings and conclusions of the measuring and monitoring efforts, the organization must identify necessary corrective and preventive actions. Clause 4.5.2 requires procedures for the following:

- Defining responsibility and authority for handling and investigating nonconformances.
- Taking action to mitigate any resulting impacts.
- Initiating and completing corrective and preventive action.

The standard emphasizes that "any corrective or preventive action to eliminate the causes of actual and potential nonconformances shall be appropriate to the magnitude of problems and commensurate with the environmental impact encountered."

Finally, Clause 4.5.2 requires organizations to implement and record any changes in the documented procedures that result from corrective and preventive action. There should be procedures in place to ensure the following:

- Those responsible for implementing the corrective actions have been notified.
- Management ensures that the corrective and preventive actions have in fact been implemented.
- There is systematic follow-up to ensure the effectiveness of corrective and preventive actions.

Environmental Records (4.5.3)

According to Clause 4.5.3, the organization must maintain appropriate records to demonstrate conformance to the requirements of the standard. This involves developing procedures for identifying, maintaining, and disposing of environmental records. This includes "training records and the results of audits and reviews."

As the ISO 14004 guidance standard states, records are evidence of the ongoing operation of the EMS. In addition to the above, records can include:

- Legislative and regulatory requirements.
- Inspection, maintenance, and calibration records.
- Incident reports.
- Reports of environmental audits and reviews.
- Contractor and supplier information.
- Emergency response records.

The standard points out that environmental records must be "legible, identifiable, traceable, readily retrievable and protected against, damage, deterioration or loss." The organization must also establish and record retention times for records.

Environmental Management System Audit (4.5.4)

The EMS standards establish the core elements of an EMS. The environmental performance evaluation (EPE) process provides guidance on measuring performance on a regular basis against objectives and targets set by the EMS. Auditing an EMS provides guidance on how to verify the existence of the EMS against agreed-upon criteria.

Clause 4.5.4 requires a program and procedures for periodic EMS auditing to achieve three goals:

1. Determine whether the EMS "conforms to planned arrangements for environmental management including the requirements of this standard."
2. Ensure that the EMS has been properly implemented and maintained.
3. Provide information from the EMS audit results to management as part of their review process.

Effective auditing can make or break an EMS. It is the nature of any system to continuously deteriorate through time. If an EMS is not monitored, it will begin to exhibit signs of chaos. Additionally, the EMS must respond to the forces of change that are constantly occurring as a result of changes in corporate expectations, technology, knowledge, market pressures, and regulations.

Finally, the environmental policy dictates a commitment to continuous improvement and the prevention of pollution. An environmental audit helps address all of these issues while keeping management informed as to how well or how poorly the EMS has been implemented and its current effectiveness. In summary, audits are needed not simply to maintain the system but to continuously improve the system.

The ISO 14001 standard emphasizes that the audit program, including its schedule, "be based on the environmental importance of the activity concerned and the results of previous audits." To be comprehensive, audit procedures should cover the audit scope, frequency, methodologies, and the responsibilities and requirements for conducting audits and reporting results. (The ISO 14010-12 series of auditing guidance standards describes the environmental auditing process in detail. See Chapter 9.)

Audit frequency will depend on past audit results, the maturity of the EMS, and the status and importance of the activity. It is best, however, to audit early and often. Audits can serve as an excellent training tool for both the auditor and auditee.

There is no need to wait until the system is fully documented to conduct the first audit. In fact, the audit team can conduct audits as the system is being implemented. All audit information and results must be presented to management for their review and appropriate corrective action. Documented results of audits allows for monitoring the progress of any corrective actions.

Independence and Objectivity

The auditing process involves a neutral, independent, or objective party who examines all aspects of the EMS to ensure that the resources, processes, and procedures correspond to meet the objectives and targets and that the objectives and targets are still applicable and work toward continual improvement of the EMS. Audits can be carried out by internal or external personnel. But since an internal audit is a verification activity, it must be assured that independence exists between the auditor and the auditee.

This essential factor can be accounted for by having a representative from another department do the audit. It is a good practice to have many people carry out internal auditing, as it increases people's knowledge about the company as a whole and removes any interdepartmental barriers. Exposing as many people as possible to the audit process will help develop an audit mentality and increase the visibility of environmental issues within the organization.

Auditors must be properly trained and able to be totally impartial to the operation being audited so that they can carry out the task objectively and effectively. This training must be documented. The auditor must be familiar with both the ISO 14001 standard and the procedures used to perform the environmental audit.

Audit Team

Auditing is a demanding, if not tedious, process. It is therefore recommended that responsibility be shared by more than one person. The exact size of the audit team will naturally vary with the size of the organization and scope of the audit. It is the responsibility of the internal audit team to not only plan and schedule the audit, but to conduct the audit, verify that the documented system matches the implemented system, and finally and most importantly, report findings to management. The audit team should submit the EMS audit report in accordance with the audit plan.

The success of an internal audit will generally depend on several key elements. The audit team must be well prepared and organized for the audit. This includes clearly defining the scope and purpose of the audit, scheduling the audit, and deciding on an audit trail method such as following the process flow. The audit team must possess the necessary interpersonal skills that will allow them to listen and obtain input on how to improve the system.

Finally, the success of an audit depends on the extent of follow-up action performed to achieve closures of nonconformities. While the environmental policy tells the environmental principles of the organization to the world, internal audits make certain that the environmental policy is actually pursued within the framework of the EMS.

Management Review (4.6)

Continual improvement is achieved by improving the operational processes in the organization and is bolstered by training. The final step in the basic EMS process is to review the EMS itself.

The basic requirement in Clause 4.6 of ISO 14001 calls on top management to review the EMS, at intervals it determines, "to ensure its continuing suitability, adequacy and effectiveness." Management must make sure it has a process for collecting the information necessary for a comprehensive evaluation and that it documents the review. The management review must address the need for changes to policy, objectives, and other elements of the EMS, based on the EMS audit results, changing circumstances, and the organization's commitment to continual improvement.

A procedure should be developed for the management review process. The ISO 14004 guidance standard suggests that the review include the following:

- A review of environmental objectives, targets, and environmental performance.
- Findings of the EMS audits (along with any corrective actions).
- Suggested changes or improvements to the system.

- Evaluation of the EMS's effectiveness.
- Evaluation of the suitability of the environmental policy and the need for changes in light of:
  - Changing legislation.
  - Changing expectations and requirements of interested parties.
  - Changes in the products or activities of the organization.
  - Advances in science and technology.
  - Lessons learned from environmental incidents.
  - Market preferences.
  - Reporting and communication.

In addition, the procedure for management review should describe how appropriate employees are involved in the process along with the views of interested parties.

The EMS belongs to top management because it has the responsibility to define it and generate the policy of operation along with the objectives. Management is intimately involved with the EMS; without management reviews, the EMS will stagnate.

During the initial stages in defining, developing, and implementing the EMS, it is necessary to schedule frequent management reviews. These reviews keep management informed of the activities concerning implementation of the EMS and help obtain their input on an ongoing basis. Monthly management reviews are recommended during the initial stages of implementation. As the EMS matures, reviews will be less frequent but still scheduled regularly. The system should allow for unscheduled reviews when warranted by a special event or condition.

Records must be established and maintained to verify that management reviews were scheduled and performed and that any findings or conclusions resulting from the reviews were documented. The details for scheduling, conducting, and recording management reviews must be documented.

The management review of the environmental management system serves many purposes. The final outcome of a management review should lead to increased effectiveness and efficiency of the EMS.

CONCLUSION

This chapter presented the basic ISO 14001 requirements and one EMS implementation strategy. Once ISO 14000 implementation is started, top management will be in a better position to evaluate what works best within its particular organization. Management should set up its internal EMS team and seek outside resources to provide impartiality and to help steer the organization towards successful ISO 14001 implementation and improved environmental performance.

BIOGRAPHIES

Reeva I. Schiffman, Esq., B. Tod Delaney, PhD, PE, DEE, and Scott Fleming

Reeva Schiffman is a regulatory specialist with First Environment. She has practiced in the environmental field for seven years, with specific emphasis on industrial audits, regulatory compliance, environmental due diligence, and strategic planning.

For the past year, Ms. Schiffman has been a member of the International Standard Organization's Technical Committee 207, as well as the official Ad Hoc Legal Issues Forum related to ISO 14000. Ms. Schiffman is an active member of the Legislative & Regulatory Work Group of the Environmental Auditing Roundtable. She is also a member of the New Jersey Bar Association's Environmental Law Section and the American Bar Association, Section of Natural Resources, Energy, and Environmental Law.

Ms. Schiffman earned a B.S. degree from the University of Vermont; a J.D. from the Benjamin N. Cardozo School of Law; and a master's degree in the Study of Environmental Law (M.S.E.L.) from the Environmental Law Center at Vermont Law School.

Tod Delaney is president of First Environment, an environmental engineering firm that provides a wide range of consulting services to private industry. He has practiced in the fields of pollution prevention and hazardous waste management for twenty-seven years, with specific emphasis on strategic planning, industrial audits, site investigations, remedial design, air pollution control, and development of new control and treatment technologies. Prior to forming First Environment, he was associated with Exxon, Fred C. Hart Associates, and CH2M Hill.

For the past year, Dr. Delaney has served on SC5A, Life Cycle Analysis Committee of the American Society of Testing Materials (ASTM), and through the ASTM Committee, he serves on ISO TC 207. He is also an active member of the Air & Waste Management Association where he served as chairman of the Hazardous Combustion Committee, and of the American Institute of Chemical Engineers where he serves as a Diplomate and as the AIChE Trustee on the Board of the American Academy of Environmental Engineers. He is also a member of the American Society of Civil Engineers.

Dr. Delaney earned B.S. and M.S. degrees in chemical engineering from the University of New Mexico; and Ph.D. in environmental health engineering from the University of Texas. He has an M.B.A. from Pepperdine University and has taught graduate and undergraduate courses in chemical and environmental engineering at the University of New Mexico, the University of Texas, Cooper Union, and Rutgers University.

Scott Fleming is a staff engineer with First Environment. He has a background in materials, manufacturing and process engineering. Prior to joining First Environment, Mr. Fleming was with the Abex Corporation Foundry Division. He is a member of the American Society of Civil Engineers, the American Ceramic Society, and the American Foundrymen's Society. Mr. Fleming earned B.S. and M.S. degrees in ceramic science and engineering from Rutgers University and holds an M.S. in environmental engineering from the New Jersey Institute of Technology.

NOTE

1. The standard mentions that when establishing objectives, an organization "shall consider financial, operational and business requirements." The annex to ISO 14001 points out that this does not imply that ISO 14001 requires the use of environmental cost-accounting methods to track the costs and benefits of environmental performance, such as the cost of pollution control, waste, and disposal. The organization, however, is free to use these techniques if it finds them useful.

CHAPTER 4

Employee Training and Awareness

W. Gary Wilson

INTRODUCTION

This chapter looks at the requirements in ISO 14001 for employee awareness and training, including documenting and measuring the effectiveness of training programs. This chapter goes beyond the general requirements of ISO 14001 and provides specific examples of how to determine levels of competence, how to design a training program, and how to implement a training session.

The central tenet of ISO 14001 is that through understanding the impacts that each operation has on the environment and the successful management of those impacts, environmental improvement is inevitable. The operational practices of individual employees are critical to the development of an EMS that succeeds in achieving environmental improvement.

The effectiveness of those practices depends on the degree of sensitivity employees have to the environmental impacts of their actions and their understanding of those impacts. ISO 14001, therefore, contains three main requirements:

1. Employees be made aware of the environmental impacts that can result from performance of their job responsibilities.

2. Management determines the levels of competence necessary to perform environmentally sensitive jobs and ensures that employees assigned to those jobs have the requisite level of competence.

3. Employees undergo training suitable to their job responsibilities.

ISO 14001 TRAINING REQUIREMENTS

An important ISO EMS concept is that employees who understand the consequences of their actions will individually make more environmentally friendly decisions. Thus, maintaining better informed and environmentally conscious employees will result in improved environmental performance. Clause 4.4.2 of ISO 14001 requires that "the organization shall identify training needs. It shall require that all personnel whose work may create a significant impact upon the environment have received appropriate training."

The requirements set forth in ISO 14001, Clause 4.4.2, for training and awareness are not lengthy or detailed but provide the general goals that training should achieve. ISO 14001 requires that an organization establish and maintain procedures that will ensure its employees' awareness in the following areas:

- The organization's environmental policy/procedures and their importance.
- The significant environmental impacts of their work activities.
- Their roles and responsibilities in achieving compliance with the environmental policy/procedures and requirements of the organization's EMS.
- The environmental benefits of improving their own performance as it relates to work activities that have, or may have, environmental impacts.
- The potential consequences of departure from any specific operating procedure.

Employee Awareness

No specific requirements for employee awareness are mandated by ISO 14001 beyond the general notion that the success of the EMS is affected by employee awareness of the principles and procedures of the EMS and an understanding of the impacts of their work activities. As discussed below, the ISO 14004 guidance standard provides additional guidance on how to assure employee awareness.

Employee Competence

Not only should employees be trained but an organization should ensure that they have the adequate education and experience to perform tasks that can have significant environmental impact. It may not be enough that an organization provides training to an employee if that employee does not have the appropriate education and experience to perform the specific assigned task.

ISO 14001, Clause 4.4.2, requires that "personnel performing the tasks which can cause significant environmental impacts shall be competent on the basis of appropriate education, training and/or experience." The annex to ISO 14001, Clause A.4.2, provides further that "management should determine the level of experience, competence and training necessary to ensure the capability of personnel, especially those carrying out specialized environmental management functions."

Contractors

ISO 14001 makes no mention of contractor responsibility. However, Section A.4.2 of the annex to ISO 14001 discusses generally that organizations should also consider contractors working on their sites and have them provide evidence that they have the knowledge, skills, and training to perform their work in an environmentally responsible manner. This is reiterated in guidance provided by ISO 14004 Clause 4.3.2.5.

Fulfillment of this requirement may be met by requiring contractors to be ISO 14001 certified. However, this may not be a realistic approach and could limit the contractor's availability to work for the organization. A less stringent approach is to set up a contractor prescreening procedure through which potential contractors can demonstrate their environmental qualifications. This type of prescreening is already common in the areas of health and safety (compliance with OSHA or use of acceptable health and safety plans) and technical competence (qualifications to perform particular tasks).

A prescreening questionnaire would include questions that will show whether a potential contractor has considered environmental impacts in the selection of employees and setting of job responsibilities. The types of environmental issues discussed below should have been considered by the potential contractor.

ENSURING EMPLOYEE AWARENESS

Employee awareness is critical to the success of the EMS. Ensuring employee awareness is the responsibility of top management. Top management must establish a set of environmental values—a corporate environmental culture—and make these values evident to employees at all levels of the organization both through effective communication and by example.

Although management may establish a very workable and comprehensive EMS manual, it is the actions of individual employees who are carrying out the day-to-day work activities of the organization that will determine the success or failure of the EMS. Therefore, employees from all levels of an organization must understand the goals and principles of the EMS and the ways in which their activities impact, both negatively and positively, on the achievement of those goals. Also, the employees must commit to the success of the EMS.

Communication plays a large role in establishing and maintaining employee awareness. Communicating successes and failures of an EMS to employees throughout the organization helps further the understanding of each employee's impact on the environment. This dissemination of information must go beyond management, beyond specific groups of employees who may have been most affected, and beyond operations.

Awareness must exist, for example, in the human resources department (where decisions are made regarding job applicants and employee performance review and incentive programs), in the purchasing department (where decisions are made regarding product selection or contractor selection), and in the maintenance department (where decisions are made that impact the operational efficiency of environmentally sensitive equipment).

ISO 14004, Clause 4.3.2.4, provides guidance to assist an organization in establishing employee environmental awareness and suggests that it consider questions such as these:

- How has top management established, reinforced, and communicated the organization's commitment to the environmental policy?
- To what extent do employees understand, accept, and share the environmental values set by the organization?
- To what extent do shared environmental values serve to motivate environmentally responsible action?
- How does the organization recognize employees' environmental achievements?

In setting up a program to develop and maintain employee awareness and commitment, consider the following suggestions:

- Provide incentives to employees who demonstrate environmental commitment. These can include awards, special recognition in company newsletters, salary increases, and so on.
- Consider environmental performance as an objective in employee performance reviews. These environmental performance objectives should be based on the degree to which each employees' job responsibilities impact environmental performance. Employees with direct environmental job activities, such as waste disposal, should be reviewed in part based on the manner in which they assured that those activities were carried out in an environmentally responsible way (i.e., wastes were disposed of in a manner having minimal impact on the environment).
- Ensure that unacceptable environmental performance is discouraged on the spot and/or punished through performance reviews or warnings/disciplinary actions. Treating instances of negative environmental impacts seriously sends a consistent message that reinforces top management commitment to the EMS and is as important as positive recognition.
- Make environmental awareness an integral part of the overall training program. Discuss and use as examples both successes and failures that have occurred in the organization's attempts to better manage its environmental performance.

ESTABLISHING LEVELS OF COMPETENCE

Competence in performing work activities that may have environmental impacts should be the main goal of a training program. This competence is based on awareness and commitment as well as in experience and education. What it takes to be competent in a particular task will, of course, vary among tasks. Some tasks will require specialized formal education, while other tasks will require hands-on experience. Defining competence requires an understanding of the work activity being considered and its relationship to environmental aspects.

Establishing the level of competence for work activities can be described in a three-step process:

1. Identify job descriptions that are environmentally sensitive (have environmental aspects).

2. Determine the skills required to perform those jobs in an environmentally responsible manner. This process should be quantitative when possible.

3. Based on the skills identified as necessary, establish minimum education and experience requirements.

Having established the appropriate levels of competence, the training program can be used to reinforce knowledge and experience for seasoned employees and to provide a baseline level of knowledge and competence for new employees or employees moving into new jobs.

Environmentally Sensitive Job Descriptions

Not every job performed within an organization has environmental aspects. Some work activities associated with environmental compliance are obviously environmentally sensitive, such as activities related to operation of treatment equipment and disposal of wastes. Other activities are not directly related to environmental performance but may have significant impacts on performance, such as operation of equipment using hazardous waste (solvent degreasers) or maintenance/janitorial activities in areas where hazardous wastes are used (mishandling of residues during facility cleaning).

Another level of work activities has no direct connection to operations but involves decisions that can significantly affect environmental performance, such as engineering (selection of processes), purchasing (selection of raw materials/chemicals), or human resources (setting hiring standards). When considering those work activities that may be environmentally sensitive, it is therefore important to involve all levels of the organization.

The process of identifying environmentally sensitive job descriptions is generally straightforward but may be quite complicated in a large organization. Consideration should be given to the organization's selected targets and objectives particular to the organization's environmental aspects. Environmentally sensitive job descriptions will involve those work activities that relate to the environmental aspects. The process then flows like this:

Environmental aspect → related work activities → jobs that perform or impact the related work activities.

Look at each environmental aspect identified. There will be a list of work activities associated with each environmental aspect. Once an organization has listed the related work activities, it can determine what job descriptions within the organization have responsibility for, or impact on, those work activities. Some job descriptions are not as obvious as others, so it is important to approach the process with an open and creative mind. Job descriptions can be later eliminated from the list of environmentally sensitive jobs if it appears that too conservative an approach was taken.

Table 4–1 works through the process for some hypothetical environmental aspects. In most cases, job descriptions that include direct supervision of workers performing environmentally sensitive work activities will also be included in the environmentally sensitive category since decisions made by supervisors, and their attitude toward environmental performance, can significantly impact the performance of their subordinates.

Determining the Required Skills

The second step in the process of establishing competence is to identify the environmentally related skills necessary to perform each environmentally sensitive work activity. For example, a buyer needs to understand the EMS requirements for selection of raw materials. This skill is in addition to those necessary to perform the function of a buyer. A laborer who is given work activities in an environmentally sensitive area may need additional skills related specifically to the area or equipment operating within

TABLE 4–1

Selection of Environmentally Sensitive Job Descriptions

Environmental Aspect	Example of Work Activities	Job Descriptions That May Be Environmentally Sensitive
Air emissions from process systems	Engineering design, emissions testing, maintenance of emission control equipment, selecting/ buying process chemicals.	Process engineer Maintenance laborer Buyer Laboratory technician
Treatment system discharge to surface water	Operation of treatment plant, selecting/buying treatment chemicals, testing of discharge, cleaning floors/equipment, and discharging to floor drains.	Treatment plant operator Buyer Laboratory technician Janitor Maintenance
Electrical energy usage	Purchase of lights and energy-efficient electrical equipment, maintenance of equipment, HVAC design and operation.	Buyer Janitor Maintenance laborer Plant engineer

the area. At a minimum, the laborer would need an awareness of the potential environmental impacts of this particular work activity and any specific requirements from the EMS.

The ease with which these additional environmentally related skills are determined will vary, depending on the sophistication of the existing job requirements. A maintenance worker needs basic skills related to working with machinery, tools, and so on and experience with the specific equipment he or she is asked to maintain. This is true whether or not operation of the equipment has environmental impacts. If the organization has defined job descriptions, it will have defined the skills necessary for maintenance personnel. The additional skills required for environmentally sensitive work activities will be few and specifically related to the environmental aspects (e.g., awareness of the environmentally sensitive nature of the activity; knowledge of specific EMS requirements, recognizing and responding to releases).

If the organization has no defined job descriptions, it will need to go through the entire process of defining the basic and environmental skill base needed. For maintenance personnel assigned environmentally sensitive work activities, the skills must include those discussed above as basic skills (knowledge of machinery and tools; experience or training on specific equipment, etc.) in addition to those related to the environmental aspects.

This determination of skills should be completed for employees at all levels, for each environmentally sensitive work activity. This skills base will form the foundation for establishing minimum education and experience requirements.

Establishing Minimum Education and Experience Requirements

The level of effort needed to establish minimum education and experience requirements will depend on the degree to which an organization has existing job descriptions. If it has job descriptions for most work activities, only additional environmentally related requirements need consideration. Performing the work activities that have a more indirect impact on environmental performance may require only awareness of environmental issues and the details of the EMS. For example, a buyer needs to have an awareness of the environmental impacts of raw material selection as well as a knowledge of the EMS and any procedures concerning selection of raw materials. A buyer's education and experience requirements are already defined by the position, independent of environmental issues.

On the other hand, a treatment plant operator should be required to have a particular education or level of experience that demonstrates his or her understanding and competence to operate the plant in an environmentally sensitive manner. Granted, many companies would require a minimum level of experience or education to operate the plant even without an EMS. What needs to be considered in the ISO 14001 context is a documented procedure demonstrating that only personnel meeting some minimum environmentally related requirements will be put into positions of operating a treatment plant that has environmental aspects. This perhaps is better illustrated when considering the laborer level. The organization should determine a minimum level of environmental education and experience for the laborer assisting with plant operation, based on the actual environmentally sensitive work activities the laborer will be asked to perform. In this case, the environmentally related requirements will be in addition to the general requirements that an organization would normally require for a laborer position.

If an organization has no existing job descriptions, it will need to develop job descriptions that specify minimum education and experience, based on the skills identified as necessary to perform the environmentally sensitive work activity. This will mean defining the necessary basic skills and the environmentally related skills. Using the laborer example, since the organization has no job description or requirements for the basic skills of a laborer, it must define them first. Then it must further define what additional skills are necessary for the laborer to perform the environmentally sensitive work activity. Defining skills for the environmentally sensitive work activity does very little good if, in fact, the organization has not ensured that the employee has the basic skills necessary to be a laborer.

ISO 14001 does not require development of job descriptions per se, but an organization should set minimum requirements. This could be accomplished by listing only those work activities that have environmental aspects and listing corresponding basic and environmentally related education and experience requirements. However, the process of determining what skills are needed leads to the development of something very close to a full job description, listing at least those work activities with environmental aspects. Therefore, for little additional effort, an organization may, if desired, find it beneficial to generate an actual set of job descriptions as part of this process.

DESIGNING AN EFFECTIVE TRAINING PROGRAM

The training program should be designed to provide employees at all levels of the organization with the skills and awareness necessary to understand the requirements of the EMS, to understand their role in assuring the success of the EMS; and to perform their work activities in an environmentally sensitive manner, consistent with the requisite education and experience requirements. The type and degree of training required will vary considerably, depending on each employee's position within the organization and the particular work activities.

Typical elements of a training program, as envisioned by ISO 14001, include the following:

- Identifying employee training needs.
- Developing a training plan specifically to address those identified needs.
- Verifying that the training program conforms to applicable regulatory or organizational requirements.
- Selecting target employee groups for training.
- Documenting that training has been performed.

Identifying Training Needs

Because training requirements will vary within an organization and numerous types of training may be needed, the first step in setting up a training program should be identifying those needs. This section discusses several considerations that should help an organization develop and understand its specific training needs.

Organization's Targets and Objectives

As with all aspects of the EMS, training needs should be considered in light of an organization's list of targets and objectives. Since ISO 14001 is a process of continuous improvement, an organization may choose to begin the process with the minimum number of objectives and targets necessary to assure a minimum level of compliance with the standard. Upon completion of each cycle through the EMS process, the organization can then amend its targets and objectives or add new targets or objectives. The training program should reflect these potential changes and course corrections and may evolve over time.

Environmental Aspects/Impacts

The training program is directly related to an organization's environmental aspects. The selection of environmentally related work activities is based on the environmental aspects identified by the organization. As with objectives and targets, as an organization identifies additional environmental aspects or eliminates environmental aspects, the training program must reflect those changes.

   The training program should provide the training necessary for an employee to meet the minimum education and experience requirements of his or her assigned work activities. Therefore, as environmental aspects change and thus environmentally related work activities change, the training program must adapt to provide the necessary type of training.

Types of Training Programs

It is convenient to group training programs into three general types:

1. Awareness training.
2. Understanding of the EMS requirements.
3. Job-specific training.

Awareness Training

Arguably, all employees in an organization need to be aware of the environmental impacts of the organization's activities. Therefore, awareness training may involve the largest number of employees within an organization. Certainly, all employees whose work activities directly or indirectly impact the environment should undergo awareness training. Likewise, supervisors and managers, including top-level executives, should be aware of the environmental impacts of the organization's activities.

Awareness training should be broad-based, focusing on the organization's environmental aspects and how they relate to environmental impacts. At all levels of the organization, employees should understand that the organization's activities can impact the environment and that there is an EMS process designed to mitigate those impacts. As one moves through the organization from executive level, administrative level, and manager level to operational level, the type of awareness varies. At the operational level, it is critical according to ISO 14001 that each employee understand the manner in which he or she has an impact on the environment. Similarly, supervisors or managers should understand how their employees' work activities can impact the environment.

Understanding of the EMS Requirements

Any employee who has a defined role and responsibilities pursuant to the organization's EMS must understand those responsibilities. This type of training is reasonably straightforward. At each level of an organization, those employees identified as having responsibilities within the EMS must be taught what those responsibilities are and how they should be carried out.

This type of training should provide, in a very specific manner, a road map of those responsibilities, including, for example, documentation, reporting, or additional ongoing training. The training should focus on providing each employee with the basis of understanding necessary to the performance of his or her EMS responsibilities.

Job-Specific Training

Job-specific training will normally apply to operational-level employees. Those employees with "front-line" work activities involving operation of equipment or machinery, monitoring of environmental indicators, maintenance of environmentally related machinery, an so on, must be trained in the appropriate procedures for performing these work activities.

This type of training is generally very practical in nature and specific to particular groups or employees. For example, those employees operating vapor degreasers must understand how to operate the equipment in an environmentally sensitive manner. They must also understand what to do when equipment fails and how to address environmental upsets and incidents. This includes knowledge of whom to contact within the organization. Job-specific training provides the training necessary to achieve the competence required by ISO 14001 and may be used to periodically refresh the knowledge of existing employees as well as to provide new employees with a baseline level of knowledge.

Employee Groups

As indicated above, grouping of employees is necessary for a cost-effective and efficient training program. Training should be targeted to those employees who need the training. There is a trade-off to be considered between the number of separate training programs developed versus the degree of inefficiency related to having diverse interests within the same training program. For SMEs, it may make sense to conduct fewer training sessions and include a more diverse group of employees. An organization with 30 employees may very well conduct all its training, except perhaps some job-specific training, in joint sessions. A large organization with hundreds of employees will have to make decisions as to grouping because of the difficulty of getting all employees together in one place at one time. Similarly, organizations with multiple facilities might have separate training programs at each facility.

In any training session, it is likely that information irrelevant to some participants will be provided. When selecting training groups, the goal is to get the most benefit from the training session with the minimum amount of irrelevant information. As discussed above, there are three general types of training: awareness, EMS requirements, and job-specific requirements. In many organizations, these will provide obvious first-level groupings. The organization should consider the advantage of selecting groups targeted for specific types of training. As discussed later in this chapter, training is a significant cost to an organization, and steps should be taken to assure the most efficient training program possible.

Frequency of Training

There are no requirements within ISO 14001 for the frequency of training. Training should occur often enough to assure that employees are aware of the environmental impacts of their work activities and competent to perform those work activities. Certainly, training is required for new employees and for employees changing job descriptions. In addition, it is reasonable to assume that some amount of refresher training would be beneficial to the successful implementation of an organization's EMS.

Training for awareness and EMS requirements should be performed for all targeted employees at least once at the initiation of the EMS. Likewise, all new employees should undergo awareness and EMS requirements training. Depending on how frequently the organization adds new hires, these training elements may be repeated at reasonable intervals, such as quarterly, semiannually, or even annually. The important consideration is that no employee be put in an environmentally sensitive work activity for an unreasonable period of time prior to receiving training.

One approach is to have a minimal training session (e.g., video, reading materials, etc.) prior to a new employee starting work, to be followed by a more intensive training session when practical. If the organization has an ongoing awareness program, there may be no need for repeated structured awareness training.

Job-specific training should include initial training and refresher training. No employee should be performing job activities, such as operation of equipment, without specific training. The training program should provide documented evidence that an employee has been provided detailed instructions relative to his or her work activity.

Refresher training should be conducted at reasonable intervals to assure continued competence; the frequency will depend on the complexity of the operation. Some level of documented training should also occur whenever modifications are made to the work activity (i.e., updated equipment, new processes, new raw materials).

Targeting Training

An organization will also need to base its training on the level of each employee within the organization. The needs, concerns, interests, and motivations are different for executives, mid-level managers, and operations employees. When establishing employee groups, it may be appropriate to use these distinctions as a basis for grouping. However, in some cases, such as in SMEs, it may be more cost-effective to have employees from different levels of the organization in the same training sessions. Either way, when developing training sessions, the organization should be aware of and consider the inherent differences between employee levels.

Executives

Executive-level employees primarily focus on the organization's profits, its reputation, and its overall health and growth. Executives are interested in the big picture. They establish policies and guidelines and consider issues in terms of concepts and goals. Their issues are global, encompassing the entire organization and its standing in the marketplace.

Executives will consider the EMS from the overall system level and expect to delegate the responsibility for implementation. Information typically needs to be in broader summary form, emphasizing the impact on the organization as a whole.

Mid-Level Managers

Mid-level managers have a somewhat narrower view because of their responsibility for a particular section of the organization. They are directly concerned with productivity and budgets. They have staffing issues to consider and customers to satisfy.

Managers will be concerned about implementation of specific EMS programs. They need to understand and establish responsibilities. They will usually have responsibility for the success of the EMS. They need to understand regulations and how they apply to the operations under their control. Managers need to maintain control of the operation's environmental compliance.

How compliance information is reported to managers (format, frequency, procedures for quality control, etc.) is critical to their control of environmental compliance. Training for managers should include an understanding of the processes within their control, of the regulatory requirements associated with those processes, of the data sources needed to maintain compliance, and of permits and reporting requirements.

Operating-Level Employees

Operating-level employees are concerned with the day-to-day operation of specific equipment and processes. They are on the "front line" of the organization's environmental performance. No matter how elaborate an EMS is in place, without knowledge, commitment, and implementation at the operating level, the EMS will not achieve improvement of environmental performance.

Training of operating-level employees needs to be "how to" tempered with "why." The training is typically more process-oriented and will often need to include very specific instruction on the operation of equipment. This level of training should describe the environmental aspects of each operational process or work activity. The discussion should include how improper operation may adversely impact the environment and the role routine maintenance plays in ensuring proper operation (and how lack of maintenance may negate the benefit of environmental equipment, leading to adverse environmental impacts), and should stress the role each employee has in achieving environmental improvement. Each employee must understand the impact of his or her own actions.

Training for Maximum Efficiency and Information Transfer

Training is expensive, in terms of actual costs associated with setting up the course (paper, space, trainers, etc.), and in terms of lost productivity while trainees are taken away from normal functions. Therefore, it is imperative that training sessions be designed for the maximum transfer of relevant information in as efficient a time frame as feasible. When setting up a training program, the organization must consider the needs of the trainees and must target the training to fulfill those needs. The organization cannot afford to spend trainee time discussing issues not relevant to the trainee. Not only does it waste precious time that could be spent more productively elsewhere, it will be of little or no interest to the trainee, who will likely not retain the information.

As discussed earlier, there are three types of training to be considered in meeting the goals of ISO 14001: awareness, understanding of the EMS, and job-specific. Employee groups, as discussed, can be selected based on their relative information needs. Having determined which information needs to be presented to a particular employee group, it is necessary to design the training program to provide that information in as efficient manner as possible.

Consider the following questions while selecting topics and designing each training session:

- Are only those issues that have bearing on the goals of this training session being addressed?

- Is the information prepared and presented in a format that fits the audience?

- Are the trainees told what they *need* to know and is information avoided that is only *nice* to know?

- Is the level of the trainee in the organization taken into consideration?

- Has the ability of the audience to absorb information been considered, rather than remaining focused on covering some predetermined amount of information?

- Is each topic interesting and relevant to the trainees?

Training is teaching. Information provided to, but not retained by, the trainees is wasted information. By reconsidering this issue of maximum transfer of information at each step of setting up a training session, it should be possible to minimize ineffective techniques.

Setting Up the Training Program

Once the organization has determined its training needs, designed a program to address those needs, and selected groups of employees for each type of training session, it still needs to consider the practical aspects of physically setting up the training program. This involves the ergonomics of the training facilities, duration of training sessions, and selection of speakers.

Ergonomic Considerations

Things like comfortable seating, proper temperature control, lighting, sound quality, and writing space are very important, but often neglected, conditions for the efficient transfer of information. It may seem to some that this is coddling the trainees; however, if the interest of management is an efficient and effective training program, proper consideration of these factors is important.

There is no right way to set up your training room or provide writing space, and so on. The point is to consider these issues, not just decide to use that room in the back of the plant because it is available. Consider the following suggestions:

- Provide ample space to avoid having trainees feel cramped; everyone needs some space of their own.
- Use tables or desks so that trainees have a surface on which to write and lay out materials; nothing is so distracting as trying to balance materials on one's lap.
- Select a quiet room with good acoustics and ample lighting.
- Ensure that the room has good temperature control.
- Provide comfortable seating, with good back support, which will help minimize fidgeting.
- Set up the room to allow access to projectors and overheads and good views of the screen for all participants.
- For large rooms, a sound system may be necessary for the trainers, with microphone access for trainees.

Duration of Training Sessions

Ample breaks for relaxation, stretching, rest room visits, and so on are necessary to a productive training session. The practice of having 50 minutes of work with 10 minute breaks is preferred. However, this requires diligence in assuring that breaks are limited to 10 minutes and that each part of the session starts and stops on schedule. Good planning of each portion of each session, with an eye to time management, can help assure that the training day progresses on schedule.

Set up the training session with ample time for each topic to be covered, time for questions and audience interaction, time for demonstrations, and time for breaks and lunch. Trying to squeeze too much activity into the session is a sure way of spending the whole day behind schedule. Each speaker should know the length of time required for a good presentation of the material. Set up demonstrations and role-playing or games with a defined time limit for each phase of the activity and then assure strict compliance to the times allotted.

Good advance planning provides confidence in the timing and makes it easy to control the session. It is each speaker's, and the moderator's, responsibility to control discussions, questions, and so on within the time allowed. This responsibility includes shutting off discussion and questions when necessary. An efficient transfer of information relies on knowing what material needs to be transferred, how that material can best be transferred, how long it should take, how many and what types of questions are likely to be asked, and how to control the audience in a way that assures the transfer can take place.

Trainers

Knowing the material is not the only prerequisite to being a good teacher. Good teachers have the ability to interest their students in the subject matter, to get them to consider the information being provided, and to help them understand the information. Trainers should first of all want to do the training. Trainers who have been drafted for the role are generally unenthusiastic and less well prepared. Good training, like anything else, requires creativity and good planning. People interested in training and the pleasures of helping people learn something new make the best trainers.

Realistically, there may not be enough people in an organization with these qualifications to meet the staffing needs of the training program. However, rather than selecting trainers by some arbitrary method, such as department heads conducting training about the activities within their departments or trainers being selected from people who have free time, give some thought to who is recruited and look throughout the organization for people who are truly interested. In the long run, providing some overhead time for an employee anywhere in the organization to prepare and provide training will be more cost-effective than training sessions that do not transfer the information desired and generally waste employees' time.

Use numerous trainers to create variability during the session. Mix the best trainers and the less-effective trainers throughout a session to prevent losing the audience for long periods of time. This procedure can have the side benefit of allowing less-effective trainers to learn the techniques of better trainers. Be aware of the effectiveness of each trainer and replace trainers who clearly are not effective. Consider having the trainees fill out trainer evaluation forms. Always ensure that all trainees submit the evaluation form at the end of a session because, if given an option, only those with strong negative or positive reactions will submit them. Further, getting evaluation forms from several training sessions will provide a better understanding of each trainer's effectiveness. Everyone can have an off day.

Testing Training Effectiveness

It is necessary to have some method for evaluating the effectiveness of information transfer. Therefore, an organization must devise ways of testing trainees' retention of the information presented in a training session. Although a very important process, developing tests is often difficult and tedious. Tests requiring rote repetition of information are the easiest to prepare but are least effective as a measure of long-term retention by trainees. Tests that require the trainee to assimilate and use the information provided are most effective but are often difficult to develop.

A test's content and structure will depend on the type of information being tested. For interactive training, such as role-playing, case studies, or demonstrations, testing may be incorporated into the training itself. For example, results of case studies can be scored. Role-playing can be individually critiqued and repeated to build skills. Demonstrations, especially involving operation of equipment, can require trainees to demonstrate their understanding by correctly operating the equipment in the presence of the trainer.

Traditional classroom instruction will typically require development of a written test. To the extent possible, the questions should elicit thoughtful answers, not just repetition. This can be accomplished by developing short scenarios followed by several questions based on each scenario. For example, a test for a session teaching the components of the EMS could include a scenario describing a particular plant operation the trainees are familiar with. The questions could require the trainee to describe different employees' responsibilities, what environmental aspects are evident, and so on. Another technique involves using actual slides of plant activities and asking questions regarding the pictured activity. Any testing technique that includes real-life elements familiar to the trainee will facilitate accurate testing and help assure the trainee's retention of the information.

Finally, testing should not be a means of disciplining the employee. Testing should identify problem areas that require additional attention. A poor test score may reflect as badly on the trainer as the trainee. Using test scores as a means of tracking effectiveness is only meaningful if it leads to improvement in the training program as well as in overall employee performance.

DOCUMENTING ENVIRONMENTAL TRAINING, COMPETENCE, AND AWARENESS

ISO 14001 certification requires documentation of many aspects of the EMS, for the purposes of demonstrating compliance with the standard and providing information for evaluation of the effectiveness of the EMS. It is not necessary to build a bureaucracy of documentation requirements. However, there are basic levels of documentation that an organization should consider. As discussed above, documentation assures compliance and provides information necessary to evaluating this phase of the EMS. Common sense should play a key role in setting up the documentation procedures. Good management practices should include developing procedures and writing them down prior to implementing any new process or operation.

Awareness

The programs that an organization institutes to create and maintain awareness of environmental aspects should be described, and ongoing aspects of the program should be documented as they occur. The environmental policy may detail particular activities that are meant to create and maintain awareness (e.g., training, awards programs, other employee incentives, objectives within employee performance requirements, etc.). The details of these programs should be written and accessible. Results of awards programs, for example, should be documented: what the criteria were, what awards were given, who received them, and why. Certainly, if the environmental policy states that some action is occurring, the organization should document that the action was in fact taken and how it was accomplished. Consider what activities are underway that are meant to create or maintain awareness. Then simply document how each of those programs was implemented and how they are proceeding.

Competence

Competence can be documented by describing the process by which environmentally sensitive job activities were identified, how minimum requirements were established, and what steps are being taken to assure employees meet those requirements. During EMS planning, an organization will usually develop a procedure for implementing the various components of the EMS. The organization may have a procedure developed for assuring competence. If so, this procedure, duly written and filed, provides the initial documentation necessary. Beyond this, the organization need only document changes, or milestones met if it is implementing a program in steps over time.

Training

Training documentation should include the following, where applicable:

- Written documentation of the overall training program, including goals, assumptions, strategy, and so on.
- Documentation of each training session that is undertaken, including purpose (awareness, EMS components, job-specific), date(s), trainers, and number of trainees attending.
- Brief summaries or outlines for each training session topic.
- Trainee testing results.
- Trainer evaluation results.

In general, documentation should be sufficient to detail what the training intended to accomplish, how training was undertaken, who was trained and when, what information was provided, and what the results of the training were.

MEASURING EFFECTIVENESS

Chapter 8 discusses in detail the process of environmental performance evaluation (EPE) as it is being developed under ISO 14000. EPE can be used to collect data to help evaluate the effectiveness of an organization's training and awareness programs and provide information for management to use for improving the EMS. Effectiveness may be measured in terms of direct information regarding how the programs function or indirectly by measuring areas of the organization's operations that are impacted by training and awareness. The final EPE standard will include examples of management system environmental performance indicators (EPIs) to help the organization develop its own EPIs. The list below provides examples of ways to measure training programs:

- Track the number of hours of training provided each employee.
- Track the amount of resources allotted to training, as a percent of the organization's total budget.
- In an evolving program, track the employees trained as a percent of those expected to be trained by each milestone date.
- For frequently repeated training programs, track the testing scores over time.
- Track the percent of employees participating in training or awareness programs, perhaps by job function or level in the organization.
- Track the percent of employees recognized for participation in environmental programs, perhaps separately for employees with environmentally sensitive job activities and for other employees.
- Track the percent of employees who have environmental responsibilities as part of their job performance.
- Track the number and type of environmental incidents traceable to inadequate employee awareness or training.
- Track the percent of employees meeting the minimum environmental job requirements at milestone dates.

These are merely examples. Think about how to measure the effectiveness of training and awareness programs in ways that provide meaningful information to the organization. Understanding the effectiveness of the programs helps an organization avoid inefficient training, which only has the effect of costing time and money. When an organization understands what is working and what is not working, it can make the changes necessary to guide it toward the most efficient and cost-effective transfer of information to its employees.

BIOGRAPHY

W. Gary Wilson, Esq.

> **W. Gary Wilson** is an associate vice president and director of NE Environmental Management Services in the Amherst, NH office of Environmental Science & Engineering, Inc. (ESE). Mr. Wilson consults with industry on environmental management services, such as compliance auditing, strategy development, training, and goal setting. He has more than 25 years of experience in environmental consulting/management, with the past 10 years including environmental law. He works with industrial clients helping them understand the implications of the impending ISO standards and helping them develop the management structures necessary for compliance with ISO 14001. Mr. Wilson is active in ISO Technical Committee 207 as a member of US Sub-Tag 4, Environmental Performance Evaluation.
>
> Mr. Wilson is a member of the Boston and Massachusetts Bar Associations, participating in their environmental sections. He is also on the Board of Directors and is president of the New England Association of Environmental Professionals. He has participated in training seminars for environmental management, including hazardous waste, industrial hygiene, and ISO 14000 development and tracking.

CHAPTER 5

Environmental Management System Documentation

W. D. Anderson

INTRODUCTION

Establishing a documented EMS within an organization provides a formal framework for tracking environmental activities. The existence of EMS documentation supports employee awareness of the requirements for achieving the organization's environmental objectives and enables the evaluation of the system and environmental performance. It demonstrates to the auditor, whether internal or external, that the EMS has been implemented. Effective documentation can also better inform the organization's stakeholders and employees of the environmental management activities. It can help an organization benchmark its environmental activities in an effort to improve environmental performance.

WHAT TO DOCUMENT

General Requirement—Clause 4.4.4

The general requirement for documentation is contained in ISO 14001 Clause 4.4.4. The organization must "establish and maintain information, in paper or electronic form" to do the following:

1. "Describe the core elements of the management system and their interaction."

2. "Provide direction to related documentation."

Note that the above requirement applies to "core elements of the management system and their interaction." The requirement does not say "every element" of the system. Also, the requirement allows for providing "direction to related documenta-tion." The implication is that the organization need not create everything from scratch or redo existing documentation that supports the EMS.

The language about documentation may reflect a desire on the part of the standards developers to avoid excessive and unnecessary documentation and to negate the automatic assumption by users of the standard that they must document everything. Thus, in many cases, the standard requires procedures but does not explicitly require "documented" procedures. A procedure can be useful and effective without being documented. However, documentation is important to demonstrate conformance with the standard, whether determined by internal or external auditors. Therefore, most organizations will want to create documented procedures.

The core elements of the EMS are, of course, those described in ISO 14001. More specifically, the ISO 14001 clauses where organizations must develop documentation are listed below. Also discussed below are areas where the standard does not explicitly state that documentation is required but where a reasonable implication is that docu-mentation will be necessary to demonstrate conformance with the standard.

Specific Documentation Requirements

The EMS model illustrated in both ISO 14001 and 14004 shows the basis for the approach to establishing an EMS. Figure 5–1 is an illustration of the EMS model presented in ISO 14001.

Organizations are not required to document the type, or types, of models used as a basis for developing their EMS or how these models will be maintained, although the organization should consider documenting the model shown in Figure 5–1. The organization does not need to follow Figure 5–1 nor the exact structure presented in ISO 14001; however, organizations seeking certification or self-declaration will need to show how their environmental documentation procedures align with the clauses in ISO 14001.

EMS documentation should at least include procedures for the following five principles:

- Principle 1   Environmental policy.
- Principle 2   Planning.
- Principle 3   Implementation and operation.
- Principle 4   Checking and corrective action.
- Principle 5   Management review.

Organizations with established quality management system documentation will notice the similarity between ISO 14001 and ISO 9001.

If organizations subscribe to other environmental management principles, such as the International Chamber of Commerce (ICC) 16 principles or the Chemical Manufacturers Association's (CMA's) Responsible Care® Codes of Management Practices, the congruency between those principles to ISO 14001 should be documented.

Environmental Management System Model

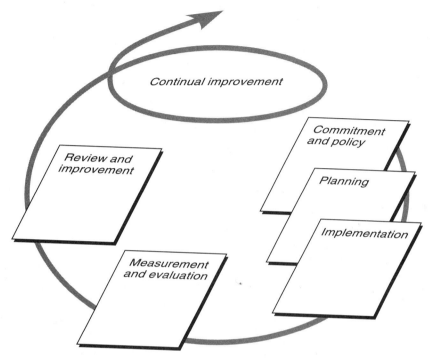

Adapted from ISO 14001

Clause 4.2 Environmental Policy

The requirements for the content of the environmental policy were described earlier in this book. The requirements emphasize that the policy must be documented, maintained as needed, communicated to all employees, and available to the public.

The organization should develop a procedure, whether documented or not, for a review of the policy, based on the results of the management review of the EMS.

Clause 4.3 Planning

Clause 4.3.1 Environmental Aspects

The organization must develop a procedure to identify significant environmental aspects and keep the information up to date.

Clause 4.3.2 Legal and Other Requirements

The environmental policy states the organization's commitment to comply with relevant legal and other requirements. Clause 4.3.2 requires procedures that describe how to identify and have access to those requirements directly applicable to the environmental aspects of the organization's activities, products, or services.

Clause 4.3.3 Objectives and Targets

This clause requires the organization to establish and maintain "documented environmental objectives and targets at each relevant function and level within the organization." The person(s)/departments responsible for achieving objectives and targets at each relevant function and level of the organization should also be documented, including the means and timeframes for achievement.

Clause 4.4 Implementation and Operation

This clause describes the details of the EMS and contains those areas associated with most of the documentation requirements. The areas that *must* be documented include the following:

- The roles, responsibilities, and authorities for everyone whose tasks are associated with significant environmental aspects.
- Procedures to cover operational control and maintenance procedures for situations where their absence could lead to deviations from the environmental policy and the objectives and targets.

The following areas *should* be documented:

- Training procedures, for both awareness and competency training.
- Procedures for internal communication regarding environmental aspects and the EMS.
- Procedures for receiving, documenting, and responding to relevant communication from external interested parties.
- A documented process, if deemed appropriate by the organization, for external communication regarding significant environmental aspects and a record of this decision.
- Procedures for controlling all documents required by ISO 14001.
- Procedures concerning the creation and modification of the various types of documents.
- Procedures related to the identifiable significant environmental aspects of goods and services used by the organization and communicating relevant procedures and requirements to suppliers and contractors.

- Procedures to identify the potential for and the response to accidents and emergency situations, and for preventing and mitigating the environmental impacts that may be associated with them.

In addition, consider documenting financial and other resources for emergency preparedness and response as part of the overall EMS system. This provides a means to evaluate the effectiveness of the environmental documentation procedures, and systems.

ISO 14004, Clause 4.3.3.2 suggests that "operational processes and procedures should be defined and appropriately documented, and updated as necessary. The organization should clearly define the various types of documents which establish and specify effective operational procedures and control."

Clause 4.4.5 Document Control

The document control procedures in ISO 14001 Clause 4.4.5 are rigorous. The procedures must ensure that documents:

- Can be located.
- Are periodically reviewed, revised as necessary, and approved for adequacy by authorized personnel.
- If current versions, are available at all locations where operations essential to the effective functioning of the system are performed.
- If obsolete, are promptly removed from all points of use or otherwise assured against unintended use.
- If obsolete but are retained for legal and/or knowledge preservation purposes, are suitably identified.
- Are legible, dated (with dates of versions), readily identifiable, maintained in an orderly manner, and retained for a specific period.

The organization must also establish procedures and responsibilities concerning the creation and modification of the various types of documents. Annex A of ISO 14001 emphasizes that the purpose of document control is to support the EMS, not to create a complex document control system for its own sake. Therefore, EMS documentation and document control should be easily understood by all levels and functions within the organization and should align with the organizations goals, objectives, and targets.

Clause 4.5 Checking and Corrective Action

The areas in this section that require documentation include the following:

- Procedures used to monitor and measure the key characteristics of operations and activities that have a significant impact on the environment.

- Procedures to record information to track performance, relevant operational controls, and conformance to objectives and targets.

- Procedures for periodically evaluating compliance with relevant environmental legislation and regulation.

Other areas where documentation would be prudent include:

- Procedures to calibrate and maintain monitoring equipment and records of the process.

- Procedures that define responsibility and authority for investigating and handling nonconformances and mitigating any impacts caused.

- Procedures for initiating and completing corrective and preventive actions and for recording changes in the documented procedures that result from corrective and preventive action.

Clause 4.5.3 Records

As mentioned in earlier chapters, Clause 4.5.3 requires procedures for identifying, maintaining, and disposing of environmental records. The records to be maintained are those that demonstrate conformance to ISO 14001. These records must include training records and the results of audits and reviews. They can also include the following, among other things:

- Legislative and regulatory requirements.

- Operating permits.

- Inspection, calibration, and maintenance activity.

- Monitoring data.

- Compliance records.

- Corrective and preventive action reports.

- Product information.

- Supplier and contractor information.

- Information on emergency preparedness and response.

While organizations may integrate their environmental records with their documentation system, the two requirements (Clauses 4.4.4 and 4.5.3) should be discernible. In other words, environmental auditors should be able to easily identify that the organization has met both documentation and records requirements.

Clause 4.5.4 Environmental Management System Audit

The organization should document its EMS audit procedures, including the schedule for audits, audit scope, frequency, methods, and responsibilities and requirements for conducting audits and reporting results. The written audit procedures should be consistent with the organization's other written environmental procedures regarding structure, format, approval, cataloging and so on.

4.6 Management Review

The management review process and its results must be documented. A final point: If there are elements within ISO 14001 that do not apply to the organization, this fact also should be documented.

DEVELOPING DOCUMENTATION PROCEDURES

Creating procedures for documenting the EMS is a vital element for organizations, especially if they want a means of verifying and improving their EMS. The organization should create environmental documentation procedures for its own benefit, not to satisfy ISO 14001 or any other standard.

Planning

Creating environmental documentation procedures should begin with planning. Typically, it is the top management of the organization that facilitates the planning process. The planning process should include consideration of the following items:

- What are the internal and external organizational needs for documentation?
- How will the organization communicate the documentation system (internally and externally)?
- What are the procedures for implementing, reviewing, measuring, and controlling the documentation system?
- What are the resources for implementing, reviewing, measuring, and controlling the documentation system?

Top Management Commitment

Developing an effective documentation system for the EMS begins with commitment from all levels and functions of the organization, especially from top management. As with the overall EMS, top management commitment is necessary for making the process work.

Allocating Resources for Developing Documentation Procedures

After the organization identifies the need to create environmental documentation procedures, it should allocate resources necessary for developing, maintaining, reviewing, controlling, and improving the environmental documentation procedures. Commitment of resources by management should include the following areas:

- Financial.
- Personnel, such as environmental, quality, etc.
- Technological, such as computers, software, etc.

Financial resources for developing environmental documentation procedures can be estimated by determining the number of environmental and other personnel and the number of computers and other technology needed.

Documentation Systems Vary

Planning and developing a documentation system for EMS will vary from organization to organization, depending upon its size and complexity. If elements of the EMS are integrated into the organization's overall management system, the environmental documentation should be integrated into existing documentation.

Documentation Gap Analysis

In setting up a system, most organizations will also evaluate their existing organizational documentation procedures. These may include the following:

- Quality documentation procedures, such as ISO 9001, 9002, and 9003.
- Financial documentation procedures, such as corporate reports.
- Management documentation procedures, such as lines of communication and employee roles and responsibilities.

By examining the existing documentation procedures, an organization can build a useful framework for creating environmental documentation procedures without unnecessary duplication of documentation.

After determining what exists, the organization will want to consider the following factors to aid in assessing congruency with ISO 14001:

- Assess the existing environmental activities from which the organization wants to formalize environmental procedures, such as environmental issues that impact the organization internally and externally. The organization can use a simple input-output matrix, as shown in Table 5–1.
- Assess the existing organizational documentation procedures such as cataloging, numbering, indexing, formatting, reporting, controlling,

TABLE 5–1

Input/Output Model

Input		Output
Environmental Activity	*Transition*	*Environmental Procedure*
Emergency response	Develop	Emergency procedure
Public communication	Develop	Communication procedure

TABLE 5–2

Examples of Existing Documentation Procedures and Examples of Existing Environmental Procedures Congruent with ISO 14001

a. Existing Documentation Procedures

Company X Documentation Procedures	*Alignment with Environmental*
Controlling quality documents	Controlling environmental documents
Cataloging quality documents	Cataloging environmental documents
Communicating quality procedures	Communicating environmental procedures

b. Existing Environmental Procedures Congruent with ISO 14001

Company X Environmental Activities	*Alignment with ISO 14001*	
Environmental policy	4.2	Environmental policy
Environmental compliance program	4.3.2	Legal and other requirements
Environmental communication procedures	4.4.3	Communication

reviewing, and approving. Assess the existing environmental procedures that apply to the organization's overall environmental goals, objectives, and targets that align with ISO 14001 clauses (Table 5–2). Develop documentation procedures and justifications for subclauses within ISO 14001 that may not apply to the organization's overall goals, objectives, and targets.

Documentation Hierarchy

Once the organization conducts a gap analysis and identifies the necessary documentation, a key challenge is to organize the basic structure of documentation. Often, organizations create an EMS Manual that provides the basics, such as the environmental policies, objectives, targets, key roles, and major responsibilities. The manual references relate documentation and other relevant aspects of the organization's management system.

An approach that has been generally favored in the ISO 9000 quality management application is a documentation hierarchy consisting of four layers. Each layer develops a steadily increasing level of detail about company operations and methods. These layers are shown in Figure 5–2 and consist of the following:

- The environmental manual.
- Company operating procedures.
- Work instructions.
- Records.

The layers in the figure are presented as a broad-based triangle. The environmental manual would generally contain the basic policies, objectives, and targets and other general information about the EMS program. The operating procedures describe the overall flow of activities. Work instructions are more detailed, activity-specific guidelines. And records include all documentation needed to demonstrate compliance with the EMS and its requirements.

Summary of Documentation/Environmental Manual

For ease of use, the organization can consider organizing and maintaining a summary of documentation. This can also be the EMS Manual. This document, manual, or summary document should accomplish the following:

- Collate the environmental policy, objectives, and targets.
- Describe the means of achieving environmental objectives and targets.
- Document the key roles, responsibilities, and procedures.
- Provide direction to related documentation and describe other elements of the organization's management system, where appropriate.
- Demonstrate that the EMS elements appropriate for the organization are implemented.

Such a summary document can serve as a reference to the implementation and maintenance of the organization's EMS.

Recommended Documentation Format

Environmental documentation procedures established by the organization should be uniform or consistent in approach, structure, and format. Therefore, the environmental documentation procedures should consider the following items:

FIGURE 5–2

Documentation Hierarchy

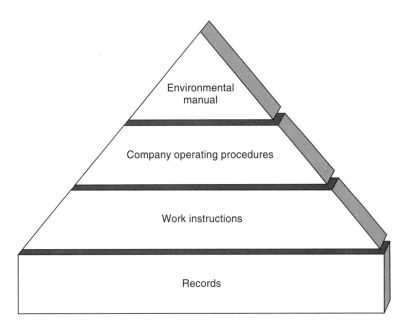

- Title of the environmental procedure.
- Purpose/objective, introduction.
- Scope.
- References.
- Definitions.
- Procedure.
- Responsibilities.
- Standard organizational format (the organization's existing format such as font type and size, document control number, document version, date, and approval).
- Request for change procedures.

An example is shown in Table 5–3.

TABLE 5-3

Sample Documentation Format

Title	Labeling of Unknown Wastes
Date and version	March 25, 1996, Ver. 1.0
Document control no.	ENV-PRO-001.001
Approval	Name of person approving this procedure
Purpose	To improve "Company X" Waste Management Program by providing instruction to and responsibilities for controlling unknown wastes
Reference	Waste Management Program
Definitions	See Corporate Environmental Definition Manual
Responsibilities	All Supervisors in Section Units A through G
Request for change	Suggestions for changing this procedure, use the request for change form
Written procedure	The written procedure needs to include specific instructions on what to do, and what not to do

Level of Detail Required/Related Documentation

According to Annex A of ISO 14001, clause A.4.4, "the level of detail of the documentation should be sufficient to describe the core elements of the environmental management system and their interaction and provide direction on where to obtain more detailed information on the operation of specific parts of the environmental management system. This documentation may be integrated with documentation of other systems implemented by the organization. It does not have to be in the form of a single manual." The annex suggests that related documentation can consist of information such as the following:

1. Process information.
2. Organizational charts.
3. Internal standards and operational procedures.
4. Site emergency plans.

CONCLUSION

Documentation has often been mentioned as one of the greatest challenges and obstacles in the ISO 9000 context. Companies implementing ISO 9000 standards have complained that it requires a "paper factory." The same could hold true in the ISO 14000 context. But ISO 14001 implementation doesn't necessarily require reams of additional documentation, nor does it require documenting everything indiscriminately. It *does* require, however, that an organization document those aspects of its operations that demonstrate first to itself that its EMS is working well and then to an auditor that an ISO 14001-compliant system is in place and functioning effectively.

BIOGRAPHY

W.D. (Doug) Anderson

W.D. (Doug) Anderson is president of Anderson Development, which specializes in business management; quality management; health, safety, and environmental program design; computer services, such as database design, software training, and programming; and research design and methodology. Prior to Anderson Development, Mr. Anderson specialized in developing and assessing health, safety, and environmental management systems for small, medium and large organizations in various industries. Mr. Anderson is a member of the U.S. Technical Advisory Group to ISO/TC 207 on Environmental Management. He is also a member of the American Society of Quality Control (ASQC) and many of its divisions, such as the Quality Management Division, Quality Audit Division, and the Energy and Environmental Division. Currently, Mr. Anderson is participating in ASQC Energy and Environmental Division's Assessment, Verification and Auditing Committee. He is a candidate to receive a master's of science degree in management from National-Louis University. He received his bachelor of science degree in geology from Indiana University of Pennsylvania. *Anderson Development, 7641 Chadds Landing Way, Manassas, Virginia 22111, Tel: 703-331-1445, Fax: 703-331-0248.*

CHAPTER 6

Information Technology and ISO 14000

David C. Roberts

INTRODUCTION

The underlying premise of the ISO 14000 standards is that effective and enlightened environmental management depends upon, and will follow naturally from, a deep and detailed understanding of one's operations and their impacts on the environment, safety, and health. This means accessing and interpreting data about real processes, systems, and materials. In all but exceptional cases, this can be done most effectively by taking advantage of modern information technology (IT).

In fact, it is only with the availability of cost-effective computing resources that a company can realistically adopt a standard such as ISO 14000 in a meaningful way. Thus ISO 14000 and IT are closely intertwined, even though the standard does not explicitly require automated information systems.

ISO 14000 asks organizations to apply a near-scientific level of rigor to the management of their operations, with the promise that this too will be paid back many times over for the cost and effort involved. The better able an organization is to master the details about a system, the better able it is to understand and hence to predict its behavior. Ultimately, the organization should influence that behavior in beneficial ways. Information technology can, often for the first time, make these details available and understandable to the decision maker.

Throughout this chapter, the term *ISO 14000* will be used without distinguishing between the different individual standards. The subject matter is geared primarily toward the ISO 14001 EMS standard, although it applies to the other standards in a more peripheral way. This chapter will examine the components of an ISO 14001 compliant EMS in the light of the most exciting recent advances in IT and will look at how these technologies can be applied to provide an advantage in implementing those components. This chapter will not review available "ISO 14000 compliance" software or other environmental management information system products and vendors although it will discuss such products generically in terms of what they offer to those seeking to implement an ISO 14001-compliant EMS. Mention of an individual product or technology in this chapter is for clarification only and should not be taken as an endorsement of that product or technology.

ISO 14000 AND CORPORATE COMPUTING

As has been made clear in earlier chapters, ISO 14000 does not prescribe any particular set of goals, policies, or processes as prerequisites for an effective EMS. Neither does the standard require use of any particular computer software or information systems; conversely, there are no software packages that, when implemented in a company, confer ISO 14000 compliance status on it. In fact, there is nothing in the standard requiring use of any kind of automated information system.

However, what the standard does require is the development of a clear, comprehensive, and detailed description of how environmental issues are managed. At the very least, going through this exercise typically reveals cases of poor management or nonmanagement, which may then be rectified.

Thus ISO 14001 compliance typically implies a certain amount of business process reengineering (BPR). Good BPR, in turn, attempts to deploy information technology to its best possible advantage. More fundamentally, an ISO 14001-compliant EMS must support effective tracking of environmental performance and provide a mechanism to continuously improve this performance over time. Tracking environmental performance in a meaningful way requires the collection, processing, and dissemination of information. Given the quantity and nature of data involved, it can be handled far more efficiently in an automated manner. Advanced information technology can provide, in addition to the automation of a given function and collection and reporting of data, a superior means of analyzing and integrating the data into meaningful information that can serve as the basis for sound decisions.

ISO 14000 Software: What Does It Do?

There are several commercially available software packages that claim to assist users in understanding, implementing, and documenting an ISO 14000-compliant EMS. In essence, these programs provide a template and guidance for constructing an electronic document that describes an EMS, and in this way function comparably to a consultant. A key question to ask is this: Should the organization use a new system or build onto its existing systems?

One product in particular provides a checklist-oriented user interface: The top level shows all the components of a fully functional EMS and displays an icon for each that shows the current status as compliant, noncompliant, or indeterminate. Moving down one level reveals all the functions within that component and their implementation status. The software typically has embedded record-keeping and data analysis functions of the sort required to show that continuous improvements are being made; for example, a complete set of employee training records can be established and maintained within the package.

These are attractive features for the smaller and less information-intensive organization, but such a package must be populated with information for it to provide value to the user. For a large organization, this can be a daunting task, and while in principle it can be performed manually, some sort of data migration or integration will prove to be a better method.

The cost of this process, however, may greatly exceed the nominal cost of the software. Another problem with such software is that it may be single-user-oriented, and not ideally suited to the sharing of information across a network.

A preferable alternative, especially for a larger facility, would be to build more effectively on existing corporate management information systems. For example, a company may already maintain a complete set of employee training records or may have a partially implemented capability to do so. For that part of the EMS, it will be more cost-effective to build onto this system than to import data into a dedicated ISO 14000 software system.

Using Existing Corporate Management Information Systems in ISO 14000 Implementation

A company's existing information systems typically will already capture, contain, and manage much of the data required to support the environmental management functions. For example, records of hazardous materials acquisition and hazardous waste disposal are both managed at least at some level by the corporate purchasing function. Thus, there will be records of materials ordered and received, along with quantities, costs, time, organization, location, and so on. The purchasing system may not contain all the information, such as material composition and how it is used, that is needed for a complete accounting of chemical substance release into the environment.

That additional information, as well as additional reporting functions, must be added to the corporate information system and integrated with the purchasing data and functions in order to achieve complete accounting. Furthermore, the purchasing system is a transaction-oriented system whose primary function is to process purchase requisitions and may not have the computing capacity to handle complex queries and statistical processing of historical data.

Many environmental software vendors and systems integrators, as well as their customers, now recognize that installing a "shrink-wrapped" environmental management information system is not in itself a realistic solution for most companies. They recognize that substantial effort must be expended in achieving both compatibility and connectivity of a new Environmental Management Information System (EMIS) functionality with the client's existing systems, and in either migrating or mapping data from those systems. It is easy for a project of this kind to get out of hand. If an organization decides to pursue this strategy, it should be careful to do the following:

1. Allow for reasonable costs and time frame for the project.

2. Select qualified and experienced vendors and systems integrators to perform the work.

3. Closely oversee the project to ensure reasonable progress.

Modify and Enhance Existing Systems

Several different strategies may be adopted to introduce environmental management functions into the corporate computing environment. One strategy is to modify and enhance the functions of the existing systems. This strategy may be appropriate for recently installed or upgraded systems. It incurs the risk, however, of exceeding the computing capacity of these systems and/or negatively impacting the performance of existing functions.

In addition, modifying these systems involves costly custom design and programming services, and the cost of doing so is difficult to estimate accurately beforehand.

Purchase and Install a Commercial System

A second strategy is to purchase and install a commercial system containing the desired functionality and then import or map data from existing systems into it. This may be appropriate for smaller organizations or those with limited environmental management requirements. This strategy requires the selection of software and a platform that can provide the desired level of connectivity to the existing systems. While this is becoming the norm for commercial software, there are many products that do not offer a high degree of connectivity and compatibility.

The Data Warehouse Strategy

A third strategy is to mirror a subset of the data in the transaction-oriented systems (e.g., purchasing, inventory) in a "data warehouse" (see Box 6–1). The data warehouse is dedicated to supporting a large subset of the environmental management functions that are largely oriented toward long-term record keeping, data aggregation and summarization, and information dissemination.

The advantage of such a strategy is that it places little additional computing load on the transaction-oriented systems and provides a backup to that system. In addition, vendors and systems integrators can preconfigure much of the functionality desired. This minimizes the cost and time commitment involved in custom on-site work.

Integrating Data across Corporate Levels

A final issue in corporate EMIS implementation is the roll-up and integration of data from shops to facilities to the corporate level. This issue is not a concern just in the environmental management area but cuts across all management functions: The reason

BOX 6–1

THE DATA WAREHOUSE

Data warehousing is a process by which data from the various transaction-oriented systems that manage the day-to-day flow of information are migrated or archived periodically to a single, separate location. The data are made available in fully integrated form for querying and analysis without significant performance or reliability impact on the other information systems. A data warehouse can be a tremendous source of value, in that it allows a company to put to strategic use the wealth of data that it accumulates in its day-to-day business. Some preprocessing and aggregation of the data is usually needed to bring data from different sources into a congruent format. However, the philosophy of data warehousing is to provide an accurate and searchable record of the data as it existed in the transaction-oriented systems. As corrections are made to the latter, they will appear in the warehouse along with their previous incorrect values.

The value of a data warehouse depends very much on the semantic normalization and integration of the data in it; that is, a data item should not mean two different things depending on what source it comes from. Much of the cost of setting up a data warehouse is in establishing a semantically consistent repository of data definitions (also called a catalog or a data dictionary), an exercise that requires broad expertise in the subject matter area and familiarity with how the transaction-oriented systems are used. For a complex data warehouse, this can be a substantial repository of information. At a minimum, the user of a data warehouse needs a comprehensive, preferably on-line catalog of the data contained in it, a means of querying the warehouse, and a means to format the results of a query. These functions may be carried out individually, using simple functions that are standard features of almost all commercial database management systems, or they can be integrated under a supplemental layer of software. The supplemental software provides the user with easy access to all data item definitions and formats in a way that is integrated with query and reporting functions and that insulates the user from the system-specific characteristics of the individual databases that feed the warehouse.

Data-querying functions for the warehouse range from the simple to the highly sophisticated. In addition to system calls and query languages, many database packages offer a "query by example" grid paradigm in which the tables and columns to be queried can be assembled via "drag and drop" into a grid-like tool. Conditions and aggregate functions are then selected or entered, and finally the query is executed. A number of front-end products are available that allow data items for a query to be selected with their definitions in view. Natural language interface tools are also available, allowing queries to be constructed in plain English. Specialized query software aimed at the needs of the data warehouse market is available.

corporations aggregate and merge is to take advantage of the economies of scale. But to do so requires a roll-up or cross-feeding of all kinds of information. To eliminate duplication of effort, the organization must identify duplication of effort. To clone a good idea from one facility to others, the organization first has to identify that good idea. So it is with corporatewide environmental management: Good data collected at the shop or facility level must be rolled up to the corporate level before they can be used, for example, to prioritize capital spending alternatives for environmental improvements. Not all environmental data, however, need to be rolled up to the corporate level; in many cases, summary information from operating units will suffice.

Requirement: Semantic Consistency

Data integration requires semantic consistency of the underlying information across all the facilities; data must be collected and processed in much the same way to be the basis for comparison between facilities. Integration also requires two important information-processing functions: periodic transmission of aggregate information from the facility level to the corporate level, and further aggregation and analysis at that level. These functions are as important for other corporate information systems functions as they are for environmental management functions.

Semantic consistency can be achieved in several ways. An organization can implement a single corporatewide information system with integrated environmental management functionality and remote access at the facility level; the same set of environmental management software can be implemented at individual facilities; or a middle layer can be implemented that maps and pipes data from each facility level system to a corporate system. Any of these methods can be the most appropriate solution depending on circumstances.

Information Systems Reengineering and Integration

Whether adopting ISO 14000 or not, a healthy company will periodically reengineer various parts of its information systems infrastructure. Doing so can yield two kinds of benefits: It can help automate and streamline existing processes, and it can provide new (and perhaps necessary) functionality that the previous system did not have. Thus, when figured in as part of a reengineering effort that would probably be performed anyway, the cost of adding environmental management functions may be relatively small.

Good reengineering is more than simply replacing a manual process with a computerized one (e.g., filling out and printing a form using a computer rather than a typewriter). It is carried out to streamline the underlying processes; for example, electronically transmitting the data from the completed form to a location where the user of the data retrieves it, or perhaps eliminating part or all of the manual keyboard entry process entirely through the use of look-up tables or bar coding.

Of course, this will change the roles of the people performing the process, so a significant information systems reengineering project is by its very nature a reengineering of the business process itself. This change, while in some ways more painful, can yield large payoffs in efficiency and quality; whereas, information technology improvements implemented without regard to the underlying processes typically fail to yield a good return on investment.

The ISO 14000 philosophy integrates environmental management functions into all relevant business processes rather than adding separate functions on top of those processes. This method offers the best promise of keeping costs down and productivity up. The same philosophy applies to the information systems component: If environmental management functions are performed in a separate computing environment or require duplicate data entry, they are likely to be viewed by employees as a separate function that has little to do with their world and that constitutes an unreasonable burden. It is far better that these functions simply become part of the employee's day-to-day business; for this to happen, a high degree of integration in the corporate computing environment is necessary.

Unfortunately, such integration poses more than just technical challenges. Corporate information system software providers frequently withhold specifications and other information about their products that is needed to achieve such integration, arguing that its public release could hurt their competitive advantage. The alternative to purchasing these high-performance proprietary products is to adopt an open-systems architecture that constructs a corporate information system from a variety of commercial products that conform to open-systems standards. But this technology lags behind proprietary technology because it is tied to the standards development process.

Customers need to weigh the advantages offered by "single-vendor integration" against long-term vendor independence and maintainability offered by an open-systems approach. Customers need to put pressure on vendors to adopt open standards and/or to provide interface specifications for specialized environmental software products.

INFORMATION TECHNOLOGY IN ENVIRONMENTAL MANAGEMENT COMMITMENT AND POLICY

Implementing an ISO 14000-compliant EMS is not a closed-ended process but is itself subject to continual improvement. This section will provide environmental managers and information systems planners with ideas about taking advantage of modern information technology to streamline environmental management functions and thereby reduce the costs and improve the effectiveness of these functions.

Initial Environmental Review

The annex to ISO 14001 recommends that an initial review be done at the outset. Existing corporate information systems can provide supporting information needed for this review. Although there may not yet be an EMIS implemented within the company, there may be individual systems that can collectively provide considerable information to support an environmental review if one knows how to obtain that information.

In addition to inventory control and purchasing systems, which can contain a lot of useful data, there may be separate systems for identifying and tracking incidents of noncompliance, for tracking emissions of contaminants into the environment that support permitting functions, or for tracking the cost of waste management and disposal. Because the review is an extraordinary function—that is, not a part of normal operations—these systems may not be able to generate automatically the kinds of reports needed for the purposes of the review. One solution is to develop customized reports in each system.

General purpose data query and integration tools are available that provide a single user interface and command set through which one can build queries and reports from data contained in these separate systems. If a system cannot be accessed over a network, it can be used to generate an export file that is moved via hard media to the analysis platform. Data-mining tools carry this one step further: An information repository that defines the data content and format of existing information systems can greatly aid in this process. This section will describe these tools and how they work.

Establishing and Disseminating Environmental Policy

A well-managed organization will have effective mechanisms in place for the dissemination of all kinds of policy and information from managers to employees. A separate mechanism for establishing and disseminating environmental policy is not needed for such a company; thus the IT solutions discussed below are not specific to the environmental domain area but apply equally well to other kinds of corporate policy and information. Also, the use of IT here is not critical, but it can greatly facilitate the process.

Both establishing policy (a process involving drafting and revision of documents) and dissemination of the policy (involving not just transmission of textual material but potentially involving more sophisticated media and training programs) can benefit from even simple automated systems. IT solutions applicable to these functions range from low-end to high-end in terms of functionality and price. At the low end are systems such as electronic mail and file sharing systems that are ubiquitous in the corporate environment, notwithstanding complaints still heard rather frequently about corporate E-mail systems not working.

Electronic bulletin boards, which are included in some electronic mail implementations, or can be implemented independently, such as on a net news server, are a more collective alternative that give employees the assurance that they are all reading the same policy and also provide a forum for responding. Typically a bulletin board provides information only when queried by the user, so there is a greater risk than is the case with E-mail that a document will go unread by some employees. A bulletin board can be configured to allow readers to post responses.

At the high end are groupware systems that provide, in addition to E-mail and bulletin boards functionality, additional capabilities and a somewhat different paradigm for sharing information. This includes management of the routing, markup, and revision of documents; management and searching of structured data (including "agents" that

BOX 6–2

KEY FEATURES OF GROUPWARE: SECURITY AND REPLICATION

Because it is a mature, widely adopted technology, groupware has developed into a computing platform in its own right in which many third-party environmental applications are currently available. Two of the features of groupware that make it extremely attractive as a mechanism for intramural corporate communications are its sophisticated security features and its replication functions. Its security features allow convenient yet fine-grained control of who has what kind of access (read, modify, delete, etc.) to what data on the network, all the way down to individual database fields and records. Its replication functions allow data to be shared among many geographical locations in near real time without the overhead and reliability problems typical of a centralized server with long-range direct network connections. Each location maintains one or more servers, which periodically update each other as data are added or modified. Mobile computing is made simple, with the subset of company databases needed by the user copied to a portable computer. Work can then be done off-line, with replication of changes occurring in both directions automatically upon remote log-in to a server.

may be programmed to periodically search databases); and sophisticated, customizable functions such as automated processing of responses to a questionnaire, automatic event notification, and powerful remote access and security features. Commercial groupware packages such as Lotus Notes® are based on proprietary networking technology and are relatively mature and robust products (see Box 6–2).

Comparable functions can be implemented through the use of the open World Wide Web technology, but this technology is less mature and is weaker in the area of security. Adequate security can be provided in many cases by isolating sensitive corporate network functions (the corporate "intranet") from the outside world, using a network fire wall that conceals all but a few heavily controlled gateway machines from direct outside access. Finally, these two technologies are beginning to converge, with the appearance of bridging applications on the market.

INFORMATION TECHNOLOGY IN EMS PLANNING

A good understanding of all facility operations is needed as the basis for planning an EMS: What components of the system are needed and how they should be implemented will depend on the perceived environmental impacts of different activities, upon the regulations to which the facility is subject, and on the environmental goals that the company sets for itself. This section describes how IT can aid in developing this understanding and thereby facilitate the planning of an effective EMS.

Identification of Environmental Aspects and Evaluation of Associated Environmental Impacts

Process modeling and simulation is another approach to identifying environmental aspects of a process. It is not exclusively oriented toward environmental issues but can be used for identifying and even simulating environmental improvements to a process. Process modeling can be performed using simple or sophisticated analysis tools; even the exercise of creating such a model can reveal previously hidden aspects of an operation. A number of modeling tools that vendors refer to as "business process modeling" or "business process reengineering" tools are available that are relatively easy to use and in some cases provide the ability to run simple simulations and monitor operating parameters. Dynamic process modeling (see Box 6–3) offers additional advantages. More complex models, with more accurate depictions of events occurring in time and space, can be created using these tools.

Life-cycle assessment, broadly defined in ISO 14040, is an effective tool for identifying hidden environmental burdens. Specialized software tools are available that conduct life-cycle assessments on a clearly defined segment of an industrial operation, product, or process. These tools lead the user through a comprehensive accounting procedure in which all material, energy, and human resource inputs and outputs are quantified and characterized. This exercise may reveal hidden factors that have an important impact on environmental burdens.

Such tools can perform a sensitivity analysis that reveals those aspects of an operation that have the greatest effect on the parameter of interest. The value of these tools and the results they produce depends heavily on the availability of reliable cost factors for each element of a process; developing or licensing a valid database of cost factors may require a substantial investment.

Legal Requirements

Careful tracking and analysis of laws and regulations is required to ensure that the company can respond in a timely manner to proposed or enacted changes. Modern information technology offers an efficient and effective means to do this. A number of commercial regulatory information products are available, furnished on one or more CD-ROM disks; a subscription to such a product typically covers periodic (e.g., quarterly) updates and may also include more frequent (e.g., daily) electronically transmitted information feeds. The user interface provides easy searching by subject and other fields, and scripting tools for automated selection and extraction of text. The data structure typically includes a "list of lists," which is a cross-reference to regulations by chemical substance. Products may vary according to what regulations are covered. The customer may wish to have state and local regulations covered as well as federal regulations, and, if so, should verify that this information is provided in the product. This information is also being offered on-line, via proprietary interfaces and increasingly on the World Wide Web. Using a groupware product or Web browser

BOX 6-3

DYNAMIC PROCESS MODELING

Dynamic process modeling involves creating a dynamic model of the process that closely represents the physical world and contains representations of all the equipment, material, power, and human resources in the process, the state-change events that occur in executing the process, and the rules that govern the frequency and interdependency of these events. Of course, no model can be an exact representation of a physical process, but a sufficiently fine-grained model will accurately represent the process for all practical purposes. Using the embedded programming language available in these tools, the modeler can create a model of any desired degree of complexity. Executing the model will reveal sources of inefficiency and waste in the process and thereby help identify environmental improvements.

Process modeling employs specialized software; creation of anything other than a very simple model typically requires sophisticated programming skills and a significant time commitment. The beauty of process modeling is that, once created, parameters in the model can be varied to test alternative ways of running the process, with no impact on the process itself. After creation of the model, it can be "run" to simulate the actual process, using different operating parameters; doing so can reveal which operating parameters work best and can help to identify ways to streamline the process. Most such packages provide some degree of animation capability. This capability is extremely useful in the process of debugging and validating the model since behavior that does not parallel the real-world system is evident in the operation, not buried in the results.

interface, software agents can be set up to search these information sources either remotely or locally on a daily basis, and identify and report back on any new information meeting defined criteria. This strategy provides almost immediate notification of changes to laws and regulations.

A "home-brew" alternative to subscribing to a commercial service is to access free government sources of legal and regulatory changes. For example, the full text of the Federal Register is now available on-line through the Library of Congress Web site. These information sources, however, will not be as broad in coverage or as frequently updated as most commercial services are. A regulatory alerting system based on publicly available information can be implemented at relatively low cost and tailored to include specific areas not included in commercial legal and regulatory tracking services, which may be desirable in specialized business areas. Software products are available that can be programmed to periodically scan specified portions of the Web and create a structured index of the scanned material. The index can then be used in combination with a search engine (many are available as freeware or shareware) to allow the user to search on a subject, title, or other field, with the results presented in various formats (e.g., keyword in context) with direct links to the original source.

However one tracks laws and regulations, human effort is required to interpret them and determine what response actions, if any, are called for in one's specific business context. Thus, having established a feed of legal and regulatory current awareness information into the company, one needs to ensure that the appropriate end-users have ready access to this information. Electronic mail, including list servers that allow easy maintenance of specialized mailing lists, is a simple and effective way to achieve this distribution electronically. Usenet news groups, proprietary groupware and bulletin boards, and Web technology are other useful means for disseminating the information. In addition, workflow tools are useful in managing the sequence of events triggered by a significant regulatory change.

Environmental Objectives and Targets and Environmental Plans and Programs

Effective environmental management means setting specific performance goals and then taking actions to achieve those goals. Managers need a mechanism to systematically examine all environmentally oriented programs against these goals to identify those programs that really do not address a current goal, and address those goals that are not being effectively addressed. Beyond this, programs that do address goals should be prioritized on the basis of estimated return on investment. One type of technology available to assist users in this area is program planning and tracking software; a full-featured program will allow goal setting and tracking progress toward achieving the goals.

This approach is probably better suited to the actual management of the individual projects. An alternative type of tool that is more appropriate for providing perspective over an entire program allows the creation of functional flow and organizational diagrams, and then permits objects in the diagram to be associated with data and business rules that operate upon the data. This type of tool is used in high-level business process reengineering and is sometimes referred to as a process-modeling or road-mapping tool.

For example, a reasonable goal might be to reduce volatile organic compound (VOC) emissions by 50 percent in five years. A given project, such as a change in a painting process, may target this and any number of other goals. The extent to which the painting process is expected to contribute to a given goal may be expressed quantitatively. Thus, making material substitutions in a small-scale painting process may contribute less to the VOC goal than making similar changes to another, larger-scale process. Alternately, the initial investment may be larger in the latter case, and the payoff realized over a longer term. Each project has attributes of this kind associated with it, and a good road-mapping tool will allow the user to create and edit these attributes for each project, link them to goals, and then compare and evaluate projects against the goals on a more objective basis.

INFORMATION TECHNOLOGY IN EMS IMPLEMENTATION

Information technology typically forms the backbone of an effective EMS. Information systems, when implemented properly, are very good at handling the kinds of repetitive bookkeeping functions that are the necessary underpinning of an EMS: the tracking of people and materiel, the summarizing and transmittal of data, the archiving and management of records, the detailed control and scheduling of operations. This section describes the specific ways in which modern IT can enhance and automate these functions.

Ensuring Capability

Capability in the ISO 14001 context refers to the necessary commitment of human and physical resources to effectively perform all functions that have a meaningful environmental impact, from routine operations to emergency response situations. Information technology offers a way to manage these resources more effectively. From the standpoint of human resources, issues to be dealt with include human resource planning and scheduling, skills evaluation and selection, and training and education. While especially important in the environmental domain, these issues are crucial to the broader context of quality management.

Human resource planning and scheduling fall under the broader umbrella of operations research, which has flourished since the appearance of recent advances in computational technologies such as fuzzy logic, neural networks, and rule-based heuristic systems.

Because this area is still relatively immature, wide acceptance of automation in this area is still years away. Specific environmental training and education is required, often by law or regulation, for many environmental functions. For example, employees handling hazardous materials must receive training in the proper handling of these materials; a well-planned employee database will track the completion of required training, identify individuals who need periodic updates in time for the training to be scheduled, and effectively document the completeness of employee training for the company as a whole. The training itself may be computer-based and can provide its own assessment, tracking, and documentation functions as well as employ effective multimedia instructional technologies.

The management of physical resources that support environmental functions, such as security or environmental monitoring should also be considered. Here, too, information technology in the form of automated reporting and notification systems can amplify the effectiveness of the isolated systems and provide a facilitywide or corporatewide perspective needed for good management.

Communication and Reporting

Network, groupware, and World Wide Web technologies offer new and enhanced means for communication and reporting of environmental information, from regulatory submissions to material safety data sheets (MSDS). Even a simple file-sharing network can be used to provide easy searching and access to the kinds of chemical hazard information, but such a network and the search and retrieval software must be able to carry the anticipated load of use.

Rather than physically maintaining and updating a large number of hard-copy sets of MSDSs, the release of MSDSs can be driven by user needs by placing this information on a Web site. Although there has been a lag in the government's ability to accept and process electronic regulatory reports, more agencies are beginning to accept submissions of this kind, and acceptance is likely to become widespread in a few years. In this case, most of the immediate advantage lies on the government's side, but to the extent that turnaround times are reduced, the submitter of information benefits as well.

Effective communication with customers is a vital part of a product stewardship program. World Wide Web technology can provide customers with instant access to up-to-date product information and other value-added information that can strengthen customer relations at the same time it reduces risks to environment, health, and safety. Simple mail-back forms on a Web site can make it easy for customers to communicate their concerns. The mail-back forms can be processed automatically into a structured format for later analysis. Alternatively, a direct Web interface to a database can be engineered using tool sets available from many database vendors, allowing essentially all desired database functions to be executed through a browser interface.

Mobile networked computing offers new and more efficient means of communication and reporting, from the shop and field operations to the facility level. Handheld computers (personal digital assistants) or terminals may be deployed with custom application software to provide specialized auditing functions. These units can store information obtained in the field and can subsequently off-load the information to another computer for processing. Equipped with wireless communications hardware and software, these units can provide robust connectivity with other systems so the transfer of data can take place in near real time.

EMS Documentation, Records, and Information Management

The value of collecting and analyzing environmental information is mostly realized over the long term, where it can be followed over time and as a function of operating conditions. Besides revealing trends and patterns that are essential to good management, historical environmental information provides a permanent record of a company's efforts to comply with regulations and be proactive in reducing environmental impacts. It provides evidence of past activities and environmental burdens needed to support permit applications so that business can continue unimpeded. It provides records of individual workers, their health histories, and their exposure to environmental and workplace contaminants that can help the company defend itself in legal actions.

Implementing a data warehouse is an excellent strategy for managing EMS-related information. Reports from such a system can reveal important trends and patterns and serve to document the effectiveness of the EMS. It can also reveal patterns in the functioning of information-processing activities upon which the EMS depends.

Operational Control

Particularly in the area of operational control, the distinction between environmental and nonenvironmental functions becomes blurred. Fundamentally, quality management of a complex operation means creating a corporate culture in which the available resources—people, materials, equipment, energy, and money—are used as efficiently and effectively as possible. While not specifically environmental in their emphasis, computer-based tools for process modeling and simulation and process engineering, and integrated systems for manufacturing operations management and enterprise resource planning, can provide valuable insight into and control over complex industrial processes that can lead to significant environmental and cost improvements.

These systems are only now beginning to be implemented. Products are not yet mature, and their implementation can incur significant risks. The true power of such systems comes not so much from the specialized functions they perform but from the degree of integration they achieve across the product life cycle: from market research through product design and development, manufacturing development, production, marketing, sales, and product stewardship.

A wide variety of products are available that claim to be useful in process modeling and simulation and process engineering. At the low end are simple flow-charting tools that allow complex and attractive, albeit static, depictions of a complex operation to be prepared. Requiring a larger investment of time and money, but with a bigger payoff, dynamic process modeling tools allow all the components of a complex system, and their possible physical states, to be specified, along with the rules defining conditions under which states changes occur.

At the high end, sophisticated process engineering tools are available that can model the behavior of complex physical systems in great detail. For example, the behavior of a reactor or heat exchanger is described as a continuous function rather than a series of discrete states. These systems approach computer-aided design (CAD) tools in their ability to provide sophisticated graphical representations of the design of a complex process and to precisely specify the physical configuration of equipment. Some offer a three-dimensional, "virtual reality" interface that allows the user to view the configuration from any point and to walk through the model of the facility.

An additional level of operational control is possible with the integration of sensors into process equipment, where the output of these sensors is tied to a computer model of the process, and the current state of the system can be monitored through the model as user interface. The ultimate degree of control, and a logical extension of this trend, is to integrate actuators into the process that directly control the operating parameters of the process. This technology has been used for many years in industries that have continuous processes that operate in a very stable manner, such as power generation and petrochemical manufacturing. With such a system in place, the operational process can be fully optimized to provide the best balance of product yield, product quality, energy consumption, and waste generation.

Emergency Preparedness and Response

For a complex manufacturing operation, emergency planning and response is a good example of an area where information technology can make a big difference. Automated detection systems employing simple or sophisticated sensor technologies can be an important part of a company's capability to identify a hazardous material release incident. Specialized equipment needed for responding to emergencies may be physically tracked and located via a computer-aided dispatch system; emergency response personnel can use such a system to immediately identify the location of the incident, identify the best route to the site, identify affected persons, manage evacuation, determine the nature of any adjacent hazards, communicate with other authorities, and generally manage the entire response function in a highly effective manner. This is a wise investment, especially where a few seconds one way or another can be a matter of life or death.

INFORMATION TECHNOLOGY IN MEASUREMENT AND EVALUATION

The ongoing monitoring, evaluation, and correction of environmental performance is a crucial part of an effective EMS. This function is not only needed to provide a way to achieve environmental improvements but is also needed to show the tangible evidence of those improvements and their beneficial effects on operating costs.

Measuring and Monitoring

Environmental monitoring is needed to document the benefits of an EMS and to show that the goals of ISO 14000 implementation are being achieved. At the business end of a monitoring system are the sensors themselves. There are currently many new developments being made in sensor technology: Products for environmental and workplace exposure monitoring are becoming less expensive, easier to maintain, more reliable, and more functional.

But measuring and monitoring is more than just the generation of data: The data frequently must be calibrated and standardized; normalized to common units of measure; stored, managed, and archived in a structured database; compared to other values; and analyzed for trends. Devices used in emissions and cleanup site monitoring must be calibrated and standardized periodically to validate and scale the data they provide. Thus complex data operations must underlie even simple interpretations of the data, and these operations are best performed using a good database management system.

Other kinds of business data, such as the usage rates of regulated chemicals and power and water utilities, and the quantities, analyses, and disposal costs of hazardous and municipal wastes, must also be gathered and managed. All of these functions require basic database management functionality at a minimum; but the monitoring function, which is interpreted here to mean the ongoing evaluation of the data as the basis for making business decisions, is greatly facilitated when modern data analysis and visualization tools are used. Such tools are now considered to be integral to a class of software called *executive information systems*. Executive information systems bring together data from many sources that describe many aspects of a company's operations, and, at a minimum, allow managers to identify, retrieve, examine, and graph the data. The more sophisticated functionality found in scientific visualization tools can more effectively help managers understand complex and diverse environmental and operational data and provide a better basis for business decisions.

Another development in this area is the use of modeling tools to manage facility emissions under a regulatory prescribed envelope. Modeling tools can identify ways to reschedule or otherwise modify operations to normalize overall facility emissions. This ensures compliance with limits specified in the permit and may allow cost recovery from sale of excess emissions credits.

Nonconformance and Corrective and Preventive Action

The basic paradigm of the environmental audit is one of problem identification, problem evaluation, corrective action, and verification that the corrective action has been accomplished. This process involves multiple persons and organizations with different responsibilities and is implemented through the creation, tracking, and resolution of action items. In this area, groupware products offer an effective solution that allows users even in geographically disperse locations to define, track, and resolve such action items, and provide an accurate log of such activities that serves to self-document the system.

These products offer highly effective and robust connectivity, structured data operations, statistical summarization, and sophisticated report-generating capabilities. The same functionality can be implemented using the open World Wide Web technology, although security is potentially a problem.

BIOGRAPHY

David C. Roberts, PhD

David C. Roberts holds a B.A. in molecular biology from the University of Wisconsin and a Ph.D. in organic chemistry from the Massachusetts Institute of Technology. He was an NIH postdoctoral fellow at UCLA, served as an assistant professor of chemistry at Rutgers University, and worked as an associate professor of chemistry at Fordham University, where he performed basic research in peptide chemistry, polymer chemistry, and chemical information science. Dr. Roberts was on the technical staff at The MITRE Corporation from 1985 until 1996, when Mitretek Systems split off as a separate company. He is currently a lead scientist in the Center for Environment, Resources, and Space at Mitretek. He has provided technical support to governmental activities in the areas of chemical risk and hazard assessment, toxic substances evaluation and control, and information management and retrieval in the environmental, chemical, and biotechnology areas. His current work focus is environmental and corporate information systems, with emphasis on design and implementation methodology, data and systems integration, commercial off-the-shelf software implementation and integration, and scientific computing.

Center for Environment, Resources, and Space
Mitretek Systems
7525 Colshire Drive
McLean, VA 22102-7400
Phone: (703) 610-2195
E-mail: droberts@mitretek.org

CHAPTER 7

Checking and Corrective Action

Jean McCreary and Libby Ford

INTRODUCTION

The ISO 14001 standard specifies that its requirements apply to all types and sizes of organizations and accommodates diverse geographical, cultural, and social conditions. The system is based on the concept of continual improvement. This, in turn, encompasses the principle of measurement and evaluation. That is, an organization should measure, monitor, and evaluate the performance of its EMS. Without measurement, improvement of the EMS and hence environmental performance is uncertain at best. According to a common business axiom, "If you can measure it, it gets done."[1] This chapter provides an overview of ISO 14001 requirements related to measuring and monitoring the functions of the EMS to ensure that the organization is performing in accordance with its environmental policy, objectives, and targets.

The objective of ISO 14001 Clause 4.5 is to ensure that the organization has a system in place that measures and monitors its actual performance against the organization's environmental objectives and targets. It is the "check" element of the overall "plan, do, check, act" philosophy of the standard. The measurement system encompasses the management system and operational processes, and includes regulatory compliance. The aim is to determine areas of success and areas that require corrective action and improvement. Clause 4.5 has four major requirements:

1. Monitoring and measurement (Clause 4.5.1).

2. Nonconformance and corrective and preventive action (Clause 4.5.2).

3. Records (Clause 4.5.3).

4. Environmental management system audit (Clause 4.5.4).

MONITORING AND MEASUREMENT

Broken into a list of elements, Clause 4.5.1 of ISO 14001 requires that an organization do the following:

- Establish and maintain documented procedures.
- To monitor and measure on a regular basis.
- The key characteristics of its operations and activities.
- That can have a significant impact on the environment.

These activities include:

- Tracking performance.
- Tracking relevant operational controls.
- Tracking conformance with the organization's objectives and targets.
- Calibrating and maintaining monitoring equipment and retaining records of this process.
- Documenting its procedure for periodically evaluating compliance with relevant environmental legislation and regulations.

Environmental Performance Indicators

Knowing that an organization must track and measure performance is one thing. Knowing how to do so is another. In the ISO 14000 pilot program experience of many organizations, determining how to measure performance or even progress toward achieving objectives and targets is one of the most difficult aspects of the management system. According to ISO 14001, Clause 4.5.1, the organization must regularly measure "the key characteristics of its operations and activities that can have a significant impact on the environment." One way to do this is to develop performance indicators for these "key characteristics."

The ISO 14004 guidance standard suggests that in addition to ensuring reliable data through equipment calibration and testing, the organization should identify "appropriate environmental performance indicators" on an ongoing basis. Such environmental performance indicators (EPIs) should be objective, verifiable, reproducible, and should be consistent with and relevant to the organization's activities and environmental policy.

Keep in mind the need to measure and evaluate when initially developing the objectives and targets. Selecting measurable objectives and targets will aid in tracking progress during the implementation and review phases of the EMS. The following are a few examples:

- The number of noncompliance incidents during the review period.
- The number of consent orders or notices of violation received within the review period.
- The increase/decrease in the volume of solid/hazardous waste generated or other emission tracking during the review period.

- The increase/decrease in the energy consumed during the review period.
- The amount of waste disposal dollars saved or dollars earned through material reclamation.
- The implementation cost increases/decreases compared to a baseline during the review period.
- The number of incidents (such as materials releases, etc.) during the review period.

     (See Chapter 8 for an extensive list of EPIs and other information about environmental performance evaluation.)

However an indicator is selected, it must relate to the legal requirements applicable to the organization, and it must be technologically feasible to measure (i.e., be objective and reproducible). In many instances, the ability to measure progress against defined criteria may be essential to making a business case for the EMS and for justifying its continued support within the organization.

In addition, since measurement and monitoring are founded on the principle of continuous improvement, the indicators and measurement procedures themselves will be subject to revision and improvement over time, both in terms of their precision and in terms of "raising the bar" as the quality of performance improves.

The ISO 14031 guidance standard under development on environmental performance evaluation (EPE) provides useful information to help an organization design and implement an environmental performance evaluation system. Although the guidance in ISO 14031 does not constitute requirements for implementing an ISO 14001-compliant EMS, EPE is a very important tool to assist management in reviewing the functionality of the EMS.

Evaluating Compliance with Regulations

Clause 4.5.1 of ISO 14001 also requires the organization to establish and maintain a documented procedure for periodically evaluating compliance with applicable environmental legislation and regulations. The standards developers deliberately crafted this clause to be general and to accommodate international differences in characterizing procedures for evaluating regulatory compliance.

In the United States, however, this requirement clearly calls for some type of compliance audit program, whether implemented using internal resources or commissioned from an external resource for internal use. In either case, the audits for the purpose of evaluating regulatory compliance must be performed by a person who is objective, impartial, and properly trained (ISO 14004, Clause 4.4.5).

Beyond Compliance Auditing

Auditing for regulatory compliance is a subset of the EMS. It encompasses those elements of an ISO 14001 EMS that relate to achieving and maintaining compliance with applicable laws and regulations. An EMS audit, however, evaluates the entire EMS program, not just compliance with regulations. Such a program under ISO 14001 goes beyond simple compliance with laws and regulations to encompass the many other environmental aspects of an organization (financial, organizational, training, energy, vendors, etc.).

It is beyond the scope of this chapter to detail all of the necessary features of an appropriate compliance audit program. The ISO 14010-12 auditing documents, however, provide useful guidance on general auditing procedures that apply not only to EMS audits but to all other types of environmental investigations, including compliance audits (see Chapter 9).

In addition, various domestic standards have emerged or are being developed on the topic of compliance audits or audit programs, such as those developed by the Environmental Auditing Roundtable (EAR) and the American Society for Testing and Materials (ASTM) (see Box 7–1). An organization that is implementing this requirement of ISO 14001 may also want to ensure that the compliance-auditing component fits other state and federal incentive programs that might provide relief from enforcement activities for findings of audit programs.

B O X   7–1

ENVIRONMENTAL AUDITING STANDARDS

The following is a partial list of useful environmental auditing standards:

ASTM E 50.04 *Standard Provisional Practice for Environmental Regulatory Compliance Audits*

ASTM Provisional Standard *Guide for the Study and Evaluation of an Organization's Environmental Management Systems*

ASTM E 1527-93 *Standard Practice for Environmental Site Assessments: Phase I Environmental Site Assessment Process*

ASTM E 1529-93 *Standard Practice for Environmental Site Assessments: Transaction Screen Process*

ASTM E 50.02 *Standard Guide for Environmental Site Assessments: Phase II Environmental Site Assessment Process*

Thrift Bulletin 16 (Federal Home Loan Bank System—Office of Regulatory Activities) *Environmental Risk and Liability*

Environmental Auditing Roundtable *Standards for Performance of Environmental Health & Safety Audits* (1993)

Environmental Auditing Roundtable *Standard for the Design and Implementation of an Environmental Health and Safety Audit Program* (1996)

ISO 14010—*Guidelines for Environmental Auditing—General Principles*

ISO 14011—*Guidelines for Environmental Auditing—Audit Procedures - Auditing of Environmental Management Systems*

NONCONFORMANCE AND CORRECTIVE AND PREVENTIVE ACTION

It is axiomatic that for audits to have true value, their findings must be addressed through some corrective actions. The vast array of environmental laws and regulations in the United States has the potential to be criminally enforced if violations, once detected, are not promptly and completely corrected. Knowledge of a noncompliance as evidenced by the audit report, coupled with a failure to correct in a timely manner, could be deemed willful and knowing noncompliance and thus a criminal offense. Thus, it is essential to establish procedures for correcting noncompliances once detected and for preventing their recurrence.

Consistent with these principles, ISO 14001, Clause 4.5.2 requires that an organization:

- Establish and maintain procedures for defining responsibility and authority for handling and investigating nonconformance.
- Take action to mitigate any impacts caused.
- Initiate and complete corrective action and preventive action commensurate with the environmental impact encountered.
- Implement and record any changes in documented procedures resulting from corrective and preventive action.

It is the responsibility of management to ensure that corrective/preventive actions have been implemented and that there are systematic follow-ups to ensure their effectiveness.

Corrective versus Preventive Action

It is important to distinguish between corrective and preventive actions. Corrective action focuses on eliminating or addressing the compliance issue (label the drum, obtain the permit, etc.). Preventive action is more prospective in nature and focuses on identifying the cause of noncompliance and the institution of procedures to ensure that noncompliances do not recur.

The first corrective attempt(s) may not reveal the causes of the deficiency, so it is a good idea for the organization to periodically recheck the status of compliance issues noted in prior audits before the subsequent periodic audits.

Appropriateness of Corrective/Preventive Actions

ISO 14001 also requires, in Clause 4.5.2, that the corrective/preventive action be "appropriate to the magnitude of problems" and "commensurate with the environmental impact encountered." Although these phrases are not defined in the standard, obviously evidence of pervasive noncompliance warrants a more aggressive response than sporadic noncompliance because it is more suggestive of a wholesale system failure than an isolated misunderstanding or misinterpretation of an applicable requirement.

Similarly, while "paperwork" violations may produce liability exposure to the company, when an audit detects evidence of substantial risk to human health or the environment, addressing the circumstances must be a priority, even absent risk of discovery or liability to third parties. Where operations result in adverse health or environmental impacts, the organization should have in place a response procedure that includes immediate elimination of the circumstances creating the impacts and investigation of the magnitude of the impacts. The organization should consider involving legal and other support resources under these circumstances.

Documenting Corrective/Preventive Actions

According to ISO 14001, it is not essential that corrective/preventive actions taken by the organization be described in any EMS documents or in compliance audit reports. But if actions are taken that result in changes in procedures that require documentation under ISO 14001, such changes must be recorded. If a company is seeking registration, however, the registrar will likely require a demonstration that corrective actions have been implemented where no documentation exists.

Not all compliance audit reports encompass corrective actions (ISO 14010 and ISO 14011 makes recording them optional). A reason is that the "independent" audit team may not determine the appropriate response to audit findings, especially if they are not sufficiently familiar with the operating needs of an organization. For example, the audit team may identify the compliance issue in the report, but the organization's counsel may make the actual determination of compliance or noncompliance. The counsel may rely not only on interpreting the regulations themselves, but also evaluating case law, interpretive policies, and other information not usually available to an audit team.

In addition, a finding of noncompliance may be referred to a team at the audited facility for a determination of the appropriate corrective action(s) because of the need for detailed operating knowledge of a process. Corrective actions could span a range of options; for example, from getting a permit to totally reconfiguring the process to avoid the need for a permit. By acquiring a totally enclosed operating system, the organization may avoid the need to take the most immediate action indicated by the regulations, based on the operation as configured at the time of the audit. Because such actions may require capital expenditures, workforce training, and so on, all of which typically are outside an audit scope, the audited facility's management may need to be involved in defining corrective actions.

Corrective Action Tracking

Although corrective actions may not be described in compliance audit reports or EMS audit reports, if corrective actions are ultimately identified as necessary to achieve or maintain compliance, some kind of a corrective action-tracking mechanism is essential. The tracking mechanism records the fact that actions committed to as part of the compliance audit process are in fact carried out. Implementation of corrective actions that have been identified will be part of both an internal EMS evaluation and any third-party (registration) verification assessment.

As discussed above, for practical or legal reasons the process of deriving the appropriate corrective action might not be articulated, nor would recommendations necessarily be sought from the audit team. But the corrective action would still take place and be verifiable as an EMS component.

It is good practice, however, to record corrective actions and track them (in the documentation) as a means of ensuring that they take place. There are legal consequences, including potential criminal liability, if necessary corrective actions are not completed.

Due to liability considerations in the United States that arise from disclosure of audit reports and corrective action plans, the organization should consider whether to involve legal counsel in interpreting suspected violations and in planning for corrective actions. For example, EPA's final audit policy stipulates that to qualify for penalty mitigation under the policy, correction action must have been completed within 60 days, although provision is made for longer periods subject to written notification to EPA (see Chapter 22 for a discussion of EPA's final audit policy).

In addition, the fact that a corrective action is not initially effective does not necessarily signal the failure of the organization's EMS. Corrective action follow-up can include identifying the root cause of compliance issues if initial corrective actions do not successfully eliminate the problem. For example, if a waste drum is found on a loading dock with improper labeling, corrective action might include noting the need to relabel the container. If subsequent verification indicates that the container is not relabeled or that other containers are mislabeled, it may be necessary to evaluate the training of persons responsible for the container and retrain them as needed.

One of the biggest failures of corrective action plans is the failure to break the necessary tasks into understandable parts. Here's a simple example. A compliance audit notes the suspected need for an air emission permit for a source. The corrective action might read "evaluate need for and obtain permit for source XX if required." If the environmental manager in charge of this operation did not understand the need for the permit in the first instance, the manager might not fully understand the subtasks implicit in the corrective action mission.

It may be necessary to identify, possibly in the corrective action plan itself, the following elements:

- Applicable provisions of the regulation.
- Evaluation of the process or operation to determine if the permit requirement applies.
- The requirement to possibly test emissions.
- How to complete a permit application.
- How to submit it to the permit-issuing agency for review.

If the subtasks are not taken into consideration in establishing the required corrective actions, the timing expectations may not be appropriate for the task. Further, some corrective actions may have significant capital or operating expenditures associated with them, which may require management approvals if the expenses are unbudgeted.

Corrective/Preventive Tracking Procedures

Corrective action tracking procedures vary from facility to facility, depending on what gets tracked and how. Some facilities track only the number of findings from year to year, some the frequency of the occurrence of the same findings. Others track findings by severity ranking or by regulatory program.

Some facilities compile a facility-specific list of the intended actions on a task-by-task basis and establish the following:

- A list of the resources needed.
- The assignments of responsible individuals.

T A B L E   7–1

Environmental, Health and Safety Corrective Action Task Chart

Issue — Environmental	Task	Responsible Individual
3. Process Wastewater a. *Leachfield Galleries:*	1. Verify that no listed, characteristic or other hazardous wastes are being discharged to Leachfield or other subsurface discharge points.	EHS Mgr. and Facilities Dept.
b. *Settling Tank:*	1. Empty contents and properly dispose of sludge.	Maintenance Dept.
c. *Wastewater Discharge Levels:*	1. Ensure that discharge levels are within parameters of Consent Order.	EHS Mgr. and WNTP Operator
4. Chemical Usage and Handling a. *Material Safety Data Sheets:*	1. Review 1993 Chemical Inventory with MSDS notebooks and segregate MSDS notebooks into those chemicals currently in use and those no longer utilized at the Facility.	Accounting Dept.
	2. Attempt to reduce amounts of chemicals used at Facility.	EHS Mgr.
b. *Secondary Containment:*	1. Apply impervious sealants to base of berming used to store chemicals.	Maintenance Dept.
c. *Labeling:*	1. Ensure that process wastewater tanks have appropriate hazard waste communication labels.	EHS Mgr.
5. Asbestos a. *Not within scope of audit.*		
6. PCBs (Polychlorinated Byphenols) a. *Transformers:*	1. Label as non-PCB containing (i.e., "non-PCB").	EHS Mgr.

- The sources of funding.
- The deadlines for commitments to complete the actions.

This format is shown in Table 7–1.

Failures to take corrective action most frequently stem from one or more of the following causes:

- A failure to understand the finding.
- A failure to understand the steps needed to correct the finding.
- A failure to assign "ownership" of the tasks.

Target Completion Date	Date Completed	Cost Category	Priority	Notes
10 Days			High	
90 Days		$1,500	Low	
15 Days, ongoing		$6,000 to acquire contin. flow monitor	High	CCWA § 22a-432
60 Days		None	Low	
Ongoing		(possible capital exp.)	Medium	
30 Days		$3,000	High	40 CFR § 264-175 (b) (1) § 22a-449-104 (a)
10 Days		None	High	
Immediate		None	High	

- Limited commitment of resources to the task.
- Failure to track follow-up actions.
- Lack of management support.

To avoid these potential barriers to implementing corrective action, the tracking format should specifically identify the following:

- The problem, the tasks, and subtasks needed to correct the problem.
- The individual (or group) accepting ownership of the task.
- Where the resources will come from (capital, operating, personnel).
- The deadlines for each subtask.

The compliance auditor should be involved at least to the point of explaining the report findings to ensure that the issues are understood. The facility management should be involved to ensure commitment of personnel and financial resources as needed and to convey the sense of consequence if there is a failure to perform.

It is a good idea to involve other EHS representatives across the audited organization to ensure that identified corrective actions can be implemented without running afoul of other regulatory issues. The participation of counterparts from other facilities within the organization offer the benefits of cross-facility fixes and preventing reinvention of the wheel on every finding. For example, a satellite waste accumulation area cannot be moved into the area under the control of the operator if it would pose a fire hazard.

Legal counsel can provide the legal interpretations and suggest defenses that might not be evident from the regulations alone, and ensure that audit findings and corrective action plans are carefully worded to minimize liability in the event of disclosure.

Evaluating Corrective Actions

Every corrective action to be taken should be evaluated from three viewpoints:

1. Does it fix the problem?
2. Does it prevent recurrence?
3. Should it be reported?

Fixing the problem may require root cause analysis. For example, if a drum is missing a label, a fix could be to place the label on the drum. Root cause analysis would examine whether there was a communication failure, a simple mistake, a failure to perform an assigned task, a failure to define responsible parties, a failure to understand the task assigned, or some other systemic cause.

In answering whether corrective action has fixed the problem, it is good idea to ask how one knows when the job is done. For example, if the finding indicates that a tank leaked and the leak had not been detected in a timely manner, the corrective action might be to improve tank inspections. But, how does one know that the improvement is sufficient to fix the problem and prevent recurrence? It is better to be precise in writing the corrective action, specifying the repairs to be done to the tank, the remedial action to be taken for the release, the modifications in the Spill Prevention Control and Countermeasure (SPCC) plan needed to ensure that daily inspections occur, the training needed on the part of the person responsible for the inspections, and so on, so that the corrective action completely addresses the finding. This example also highlights the preventive nature of corrective actions.

Reporting Requirements

There are literally hundreds of reporting requirements under various federal regulations, ranging from release reporting (spills) to mandated reporting of passthroughs and exceedences to the Publicly Owned Treatment Works, toxic release inventories, and discharge monitoring. As part of an effective preventive program, it is a good idea to maintain a list of applicable reporting requirements under state, federal, and local law since some requirements impose "immediate" and "two-hour" time frames in the case of releases, and 30-day EPA policy and even ten-day time frames for some written notifications.

Verification

There should also be a component that verifies that the measures taken to correct the violation have worked and are preventing recurrences—This may mean periodic spot-checking in the field or, in significant situations, verification audits (re-audits).

Performance Evaluation

Performance on corrective action plans (including timeliness and completeness) should be part of the facility manager's performance evaluation process and should be tied to compensation, bonus benefits, and other management incentives. These verify ownership of the responsibility and reward follow-up on corrective actions.

RECORDS

Clause 4.5.3 of ISO 14001 requires the organization to establish and maintain procedures for identifying, maintaining, and disposing of environmental records. Records are evidence of the ongoing operation of the EMS. As described in ISO 14004 Clause 4.4.4, the records should cover the following:

- Legislative and regulatory requirements.
- Permits.
- Environmental aspects and their associated impacts.

- Environmental training activity.
- Inspection, calibration, and maintenance activity.
- Monitoring data.
- Details of nonconformance: incidents, complaints, and follow-up actions.
- Product identification: composition and property data.
- Supplier and contractor information.
- Environmental audits and reviews.

In implementing this provision, the organization should determine which records need to be managed and what data must be tracked to achieve the defined objectives and targets (including measurement of progress on indicators).

Demonstrating Conformance

It is necessary to maintain records that demonstrate conformance to the standard. This is true whether there is a self-declaration of conformity or whether a registrar performs a third-party registration audit. In terms of records that "demonstrate conformance to the standard," some companies will develop EMS "signpost" documents, that is, documents that will articulate how the company is implementing key components of the EMS program. These will be auditable records for review by the registrar or third-party verifier, although ISO 14001 does not mandate any specific documentation. Nevertheless, documentation will likely be desired by registrars since records are easier to audit than other ways of demonstrating conformity (e.g., through interviews).

Legible/Identifiable/Traceable

The ISO 14001 standard requires records to be "legible, identifiable and traceable to the activity, product or service involved" and "readily retrievable." They should also be stored in a way that protects against damage or loss.

Record Retention

Procedures should be developed to ensure that records are retained at least as long as required by any applicable regulation. Record-retention periods are specified by laws, running from a few years (usually 3) to as many as 10 years and in some cases "forever." The requirements vary by regulatory program (see Table 7–2).

Accessibility of Information

Accessibility of the information is a crucial issue—some elements of the EMS may require public access to certain information, while other applicable legal requirements may specify access to employees or availability on demand to government inspectors.

TABLE 7–2

Sample Record Retention Form

Type of Record	Required Retention Period	Authority
For generators of hazardous waste which is restricted from land disposal (6 NYCRR Pt. 376):		
• Copy of all notices, certifications, demonstrations, waste analysis data, or other documentation required under §376.1.	5 yrs.	6 NYCRR § 376.1 (g) (1) (vii)
For low-level radioactive waste transporters:		
• Copy of manifests and records on which annual reports are based.	3 yrs.	6 NYCRR § 381.11 (h), 381.15 (a)
Solid Waste		
For solid waste management facilities, including storage areas:		
• Inspection records, operational records, records of all monitoring information.	7 yrs.	6 NYCRR § 360-1.14 (h) (3), (j) (1), (j) (2)
• Records of data used to develop/ support permit applications, other compliance information, construction information and existing water quality records.	Until end of postclosure period	6 NYCRR § 360-1.14 (j) (1) and (j) (2)
Petroleum Bulk Storage and Underground Storage Tanks (USTs):		
• For metal USTs without additional corrosion protection, records demonstrating compliance with EPA corrosion requirements.	For life of tank	40 CFR § 280.20 (a) (4) (ii) (ii)
• For USTs using cathodic protection, records of operation of cathodic protection to demonstrate compliance with performance standards and records of inspection and testing records.	Not stated	40 CFR § 280.31 (d)
• Repair records.	For life of tank	40 CFR § 280.33 (f)

According to ISO 14001 Clause 4.1(f), public access is required for the environmental policy, and perhaps for certain environmental emergency preparedness aspects (see ISO 14004, Clause 4.3.3.4).

Disclosure of Information

Encompassed in the accessibility requirement is the issue of whether there is information that should be protected from disclosure and how to reconcile the needs of access with those of protection.

The basic rule is that an organization cannot protect documents that may be part of a possible registration process since they are intended for possible disclosure and third-party verification either by an auditor working for a registrar or someone verifying self-declaration of conformity to ISO 14001. However, the process through which the disclosable documents themselves are prepared (i.e., the internal process of identifying environmental aspects and impacts, or the process of designing, developing, and initially implementing the compliance program) may be protected from disclosure if various conditions are met.

Thus, when considering the need to protect certain EMS documents, it is important to be aware of the status of legislation related to the disclosure and use of such documents in the state of the facility being audited (or, possibly, the organization itself). The organization should also consider other traditional privileges, including attorney–client communications, attorney work-product doctrines, and business confidentiality (proprietary information). These issues are best resolved as part of the EMS planning stage. (These issues are also described in greater detail in Chapters 10 and 11.)

Access to Legal and Other Requirements

Clause 4.3.2 of ISO 14001 requires an organization "to maintain a procedure to identify and have access to legal and other requirements to which the organization subscribes" that are directly applicable to the environmental aspects of its activities, products, or services. Legal requirements can be accessed through a legislative and regulatory information service such as that provided by The Federal Register, its state counterparts, BNA or various on-line services. In any case, the organization should be able to learn about new regulatory programs that may apply to it, as well as to monitor periodic changes to those regulations.

ENVIRONMENTAL MANAGEMENT SYSTEM AUDIT

The EMS audit required in Clause 4.5.4 is distinct from the compliance audit that is one element of ISO 14001's monitoring and measurement requirement. The EMS audit evaluates more than compliance with applicable legislative and regulatory requirements. Essentially, the EMS audit is the process (internal to the organization, even if external auditors are used for the function) by which the organization periodically determines whether or not the EMS conforms to requirements established by the organization, including the requirements of ISO 14001, and whether the EMS has been properly implemented and maintained.

The audit also provides information by which management can review the EMS system with the aim of ensuring suitability, adequacy, and effectiveness of the system toward the goal of continual improvement. The EMS audit should take into account the results of previous audits, and the audit procedures should be consistent with the guidance in ISO 14010, 14011, and 14012. (Chapter 9 discusses EMS auditing in detail.)

Conformance versus Effectiveness?

Many organizations have questioned the depth of the EMS audit—must it ensure that the program elements exist and are functional, or must it effectively evaluate the judgment of the EMS planners who developed the objectives and targets based on the organization's environmental aspects? Must the EMS audit confirm that the organization is in full compliance with all applicable regulations, or can a compliance system be evaluated for functionality by a "sampling" of compliance status and corrective action implementation?

The simple answer is that the EMS audit must be sufficient to ensure that the organization's EMS will pass muster for conformity to ISO 14001 for purposes of either registration or self-declaration. Since the registration program is currently under development, a more specific response is not possible as of this writing. As a practical matter, the EMS audit itself is an element subject to continual improvement. As the organization's EMS reaches differing levels of performance, so too must the EMS audit adjust to measure the improved performance.

In the conformity assessment context, the Registrar Accreditation Board (RAB) draft document setting forth criteria for registrars seeking accreditation by RAB would appear to adopt the view that the registrar must:

1. Evaluate the appropriateness of the environmental aspects identified by an organization and the suitability of the objectives and targets developed by the organization with respect to the environmental aspects of its operations; and

2. That for an organization to become registered to ISO 14001, all significant nonconformances with applicable requirements must be rectified through corrective action.

The American National Standards Institute (ANSI) draft document takes a more general approach and would not require a registrar to substitute its judgment for the organization's judgment, or to verify compliance with all applicable requirements. The ANSI approach would enable an organization to register an ISO 14001 EMS system if it was effectively aimed at achieving those goals through the continual improvement process.

However, these questions pertain to organizations that demonstrate conformity to ISO 14001 for registration purposes, where auditors working for a registrar will perform a conformity assessment EMS audit. They are less significant for organizations that implement an EMS program without intending to eventually seek ISO 14001 registration. (See Chapter 19 for a discussion of RAB, ANSI and other draft registrar accreditation criteria.)

Use of the ISO 14010-12 Auditing Standards

The ISO 14010-12 series of environmental auditing standards describes the general principles of environmental auditing, EMS auditing procedures, and qualifications for environmental auditors.

A key issue not clarified in the ISO 14010-12 guidance standards is the interplay between the following:

- The auditing process that an organization would employ internally to ensure that it achieves and maintains compliance with applicable laws and regulations.

- The auditing process that an organization undergoes to evaluate whether its EMS is working.

- The process that the registration auditor will follow during the third-party registration ("conformity assessment") audit.

All three audit components would, in theory, be covered by ISO 14010/11/12, yet there is not much specificity to help an organization apply the general requirements of the auditing standards in these contexts. The question remains: Will the criteria needed to qualify an EMS auditor for ISO 14001 registrations be the same as the criteria for performing internal EMS audits or for performing compliance audits? One place to turn for guidance in this area is existing domestic auditing standards, such as those of the Environmental Auditing Roundtable (EAR) and the American Society for Testing and Materials (ASTM) mentioned earlier in this chapter. These standards can help apply the general ISO 14000 standards in specific auditing contexts.

Management versus Environmental Experience?

A debate is also raging about the amount of "management system" expertise that is needed for EMS auditors (i.e., obtained from QMS auditing for ISO 9000) versus how much environmental regulatory and technical knowledge is needed. In theory, the management system background is more significant since the EMS auditor evaluates the functionality of the compliance system, not compliance status. In practice, however, this distinction is hard to maintain since the functionality of a system is very hard to critically determine without working knowledge of the impact of regulatory programs on the organization. Discussions are underway to try to arrive at a harmonized view of these issues.

Small and Medium-Size Enterprises

Another key issue in this area of ISO 14001 implementation concerns small and medium-size enterprises (SMEs) and their motivation to conduct internal audits. Evidence indicates that SMEs have low probability of detection of violations and/or management problems through regulatory inspection, which is a primary motivator of auditing behavior in larger enterprises. Thus SMEs have not, historically, recognized the cost benefits of auditing.

The size of the enterprise, however, does not correspond with its potential to impact the environment, nor is liability for releases to the environment limited to the amount of investment in an enterprise. Thus, for SMEs, the risk of environmental issues eclipsing the assets of the enterprise is greater. These factors, if fully appreciated, should motivate more frequent auditing among SMEs. They rarely do, however, due to other perceived risks and costs of auditing, including perceived potential adverse use of audit reports, whether or not they are supported by actual experience.

In light of these trends, SMEs should consider a phased implementation of ISO 14001—They should focus first on major components, such as the compliance program element. This will reap other rewards, such as risk minimization, waste minimization, process efficiencies, and so on. Then, once all the programs are in place and justified by their own merits, the organization can work towards eventual self-declaration or third-party registration of its environmental management system.

CONCLUSION

Organizations deciding to implement an EMS system should consider the issues posed by the checking and corrective action program elements from the earliest stages of the planning process. By knowing where it has to go, the organization can design the process of getting there more effectively.

BIOGRAPHIES

Jean Hutchinson McCreary, Esq., and Mary Elizabeth (Libby) Ford, CHMM, QEP, Esq.

Jean McCreary is a partner in the law firm of Nixon, Hargrave, Devans & Doyle, LLP, and has coordinated and conducted environmental compliance and preacquisition audits throughout the United States and internationally. She serves as president of the Environmental Auditing Roundtable. Ms. McCreary also chairs the Work Group on General Auditing Principles on the ISO 14000 environmental management system standards (ISO 14010) and she served as the U.S. expert on this subject at the TC-207 meeting in Oslo, Norway. She has been appointed to the Environmental Management Systems Council of the National Accreditation Program for ISO 14000 by the American National Standards Institute.

Libby Ford is a senior environmental health engineer and coordinator of the Environmental Technical and Water teams with the law firm of Nixon, Hargrave, Devans

& Doyle, LLP. Ms. Ford has extensive working knowledge of a broad range of federal, state, and local environmental regulations; among her areas of expertise are environmental auditing, industrial environmental management, and negotiation. She has performed environmental audits throughout the United States and internationally, including environmental management system reviews. She has a B.S. in biology and an M.S. in environmental engineering from the University of Notre Dame in Indiana.

NOTE

1. A. Marlin, President, Council on Economic Priorities, quoted in *Hemispheres,* 11/95, p. 25.

CHAPTER 8

Practical Issues in Environmental Performance Evaluation

Joseph Fiksel

INTRODUCTION

Leading organizations are beginning to recognize that environmental excellence is a significant element of business strategy. The development of the ISO 14000 series of environmental management standards is but one aspect of a worldwide paradigm shift from viewing environmental responsibility as a compliance burden to viewing it as a customer need. As evidence of this, dozens of major organizations have recently begun to measure and report their annual environmental performance for the benefit of customers, stockholders, and other interested parties. The many driving forces that are influencing enterprises to focus on their environmental performance are depicted in Figure 8–1. These driving forces include the following:

Customer Expectations   Customers are increasingly concerned about the environmental quality of the products they use, and major organizations are beginning to systematically review the environmental performance of their suppliers.

Environmental Regulations   Both in the United States and abroad, government regulations regarding the environmental impacts of products and production processes are becoming more stringent, especially regarding the disposal and recycling of products at the end of their useful life.

Environmental Stewardship   The notion of "stewardship" involves an ethical commitment by businesses to maintain integrity and care in the management of their assets and products. This commitment extends to all phases of manufacturing and distribution. The U.S. Chemical Manufacturers' Association (CMA) has codified this approach in its Responsible Care® program, which has also served as a model for other industries. In the United Kingdom, a similar concept has evolved, called Duty of Care.

FIGURE 8–1

Driving Forces for Environmental Performance Improvement

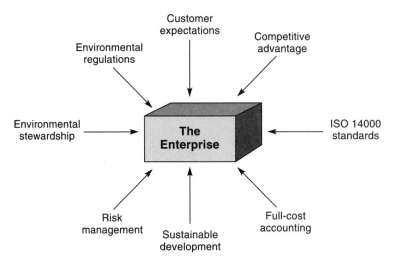

Risk Management   An important element of environmental stewardship programs is active risk management. This involves going beyond simply purchasing insurance, to assessing and mitigating the potential adverse environmental, health, and safety impacts of an organization's operations.

Sustainable Development   Sustainable development is industrial progress that meets present needs without compromising the ability of future generations to do the same. The implied question of how to assure continued industrial growth without adverse ecological impacts was a major theme of the 1992 Earth Summit in Brazil. Leading companies are now beginning to embrace "industrial ecology," which broadens their economic view of industrial management to include the natural ecosystems in which they operate.

Eco-Labeling Programs   A number of eco-labeling initiatives, which rate the environmental sensitivity of products, have arisen both in the United States and abroad, and the European Union is moving toward an eco-labeling standard. There is still considerable debate over appropriate measures of environmental performance for eco-labeling purposes.

ISO 14000 Standards   The development of international standards has created a wake-up call for many organizations who have already experienced the emergence of ISO 9000 standards as a potent force in international markets. In addition, a number of earlier standards efforts, such as BS 7750, have attracted considerable participation from industry.

Competitive Advantage   Improving the environmental performance of a company's products and processes can have a significant impact on reducing manufacturing and other operating costs, as well as increasing market share. Product designs that consider environmental issues will generally be superior in terms of elegance, energy efficiency, and cost of ownership and can frequently sway a purchase decision if price and performance are comparable.

Profitability   Perhaps the most important factor in focusing industry attention on environmental performance has been the realization that it can actually increase profitability. Reducing pollution at the source and designing products and processes in ways that enhance environmental quality will generally result in increased efficiency and reduced operating costs.

WHAT IS EPE?

ISO 14001 sets forth the basic elements that constitute an EMS and enables companies to certify themselves as having those elements in place. While the standard does not attempt to mandate performance levels, it does require that senior management establish environmental performance goals and monitor progress toward these goals. Therefore, one of the key elements of an EMS is the environmental performance evaluation (EPE) system, which is addressed by the draft standard ISO 14031.

EPE is defined in the draft version of ISO 14031 simply as a tool to review an organization's environmental aspects to determine whether objectives are met. Here, environmental aspects are defined broadly as any elements of the organization's activities, products, or services that can interact with the environment. This encompasses not only waste and emissions, but also utilization of energy, water, land, and other natural resources. For private sector organizations, EPE should be treated like any other business process and indeed should be integrated with the organization's planning and performance measurement systems at an individual, departmental, and enterprise level.

According to ISO 14031, EPE is a management tool that can provide an organization with reliable, objective and verifiable information to focus on and improve its environmental performance. EPE uses selected indicators to measure and communicate the organization's environmental performance relative to objectives set by management. The information obtained through EPE enables management to determine necessary actions to achieve its environmental policy, objectives, and targets and to communicate with interested parties as appropriate. The following principles illustrate current ISO thinking, as expressed in ISO 14031, about the practice of EPE:

- EPE should have the full commitment of senior management.
- EPE should be compatible with existing business functions and activities.
- EPE should be based on accurate, objective, and verifiable data.
- EPE should generate understandable and reliable information.

- EPE should appropriately consider interested parties' expectations and concerns, as well as regional, cultural, and socioeconomic factors.
- EPE should consider life-cycle concepts, as appropriate.

THE EPE PROCESS

The draft ISO 14031 standard defines the following three basic steps in the EPE process:

1. **Planning for EPE**   Establishing the EPE objectives, scope, supporting information, available resources, and appropriate EPIs.

2. **Evaluating EPE**   Collecting, analyzing, and evaluating the environmental performance data and reporting and communicating the results.

3. **Reviewing and Improving EPE**   Enhancing the effectiveness of the EPE process, contributing to the EMS, and improving environmental performance.

Thus, like any other business process, EPE should strive for continuous improvement at each iteration. The EMS as a whole and EPE in particular need to be dynamic and flexible in order to respond to changing technologies, external forces, and market conditions. In practice, it is important to implement EPE in a way that reflects the intended use and audience for the performance results. The following are three primary uses of environmental performance information:

1. Internal reporting to guide business process changes, profitability enhancement, and management decision making.

2. External reporting and communication with stakeholders in the public domain. Stakeholders may include customers, shareholders, regulatory agencies, local communities, environmental interest groups, and employees.

3. Benchmarking of performance with respect to competitors, peers, or companies in other industries.

The choice of appropriate environmental performance objectives and indicators can vary depending upon which of these uses are intended. The steps involved in implementing an EPE are depicted in Figure 8–2.

Policy, Principles, Objectives

The basis of the entire EMS implementation is the organization's environmental policy and principles. To focus on key areas of performance, the EMS must conduct a review of its environmental aspects and select high-priority aspects for environmental performance evaluation.

Implementing an Environmental Performance Evaluation System

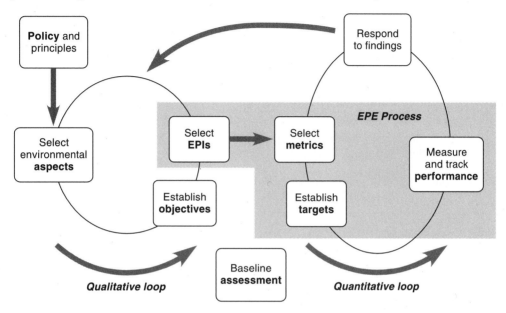

Management must then establish qualitative objectives for the selected aspects to provide guidance to the EPE process. These might range from straightforward operational improvements to strategic imperatives. The following are examples of environmental objectives:

- Improve energy efficiency at all company facilities.
- Reuse or recycle waste materials wherever feasible.
- Improve relationships with local communities.
- Use environmental technology to increase shareholder value.

Once management's objectives are established, the EPE process actually begins.

Planning and Selecting EPIs

The planning step involves selecting appropriate EPIs that are relevant to the objectives. EPIs are stated initially in qualitative terms (e.g., energy usage), but to support measurement they must be quantified in specific units (e.g., energy consumed per unit of operating output). The latter is often referred to in practice as an *environmental performance metric,* although ISO 14031 does not explicitly use that term.

Defining such metrics permits the establishment of quantitative targets, the calculation of performance measures and, if desired, the calculation of a baseline against which future performance improvements are measured. At this point, the EPE process is used iteratively to evaluate performance results and to revise the metrics and targets as necessary. In addition, management may respond to the EPE findings by changing its objectives or priorities, which in turn will influence the choice of EPIs and subsequent EPE activities.

IMPLEMENTING THE EPE PROCESS

This section discusses the three major technical aspects of the EPE process described above:

- Selecting environmental aspects and setting objectives.
- Selecting environmental performance indicators.
- Selecting environmental performance metrics.

The concluding sections discuss how life-cycle thinking can influence EPE and the role that EPE can play in seeking competitive advantage.

Selecting Environmental Aspects and Setting Objectives

The EMS standard, ISO 14001, defines an environmental aspect as "an element of an organization's activities, products, or services that can interact with the environment." It further states in Clause 4.3.1 the following EMS requirement: "The organization shall establish and maintain a procedure to identify the environmental aspects of its activities, products or services that it can control and over which it can be expected to have an influence, in order to determine those which have or can have significant impacts on the environment. The organization shall ensure that the aspects related to these significant impacts are considered in setting its environmental objectives."

Environmental Aspects Review

As further guidance, Annex A of ISO 14001 recommends that prior to establishing an EMS, an organization should undertake an environmental review that would include an identification of significant environmental aspects. This review should consider not only normal operating conditions but also the potential environmental interactions during abnormal conditions (e.g., start-up or shutdown) as well as emergency situations. It should also consider the environmental aspects of product use or service delivery in environments beyond the organization's facilities.

Environmental aspect reviews can be performed in a variety of ways, but the end result will be the identification of important cause-effect links between the organization's activities and known, perceived, or potential environmental impacts. It is often helpful to organize the identification of environmental aspects by considering the different life-cycle stages associated with the organization's products and processes. An example of environmental aspects that might emerge from an environmental review is presented in Figure 8–3. Here, a hypothetical consumer products manufacturer has identified the aspects associated with four major stages in the product life cycle: raw material acquisition, manufacturing, distribution and use, and disposal or recovery. Many of these aspects, such as energy usage, are common to several stages.

Note that the review includes not only tangible impacts but also stakeholder perceptions. The term *aspect* literally means "face," and an organization should consider the face that it presents to each of its stakeholder groups: shareholders, customers, suppliers, regulators, competitors, local communities, and public interest groups.

Finally, it should be noted that the ISO 14001 standard is nonprescriptive and allows great latitude in how environmental aspects are described and characterized. While one organization might describe its environmental aspects in general terms such as consumer health and safety, another organization might select very specific issues that are known concerns, such as chronic exposure by children to trace metals.

FIGURE   8–3

Environmental Aspects for a Consumer Product Manufacturer

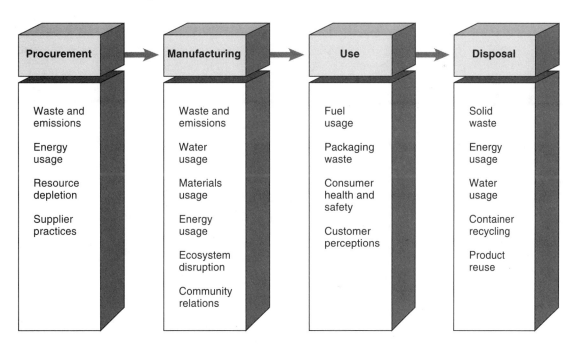

Selecting Environmental Performance Indicators

An environmental performance indicator is any quantifiable attribute of an organization's activities that characterizes the potential environmental implications of these activities. The current draft of ISO 14031 defines three major "evaluation areas" for selecting EPIs: the management system, the operational system, and the environment.

Management System

The management system includes business processes related to the organization, planning, resource allocation, control of operational processes, feedback, and verification of performance results. Management-related types of EPIs include:

- Maturity and effectiveness of existing environmental management processes.
- Extent and quality of resources, training, and expenditures assigned to environmental activities such as compliance, auditing, and pollution prevention.
- Evidence of stakeholder satisfaction, encompassing customers, stockholders, employees, communities, regulators, and environmental interest groups.

Operational System

The operational system includes the design and operation of physical plants and equipment, and the physical material and energy flows required for generation of products and services. Operational types of EPIs include:

- Resource efficiency with regard to utilization and conservation of electricity, fuel, water, raw materials, and land.
- Waste characteristics, including hazardous constituents and quantities of wastes, effluents, or emissions from manufacturing processes, as well as product disposal.
- Environmental disturbances, such as accidental releases, noise, visibility impairment, biodiversity reduction, or ecosystem disruption.
- Life-cycle indicators that track material and energy flows over multiple stages, including extraction, transport, manufacture, distribution, use, and disposal.

The Environment

The environment encompasses external systems, both physical and socioeconomic, (air, water, land, plant and animal life, human health, and natural resources) on which the organization's activities may have an impact. Examples of environmental indicators include aquatic ecosystem impacts, air quality, and global impacts such as climate change. However, evaluating the relationship of such indicators to any single organization's activities is extremely challenging, unless the operational system and the environmental medium of interest are virtually isolated from other systems.

Although the boundaries between these three areas are not definitive, they provide a conceptual framework that helps an organization select appropriate EPIs. As illustrated in Figure 8–4, the three areas are closely interrelated, since the management system organizes and controls the operational system, which in turn may influence the environment. Moreover, the operational system of a company is linked to those of its suppliers and customers, forming a "value chain."

Factors in Selecting EPIs

For a given organization, such as a manufacturing organization, the choice of EPIs should be driven by a number of factors:

- The organization's policies and performance goals.
- Whether the environmental impacts of its products and services are manufacturing-intensive (e.g., semiconductor devices) or dependent on upstream supplier performance and downstream customer behavior (e.g., personal computers).

FIGURE 8–4

Environmental Performance from a Supply Chain Perspective

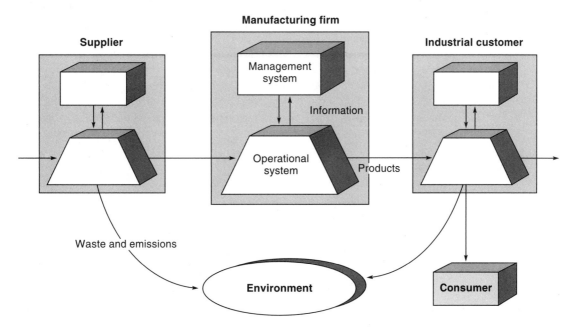

- The potential contributions of environmental performance improvement to competitive advantage with regard to critical success factors, including profitability improvement, regulatory positioning, market access, and stakeholder satisfaction.
- Existing industry performance benchmarks, best practices of competitors, and customer expectations.

A number of leading companies, including 3M, Polaroid, Xerox, and Duke Power, have established successful EPE programs. Each program is highly tailored to the needs, resources, and business characteristics of the individual company.

For example, 3M has developed an indicator of eco-efficiency called a *waste ratio* that is useful for application to manufacturing facilities.[1] It is defined as follows:

$$\text{Waste ratio} = \frac{\text{Waste}}{\text{Product} + \text{Byproduct} + \text{Waste}}$$

This indicator focuses on the quantity of waste generated relative to the total material output of the plant. The waste quantity is measured prior to treatment, thus encouraging pollution prevention. In order to minimize the waste ratio, plant engineers can either convert waste to useful byproducts or reduce the waste generated.

Selecting Environmental Performance Metrics

Environmental performance metrics are the quantified parameters used to measure improvement with respect to environmental performance indicators. Although ISO 14031 does not explicitly define the concept of metrics, they are critical to the practical implementation of an EPE program.

Environmental performance metrics can be classified in several ways. For example, qualitative metrics rely upon semantic distinctions based on observation and judgment, while quantitative metrics are those that rely upon empirical data and derive numerical results. Absolute metrics are defined with respect to a fixed measurement scale, such as "total annual hazardous waste generated." Relative metrics are defined with respect to another metric or variable, as in the 3M waste ratio mentioned above. A common approach is to use time-based relative metrics, that is, those that compute the change in a particular quantitative metric over a given time period, for example, "percentage reduction from 1992 to 1993 in total hazardous waste per unit output."

The following are examples of environmental performance metrics for the major evaluation areas described above; note that many of them can be normalized by facility output to enable internal comparisons.

Management System Metrics

- Frequency or intensity of training, auditing, and other preventive measures.
- Number of notices of violation, compliance-related fines, or other penalties.
- Capital or other expenditures on environmental improvement initiatives.

- Life-cycle cost savings achieved through environmental initiatives.
- Fraction of suppliers receiving environmental performance approval rating.
- Number of environmentally related external complaints received.

Operational Metrics

- Total energy consumed during the product life cycle.
- Total fresh water consumed during manufacturing.
- Toxic or hazardous materials used in production.
- Hazardous waste generated during production or use.
- Air emissions, water effluents, or solid waste generated during production.
- Greenhouse gases or ozone-depleting substances released over life cycle.
- Percent of product recovered and recycled or reused at end of life.
- Percent of recycled materials used as input to product.
- Fraction of packaging or containers recycled.

Environmental Metrics

- Depletion rate of nonrenewable natural resources.
- Impacts on wetlands or other ecosystems of concern.
- Acute lethal or sublethal effects on fish or wildlife populations.
- Estimated increase in annual incidence of chronic effects in humans or biota.
- Ambient concentrations of hazardous by-products in various media.
- Reductions in air quality or visibility.
- Global climate impacts.

It should be noted that evaluating the relationship of environmental metrics to any single organization's activities is extremely challenging unless the operational system and the environmental medium of interest are virtually isolated from other systems. In most cases, it is scientifically impossible to quantify the causal linkages between releases and consequences. Nevertheless, the environmental aspect review may determine that it is important to track certain environmental indicators that are of concern to key stakeholders and are believed to be linked to the organization's activities.

Relationship of Metrics to Aspects, Indicators, and Objectives

The relationship of metrics to aspects, indicators, objectives, and targets is illustrated in Table 8–1. Once the important aspects are selected, objectives represent a qualitative statement of intent, indicators designate a measurable dimension of improvement, metrics provide a means of quantifying the indicators, and targets provide a basis for tracking and assessing improvement.

Aggregation of Metrics

A common practice in EPE is to use scaling or weighting techniques to aggregate various specific performance metrics. Weighting schemes may reflect a variety of different considerations, including the following:

- Values of different stakeholder groups (e.g., customers versus community).
- Relative importance of environmental impacts (e.g., human health versus ecology).
- Internal business priorities (e.g., strategic advantage).

TABLE 8–1

Examples of Environmental Objectives and Corresponding Indicators, Metrics, and Targets

Objectives for Selected Aspects	Environmental Performance Indicators	Examples of Quantifiable Metrics	Examples of Specific Performance Targets
Reduce or eliminate waste	Waste and emissions from products and processes	• lb. of emissions over the life cycle • % of product weight disposed in landfills	• Reduce life-cycle emissions by 30% annually • Reduce solid waste disposed to 1 lb. per product unit
Develop "green" products	Recyclability of obsolete products	• % of product weight recovered and recycled • lb. of solid waste	• Achieve 95% recycling • Eliminate end-of-life waste disposal
Reduce life-cycle cost of products	Costs incurred at each stage of life cycle	• Manufacturing cost • Distribution and support cost • End-of-life cost	• Reduce total life-cycle cost to $7,500 per product unit • Reduce end-of-life cost (or increase value) by 20%
Conserve energy	Energy usage over the life cycle	• Total energy (BTU) to produce one unit • Average power use	• Reduce to 1,000 BTU • Reduce by 10% annually • Power less than 30 watts
Conserve natural resources	Recycled content in products	• % by weight of product materials that is recycled	• Achieve 20% or greater total recycled content • Achieve 30% recycled plastics

In general, as there is no universal weighting scheme that will suit the needs of diverse organizations, each organization should develop a scheme that fits its particular needs. Exercise caution in developing such weighting schemes because implicit value judgments may skew the results in unintended ways. Moreover, the significance of improvement in an aggregated score is difficult to communicate both to employees and external audiences. In fact, aggregated measures may invite unfair comparisons among dissimilar products or facilities.

Environmental metrics ideally should be assessed with respect to the life cycle of the product or process being developed. Table 8–2 illustrates how various types of metrics are typically related to life-cycle stages. Each row represents a class of primary environmental metrics; the arrows represent the direction of desired improvement (up or down). A star in a given cell indicates that the corresponding metric is relevant to the life-cycle stage.

In many cases, practical limitations of data resources or methodology may hinder the ability of a development team to evaluate all of the relevant cells. In other cases, organizations may wish to exclude certain life-cycle stages from consideration because they are not relevant to business decision making. Therefore, the intended scope and rationale for metrics should always be clarified. For example, rather than speaking of "energy use reduction," specify "reduction in energy use during manufacturing and distribution" or "reduction in energy consumption during product end use."

At the aggregate level, metrics represent the overall performance of an organization. However, in order to support data collection and process improvement, metrics need to be decomposed into observable and verifiable measures associated with particular activities and business processes. At that level, metrics can be used not only to monitor continuous improvement but also to develop employee incentives and reward systems. Because of the obvious data-management challenges, information technology must be deployed for computing, tracking, and converting these metrics to meet various needs.

T A B L E   8–2

Environmental Performance Metrics Relevant to Each Life-Cycle Stage

	Materials	Fabrication	Transport	End Use	Disposal
Energy usage $\downarrow$	★	★	★	★	★
Water usage $\downarrow$	★	★		★	
Source volume $\downarrow$	★	★	★	★	★
Recycling & reuse $\uparrow$		★		★	★
Waste & emissions $\downarrow$	★	★	★	★	★
Recycled materials $\uparrow$	★	★			

B O X   8–1

EXAMPLES OF ENVIRONMENTAL PERFORMANCE INDICATORS

The following examples of environmental performance indicators (EPIs) have been adapted from the proposed annexes to ISO 14031, from comments submitted to Subcommittee 4 (SC4) on environmental performance evaluation regarding the development of the annexes, and from other materials used by SC4 to develop the ISO 14031 EPE standard.

EXAMPLES OF MANAGEMENT SYSTEM EPIs

Training

- Resources allocated to training as a percent of total environmental budget.
- Hours of environmental training per employee.
- Percent of employees receiving environmental awareness training.
- Number and type of environmental incidents traceable to inadequate training.
- Percent of employees meeting specified levels of knowledge of environmental issues.

Integrating Environmental Issues into Corporate Management

- Number, type, and level of nonenvironmental staff with environmental elements in their job descriptions.
- Number of senior managers whose compensation is affected by their unit's environmental performance.

Pollution Prevention

- Percent of budget devoted to development of pollution-prevention processes and products.
- Percent of capital budget assigned to prevention versus end-of-pipe treatment.

Environmental Costs/Benefits

- Environmental costs as a percentage of total capital, operations and maintenance costs.
- Costs associated with prevention activities.
- Costs associated with checking and monitoring.
- Costs of external failures, such as fines, violations, liabilities, etc.
- Savings associated with environmental activities.

Implementation of EMS

- Percent of targets and objectives achieved.
- Percent of operations that have implemented specific EMS tasks.

Checking and Corrective Action

- Number and frequency of audits.
- Number of corrective actions and incident response time.
- Timeliness of response to environmental problems (length of time from notification of problem to actions taken).

EXAMPLES OF OPERATIONAL SYSTEM EPIs

Raw Material Use

- Units of raw materials per unit of product (i.e., in tons).
- Number of different raw materials used.
- Units of nonrenewable raw materials used per unit of product.
- Units of renewable raw materials used per unit of product.
- Cost of raw materials used per unit of product.
- Units of raw material reused in production process.
- Percent of recycled content in product.
- Cost of recycled raw material used per unit of product.

Energy Use

- Energy units (e.g., BTUs) used per year.
- Energy units per unit of product.
- Energy units of each source of energy used.
- Energy units consumed by product units.
- Energy units or renewable energy used during a given time frame.
- Percentage of energy units saved by scheduling energy usage.

Waste Generation

- Units (e.g., tons) of waste generated per year.
- Units of waste generated per unit of product.
- Percentage of waste reduction per unit of product.
- Cost of waste disposal.

Waste Disposal

- Units of waste disposed per year.
- Units of waste recycled per year.
- Units of waste reclaimed per year.
- Units of waste sold as secondary material per year.
- Units of waste used as raw material for a process.

(Continued)

B O X   8–1 *(Concluded)*

Controlling Environmental Aspects
- Percentage of products with zero emissions discharge.
- Number of days with no spills, upsets or incidents.
- Number of days in compliance with regulations.

AREAS IN WHICH ENVIRONMENT INDICATORS CAN BE DEVELOPED

Natural Resources
- Nonrenewable resources.
- Energy.
- Water.
- Raw material usage.
- Desertification and erosion.
- Wetlands.
- Land use.

Ecology
- Biological diversity.
- Habitat.
- Rare and endangered species.
- Ecologically sensitive areas.
- Food chain issues.
- Flora and fauna population health.

Water Quality
- Eutrophication.
- Toxic chemicals.
- Sediments.
- Drinking water properties.
- Recreational parameters.
- Navigable waters' properties.

Air Quality
- Particulates and smog.
- Toxic chemicals.
- Odors & aesthetic qualities.
- Characteristics affecting human health.
- Acid rain.

LIFE-CYCLE THINKING

Many of the examples given above reflect the use of life-cycle concepts. However, there has been considerable debate within the ISO 14000 standard-setting process regarding the appropriate use of life-cycle assessment (LCA), especially with regard to environmental performance evaluation. Proponents of LCA argue that it is the only meaningful way to understand the environmental impacts of industrial activities. Yet the ISO 14000 subcommittee working on LCA has recognized that existing methodologies are inadequate for impact assessment and is exploring alternative approaches.

Meanwhile, the position of the EPE subcommittee is that the EPE standard should encourage life-cycle thinking but should not endorse LCA or any other specific methodology. This is consistent with the basic principle that ISO 14000 should address only processes and should be independent of implementation technology. Similarly, the EMS standard, ISO 14001, states that the environmental review process does not require a detailed life-cycle assessment.

In practice, the term *life cycle* is used frequently in the context of environmental management, yet it has widely differing interpretations. A business life cycle is a sequence of business processes including the initial design of a product or process, its development, launch, production, maintenance and support, reevaluation, and renewal as a next-generation product or process. In contrast, a physical life cycle is a sequence of transformations in materials and energy that includes extraction and processing of materials, product manufacture and assembly, distribution, use, and recovery or recycling of product materials.

As illustrated in Figure 8–5, the concept of design for environment (alternatively called life-cycle design) is being adopted by progressive organizations that are changing their business processes to design not just a product but the entire physical life cycle. For example, Xerox Corporation deliberately designs its photocopiers for

FIGURE   8–5

Designing a Product Life Cycle

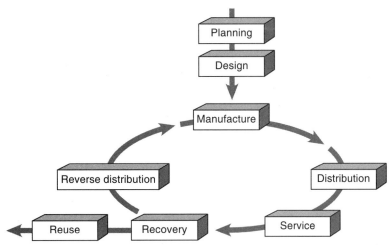

remanufacturing and has developed an efficient reverse distribution system for obsolete parts and equipment. Although full-scale, quantitative LCA is seldom pursued under these initiatives, life-cycle thinking is clearly a driving force.

Note that the responsibility for the business life cycle and the business impacts (profits or losses incurred) are borne fully by the producing organization; whereas, the responsibility for the physical life cycle and its associated impacts is distributed among many organizations or individuals involved at different stages of the value chain, and in some cases the responsibility for adverse impacts may be ambiguous (e.g., liability for waste disposal). LCA results regarding environmental burdens, to the extent they reflect customer needs or organizational objectives, may certainly be factored into a business analysis, but the decision framework must have a "return on investment" perspective.

It is no wonder, then, that business managers are often puzzled by the calculus of LCA, which seeks to quantify the "cradle to grave" impacts of the physical life cycle. While it is relevant to sustainability, this type of life-cycle assessment may be quite unrelated to the decisions addressed by business teams, in which life-cycle thinking focuses on cost and performance trade-offs; for example, the increased cost of making a product more durable may be offset by reduced warranty costs. This suggests the need for a greater emphasis on the emerging field of environmental accounting (alternatively called life-cycle accounting).

It is widely recognized that most current accounting methods do not properly capture and internalize the costs or revenues associated with environmental management efforts. Because environmental budgets are usually assigned to overhead accounts, product or process improvement initiatives cannot easily be credited for their monetary benefits. In particular, impacts upon resources such as materials, water, soil, or energy are difficult to evaluate because market value based on classical supply and demand mechanisms fails to reflect the true societal value of these resources.

However, by following the principles of activity-based costing, it is possible to capture the contribution of environmental improvements with regard to increased profitability. For example, recent EPA-sponsored work has shown that when savings associated with reduced energy use, reduced waste management expenses, and salvage values of recycled materials are taken into account, pollution prevention projects become much more financially attractive. This type of environmental accounting is the missing link that will make life-cycle thinking relevant to business decision making.

CONCLUSIONS

In summary, EPE can be a valuable management tool for improving the profitability, competitiveness, and sustainability of a business organization, while meeting broader societal needs. However, the results of EPE must be communicated with great care to avoid misinterpretation or misuse by employees or third parties. When properly implemented, EPE will become a continuous improvement process, like any other

EPM as a Continuous Improvement Process

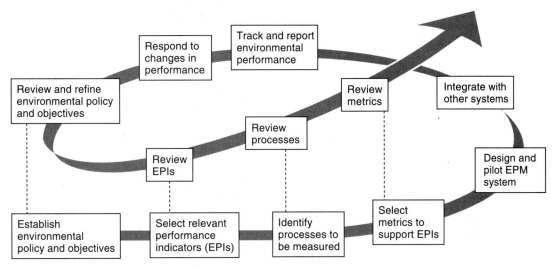

quality-oriented process. As illustrated in Figure 8–6, the continuous improvement model assumes that performance indicators and targets will repeatedly be reevaluated in the light of changing socioeconomic conditions.

On the basis of the organization's environmental policy, strategic environmental objectives and corresponding corporate-level environmental performance indicators (EPIs) are identified. The core business processes (e.g., generation) are reviewed to identify specific activities that have a significant impact on the EPIs, and appropriate metrics and goals corresponding to these activities are selected. Next, a system is developed for collecting and reporting environmental performance data. After an initial, pilot implementation period, the system is integrated with existing business systems and procedures. The EPM process then tracks environmental performance results, and tactical responses are undertaken to improve performance. As the cycle continues, information about overall performance is fed back to support periodic reviews of the corporate environmental policy, strategy, and objectives.

Finally, it is important to note that the ISO 14000 standard-setting process is not concerned with the concept of competitive advantage. However, it is critical that organizations reflect on how they can utilize the new standards to their advantage or at least avoid a decline in competitiveness. In order to use EPE effectively as a business tool, there are a number of implementation issues that organizations should address:

- The organization's EMS should be integrated with existing business processes, as opposed to being a stand-alone appendage.

- The organization should strive to select environmental aspects and performance metrics that are relevant to economic competitiveness (e.g., resource consumption, waste recovery, compliance costs).

- The organization should use an activity-based life-cycle accounting approach to identify and reward activities that add economic value.

- The organization should deploy enabling information technology to support the efficient implementation of the EMS.

It is becoming clear that eco-efficient, sustainable organizations will be more competitive over the long run. Since organizations with competitive advantage will survive through evolutionary selection, the only way to achieve worldwide sustainable development is to encourage competitive advantage through environmental performance improvement. This is an important message not only for managers but also for environmentalists who confuse the profit motive with an imagined environmental threat. Enlightened firms today are accomplishing more for the environment through internal performance improvements than could ever be achieved through obstructive political tactics.[2]

BIOGRAPHY

Joseph Fiksel, PhD

Joseph Fiksel is a senior director in the Strategic Environmental Management practice of Battelle Memorial Institute, where his work involves assisting clients to achieve competitive advantage through environmental excellence. His 20-year consulting career has spanned a variety of different industries, including chemicals, electronics, automobiles, consumer products, and electric power. Previously he was a vice president at Decision Focus Incorporated, where he specialized in Design for Environment and Environmental Performance Evaluation.

Dr. Fiksel is an active member of the U.S. Technical Advisory Group for ISO TC 207, the IEEE Technical Advisory Board on Environmental Health and Safety, and numerous other professional organizations. He holds a B.Sc. in electrical engineering from MIT and a Ph.D. from Stanford University in operations research, as well as a postgraduate degree in applied mathematics from La Sorbonne in Paris, France. As a recognized expert in the field of health and safety risk analysis, Dr. Fiksel has testified before Congressional and White House committees.

Dr. Fiksel has published extensively, and is the principal author and editor of a recent book entitled *Design for Environment: Creating Eco-Efficient Products and Processes,* published by McGraw-Hill in October, 1995. This comprehensive guide to the principles and practices of DFE features contributions by a dozen major U.S. companies who are acknowledged leaders in environmental excellence, including chapters by Frank Popoff of Dow Chemical and Brad Allenby of AT&T.

NOTES

1. Thomas, W. Zosel, *Developing Company Specific Environmental Performance Metrics,* presented at Environmental Excellence Through Measurement conference, San Francisco, CA, October, 1993.

2. Portions of the above are based on the author's book, *Design for Environment: Creating Eco-Efficient Products and Processes,* McGraw-Hill, October 1995.

CHAPTER 9

EMS Auditing and Management Review

Anton Camarota

INTRODUCTION

Since the early 1970s, the growing body of environmental law and regulation has played an important part in the lives of most organizations in the United States. Most recently, the ISO 14001 EMS standard has provided a mechanism for integrating environmental decision making into routine business planning. ISO 14001 establishes a framework for proactively managing and controlling environmental impacts throughout the organization. This framework, however, depends heavily on the results of management systems audits as well as management reviews to ensure continual improvement of the management system throughout the organization.

Environmental audits, while originally intended to ensure regulatory compliance, have expanded in scope and purpose to include evaluations of management systems and risk assessments of unregulated activities (Figure 9–1). The ISO 14010-12

FIGURE 9–1

Types of Environmental Audits

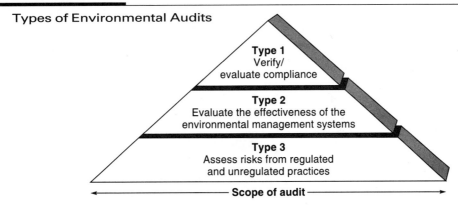

Type 1
Verify/
evaluate compliance

Type 2
Evaluate the effectiveness of the
environmental management systems

Type 3
Assess risks from regulated
and unregulated practices

← ──────────── **Scope of audit** ──────────── →

environmental auditing standards provide the basis for developing an environmental audit program that serves to gather and distribute information related to an organization's EMS. These standards set the stage for audits that evaluate the management systems used for establishing compliance with legal requirements, controlling environmental impacts, and minimizing the risks from unregulated activities.

EMS AUDIT VERSUS MANAGEMENT REVIEW

The EMS audit and the management review are two key activities that determine the effectiveness of an organization's EMS as well as its degree of commitment to continual improvement.

In Clause 4.5.4, ISO 14001 requires the company to carry out periodic audits of the environmental management system. This is a system audit, not an audit for technical compliance with laws and regulations. The aim is to make sure that the EMS "conforms to planned arrangements for environmental management including the requirements of this standard and has been properly implemented and maintained." The other aim of the EMS audit is to provide information on its results to management for review.

The basic management review requirement in Clause 4.6 of ISO 14001 calls on top management to review the EMS, whenever it determines appropriate, "to ensure its continuing suitability, adequacy and effectiveness." Management must make sure that it has collected the information necessary for a comprehensive evaluation and that it documents the review. The primary purpose of both audits and reviews is to evaluate the management systems used to fulfill the organization's environmental policy and achieve its environmental objectives and targets. There are, however, differences as well as similarities between them.

Regarding similarities, audits and reviews are both activities to evaluate how well an organization manages its environmental performance. Second, they use similar techniques and methods, such as gathering and evaluating objective evidence of performance in many organizational areas. Third, they each result in recommendations for corrective action. Finally, they are both tools for gaining more management control over environmental problems, concerns, and issues.

The primary difference between an EMS audit and a management review is scope. An EMS audit focuses on the management systems used to control organizational performance as they relate to the stated policy, objectives, and targets. These include aspects such as operational controls, training, document control, and other implementation activities. The management review assesses management systems, but at a programmatic level, and includes a review of each of the environmental program elements, including the need to adjust them in light of changing external conditions such as new legislation, changed customer requirements, or increased community involvement.

Many, if not most, of the organization's routine specific corrective actions will be generated by a good audit program; the management review, however, functions at a higher level to adjust and improve the environmental program as a whole. The

EMS audit addresses the need for functional change within the organization; the management review looks at broad, strategic environmental issues and the organization's response to those issues. Changes resulting from EMS audits will tend to be adjustments within the separate operational systems that make up the EMS; management reviews will generate changes that involve multiple systems, their interactions, and their interfaces with other organizational systems, goals, and objectives.

ISO 14010-12 AUDITING STANDARDS

The ISO 14010-12 auditing standards were developed by Subcommittee 2 of TC 207. Its official scope is "standardization in the field of environmental auditing and related environmental investigations." This is a broad statement that can cover not only compliance auditing and EMS auditing but also areas such as site assessments, initial reviews, environmental statements, decommissioning audits, and other evaluative activities.

SC2 has developed three auditing standards to this point. *ISO 14010 Guidelines for environmental auditing—general principles* describes general principles common to all types of environmental auditing. *ISO 14011 Guidelines for environmental auditing—Audit procedures - Auditing of environmental management systems* looks at specific procedures for auditing environmental management systems. *ISO 14012 Guidelines for environmental auditing—Qualification criteria for environmental auditors* sets out specific qualifications for environmental auditors.

Applicability

The standards apply to any environmental audit, whether a compliance or management system, whether conducted internally or commissioned externally. They can be used internally (first-party), in contract situations (second-party) and for external, (third-party) audits. The auditing standards apply to all types of organizations. Any company can use the guidance in the ISO 14010-12 series to set up its auditing program.

Guidance, Not Specifications

The ISO 14010–14012 series are guidance standards, not specification standards. That is, they are not requirements of an ISO 14001 EMS, either for self-declaration or third-party registration (certification) purposes. Although ISO 14001, in Clause 4.5.4, requires EMS audits, these audits need not be performed in conformance with ISO 14011. A company can select ISO 14011 to guide its EMS audit program, but this is not an express requirement of ISO 14001.

Auditing Principles (ISO 14010)

This standard is a generic "umbrella" document that provides general principles for all types of activities that can be considered environmental audits.

What Is an Environmental Audit?

As defined in Clause 3.9 of ISO 14010, an environmental audit is "a systematic, documented verification process of objectively obtaining and evaluating audit evidence to determine whether specified environmental activities, events, conditions, management systems, or information about these matters conform with audit criteria, and communicating the results of this process to the client."

As shown in Figure 9–2, ISO 14010 describes key audit principles applicable to many types of activities. Environmental audits are, at their core, verification processes to determine by examination of objective evidence whether or not the subject matter conforms with the predetermined criteria. In the case of ISO 14010, the verification process could include evaluations of environmental management systems, evaluations of environmental performance of the operations, or evaluations of operations and performance based on information included in an environmental statement.

F I G U R E   9–2

Generic Environmental Audit Process

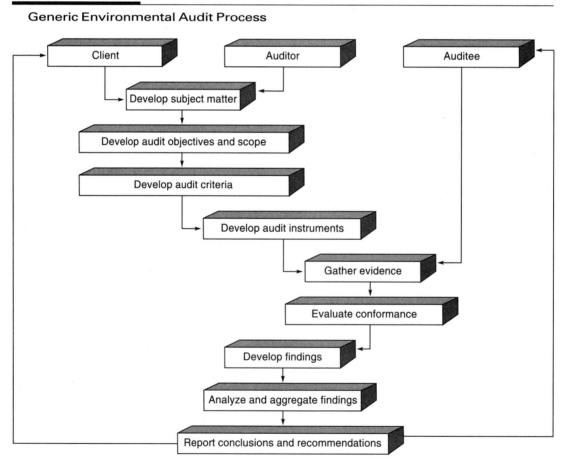

Types of Auditing Activities

Types of auditing activities that are covered by this standard include the following:

- Environmental management systems audits.
- Environmental statement audits.
- Environmental legislation compliance audits.
- Decommissioning/decontamination audits.
- Site assessments.
- Initial reviews.

Prerequisites for Auditing

These audits should only be performed if certain requirements surrounding them have been met. These requirements include:

- A clearly defined and documented subject matter, including identification of the parties responsible for the subject matter.
- "Sufficient and appropriate" information available about the activity, facility, or organization to be audited.
- Adequate resources to support the audit.
- Cooperation from the auditee so that the audit may proceed without undue difficulty or delay.

If these conditions do not exist, the audit should not take place.

Base Audit on Defined Objectives

The audit should be based on defined objectives as agreed to by the client. The auditee is the organization to be audited. The client is the organization commissioning the audit. Therefore, the client may be, in many cases, a different person or organization than the auditee.

The scope of the activity should be determined by the lead auditor in conjunction with the client and must be sufficient to meet the defined audit objectives. For example, if the objective of an audit was to determine the compliance status of an entire organization but the scope was limited to a single division, the audit would be insufficient. Finally, the objectives and scope should be communicated to the auditee to obtain agreement and understanding on what will occur during the audit and why it will happen.

Key Characteristics of Environmental Auditors

Key characteristics for environmental auditors include objectivity, independence, and competence. Auditors should be functionally independent of the activities they audit. This ensures objectivity and integrity of the audit process, including the development of findings and conclusions. They should be objective and free from bias and conflicts of interest.

Clause 5.2 of ISO 14010 notes that the organization can use external or internal audit team members. Audit team members chosen from within the organization, however, "should not be accountable to those directly responsible for the subject matter being audited."

Finally, all members of the audit team should have "an appropriate combination of knowledge, skills, and experience" to perform their activities successfully. Specific auditor qualification criteria are detailed in ISO 14012.

Due Professional Care

Auditors should also exercise "due professional care" during the planning, performance, and reporting of the audit. According to ISO 14010, this requires establishing a client–auditor relationship based on confidentiality and discretion. Auditors must not disclose any information or documents obtained during the audit without the express approval of the client.

The exception, of course, is when such disclosure is required by law or when the auditor discovers what he or she considers to be blatant criminal behavior. In such cases, it is advisable for the auditor to first consult with an attorney to determine the appropriate course of action.

The final component of due professional care is quality assurance (QA). The auditor should follow applicable QA procedures and methods to ensure the integrity of audit evidence and findings.

Systematic Procedures

The environmental audit should be conducted according to "documented and well-defined methodologies and systematic procedures." These procedures should be consistent among the different types of audits, with just enough variation in requirements to allow for the different technical makeup of the particular audit. These procedures allow for consistent information gathering and interpretation and provide a baseline to ensure that the audit activities are complete and comparable among different locations, times, or organizations.

Determining Audit Criteria

A key step in the audit process is determining the audit criteria, which according to ISO 14010 should be "at an appropriate level of detail" and agreed to "between the lead auditor and the client, and communicated to the auditee." This means that audit criteria must be clearly defined, leaving no room for ambiguous interpretation, and that all parties involved with the audit must agree on the intent, extent, and exact meaning of what will be used by the auditors to evaluate the facility, activity, or organization.

Collecting Evidence

The standard requires that the auditor collect, analyze, interpret, and document evidence sufficient to determine whether the facility, activity, or organization conforms to the agreed criteria. This requires the development of audit instruments such as checklists and may require judgment calls on the part of the auditor. ISO 14010 additionally requires the audit evidence to "be of such a quality and quantity that competent environmental auditors working independently of each other would reach similar audit findings from evaluating the same audit evidence against the same audit criteria." This means that the evidence must be objective; complete; verifiable; traceable; relevant to the facility, activity, or location; direct or obtained from first-party observation or recording; and unbiased.

Reliability of Audit Findings

Another important consideration is the reliability of audit findings, which is determined by taking into account the limitations associated with obtaining samples of evidence. In certain audits, such as phase two property assessments, statistical sampling may be used to obtain a desired level of confidence about the subject matter of the audit. In other cases, a nonrepresentative or judgment sample may be used to determine conformance. In either case, ISO 14010 requires the audit process to be designed such that the uncertainty involved in the sampling is considered when planning and executing the audit, and is also defined and communicated to users of the audit report.

Also, findings should consist of either a standalone major finding or findings capable of being aggregated into a major finding. This ensures that the findings are representative of actual conditions and that they can be used as evidence of systemic failures that may occur at widely varying times and places.

Reporting Audit Results

Finally, the results of audits should be reported in a complete and consistent manner. ISO 14010 recommends that the lead auditor, in consultation with the client, determine which reporting elements should be selected from the following:

- Identification of the audited organization and the client.
- Agreed audit objectives and scope.
- Agreed criteria used for conformance evaluation.
- Period covered by the audit and the date(s) the audit was conducted.
- Identification of audit team members.
- Identification of the auditee's representatives participating in the audit.
- Summary of the audit process, including any obstacles or unusual difficulties encountered.
- Audit conclusions.

- Statement of the confidential nature of the contents.
- Report distribution list.

A note to the standard emphasizes that it is the responsibility of the client or the auditee to determine if any corrective actions are needed to respond to the findings. The auditor, however, can provide recommendations upon prior agreement with the client.

THE ISO 14011 STANDARD—EMS AUDIT PROCEDURES

The ISO 14011 standard, *Guidelines for environmental auditing—Auditing of environmental management systems* describes the basic elements of an effective environmental management systems audit program. These elements, when developed fully, can provide management with a series of "snapshots" of the individual systems that comprise its EMS. Management must require that trained and experienced auditors evaluate the organization's environmental management systems at predetermined times and according to established criteria. In addition, the results of these audits must be reported to operational management responsible for performing corrective actions, and corrective actions must be implemented and verified as effective.

The elements of the ISO 14011 standard prescribe basic activities that comprise an EMS audit program. These activities include the following:

- Determining the audit objectives and purposes.
- Assigning roles and responsibilities for the lead auditor, team auditor(s), client, and auditee.
- Defining the audit scope.
- Reviewing preliminary organizational documents.
- Preparing an audit plan.
- Assigning audit team members.
- Developing working documents to be used during the audit.
- Conducting the opening meeting.
- Collecting objective evidence about management systems.
- Determining EMS conformance and developing audit findings.
- Conducting the closing meeting.
- Preparing and distributing the audit report.
- Retaining audit documents.

The EMS Audit Process and Procedures

Where the ISO 14010 standard applies to all types of environmental audits, the ISO 14011 standard is meant to apply only to audits of environmental management systems.

These audits evaluate three critical aspects of the EMS:

1. Does a system exist that conforms to organizational, regulatory, or other environmental requirements?
2. Is the existing system implemented as required by its nature and scope?
3. Is the implemented system achieving what it is supposed to achieve?

These three aspects are used by the lead auditor throughout the audit process to determine the development of objectives, scope, criteria, instruments, plans, findings, and reported conclusions and recommendations.

Focus on Systems, Not Performance

The key distinguishing characteristic of EMS audits is that they focus on management planning and control activities related to environmental performance, not on environmental performance specifically. The intent is to determine the existence, implementation, and effectiveness of the management systems used to control environmental performance. Where an environmental compliance audit would determine if emission levels exceeded a specific regulatory threshold, an environmental management systems audit would look at the control mechanisms used to ensure that the regulatory emission limit was not exceeded (see Box 9–1).

The difference in focus is subtle but critical: Management systems audits are part of the core requirements for an EMS. Other types of audits may be performed but are not a requirement of ISO 14001.

B O X   9–1

EMS AUDITING VERSUS COMPLIANCE AUDITING

Compliance auditing is designed to check for compliance against prescribed activities that are contained in permits, regulations, internal standards, and other requirements. The auditor wants to know whether performance deviates from requirements. The auditor is checking to see if one follows the rules, not so much how one does it, who does it, or how efficiently or effectively it's done. The EMS auditor is interested, however, in how, not just what, is done. The EMS auditor must make some judgments: Is the system effective and resulting in continual improvement? EMS auditors deal with many departments, not just the environmental staff. For example, do operations personnel have control over environmental aspects of their jobs that have been defined? Are adequate resources allocated to the EMS? How does the auditor know this? He or she must interview business managers and others who control funds. To judge the effectiveness of management review, the auditor talks extensively with top management. EMS audits should be repeated several times to establish a management review process.

Determining Audit Objectives and Scope

The first step in the EMS audit is determining the audit scope, objectives, and purpose. The lead auditor, in conjunction with the client, should define why the audit is being performed and what it will accomplish. Once these purposes are defined, the lead auditor and the client can determine the resources that will be required, the duration of the audit, and where it will take place. Without a carefully crafted backdrop of defined objectives and purposes, the auditor runs the risk of wasting valuable resources on activities that may not meet the needs of management, especially if the audit is internal.

The following are some examples of typical EMS audit objectives defined in ISO 14011:

- Determine conformance of an auditee's EMS against defined criteria.
- Determine if the auditee's EMS has been properly implemented and maintained.
- Identify potential areas of EMS improvement.
- Assess the effectiveness of the management review process in establishing continual improvement.
- Evaluate the overall EMS of a supplier or potential partner organization in order to establish a contractual relationship.

Once the purpose of the audit has been established, the lead auditor in consultation with the client and the auditee should define the extent and boundaries of the auditing activity required. Once a scope has been defined, any subsequent changes need to be agreed to by the client and the lead auditor.

Scope factors that need to be defined include physical location(s), organizational activities and functions, and how the audit results will be reported. These factors control the resources required for the audit; therefore, they must be defined carefully and accurately.

Defining Audit Roles, Responsibilities, and Activities

The next major step is to clearly define the roles and responsibilities of the audit team, especially if the client and the auditee are not the same person or organization. The audit team composition will vary with the objectives, scope, industry, location, and timing. Generally, the lead auditor is responsible for managing the audit process from inception until closing according to the scope and plan as approved by the client. Lead auditor responsibilities include the following:

- Determining the objectives and scope of the audit in consultation with the client.
- Determining whether enough information exists to perform an environmental audit.

- Forming the audit team and assigning responsibilities to team members.
- Directing the activities of the team and coordinating activities with the client and auditee.
- Preparing an audit plan and communicating it to the client, auditee, and team members.
- Ensuring that audit team members follow approved procedures for performance and reporting.
- Acting as the representative for the audit team in communications with the client and the auditee.
- Reporting the results of the audit, including any recommendations for improvements.
- Notifying the client of any critical nonconformities, including possible criminal activities, without delay.

The team auditor's responsibilities include following the direction of the lead auditor for gathering information, analyzing evidence, preparing working documents, and assisting in writing the final audit report. Team members must be experienced in carrying out their responsibilities; ISO 14012 provides some guidelines in this regard.

The audit team should, as a whole, have both industry-specific and generic auditing knowledge and skills. The team may also contain auditors-in-training and specific technical experts, who are consulted as necessary. The keys to team formation are acceptance and approval by the client and the auditee, as well as technical proficiency in the industry in which the audit takes place. The team will provide answers to questions such as these:

- Is the policy appropriate to the nature and extent of the organization's activities?
- Have all the significant environmental aspects of the organization been identified?
- What is the extent of regulated and nonregulated activities that this organization engages in that may impact the environment?

Industry-specific experience, coupled with an understanding of environmental science and regulations, are critical in ensuring complete, accurate, and reasonable answers to the above questions.

Client Responsibilities

The client should help the lead auditor define the objectives, goals, and scope of the audit as well as review the composition of the audit team. The client should approve the audit plan and assist in the performance of the audit by providing required resources.

Auditee Responsibilities

The auditee must provide access to facilities and locations where the audit will be conducted, as well as provide competent staff to support the audit information-gathering process. The auditee also should notify the lead auditor of any health, safety, or special access requirements and should act as a guide or escort for the team during the audit performance.

Initiating the Audit

The four basic activities required for initiating the audit process are as follows:

1. Review preliminary documents from the organization.
2. Prepare an audit plan.
3. Assign audit team members.
4. Develop specific audit instruments/working documents such as checklists.

Review Preliminary Documents

The lead auditor must obtain and review documents relevant to the environmental performance of the organization, such as:

- Policy statements.
- Program descriptions.
- Procedure manuals for environmentally related activities.
- Records such as permit applications or discharge certificates.

If the lead auditor determines from this review that the existing documentation is insufficient to support the agreed-upon audit activities, he or she should notify the client and stop any further audit activity.

Prepare the Audit Plan

The lead auditor, in conjunction with appropriate team members, should prepare a comprehensive yet flexible audit plan. The purpose of this plan is to formalize the scope, purpose, objectives, roles and responsibilities, and required audit activities so that they may be communicated clearly and unambiguously to the audit team members, the client, and the auditee. There should be no question as to what will be done, why it will be done, where and when the activities will take place, and who is responsible for performing what activity. Any objections or questions regarding any provisions of the audit plan should be made known to the lead auditor, who should resolve them prior to performing the audit.

Elements for inclusion in the audit plan should include the following:

- Audit objectives, scope, and criteria.
- Identification of the auditee's organizational and functional units to be audited.
- Identification of responsible individuals within the EMS.
- Identification of those EMS elements that are of high audit priority.
- Procedures for performing and reporting.
- Working and reporting languages for the audit (especially for multinational organizations).
- Identification of reference documents.
- Expected dates, times, durations, and locations for major audit activities.
- Identification of audit team members.
- Schedule of meetings to be held with the auditee's management.
- Confidentiality requirements.
- Reporting and document-retention requirements.

Assign Audit Team Members

The next step is to assign each team member specific tasks to assist in completion of the audit. An auditor may be assigned to evaluate a functional area, such as shipping; a specific activity, such as cleaning and repair; or an EMS element, such as policy development and implementation. Regardless of the assignment, the lead auditor must monitor audit performance and change assignments as appropriate to ensure optimal achievement of audit objectives.

Prepare Audit Tools

The lead auditor should, in conjunction with the team members, prepare any required working documents for the audit. These documents could include the following:

- Checklists and forms for documenting supporting evidence and audit findings.
- Procedures for performance of audit tasks, such as reporting.
- Forms for meeting records.

The working documents will be used during the audit and should be retained at least until audit completion or as required by law or other client requirements. The team should take care to protect confidential or proprietary information until it has been returned to the client.

Performing the Audit

The audit itself consists of four basic activities:

1. Conducting an opening meeting with the client and auditee.
2. Collecting objective evidence about management systems.
3. Determining EMS conformance and developing audit findings.
4. Conducting a closing meeting.

The Opening Meeting

The opening meeting is held to review the audit plan with the auditee's management and to introduce them to the audit team. The lead auditor usually conducts this meeting and establishes himself or herself as the official communication link for the audit team. The lead auditor should provide a short summary of what will happen during the audit, including methods, procedures, times and places, and should confirm that the resources and facilities needed by the audit team are available. Especially important is the review of safety and emergency procedures for the audit team: Each person should know what his or her responsibilities are when entering, occupying, or leaving the auditee's facilities.

Collecting Evidence

Evidence is collected during the audit from a number of different sources, including: interviews, observations, and document reviews. Evidence collection should be sufficient to determine whether the auditee's EMS conforms to the EMS audit criteria. This is a judgment call, but evidence should show the same characteristics as specified in ISO 14010 for completeness, accuracy, representativeness, and comparability.

Additionally, all evidence should be either verified from an independent source or recorded as nonverifiable. The standard also requires the auditors to look at the basis of sampling programs and the procedures for quality control of the sampling and measurement processes.

Auditors should record instances where the evidence indicates that the EMS does not conform with applicable criteria on the working documents. This documentation is especially critical, as these statements will be used to develop the audit findings.

Determining EMS Conformance

After the team has collected and verified all of the evidence, it must determine whether the EMS conforms to the EMS audit criteria. They must then ensure that their findings of nonconformity are documented in a clear, concise way and are completely supported by the available audit evidence. The findings should be reviewed with the responsible manager to obtain acknowledgment of their factual basis; that is, to determine whether the finding is true and accurate in all respects.

The Closing Meeting

After the auditors have gathered the evidence and developed the findings, they should hold a closing meeting with the auditee's management to present a summary of the noted findings. The objective here is to obtain the clear understanding and acknowledgment of all individuals involved with the audit regarding exactly what the findings or nonconformities are, what the factual basis of each is, and where and when each was noted.

This is the time to resolve any disagreements before the lead auditor issues the final report. Often, there may be disagreement between the auditee's management and the audit team as to the significance and description of the findings. To the extent possible, the lead auditor must explain the basis for the findings to the auditee's management and ensure that all present know why the findings were so stated and their importance to the effective functioning of the EMS.

Preparing the Audit Report

The lead auditor prepares the final audit report with the assistance of the team members but is ultimately responsible for its accuracy and completeness. The report should reflect the topics required by the audit plan and may contain restatements of many plan elements in addition to the findings generated during the audit. If the report changes in content or format from that agreed on in the audit plan, those changes must be approved by the parties involved with the change. The basic purpose of the report is to provide a written description of the audit findings or a summary of them, with complete references to supporting evidence. The report may also contain the following:

- A description of any obstacles encountered during the audit.
- A distribution list for the report.
- Statements of EMS conformance to EMS audit criteria.
- Statements related to the proper implementation and maintenance of the EMS.
- Statements related to the ability of the management review process to ensure the continuing suitability and effectiveness of the EMS.

Distribution Report

Distribution of the report should follow the audit plan but should always include the client. Unless specifically excluded by the client, the auditee should also receive a copy of the audit report. Additional distribution beyond the client or auditee's organization requires the client's permission. The audit team must remember that audit reports are the sole property of the client, and confidentiality should be respected and appropriately safeguarded by the auditors. Any delays in issuing the report should be formally communicated to the client and the auditee, as should the revised issuance date.

Audit documents should be retained in accordance with the agreement developed between the client, the auditee, and the audit team.

AUDITOR QUALIFICATIONS (ISO 14012)

As noted earlier, many audit decisions require the judgment and experience of an environmental auditing professional. The ISO 14012 standard establishes the minimum requirements for such individuals in addition to providing requirements that can be used to certify both environmental auditors and lead auditors. This standard applies to individual auditors rather than to audit teams, as does ISO 14011, and it applies to both internal and external auditors.

The ISO 14012 standard, however, sets apart internal auditors by recognizing that they may not meet all of the detailed requirements for external auditors, depending on the following variables:

- The size, nature, complexity, and environmental impacts of their organization.

- The rate of development of relevant expertise and experience within their organization.

These provisions allow employees of small to medium-size enterprises to be considered qualified and allows these types of organizations the flexibility of using their existing personnel without having to resort to massive training and education efforts or extensive hiring of new auditing personnel.

Auditor qualifications consist of demonstrated achievement in each of the following areas: education, work experience, and training.

Education

Auditors should have completed at least a secondary education or the equivalent. The ISO 14012 standard defines *secondary education* as "that part of the national education system that comes after the primary or elementary stage, but that is completed immediately prior to entrance to a university or similar establishment."

Achievement of successful completion of post-secondary education is generally evidenced by the awarding of a degree, which ISO 14012 defines as a "recognized national or international degree obtained after secondary education, through a minimum of three years formal full-time, or equivalent part-time, study."

Work Experience

The requirements for work experience allow for some additional combinations of education and work experience, but auditors who have only secondary education or the equivalent should have a minimum of five years appropriate work experience. This experience should have contributed to the development of skills and understanding in some or all of the following areas:

- Environmental science and technology.
- Technical and environmental aspects of facility operations.
- Relevant requirements of environmental laws, regulations, and related documents.
- Environmental management systems standards.
- Audit procedures, processes, and techniques.

The standard allows for a one- or two-year reduction in the five-year work experience requirement for auditors that have demonstrated satisfactory completion of formal post-secondary full-time or part-time education that addresses some or all of the topics listed above, as evidenced by the holding of a degree.

Training

In addition to education and relevant work experience, auditors need to have completed both formal and on-the-job training. This type of training can be provided by either the auditor's own organization or an external organization. The key here is the accreditation of such training. Some sort of national accreditation body must have approved the auditor training course to ensure that the course meets a minimum standard for achieving and evaluating auditor competence.

Formal training should address the same topics as listed above for work experience.

On-the-job training should enable the auditor to demonstrate that he or she has participated in a total of 20 equivalent workdays of environmental auditing for a minimum of four environmental audits. This training should include involvement in the entire audit process under the supervision and guidance of a lead auditor and should occur within a period of not more than three consecutive years.

Personal Characteristics

In addition to education, experience, and training, auditors should possess the following personal characteristics:

- Competence in clearly expressing concepts and ideas, orally and in writing.
- Interpersonal skills such as diplomacy, tact, and the ability to listen.
- The ability to maintain independence and objectivity during the audit performance.
- Personal organization and orderliness.
- The ability to reach sound judgments based on objective evidence.
- The ability to be culturally sensitive to the conventions and creeds of the country or region in which the audit is performed.

In addition to all of the above qualifications, lead auditors must demonstrate personal attributes and skills that enable them to effectively manage the audit process. The key here is demonstrated audit leadership skills and experience:

- Either by participation in the entire audit process for a total of 15 additional equivalent workdays, for a minimum of three additional complete environmental audits, and participation as an acting lead auditor under the supervision and guidance of a lead auditor for at least one of these three audits;
- Or demonstration of these attributes and skills to the audit program management or others, by means such as interviews, observations, references and/or assessments of environmental auditing performance made under quality assurance programs.

The lead auditor should meet these additional criteria within a period of not more than three consecutive years.

Maintaining Competence

Auditors must maintain their competence by keeping their knowledge current in all fields relating to environmental auditing, as stated above in the work-experience categories. It is up to each auditor to ensure that he or she participates in current environmental audits as well as relevant training activities.

Due Professional Care

Auditors must also exercise due professional care, as defined in Clause 5.3 of ISO 14010 and should adhere to an appropriate code of ethics such as those promulgated by professional societies or organizations such as the Institute for Environmental Auditing in the United States or the Institute for Environmental Assessment in the United Kingdom.

Language Competence

A unique ISO 14012 requirement is language competency. The standard requires that auditors should not participate in audits when they are unable to communicate effectively in the language necessary for performing the required activities as noted in the audit plan. The standard does allow for support from a person or persons with the necessary language skills, but this person must not be subject to pressures that would affect the performance of the audit. This means that the audit team may want to consider having an interpreter available who is not an employee of the auditee's organization.

ISO 14012 ANNEXES

There are two annexes to ISO 14012 that define a method for evaluating the qualifications of environmental auditors and describe the techniques used by an environmental auditor registration body to register auditors. The first annex describes the evaluation process for determining auditor qualifications. This process should include some of the following methods:

- Interviews with candidates.
- Written and/or oral assessment.
- Review of candidate's written work.
- Discussions with former employers and colleagues.
- Role-playing.
- Peer observation under actual audit conditions.
- Reviewing records of education, experience, and training.
- Consideration of other professional certifications and qualifications.

This process could be used internally as well as by an external organization, such as a training organization that offers a class with a written exam. The idea is to promote consistent and adequate evaluations of an auditor's qualifications.

Organizations such as the Environmental Auditors Registration Association (EARA) ensure that environmental auditors are registered in a consistent manner, according to Annex B of 14012. These organizations act to accredit environmental auditors at different levels depending upon qualifications, and use an evaluation process commensurate with the requirements of Annex A.

MANAGEMENT REVIEW OF THE ENVIRONMENTAL MANAGEMENT SYSTEM

Management reviews are a cornerstone of any environmental management program. These reviews allow top management to become involved with the program and to demonstrate their commitment to environmental excellence. While these types of assessments may follow the generic audit process described in Figure 9–2, they are much more strategic in nature and are generally much broader in scope than an EMS audit. These reviews seek to answer the basic question: "How can management improve the EMS to get an improvement in overall environmental performance?"

Management reviews periodically ensure that the EMS is continuing to function effectively and that it is appropriate for the organization based on current internal and external conditions. These reviews are especially important in identifying new issues that the organization may have to deal with as well as establishing what effect the EMS may have had or is having on the organization's competitive position. The management reviews should be conducted periodically. Organizations that become registered to ISO 14001 should look at the entire EMS at least every three years, which is the recertification period.

Scope of the Management Review

The scope of management reviews should be broad and should encompass the environmental dimensions of all activities, products, and services of the organization.

Management should consider the impact of the EMS on the financial status of the organization as well as its interaction with other organizational management systems, such as marketing, finance, or research and development.

ISO 14004 suggests that a typical management review would look at the following:

- The environmental objectives, targets, and environmental performance.
- Findings of EMS audits.
- An evaluation of the EMS's effectiveness.
- An evaluation of the suitability of the environmental policy and the need for changes in light of the following:
  - Changing legislation.
  - Changing expectations and requirements of interested parties.
  - Changes in the products, services, or activities of the organization.
  - Advances in science and technology.
  - Lessons learned from environmental incidents.
  - Market preferences and consumer trends.
  - Reporting and communication requirements.

The management review should consider the views of interested parties to ensure that it captures any emerging local, national, or international issues. Management reviews can internalize the organizational process of continual improvement. By performing regular and comprehensive reviews of the EMS, management should be able to spot opportunities to improve its performance which in turn should lead to improved environmental performance.

Consequently, ISO 14004 suggests that management reviews include the following:

- Determinations of the root cause or causes of nonconformances.
- Development and implementation of a plan or plans of corrective and preventive action to address root causes.
- Verification of the effectiveness of previous corrective and preventive actions.
- Comparisons between actual results and predetermined objectives and targets.
- Determinations of required changes to existing EMS elements.

CONCLUSION

The information gained from environmental auditing is critical to developing, maintaining and improving an environmental management system. Auditing provides critical information for use in a management review of the EMS. The results of the management review brings the "plan-do-check-review" cycle full circle and launches the organization's EMS to a higher level of performance.

BIOGRAPHY

Anton G. Camarota, MBA

Anton G. Camarota is currently a Principal in QUEST Management International, a consulting firm dedicated to building management systems for performance excellence. Mr. Camarota has fifteen years of technical and professional experience in management planning and program development, ISO management systems analysis and auditing, and training program development and presentation for non-profit, commercial, government, educational, and nuclear industries. Mr. Camarota has developed quality management programs for manufacturing, engineering, environmental, information systems, waste management, geological exploration, and recycling businesses. He has analyzed and audited management processes in all areas of business including finance, manufacturing, design, procurement, information systems, quality assurance, marketing and sales, facility maintenance, health and safety, and environmental compliance.

Mr. Camarota has developed and presented five courses for quality and environmental management systems, and is an adjunct faculty member at the University of Denver and George Washington University. He is an active member of the U. S. TAG to ISO TC 207, and has actively participated in the development of the ISO 14010, 14011, and 14012 standards for environmental auditing at both the national and international levels. He holds a bachelor of science in information systems, summa cum laude, from the Metropolitan State College of Denver, and an MBA from the University of Denver.

CHAPTER 10

Important Legal Considerations in Implementing ISO 14001

Marc E. Gold

INTRODUCTION

The ISO 14000 series of environmental management standards is proceeding through the review and approval process of the International Organization of Standardization (ISO). Some of the countries participating in the ISO 14000 development process will use the ISO 14000 series as a principal means of achieving environmental improvement, thereby avoiding, to a large extent, command and control statutory and regulatory schemes.

In the United States, however, organizations implementing ISO 14000 face a substantially different legal framework. Our prescriptive legal and regulatory system raises numerous legal issues that may disfavor the broad-based endorsement of international environmental standards. This chapter identifies many of these legal issues and offers insights into the manner in which to weigh the legal risks against the potential environmental benefits and the costs savings that may be achieved through ISO 14001 implementation.

Despite these legal risks, it is possible that the world marketplace will compel domestic companies to implement ISO 14001.[1] In that event, careful advance analysis and planning to manage the risks associated with these legal issues will be imperative for any company contemplating the development of an ISO 14001-compliant EMS.

Reasons to Comply with ISO 14001

Before evaluating the legal considerations associated with the implementation of ISO 14001, it is helpful to identify the significant legal benefits that can be achieved by developing and implementing an environmental management system such as ISO 14001. Some of these benefits are as follows:

- Establishing a systematic program to achieve and maintain compliance with environmental laws and regulations.

- Identifying in advance future obligations under environmental laws and regulations.

- Managing proactively on-site and off-site environmental liabilities.

- Identifying opportunities for increased employee training.

- Achieving greater environmental improvement.

- Facilitating compliance with related legal requirements such as those administered by the Securities and Exchange Commission (SEC).

- Positioning the company for more favorable treatment by regulatory and enforcement authorities.

The extent to which ISO 14001 will result in any of these benefits or further progress toward environmental improvement depends entirely on the scope and objectives of an organization's environmental policy.

The basic concept of an EMS is certainly not foreign to U.S. industry. Well-developed EMSs have been used by many companies for years, either built around trade association initiatives such as the chemical industry's Responsible Care® program or the textile industry's Encouraging Environmental Excellence (E3) program, or based on an individual company's own environmental vision. Likewise, environmental auditing, at least as it relates to legal and regulatory compliance, has been a common industry tool since the early stages of the environmental movement. What is different about the ISO 14001 EMS standard is its potentially far-reaching scope, which extends beyond mere regulatory compliance, and its uneasy fit with the current environmental legal scheme and jurisprudence in the United States.

LEGAL ISSUES PRESENTED BY THE ISO 14001 EMS STANDARD

The momentum supporting the adoption of a worldwide environmental management system standard continues to grow as the legal community in the United States continues to cautiously assess the strengths and weaknesses of the program. The major legal issues break down essentially into three broad categories:

1. Issues related to the collection, management, and dissemination of information about a company's environmental compliance status and its environmental aspects and impacts.

2. Issues related to the integration of ISO 14001 into the current environmental legal system in the United States.

3. Issues related to the potential liabilities caused by the mere existence of a global EMS standard.

A more detailed discussion of each of these key legal issues follows.

Collecting Sensitive Information about an Organization's Environmental Aspects and Impacts

The environmental policy required under ISO 14001 must demonstrate a commitment to compliance with legal requirements and any other voluntary standards to which the company subscribes and to "continual improvement and prevention of pollution" (ISO 14001, Clause 4.2[b]). Within these broad guidelines, the organization is free to identify the most important environmental aspects of its operations, their corresponding environmental impacts, and the goals which they intend to be achieved.

No specific environmental performance standards are established under ISO 14001. Instead, through its environmental policy, the organization defines measurable objectives to address these environmental impacts. Senior management must participate in defining the environmental policy based on the company's size and an understanding of the company's potential environmental impacts. The standard requires that the corporate environmental policy statement must be communicated to employees and made available to the public.

The environmental aspects and impacts assessment is the critical first step in implementing ISO 14001 since it provides the environmental and operational baseline upon which the company's environmental programs are developed to implement the corporate environmental policy and against which continuous improvement is evaluated. Included as part of the information to be gathered is the identification of legal requirements that the company must meet and an evaluation of its current compliance status.

The collection of this information, its review, distribution, and use will require the company to first consider the need for confidentiality and then to evaluate the mechanisms available, if any, to meet those needs. This is particularly important for industry in the United States due to the breadth of the regulatory agencies' statutory authority to obtain information and the legal framework that facilitates the initiation of citizen suits.

Many organizations already have sophisticated environmental auditing programs that are designed primarily to elicit relevant information on a facility's current environmental compliance status and to assure compliance with future environmental requirements (e.g., periodic reporting deadlines, permit expiration dates, proposed legislation, and emerging regulatory programs).

The scope of an ISO 14001 EMS and the initial assessment of environmental aspects and impacts it requires will extend much further than mere compliance with environmental laws and regulations and will likely include activities that are not regulated. For example, in setting corporate environmental policy and evaluating environmental aspects and impacts, a company is likely to examine measures to address energy and water conservation, pollution prevention, and recycling. This provides the appropriate backdrop to consider the available legal privileges.

Legal Privileges

Common-law legal privileges such as the attorney–client privilege, the attorney work-product privilege and, in some jurisdictions, the self-evaluative privilege may be available to protect certain information under specified circumstances but only when the requisite procedures are properly established at the outset and steadfastly followed. The need to assert a legal privilege may arise in the context of litigation with the government or a third party or in connection with agency requests for information.

Extreme care is necessary to evaluate in advance the overall objectives of the proposed environmental assessment, whether it be the aspects and impacts analysis or an evaluation of the EMS, and the company's sensitivity to current and prospective disclosure obligations. Unless the issue of confidentiality and privilege is fully evaluated and addressed at the outset, it is likely that none of the common law privileges will be available.

Attorney–Client Privilege

The attorney–client privilege has long been recognized as a means to foster the full and free disclosure of information between clients and attorneys. As a policy matter, it is generally recognized that clients should have the ability to speak freely with their attorneys when seeking legal advice, without fear that such communications will later be disclosed and potentially be used against them.

For a communication to be protected by the attorney–client privilege, it must meet a variety of requirements. For example, the communication between the client and the attorney must be for the purpose of obtaining legal advice. Communications directed to an attorney for other purposes, such as soliciting business advice, may not be subject to protection. Moreover, the communication must have been made in confidence (generally outside the presence of third parties) and made by the client. The privilege may also be lost if appropriate steps are not taken to prevent the waiver of the privilege by disclosure of the communication to a third party.

In the context of ISO 14001, pitfalls with the attorney–client privilege are obvious. Many elements necessary to claim the privilege may not be possible to achieve. That could lead to a strategy where certain types of information (e.g., regulatory compliance) is sought to be protected while information about business activities is not. The prospect of third-party certification introduces an additional complicating factor.

Attorney Work-Product Privilege

The attorney work-product privilege offers a second potential avenue for protecting the results of an environmental assessment. Under the work-product doctrine, the mental impressions, conclusions, opinions, and legal theories of an attorney or other representative of a party concerning actual or anticipated litigation are generally subject to a qualified immunity from discovery. Unlike the attorney–client privilege, this immunity may be overcome by a showing of sufficient need.

The principles undergirding the work-product doctrine were articulated in *Hickman v. Taylor,* 329 U.S. 495 (1947) and have been incorporated into Fed. R. Civ. P. 26(b)(3), which provides in pertinent part as follows:

[A] party may obtain discovery of documents and tangible things otherwise discoverable and prepared in anticipation of litigation or for trial by or for another party or by or for that other party's representative (including the other party's attorney, consultant, surety, indemnitor, insurer or agent) only upon a showing that the party seeking discovery has substantial need of the materials in the preparation of the party's case and that the party is unable without undue hardship to obtain the substantial equivalent of the materials by other means. In ordering discovery of such materials when the required showing has been made, the court shall protect against disclosure of the mental impressions, conclusions, opinions, or legal theories of an attorney or other representative of a party concerning the litigation.

The work-product doctrine is limited in that it applies only to work performed "in anticipation of litigation." Accordingly, in the absence of litigation or anticipated litigation, the work-product doctrine does not offer protection for environmental assessments. Even when an environmental assessment is conducted "in anticipation of litigation," the attorney work-product privilege generally cannot be asserted to protect underlying facts but only the conclusions and impressions that are drawn from those facts.

Self-Evaluative Privilege

Over the past two decades, the courts have begun to recognize that in certain instances, it is sound public policy to encourage candid and frank self-evaluation, which can lead to the identification and correction of internal problems. Accordingly, in certain instances, the courts have insulated reports and documents from disclosure, relying on a concept called the *self-evaluative privilege* or the *critical self-analysis doctrine.*

The self-evaluative privilege was first recognized in a medical malpractice case where the court ruled that confidential hospital staff meeting minutes, recorded for the purpose of self-improvement, were entitled to a qualified privilege on the basis of the compelling public interest in facilitating peer review of physician performance.[2] Since that time, the self-evaluative privilege has been examined in other contexts including auditing functions to enhance environmental compliance.

In *Reichhold Chemicals, Inc. v. Textron, Inc.,*[3] the court held that the self-evaluative privilege protected reports concerning retrospective analyses of past conduct, practices, and occurrences, and the resulting environmental consequences, as long as the reports were prepared for the purpose of candid self-evaluation, with the expectation that the reports would remain confidential and such confidentiality was in fact maintained. The court also found that the privilege was a qualified rather than an absolute privilege, which could be overcome by a showing of extraordinary circumstances or special need.

The court noted that the self-evaluative privilege was rooted in public policy considerations designed to allow individuals or businesses to candidly assess their compliance with regulatory and legal requirements without creating evidence that might be used against them by their opponents in future litigation. The court indicated that the privilege protects an organization or individual from following the Hobson's choice—

> Aggressively investigating accidents or possible regulatory violations, ascertaining the causes and results, and correcting any violations or dangerous conditions creates a self-incriminating record that could be evidence of liability; or

> Deliberately avoiding an inquiry so as not to obtain information (and possibly leaving the public exposed to danger) in order to lessen the risk of liability even though a problem, once identified, could be addressed.

The court enunciated a four-part test for determining whether to protect self-evaluative materials from disclosure:

1. The information must result from a critical self-analysis undertaken by the party seeking protection.

2. The public must have a strong interest in preserving the free flow of the information sought.

3. The information must be of a type whose flow would be curtailed if discovery were allowed.

4. The information must be generated with the expectation that it will be kept confidential, and the information must be so maintained.

In contrast to the *Reichhold Chemicals* decision, certain other courts have taken a narrow view of the self-evaluative privilege in the context of environmental reports and documentation. In *Koppers Company, Inc. v. Aetna Casualty and Surety Company,*[4] the court held that the self-evaluative privilege "does not apply *a fortiori* to environmental reports, records, and memoranda. Indeed, we disagree that a corporation would face a Hobson's choice between due diligence and self-incrimination in the tightly regulated environmental context, for that context requires strict attention to environmental affairs. We doubt that today potential polluters will violate regulations requiring environmental diligence for fear of these documents being used against them tomorrow."

In *In re Grand Jury Proceedings,*[5] the court refused to protect audits conducted by a company to determine whether it was in compliance with requirements under the Food, Drug, and Cosmetics Act. The court held that the results of such audits had to be produced in response to a grand jury subpoena. In reaching this decision, the court indicated that it was aware of no case in which the self-evaluative privilege had been applied to thwart a governmental request for documents. If this aspect of the decision is followed, it may severely undercut the utility of the self-evaluative privilege as fashioned by the courts in the context of environmental audits.[6]

It remains questionable whether there is any reason to rely on a common-law legal privilege fashioned from the doctrines supporting the *Reichhold Chemicals* decision. In some jurisdictions, therefore, state legislatures have attempted to provide some measure of protection by enacting privilege laws intended to encourage self-evaluation.

State Legislative Initiatives

The use of environmental assessments to facilitate compliance with environmental requirements has increased, as have concerns relating to the potential disclosure of the results of such assessments and the mixed results that businesses and individuals have experienced in seeking to protect the results of environmental assessments under the traditional common-law concepts described above. In response, a number of states have intervened and adopted statutes recognizing the self-evaluative privilege for environmental assessments. Typically, these statutes have been designed to cover formal voluntary environmental compliance audits. However, the definitions and scope of each state law differs slightly and needs to be carefully evaluated.

In 1993, Oregon became the first state to legislatively create a qualified privilege for voluntary environmental audits. The law was adopted as part of an omnibus environmental crimes package, and the audit provisions were considered part of an overall systemic solution to the need to reform Oregon's environmental requirements. Since Oregon took action in 1993, many other states have followed suit. Legislation has been passed in several states creating a self-evaluative privilege for environmental audits including Arizona, Colorado, Idaho, Illinois, Indiana, Kansas, Kentucky, Minnesota, Mississippi, Texas, Utah, Virginia, and Wyoming. Similar legislation is under consideration in a large number of additional states as well as at the federal level, while other states have entertained and rejected such legislation.

Government Initiatives

In addition to the possible availability of legal privileges both under common law and state statutes, state and federal regulatory agencies have developed policies intended to encourage environmental assessments that focus not only on regulatory requirements but on overall environmental improvement. These policies offer some relief from penalties and other enforcement remedies upon the implementation of an environmental audit and the disclosure and correction of violations. They are helpful in providing some legal incentive for a company to embark on an ISO 14001 environmental management system program but appear to be insufficient alone.

U.S. Sentencing Commission's Draft Sentencing Guidelines for Environmental Offenses

In the event of a criminal prosecution for violation of environmental laws, the Draft Sentencing Guidelines (1993) strongly favor the organization that has a program in place that is aimed at environmental compliance, awareness, and improvement—not merely minimum compliance, but a comprehensive, documented EMS founded on a clear commitment from management and supported by adequate training, follow-up, and disciplinary procedures for noncompliance. Thus, in the event of a criminal prosecution, some measure of protection is provided by a company's demonstrated, systematic, and documented commitment to environmental compliance and continuous improvement. (See Chapter 23 for the nature of the EMS suggested by the U.S. Sentencing Commission's guidelines.)

EPA's Policy on Incentives for Self-Policing: Discovery, Disclosure, Correction, and Prevention of Violations

EPA's Policy on Incentives for Self-Policing[7] was developed through dialogue with the regulated community as well as other key stakeholders. The policy provides three major incentives for the regulated community to develop environmental management systems designed to discover, disclose, correct, and prevent violations of federal environmental requirements.

First, EPA will not seek or will substantially reduce (up to 75 percent) the gravity component of civil penalties assessed for violations discovered during an environmental audit or as a result of due diligence efforts and promptly disclosed to EPA. Under the policy, EPA may still pursue the disclosing entity for the economic benefit component of the penalty, provided that the disclosing entity actually realized an economic gain as a result of noncompliance.

Second, EPA will not recommend criminal prosecution of the disclosing entity as long as the disclosed violation is not indicative of either of the following:

1. Management's philosophy to conceal or condone environmental violations.

2. Management's involvement in or willful ignorance of environmental violations.

EPA reserves the right to recommend prosecution of individual employees for their criminal acts.

Third, EPA will not request or use an environmental audit report to initiate a civil or criminal investigation of the disclosing entity unless EPA has an independent basis for believing that a violation has occurred.

To qualify for these incentives, a regulated entity must demonstrate the following:

1. The violation was discovered through an environmental audit or other due diligence measures.[8]

2. Discovery must be voluntary, for example, not the result of a legal monitoring or sampling requirement.

3. The violation must be disclosed in writing to EPA within 10 days of discovery unless a shorter period is required by reporting requirements.

4. Discovery and disclosure must occur prior to a government inspection, investigation, or information request, citizen suit, or other third-party action.

5. The violation must be corrected within 60 days and appropriate measures must be taken to remedy any harm (additional time may be requested).

6. The disclosing entity must agree in writing to prevent recurrence.

7. The violation is not a repeat violation.[9]

8. The violation did not result in serious harm or present an imminent and substantial endangerment and did not violate an order or consent agreement.

9. The regulated entity must fully cooperate with EPA. Significantly, the policy also applies to disclosures made to EPA pursuant to legal reporting requirements.

If a regulated entity cannot demonstrate that the violation disclosed to EPA was discovered through either an environmental audit or due diligence efforts as defined in the policy, the disclosing entity can still qualify for up to a 75 percent reduction in the gravity component of the penalty, provided that the disclosing entity meets the remaining conditions. Members of the regulated community who closely tailor their environmental management systems to the criteria set forth in the policy stand to gain significant benefits over their competitors in terms of fewer enforcement actions and lower penalties.

Statutory and Regulatory Reporting Requirements

Legal requirements to report to regulatory authorities certain environmental conditions discovered at a facility create additional legal tensions between the desire to protect and control the dissemination of environmental information and the independent legal obligations to notify regulatory authorities.

Federal and state laws, as well as individual facility permits and approvals, are replete with mandatory reporting obligations where substantial penalties are at risk for noncompliance. The initial review suggested in ISO 14001 to establish an environmental baseline, upon which the environmental policy is crafted and the EMS is developed, could be expected to uncover areas of noncompliance or past releases, thereby creating a legal dilemma for the company. Recently, those companies with sophisticated EMSs have dealt with this issue as a matter of routine corporate practice. For others, ISO 14001 may create the impetus to face this dilemma for the first time.

The establishment of a sophisticated EMS sufficient to obtain third-party certification under ISO 14001 may also lead to additional reporting requirements under the laws and regulations of the SEC. These reporting requirements focus on the obligation to disclose areas of liability that may have an adverse impact on the financial strength of a company. In this instance, the stakeholders are somewhat different, which can make reporting all the more difficult. Generally, the SEC requires public companies to report both of the following:

1. Material impacts on the company of environmental compliance, including material capital expenditures.

2. Environmental legal proceedings.

Given the emphasis by the SEC on costs and legal liabilities as they may impact the financial well-being of a organization, the requirements appear to be more narrowly focused than the extent of an ISO 14001 EMS and an organization's identified impacts and effects. Moreover, to the extent the implementation of an ISO 14001 EMS could result in cost savings and increased profitability, the SEC requirements could ultimately turn out to be a lesser concern.

Public Disclosure

One area of potential concern to industry in the United States is avoided because ISO 14001 does *not* require public disclosure of an organization's environmental aspects, impacts or the details of its environmental management system. Instead, ISO 14001 requires the organization to make available to the public only the environmental policy document and merely to "consider" a procedure for external communication of "significant environmental aspects" and to document that decision.

Organizations will respond to this element of ISO 14001 in different ways. The internal corporate decision-making process may distinguish between external reporting to regulatory agencies or to local emergency response authorities as opposed to the public at large. However, the legal process in the United States may make it impossible to shield sensitive environmental information, and the public perception of an organization attempting to do so may render moot the voluntary nature of public disclosure under ISO 14001. Requiring an organization to "consider" more complete public disclosure and to document that decision may tilt the balance in favor of more detailed public disclosure.

Identifying Environmental Priorities

In countries where the environmental legal system is not already developed on a media-by-media basis (i.e., air, water, and waste regulated under separate statutes and regulatory programs), the organization can prioritize the information gathered through the environmental aspects assessment, taking into account both the goals and objectives of the organization's environmental policy and the relative environmental risks posed by the conditions found.

Ideally, an organization will prioritize its environmental corrective actions to address first those conditions that present the most risk. In the United States, however, given the compartmentalized legal structure in which industry must operate, that flexibility is absent or at least substantially limited. The operating conditions that may cause the most significant environmental impacts or pose the greatest risks often do not correlate to mandatory legal requirements or areas of potential noncompliance. An organization can perhaps achieve greater environmental improvement cost-effectively by controlling the pollution from sources that are not regulated rather than those that are regulated. The interrelationship between current legal and regulatory requirements and the ability to establish priorities based upon risk is an issue that industry in the United States will have to work through as part of the ISO 14001 process.

EPA appears to have recognized some of the weaknesses of the current media-by-media regulatory schemes and has been working with specific industry sectors in an effort to identify and address regulatory inefficiencies. The Common Sense Initiative, launched by EPA in 1995, is an ambitious effort that brings together affected stakeholders to closely examine the overall environmental impacts of a particular industry group. The goal, as stated by EPA, is to find a "cleaner, cheaper and smarter" method of achieving further environmental improvement. (A similar description also could be used to describe one of the primary goals of ISO 14001.) Phase I of the Common Sense Initiative focuses on the following industries: automobile assembly, computer and electronics, iron and steel metal plating and finishing, petroleum refining, and printing. EPA believes that through this process, a new prescription, tailored to a specific industry segment, will emerge that will both simplify environmental regulation and lead to well-conceived programs to achieve further environmental improvement.

Third-Party Registration

Some observers believe that ISO 14001 will be rejected in the United States if the competitive marketplace or other potential stakeholders (e.g., shareholders, consumers, environmental groups, or regulatory agencies) demand third-party registration. Others contend that without third-party registration, ISO 14001 will serve no real purpose and will simply enable companies to make unsubstantiated claims about environmental performance.

Given the worldwide support for the ISO 9000 standards, many believe that the ISO 14000 series will enjoy the same favorable spotlight. While that result is possible, it is far from certain. The incentives, market drivers, and potential advantages of ISO 9001 registration (e.g., meeting both customer specifications and objective product quality standards) are somewhat different from the motivators linked to ISO 14001.

The concern about ISO 14000 third-party registration is not unfounded. As currently drafted, ISO 14001 provides for either third-party registration or self-declaration; in either event, it is based on periodic audits of the environmental management system. Despite the two options expressly provided by ISO 14001, pressure for third-party registration is substantial and may be essential to provide the external program verification necessary to legitimize ISO 14001. The existing environmental statutory and regulatory schemes in the United States are not geared to a voluntary standard that depends on formal review, registration, and periodic reregistration by an independent third party. The most analogous circumstances are compliance inspections by regulatory agencies under specific statutory authority, or audits by internal corporate personnel or outside consultants retained by a company that are often subject to a variety of confidentiality agreements or legal privileges. Neither of these common practices compares to the third-party certification of an environmental management system contemplated by ISO 14001.

Set out below are other meaningful distinctions between ISO 9000 and ISO 14000 that are likely to influence a company already certified under ISO 9001 to evaluate whether to proceed to implement ISO 14001:

- Unlike in the environmental field, current laws and regulations do not occupy the product-quality arena which is primarily driven by manufacturers' specifications and customer needs.

- Market forces have not made environmental performance mandatory (except in the environmental services industry).

- Environmental management systems have no direct bearing on product quality.

- Environmental awareness and perceived needs differ throughout the world and, due to disparate legal and regulatory systems, are not as susceptible to uniform schemes of review and assessment.

Each of these factors favors ISO 9000 but provides no real incentive to support ISO 14000. Until a company's environmental performance becomes a marketing consideration on par with product quality, it will not be easy, at least philosophically, merely to piggyback ISO 14001 onto an existing ISO 9000 program despite any similarities or apparent efficiencies there may be in meeting the procedural requirements of each standard.

Integrating ISO 14001 with Current Legal Requirements

Perhaps the most challenging legal issue for domestic industry is the manner in which ISO 14001 can be integrated with current environmental laws and regulations in the United States. Over the past 25 years, the environmental legal structure in the United States has developed on a media-by-media basis with a disjointed web of operational requirements, compliance obligations, and liabilities. In addition to the extensive regulatory compliance programs, the liability scheme set forth in the Comprehensive Environmental Response, Compensation, and Liability Act (commonly known as Superfund) of strict joint and several liability has become the common denominator for government litigation and third-party claims relating to the remediation of contaminated sites.

This comprehensive legal framework targeting past, present, and future environmental liabilities creates an imposing domestic obstacle to the unconditional endorsement of a global environmental management system standard driven by priorities established by corporate policy and coordinated multimedia risk evaluations. If ISO 14001 is to succeed, regulatory agencies (or the state and federal legislatures) may need to develop new mechanisms that are accepted by the public to temper the inflexible requirements of the environmental laws and regulations in the United States.

There is a strong case to be made that substantial environmental improvement will be achieved through the implementation of a comprehensive environmental management system, endorsed by senior corporate management and containing measurable goals and objectives. Part of the premise, however, is that the current command and control environmental strategy is exhausted, having reached the point of diminishing returns. There is a fundamental need, therefore, to reexamine the manner in which environmental improvement will be accomplished over the next decade and to create sufficient legal incentives to encourage industry to invest the additional sums necessary to continue the substantial progress that has been made.

The regulatory agencies have responded tentatively with a series of pilot programs and experiments aimed at defining the benefits of comprehensive environmental management systems. For example, some state regulatory agencies have attempted to implement facilitywide permitting programs, and others are beginning to sort out the issues, impediments, and opportunities presented by ISO 14001 to chart a new course. Not to be outpaced by the states, EPA has embarked on an aggressive program of experiments through initiatives such as Project XL and the Environmental Leadership Program, seeking to work with industry and other stakeholders to find a new formula.

EPA regions are likewise searching for answers. EPA Region I has initiated StarTrack (formerly the "3PC Program"), intended to entice environmentally superior companies to develop and implement certain environmental programs to be verified by a third party. EPA Region IX has implemented its Merit Partnership program built around a liberal interpretation of the principles of ISO 14001, plus other environmental excellence criteria. For environmentally superior companies, EPA offers regulatory incentives and streamlined permitting programs to encourage the implementation of environmental management systems.

The results of these agency initiatives remain to be seen, as does the manner in which the regulatory authorities will try to weave into current law and regulations (or will support new legislation) legal mechanisms for industry to evaluate the environmental impacts of their operations and to address those impacts on a priority basis, taking into account the risks posed by the conditions discovered.

An entirely new statutory program may need to be developed to replace the current system in order to reap the full benefits of ISO 14001. The worst of both worlds would result, however, from a system that wraps ISO 14001 around the hardened core of our historical command-and-control approach. In that event, neither approach would be improved. Unfortunately, the vision of our future environmental landscape remains blurred.

Establishing an Industrywide Standard of Care

A longer-term legal issue to consider as the ISO 14000 series of standards is evaluated is the potential for those standards to become the environmental performance benchmark against which all industry will be judged in the context of government enforcement, citizen suits, and third-party damage claims. Through adoption of ISO 14001 (and the likelihood is that additional environmental standards in the ISO 14000 environmental series will be adopted in the future), the industry standard of care with respect to the management of environmental risks and liabilities could be redefined. This could be the result even though ISO 14001 steadfastly avoids establishing performance standards in any respect. Such a standard of care would then be used by those claiming injury or seeking damages from environmental exposures to strengthen their claims if industry defendants have not subscribed to the ISO 14000 standards.

Voluntary industry standards have been held by many state courts to be relevant factors in determining whether a company has acted negligently. In fact, in *Kent Village Associates v. Smith*[10] and *Hansen v. Abrasive Engineering and Manufacturing,*[11] consensus standards developed by the American National Standards Institute were held to be admissible in defining an industry standard of care. This result, while perhaps unintended, may already have occurred as trade associations have established core environmental principles that are intended to provide guidance to their members and serve as a public commitment to environmental protection and improvement. As a legal matter, when a voluntary code or standard is widely adopted, it becomes a bit more mandatory.

In light of the general nature of ISO 14001, however, much of the legal precedent on the standard of care issue arguably may be inapplicable since it may be difficult to fashion a particular standard of behavior or care out of the broad language of ISO 14001. Nevertheless, it is an extremely important legal issue that warrants close evaluation over time.

CONCLUSION

Despite these significant legal issues, which are particularly relevant for firms contemplating applying ISO 14001 to operations in the United States, the world marketplace or other stakeholders may dictate that companies adopt ISO 14001 as a means of either maintaining a competitive position or establishing a new competitive advantage. In addition, the movement toward EMSs may provide the impetus for redefining the current environmental legal and regulatory scheme in the United States.

Given the current political climate and the trend toward reducing federal and state bureaucracies, the time may be right for government, industry, and citizens to work together to forge a cooperative program that will build upon the principles of ISO 14001 to achieve continuous improvement in environmental protection and risk reduction. If the benefits to be achieved are compelling enough, it seems likely that the environmental legal framework in the United States, which is largely out of step with this new approach, will gradually adjust.

Combining the financial incentives, business opportunities, and public sentiment supporting environmental programs worldwide, government authorities in the United States and domestic industry may well find themselves on the doorstep of new opportunities to build upon the environmental protection gains of the first 25 years of the modern environmental movement and to enter the 21st century with a renewed environmental spirit and a brighter environmental future. ISO 14001 appears to be the vehicle designed to fuel this new approach on a global scale.

BIOGRAPHY

Marc E. Gold, Esq.

Marc E. Gold is a founding partner of Manko, Gold & Katcher, a twenty-two lawyer firm that concentrates its practice exclusively in environmental law. Formerly, Mr. Gold served as a section chief in the Legal Branch of the United States Environmental Protection Agency, Region III, and was a partner in the Environmental Department of a major Philadelphia law firm. In addition, Mr. Gold was an Adjunct Assistant Professor at Temple University's School of Engineering where he taught environmental regulation.

Mr. Gold has more than 20 years of experience in environmental law. His practice focuses on all aspects of environmental regulation and counseling covering hazardous waste, air and water pollution, and site remediation issues. Mr. Gold has been involved in several procedures, developing Pennsylvania's 1995 Brownfields legislation, and handling the environmental aspects of major national and international corporate transactions. He has been listed in *The Best Lawyers in America* since 1989, and is also listed in *International Corporate Law's Guide to Environmental Law Experts*.

Mr. Gold received his J.D. from Villanova University School of Law and his B.A. from The American University.

NOTES

1. In focusing on the legal issues raised by the ISO 14001 EMS standard, this chapter will not evaluate or consider other potential advantages of the ISO 14000 standards (e.g., competitive market advantage, shareholder satisfaction, and benefits from employee training, among others).

2. *Bredice v. Doctor's Hospital, Inc.,* 50 F.R.D. 249 (D.D.C. 1970), *aff'd,* 479 F.2d 920 (D.C. Cir. 1973).

3. 157 F.R.D. 522, 39 E.R.C. 1328 (N.D. Fla. 1994).

4. 847 F. Supp. 361, 364 (W.D. Pa. 1994).

5. 861 F. Supp. 386 (D. Md. 1994).

6. See also *Reich v. Hercules, Inc.,* 857 F. Supp. 367 (D.N.J. 1994) (enforcing on similar grounds a subpoena duces tecum issued by the Occupational Safety and Health Administration seeking the results of safety audits conducted by Hercules).

7. 60 Fed. Reg. 66076 (December 22, 1995).

8. The policy defines an environmental audit as a "systematic, documented, periodic and objective review by regulated entities of facility operations and practices related to meeting environmental requirements." Due diligence is defined as "systematic efforts, appropriate to the size and nature of [the regulated entity's] business, designed to prevent, detect and correct violations." Six criteria, contained in the definition, set forth standards that the due diligence efforts must meet to qualify for the policy's exceptions. These criteria were largely adopted from the Draft Sentencing Guidelines, which provide for the mitigation of penalties if the prosecuted entity has an environmental management system in place.

9. To demonstrate that a violation is not a repeat violation, the disclosing entity must show that the specific violation or a closely related violation has not occurred, within the past three years at the same facility or that the violation is not part of a pattern of federal, state, or local violations by the facility's parent organization.

10. 657 A.2d 330 (Md. Ct. Spec. App. 1995).

11. 856 P.2d 625 (Or. 1993).

CHAPTER 11

ISO 14000 and Environmental Audits: A Legal Perspective

Catherine W. Johnson

INTRODUCTION

Under ISO 14001, companies must establish an EMS and conduct environmental audits to determine whether the EMS is properly implemented and maintained. ISO 14001 establishes the criteria for conducting an EMS audit for ISO 14001 implementation. Many companies have been conducting environmental audits for the purpose of evaluating their facilities' compliance with environmental laws. With the advent of ISO 14000, however, many companies will be conducting environmental audits for the first time.

If conducted properly and used appropriately, an environmental audit serves to minimize liabilities and can confer significant benefits, such as protecting management from personal liability for unknown environmental problems. Disclosure of an audit report to environmental enforcement authorities, however, may subject a company to fines and liabilities. If improperly managed, an environmental audit can expose a company to serious liabilities.

This chapter provides practical suggestions, from the legal perspective, for managing the environmental audit, for protecting the confidentiality of the report, and for correcting violations identified in the audit.

PREPARING FOR THE AUDIT

Clause 4.5.4 of ISO 14001 requires that a company perform an EMS audit. The requirements in Clause 4.5.4 are quite general. The EMS audit program, including its schedule, must "be based on the environmental importance of the activity concerned and the results of previous audits." Audit procedures should cover the audit scope, frequency, methodologies, and the responsibilities and requirements for conducting audits and reporting results. The frequency of audits will depend on past audit results, the maturity of the EMS, and the status and importance of the activity.

In Clause 4.5.1, the standard also requires the company to establish procedures to periodically evaluate compliance with relevant environmental legislation and regulations. Although this clause does not explicitly use the term *compliance audit,* the requirement for U.S. companies, at least, would translate into conducting a compliance audit.

Additional guidance in conducting environmental audits, no matter what type, are contained in the ISO 14010-12 auditing standards. ISO 14011 focuses specifically on EMS auditing procedures. Since the ISO 14001 auditing requirements are general rather than detailed and specific, organizations will have great flexibility in structuring and managing the audit to minimize the company's exposure to liability.

Under ISO 14011, Clause 5.1, the objectives and scope of the audit are defined by the client. The client should "communicate" these objectives to the auditor, and the objectives must be identified in a written report. The first important step a company should take to limit its liabilities is to establish the objectives and scope of the audit before conducting the audit.

Selecting the Scope of an Audit

If the planned audit is an EMS audit, it will probably not be protected by any available legal doctrine; however, this type of audit is also less likely to contain any damaging information. Depending on a company's EMS, even this approach to an audit, however, may contain information that exposes a company to liability. For example, the EMS may provide that any environmental violations must be promptly reported to management and corrected. Thus, an audit of such a system might identify environmental violations that were not corrected—although the audit might not identify the actual violations. A meaningful audit, however, would go further and identify environmental violations.

Before deciding on the scope of an audit, a company should consider directing an environmental attorney to interview company employees and review relevant records. Under the conventional attorney–client privilege doctrine, these communications and review should be protected by the attorney–client privilege and will enable the company to flesh out any major problems before directing an auditor to conduct an audit. The auditor's communications and reports may not be privileged.

The attorney should also take steps to position the company to take advantage of EPA's new audit policy. (See Chapter 22 for an explanation of EPA's new audit policy.) If the attorney discovers a significant violation during the course of this pre-audit, the company should consider reporting the violation to EPA (within the 10 days set forth by the new policy). The attorney should also be prepared to document that the pre-audit conducted by the attorney was indeed a pre-audit and meets EPA's definition of an environmental audit.

Alternately, the attorney may discover that the violation in question will not satisfy EPA's new audit criteria (e.g., a significant harm to the environment has resulted), and the company may decide either not to report the violation but instead to correct it before the actual EMS audit is conducted, or to limit the scope of the EMS audit to addressing the procedures established by the EMS. (The company may also consider including the attorney' pre-audit as part of the EMS.)

For example, large companies or companies with relatively new environmental managers or legal counsel should research past enforcement issues in advance of the audit. These issues will be sensitive during the audit and may also mean that the company is disqualified from the EPA audit policy if a similar violation is detected during the course of the audit. Because the EPA audit policy requires that companies report the violation within 10 days of discovery, companies will have very little time to research these issues after receiving the audit results.[1]

CONDUCTING THE AUDIT

Environmental audits generally are conducted by an environmental consulting company or an in-house environmental manager under the direction of an environmental attorney. As a threshold matter, companies should consider the advantages and drawbacks from the legal perspective of using in-house environmental managers and attorneys versus outside managers and attorneys.

Selecting an Attorney

Large companies with an in-house environmental attorney will want to consider whether they should retain counsel or use in-house counsel as the attorney team member of the audit.

There are some advantages to retaining corporate counsel. First, the external environmental attorney may be a more objective party, which could be an important issue if the audit involves decisions that the in-house environmental attorney may have been responsible for making. Indeed, the company may compromise its ability to qualify under the EPA audit policy if the party conducting the audit is not an "objective" party.

Second, courts have recognized that in-house counsel often function in a nonlegal capacity for a corporation. Thus, courts have scrutinized the attorney–client privilege more carefully in the context of in-house attorney communications with their corporate client.

There are drawbacks, however, to retaining corporate counsel. A company may prefer to use in-house counsel who are more experienced with the particular environmental laws applicable to its facilities. For example, some environmental laws are specific to particular industries, and even the most experienced corporate environmental attorney will not be as familiar with these regulations as is an experienced in-house staff.

An in-house attorney will also be able to assert the attorney–client privilege in a broader range of situations (e.g., communications made by the attorney when attending board meetings) than can the corporate attorney (despite the possibility that courts will scrutinize this claim to the privilege more closely).

Selecting an Auditor

Some companies retain third-party consulting firms to conduct an environmental audit. Other companies use in-house environmental managers or other qualified employees to conduct the audit.

ISO 14011 states that it is at the discretion of the client to use either an external or internal auditor. If, however, the auditor is chosen from within the organization, the auditor "should not be accountable to those directly responsible for the subject matter being audited." (ISO 14010, Clause 5.2). In addition, the auditor should possess the appropriate knowledge, skills, and experience to conduct the audit.

Because a company employee can take advantage of the attorney–client privilege by relating confidential matters to the attorney, there are some advantages from the perspective of confidentiality to using an in-house auditor to conduct the audit. For example, during the course of the audit, the in-house auditor may report orally to the attorney about a potential violation. The attorney may defer the preparation of a written report until the violation is corrected.

For companies with small environmental departments, however, it may be impossible to find an objective person capable of conducting the audit. As noted above, under the EPA audit policy, the audit must be conducted by an "objective" party. Nonetheless, a company may still take advantage of the substantial reduction for penalties under the EPA policy simply by reporting the violation, even though EPA may decide the audit did not qualify as an audit for purposes of their policy.

Audit Reports

ISO 14011 states that the audit findings must be communicated to the client in a written report. The report "may" include, but is not limited to, information about those conducting and participating in the report, the objectives and scope of the audit, the criteria, a summary of the audit process, and conclusions. In addition, where there has been a prior agreement with the client, the audit may include recommendations or opinions.

As a preliminary decision, the company must decide whether to ask for a report with written recommendations or opinions. Without recommendations or opinions, the audit may be less useful to the company. In fact, given the complexity of many environmental laws, it may be almost impossible for the company to understand how best to proceed without written recommendations.

With the written recommendations and opinions, however, the company is compromised if it elects not to follow the recommendations. There may be a wide variety of reasons why a company elects not to follow these recommendations, including an inaccurate conclusion made by an auditor.

Another factor to consider is the availability of the EPA audit policy or the applicable state audit policy. Under the EPA policy, companies must report a violation in writing to EPA within 10 days of discovering the violation. This hardly gives the company time to investigate the nature of the violation. In addition, however, if the company intends to report the violation, the company should be documenting all facts and circumstances surrounding the audit and the discovery to support the availability of the EPA policy (e.g., no similar violations in the last few years, no substantial threat to the environment).

An oral report of preliminary findings may give the attorney more time to investigate the surrounding facts and prepare for a report to EPA. For example, an attorney may want to place a confidential call to an agency to determine whether they believe that this particular type of violation is considered a substantial threat to the environment. (A corporate attorney, who can interview agency employees about the applicability of particular policy provisions without revealing the name of the company, may be useful for this purpose.)

In that case, however, the attorney may want to ask the auditor to report possible violations and not present final conclusions to the attorney, which may trigger the 10-day reporting period under the EPA audit policy.

AFTER THE AUDIT

As a preliminary matter, a company should consider steps to control the content of the final report, either by first reviewing a draft report or providing for oral reports. Without such control, the report may contain inaccuracies, which, once committed to paper, will be difficult to deny later. Second, the company should consider how to preserve the possibility of taking advantage of the EPA audit policy. Finally, whether or not a company takes advantage of the EPA audit policy, the company should consider how to minimize the possibility that a reported violation will be subject to penalties as a willful violation.

Oral or Draft Report

By providing for an oral report, a draft written report, or both, a company may protect itself from the inaccuracies contained in a final written report—or even direct that the final report should not include information reported in the oral report or draft written report.

Inaccuracies in audit reports are common. These include factual inaccuracies (e.g., the date on which the company learned about a violation), which have significant legal consequences.

To take advantage of the attorney–client privilege, the oral or written draft report should be made to the attorney overseeing the audit on behalf of the corporation; however, a company will be in a better position to assert a privilege when an oral or written report is made by an internal employee conducting the audit to an attorney rather than between a nonclient (i.e., an independent consultant) and an attorney.

If the communication is between an independent consultant and an attorney, a work-product privilege will apply only if litigation is anticipated.

It is preferable to first obtain an oral report about the audit. In some cases, a company may decide that it does not want to authorize the auditor to complete the report, that instead it needs more time to assess these matters internally without the presence of a written report.

Finally, the draft written report must be carefully reviewed for inaccuracies and it must be done quickly, as noted above, if the company intends to report the violation under the EPA audit policy.

Companies that intend to take advantage of EPA's new audit policy must report any violations within ten days of their discovery. This time frame gives companies very little time to read and digest the audit report, evaluate the accuracy of the report, evaluate the steps that must be taken to correct the violation (and the costs incident thereto), and report the violation to EPA. Thus, companies that believe they may want to take advantage of the audit policy should be poised to deal with the audit immediately after it is completed.

The company should take the following steps to ensure that they are able to respond to the audit report as soon as it is complete:

1. Require that the consultant or in-house manager alert the environmental attorney or company representative responsible for reviewing the report on behalf of management to the exact date that it will produce the report—and notify that person of any delays so that the company can plan to be available to respond to the report.

2. Require that the consultant or in-house manager be available during the week after the audit is finished.

3. Plan a meeting with management within a week after the report is finished to discuss the advantages and disadvantages of reporting the violation and taking advantage of the EPA audit policy.

In addition, companies should document all the facts that will enable them to qualify for the audit policy, including the following:

• The date on which the company learned about the violation.

• Plans for corrective action.

• Evidence that no harm to the environment resulted.

• Evidence that the company has not been responsible for similar violations during the last few years.

Companies may not, of course, want to take advantage of the EPA audit policy. For example, there may be cases in which a company may be in a better position to think through the factual and legal issues associated with a violation even if they forfeit the right to qualify for the audit privilege.

Moreover, if significant harm has occurred to the environment, the company will be unable to qualify for the audit policy. In that case, a company will want to evaluate whether it should report the violation even without a legal obligation to do so or whether it should simply correct the violation quietly and not report it. Note that some environmental laws require that violations be reported (e.g., discharges in excess of a company's NPDES permit).

Correcting a Violation

Even if EPA's audit policy is not a driving force behind a company's audit, the company should correct any violations and document the steps taken to correct the violation. The documentation should establish that the company took reasonable steps within a reasonable period of time to correct the violation. Any privileged communications about the violation should be made with or to the attorney to take advantage of the attorney–client privilege.

CONCLUSION

Companies conducting audits for ISO 14001 certification should carefully plan the audit to protect the company from any liabilities. ISO certification does not require that an audit identify all environmental laws; the audit may be conducted only for the purpose of identifying a company's compliance with an EMS. An audit conducted for the purpose of identifying any environmental liabilities should be performed only if a company is willing and able to correct any violations detected during the course of the audit. In either case, the company should carefully plan the scope of the audit, protect the confidentiality of the audit report, and correct violations identified by the audit report.

BIOGRAPHY

Catherine W. Johnson, Esq.

Catherine Johnson is an environmental lawyer based in California. Ms. Johnson specializes in environmental due diligence associated with facility acquisitions, underground storage tanks, contaminated sites, transactions involving contaminated property, solid and hazardous waste issues and other general environmental compliance issues. From 1986–1988, Ms. Johnson worked for a consulting firm in Washington, D.C. where she assisted the U.S. EPA, the Atomic Energy Commission, and various state and local governments to develop environmental regulations and policy documents for a range of environmental programs, including the Comprehensive Environment Response, Compensation & Liability Act and the Resource Conservation & Recovery Act.

Ms. Johnson was chair, Environment and Real Estate Section, Bar Association of San Francisco's Barristers' Club, 1991–1992, and participates in the Technical Assistance Team for ISO 14000 for the American Society for Testing and Materials (ASTM). Ms. Johnson received her J.D. from The University of Virginia School of Law in 1985.

NOTE

1. In addition to the EPA audit policy, many states have adopted their own audit policies. Companies should be familiar with every audit policy possibly applicable to its facilities before beginning the audit, to ensure that the audit is conducted to conform to these policies if possible.

CHAPTER 12

Case Study: Developing and Implementing an Environment, Health and Safety Management System Using Process Management and ISO Principles

Joseph Roitz

INTRODUCTION

Within AT&T Network Services Division (NSD), environment, health, and safety (EH&S) is managed as a management process within our quality management system, using ISO 14000 and principles drawn from the Malcolm Baldrige National Quality Award criteria. Our quality management system, or QMS, is the basis for our 1994 Malcolm Baldrige award and our current ISO 9000 registration effort.

We have redesigned the EH&S process and developed an organizational structure that does two things:

- Greatly facilitates compliance with ISO 14000 principles.
- Ensures that improvement is continual.

The purpose of this chapter is to explore how process management works, describe NSD's new EH&S management system, and show how process management and an existing quality management system can support best-in-class EH&S performance. Health and safety standards BS 8750 and OSHA's Voluntary Protection Program (VPP) were also used as guidelines for our redesign, but the focus of this chapter will be on ISO 14000.

Our existing organizational structure was replaced with the higher performing one described here, without increasing our current budget, by focusing on the following:

- Linkages with other processes and organizations.
- Measurable inputs, outputs, and expectations of all parties.
- Information movement and management.
- Balancing and satisfying the needs of our three key stakeholder groups: employees, assets (or stockholders), and customers (or the external world).

BACKGROUND: AT&T NETWORK SERVICES DIVISION

AT&T Network Services Division (NSD) is the part of AT&T that operates, maintains, and improves the Worldwide Intelligent Network. It has about 17,000 people reporting to over 600 facilities, with another 4,500 unmanned buildings. The facilities include construction sites, towers, underground vaults, multistory switching offices, and large office buildings.

NSD's QMS structure is made up of 13 processes, crossing over hundreds of organizations. The processes operate according to AT&T's quality principles:

- The customer comes first.
- Quality happens through people.
- All work is part of a process.
- Suppliers are an integral part of our business.
- Prevention is achieved through planning.
- Quality improvement never ends.

Our EH&S process operates according to "workplace-of-the-future principles." This essentially means that all teams have union representation, with joint decision making.

THE PROCESS MANAGEMENT APPROACH

A *process* is defined as a natural set of activities that involves taking an input; adding value in the form of knowledge, labor, or both; and producing an output for a given set of "customers."

The scope of a management system is larger than that of a process, although it will typically include many processes. A management system encompasses such arenas as training and development, communications, roles, and responsibilities. A process is simply *how* work gets done. A quality or environmental management system encompasses all processes within a business, for example, in the sense that the actions of all employees influence both quality and the environment.

When we focus on aligning the outputs of a process with customer requirements, we expose improvement opportunities and performance gaps. The result is that we achieve continual improvement more easily.

Processes may be broken down into subprocesses, with the output of one serving as the input of another. This again facilitates continual improvement, as further inefficiencies are exposed and eliminated. Each process and subprocess must have clearly defined boundaries and input, output, and in-process metrics or measures.

Process versus Hierarchy

In a large corporation, or a division within a corporation, there are hundreds of little hierarchies, or traditional organizations. Work is driven by whom you work for; their work, in turn, is driven by whom they work for, and so on. This hierarchical approach leads to a shift of focus away from pleasing your customers and toward pleasing your manager.

In a process-managed organization, the roles of support manager (whom you work for) and process manager are different. The process manager, or team leader, determines how the work gets done. The support manager supplies the resources for those process managers or team leaders that report to him or her. Both positions are necessary.

Cross Functional Teams (PMTs)

Managing by process means we must assemble the various organizations that contribute in various ways to the process outputs together, across organizational lines. For example, the property management, purchasing, and training organizations all play a key role in optimizing EH&S performance at a macro level. These other functions are known as "business partners."

Customers and Stakeholders

The EH&S organization traditionally viewed employees and the external world as third-party beneficiaries of their activities, which were primarily based around providing direction to people doing EH&S work, with little upward feedback. Process management dictated that we take a different approach to managing the business.

For a line or operational function, the customers are readily identified. For a management function, the task is more difficult. Instead, the concept of *stakeholders* is used. For the environment, health and safety process, three key stakeholder groups can be identified: employees, stockholders, and the surrounding world. The EH&S process has a responsibility to balance the needs of each of these stakeholders. These needs can be measured by injury and accident rates, improvements to our identified environmental effects, and financial performance. Our redesigned process was developed by analyzing stakeholder requirements.

Management and Operational Processes

There are two basic types of processes: *management* and *operational*. Management processes can be characterized in a positive light as the leadership of the business, or in a less positive light, as overhead. In any case, they are administrative or staff functions—such as environment, health and safety, finance, human resources, or legal—that are necessary, encompass all employees, and can either support business success or hinder it. The output of a management process is traditionally thought of as information, policies, or procedures.

Operational processes are those that directly tie to an external customer. They are the line functions of a business—the traditional focus of process management. Operational processes depend on the management processes for efficient and effective support; that is, they are the customers of staff functions.

The Role of Information Movement and Management

In managing a process, we rely heavily on information technology, or movement and management of information, AT&T's core business. In a sense, the majority of EH&S functions consist of moving and managing information, for example: whether that information is designed to increase awareness or is associated with permitting. The business of EH&S is actually the information management and movement business (IM&M), with EH&S being one of many applications.

Our process, then, is designed around information flow, with the key platform being the World Wide Web. The communications function, which includes IM&M, lives at the entry point to the process. The use of paper is strongly discouraged; on-line documentation is always the most accurate.

All associates use E-mail as the primary means of rapid and responsive communication. Full-time EH&S associates are dispersed throughout the country, with our technical and business knowledge residing in the network, independent of geography. We use information technology, such as video conferencing, to bring us together as much as possible. This allows us to get closer to our employees and to the surrounding communities, instead of being clustered in one place. It also supports the cross-functional nature of process.

NSD's Quality Management System

Within AT&T Network Services Division, there are seven management processes and six operational processes. Each process is managed by a cross-functional process management team (PMT). A PMT has day-to-day responsibility for process performance, and has a formally defined leader and membership. Subprocess PMTs may exist to manage smaller parts of the overall process.

Strategic direction for a process is provided by a quality council, acting as a board of directors or policy board. It is comprised of leaders or stakeholders from across the business, who can serve both as an escalation point and as a strategic planning body.

Each process has formally defined roles and responsibilities for the following positions:

- Process champion, responsible for executive oversight and sponsorship.
- Process owner, accountable for the ultimate success and performance of the process.
- Process, or subprocess, leader responsible for the day-to-day execution of the process and for PMT leadership.

Key business partners within the scope of the process are represented on the PMT. Linkages and deliverables between the EH&S process and its partners are clearly delineated, with written agreements for documenting handoffs of roles and responsibilities. Goals can then be set for the PMT and linked to compensation, driving the right behaviors and ensuring continual improvement.

Redesigning a New Management System for EH&S

In pursuit of continual improvement beyond compliance, the environment, health, and safety process was redesigned in the fourth quarter of 1994 and the first quarter of 1995. A large number of interviews were conducted, with the technicians and supervisors actually doing the work to determine what needs were and were not being met. Data from various reviews were gathered and analyzed. Current activities, down to the specific media level, were documented. The ISO 14001 draft EMS standard and the Malcolm Baldrige National Quality Award criteria were used as guidelines.

Development of a Management System Solution

Environment, health, and safety is a very technical field. We sought to apply the discipline of continuous quality improvement and business know-how to the technical arena by developing a process, or way of doing work, that moves programs though a structured cycle similar to the familiar Shewhart "plan, do, check, act" cycle.

We turbocharged this cycle, however, by developing an input process that actively and continually gathers opportunities for improvement based on customer feedback, analyzes this information, and feeds it into the process. Also, we took into account the other elements of a holistic management system, including people and cultural factors such as values and principles, development (both personal and job-related), information content and flow, and leadership.

The redesigned EH&S structure (see Figure 12–1) consists of an EH&S quality council, a process management team, and four subprocess management teams. This configuration was designed to address specific business needs identified during the data-gathering activities. These four subprocesses are supported by a professional team comprised of experts in environmental engineering, industrial hygiene, safety, quality, and communications (including training development and information technology).

The redesigned structure will be described from the ground up, that is, starting with the subprocesses, to better explain how it focuses on supporting the people who actually do the work.

For each of the subprocesses, a subprocess PMT was formed, consisting of a full-time leader from within the EH&S organization, involved members of the professional team, and key business partners for that function.

In some cases, these other members represent an organization that is a supplier to the EH&S process, such as training services. In other cases, the other organizations may be doing work actually within the scope of the EH&S process, such as maintenance on equipment driven by the Clean Air Act amendments.

The Stakeholder Interface Subprocess

The stakeholder interface PMT is the front end of our process. It is designed to continually seek and gather perceived opportunities for improvement from our three key stakeholder groups. Various mechanisms are utilized to gather this data, such as

FIGURE 12–1

EH&S Process Management Structure

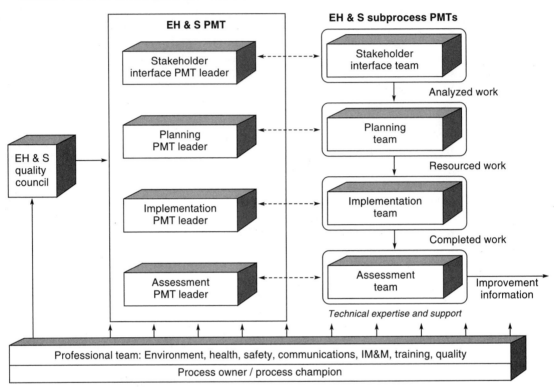

environmental aspect reviews, telephone hotlines, the Internet, employee survey data, review results, and the like, as well as more traditional "opportunities" such as reviews of new regulations and legislation.

The incoming data is analyzed and turned into information. Triage is performed to determine the relative priority and urgency. This team also ensures that legal requirements are identified and accessible. Communications is a key function of this subprocess, as it functions as a window to both the internal and external world. Strategies to increase awareness are developed based on feedback into the process. Audit or review findings are input to the process as further fuel for improvement, strengthening our ability to perform nonconformance, corrective, and preventive action.

The Planning Subprocess

The planning subprocess is where program development begins. All budgeting and resourcing (as defined by the ISO 14001 standard within structure and responsibility) is performed as a function of the planning PMT, as is goal setting—objectives and targets.

The true impact of incoming work, whether in cost or labor or other, is calculated and budgeted for. If training is needed, development begins. For major initiatives or programs, agreements are executed with business partners to ensure effective cross-functional planning and implementation. Preventive maintenance routines (fire extinguisher inspections, for example) or other operational control requirements are developed. When the program is approved, it leaves the planning process and is fully implementable.

The Implementation Subprocess

The implementation subprocess is "where the rubber meets the road," and program implementation is executed. The implementation PMT is composed of our "process representatives"—people who are responsible for implementation of EH&S programs within a certain organization.

These people usually do not report to the EH&S organization but to the organization they support. The local management is responsible for support management (such as development of an individual's personal effectiveness), while the EH&S process specifies how the EH&S work gets done in that organization. The process representative, working as part of the EH&S process, is the channel to and from the local organization.

The process representatives provide timely information to their organizations and back to the process leadership. While the implementation process representatives are accountable for successful performance within their organizations, they in turn hold the upstream EH&S subprocess teams accountable, with measurable expectations, for delivering the proper support. For example, the planning subprocess receives feedback about the effectiveness of programs that it has developed and resourced. The process representatives monitor the success of business partner agreements at a tactical level and are also responsible for corrective action within their organizations.

The Assessment Subprocess

The assessment subprocess team manages both compliance and management system audits. Members include representatives from other auditing groups, such as our internal network quality review group, to increase the opportunity for synergies. This team ensures that EH&S auditing is cost-effective and statistically valid, and that it produces value-added information. Metrics are developed, compiled, and published. Depending on the cause, areas for improvement are either handed off to the responsible subprocess or sent to the stakeholder interface team for processing.

The Professional Team

The professional team supplies the technical expertise required to execute the process, whether in the classic areas of environment, health, or safety program development or in areas such as communications, continual improvement/quality, training, or information technology. The members of this team do their technical work through the subprocesses and process management teams, supplying the underlying knowledge and necessary skills to the workforce in a structured manner.

This creates a focus on value-added program development and implementation. Technical applications move through the continual improvement cycle: Needs are prioritized; then programs are developed, fully resourced, and planned, implemented, and assessed for effectiveness and efficiency.

The Environment, Health, and Safety Process Management Team (PMT)

The EH&S PMT is made up of the leaders of the four subprocess teams, the professional team on an ad hoc basis, and business partners from organizations having a large scope of influence on EH&S matters. Initiatives with a large impact or scope of influence, such as validation and concurrence on goal setting, are brought to this team to be worked across the process simultaneously. The EH&S PMT primarily addresses issues involving three or more of the four subprocesses and serves to ensure that subprocess suboptimization does not occur. It currently is a self-directed team.

The Environment, Health, and Safety Quality Council

The EH&S PMT is supported by the EH&S quality council, the senior board of directors for the process. Comprised of leaders from across the business, it sets policy and strategic direction, serves as an escalation point, and helps gain high-level buy-in for EH&S initiatives. It creates the environment for success, monitors measures of performance and management system improvement, and ensures that the process is operating according to strategic direction.

LINKAGES WITH THE QUALITY MANAGEMENT SYSTEM

ISO 14001 shares many elements with the ISO 9000 series of standards, which is one of the platforms for our quality management system (QMS). Therefore, most of the structure already existed for elements such as management review, which is required to be performed by our vice president and general manager and his executive quality council.

Roles, responsibilities, and authorities for process champions, owners, leaders, and process management teams are defined as part of our QMS. Management system documentation is developed per QMS standards. Document control procedures and a World Wide Web (Internet) platform allowing access by all associates are usable for EH&S documentation.

Emergency preparedness and response procedures are in place. Nonconformance and corrective and preventive action policies currently exist, as do management system audits and the associated management reviews. Documented policies and procedures for compensation, goal setting, development, and budgeting exist as part of other processes.

A CLOSER LOOK: APPROACH TO EACH ISO 14001 ELEMENT

Table 12–1 shows how the elements of ISO 14001 map to our new process structure. Note that the EH&S PMT is not shown. The functions of this body are a composite of the functions performed by the subprocess teams. Following is an element-by-element description of our approach to each ISO 14001 element.

T A B L E   12–1

Mapping of EH&S Process Structure to ISO 14001 Elements

ISO 14001 Element	Stakeholder Interface Subprocess	Planning Subprocess	Implementation Subprocess	Assessment Subprocess	Quality Council
General	X	X	X	X	X
Policy					X
Planning					
• Aspects	X				
• Legal	X				
• Objectives and targets	X	X			X
• Programs		X	X		
Implementation and operation					
• Structure and responsibility		X	X	X	
• Training/awareness/competence		X	X		
• Communication	X	X	X		X
• Documentation (MS/controlled)	X	X	X		X
• Operational control		X	X		
• Emergency preparedness and response		X	X		
Checking and corrective action					
• Monitoring and measurement			X	X	X
• Nonconformance and correction and preventive action	X	X	X	X	X
• Records	X	X	X	X	
• EMS audit				X	X
Management review				X	X

General Requirements

Establishment and maintenance of a management system is simply part of the existence within AT&T NSD. Our quality management system provides a platform for our EH&S management system. As part of the professional team, the quality group is accountable for the successful implementation and improvement of our EH&S management system as well as our QMS.

Policy

The environmental policy is set by the quality council, using data supplied to it by the various subprocesses. Current plans are to make it available to the external world on our World Wide Web site.

Planning

Aspects

We consider aspects for health and safety to be those that contribute to injuries and accidents and other measurable indicators, that is, root causes. We look at both positive and negative aspects for environment, health, and safety impacts, then seek to maximize the benefit and minimize the risk to our three key stakeholder groups, as measured by EVA (economic value added), PVA (people value added), and CVA (customer, or external stakeholder, value added).

Legal and Other Requirements

Establishing and maintaining a procedure for EH&S federal, state, and local legislation and regulation is the responsibility of the stakeholder interface team.

Objectives and Targets

Compensation is a key driver for achieving objectives. We tie compensation to EH&S results across a large percentage of the 16,000 employees within NSD. These objectives and targets are developed by the planning PMT, based on analysis made by the stakeholder interface team. We also link compensation to performance at the process management team level, with measurable goals for each team.

Programs

Program development is performed within the planning subprocess, using the professional team for specific expertise under the leadership of the PMT and team leader. Responsibility for achievement is already designated through our defined process structure. We achieve primary linkages with other planning organizations, such as product or service development or engineering, within the planning subprocess as well.

Implementation and Operation

Structure and Responsibility

Program execution occurs within the implementation subprocess, but the planning PMT is accountable for ensuring that resources are sufficient and that all parties are aware of their responsibilities. The EH&S process representative within a specific organization is responsible for supporting the rollout of new initiatives with their organization. The process owner is the management representative as defined by the standard.

Training, Awareness, and Competence

In conjunction with the human resources training organization, training needs and paths have been identified to ensure that appropriate training takes place. We seek to embed EH&S elements into other training courses. For example, a training class on a maintenance procedure can include information on safely performing that procedure.

Awareness is a key strategy. We publish a monthly newsletter on EH&S. We embed EH&S goals in compensation across the business, and we have extremely strong executive sponsorship, which facilitates awareness of EH&S. Our communications professional has developed both an internal and external (to AT&T) World Wide Web page, using an interactive, entertaining format, to encourage "surfing." When the employee is taking a break and accessing the page, he or she is in fact learning about EH&S.

Communications

The stakeholder interface team is where the communication element of our process primarily resides. Prompt feedback must be given to the sender of the incoming information to ensure that referred issues are not perceived as lost. Information technology and the content carried on that technology must both be located, in terms of organizational structure, at the front end of our process. This ensures that streamlined, proper procedures for communication are developed up-front.

Management System Documentation and Document Control

All required documentation will soon be available on the internal World Wide Web, with pointers to other relevant documentation such as that "owned" by other organizations. This ensures that the latest version is always known and available, and trains the workforce to favor electronic over paper communication. We use a standard process management improvement cyclical tool so that the management system documentation for all subprocesses is developed in a standard manner as the quality journey continues. Document control, including records, is considered the responsibility of all subprocesses and professionals, depending on the document.

Operational Control

We identify affected operations and activities—business partners—during the planning subprocess and ensure that implementation takes place in a controlled manner. For example, we create preventive maintenance routines for inclusion in work management systems or develop business partner agreements with organizations such as procurement, which manages external suppliers.

Emergency Preparedness and Response

For AT&T NSD, the reliability of our network is of utmost concern. In the event of an emergency, communication is critical. Emergency preparedness and response is ingrained in our culture, with the corresponding procedures.

Checking and Corrective Action

Monitoring and Measurement

Metrics and measures, which track performance towards goals and objectives and include reviews and audits, are electronically published weekly by the metrics professional and assessment PMT. This increases awareness and drives the desired behavior. Metrics have two uses: to measure performance and to drive behavior. The soft, behavioral, issues must be addressed during metric design.

Nonconformance and Corrective and Preventive Action

Our QMS specifies a divisionwide policy for this area. We have implemented this policy by basing our structure on continual improvement. The stakeholder interface PMT is constantly evaluating new areas for improvement, including feedback from the assessment subprocess. Corrective action, based on feedback from assessment, is performed by the responsible organization, working within the boundaries of the implementation subprocess.

Records

Records are maintained according to our documentation control policy and procedure by the responsible organization.

Management System Audit

Management system audits are performed in several ways. NSD has an internal quality auditing group that performs ISO 9000 management system auditing and assessment services, as required by our QMS. We are also assessed against Malcolm Baldrige National Quality Award criteria by submitting for the Chairman's Quality Award, an

AT&T internal measure of organizational excellence. The assessment PMT has not yet made the final decision regarding ISO 14000 management system auditing.

Management Review

Management review is performed for each of the processes within our division by the process owner and NSD's vice president and general manager and his executive quality council, as required by our quality management system. We place emphasis on an effective review, focusing on areas for improvement and the time frames required.

CONCLUSION: PROCESS MANAGEMENT / QMS / ISO 14000 SYNERGIES

Applying process management techniques to Environment, Health, and Safety leads to a enhanced focus on delivering measurable, value-added products and services. Configuring this process into a structure that essentially *demands* continual improvement causes us to never lose that focus.

Having an existing quality management system allows speedy implementation of an EH&S Management System—a lot of the work has already been completed. As we deployed our new process we learned the following lessons:

- *Management commitment is paramount.* This support is critical to implementing management across organizational lines. Without the ability to drive behavior at the working level of the enterprise to all people touched by a process, any management system will fail.

- *Start with a thorough and rigorous approach to understanding the needs of customers or stakeholders.* Use a grounds-up approach to solving problems. Understand the risks, costs, and benefits of meeting a perceived need. Once the needs are understood, analyze, act, and assess. The more the actual organizational structure drives this, the quicker the process improves.

- *Maintain a constant focus on value-added, cross-functional, measurable inputs and outputs.* This will help the organization to continually improve, by reducing effects, defects, the budget, or cycle time. End-to-end processes, which have been broken apart by organizational boundaries, are put back together. Environment, health, and safety work may be performed by organizations such as procurement, human resources, engineering, and property management. Only a focus on cross-functional teams and clear goals and objectives linked to compensation can align the enterprise with what needs to be done.

- *Focus on knowledge transfer to drive behavior.* All employees have an influence on the success of the business, their health and safety, and the environmental impact they produce. By seeking to understand the wants and needs of all employees, we can produce programs designed to make a difference in behavior, using the continuum of *awareness to knowledge to wisdom*. Use targeted communications messages and vehicles. If the EH&S message is not understood, the problem is with EH&S, not the individual.

BIOGRAPHY

Joseph Roitz, PE

Joseph Roitz is currently the EH&S Management System Improvement Manager for the restructured AT&T, having served on the team that developed their Environment, Health and Safety organization. At the time this chapter was written, Mr. Roitz was the Lead Quality Professional for the Environment, Health and Safety Process within the Network Services Division (NSD) of AT&T, a Malcolm Baldrige National Quality Award winning organization.

Following a position with Dow Chemical in Freeport, Texas as a mechanical engineer, he began his career with AT&T as a planning engineer and member of the technical staff in the Little Rock factory, developing circuit card assembly processes.

Later, he became a process improvement project leader within AT&T NSD's Asset and Financial Management organization, where his team was recognized with the highest attainable internal quality award.

CHAPTER 13

Practical Guidance for Implementing an EMS

John Kinsella

INTRODUCTION

In the past, a company managed its environmental problems largely in reaction to outside pressures. These pressures came from government agencies, environmental interest groups, and citizens. Internal environmental managers were often part of the legal department and obtained their funds to comply with or resist imposed rules and regulations. The company regarded environmental management as a cost center (negative) versus a revenue-generating profit center (positive).

Today, that way of thinking has been replaced by a recognition that environmental management is an integral part of business. Companies have become more efficient, responsive, and more tightly managed. As a result, companies that do not have a system for managing their environmental issues and opportunities will be less efficient than their competitors.

Leading companies have quantified their environmental costs and have implemented an EMS to manage those costs. The EMS guides the company towards continual environmental improvement. In the beginning, it deals with the basics: assuring regulatory compliance and limiting sources of liability. It can then advance beyond minimum regulatory standards and focus on pollution prevention, waste minimization and more efficient use of materials and energy. The key components of an EMS are the following:

- Continuous improvement.

- Prevention of pollution.

- Integration of environmental management principles into all areas of an organization's management and operations.

ISO 14001

ISO 14001 sets compliance with regulations as a baseline and then focuses on the reduction of impacts through planning and implementation. An initial evaluation should be conducted to establish targets for pollution reduction. This initial evaluation serves as a baseline measurement against which to measure progress. The certification audit reviews environmental results compared to initial targets and evaluates the capability of management systems to achieve projected goals.

ISO 14001 contains no numerical emission standards to be satisfied, nor does it establish specific management practices to be employed. ISO 14001 addresses itself to the structure and performance of "institutional" arrangements, not "hardware." It is possible that an organization could be in full compliance with existing environmental standards but yet not have an acceptable EMS.

The EMS may have no elements evaluating and encouraging improvements beyond minimum compliance. It is also possible that an organization could have compliance problems and yet have an acceptable EMS. The most likely scenario where this apparent contradiction could develop is in the early stages of an EMS. If compliance problems continue to exist, one would consider them evidence of an inadequate EMS.

Why Have an EMS?

Having an EMS makes good business sense. It requires management to address compliance in a systematic manner and puts the company on a path of continuous improvement. To illustrate how companies have implemented an EMS within the organization, two companies are profiled below. Both companies initiated these systems independently of ISO 14000 but plan to integrate the standard into their operations.

Company A is a computer software company. It is an international leader, with a high-profile, young workforce and is environmentally aware. It has packaging plants in the United States, Europe and Puerto Rico. It is a leader in the computer software industry. Consumers of its products include corporations, civil institutions, and individuals. Company A wants to take a proactive approach to environmental issues.

Company B is an electronics manufacturing company. It is a local family firm, now public, that produces specialty electronics equipment for industry. It manufactures in the United States and Europe. Company B has a strong environmental ethic and quality systems pervade everything it does. Company B has manufactured electronic testing equipment since 1950. The company is a leader and innovator in the industry and has carried this philosophy forward into its environmental management program.

PROFILE OF THE TWO COMPANIES' EMSs

This profile will involve a discussion of each company's system under the following headings. Differences and similarities in approach will be discussed.

1. Policy.

2. Organization and personnel.

3. Objectives and targets.

4. Program implementation.

5. Control procedures.

6. Emergency preparedness and response.

7. Verification and review.

8. Documentation.

9. Communications.

1. Policy

A written, corporate environmental policy is the basis of an EMS. It guides the establishment and execution of initiatives, empowers the managers, and conveys to employees, owners, and customers that the company takes its environmental commitment seriously.

At Company A, there are no barriers to having and maintaining a written environmental policy; the company enjoys the freedom of its open environmental commitment. Personnel believe that a written policy would invite hypocrisy and hamper innovation. The company has a general commitment to the environment that guides its performance.

The company's environmental commitment provides flexibility but does not provide a foundation for an EMS. A written environmental policy would promote continued environmental improvements at all levels of the organization.

Company B has successfully implemented a companywide environmental policy that encompasses all aspects of its activities, products, and services. There are no barriers to having and maintaining this policy. Positive financial impacts have resulted from implementing this policy: e.g., cost savings in waste disposal, water use, and energy consumption. No negative impacts have been reported.

2. Organization and Personnel

An environmental management group ensures that every facet of a corporation is within regulatory compliance and can provide advice about the purchase of less-hazardous products, new technologies, suppliers, subcontractors, and so on. It relieves the workload of facilities operations personnel responsible for environmental issues and thereby ensures adequate coverage of those topics.

At both companies, there is no formal environmental management hierarchy. Operations personnel are responsible for environmental management of their processes. Environmental improvements have resulted from innovation and conscientious effort by small quality teams. A positive impact has been "ownership" of environmental issues by all teams. A negative impact of no formal structure is the lack of specific corporate environmental goals and objectives. It is recommended that environmental management be identified in the corporate structure of both firms. Both companies are growing, and this change will become a necessity. By establishing an environmental management group, the companies can forestall the difficulties of later reorganizing an elaborate web of intertwined environmental and non-environmental disciplines.

3. Objectives and Targets

Setting objectives and targets for environmental initiatives focuses action where improvements are needed most and where the company will have the highest return on its action spent.

Company A does not set environmental targets at the corporate level. Facilities engineering has been very successful at improving the corporation's environmental performance (reduced resource use and waste generation). Targets have been identified through a waste audit.

Landscape maintenance at Company A employs an irrigation system that is up to 40 percent more efficient and helps conserve fertilizer and pesticides by not washing them away. Horticultural practices ensure that fertilizers and pesticides are only used when absolutely necessary. Informal fountains and other water features are kept cleaner by microbial filtration. Trees and plants displaced by new construction are stored and replanted as needed, and yard waste is collected by a contractor and composted into topsoil. To complete the cycle, Company A makes a point of purchasing topsoil from this composting company. Many outdoor benches at the corporate campus are made of recycled materials.

Company B has reduced its solid waste stream by 50 percent and electrical use by 14 percent. In fiscal year 1994, employee recycling kept 3,200 tons of material from being landfilled and saved the company $215,000.

The packaging facility at Company B reduced its solid waste stream by 70 percent. The company is reducing the amount of shrink-wrap in the packaging process. Programs on compact disk have on-line, paperless manuals and fewer packaging materials.

General construction contractors have been challenged to reduce their waste. During construction of a new building in 1995, 47 percent of the waste (2,600 cubic yards) was recycled, including wood, drywall, cardboard, asphalt, concrete, and some ferrous metals. This effort saved $32,000.

Environmental programs should be corporate sanctioned through the establishment of corporate objectives and targets in order to increase the incentive to succeed and to attain ISO 14000 certification. It is recommended that corporate environmental objectives and targets be set at the beginning of each fiscal year and be kept general.

Although Company B does not set specific environmental targets at the corporate level, individual work teams have been very successful at improving their environmental performance (reduction of overall volumes of waste generated). The positive impacts have been substantial. They include the following:

- The elimination of ozone-depleting chemicals, hazardous materials used in inks for product packaging, and toxic additives in molded plastic components.
- A 44 percent reduction in the volume of solid waste sent to local landfills from 1989 to 1995.
- A reduction in process water consumption by 2.6 million gallons per month.
- A reduction in electrical consumption by 2.2 million kilowatt hours per year.
- An increase in the percentage of recycled material used in product packaging.
- A reduction in the amount of hazardous waste generated, from 850 tons in 1986 to 585 tons in 1995.

Since September 1991, Company B has shipped 240 drums of sulfuric acid to a local recycling facility. The company uses sulfuric acid in the circuit board process; the recycling facility uses it to neutralize their customers' wastes. Before this arrangement, it cost over $200 per drum to dispose of the acid as hazardous waste. To date, savings amount to almost $50,000.

The reductions made in shipping materials off-site have greatly reduced the company's expenses, with out-of-pocket savings estimated at over $500,000 per year. In addition, long-term liability for potential clean-up costs has been greatly reduced.

Environmental risks have been reduced since the implementation of a circuit board scrap disposal project in 1990. In that year, the Environmental Protection Agency labeled the lead content on printed circuit boards hazardous waste. Company B now pays a processing fee (which is offset by reduced garbage disposal costs and precious metal reclamation credits as well as liability reduction) to recycle circuit board scrap and keep the hazardous material out of landfills. The company has also managed to reduce the annual volume of circuit board scrap from 63,000 lbs./year in 1991 to 31,000 lbs./year in 1995.

Under ISO 14001, a company must identify the environmental aspects of its activities, products, or services and determine the impact of these aspects. Both companies have done this under their current programs. Examples of environmental aspects and related impacts at both companies are shown in Table 13–1.

T A B L E   13–1

Environmental Aspects and Impacts

Activity	Aspect	Impact
Packaging	Solid waste generation	Landfill capacity
Circuit boards, wastewater sludge	Hazardous waste generation	Landfill capacity
Molding, inks	CFC/solvent use	Air pollution/ozone depletion
Landscape maintenance	Pesticides/herbicide use	Water pollution

4. Program Implementation

Both firms have implemented some form of EMS. Since 1990, Company B has implemented a series of management programs to achieve its environmental objectives and targets. For example, the reduction and eventual elimination of CFCs from its operations were identified as major goals. The company achieved these goals in 1992 when use of CFCs ceased. There have been significant, positive impacts of implementing specific environmental management programs. These have included a Governor's Award for pollution prevention and recognition from the state environmental agency.

At Company A in 1995, employee recycle and reuse efforts diverted 3,400 tons of solid waste from landfills, saving the company $220,000. The company's recycling program has received numerous state and local environmental awards.

Both company's current programs could benefit from a firmer foundation provided by a formal EMS, which would include a corporate environmental policy, objectives, and targets, and an environmental management group. Establishing an EMS would largely amount to modifications to the current systems. It would underscore their belief in the importance of environmental responsibility and would satisfy several ISO 14001 requirements.

The cost of implementing an EMS would not be substantial and should more than pay for itself since the intent of the EMS is to increase the efficiency and scope of environmental programs.

5. Control Procedures

Control procedures ensure that systems work well by adjusting them or providing information when they are not working correctly. Automated control ensures immediate response to changing conditions. Company A's main applications for control procedures are its heating/ventilation/air conditioning (HVAC) system and its grounds irrigation system.

The grounds irrigation system is centrally controlled. It provides water based on the temperature, humidity, plant type (grass or shrub), evaporation, and transpiration in the previous 24 hours. Overwatering is eliminated, resulting in less fertilizer and pesticide use.

Centrally controlled HVAC systems monitor interior and exterior temperatures at various points, and use variable-speed motors that run slowly when demand is low. Capital expenditures are returned through savings of water, energy, materials, and avoided disposal costs.

Company B has successfully implemented procedures for monitoring and controlling activities that impact the environment. These procedures ensure that the company is in compliance with (or exceeding) regulatory standards. There are no known barriers to implementing control procedures. The company recognizes that not having adequate environmental control procedures will result in regulatory infractions, monetary costs and poor public image.

Both companies maintain and upgrade existing control procedures and work with system designers and architects to develop efficient facilities system controls and to retrofit older buildings/processes with new designs.

6. Emergency Preparedness and Response

Emergency preparedness is best accomplished through preparation of an emergency response plan (ERP). An ERP is a guidance document providing specific instructions and information that can be used to coordinate an effective response to any emergency. Both companies already have extensive ERPs.

The plans ensure that in the case of an emergency, there will be a minimum of confusion and risk of injury. The ERPs also have a positive impact on employee morale; they know the company is concerned with their welfare. No negative impacts have been identified.

Company A's ERP is communicated to all personnel: It is included in the employee handbook, and managers have even more comprehensive versions. The plan includes a phone list, site maps, life safety maps, additional security information, and emergency response information for the following:

- Injury/accident
- Emergency evacuation
- Electrical
- HVAC
- Domestic water
- Irrigation and water
- Halon

Company B has an overall emergency preparedness plan that is a collection of plans and procedures covering fire, chemical, earthquake, medical, utility disruption, bomb threat, and hostile intruder emergencies.

The plan is designed to protect the safety and well-being of employees and others and to minimize business disruption and property damage that adversely affect the company's assets or the community and environment. The primary users of the plan are the various emergency response teams that are described in the plan. The plan provides each individual on the teams with a detailed list of actions to be performed in the event of each type of emergency.

To provide an immediate, coordinated, and effective response to an emergency, an emergency command team has been established. The emergency command team has a functional, task-oriented structure that is independent of the company's normal management structure. The mission of this group is to ensure the successful implementation of this plan in response to an emergency situation. The team consists of the following:

Company president.   Is able to order plant closure or send uninjured employees home and to make discretionary evacuations and major financial decisions.

Emergency coordinator.   The focal point and information conduit between the president and other emergency command team members.

Safety engineer.   Advises on safety issues; reports to safety regulatory agencies.

Facilities response team manager.   Recruits provisions, area monitors, facilities engineering, and facilities maintenance team members.

Environmental manager.   Advises and counsels emergency command team on environmental issues; reports to environmental regulatory agencies.

The plan has had a very positive impact on employee morale; they know the company is concerned with their welfare. The company invested over $250,000 in team training and equipment, a $75,000 earthquake simulation model and structural building upgrades and emergency food supplies (three days) for employees.

7. Verification and Review

Verification and review of the EMS is important to ensure that it is effectively implemented. This is done by audit. Audits are also crucial to assessing the effectiveness of individual environmental programs, and they make it possible to fine-tune systems. Baseline information is required to determine preexisting conditions.

Neither company has an EMS to review, but there are no barriers to verification and review of environmental initiatives.

Company A undertakes environmental programs that are financially beneficial. As a result, the programs are tracked closely to ensure they are earning a return. In 1990, they participated with the local county waste department to perform a baseline waste audit. Waste streams identified in that audit have been targeted and reduced. They intend to perform another audit in the near future.

Company B performed a comprehensive baseline compliance and risk audit of all operating facilities in 1990. Certain recommendations from that audit have been implemented. No formal, comprehensive audits have been completed since that time. It is recommended that a schedule of routine audits be instituted. It is also recommended that a formal EMS be implemented and that a regular review of the EMS be conducted.

Based on the company's leading position with environmental management, no barriers have been identified. Routine audits will provide management with an objective (third-party) evaluation of environmental performance. This will enable management to make changes to operating systems and reporting procedures as necessary. There are no perceived negative impacts of implementing this program. Periodic review of the EMS will also provide management with feedback on how well the system is performing.

8. Documentation

Documenting the volume of materials and resources consumed is vital to assessing the success of an EMS. Proper documentation of water and energy consumption and waste-stream volumes provide the opportunity to constantly review performance. There should also be formal procedures for managing, reviewing, and revising these documents.

There may be a barrier at both companies to implementing a document control process, as it may be viewed as unnecessary and overly burdensome. Benefits would need to be demonstrated. By having environmental documents managed and controlled under the EMS, the environmental management group will be able to retrieve environmental performance/compliance data quickly and easily.

Company A documents the progress of its recycling programs through monthly reports based on information from recycling contractors. At their packaging facility, a comprehensive file of Material Safety Data Sheets is maintained. The facility is registered with the state as a small-quantity generator of hazardous waste and files annually with this agency.

Company B documents the environmental impact of its operations via state air and waste permits. The volumes of waste generated and treated, levels of water, and energy consumption are documented. However, there are no formal procedures for managing, reviewing, and revising these documents.

Both companies should consider installing a formal document database and review process to cover waste streams, water and energy use, and any regulatory compliance issues. Costs involved would include personnel time to identify needed documents, define reporting procedures, and generate a historical database.

9. Communications

Communication is vital to ensuring the smooth operation of an EMS and its environmental programs. It ensures a transfer of information from the source to receivers, which improves efficiency. It empowers all who are involved. For the purpose of good public relations, the success of the EMS can be communicated to the employees, shareholders, and the community.

There are no barriers to communications at Company A. However, personnel feel that the company's focus on software development should not be distracted by a large, environmental-management effort. The company prefers environmental management for efficiency and thrift rather than for public relations.

The company's public relations department has available a description of the company's environmental commitment: its recycling program, energy and water reduction program, and other environmental programs. All new employees are apprised of these issues and of how they can participate. Information is available to employees on-line and in hard copy. The company has an excellent system of interoffice electronic mail and voice messaging. The employee newsletter features articles about the company's environmental programs. Series articles are run often to reach even occasional readers.

Company B has a series of environmental principles that have been made available to all employees and are included in all new-employee packages. There is a very strong commitment by the company CEO to communicate the environmental principles and achievements of the company. Regulatory articles in the company's internal newspaper have featured environmental achievements. There are no perceived barriers to communications. The positive impacts have resulted in a perception by the employees and local community that the company has a progressive environmental management program.

BARRIERS TO IMPLEMENTING AN EMS

From the above discussion, it is apparent that the benefits of having an EMS far outweigh those of not having one. Why then are many organizations reluctant to implement an EMS? What are some of the barriers to implementation? In interviews with organizations, the following main reasons were cited:

- Environmental management was not perceived as a critical issue.
- No budget was available to change the status quo.
- The organization wanted to wait and see what everyone else was doing.
- The organization wanted to wait and respond to customer pressure to adopt an ISO 14001-type EMS.

In addition, the majority of those responsible for dealing with environmental issues in several companies said that senior management did not view having an EMS as a priority.

How You Can Begin

How can an organization develop an EMS and prepare for ISO 14001? The following three steps are being pursued by several forward-thinking firms:

1. Gap analysis
2. Internal program
3. Self declaration/Registration

Gap Analysis

A gap analysis, as discussed in detail earlier in this book, measures the difference between how the business is currently managed and the requirements of the ISO 14001 standard. It is a good way to evaluate procedures and identify those areas that need attention. It is often beneficial to have a third party perform a gap analysis for objectivity.

Internal Program

Using the gap analysis, implement a program to improve the EMS under a predetermined timetable. The ultimate goal is to introduce efficiency into the business. Only the organization can set these goals and objectives.

Self-Declaration/Registration

The decision whether to self-declare conformance to ISO 14001 and/or to seek third-party registration depends on the type of business and its customers. Many organizations have decided that a two-step process will allow them to implement change more effectively into their operations. The decision to seek third-party registration against the standard will be driven by customer demand and market advantage.

CONCLUSIONS

Environmental management is an integral part of business. Companies have become more efficient, responsive, and more tightly managed. Those companies that do not have an EMS for managing their environmental issues and opportunities will be less efficient than their competitors. Having an EMS makes good business sense. It requires management to address compliance in a systematic manner and puts the company on a path of continuous improvement. Companies have recognized that having an EMS improves their operations and reduces costs. ISO 14001 offers a foundation on which an organization can build its EMS.

BIOGRAPHY

John Kinsella

John Kinsella is vice president of SCS Engineers, an environmental management firm. Mr. Kinsella has a bachelor's degree in geology from the University of Dublin, Ireland and a master's degree from the University of London, U.K. He has 15 years experience with the environmental management of private and government facilities throughout the United States and the Pacific Rim. Mr. Kinsella is an ISO 9000 internal auditor and a member of the U.S. ISO 14000 Technical Advisory Group that is participating in the development of the ISO 14000 series of environmental management standards. He is currently working with several firms nationally and internationally to prepare them for ISO 14001.

John Kinsella
SCS Engineers
2405 140th Avenue, NE, Suite 107
Bellevue, Washington 98005
Phone: (206) 746-4600
Fax: (206) 746-6747

PART THREE

ISO 14000 and ISO 9000 Integration

CHAPTER 14

ISO 14000/ISO 9000: Integration, Conformity Assessment, and Auditing Skills

Ron Black

INTRODUCTION

In terms of resource savings and improvement in environment responsibility, there is value in integrating ISO 14001 environmental and ISO 9000 quality standards. Success in integration will depend on cross-training of managers and skilled support groups to maintain the systems. The value of ISO 14001 in terms of stakeholder confidence in the process will significantly depend on the integrity of the registration process and the skills of the auditors. Because the lines of communication between stakeholders and facility are more limited in the environmental process than in the quality process, environmental stakeholders must be provided with a high level of confidence in the third-party evaluation process. Therefore, the third-party process for registration cannot fail to accurately define the degree to which an organization conforms to the ISO 14001 requirements.

The ISO 14001 Environmental Management System (EMS) standard and the companion guideline are believed to have evolved as a natural adjunct to the ISO 9000 series of quality management standards (QMS). While there was an early attempt to model the EMS standard after the QMS standard, international environmental experts saw a need to significantly depart from this standard, both in terms of specific elements and less detail in the ISO 14000 standards. As one of several ISO 14000 approaches, integration with ISO 9000 has many logical advantages. This chapter explores the standards and their differences and what is meant in terms of standards integration, conformity assessment, and the skills necessary for providing credible objective audits of facilities seeking registrations.

A better return on environmental investment will come from implementing systems that will identify the environmental aspects of industrial activities, processes, and products and from implementing practices to provide for the continual reduction of the environmental impact these aspects have. ISO 14000 simply harmonizes these efforts and provides for global normalization of environmental management practices without the constraints on innovation that are endemic to prescriptive regulations. Continued residual improvements in environmental performance cannot be legislated. They must come from those who understand and manage the processes.

There are many hurdles to overcome before the ISO 14000 standards are accepted by stakeholders. If regulatory agencies intend to use ISO 14000 to identify environmentally responsible companies, the registration criteria will need to include a highly defined compliance system, and the agencies will need to shift from command and control to service. Several state agencies, such as Pennsylvania and Wisconsin, have initiated this change.

The registration process must be designed to ensure that registered companies are capable of maintaining a high level of environmental performance and have programs in place to improve on that performance. The values of the ISO 14001 registrations need to be marketed so that communities develop a sense of confidence in the companies that are registered.

There are three apparent driving forces that could launch ISO 14001: state and federal regulatory agencies, market forces, and community. Recognizing that most companies have had highly defined systems in place for several years and that others are in the process of implementing systems, it is not surprising that broad-based ISO 14001 registrations by industry in the United States will require that there be added value not withstanding market forces. In part, added value may be found in the possibility of integrating the quality and environmental systems.

ISO 14001/ISO 9000 GAP ANALYSIS

Registration under either ISO 9000 or ISO 14001 will require that the applicant conform with the specifications of each standard. This discussion assumes registration is desired under both standards. The question is whether efficiencies and cost savings will result from integrating systems. This could be evaluated in terms of integrated implementation and management of the systems elements and/or reducing the cost of the third-party review process. Of the ISO 9000 series of standards, ISO 9001 will be evaluated because it is the most comprehensive.

The ISO 9001 standard includes 20 paragraphs, which are listed in Table 14–1, and the ISO 14001 standard has 6 paragraphs, which are listed in Table 14–2. Of the 20 paragraphs in ISO 9001, 11 demonstrate sufficient similarity to evaluate the possibility that QMS and EMS could be concurrently audited for registration purposes. The first part of the analysis will focus on this comparison. The nine remaining ISO 9001 paragraphs do not appear necessary to meet EMS registration but do provide opportunities to enhance the EMS or in some cases be considered by registrars as logical and necessary extensions of the EMS specifications.

T A B L E 14–1

ISO 9001 Paragraph Titles

No.	Title	EMS Equivalent
4.1	Management responsibility	Yes
4.2	Quality systems	Yes (i.e., EMS)
4.3	Contract review	No
4.4	Design control	No
4.5	Document and data control	Yes
4.6	Purchasing	No
4.7	Control of customer-supplied product	No
4.8	Product identification and traceability	No
4.9	Process control	Yes
4.10	Inspection and testing	Yes
4.11	Inspection, measuring, and test equipment	Yes
4.12	Inspection and test status	Yes
4.13	Control of nonconforming product	No
4.14	Corrective and preventive action	Yes
4.15	Handling, storage, packaging, preservation, and delivery	No
4.16	Quality records	Yes
4.17	Internal quality audits	Yes
4.18	Training	Yes
4.19	Servicing	No
4.20	Statistical techniques	No

T A B L E 14–2

Six ISO 14001 Paragraph Titles

No.	Title
4.1	General requirements
4.2	Environmental policy
4.3	Planning
4.4	Implementation and operation
4.5	Checking and corrective action
4.6	Management review

The analysis will be based on the six ISO 14001 paragraphs and will assume facilities of medium to large size that are reasonably staffed to assume responsibility for implementation of both standards. Until model programs can be developed against which small facilities can benchmark, the value and applicability of integrated quality and environmental systems will be difficult to predict. Small independent facilities or those that depend on a central staff may find the cost of implementation and maintenance of EMS prohibitive. Small facilities operating a single, noncomplex process or service may find it difficult to justify the cost of a formal registration. The 14001 EMS companion document ISO 14004 provides guidance on interpretation and implementation of the ISO 14001 specifications. This document was reviewed but not considered in this analysis because it would have limited options for potential integration of the QMS and EMS standards.

4.1 General Requirements

This paragraph requires that the standards' specifications be implemented and maintained. This is also covered under Clause 4.2.1 of the quality standard. Both standards require commitment of workforce, capital and workforce resources, and top management.

4.2 Environmental Policy

Conceptually, the policy requirements of the two standards are similar. Both seek design of the system to meet stakeholder needs. The scope of the environmental policy, however, is broader in scope in two respects. First, the policy addresses a greater number of stakeholders, who have a variety of concerns (Table 14–3). The environmental policy considers the concerns of customers, suppliers, community, and government, all seeking different levels of assurance that systems are in place to ensure compliance with laws and regulation and beyond. The quality system policy focuses on customer/supplier needs.

Second, the matrix of skills and site parameters that need to be considered in developing the environmental policy are more complex than those of the ISO 9001 policy. This should not be construed as meaning implementation and management of the quality systems are not complex; QMS is more complex in the design, development, and implementation stages. It then settles into a long-term operational phase. But the environmental policy element is designed to specifically drive identification of environmental issues, their associative risk, and continual reduction in risk levels. Many factors constantly drive environmental risk reduction, including government limits, new scientific data, public demands, and the overriding sense that all risk should be eliminated.

One value of fully integrating EMS and QMS policies comes from demonstrating that environmental performance is given equal weight to business/operations considerations. An integrated policy must not only meet the specifications of both standards, it must also meet the need of all stakeholders. The policies serve different stakeholders and are implemented by different personnel with different skills. Significant knowledge of environmental practices and to some extent process knowledge would be needed

TABLE 14–3

Quality and Environmental Policy Requirements to Meet Stakeholder Needs

| | Stakeholders | | | | |
Policy Elements	State/Federal and Local Government	Community	Environmental Activist	Customer or Supplier	Employees
Regulations	14001	14001	14001	14001	14001
Environmental risk	14001	14001	14001	14001	14001
Industry initiative	14001	14001	14001	14001	14001
Process complexity	14001	9001	14001	14001/9001	14001/9001
Pollution prevention	14001	14001	14001	14001	14001
Continual improvement	14001	14001	14001	14001/9001	14001
Available to stakeholders	14001	14001	14001	14001/9001	14001
Setting objectives	14001	14001	14001	14001/9001	14001
Documented and implemented	14001	14001	14001	14001/9001	14001

to assess conformance with this aspect of the standard. At present, most organizations have specific policies on the environment. Having independent policies does not preclude integration of other parts of the two standards, but a commitment to environmental performance that equals that of business objectives is a compelling reason for a single policy.

4.3 Planning

The planning element of the ISO 14001 and ISO 9001 standards (Table 14–4) serves as a basis for establishing systems for meeting stakeholder expectations. The environment planning element requires site management to develop procedures to identify environmental manifestations of product, processes, and site activities and to establish management programs that will drive minimization or elimination of environmental impacts. Similarly, quality planning focuses on the design of process equipment, controls, and measurement factors that need to be in place to provide consistent quality product to customers.

TABLE 14–4

ISO 14001 and 9001 Planning

ISO 14001 Sub-Clause	Description	ISO 9001 Equivalent
4.3.1	**Environmental aspects.** Addresses the need to identify all environmental aspects of activities, products, or services in order to set environmental objectives that satisfy stakeholder concerns.	4.2.3 The supplier shall define and document how the requirements for quality will be met. Addresses the need to identify aspects of the product/ service process that need to be addressed in order to meet customer quality specifications.
4.3.2	**Legal and other requirements.** This subparagraph can be considered baseline aspects. That is, society identifies general areas for which baseline performance is expected	No direct equivalent.
4.3.3	**Objectives and targets.** Based on policy requirements and the need to reduce the impact of environmental aspects.	No direct equivalent.
4.3.4	**Environmental management programs.** Establishes programs for achieving objectives, including defining responsibilities and the means and time frame by which they are to be achieved.	Generally incorporated into 4.2.3, Quality planning.

There are striking differences in these systems that need to be considered if integration of systems or systems audit is contemplated. The core value of a quality system is to provide the customer assurances that systems dynamics are in place to respond to customer specifications. That is, the system is designed to develop a means to track conformance with specifications. With quality systems, the product is a constant within tolerance limits. The value of environmental systems is to ensure a variety of stakeholders that environmental performance meets their expectations, is maintained, and is continually improved. Recognizing that compliance with regulations is the baseline design, the challenge is to decide on what mix of stakeholder specifications to meet. This will depend on a number of factors. Size and location of the facility, industry sector, public perceptions of industrial activities, product/service customers, and internal goals are among the factors that will shape the design of an EMS.

While both systems share the concept of targets and tolerances, they differ in the variability of demands placed on the systems. In quality systems, a strong line of communication is established between customer and supplier. This line of communication provides for the flow of information between customer and supplier. The registration systems provide for assurances to the customer that systems are in place to respond to customer needs. This linking of suppliers and customers in theory establishes a system where quality is maintained from the raw-material phase through intermediate processing to consumer end product. The process is by design maintained within the global industrial community. Although, one could argue that consumers are part of the process, they are not part of the formal quality system. If a product or service that is unreliable or does not meet specifications reaches the consumer, the quality system has failed.

The EMS standard is not yet entirely clear. First, the lines of communications between stakeholders and the registered facility are not clearly defined. The three specific requirements in ISO 14001 on communication outside the organization are as follows:

1. 4.2 (f): "The policy is available to the public."

2. 4.3.3: "When establishing and reviewing its objectives, an organization shall consider . . . the views of interested parties."

3. 4.4.3: "The organization shall establish and maintain procedures for . . . receiving, documenting and responding to relevant communications from external interested parties".

These three areas addressing communications with external stakeholders do not collectively appear as strong as the customer and supplier communication requirements found in the ISO 9001 quality standard. Under the ISO 14001 EMS standard, the facility need only make the policy available to the public. This could range from putting it in the visitors center to publishing it in the paper. Because the policy is general, it does not offer external customers a significant basis for input.

This is an important distinction. First, unlike the ISO 9001 standard implementation, which is constantly monitored by the customer through product quality delivered by the supplier, there is no dynamic for keeping ISO 14001 stakeholders informed of systems performance. For environmental objectives, the facility need only "consider" the views of external parties. Since the specifications do not require input from stakeholders, a significant variation in the setting of facility objectives is expected because the interest level of stakeholders will vary, depending on such variables as industry, governmental jurisdictions, location, population, or media focus. In the communications subparagraph, procedures are required to receive, document, and respond to relevant communications from external parties. This requirement appears strong, but in the absence of the external parties' awareness of internal environmental activities it raises questions regarding whether external stakeholders have sufficient awareness of environmental activities at a particular facility to provide informed and relevant input. Note that Clause 4.4.2, Training, awareness and competence, only addresses internal stakeholders; nowhere in the specification are there provisions for external stakeholder awareness.

Second, the ISO 14001 specification standard requires compliance with laws and regulations. This introduces variation in baseline performance at local, state, and country levels. It would also affect the level of stakeholder interest in environmental performance. That is, the less regulated the activity, the greater the chance nonregulatory stakeholders may intervene in the process. In theory, one can argue that the ISO 14001 standard adjusts for these differences through the process of defining environmental aspects. That is, whether environmental laws are comprehensive or not, the requirement that all environmental aspects be addressed would level the differences. If this is the desired outcome, the system for identifying environmental aspects and associative impacts is a *critical activity* in the process.

Despite these significant differences in information flow for the two standards, there is value in integrating quality and environmental management. In the quality management system, environmental aspects are more likely to be identified when processes are changed to meet customer specifications. The quality management standard requires the establishment of management systems throughout the product cycle. It is through management of these systems that the changes in the life cycle of the product or service that impact the environment can be identified.

4.4 Implementation and Operation

Three elements defined in both the ISO 9001 and ISO 14001 standards are essential to implement and support improvement in management systems: assignment of responsibility, authority, and resources (Table 14–5). Both standards also require that systems performance be periodically reported to top management. This requirement is repeated in several sections of both standards, suggesting that the information flow to top management is essential to the implementation and improvement of both QMS and EMS systems.

It is conceivable that for most facilities assignees could assume responsibility for both QMS and EMS, resulting in potential efficiencies in human resourcing. For those organizations seeking to fully integrate environmental responsibility into the business/operational functions, this multitasking is critical. Centralizing authority and responsibility ensures that as process changes are made that affect the environment, procedures are triggered that identify the associative risk, and risk reduction designs are completed and resources provided.

Both standards require that all employees associated with the standards receive training and demonstrate competence in carrying out systems responsibilities. The training function can be integrated if appropriate training expertise is provided to meet the needs of both systems.

Identification of environmental training and target individuals will need to be more closely monitored because there is a broader scope of inputs from a variety of stakeholders. Once the operational process is established, change to the process is facilitated by the customer. These process changes can result in a complex matrix of environmental changes necessary to meet a variety of stakeholder needs (e.g., air and water emissions, solid waste disposal, employee exposure, or operational hazards). Therefore significant and complex changes in training must be addressed.

For example, suppose a customer wants to change a dispersion solvent of an intermediate product to meet its customer needs. The operational process review would look at the compatibility of the present process equipment and design with the new solvent and would make the appropriate changes. These would include modifications to ensure safe practices and employee protection. Except for the initial customer request for change, all of these efforts are initiated internally and are driven by organizational business objectives.

The environmental aspects are more complex, driven not only by organizational objectives but also by the needs of a multitude of stakeholders. Also, environmental initiatives do not always enjoy the pure motivation provided by organizational business objectives. Under the previous example, the new solvent needs to be managed throughout the production and distribution phases. Air and water emission, containment procedures, emergency response, and waste management issues need to be addressed in terms of risk levels, procedures for reducing risk, and establishing a dialogue on residual risk with stakeholders. Training facilitators will need to identify a variety of training modules to ensure that all of these environmental variables are appropriately addressed.

ISO 9001 has no specific language on communications although it is implied that continual communication between customer and supplier is critical to the QMS process. Communication with stakeholders is specifically identified in the ISO 14001 EMS. It has been stressed throughout this analysis that two-way communication between an organization and its stakeholders is important if systems are to continually improve.

The ISO 14001 standard requires that systems be in place for receiving information from stakeholders, but systems for information flow to external stakeholders is optional. This potential imbalance in flow of information represents a weakness in the EMS standard, which will minimize the rate of improvement in the environmental systems and therefore the rate of improvement in environmental quality. A single QMS/EMS coordinator can manage all communications systems, provided they are trained to manage both the output and input of customers and environmental stakeholders.

Documentation requirements and control systems are prominent throughout both standards and need to be woven throughout both processes. Documentation is necessary to identify change and track progress. Obviously, it is critical to the registration process, for without it the client could not demonstrate conformance with either standard. Integrated management of records is not only possible but preferred because systems reviewers need to understand the sequencing of process change, the resulting environmental aspects, and the way in which those aspects are managed.

Under ISO 9001, operational control seeks to identify and plan production and, where applicable, processes that directly affect quality. The EMS standard seeks to identify environmental aspects of the operation that affect the environment. Both elements are open-ended. The questions to ask are: What affects quality and which

TABLE 14-5

Implementation and Operation

ISO 14001 Subparagraph	Description	ISO 9001 Equivalent
4.4.1	**Structure and responsibility.** Assign, document, and communicate responsibility and authority to ensure that management systems are implemented and systems performance is reported to top management. Provide resources to meet these requirements.	4.1.2.1 Responsibility and authority 4.1.2.2 Resources 4.1.2.3 Management representative 4.1.2.4 Management review There are no substantive differences between the two standards.
4.4.2	**Training, awareness, and competence.** All employees associated with environmental systems need to understand how their work impacts the environment and the consequence if they do not follow procedures. Employees need to receive training in the skills necessary to carry out their work.	4.18 Training There are no substantive differences between the two standards.
4.4.3	**Communication.** Establish procedures for communicating environmental information to employees and procedures for receiving input from external parties. Consider implementation of a process for providing information to external parties.	No equivalent language.
4.4.4	**Environmental management systems documentation.** Establish documentation system to describe systems and their interaction.	4.2.1 without first sentence.
4.4.5	**Document control.** Ensure documents are available, current, comprehensive, and controlled. Documents held for legal purposes should be so marked.	4.5 Document and data control. The three subparagraphs closely parallel the 14001 requirements.
4.4.6	**Operational control.** Requires the implementation of procedures to manage and control environmental aspects of activities. Also provides for communicating relevant procedures to suppliers and customers.	Covered under 4.9, Process control, but also to some extent under 4.7, 4.8 and 4.10. Generally, quality systems controls are broader in scope and more readily expanded to cover suppliers and customers.
4.4.7	**Emergency preparedness and response.** Provides systems and procedures for preventing environmental impacts and responding to releases.	No equivalent.

aspects impact the environment? In the QMS process, the direct communications link with the customer ensures that any problems will be corrected. If a product or service does not meet customer expectations, the ISO 9001 system provides direct and timely action by the supplier.

The EMS does not enjoy this level of assurance. Failure by the organization to identify an environmental aspect and its significance in terms of impact on the environment could not be known by environmental stakeholders unless the policy is extended beyond that required by the EMS standard. This is of special concern where organizations fail to establish two-way communications with stakeholders. Complete integration of these systems may not be possible because the stakeholders, their sensitivities, and knowledge bases are vastly different. Also, identification of environmental aspects and their significance will require ongoing monitoring by individuals with environmental expertise. However, management of processes and procedures to control environmental impacts to acceptable risk levels can be integrated into the QMS management process.

Emergency preparedness has no equivalent in the ISO 9000 system. Under this system, the potential for inadvertent releases needs to be identified and procedures put in place to minimize or eliminate impacts on the environment. This is a purely environmental issue requiring development of emergency procedures by environmental and safety experts, and requiring highly trained specialists to respond to emergencies.

4.5 Checking and Corrective Action

Monitoring and measurement are essential elements of both systems. Data generated through these systems provide the organization with benchmarks on meeting specifications and objectives. Design and implementation of the monitoring and measurement systems and procedures will require specialists. Once in place, management of the systems and procedures can be fully integrated.

Systems for checking and corrective action can also be fully integrated. In terms of pacing corrective action, the expectation is that corrective action of nonconformance with the quality standard, or deviation from specifications or nonconformance with environmental regulations or standards, should be immediate. Response to nonregulatory issues may result in longer-term solutions and require input from external stakeholders to determine pacing.

This is an important distinction. As mentioned earlier, the EMS standard does not require proactive sharing of environmental information with stakeholders. Therefore, decisions on corrective action for nonregulatory issues are left to internal management. This will pose a difficult problem for registration auditors. They will look for documented corrective action schedules, but will be compelled to judge the reasonableness of the action and the pacing. Some interested parties argue that these judgments are beyond the scope of the systems auditors. In evaluating this position, consider that unreasonable corrections to a QMS will be detected and reported by the customer. No such guarantee is present in the EMS process.

Records Management

Records management systems must be developed independently to meet a variety of internal and external stakeholder needs. Records management under the EMS standard must take into account the issue of liability and compliance with environmental regulations. This is probably of greater concern in the United States than in any other country. Recent initiatives such as privilege legislation in many states and the new EPA audit policy should enable organizations to establish more liberal recordkeeping programs. There is no apparent restriction on the quality of records in terms of what records are kept or how long they are maintained.

Audit Systems

Audit systems may be organizationally integrated but will need to include specialists qualified in each area. As discussed throughout this analysis, the evaluation of performance in the environmental area is sensitive not only to specialty knowledge of a technical nature but also to an understanding of the dynamics of the relationship of internal and external stakeholder needs.

In terms of qualifications of registration auditors, this is clearly an area that requires a high level of environmental expertise. Both standards will require auditors trained in systems auditing. EMS auditors will also need experience and background in evaluating a system's ability to identify all environmental aspects, significant impacts, and risk levels of processes, and, as noted, the reasonableness of corrective action programs.

4.6 Management Review

This element in ISO 14001 closely parallels that in ISO 9001. The objective is to periodically review management systems to continually ensure that they are appropriate in terms of suitability, adequacy, and effectiveness for the operation, and that they meet stakeholder needs. The quality and environmental management of this element can be fully integrated. That is, the review of both would be the responsibility of the same manager(s). The input for management review of environmental systems, however, may require more careful study and review by specialists.

Quality systems should be self-adjusting. Customers provide input to the supplier, who should respond by adjusting the system to conform to customer specifications. Reports to management then should primarily consist of shifts in the systems to accommodate changing customer specifications. The need for shifts in environmental systems are more complex and not only depend on input from a variety of stakeholders but also are subject to a matrix of management decisions that take into account risk analysis, cost, and pacing of implementation. One would also expect that internal and/or external specialist input to the analysis to management would be necessary for management to make changes in systems.

TABLE 14-6

Checking and Corrective Action

ISO 14001 Sub-clause	Description	ISO 9001
4.5.1	**Monitoring and measurement.** Requires monitoring and measurement of key characteristics of its operation that have a significant impact on the environment for the purpose of tracking performance, operational controls, and conformance with the organization's targets and objectives.	Equivalent requirements identified under 4.11, control of inspection, measuring, and test equipment.
4.5.2	**Nonconformance and corrective and preventive action.** Requires procedures, defined responsibility, and authority for managing nonconformance in terms of identification, mitigation, and correction of nonconformance.	Equivalent language under 4.14.
4.5.3	**Records.** Requires procedures for identification, maintenance, and control of environmental records appropriate to demonstrate conformance with this standard.	Equivalent language under 4.16.
4.5.4	**Environmental management system audit.** The organization needs to establish a program and procedures for periodic EMS audits to measure conformance with this standard and report results to management. Management should use the results of these audits to address the need to change policy, objectives, and elements of the EMS.	Equivalent language under 4.17.

TABLE 14-7

Management Review

ISO 14001 Clause	Description	ISO 9001
4.6	**Management Review.** Management shall periodically review the EMS to determine its suitability, adequacy, and effectiveness in order to address the need for changes to policy, objectives, and elements of the EMS.	Equivalent language under 4.1.3.

EXTENDED ANALYSIS OF ISO 9001 ELEMENTS FOR EMS VALUE

Following is an analysis of nine ISO 9001 paragraphs that do not appear necessary to implement ISO 14001 for registration purposes, but do provide opportunities to enhance the EMS or in some cases be considered by registrars as logical and necessary extensions of the EMS specifications.

4.3	Contract review.
4.4	Design control.
4.6	Purchasing.
4.7	Control of customer-supplied product.
4.8	Product identification and traceability.
4.13	Control of nonconforming product.
4.15	Handling, storage, packaging, preservation, and delivery.
4.19	Servicing.
4.20	Statistical techniques.

4.3 Contract Review

There are a number of programs undertaken by organizations that can be interpreted as EMS contract-like. These include all programs to which a company subscribes and commits to under its policy. Such programs as Responsible Care®, CERES Principles, ICC Charter on Sustainable Development, and the EPA Environmental Leadership program define contractual-type parameters that an organization needs to achieve to be recognized as a subscriber. Programs such as community advisory panels and environmental conservation programs will also be viewed by registration auditors as contracts with stakeholders and will be evaluated as to the extent to which the organization is resourced and committed to meet the terms of the contract.

4.4 Design Control

The purpose of this ISO 9001 paragraph is to develop and maintain procedures to ensure the design of the product meets specific customer requirements. While not explicitly included in the EMS standard, this process offers an opportunity to the organization to merge product design with environmental responsibility. It offers the first opportunity to design for the environment so that raw materials used, the production process, and the final product have a minimal impact on the environment.

4.6 Purchasing

Under ISO 9001, the purchasing function is critical to supplier control of purchased product quality. This function can also be used as a first-line system for monitoring receipt of materials that impact the environment. As new materials are imported into the quality process through the purchasing system to meet changing specifications, the purchasing system can identify the need for control systems to minimize the impact of new materials on the environment.

4.7 Control of Customer-Supplied Product

This clause is designed to ensure that subsuppliers to an ISO 9001 supplier control the quality of their product. This particular element in the ISO 9001 standard drives registrations. Registered organizations are more likely to provide quality product consistently if their suppliers are operating under the same control system. While most organizations require suppliers to be environmentally responsible, requiring ISO 14001 registrations or declarations of conformance is not likely to be a prerequisite for doing business.

Demand for product performance down the line is also likely to slow the pace of environmental improvement. Market-driven mechanisms for conformance with the EMS standard will not develop quickly, especially in the United States. State and local government policy or legislative initiatives would significantly affect registrations.

4.8 Product Identification and Traceability

The ISO 9001 standard suggest that suppliers track the product at least to the primary customer. The ISO 14001 standard suggests that the product environmental impact be tracked throughout its life cycle. Environmental responsibility throughout a life cycle has yet to be defined. At a minimum, responsibility appears to be in the hands of the producer until the product is altered. Future interpretations may expand this responsibility.

4.13 Control of Nonconforming Product

This clause requires procedures for distribution control of a nonconforming product. To the extent that the nonconforming product includes variations that represent new environmental impacts, the QMS procedures should be applied to this concern to ensure that these impacts are communicated and that steps are taken to minimize the impact in all distribution processes, including disposal, rework, or secondary-market distributions.

4.15 Handling, Storage, Packaging, Preservation, and Delivery

This paragraph provides procedures to ensure that the integrity of a product meeting customer specifications is not compromised during handling, storage, packaging, preservation, and delivery. The EMS standard is questionably mute on the potential for environmental impact of failures during these activities. This may be because the authors deferred this area to other ISO 14000 standards under development, such as labeling or life-cycle assessment or proposed standards addressing health and safety. However, until these standards are available, organizations should implement systems to monitor potential environmental impacts that could occur during handling, storage, packaging, preservation, and delivery.

4.19 Servicing

The ISO 9001 standard component "Servicing" applies to suppliers who contractually agree to provide specified services. Those suppliers who provide contractual services must implement procedures to meet contractual obligations. The concept provides environmental opportunities for large organizations to provide reasonably low-cost or free environmental services associated with the product provided by smaller subcontractors. With continual movement toward outsourcing, the distribution of environmental responsibility will come under stakeholder scrutiny.

4.20 Statistical Techniques

The ISO 9001 standard recommends the use of statistical process control (SPC) techniques by suppliers to verify process capability and product conformity to specifications. Statistical techniques are not specifically addressed in the ISO 14001 standard, but it should be assumed that application of these techniques is a necessary tool for measuring performance. It is likely that SPC will be addressed in the ISO 14031 environmental performance evaluation standard.

CONFORMITY ASSESSMENT

All potential stakeholders in the ISO 14001 process need assurance that organizations committing to conformance with ISO 14001 specifications can demonstrate conformance through third-party verification and the absence of environment incidences. Development of the ISO 14012 auditing guidelines on EMS auditor qualifications paralleled development of the ISO 14001 EMS specification standard and the ISO 14004 EMS guidance standard. TC 207 leadership monitored the development of drafts to further ensure that the EMS specification, guidance document, and audit guidelines were synergistic. The ISO 14012 guidelines for auditor qualification can be assumed as intended to certify auditors for EMS registration purposes.

ISO 10011 standards on auditor qualifications for auditing ISO 9000 registrations are more general than those of ISO 14010-12. The QMS auditor guidelines more closely parallel general auditing qualifications of most auditing disciplines. The ISO 14012 guidelines, on the other hand, recommend specific experience in the following areas:

- Environmental science and technology.
- Technical and environmental aspects of facility operations.
- Relevant requirements of environmental laws, regulations, and related documents.
- Environmental management systems and standards.
- Audit procedures, processes, and techniques.

All other qualifications in 14012 are either generic to other audit disciplines (e.g., HS&E, financial, or QMS) or can be acquired within a reasonable period of time.

Varying points of view persist regarding the necessary skills for successfully auditing an EMS. Some commentators stress that ISO 14001 is a management standard and thus requires little or no environmental expertise. Some QMS auditors even say that environmental expertise encumbers system evaluation because that expertise will draw the auditor into a compliance audit mode rather than focusing on the management system.

Others counter that an effective EMS audit cannot be performed by auditors who lack an environmental background. According to this view, there are some clauses in ISO 14001, such as identifying environmental aspects and significant impacts, that require a person with environmental expertise. So the obvious response to the question of "What additional qualifications will a quality management systems auditor need to effectively audit environmental management systems?" is that they will need to acquire at a minimum those skills identified in the ISO 14012 guidelines that exceed those in ISO 11011.

However, the extent to which these skills are necessary to audit a facility for registration will depend on how the standard is interpreted. If, as in the QMS registration requirements, the systems need only be in place and conform with the ISO 14001 requirements, then most auditors who have general skills such as interviewing and document review should qualify, especially if supported by the type of training QMS auditors are required to take. Under these conditions, most auditors—financial, environmental, or QMS—will qualify.

But many ISO 14001 stakeholders believe that to qualify for registration, facilities will be required to have more than just systems in place to meet the basic tenants of the standard. For example, one higher level of conformity to the standard would require a determination regarding whether the EMS is designed to effectively manage environmental aspects appropriate to the size and activities of the operation.

A second level of analysis would address the impact of these aspects on the environment and the ability of the systems to classify their significance. Both of these investigative extensions would require significant environmental training and experience. In addition, ISO 14001 requires a system component that ensures legal compliance. Environmental regulations in the United States (exceeding 20,000 pages) are extensive and complex. How much regulatory experience, knowledge, and training does an auditor need to evaluate a system to ensure that the system is capable of sustaining compliance with laws and regulations? Many countries have already indicated they will ratchet up the baseline qualifications identified in ISO 14012, including advanced educational degrees.

In conclusion, the additional qualifications needed by QMS auditors or other nonenvironmental auditors who do not have environmental experience and training will depend on what the certification bodies decide are necessary qualifications. Their decisions will be influenced by a broad spectrum of stakeholders.

Auditor Accreditation

Who is most likely qualified to audit an EMS for registration without the need for extensive training? The fact is that many companies have implemented EMSs over the last five years. These systems are audited by internal environmental auditors who are trained in auditor skills and who have the knowledge and instincts to not only verify that the system is in place but to provide insights into that system's operability.

QMS auditors are also trained in auditor skills and have demonstrated an ability to focus on the presence of systems that ensure customer satisfaction by preventing nonconformity. The question of which type of auditing skills or combination is best for ISO 14001 audits will depend on what the stakeholders want from the process. What level of comfort will government agencies have in knowing simply that systems are in place? Will they need to know that a system has been tested to determine its ability to identify environmental aspects or significant impacts or appropriate training? Will industry want to coordinate QMS and EMS audits, or is there more value and efficiency in coordinating EMS with HS&E compliance audits? These questions are best answered by the stakeholders. In making a reasonable guess regarding stakeholder expectations, the current community of environmental auditors is best prepared to meet these expectations.

CONCLUSION

There is a great deal of synergy between ISO 9001 and ISO 14001 in terms of multitask management of fully implemented QMS and EMS standards. Integrated systems provide opportunities for resource efficiencies in terms of personnel and cost. But more importantly, QMS management can drive improvements in environmental performance. Both implementation and support of systems will require a high degree of expertise. While not a required element in the EMS standard, systems that encourage sharing of information with external stakeholders will help drive continual improvement.

The extent to which EMS auditors judge reasonableness of systems implementation and performance needs to be addressed. Unlike QMS, where performance is constantly driven by the customer, the EMS's performance measurement is internal and subjective unless third-party auditors are provided some latitude in evaluating the reasonableness of systems performance and provided with training in this area. The quality of registration audits will suffer if a high level of environmental skills is not included on the EMS audit team. Skilled environmental auditors, in turn, will need to have training in auditing systems.

BIOGRAPHY

Ron Black

Ron Black is Director of Health, Safety and Environmental Systems at the B.F. Goodrich Company. Previously he was Director of the International Audit Department at the Rohm and Haas Company. Ron is currently chairman of the ISO TC207 work group on Audit Procedures. He also chaired the US TAG work group on audits and was a member of the Chairman's Advisory Group. He is the recent past president of the Environmental Audit Round Table, a board member and Director of the Compliance Programs Committee. Mr. Black has a B.S. degree in analytical chemistry from LaSalle University and a master's degree from Temple University.

CHAPTER 15

Integrating the ISO 14001 Environmental Management System with the Chemical Manufacturers Association's Responsible Care®

John (Jack) McVaugh

INTRODUCTION

There is a tendency among environmental professionals working in industry to view every new environmental initiative, voluntary or mandated, as adding another onerous burden. This tendency is only natural since virtually every program, law, regulation, management program, and so on, over the last 25 years has presented another such burden.

As chemical companies rush to implement an EMS modeled on the ISO 14001 standard, it is important to consider every opportunity to embrace and harmonize existing requirements, programs, and systems with their EMS. This will facilitate integration of environmental management into the strategic business process—an activity many companies would like to accomplish but few have successfully achieved.

Integrating management systems is of prime importance since the benefits can be tangible and immediate. One chemical plant environmental manager reported seeing opportunity in the fact that nine separate corporate groups perform audits at his facility. Another reported reductions in corporate auditing worker hours from 6,000 per year to 2,000 per year by combining various audits.

The ISO 14001 EMS standard presents many opportunities for integration with existing activities because it consists of a basic management system applied to the environmental aspects of the organization's business. Since several regulations require at least some elements of a management system (EPA's Resource Conservation and Recovery Act, Pollution Prevention Act, and stormwater regulations, for instance, as well as OSHA's Process Safety Management), greater operating efficiencies can be realized by managing them under one system.

The chemical industry's initiative, Responsible Care®, is intended to be a complete management system focusing on the health, safety and environmental aspects of the chemical product life cycle, from design and production through distribution and use. (See Box 15–1.) The course of its development also illustrates one of the principles of total quality management: it is essential to find out what your customers (internal and external) expect and to strive to meet those expectations.

HISTORY OF RESPONSIBLE CARE

In early 1985 the chemical industry reeled from the news that a catastrophic release of chemicals had killed and injured thousands of people in Bhopal, India. In response to anxious questions from U.S. communities about the possibility of such an accident closer to home, the Chemical Manufacturers Association (CMA) launched the Community Awareness and Emergency Response (CAER) Program. This voluntary initiative called for chemical facilities to facilitate outreach to their respective communities and provide leadership in the development and/or improvement of local emergency plans.

But, perhaps due to the spread of total quality thinking among chemical companies in the mid-1980s, CMA management went to one of their "customers," the public, to see how well the CAER Program met their expectations. The response was that the CAER Program was good, as far as it went, but did not address all of the public's concerns about the chemical industry.

The public was concerned not only with emergency planning, but also with the wastes produced, the safety of chemical transportation and warehousing in their communities, the safety of manufacturing processes and worker health, and the safety of the products they purchased. When these concerns were tallied, a program developed by the Canadian Chemical Producers Association, called Responsible Care, appeared to meet public and employee expectations, and was adopted by CMA.

Recognition and response to community concerns about chemicals and chemical operations is listed first among the Guiding Principles of Responsible Care, and public input is a built-in feature throughout the process. Moreover, each of the six Codes of Management Practices addresses one area of public and employee concern about the chemical business and the life cycle of chemical products.

THE STRUCTURE OF AN ISO 14001 ENVIRONMENTAL MANAGEMENT SYSTEM

The elements of ISO 14001 are arranged to describe a five-step iterative process similar to the process used for managing a business:

1. Management establishes an environmental policy and makes commitments to compliance, to continuous improvement of the system, and to the prevention of pollution.

2. The organization develops a plan to carry out the environmental policy.

3. The organization sets up a structure and an operational system to implement the plan.

B O X   15–1

RESPONSIBLE CARE

While TC 207 works to develop comprehensive guidelines for environmental management systems, perhaps the most complete set of guidelines already in place is the product of the Chemical Manufacturers Association (CMA). The CMA's program is called Responsible Care, and participation by individual businesses is an obligation of membership in the CMA.

Responsible Care, which was adopted by the CMA Board of Directors in 1988, was launched as a response to public concerns that the chemical industry was a potential threat to health and safety. Believing that self-imposed industry-driven guidelines would be preferable to externally imposed ones, the chemical industry's leaders began a search in the early 1980s for a program that would at once make the industry safer, address public fears, and not impinge too much on the industry's ability to turn a profit.

CMA's Responsible Care program establishes the following goals:

- Improved chemical process.
- Enhanced practices and procedures.
- Reduction of every kind of waste, accident, incident, and emission.
- Reliable communication and dialogue.
- Heightened public involvement and input.

Responsible Care is built around six Codes of Management Practices and 10 Guiding Principles. Following the six codes will automatically result in the guiding principles being followed as well. These six codes are the following:

1. Product Stewardship.
2. Community Awareness and Emergency Response.
3. Process Safety.
4. Employee Health and Safety.
5. Pollution Prevention.
6. Distribution.

Responsible Care's 10 Guiding Principles are as follows:

1. To recognize and respond to community concerns about chemicals and company operations.
2. To develop and produce chemicals that can be manufactured, transported, used, and disposed of safely.

(Continued)

3. To make health, safety, and environmental considerations a priority in planning for all existing and new products and processes.

4. To report promptly to officials, employees, customers, and the public, information on chemical-related health or environmental hazards and to recommend protective measures.

5. To counsel customers on the safe use, transportation, and disposal of chemicals.

6. To operate plants and facilities in a manner that protects the environment and the health and safety of employees and the public.

7. To extend knowledge by conducting or supporting research on the health, safety, and environmental effects of products, processes, and waste materials.

8. To work with others to resolve problems created by past handling and disposal of hazardous substances.

9. To participate with government and others in creating responsible laws, regulations, and standards to safeguard the community, workplace, and environment.

10. To promote the principles and practices of Responsible Care by sharing experiences and offering assistance to others who produce, handle, use, transport, or dispose of chemicals.

One of Responsible Care's fundamental themes is that the implementation of the program will never be complete at any site. It is designed to be approached as an ongoing way of managing a chemical company's environmental impact. Four other themes are consistently stressed in each of the six codes that make up Responsible Care:

Accountability. The program both recognizes the need for and broadens the definition of accountability. Traditionally, product accountability lasted only until the point of sale. In the Responsible Care program, members are expected to take responsibility for their product's performance during and after its use, including its performance as a recyclable and its suitability for disposal.

Dialogue. The program helps businesses realize that the chemical industry does not function in a vacuum. It is interrelated with suppliers of raw materials, end users, regulators, lawmakers, shareholders, and employees. The importance of effective communication and mutually beneficial dialogue is paramount.

(Continued)

B O X   15–1 *(Concluded)*

> **Teamwork.** Just as Responsible Care puts an emphasis on working closely with those outside the chemical industry, it also stresses the need for cooperation within it.
>
> **Continuous Improvement.** Responsible Care is designed to be an ongoing commitment for those who undertake it. It is a way of doing business, not an end result.
>
> In addition to the codes, principles, and themes of Responsible Care, the program includes several adjunct panels, processes, and groups responsible for keeping Responsible Care current and continuously improving. These include the following:
>
> - A Public Advisory Panel designed to critique the development and implementation of the program and to provide public feedback.
> - Executive Leadership Groups that provide a forum where senior management can exchange information.
> - A mutual assistance strategy designed to identify and address the mutual assistance needs of member companies.
> - A self-evaluation process designed to determine how well member companies are applying the codes and to evaluate the performance of the industry as a whole.
>
> Another important aspect of the Responsible Care program is that it incorporates the management aspects of quality, environmental protection, and health and safety into one overall management system.

4. It tracks performance to spot deviations from the plan.
5. Management periodically reviews the entire system to assure its continuing adequacy and improvement; the plan is revised, and the next iteration begins.

This arrangement of elements is often referred to as a total quality management (TQM) approach because TQM requires you to "plan, implement, track, improve."

COMPARING ISO 14001 AND RESPONSIBLE CARE

Both Responsible Care and ISO 14001 heavily emphasize the concept of continuous improvement. The Chemical Manufacturers Association (CMA) declares continuous improvement in health, safety, and environmental performance throughout the chemical industry to be the overriding goal of Responsible Care. ISO 14001, however, defines *continual improvement* as the "process of enhancing the environmental management system to achieve improvements in overall environmental performance."

Each of the six Responsible Care Codes of Management Practices describes a process for managing the health, safety, and environmental aspects of a component of the chemical business, from manufacture through distribution and safe use. This chapter uses the Pollution Prevention Code for illustration purposes since it most closely parallels ISO 14001 and is the code with which environmental professionals are most familiar. There are 14 management practices listed in this code, which are described as required elements of a pollution prevention program. The following is a list of some of these practices and then a description of the corresponding requirements in ISO 14001.

1. *A clear commitment by senior management through policy, communications, and resources to ongoing reductions at each of the company's facilities, in releases to the air, water, and land and in the generation of wastes.* ISO 14001, Clause 4.2, Environmental policy, requires top management to commit to prevention of pollution as well as to compliance and continuous improvement. The policy must be communicated and available to the public. ISO 14001, Clause 4.4.1, Structure and responsibility, requires top management to provide adequate resources, including technological, work force, and specialized skills, to operate the EMS and meet objectives and targets.

3. *Evaluation, sufficient to assist in establishing reduction priorities, of the potential impact of releases on the environment and the health and safety of employees and the public.* Implicit in ISO 14001, Clause 4.3, Planning, is that environmental management priorities will be set using some kind of ranking process, based on the severity of actual or potential adverse environmental impacts caused by the business.

5. *Establishment of priorities, goals, and plans for waste and release reduction, taking into account both community concerns and the potential health, safety, and environmental impacts as determined under Practices 3 and 4.* The ISO 14001 planning process includes provisions for determining the following:

- Legal and regulatory compliance and other requirements.
- The environmental aspects of the business and their impacts on the environment.
- Organizational objectives and targets that may go beyond regulatory compliance.
- Action plans to meet these goals.

Moreover, ISO 14001, in Clause 4.3.3, Objectives and targets, calls for these goals to be set after taking into account the views of "interested parties," which may include employees and members of the public.

6. *Ongoing reduction of wastes and releases, giving preference first to source reduction, second to recycle/reuse, and third to treatment.* By its iterative nature and commitment to pollution prevention and continuous improvement, the ISO 14001 EMS specification standard is capable of promoting the ongoing reduction of wastes and releases. And since top management is required to provide adequate resources to accomplish its stated objectives and targets, these goals will probably be met in the most technologically and financially effective manner, which will tend to favor the hierarchy of actions stated in management practice number 6. ISO 14001 also places emphasis on preventive measures instead of merely reacting to problems after they occur.

7. *Measurement of progress at each facility in reducing the generation of wastes and in reducing releases to the air, water, and land, by updating the quantitative inventory at least annually.* Measurement of progress in meeting policy commitments, as well as objectives and targets, is essential information for the management review process (ISO 14001 Clause 4.6, Management review). Such information will be used by top management to determine which aspects of the EMS are working and which aspects need adjustment to be more effective. It will also be used to set new objectives and targets during the next EMS cycle. On a related subject, the developing ISO 14031 standard for environmental performance evaluation (EPE) provides guidance on measuring performance and setting up an EPE system.

8. *Ongoing dialogue with employees and members of the public regarding waste and release information, progress in achieving reductions, and future plans.* Because the ISO 14001 EMS is a cyclical process, new objectives and targets may be set each time management reviews the system. And since the views of interested parties must be taken into account each time objectives and targets are set, this will have the effect of creating an ongoing dialogue with employees, members of the public, and others.

9. *Inclusion of waste and release prevention objectives in research and in design of new or modified facilities, processes, and products.* ISO 14001 Clause 4.3.4, Environmental management programs, requires that environmental management principles be applied on projects relating "to new developments and new or modified activities, products or services."

11. *Periodic evaluation of waste management practices associated with operations and equipment at each member company facility, taking into account community concerns and health, safety, and environmental impacts and implementation of ongoing improvements.* Once again, this describes several provisions found under ISO 14001 Clause 4.6, Management review.

13. *Implementation of engineering and operating controls at each member company facility to improve prevention of and early detection of releases that may contaminate groundwater.* While this management practice focuses on groundwater contamination, similar provisions, but with a more general focus, are found in ISO 14001, Clause 4.4.6, Operational control. In the standard, operations and activities associated with all of the identified significant environmental aspects shall be planned to ensure that they are carried out under specified conditions.

SUMMARY

There are strong similarities in both structure and purpose between the ISO 14001 EMS standard and the Responsible Care Pollution Prevention Code. Both require senior management commitment; a planning process, including prioritization and goal setting; implementation and continuous improvement; measurement of progress; periodic evaluation of practices; and control of critical operations. And while both require input from interested parties, Responsible Care puts a great deal more emphasis on this aspect.

This author also believes that ISO 14001 will help companies accomplish some of the Responsible Care management practices that have presented difficulties or that have prevented the program from achieving its full potential. Responsible Care has not achieved the desired credibility with the public, according to some environmental groups, because there has never been an objective verification mechanism put in place to prove that companies were truly following all the management practices. Although a company may self-declare conformance with the ISO 14001 standard, independent, third-party certification of conformance is also an option, and this may provide stakeholders with the verification they seek.

Finally, management practice number 12, under the Pollution Prevention Code, requires "implementation of a process for selecting, retaining, and reviewing contractors and toll manufacturers, taking into account sound waste management practices that protect the environment and the health and safety of employees and the public." This has often meant costly and time-consuming audits of the operations of suppliers, contractors, and toll processors. Many companies will opt to implement this practice more simply and efficiently by making ISO 14001 registration a procurement contract requirement.

The ISO 14000 series of environmental management standards promises to be the most significant development in the history of environmental management. It is important to be sure that all concerned view their adoption as a "win–win" situation, a useful tool rather than another onerous burden. By breaking down ISO 14001, as well as existing regulatory and industry initiatives, into basic management system elements and looking for points of commonality among these elements, organizations can maximize their operating efficiency.

BIOGRAPHY

John (Jack) McVaugh, PE, REM

Jack McVaugh is a chemical engineer with a master's degree in environmental engineering. His early career involved industrial wastewater treatment process design, start-up, and troubleshooting, as well as regulatory compliance management. As manager, environmental affairs for Akzo Chemicals Inc., he headed a group that developed a highly successful waste elimination program, carried on a vigorous environmental auditing activity, managed environmental control projects in the United States, Canada, and Brazil, and obtained the first RCRA Part B Incinerator Permit in EPA Region V. Also at Akzo, he held several other management positions, including purchasing, logistics, quality assurance, customer service, commercial development, and business management. In 1994, Mr. McVaugh founded Environmental Technology & Management. Its mission is to use industrial experience in environmental, quality, and operations management to help companies gain control of their environmental affairs. He is also pleased to be involved with the development of the ISO 14000 series of international environmental management standards through membership on the U.S. Technical Advisory Group to ISO Technical Committee 207.

CHAPTER 16

Overview of the Eco-Management and Audit Scheme

Tom Tibor and Ira Feldman

INTRODUCTION

As mentioned earlier in this book, ISO 14000 has been developed in the context of other EMS initiatives, such as the United Kingdom's BS 7750 EMS standard and the European Union's Eco-Management and Audit scheme regulation (EMAS). Many companies worldwide have registered facilities to the U.K.'s BS 7750 EMS standard, and companies with EU sites are developing EMS and auditing programs that will fulfill the requirements of the EMAS regulation. How are ISO 14001, BS 7750, and EMAS similar? How do they differ? How do they fit together? A detailed discussion of every EMS-related initiative goes beyond the scope of this book. This chapter, however, briefly describes the Eco-Management and Audit Scheme regulation. The next chapter offers an analysis and comparison of EMAS and ISO 14001.

The European Union and Environmental Protection

A major factor in the development of EMAS has been the formation of the European Union (EU) and the nature of the European Union's approach to environmental regulation. (See Box 16–1.)

A key goal of the EU's 1992 initiative was to expand trade in the European Union and to reduce trade barriers among the member states. At the same time, as with other regions of the world, the EU faces environmental challenges. Environmental protection and enforcement in the European Union varies by member state. In response to environmental concerns, the EU has been looking for communitywide solutions to complement national legislation. (The enforcement of environmental legislation, whether it is developed at the EU level or at the national level, is enforced at the national level.)

BOX 16–1

DEVELOPMENT OF THE EUROPEAN UNION

The full members of the European Union are Austria, Belgium, Denmark, Finland, France, Germany, Greece, Ireland, Italy, Luxembourg, Netherlands, Portugal, Spain, Sweden, and the United Kingdom. The European Union (EU) originated with the 1957 Treaty of Rome, which was established to abolish tariffs and quotas among its six member states and to stimulate economic growth in Europe. Differing national product certification requirements, however, made selling products in multiple national markets in the European Community a costly and complex process. In addition, Europe feared that competition from the United States and the Pacific Rim would slow European economic growth.

In response, the EU called for a greater push toward a single internal market and for the removal of physical, technical, and fiscal barriers to trade. In 1985, the EC Commission presented a program for establishing a single internal market, and this goal was further expedited by the Single European Act, adopted in February 1986. The goal of this legislation was to abolish barriers to trade among the 12 member states (at the time) and to complete an internal European market by the end of 1992. The single market became effective at midnight on December 31, 1992.

The Single European Act of 1986 also recognized the EU's involvement in environmental matters by adding environmental chapters to the original treaties. By 1993, up to 400 separate items of European environmental legislation had been developed, and more than 200 pieces of legislation had been adopted in the field of environmental protection.

The goal is to develop EU-wide environmental policies that protect the environment but allow for free trade and regional differences. The ultimate aim is to work toward sustainable development. To achieve this goal, the EU is looking beyond the traditional command-and-control approach to environmental regulation. Alternatives include various market-based programs that reward environmentally responsible behavior by industry and bring public attention and pressure to bear on environmental problems. Such approaches can also improve the enforcement of environmental laws and reduce the high cost of environmental regulation and enforcement.

The main obstacle to EU-wide approaches is that the EU legislative system is not strong and cannot do much to enforce environmental protection at the member-state level. It is difficult for the EU to pass detailed legislation and, once adopted, such legislation is difficult to enforce. Thus, the EU is looking for other ways to achieve its environmental goals. The voluntary EMAS scheme is one such method.

THE ECO-MANAGEMENT AND AUDIT SCHEME (EMAS)

The eco-management and audit regulation was first released in December 1990 as a mandatory requirement that was to apply to the most polluting industries in the EU.

BOX 16–2

EU STANDARDS AND REGIONAL STANDARDIZATION ORGANIZATIONS

A key goal of the European Union is to develop EU-wide, harmonized standards to replace differing national standards. EU legislation, such as the EMAS regulation, does not contain such standards but references them instead. The task of developing specific standards is carried out primarily by three European standard-setting organizations. These include the Committee for European Standardization (or Normalization, hence the *N* in CEN), the European Committee for Electrotechnical Standardization (CENELEC), and the European Telecommunications Standards Institute (ETSI).

These organizations develop standards according to priorities set by the European Union and its member states. They also consult with existing national and international standardization organizations. CEN and CENELEC have negotiated agreements with the two international standards organizations, ISO and IEC, to develop new standards.

CEN is comprised of delegates from the national standardization organizations of 18 European countries. CENELEC is CEN's sister organization. While CEN works closely with ISO, CENELEC works with its international counterpart, the International Electrotechnical Committee (IEC). The European Telecommunications Standardization Institute (ETSI) promotes European standards for a unified telecommunications system.

The procedures for the development of CENELEC standards and CEN standards are similar. Published European standards are referred to as EN standards (for European norms). CEN and CENELEC will develop a new standard when:

- A standard does not already exist under ISO or IEC auspices.
- The standard cannot be developed at the international level.
- The standard cannot be developed at the international level within a specific time frame.

All member states are obligated to adopt an EN standard as their national standard by withdrawing the conflicting national standard. If the ISO 14000 standards are adopted by the European Union, they will be adopted as EN standards, just as the ISO 9000 series was adopted as the EN 29000 series by the European Union.

After protests involving the companies and the sites affected and the mandatory nature of the regulation, the regulation was withdrawn and republished in March 1992 as a voluntary scheme. EMAS became official in July 1993 as *"Council regulation (EEC) No. 1836/93 allowing voluntary participation by companies in the industrial sector in a Community eco-management and audit scheme."*[1] The EMAS regulation opened for participation on April 10, 1995. It is a communitywide scheme that allows voluntary participation by industrial companies for the evaluation and improvement of their environmental performance and the provision of relevant information to the public.

Basic Purpose

Adherence to a formal environmental management system and auditing procedure is mandatory under EMAS. EMAS also requires that organizations make independently verifiable public statements regarding their environmental performance. Participation in the program entitles a company to register a site on an EU-authorized list of participating sites and to use an EU-approved statement of participation and graphic to publicize inclusion in the program.

The specific objectives of EMAS are as follows:

- To promote continuous improvements in environmental performance by establishing policies, programs, and management systems.
- To perform systematic, objective, and periodic evaluation of these elements.
- To provide relevant information about these activities to the public.

Voluntary or Mandatory?

Although the program is currently voluntary, EU organizations, as well as non-EU based companies with EU sites, are concerned that EMAS could become mandatory. The EC's Environmental Commission hopes market pressures will act as an inducement. Within five years of the regulation coming into force (1998), the EU will reevaluate participation in the scheme and decide whether to make it compulsory.

As an EC regulation, EMAS is directly applicable within the national laws of the member states. Each EU member state is required to set up a structure to allow for EMAS participation.

Applies to Industrial Firms

Participation in the scheme is site-based and open to companies operating industrial activities, as defined in the EU's NACE classification of industries. (This is similar to the Standard Industrial Classification Code.) In addition to manufacturing industries, the scheme also applies to the electrical, gas, steam, and waste disposal sectors. Retail industries can also get involved in EMAS on a voluntary basis. In addition, the member states can extend the scheme's provisions on an experimental basis to other sectors, such as government agencies.

Reasons to Participate

In addition to the possibility that EMAS may become mandatory, another reason to participate is market pressure. Organizations with European sites may be encouraged to participate for competitive reasons and to achieve recognition in the EU marketplace.

Organizations that choose not to seek ISO 14001 registration for non-European sites may nevertheless register their EU sites to ISO 14001 as part of EMAS participation.

Another reason to participate is the possible role of EMAS participation in public procurement. Several countries are looking at EMS registration to ISO 14001 and/or EMAS as a precondition for receiving contracts and permits.

CEN's Vote to Select Standard to Support EMAS

EMAS is designed as a stand-alone scheme. That is, companies can meet the requirements of EMAS and seek verification of compliance with EMAS without implementing other EMS standards and achieving registration.

Article 12 of the EMAS regulation, *Relationship with national, European and international standards,* however, offers organizations another option. It states that companies that have implemented national, European, or international standards for environmental management systems and audits and are certified to one of these standards would be considered to meet the corresponding requirements of the EMAS regulation. For example, a company registered to ISO 14001 would be considered to be in compliance with corresponding EMS requirements in EMAS.

The EC commission has issued a draft mandate to the Committee for European Standardization (CEN) to produce or adopt existing standards to support EMAS.

CEN is likely to recognize ISO 14001 as meeting most of the EMS requirements of EMAS. Some of the differences will be resolved by a "bridge" document.[2] (See Chapter 17 for a discussion of the proposed bridge document.)

GENERAL REQUIREMENTS OF EMAS

This section is a description of EMAS requirements. Where appropriate, it points out differences between ISO 14001 and EMAS requirements. (The appendix to this chapter includes a more detailed description of EMAS requirements.)

EMAS calls for firms to establish management systems and programs to periodically and systematically audit their environmental performance, to strive for continuous improvement, and to inform the public of their results.

EMAS consists of 21 articles and five annexes. The detailed requirements start with Article 3. The scheme is open to companies that implement the following requirements.

Adopt an Environmental Policy

The company must adopt a company environmental policy that provides for compliance with all regulatory requirements regarding the environment and includes a commitment to achieve "reasonable continuous improvement of environmental performance, with a view to reducing environmental impacts to levels not exceeding those corresponding to economically viable application of best available technology (EVABAT)."

Note that this requirement, unlike ISO 14001, is performance oriented and refers explicitly to EVABAT. The issue of best available technology is mentioned in ISO 14001 but only in the informative annex to ISO 14001.

EMAS prescribes several principles on which the environmental policy must be based, including, among others, assessing the environmental impact of all current activities on the environment, implementing pollution prevention, providing information to the public about the environmental impact of the company's activities, and providing advice to customers about the environmental aspects of the handling, use, and disposal of its products.

EMAS also prescribes a list of issues that the policy, EMS program, and audits must address, including energy management, environmental impact reduction, raw materials management, waste avoidance, product planning, and so on.

Set Environmental Objectives

Like ISO 14001, EMAS requires the company to specify environmental objectives at all relevant levels within the company that are consistent with its policies. The objectives must be set "at the highest appropriate management level, aimed at the continuous improvement of environmental performance . . .". Based on findings from the audit, EMAS requires management to set higher objectives and to revise the environmental program to be able to achieve those objectives. This step is analogous to the management review of ISO 14001.

Conduct an Environmental Review

EMAS calls for an initial environmental review that focuses on the issues addressed by the environmental policy. This sets the stage for the EMS system. Of course, if the organization already has an EMS in place, its environmental review would not be initial but would likely check to make sure the organization addresses the issues described in EMAS.

Introduce an Environmental Program and EMS

In light of the results of the environmental review, the company sets up an environmental program applicable to all activities at the site and aimed at achieving the commitments in the environmental policy. In general, these requirements are similar to those in ISO 14001.

Environmental Effects Register

EMAS requires the company to examine and assess the environmental effects of its activities at the site and to compile a register of significant effects. This register is not required in ISO 14001.

The company must also establish and maintain procedures to record all legislative, regulatory, and other policy requirements pertaining to the environmental aspects of its activities, products, and services.

Set Up an Environmental Auditing Program

EMAS prescribes relatively detailed auditing requirements. It calls for the organization to set up, implement, and revise a systematic and periodic program of environmental audits concerning:

- Whether or not the environmental management activities conform to the environmental program and are implemented effectively.
- How effective the EMS is in fulfilling the company's environmental policy.

It must then carry out, or cause to be carried out, environmental audits at the site. The audits may be conducted by either company auditors or external auditors acting on the company's behalf. The criteria for the auditing are the same issues mentioned above.

EMAS requires that the audit frequency or the audit cycle be completed at intervals of no longer than three years.

ISO 14001's auditing requirement relates specifically to environmental management system auditing. Extensive guidance in performing the auditing is contained in the ISO 14010-12 series of guidance standards.

Prepare an Environmental Statement

EMAS requires that the company prepare an environmental statement "specific to each site audited." This is done when the initial environmental review and subsequent audits or audit cycles are completed. This public environmental statement and its validation are key goals of the entire EMAS effort.

After the first statement is issued, companies must produce simplified annual statements in the intervening years between the audits. There are two exceptions: where the nature and scale of the operations are such that no additional statements are necessary until the next audit, and where there have been few significant changes since the last environmental statement.

Verification and Validation

The company must have its policy, program, management system, review, or audit program examined by an external accredited verifier, who validates the environmental statement(s) to ensure that they meet the requirements of EMAS. The verifier is "any person or organization independent of the company being verified" who is accredited. Regarding verification, the verifier checks whether:

- The environmental policy has been established and whether it meets the requirements of EMAS.

- An EMS is in place at the site, in operation and in compliance with relevant EMAS requirements.
- The environmental review and audit is carried out in accordance with EMAS requirements.
- The data and information in the environmental statement are reliable and the statement adequately covers all the significant and relevant environmental issues. If all of these requirements are met, the statement is validated.

Verifier Does Not Duplicate Company's Internal Procedures

Does the verifier comes in and redo the company's audit? Not as envisioned. The verifier does not duplicate, substitute for, or complement the company's internal assessment procedures. Basically, the verifier is to "investigate in a sound professional manner, the technical validity of the environmental review or audit or other procedures carried out by the company, without unnecessarily duplicating those procedures." The verifier examines documentation before visiting the site. At the site, the verifier interviews personnel and prepares a report to the company management that specifies the following:

- (In general,) cases of noncompliance with the provisions of EMAS.
- (And in particular) technical defects in the environmental review, audit method, environmental management system, or any other relevant process.
- Points of disagreement with the draft environmental statement and details of the amendments or additions that should be made to the environmental statement.

If the environmental policy has not been established, the environmental review or audit is not technically satisfactory, or the environmental program or EMS doesn't meet EMAS requirements, the verifier makes appropriate recommendations to the company's management and will not validate the environmental statement until the problems have been corrected.

If the only problem is that the environmental statement must be revised, the verifier discusses the changes with the company management and validates the statement when the company makes the appropriate additions and/or amendments.

Sites That Are Registered to an EMS Standard

In cases where the site has been registered to an EMS standard, such as ISO 14001, the verifier limits verification to confirming the validity of the EMS certification, checking the environmental policies and programs, reviewing the audit procedures, and examining the environmental statement to ensure that it is complete, fair, and balanced in light of the results from the internal audit and internal monitoring procedures. The verifier examines the conclusions from the internal audit concerning compliance with the regulation's requirements, including the environmental policy and its conformity with the company's objectives and standards.

If the company does not have an EMS in place and wants to participate in EMAS, the verifier will perform a dual role: audit the facility against the requirements of EMAS (as described above) and perform the verification and validation process.

Distribute and Disseminate the Environmental Statement

The company forwards the validated environmental statement to the competent authority of the member state where the site is located and disseminates it, as appropriate, to the public in that state after the site is registered.(See Box 16–3 for description of a competent authority.)

Site Registration

Site registration occurs when the competent authority, designated by the member state, receives a validated environmental statement, levies a registration fee, and is satisfied that the site meets the regulation's requirements, including complying with all relevant environmental legislation. What happens if the verifier doesn't validate the statement? The company must take action to remedy audit defaults and/or noncompliance reports/presentation defaults.

Listing of the Registration

Each year, the lists of registered sites from the 15 member states will be communicated to the commission and a complete list published in the official journal of the EU. To promote their involvement in the scheme, companies can use a graphic symbol linked to statements of participation, which lists the site, within a company, that is registered to the scheme. It cannot be used in product advertising or on products or their packaging. The graphic symbol cannot be used on its own.

B O X   16–3

WHAT IS A COMPETENT AUTHORITY?

Each member state of the EU is responsible for designating an independent and neutral competent body within 12 months of the EMAS regulation entering into force. A competent authority or competent body is the national authority in each member country that has overall responsibility for the safety of products. A competent body can be either a government agency or independent organization that has the authority to recognize accreditation bodies. For example, in the United Kingdom, the Department of the Environment has been designated as the competent body. The competent body must also inform companies in the member state of the regulation and inform the public of the objectives and principles of the EMAS regulation.

Summary—Basic Differences between EMAS and ISO 14000

Now that we have described the requirements of EMAS, it is useful to point out the basic differences between ISO 14001 and EMAS requirements. The most obvious difference is that EMAS is a voluntary regulation while ISO 14001 is an international standard. Thus, where EMAS applies only to sites within the EU, ISO 14001 is applicable worldwide. Other key differences include the following:

- EMAS is site-specific and relates to industrial activities, whereas ISO 14001 applies to activities, products, and services across all sectors, including nonindustrial activities such as government. Note, however, that under EMAS, nonindustrial activities are being included on an experimental basis.

- EMAS requires an extensive initial environmental review as part of the EMS. This is not specifically required in ISO 14001 although it is suggested in Annex A.3.1 of ISO 14001.

- As mentioned above, EMAS focuses more directly on the improvement of environmental performance than does ISO 14001, which places more emphasis on establishing and improving the EMS, with environmental performance improvement as an implied, not a prescribed, result.[3]

- EMAS requires the publication of a validated public environmental statement and an annual simplified statement. ISO 14001 does not require a public statement. In Clause 4.4.3, it simply calls on companies to consider external communication. It is up to the company to decide what information to communicate. In addition, while EMAS requires the company to make publicly available its policies, programs, and EMS system, ISO 14001 only requires that the environmental policy be available to the public.

- EMAS calls for more extensive auditing than does ISO 14001, which only requires EMS auditing (although the organization under ISO 14001 must evaluate compliance with its requirements). EMAS, unlike ISO 14001, also specifies a maximum audit frequency of three years.

- The EMS requirements in EMAS require the preparation of an environmental effects register, which is not required in ISO 14001.

CONCLUSION

Since the EMAS regulation is fairly new and the system for verification and validation is only now being set up, many issues surrounding EMAS implementation will be resolved only through application. The following are a few of these issues:

- The exact nature and scope of the activities performed by the EMAS verifier.

- The experience and qualifications required of an effective EMAS verifier.

- The precise applicability of ISO 14001 and the ISO 14010-12 auditing standards within the EMAS context.

- The possibility that EMAS, if adopted as a de facto marketplace requirement in the EU might pose a trade barrier to companies with non-EU sites.
- The nature of the continual improvement of performance specified by EMAS.

In the meantime, companies with sites in Europe that may be interested in EMAS participation should note the above requirements, examine the EMAS regulation in detail, and monitor developments in the European Union.

APPENDIX: ECO-MANAGEMENT AND AUDIT SCHEME REQUIREMENTS

The following are the detailed requirements of EMAS. These requirements augment the discussion in the chapter.

Definitions

Article 2 contains definitions for key terms. A few of these are as follows:

- **Environmental review.** This means "an initial comprehensive analysis of the environmental issues, impacts and performance related to a site."
- **Company.** Company refers to the "organization which has overall management control over activities at a given site." This may be more site-specific than the reference in ISO 14001.
- **Site.** A site, according to EMAS, refers to "all land on which the industrial activity under the control of a company at a given location are carried out." EMAS is more site-specific than the ISO 14000's reference to organization.
- **Environmental statement.** This is a statement prepared by the company that is validated by the EMAS verifier. A publicly distributed and verified environmental statement is not required by ISO 14001; this is a key difference between the two systems.

Detailed Requirements

The detailed requirements of EMAS start with Article 3.

Environmental Policy

The company environmental policy, and the EMS program for the site, must be established in writing, adopted and periodically reviewed in light of environmental audits by management, and revised as appropriate. The policy must be communicated to the company's personnel and be available to the public.

The EMAS regulation states that the environmental policy must be based on the following set of principles, so that a company will:

- Foster a sense of responsibility for the environment among employees at all levels.

- Assess the environmental impact of all new activities, products, and processes in advance.

- Assess and monitor the impact of current activities on the local environment. It must examine the significant impact of these activities on the environment in general.

- Take measures necessary to prevent or eliminate pollution and, where this is not feasible, reduce pollutant emissions and waste generation to a minimum and conserve resources. These measures shall take into account possible clean technologies.

- Take measures necessary to prevent accidental emissions of materials or energy.

- Establish and apply monitoring procedures to check compliance with the environmental policy. Where these procedures require measurement and testing, establish and update records of the results.

- Establish and update procedures and actions to be pursued if it detects noncompliance with its environmental policy, objectives, or targets.

- Cooperate with the public to establish and update contingency procedures to minimize the impact of any accidental discharges to the environmental.

- Provide to the public information necessary to understanding the environmental impact of the company's activities and pursue an open dialogue with the public.

- Provide appropriate advice to customers on the relevant environmental aspects of the handling, use, and disposal of its products.(Note: ISO 14001 does not provide explicit requirements to provide advice to customers.)

- Make sure that contractors working at the site on the company's behalf apply environmental standards equivalent to those of the company.

Issues the Policy and Program Must Address

The environmental policy, program, and environmental audits must address the following 12 issues:

1. Assessment, control, and reduction of the impact of the activity concerned on the various sectors of the environment.

2. Energy management, savings, and choice.

3. Raw materials management, savings, choice and transportation, water management, and savings.

4. Waste avoidance, recycling, reuse, transportation, and disposal.

5. Evaluation, control, and reduction of noise within and outside the site.

6. Selection of new production processes and changes to production processes.

7. Product planning (design, packaging, transportation, use, and disposal)

8. Environmental performance and practices of contractors, subcontractors, and suppliers.

9. Prevention and limitation of environmental accidents.

10. Contingency procedures for environmental accidents.

11. Staff information and training on environmental issues.

12. External information on environmental issues.

Environmental Objectives

EMAS requires the company to specify environmental objectives at all relevant levels within the company and quantify wherever practical its commitment to continual improvement in environmental performance over defined time scales.

Conduct an Environmental Review

EMAS calls for an initial environmental review that focuses on the 12 areas described above.

Introduce an Environmental Program and EMS

The environmental program and EMS must be applicable to all activities at the site. It must designate responsibility for objectives at each function and level of the company and describe the means by which they are to be achieved.

EMAS also calls for separate programs relating to new or modified products, services, or processes. The programs must define the following:

- The environmental objectives to achieve.

- How to achieve them.

- Procedures for dealing with changes and modifications as projects proceed.

- Corrective mechanisms to employ, if the need arises, how to activate them, and how to measure their adequacy in particular situations.

The specific elements of an EMS program required by EMAS include the following:

- Establish, review, and revise its policy, objectives, and programs for the site.

- Define and document the responsibility, authority, and interrelations of key personnel who manage, perform, and monitor work affecting the environment.

- Appoint a management representative who has authority and responsibility for ensuring that the management system is implemented and maintained.
- Ensure that employees understand the importance of complying with EMS requirements and are aware of the environmental effects of their work, their roles and responsibilities, and the consequences of violating procedures.
- Identify training needs and provide appropriate training.
- Establish and maintain procedures for receiving, documenting, and responding to communications, both internal and external, from relevant interested parties concerning its environmental effects and management.
- Examine its environmental effects and compile a register of significant effects.
- Establish operating procedures to plan and control activities and processes that affect or potentially affect the environment.
- Develop documented work instructions that define the work of employees and others acting on the company's behalf.
- Develop procurement/contracting procedures to ensure that suppliers and those acting on their behalf comply with the company's policies.
- Monitor and control relevant process characteristics (such as effluent streams and waste disposal).
- Monitor each activity, including establishing and maintaining records of the results.
- Investigate and correct noncompliances with environmental policies, objectives, and standards.
- Apply controls to ensure that preventive actions are effective and record changes in procedures that result from corrective action.
- Establish documentation that describes its policies, objectives, and programs, the key roles and responsibilities of personnel, and the interactions of the EMS system elements.
- Establish records to demonstrate compliance with the requirements of the environmental management system and record the extent to which planned environmental objectives have been met.
- Set up, implement, and revise a systematic and periodic program of environmental audits.

Environmental Effects Register

EMAS requires the company to compile a register of significant environmental effects. The register must consider the following, where appropriate:

- Controlled and uncontrolled emissions to atmosphere.
- Controlled and uncontrolled discharges to water or sewers.
- Solid and other wastes, particularly hazardous wastes.

- Contamination of land.
- Use of land, water, fuels, and energy, and other natural resources.
- Discharge of thermal energy, noise, odor, dust, vibration, and visual impact.
- Effects on specific parts of the environment and ecosystems. This includes effects arising or likely to arise, due to:
  - Normal operating conditions.
  - Abnormal operating conditions.
  - Incidents, accidents, and potential emergency situations.
  - Past activities, current activities, and planned activities.

Conduct Environmental Auditing

EMAS calls for the organization to set up, implement, and revise a systematic and periodic program of environmental audits concerning:

- Whether or not the environmental management activities conform to the environmental program and are implemented effectively.
- How effective the EMS is in fulfilling the company's environmental policy.

It must then carry out or cause to be carried out environmental audits at the site. The audits may be conducted by either company auditors or external auditors acting on the company's behalf. The criteria for the auditing are the same 12 issues mentioned above. The audit checks to make sure the 12 issues were addressed by the EMS program.

EMAS requires that the audit frequency or the audit cycle is completed at intervals of no longer than three years. Top management decides the frequency of the audits for each activity at the site, taking into account the following:

- Potential overall environment impact of the activities at the site.
- Nature, scale, and complexity of the activities.
- Nature and scale of emissions, waste raw material, and energy consumption and, in general, the nature and scale of the activity's interaction with the environment.
- Importance and urgency of the problems detected following the initial environmental review or the previous audit.
- History of environmental problems.

Set High Objectives and Revise the Program

Based on its audit findings, the company must set objectives at the highest appropriate management level, "aimed at the continuous improvement of environmental performance," and it must revise the environmental program to be able to achieve the objectives.

The Environmental Statement

The company must prepare an environmental statement specific to each site audited when the initial environmental review and subsequent audits or audit cycles are completed. The first such environmental statement must include the following information:

- Description of the site's activities.
- Assessment of all significant environmental issues relevant to the activities at the site.
- Summary of figures on pollution emissions; waste production; consumption of raw material, energy, and water; noise; and other significant and appropriate environmental aspects.
- Other factors regarding environmental performance.
- Presentation of the environmental policy, program, and the management system implemented at the site.
- Deadline for submission of the next statement.
- Name of the accredited environmental verifier.
- Significant changes since the previous statement.

Verification and Validation

The company must have its system examined by an external accredited verifier and its environmental statement validated to ensure that they meet the requirements of EMAS. The verifier checks whether:

- The environmental policy has been established and whether it meets the requirements of EMAS.
- An EMS is in place at the site, in operation, and in compliance with relevant EMAS requirements.
- The environmental review and audit is carried out in accordance with EMAS requirements.
- The data and information in the environmental statement are reliable and the statement adequately covers all the significant and relevant environmental issues. If all of these requirements are met, the statement is validated.

The regulation includes a nondisclosure clause. The auditors and verifiers cannot divulge, without authorization from company management, any information or data obtained in the course of their activities.

The First Verification and Validation

The verifier can encounter two situations when performing the first verification and validation. The site may already have a well-developed, operating EMS in place. Or the site may have just implemented a new EMS. In the first situation, the verifier checks compliance by examining the initial review, any internal audit, and other internal monitoring procedures. In the second situation, the focus is on the initial environmental review, its organization, execution, and results.

A guidance document published by the European Commission to the verification and validation process points out that verification does not involve value judgments of the specific policy objectives, performance targets, and standards established by the company itself but is only a check to ensure that these are in conformity with the regulation.[4]

The verifier checks to make sure the company's policy is in compliance with all the relevant requirements of the regulation, including, and in particular, commitments aimed at reasonable continuous environmental improvement. The verifier will not independently assess environmental impacts and issues. That is the company's job, as part of its environmental review.

Site Registration

Site registration occurs when the competent body, designated by the member state, receives a validated environmental statement, levies a registration fee, and is satisfied the site meets the regulation's requirements, including complying with all relevant environmental legislation.

A site can lose its registration in the EMAS scheme under the following conditions:

- If it fails to submit a validated environmental statement and registration fee within three months of the deadline specified in its previous statement.

- If a competent body becomes aware that the site is no longer in compliance with the requirements of the regulation.

- If an enforcement authority informs a competent body that the site is no longer in compliance with relevant environmental legislation.

NOTES

1. *The Official Journal of the European Communities,* July 10, 1993, No L 168/1-18.

2. The "bridge" document may consist of references, for example, to elements mentioned in Annex A of ISO 14001 as required for EMAS participation, such as an initial environmental review.

3. In the negotiations leading up to the acceptance of ISO 14001 as a Draft International Standard, delegates from the European Union sought to make the standard more comparable to the EMAS regulation. Much of this effort played out in the definitions of concepts such as *continual improvement* and *environmental performance.* There was the concern among European delegates that the existing ISO 14001 is too weak for use in the EMAS system and that it should be more prescriptive and explicit in demanding environmental performance improvement. This is the reason that certain aspects of the EMAS regulation are referenced in the annex to ISO 14001. At a minimum, SCI sought to minimize any contradictions between ISO 14001 and EMAS.

4. European Commission, Directorate-General XI Environment, Nuclear Safety and Civil Protection *Draft 2 Guidance Document on the Verification and Validation Approach under Regulation 1836/93 on the EC-EMAS,* Document No. XI/205/94 - Rev 2 June 1994, Brussels, Belgium.

CHAPTER 17

ISO 14001/BS 7750/EMAS—
A Comparison

Dick Hortensius, J. W. Gunster, and J. C. Stans[1]

INTRODUCTION

Since 1991 ISO, the International Organization for Standardization, has been working on a series of international standards for environmental management systems (EMSs). With the publication of the ISO 14001 specification standard in 1996, worldwide agreement will now exist regarding the requirements for an environmental management system.

At present, many companies in The Netherlands apply the British standard BS 7750 when setting up an EMS. The Dutch Ministry of Housing, Regional Planning, and the Environment also more or less accepts this standard, and the Dutch Accreditation Council (Raad voor de Accreditatie [RvA]) has accredited a number of certifying bodies for certification on the basis of BS 7750. These organizations use the harmonized certification scheme developed by the Dutch Organization for Coordination of Environmental Management Certification (Stichting Coördinatie Certificatie Milieuzorg [SCCM])[2].

In addition, there is the European EMAS regulation; industrial companies can obtain an EMAS registration on a voluntary basis, provided they introduce an EMS, regularly carry out, or cause to be carried out, environmental audits, and periodically publish an environmental statement in accordance with the requirements given in EMAS.

A question often asked is whether there are big differences between BS 7750 and EMAS on the one hand, and ISO 14001 on the other. Should those companies that have or are implementing BS 7750 and/or EMAS worry about possible problems upon the transition to the ISO 14001 system? Does the application of the ISO 14001 standard result in a lower quality system? The aim of this chapter is to provide some answers to these questions.

First, the background and development of the three standards is briefly set out. After an outline comparison, the most significant aspects are further elucidated.

BACKGROUND STRUCTURE AND OVERALL COMPARISON

BS 7750

BS 7750 was published in 1992 and was the first *official* worldwide standard for environmental management systems. Six years earlier, the Dutch Confederation of Industries and Employers, VNO/NCW, published the first edition of the brochure "Environmental Management in Companies" in The Netherlands. This brochure already contained clear guidance for systematic environmental management by companies. In the development of BS 7750, grateful use was made of this VNO/NCW publication and the 1989 policy paper *In-company Environmental Management Systems* of the Dutch government.

A pilot program extensively tested BS 7750; based on experience gained from the pilot program, a second edition was published in 1994. At the same time, it was harmonized with the final version of the EMAS regulation, which was published in 1993. BS 7750 served as the model for a number of other national standards, such as the French, Spanish, and Irish standards, and formed a significant starting point for the discussions in the ISO TC 207 context.

EMAS Regulation

In the early 1990s, the European Union (EU) prepared the EMAS regulation. At first the idea was for a compulsory system of environmental audits for certain types of companies, and environmental statements based on the audit results. At a later stage, the emphasis was shifted to the introduction of an environmental management system, and the regulation took on a voluntary character. In describing the requirements that an EMAS environmental management system must comply with, extensive use was made of BS 7750. EMAS and BS 7750 can therefore be regarded as identical in that respect.

In the development of EMAS, the business community pleaded for good harmonization with the standard-based certification of environmental management systems (EMS). Therefore, the EMAS regulation offers companies the opportunity to base the EMS and the environmental audits on standards recognized by the European Union. For The Netherlands, BS 7750 is the recognized standard. The two different routes to obtaining an EMAS registration are shown in Figure 17–1.

In 1994, the EU gave the European standards organization, CEN, a mandate (standardization assignment) to develop standards for environmental management systems and environmental audits. The aim of the EU was to promote the implementation of EMAS and also to curb the proliferation of national standards for environmental management systems.[3] Via the so-called Vienna agreement between CEN and ISO, CEN wished to fulfill its obligations towards the EU by implementing the ISO

FIGURE   17–1

Two Possibilities for EMAS Registration

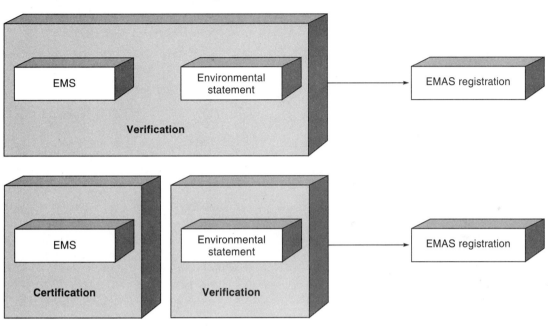

standards for environmental management systems and environmental auditing as European standards, preferably without making any alterations.

ISO 14001

As indicated above, since 1993 ISO/TC 207 has been preparing a standard for environmental management systems. This official ISO work was preceded by two years of informal discussions. The United Kingdom played a leading part in developing the environmental management systems draft, and BS 7750 formed the most significant starting point for the discussions.

Recent experience has shown that it is not easy to develop a standard for environmental management systems that will be accepted worldwide. This is because, in the area of environmental problems, countries vary in terms of the relations between the business community, government, and the general public. The ISO 14001 standard must, on the one hand, be flexible enough to be applied in many different situations by all types of companies, but on the other hand be stringent enough to provide for a system that leads to improved environmental performance. For the European countries involved, this also means that the ISO 14001 standard must fit with the objectives and requirements of EMAS. Only then will ISO 14001 be accepted by the EU as a standard recognized within the framework of EMAS.

FIGURE   17–2

Evolution of Standardization of Environmental Management Systems

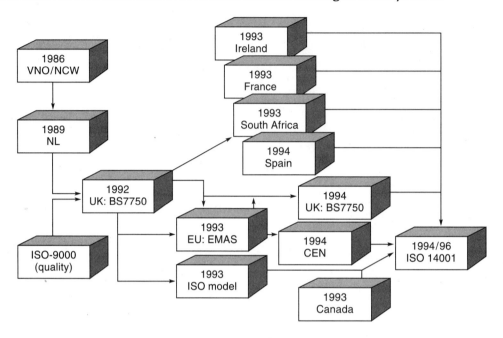

Figure 17–2 summarizes the developments and relations described above. It appears somewhat complex, but should result in ISO 14001 becoming the sole standard for environmental management systems accepted worldwide, replacing all the existing national standards and presumably recognized by the European Union as appropriate for application within the framework of EMAS.

STRUCTURE AND BASIC ELEMENTS OF THE THREE SYSTEMS

Before comparing the three systems in detail, consider the structure and basic elements of each document.

The principal part of BS 7750 is the set of requirements for an environmental management system. In addition, BS 7750 also contains two informative annexes; these annexes do not contain any requirements but are intended to give the user of the standard further information. The first annex gives a detailed explanation of the requirements of the standard and provides guidelines for carrying out an initial review. The initial review is not a compulsory part of BS 7750, but is recommended as the first step for organizations that do not yet have an EMS. The second annex compares the requirements of BS 7750 to the requirements specified in ISO 9001 for a quality management system.

The EMAS Regulation contains 21 articles and four annexes with further requirements. As stated before, participation of companies in the EMAS scheme is voluntary. In the regulation, a number of obligations are established for the EU Member States: They must take the necessary steps to make the scheme operational at the national level.

For companies, Articles 3, 4, 5, and 12 are the most important. Articles 3 and 4 contain the basic requirements for participation in the scheme, such as establishing and implementing an EMS, the conduct of environmental audits, and the preparation of an environmental statement. Article 5 describes the requirements for the environmental statement, and Article 12 contains the option of using recognized standards for the EMS and the environmental audits.

For companies that do not want to use this option, Annex I contains the requirements established for an EMS and Annex II contains the requirements for environmental audits.

Annex III contains accreditation requirements for environmental verifiers and requirements relating to the execution of their duties. Annex IV contains the various options for statements of participation in the EMAS scheme.

For drawing up the system requirements in Annex I, extensive use was made of the first edition of BS 7750. The annex is, however, quite muddled; as a result, it is difficult to determine which requirements relate to which elements of the EMS.

ISO 14001 has the same basic structure as BS 7750: the actual text of the standard (specification) and three informative annexes. The first annex contains an explanation of the requirements of the standard. The introduction to this annex states that the additional information is intended to avoid misinterpretation of the specification (for example, for certification purposes). The European countries have ensured that this annex contains many "shopping lists" from BS 7750 so that the "official" interpretation of the ISO 14001 requirements harmonizes with EMAS.

An Overall Comparison

In Table 17–1, the system elements from ISO 14001 and BS 7750 are set against one another and reference is made to where the corresponding requirements in the EMAS regulation can be found. In the table, a couple of things are noticeable:

- In ISO 14001, a logical arrangement of the system elements has been chosen, according to the so-called Deming cycle of "Plan, Do, Check and Act".

- BS 7750 and ISO 14001 contain more or less the same system elements.

- The management review, an important element of BS 7750 and ISO 14001, is missing from EMAS.

- In ISO 14001, separate requirements are laid down for emergency procedures.

TABLE 17–1

Comparison of ISO 14001, BS 7750, and EMAS

Elements from ISO 14001 (Section 4)	Elements from BS 7750 (Section 4)		Corresponding Sections from EMAS (Annex I and II)
Policy			
4.2 Environmental policy	2	Environmental policy	I.A.1, 2 and 3 I.C and D
Planning			
4.31 Environmental aspects	4.2	Environmental effects evaluation, and register	I.B.3
4.32 Legal and other requirements	4.3	Register of legislative, regulatory, and other requirements	I.B.3
4.3.3 Objectives and targets	5	Objectives and targets	I.A.4
4.3.4 Environmental management program(s)	6	Environmental management program	I.A.5 I.C
Implementation and Operation			
4.4.1 Structure and responsibility	3.1	Responsibility, authority, and resources	I.B.2
4.4.2 Training, awareness, and competence	3.4	Personnel, communication, and training	I.A.2
4.4.3 Communication	3.4	Personnel, communication, and training	I.B.2
	4.1	Communications	
4.4.4 Environmental management system documentation	7.1	Environmental management manual	——
4.4.5 Document control	7.2	Documentation	——
4.4.6 Operational control	8	Operational control	I.B.4
4.4.7 Emergency preparedness and response			I.C.10
Checking and Corrective Action			
4.5.1 Monitoring and measurement	8.3	Verification, measurement, and testing	I.B.4
4.5.2 Nonconformance and corrective and preventive action	8.4	Noncompliance and corrective action	I.B.4
4.5.3 Records	9	Environmental management records	I.B.5
4.5.4 EMS audits	10	EMS audits	I.B.6 and II
Management Review			
4.6 Management review	11	Management review	——

IN-DEPTH COMPARATIVE ANALYSIS OF THE THREE SYSTEMS

The comparison of the system elements of BS 7750 and ISO 14001 shows relatively few differences in outline. For this comparison, only that part of EMAS which relates to the EMS is considered. To check whether the objectives of the ISO 14001 system are comparable to those of BS 7750 and hence the EMAS regulation, consider the detailed requirements for a number of system elements.

In this respect, the following issues are dealt with:

- The definition of an *environmental management system.*

- The requirements for the environmental policy of an organization.

- The principle of continual improvement.

- The definition of *environmental performance.*

- The way in which reference is made to "Economically Viable Application of Best Available Technology" (EVABAT) in ISO 14001.

- The difference between *environmental aspects* and *impacts* (ISO 14001), and *environmental effects* (BS 7750).

- Attention to prevention of pollution in ISO 14001.

- The role of the initial review.

- Suppliers and contractors.

- External communication.

- The relation between the text of the standard in ISO 14001 and the informative annex, and the significance of this for compatibility with the EMAS regulation.

In the following, ISO 14001 is generally compared to BS 7750. As already indicated above, since BS 7750 and EMAS can be regarded as identical, the majority of the statements made below are also valid when comparing ISO 14001 and EMAS.

The Definition of an Environmental Management System

In BS 7750, an EMS is defined as "the organizational structure, responsibilities, practices, procedures, processes, and resources for implementing environmental management." In ISO 14001, the EMS is defined as "the part of the overall management system that includes organizational structure, planning activities, responsibilities, practices, procedures, processes and resources for developing, implementing, achieving, reviewing and maintaining the environmental policy."

The definition of an environmental management system in BS 7750 leaves some vagueness as to whether the environmental policy and the environmental objectives derived from it are part of the system or are a driving force. The EMS in BS 7750 seems to refer to the system "in the restricted sense," that is, the totality of the control mechanisms necessary to achieve the environmental objectives that are established. In the EMAS regulation, a more explicit distinction is made between environmental policy, environmental program, and environmental objectives on the one hand, and the environmental management system on the other.

The term *environmental management system* has a broader interpretation in ISO 14001; here, the planning activities also form an explicit part of the system. These planning activities include the environmental objectives and the environmental program, but not the environmental policy. This broad definition is important for the scope of the system audits and the principle of continual improvement (see below). A schematic representation of the difference between BS 7750 and ISO 14001 is shown in Figure 17–3.

The Requirements for the Environmental Policy of an Organization

As a performance-level determining element of the environmental policy, BS 7750 mentions the commitment to continual improvement. EMAS adds to this element the compliance with all relevant environmental regulatory requirements.[4] In addition to these elements, ISO 14001 states that an organization shall commit itself to prevention of pollution. ISO 14001 thus contains the largest number of requirements with regard to the content of an organization's environmental policy.

FIGURE 17–3

Difference in Definition of an Environmental Management System in BS 7750, EMAS, and ISO 14001

The system

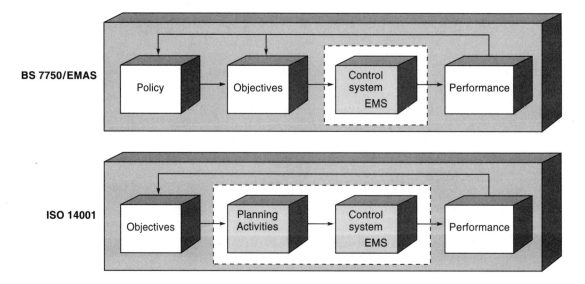

The Principle of Continual Improvement

This has been a controversial issue in the development of ISO 14001. A few countries, in particular Canada, were of the opinion that the commitment to continual improvement should not be a part of the ISO standard at all. In contrast, a number of European countries expressed the opinion that in addition to the systematic control of the environmental aspects of business management, a "driving force" should also be included in an EMS: Contrary to many quality systems, an EMS should be a dynamic system, not a static control of the status quo, but aimed at improvement. In addition, for Europe, the fact that the commitment to continual improvement is a part of BS 7750 and the EMAS regulation also played a role.

In BS 7750, the core of the definition of *continual improvement* is as follows: "Year-on-year enhancement of overall environmental performance...resulting from continuous efforts to improve in line with environmental policy." Continuous improvement therefore involves improving the *environmental performance*. In ISO 14001, the definition is as follows: "Process of enhancing the environmental management system to achieve improvements in overall environmental performance in line with the organization's environmental policy."

At first glance, there seems to be a substantial difference between BS 7750 and ISO 14001: improvement of *environmental performance* as against improvement of the *management system* (with a view to improvement of environmental performance). This has resulted in fierce disputes in Europe regarding whether ISO 14001 actually aims at the improvement of the impact of company activities on the environment or only at improvement of the operational control within stated company objectives, which may in themselves be minimal ("rubbish in, rubbish out").

It is important to realize that ISO 14001 focuses on the management system itself: That system is the management toolbox a company uses to implement its environmental policy. Every improvement in environmental performance must be made via that management instrument. Continuous improvement of that system should lead to increasingly better environmental performance.

For a sound understanding of the improvement process, it is important to reconsider the definition of environmental management system in ISO 14001; its scope is broader than the definition in BS 7750, as indicated above. The planning of environmental management, environmental objectives and targets, and the environmental program are inseparable parts of the system. Thus, the environmental objectives are also subject to improvement or refinement. In principle, this refinement takes place continually until the environmental policy of the company has been fully implemented.

The improvement process comes up again in the management review. As part of this management review, the environmental policy is from time to time reconsidered or adjusted with a view to external developments and the commitment to continual improvement. This breaks through the improvement cycle within the limits of the environmental policy that is established, and, as a result the continual improvement is aimed at achieving the new policy objectives at a higher level of ambition. This shows the importance of the management review in the overall improvement process. The double improvement cycle in ISO 14001 is shown in Figure 17–4.

FIGURE   17–4

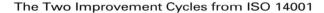

The Two Improvement Cycles from ISO 14001

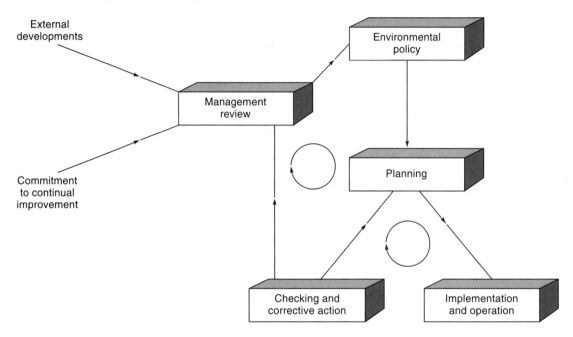

The Definition of Environmental Performance

For a correct interpretation of the improvement principle, the definition of environmental performance is also very important. When the texts for the ISO 14001 standard were prepared, it was realized that the term *environmental performance* can be interpreted in various ways, partly depending on the context in which it is used.

For this reason, in ISO 14001, contrary to BS 7750 and EMAS, a definition of the term *environmental performance* is included: "Measurable results of the environmental management system, related to an organization's control of its environmental aspects, based on its environmental policy, objectives and targets." Here again, it is clear that the ISO 14001 standard focuses on the system and therefore the term performance relates to the performance of the system.

The definition is the result of lengthy discussions in the ISO 14001 context. The measurable results of the system must be understood to include emissions to the environment, so that these measurable system results do indeed (also) involve the actual environmental effects. Other measurable results of the system may, for example, relate to organizational matters such as the number of training courses on environmental policy attended by the company staff. Performance must always be measured against something; the reference point here is the environmental policy of the organization and the objectives and targets based on it. The closer the objectives are to being met, the better the environmental performance. This may result in the misconception that a company that has achieved its own (and maybe miserable) environmental objectives has also achieved perfect environmental performance. This belief simply will not do because within the framework of the management review the environmental policy is itself subject to the improvement process.

Whether good environmental performance in the eyes of an outside party is really "good," in any case depends on the level of ambition of the environmental policy and the environmental objectives of the organization.

EVABAT

The term *EVABAT,* the Economically Viable Application of Best Available Technology, was also a serious point for discussion in the development of ISO 14001. The concept comes from the EMAS Regulation (and is therefore part of the second edition of BS 7750 as well) and was included as a yardstick for striving towards continual improvement. The background to this was the fear of some delegations to TC 207 that for companies in countries with less stringent environmental legislation, it would be easier to comply with EMAS. Indicating a direction for the process of continual improvement would prevent firms in countries with a lower starting point (namely having the less stringent legislative and regulatory environmental requirements with which they must comply), from also achieving a systematically higher level of environmental performance in the improvement process.

In any case, EVABAT by definition is also a relative concept since "economic viability" may differ from country to country. The result of the introduction of EVABAT in EMAS (and BS 7750) is that the environmental performance of a company in principle has a minimum requirement (to comply with the legislation and regulations) and a maximum goal (EVABAT).

In ISO 14001, the concept of EVABAT is less prominent. It was argued by the developing countries that the inclusion of a commitment to aim for the application of EVABAT would set up barriers to trade, as best available technology (whether or not economically viable and applicable) is often not available in developing countries. It was argued from the United States that application of EVABAT will not always give the most environmental benefits: Reducing environmental pollution to levels below what can be regarded as environmentally safe is a waste of money that can better be invested elsewhere.

ISO 14001 requires an organization to consider its technological options when establishing and reviewing its environmental objectives; the Annex to ISO 14001 explains that this also may include considering the application of EVABAT.

Where EMAS and BS 7750 set an upper limit for the process of continual improvement, this upper limit is missing in ISO 14001, and firms are thus obliged to make continual improvement ad infinitum. In this respect, ISO 14001 can be regarded as more stringent than the EMAS Regulation and BS 7750. The issue of performance levels is illustrated in Figure 17–5.

F I G U R E   17–5

The Minimum and Maximum Performance Level in BS 7750, EMAS, and ISO 14001

ISO 14001 / BS 7750 / EMAS

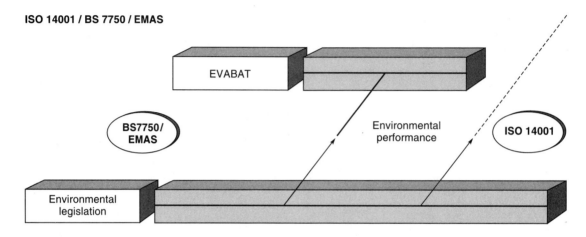

The Difference between Aspects and Impacts (ISO 14001) and Environmental Effects (BS 7750 and EMAS)

BS 7750 requires that an organization identify, examine, and evaluate its environmental effects and compile a register of those identified as significant. The significant environmental effects should then be taken into account when establishing the environmental objectives. Environmental effects in BS 7750 are defined as "any direct or indirect impingement of the activities, products and services of an organization on the environment, whether adverse or beneficial." This aspect of BS 7750 has often been the subject of discussion. Are organizations really in a position to list and evaluate all their environmental effects and, if so, how far should they go?

In the Dutch harmonized certification scheme for BS 7750 that was referred to earlier, a further explanation/interpretation of this environmental effects evaluation is given so that companies can avoid conducting a full-scale environmental impact assessment.

In ISO 14001, another approach is chosen: An organization shall identify the environmental aspects of its activities, products, and services that it can control and over which it can be expected to have an influence, in order to determine those that have or can have significant impacts on the environment. These environmental aspects that have or can have a *significant* environmental impact must be considered when setting the environmental objectives. Environmental aspects are defined in ISO 14001 as those elements of an organization's activities, products, and services that can interact with the environment.

ISO 14001 thus chooses a practical approach. First, the organization lists all of its interaction possibilities with the environment (e.g. emission sources). Next, it

FIGURE 17–6

The Concepts of Environmental Effects versus Environmental Aspects/Impacts

ISO 14001 / BS 7750 / EMAS — Effects versus aspects / impacts

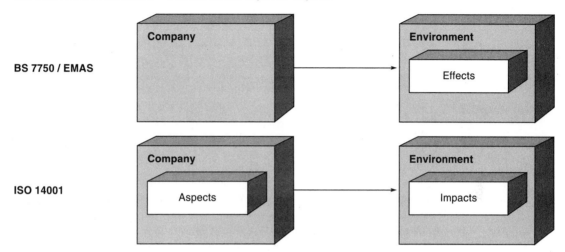

investigates controllable aspects to determine whether they have a significant environmental impact, whereby environmental impact is defined as any change to the environment, whether adverse or beneficial, wholly or partially resulting from an organization's activities, products, or services. The difference in approach between BS 7750 and EMAS on the one hand and ISO 14001 on the other is visualized in Figure 17–6.

The ultimate results of the requirements in BS 7750 and ISO 14001 will be the same. BS 7750 gives a list of environmental effects that must be considered, where applicable for the organization, while ISO 14001 gives a good generic description of the term *environmental aspects*. In the annex to ISO 14001 a number of the environmental effects mentioned in BS 7750 are listed as examples. By doing so, ISO 14001 does not include or exclude anything. BS 7750 also explicitly indicates that attention must be paid to environmental effects of abnormal operating conditions, incidents, potential emergency situations, and past and planned activities. In ISO 14001, this is done both in the annex and in a separate paragraph on emergency preparedness.

ISO 14001 has therefore chosen more generic descriptions which, certainly in combination with the use of the annex, will give the same result as BS 7750.

Prevention of Pollution in ISO 14001

The concept of prevention of pollution as a compulsory part of an organization's environmental policy (and thus also part of its environmental objectives) was introduced by the United States and in particular, the U.S. EPA. *Prevention of pollution* is defined as the "use of processes, practices, materials or products that avoid, reduce or control pollution, which may include recycling, treatment, process changes, control mechanisms, efficient use of resources and material substitution." This can be regarded as a further technical development of the concept of continual improvement of environmental performance.

Initial Review

The initial review in EMAS is a compulsory first step that companies must take before they establish their environmental objectives and EMS. Companies with an EMS that functions well have already carried out such a review or have collected comparable information within the framework of their internal environmental management.

In ISO 14001 and BS 7550, the initial review is therefore mentioned as an option for companies setting up an environmental management system for the first time. In any event, the information emerging from an initial review seems to be almost identical with the combination of registering the environmental aspects and environmental impacts and the regulatory obligations with which a company must comply. The difference is that EMAS clearly indicates a pathway to be followed (and therefore is more rigid), while ISO 14001 and BS 7750 focus on the type of information that a company must have available; it is left up to the organization how this information is gathered.

Suppliers and Contractors

This aspect generated heated debates in the ISO 14001 context. Stringent requirements on suppliers and contractors could result in trade barriers between developed and developing nations, and between large and small companies. The question of whether small companies or companies from less-developed countries can and must meet the same environmental requirements as large companies in developed countries played a part here.

ISO 14001 obliges an organization to identify the significant environmental aspects of the goods and services it uses. The suppliers and contractors must be informed of the procedures and requirements applicable to them within the framework of the EMS. However, the company ultimately remains responsible that all the activities actually are carried out under specified conditions; therefore, inspection of suppliers and contractors has to be carried out.

External Communication

ISO 14001 specifies that an organization shall consider processes for external communication regarding its significant environmental aspects. The organization shall make an explicit decision on the matter and record it. If the organization decides, for example, to publish an annual environmental report, the way in which and the frequency with which external information is distributed is then established. BS 7750 does not contain such a requirement, and in EMAS the external communication is regulated separately from the EMS in the form of the compulsory environmental statement.

The Relation between the Text of ISO 14001 and Its Informative Annex and Its Significance for Compatibility with the EMAS Regulation

ISO 14001, like BS 7750, consists of the actual standard (specification), in which the requirements for the EMS are specified, and an informative annex with a further explanation of these requirements. The introduction to the annex in ISO 14001 states that it provides additional information about the EMS requirements with the intention of avoiding misinterpretation of the ISO 14001 specification. It may be deduced from this that the annex gives the correct interpretation as intended by the authors of the standard. This makes it clear that, although the annex is informative, it is a worldwide accepted interpretation of the standard and therefore certainly of high value. From a European viewpoint, this is important because in the annex the standard is interpreted in a number of places in a way that clearly harmonizes its requirements with the intentions of the EMAS regulation.

Therefore one might argue that the requirements in ISO 14001, interpreted according to the guidance given in its annex, together with the ISO guidelines on environmental auditing (ISO 14010, ISO 14011 and ISO 14012) fully cover the system and audit requirements of EMAS. In addition, EMAS does of course also contain the obligation to publish an environmental statement.

RECENT DEVELOPMENTS IN EUROPE

As mentioned above, the European Commission gave CEN a mandate to develop standards on environmental management systems and environmental auditing that cover the corresponding EMAS requirements. This can be regarded as a tactical move by the European Commission.

First, further proliferation of national standards at the European level was blocked because CEN rules prohibit the starting of new national standardization projects when a CEN project has been announced.

Second, existing national standards such as BS 7750, the Irish, Spanish, and French standards, would cease to exist as soon as the European standard is available, again as a result of CEN rules. Finally, the ISO developments were heavily influenced by EMAS requirements, because the Commission knew that CEN would use its agreement with ISO to develop the requested European standards in parallel with the ISO 14000 series. In the mandate to CEN, the European Commission even required that the standards should be consistent with the future ISO standards. As a result, most European members of ISO/TC 207 made efforts to align the wording of ISO 14001 to be compatible with the system elements of EMAS.

The formal work related to CEN's mandate was entrusted to the CEN Programming Committee on Environment. This committee established a working group to look at the draft ISO 14000 standards in detail and at EMAS. After long deliberations it has decided to draft three documents:

1. A comparison document giving a clause-by-clause comparison between EMAS requirements and the corresponding ISO 14001 requirements; in a third column the document provides the related informative text of ISO 14001, Annex A of ISO 14001 and the ISO auditing guidelines.

2. A bridging document that identifies areas where EMAS establishes detailed system and auditing requirements that are not specifically covered by the ISO 14000 standards or where the agreements between EMAS and ISO 14001 may not be readily apparent.

3. An explanatory note that contains some information on the possible use of the bridging document.

The most interesting and controversial document is the bridging document. Although some CEN members agree with the statement that the ISO 14001 requirements adequately cover corresponding EMAS requirements, others do not. Among others, Germany, Denmark and Ireland believe that ISO 14001 has serious shortcomings compared to EMAS. The current bridging document can be seen as a compromise between the CEN members to bridge the perceived gap between ISO 14001 and EMAS.

The bridging document contains guidance on a number of EMS-related elements that companies should take into account when implementing ISO 14001 to ensure that they also meet corresponding EMAS requirements. The substantial issues dealt with in the bridging document are the following:

- Application of EVABAT.
- Scope of environmental management system audits.
- Audit frequency.
- Environmental review.
- Good management practices.

These issues are briefly described and commented upon below.

Application of EVABAT

The bridging document advises companies to be able to demonstrate that they are committed to an EMS that will lead to continual improvement of environmental performance towards EVABAT. As argued above, ISO 14001 requirements also result in continual improvement of environmental performance. Due to the absence of a perspective requirement for EVABAT in ISO 14001, ISO 14001 can be regarded as even more stringent than EMAS.

Scope of Environmental Audits

The bridging document advises companies to include an evaluation of overall environmental performance and to conduct its audits in compliance with Annex II of EMAS. According to ISO 14001, the EMS audits should be carried out to determine whether the EMS has been properly implemented and maintained. One way to check the proper implementation of the system is to check whether environmental performance objectives are indeed met. As part of a system audit this will normally only be done by making spot checks. The ISO 14010-12 guidelines on auditing adequately cover the Annex II requirements of EMAS.

Audit Frequency

The bridging document advises audits to be carried out at least every three years. ISO 14001 does not specify any audit frequency. It only requires that any audit schedule be based on the environmental importance of the activity concerned and on the results of previous audits. This seems to be a more logical requirement than a generic frequency of three years.

Environmental Review

The bridging document advises companies to be able to demonstrate that they have conducted such a review. As stated above, the EMAS requirement to carry out an environmental review seems to be superfluous and unnecessarily rigid for companies that already have a well-functioning EMS. These companies usually will have equivalent information available as part of their EMS records and registers.

Good Management Practices

The bridging document makes reference to various detailed principles of action set out in EMAS, Annex I.D. Not all of those are explicitly covered by ISO 14001. This section on good management practices is one area where EMAS takes a very prescriptive approach. All practices mentioned are fully in line with the basic philosophy of ISO 14001; ISO 14001, however, does not specify details but leaves more responsibility to companies to give shape to responsible environmental management.

Status of Bridging Document

The bridging document has been finalized by the CEN working group and has been presented to the CEN Programming Committee on Environment for approval. After this approval is obtained, the CEN Technical Management Board has to decide on its final publication. The current position of most CEN members is that the bridging document should be published as a CEN Technical Report and not as a CEN standard. The purpose of the document is not to provide additional EMS requirements but to guide companies to implement ISO 14001 is such a way to meet corresponding EMAS requirements.

Use of Bridging Document

Finally, it will be interesting to see how the bridging document will be used in practice. (See Figure 17–7.) As part of the recognition procedure for ISO 14001, the European Commission will decide which articles of EMAS are covered by an ISO 14001 certificate. All remaining issues will have to be dealt with by the environmental verifier. Ideally this verifier only needs to validate the environmental statement and not to audit any system elements. It seems more realistic to assume, however, that ISO 14001 will only be recognized as covering part of the EMAS system requirements. The bridging document is meant to cover the remaining EMAS system requirements.

The responsible CEN working group recognized two possibilities for using the bridging document. A company that is certified on the basis of ISO 14001, and which might apply for EMAS registration in the future, could request the certification auditor to also take into account the additional guidance of the bridging document. The results of this additional check can be included in the audit report. Later, the environmental verifier for EMAS could rely on this audit report and decide that an additional system check is not necessary. This strategy would concur with the general understanding that verifiers should not duplicate work.

Alternatively, companies may choose to leave the use of the bridging document to the verifier. These two possibilities are visualized in Figure 17–7. The advantage

F I G U R E   17–7

Two Possibilities for Using the Bridge Document

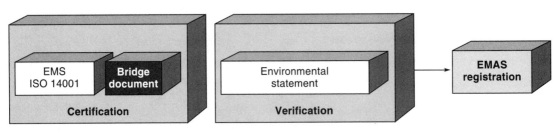

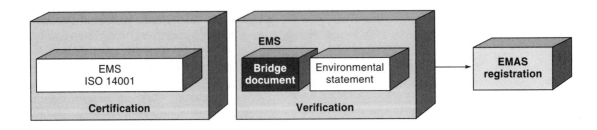

of the first alternative seems to be that the company's EMS is only audited once and that the activities of the verifier are restricted to the validation of the environmental statement.

It will take some time before it is fully clear how EN/ISO 14001 will be used in the EMAS framework. The European Commission decision on the recognition of ISO 14001 will not be taken before the end of 1996.

CONCLUSIONS AND RECOMMENDATIONS

This chapter has outlined the context in which various standards in recent years have been developed for environmental management systems. From the comparison of the EMS standards and the EMAS regulation, it appears that the objectives of the systems are the same: a management instrument to control, reduce, and prevent the environmental effects associated with the activities of an organization, aiming for continual improvement of environmental performance.

The EMAS regulation has the additional aim of encouraging companies to prepare an environmental statement and to have this verified by an independent party. The two standards are limited currently to the "internal dimension" of environmental management. Through certification, this internal dimension also takes on an external significance, and the standards offer sufficient points of departure to encourage companies to communicate with the outside world about their environmental management.

The description of the EMS in EMAS is unclear compared to the "real" standards, BS 7750 and ISO 14001. It is therefore beneficial that EMAS gives companies the opportunity to use recognized standards as a basis for their system. BS 7750 offers an extensive system description and is hence an excellent basis for certification activities; the standard, however, has an illogical structure. In addition, the standard is clearly intended to be compatible with EMAS and is consequently a typical European product.

ISO 14001 offers the best system description and harmonizes the broadly accepted management principles of Deming (plan, do, check, act). ISO 14001 can therefore serve as a good example for a new generation of ISO 9000 standards for quality control. The standard is more concise than BS 7750, but also more flexible for worldwide applications in very different situations.

Regarding the level of requirements, ISO 14001 is certainly not inferior to BS 7750. More involved parties have given lengthy consideration to the contents of ISO 14001 than was the case for BS 7750 and EMAS. This has resulted in the further development of key concepts. With the present-day understanding, the system requirements from BS 7750 and EMAS would be specified differently. As the most up-to-date, worldwide, flexible but also stringent standard, ISO 14001 deserves to be recognized by the EU within the framework of EMAS. It will be beneficial to those in the business community who want to pursue EMAS registration, and it is in line with the desire of industry to have a single universal standard for environmental management systems.

Bibliography

BS 7750 Specification for environmental management systems, British Standards Institution, 1994.

EEC Council Regulation No 1836/93 Community Eco-Management and Audit Scheme, Official Journal of the European Communities, No L 168, 10.07.93

ISO 14001 Environmental management systems—Specification with guidance for use, 1996.

ISO 14004 Environmental management systems—General guidelines on principles, systems and supporting techniques, 1996.

ISO 14010 Guidelines for environmental auditing—General principles, 1996.

ISO 14011 Guidelines for environmental auditing—Audit procedures—Auditing of environmental management systems, 1996.

ISO 14012 Guidelines for environmental auditing—Qualification criteria for environmental auditors, 1996.

BIOGRAPHIES

Dick Hortensius, J. W. Gunster, and J. C. Stans

Dick Hortensius received a master's degree in analytical chemistry at the University of Utrecht in 1983. He worked for various years with the Research Unit on Science & Society of the University of Utrecht. In that position he was involved in research projects regarding socioeconomic, toxicological, and regulatory aspects of soil clean-up policies and activities in The Netherlands.

Since 1985 he has worked for the Netherlands Standards Institute. He has been involved in many standardization projects, e.g., in the field of water and soil quality. He served as the secretary of the ISO Technical Committee on Soil Quality from its inauguration in 1986 until 1995. His present focus is on standardization of environmental management tools. He is responsible for the ISO subcommittee on Environmental Auditing and is involved in the management of ISO/TC 207. He is also closely involved in the activities of the European Standards Organization CEN directed at implementing ISO 14001 as the European Standard within the framework of the EMAS Regulation.

His current position at NNI is Senior Standardization Consultant and he is the coordinator of NNI's standards program in the field of environment. He also coordinates standardization activities in the field of management systems.

Over the last few years he has given many presentations on environmental management standardization, and on behalf of NNI he teaches courses on environmental management systems and integration of management systems for quality, environment, and occupational health and safety.

J. W. Gunster works as a secretary for environmental affairs with the Confederation of The Netherlands' Industries and Employers.

J. C. Stans is a project manager with Det Norske Veritas.

All three authors have been closely involved in the development of the ISO standards for environmental management systems and environmental auditing.

NOTES

1. An earlier, abridged version of this chapter was published as an article in the Dutch journal *Milieustrategie,* October 1995.
2. This harmonized scheme includes interpretative guidance on BS 7750, where considered necessary (e.g., on the scope of the environmental effects evaluation and the mechanism of continual improvement), directives on the organization of the certifying bodies (e.g., the qualifications and, composition of the audit team), and directives on the operating procedures of the certifying bodies (e.g., the frequencies of control and reassessments). The aim of this harmonized scheme is to ensure an equal and high level of certification of environmental management systems in The Netherlands.
3. As soon as a CEN standards project starts, the members of CEN (being national standards institutes) are no longer allowed to start national standardization projects on the same issue. As soon as a CEN standard is published, members of CEN are obliged to withdraw any national standards covering the same subject. This means that as soon as ISO 14001 is accepted as a European standard, BS 7750 and the other national standards have to be withdrawn within half a year.
4. In EMAS, in Annexes I.C and I.D, a number of other issues and good management practices are mentioned that must be addressed within the framework of the environmental policy, among other things. These are in part quite detailed issues, which seem to fit in better with the objectives and terms of references and the environmental program than with the general environmental policy itself.

CHAPTER 18

An ISO Occupational Health and Safety Management System

Charles F. Redinger and Steven P. Levine

INTRODUCTION

The focus of this book thus far has been the ISO 14000 standards. This chapter addresses the potential development of an Occupational Health and Safety Management System standard (OHSMS) by ISO. Formal consideration of an ISO OHSMS began in 1995 and will continue until ISO makes a decision regarding the need for an ISO standard. The application of the ISO management-systems model to occupational, health, and safety (OHS) has intrigued many. This approach appears to offer the seeds of a new regulatory/management instrument that can address some of the inefficiencies of traditional command-and-control instruments in occupational health and safety (OHS) control. This section addresses several theoretical and practical aspects of ISO's venture into OHS control and management. While connections to ISO 14000 are made, the emphasis is on the development of an ISO OHSMS.

OHSMS OVERVIEW

As has been mentioned in other portions of this book, the ISO Technical Management Board created Technical Committee 207 (TC 207) in 1993 to develop internationally recognized environmental management standards. Recently, TC 207 voted on final standards for environmental management systems (EMS) and environmental auditing.

Concurrent with TC 207 efforts, published articles have posed questions regarding the applicability of the ISO 9000 quality system standards and their potential benefits to health and safety management systems.[1] Some organizations recognize a compatibility and have subsequently integrated occupational safety and health within the framework of their respective ISO 9000-based systems.[2,3] Irrespective of which standard or practice is employed, there appears to be an increasing trend within industry to link quality, productivity, and occupational health with emphasis on sound managerial systems. Furthermore, businesses are increasingly managing health and safety not simply to comply with statutory requirements but to achieve a marketplace advantage through gains in efficiency.[4]

Rationale for an OHSMS

A novel approach to international organization and coordination was introduced with the management-systems methods embodied in ISO 9000 and ISO 14000. Some commentators believe that the ISO management-systems model may provide the necessary bridge between trade, environmental protection, and sustainable development.[5] By examining some of the basic tenets of the ISO management-systems approach, an emerging theme is that this approach may be applicable not only to occupational health and safety but also to other areas of social regulation where command-and-control instruments have been extensively used.

Numerous economists have been critical of the command-and-control approach to environmental, health, and safety regulations.[6] Arguments have been presented showing that the inefficiencies of the command-and-control approach should be taken more seriously. Other instruments, such as taxation, pollution credits, and market incentives, also have shortcomings and are not always widely applicable because of ethical concerns. Conversely, the management systems approach appears to offer an instrument through which negative externalities can be internalized by a system of modified market incentives; namely by tying environmental, health, and safety performance to market participation and procurement contract language.

An important component of the ISO quality management-systems model is the manner in which a quality system is verified, that is, either through first-, second-, or third-party registration. The concept of third-party registration of management systems has been used throughout industry and commerce with increased frequency over the past decade.[7] Critics of the third-party registration process argue that it creates high costs for companies. A suggested alternative is to incorporate either a first- or second-party auditing process. Briefly, a first-party system, which would result in self-declaration of conformity to the ISO standard, essentially involves internal self-auditing, while a second-party system involves purchaser audits of its suppliers. Critics of a third-party registration system have voiced support for first- or second-party auditing/qualification systems.[8]

Domestically, third-party verification of environmental, safety, and health program adequacy has been promoted as a possible mechanism to assist the Environmental Protection Agency (EPA) and the Occupational Health and Safety Administration (OSHA) in achieving their goals. The EPA recognizes the development of and growing reliance on international voluntary management standards . . . [which] . . . if properly crafted and implemented, can provide a powerful tool for organizations to improve . . . compliance with [regulatory] requirements and move beyond compliance through [innovation].[9]

The implementation of a management systems policy of OSHA, for instance, would represent a new policy approach that would augment and depart from the agency's command-and-control tradition. Such a policy shift would offer opportunities for encouraging innovation by focusing on occupational safety and health management systems.[10]

In 1993, the National Performance Review (NPR), conducted by the U.S. government to evaluate the efficiency and effectiveness of the federal bureaucracy, stated as a goal that OSHA would utilize third-party certification mechanisms to fulfill part of the Clinton administration's "reinvention" plan.[11] Since the announcement, OSHA, its stakeholders, and academics have been discussing the viability of this NPR recommendation. Assistant Secretary of Labor for Occupational Safety and Health Joe Dear has stated on a number of occasions that OSHA is interested in pursuing the third-party certification concept as part of the agency's reinvention activities.[12]

To this end, the concept of third-party certification was discussed at an OSHA stakeholders' meeting in Washington, D.C. on July 20–21, 1994. Some stakeholders voiced concerns about the concept. In response to stakeholder feedback, OSHA is still considering a third-party certification policy;[13] however, the policy was not directly mentioned in the agency's May 16, 1995 reinvention plan.[14]

An OHSMS in the Context of Traditional Command-and-Control Approaches

During the late 1960s and early 1970s, a wave of regulations were introduced that affected American society in ways that previous regulations had not. Some scholars asserted that these regulations controlled Americans in ways that inappropriately attempted to modify behavior.[15] The Occupational Safety and Health Act was one of the regulations in the wave, and had a significant impact on the American workplace. It can be inferred that both the criticisms of scholars regarding agency capture and the response of the judiciary had an effect on the manner in which the social regulations of the late 1960s and early 1970s were implemented. While the command-and-control instruments used by OSHA have come under intense scrutiny over the past decade, based on the political and legal environment in their early years, one can see the origins of the use of these instruments.[16]

Command-and-control regulations have been widely used throughout the United States to control environmental, health, and safety externalities. The basic mechanism involved is the following: A governmental agency sets a standard that must be met by the producer of a good or service. Parties who are affected by command-and-control standards are required to meet the minimum requirements of the standards or face some sort of punitive action, typically in the form of monetary fines.

Compliance with command-and-control standards is usually enforced through mandatory self-monitoring, agency inspection, or third-party complaints. A potential problem with market-based approaches is that they must base their outcomes on a consumer's willingness to pay. With occupational health and safety, willingness to pay equates to willingness to diminish one's own health and well-being.

Some economists suggest that willingness-to-pay considerations are the most efficient means of addressing occupational health and safety externalities.[17] In these cases, an employee can accept or decline a job if the wage does not fairly reflect the hazards. There are significant social and ethical problems with this rationale, including problems with unequal distribution of information and "ability-to-pay" considerations.

The application of an ISO-harmonized first-, second-, and third-party registration system, when combined with the voluntary compliance programs presented in OSHA's reinvention plan, represents a potentially powerful market-based policy. This approach would reflect the differences in marginal costs among different worksites and would allow those most familiar with the site—the employer and employees—the opportunity to develop a site-specific occupational safety and health management system, which would reflect the site-specific marginal costs. These programs, if ISO-compatible, would in turn be certified by an accredited third-party registrar. In the case of employers who choose not to participate in such a market-based approach, the traditional OSHA command-and-control regulatory structure would remain in place.[18]

EXPECTED BENEFITS OF AN OHSMS

Some of the benefits and open issues identified in ISO's formal consideration of an OHSMS are summarized in this subsection.[19]

National/International Benefits

ISO OHSMS consensus standards could benefit domestic and international workers. The development of these standards could alleviate some of the inequities inherent in OHS regulations and governmental compliance activities that differ from country to country. Relevant national specification standards for OHSMS could be nested in the program requirements of such an ISO-type standard. Conformance to the ISO standard requires compliance with relevant national and local standards.

Prevention-oriented OHSMS programs should be integrated with the design phases of industrial processes not treated as separate entities. As such, an ISO OHSMS standard would be compatible with the scope of ISO 9001, with the net effect of minimizing the number of internal and external audits companies are subjected to. By harmonizing an ISO 9000 quality management system and an ISO 14000 environmental management system, companies could address the logistical and financial barriers associated with multiple external evaluations.

Multinational corporations may benefit from the evolution of multiple national philosophies toward a singular health and safety approach. Exchanges of expertise (within the same organization) in OHS, resulting in substantial cross-training, might be encouraged since OHS professionals would be using similar procedures to resolve similar problems. ISO 9000 does not specify how companies must design quality systems, nor would an environmental, safety and health management system.

Other incentives could also be built into the system for attaining registration. Contractual language could require that trade partners be OHSMS registered to be considered for major business contracts. This could also apply to U.S. federal contract awards. Also, corporate insurance premiums could be reduced by participation in an OHSMS.

The language of the World Trade Organization (WTO) agreement supports creation of, and participation in, development of international conformity assessment standards. The agreement also suggests that developed countries, when requested, assist developing trade partners (less-developed countries, or LDCs) in their efforts to comply with technical standards and give them special consideration with conformance.

If the spirit and intent of the WTO are applied to an ISO OHSMS, LDCs could be provided time and technical assistance, without fear of trade retaliation, to develop conformance strategies suitable to local social and political conditions. Finally, the WTO as currently drafted would not interfere with U.S. public or private standards-making activities.

Industry and Governmental Benefits

By promoting the use of industry-driven OHS management systems, an OHSMS policy reaffirms the belief that industry is the main engine of sustained economic growth that should be unfettered by specification standards. Third-party registration is a market-based strategy for compliance, which thereby creates flexibility and incentives for innovation.

Benefits could also be built into the system that would be favorable to small ISO OHSMS registrants. Several large U.S. firms are already showing a preference for using suppliers who conform to the principles, and have ISO 9000 registrations. Small ISO registered firms, traditionally outside of EPA and OSHA oversight, could be brought into progressive mainline ES&H management.

An ISO OHSMS model of independent third-party inspectors could potentially provide a value-added service to federal OSHA and its state partners. First, the registration process would not interfere with OSHA enforcement activities. Second, firms that receive ISO OHSMS registration could potentially be removed from OSHA's programmed inspection schedule, thus reducing some of the workload from their compliance personnel. As a consequence, OSHA could focus their limited resources on the most immediate health threats to U.S. workers and dangers to the environment.

This policy reform fits into the category of applying existing knowledge in pioneering attempts to effect institutional change to promote innovation. This is a shift in protection strategies from the pollutant-by-pollutant, end-of-pipe, command-and-control approach to a prevention system-oriented approach. Provisions would be incorporated into new and existing regulations and programs, maximizing flexibility for industry.

Many environmental and public health professionals may take for granted the significant contributions third-party certification has already made toward the protection of public safety, public health, and the environment during the last century. The reliance on third-party certification has been important as an adjunct to regulatory oversight in all developed countries including the United States.

CURRENT STATUS OF DEVELOPMENT

As this book goes to press, ISO is preparing to determine whether or not it will pursue the development of OHSMS standards in the near future. To aid in this process, ANSI sponsored a meeting to provide a forum for stakeholder groups and interested parties to express their viewpoints on the development of both an ANSI and ISO OHSMS.[20] The five stakeholder groups identified by ANSI for participation in the workshop are business and industry, labor, government, standards-developing organizations, and the insurance industry. While the response to an ISO OHSMS set of standards is mixed, a trend appears to be evolving: As a greater understanding of the issues in gained, support for such standards increases. A brief discussion of the various stakeholder groups' interests and related issues follows.

Business and Industry

Support for ISO OHSMS standards in business and industry is mixed. Some observers would say that this stakeholder group is clearly against the development of an OHSMS standard. This observation is tempered by the fact that numerous firms, independent of the ISO standards development process, have already begun to restructure their OHS programs to conform with the ISO 9000 model. Preliminary information indicates that these firms are realizing greater efficiencies as well as reduced illness and injury rates.

Organizations that support the development of an ISO OHSMS view a potential standard as logical, efficient, and effective. Many of these firms have, or are in the process of obtaining, ISO 9000 certifications, which include OHS programs. Several organizations that are supportive and have begun to incorporate an ISO-compatible OHSMS include IBM, Raychem, Monsanto-Canada, and Kajima Construction.

A chief concern of industry is that an ISO OHSMS standard will add another layer of expense and effort on top of existing OSHA regulations; that is, there will be more "outsiders" telling them what to do. Further, there is doubt and suspicion regarding whether overseas competitors will faithfully comply. Another concern is the third-party registration aspect of a potential ISO OHSMS.

In addition, industry is concerned about the effect that an ISO OHSMS would have on labor relations. Many of the concerns expressed during OSHA's efforts to develop a comprehensive occupational health and safety program standard are germane to this point.

Another important issue associated with the ISO management standards is whether small and medium-size organizations with modest capital resources can afford to invest critical time and money to acquire registration. If the OHSMS standard is overly complex and registration excessively time-consuming or expensive, many small or financially unstable organizations will undoubtedly question their ability to achieve registration. However, the potential for a negative impact on the health of workers and the attendant liability exposure may be of importance equal to or greater than the cost of registration.

Consequently, it is these smaller firms that may achieve the greatest health and safety improvements by submitting the organization to a comprehensive health and safety management systems analysis. In recognition of the worldwide trend towards the formation of smaller organizations, accommodations for their needs should be considered prior to development of audit tools and procedures.

Labor

As with business and industry, labor support for an ISO OHSMS standard is mixed. However, the observed trend is that as this stakeholder group gains a greater understanding of OHSMS concepts, support follows. An evolving position within labor is that an ISO OHSMS represents a possible means to improve occupational health and safety since it appears that industry has effectively stalemated the development of specification standards. Further, if a reliable third-party verification mechanism is part of the system, it would allow OSHA compliance officers an expanded opportunity to focus on industries and organizations with the most serious compliance problems.

Labor's primary concern is that an ISO OHSMS might in some way weaken or undermine past gains in worker health and safety standards and regulations. If implemented, the existence of an ISO OHSMS might be used as an argument by industry to eliminate the OSHA field compliance staff. Further, if employee input is not encouraged or allowed, organizations may in effect hire auditors who will not be objective.

Government

Over the past several years, OSHA has expressed interest in a potential ISO OHSMS as the agency has considered a third-party registration policy. Specifically, at the American Industrial Hygiene Association Conference in May 1994, Assistant Secretary Joe Dear said, "If we were to have independent third parties certify workplaces, who would do the certifications? What would be their qualifications? How would we ensure program integrity? What incentives could be developed to move in that direction?"[21]

On other occasions, Dear has stated that OSHA is interested in pursuing the third-party concept as part of the agency's reinvention activities. To this end, the concept of third-party certification was discussed at the OSHA stakeholders 1994 meeting in Washington, D.C. Some stakeholders voiced concern about the concept. The discussion of a third-party registration policy at the stakeholders meeting was not connected to an ISO OHSMS. Since the stakeholders' meeting, important distinctions between third-party registration and OHSMS have evolved. As these distinctions have been refined, a number of stakeholders who originally voiced opposition are currently supportive.

ISO OHSMS Development

Many of the core principles of an ISO OHSMS are embodied in Vice President Gore's National Performance Review (NPR). Among its recommendations, the NPR addresses regulatory reform in a number of respects. Action steps that support a core principle—

customer satisfaction—call for the elimination of so-called "regulatory overkill." One specific action term calls for "the Secretary of Labor [to] issue new regulations for worksite safety and health, relying on private inspection companies or nonmanagement companies."[22]

In response to the NPR, OSHA developed an agency-specific reinvention plan. Two regulatory approaches are presented in the plan. The first is a choice of partnership with OSHA for firms with strong and effective health and safety programs. The second is traditional OSHA enforcement for firms that do not implement strong and effective health and safety programs. Organizations that have implemented strong health and safety programs will be "given the lowest priority of enforcement inspection, the highest priority for assistance, appropriate regulatory relief, and penalty reductions up to 100%."[23]

The plan's recommendations are based on six principles "for the protection of America's workers." The third principle states that "OSHA will initiate strategic, public-private partnerships to identify and encourage the spread of industry best practices to solve national problems." This principle is similar to the ISO quality management approach, which is based on management commitment and employee involvement.

Standards-Developing Organizations

Three standards-developing organizations have been active within this stakeholder group. The American Industrial Hygiene Association (AIHA) has taken a lead role in developing a consensus on a potential ISO OHSMS. In addition to the American Society of Safety Engineers (ASSE) and the American Society for Quality Control (ASQC), the AIHA has observed the ISO 9000 and ISO 14000 developments to determine if these existing standards will facilitate improvement in work conditions. These organizations have concluded that a set of separate standards, one that focuses on the unique aspects of occupational safety and health management systems, would be beneficial. Consequently, AIHA has led a collaborative effort with partner organizations, public and private, to develop an ISO 9000/ISO 14000-compatible occupational safety and health management system (OHSMS) standard. If ANSI elects to move forward with the development of a U.S. OHSMS standard, the AIHA OHSMS could serve as the initial working document for use in the ANSI consensus process.

The Insurance Industry

The best way to summarize this stakeholder group position is that they favor any standard or policy that reduces illness and injury. To the extent that an ISO standard does this, they will support it; to the extent that it does not, they will oppose it. This stakeholder group's customer base is industry. As such, it is anticipated that they will align with the positions of industry. Insurance is intrigued with the potential assessment tools and protocols that may be used in an ISO OHSMS. Interest has been expressed in the use of universally accepted auditing tools; the use of which could result in a database of validated leading indicators of workplace health and safety.

AN OHSMS AND ITS RELATION TO EXISTING STANDARDS/POLICIES

Within the ISO Framework

TC 207 structured the ISO 14000 standards so that they are, to the extent feasible, compatible with the ISO 9000 series.[24] This precedent and the current development of an OHSMS congruent with ISO 9001 and ISO 14001 suggest that critical features of an OHSMS standard would likely parallel those found in ISO 9001 and ISO 14001.[25]

Traditional environmental health and safety audits are conducted to assess numerous results. These include regulatory compliance assurance, program effectiveness, training adequacy, liability identification, and appropriate resource allocation.[26]

Alternately, ISO 9000 and ISO 14000 conformity assessments evaluate the extent to which an organization maintains and documents its management system, not necessarily the results of its system. For example, an ISO 14001 audit would verify that the organization maintains a system that ensures environmental regulatory compliance. The audit would not verify compliance in and of itself.

A formal OHSMS is an orderly arrangement of interdependent activities and related procedures that drive an organization's occupational health performance. An OHSMS standard would need to evaluate these system features. As such, the standard would not require the capture, analysis, or evaluation of exposure samples.

An ISO 9000/ISO 14000-harmonized OHSMS standard would likely contain five major elements. These elements are presented below, accompanied by the implications for a standard. The standard would evaluate the following:[27]

1. The presence of an occupational safety and health policy and performance objectives.

A standard would have to contain elements that evaluate whether the safety and health policy legitimately addresses relevant site conditions and activities. Does the policy guide the setting of appropriate performance objectives? Is there a written commitment to comply with statutory requirements and industry practices?

2. The adequacy of the occupational health management systems to achieve the policy objectives.

The management systems review would examine factors such as planning and organizational procedures. The effective presence of these two factors should indicate whether the organization has deliberate, viable mechanisms to achieve health and safety policy objectives.

3. The competency of individuals who implement the systems.

The best designed systems may be poorly implemented unless capable individuals ensure maximum performance. The standard contents would have to include an evaluation of personnel adequacy.

4. Risk assessment, risk management, risk communication, and risk documentation.

The standard should evaluate the effectiveness of the company's efforts to assess environmental working conditions. The adequacy of the management system would be evaluated in light of policy objectives and statutory requirements. The assessment instrument would also contain instructions to auditors to verify that root causes of identified health and safety problems are methodically mitigated. Company communication efforts, to both internal and external stakeholders, would also be assessed. Finally, information management systems and support documentation would be examined.

5. Continuous review and improvement.

An important component of ISO 14000 currently absent in ISO 9000 is the continuous improvement feature. An ISO OHSMS would likely require continuous improvement of the system. The OHSMS standard would evaluate the effectiveness of organizational efforts to continuously review and improve working conditions.

The standard would ideally contain auditor instructions to evaluate the company's compliance with applicable governmental specification standards, without listing the standards individually. Ironically, ISO 14001 does not mandate compliance with statutory requirements. Under the ISO 14000 model, companies are required to show "commitment" to compliance with governmental environmental regulations.[28]

Compliance with applicable regulation is always viewed as the minimal requirement for conformance with an ISO-harmonized management system standard.

Comparison with Public and Private Assessment Instruments

Numerous public and private health and safety assessment instruments currently exist.[29] While some reflect unique corporate philosophies and appear compliance-driven, some, such as the federal Voluntary Protection Programs (VPP) and the International Loss Control Institute's International Safety Rating System (ILCI-ISRS), merit closer inspection due to their systems-based, non-industry-specific assessment approach.

The ILCI-ISRS is a comprehensive health and safety assessment instrument that uses a numerical scoring system to rate organizational conformance to safety systems and practices that ILCI considers important. The auditing tool contains 20 basic element areas, which cover issues including accident/incident investigations, communications, and management of change.

An ISO OHSMS standard would likely evaluate similar factors. The ILCI-ISRS also attempts to measure specifics that fall outside the purview of an OHSMS standard. For example, the ILCI-ISRS requires the presence of loss-control bulletin boards, an off-the-job-safety program, and detailed safety and health training for senior management. The ISRS uses weighting factors for each auditable item and applies these factors and scores to all applications of the system. This practice is also not in accordance with an ISO-harmonized model.

Where the ILCI-ISRS is very detailed, the federal VPP is considerably more general and will likely be compatible with the forthcoming OHSMS. Under the VPP model, participant companies must adequately implement comprehensive safety and health management systems that contain six major areas of emphasis. These include management commitment and planning, hazard prevention and control, worksite analysis, safety and health training, employee involvement in program planning, and annual evaluation of health and safety management systems.[30]

Additionally, companies must over the three years preceding the site inspection maintain an average of lost workdays and injury case rates at or below the rates of the most specific industry national average published by the Bureau of Labor statistics. Federal OSHA conducts on-site reviews every three years to ensure that participant companies are committed to continuous health and safety improvement.

Although the VPP is broadly compatible with the OHSMS concept, size assessments would likely differ from OHSMS conformity assessment in several key areas. First, the OHSMS standard would probably not mandate employee participation in health and safety program planning. Second, the OHSMS standard would not prescribe acceptable specific lost workday rates. Third, some system elements required under VPP need to be implemented for at least a year prior to the site inspection. Specific time constraints would not be part of an OHSMS model. Fourth, VPP site inspectors do not utilize a formal assessment instrument. Size evaluation is conducted by answering broad-based, open-ended questions that evaluate the six major program elements.[31]

Perhaps the most vexing questions about an OHSMS assessment instrument pertain to instrument validity and reliability. Researchers have been unable to identify published studies that have evaluated the accuracy and repeatability of either publicly or privately held occupational safety and health assessment instruments. These attributes would facilitate parity among conformance evaluations, generate user confidence, and assist in outcomes research.[32]

The ISO 14010-12 auditing standards promote consistency and reliability by suggesting that audits be conducted by "well-defined methodologies and systematic procedures." However, it later states that "different audits may require different procedures." This vague guidance, coupled with the inherent difficulties associated with interpreting the intent of the standard, may lead to uneven interpretation and place companies at "audit risk."

Audit risk refers to the depth of detail that site assessors may require in their data-collection efforts. For example, if a U.S. site auditor is assessing the adequacy of a company's respiratory protection program (CFR 1910.134), how much data should he or she reasonably review? A respiratory protection program should contain at the minimum, 10 basic components. Should the auditor review all 10 or terminate actions after assessing the written operating procedures? (Recall, ISO 9000/ISO 14001 are management, not performance, standards.) What if one auditor examines all 10 parts of the program while a second reviews only written operating procedures? The conclusions drawn from the differing approaches may not coincide.

Under an OHSMS standard, health and safety auditors would also have to rethink traditional approaches to site assessments. Many U.S. federal and state health and safety inspections and private-sector audits tend to be reactive and prescriptive. Alternately, an OHSMS conformity assessment would evaluate proactive management systems in an approach somewhat similar to the federal VPP.[33]

Another issue associated with the ISO OHSMS is achievability. Can organizations with modest resources invest critical time and financial resources to achieve registration? If the OHSMS is overly complex, and registration is excessively time-consuming or expensive, many small or financially unstable organizations will undoubtedly question their ability to achieve registration.

By nature, small and medium-size firms often do not have a large pool of resources dedicated to OHS issues. Consequently, it is these firms that may achieve major health and safety improvements by submitting the organization to a comprehensive safety and health management-systems analysis. Accommodations for small or poorly capitalized organizations should be considered prior to development of audit tools and audit procedures.

The European study suggesting that customers generally do not perceive a difference between ISO 9000-registered and nonregistered suppliers raises an interesting question. If stakeholders do not perceive a benefit from conducting business with an OHSMS registered company, can the expense associated with acquiring registration be rationalized? If employee working conditions do not continuously improve to stakeholder satisfaction, the credibility of the entire process may fall suspect.[34]

Modifications to the Occupational Safety and Health Act of 1970 (i.e., OSHA reform) currently under consideration include proposals that exempt employers from routine OSHA inspections if the place of employment has received a workplace review provided by a "certified person."[35] If this amendment is approved as drafted, a well-designed, nationally accepted health and safety assessment instrument may be useful for both governmental and nongovernmental purposes.

Ultimately, development of an organizationwide management system assessment instrument might be practical. The assessment instrument would integrate all features of organizational performance. Elements such as accounting, personnel, environmental aspects, occupational health, information systems, and quality system considerations would necessarily be included in one seamless assessment instrument. This would reduce the need for multiple-site assessments and place employee health and safety alongside business aspects as equals in organizational priorities.

The Occupational Safety and Health Administration

Amid intense debate, the Occupational Safety and Health Act was passed in 1970 as Public Law 91-596. The goal of the act was "to assure as far as possible every working man and woman in the Nation safe and healthful working conditions and to preserve our human resources . . . by providing for the development and promulgation of occupational safety and health standards."[36]

The act was one of numerous statutes that have been called the "fourth wave" of social regulations. This group of regulations received criticism because of their far-reaching effect on American life.[37] As the federal deficit has steadily increased over the past several decades—some would say partially as a result of the social regulations of the 1960s and 1970s[38]—public administrators have been exploring ways to accomplish statutory mandates with fewer resources.

With respect to OSHA and the third-party policy, Assistant Secretary of Labor Joe Dear has stated "to me, it's the resource question which is compelling us to think differently about how we're going to encourage voluntary cooperation efforts."[39] To this end, since 1980, OSHA's FTEs (full-time equivalents) have been reduced 40 percent, while the U.S. workforce has increased by 21 percent.[40] Based on the initial signals of the 104th Congress, OSHA's future funding prospects are not encouraging.

In July 1994, OSHA brought together a diverse group of stakeholders from industry, labor, unions, and different sectors of government to discuss OSHA's future. At the meeting, Assistant Secretary Dear said:

> I believe programs like OSHA are at a critical juncture. We know what our resource picture is like. It's totally inadequate for the job at hand, but we have to live with that. And there's great public doubt and lack of confidence in programs like ours, rightly or wrongly. Maybe we haven't done a good job of communicating our message, but failure to address that issue will further undermine confidence.[41]

It was in front of this backdrop that OSHA and its stakeholders discussed a number of reinvention ideas to support the agency's original statutory mandate. Two of the issues discussed included the third-party registration policy and a focused inspection program.

From a policy formulation perspective, the development of an ISO OHSMS standard presents OSHA with an intriguing framework from which it can reexamine proposed and existing policy development activities in the agency. Two distinct aspects of the standards process discussed here are the development of an OHSMS standard and the use of third-party registrars.

It is possible that an OHSMS standard could be developed that would not include the same third-party registration mechanism used in the ISO 9000 standards. However, if the third-party registration aspect is included, it will provide OSHA with a viable model.

The development of an ISO-harmonized third party registration policy, combined with the voluntary compliance programs presented in OSHA's reinvention plan, would represent a significant paradigm shift from the agency's traditional command-and-control regulatory approach. The use of third-party registrars who have been accredited would reflect a unique combination of privatization and deregulation. Such an approach would be consistent with the principles of the National Performance Review and could support OSHA in successfully meeting both its short- and long-term challenges.

It is important to recognize that an OSHA/ISO OHSMS harmonized third-party registration policy would not represent a voluntary program unto itself, nor would it represent regulation by the least common denominator. When implemented in conjunction with voluntary compliance programs that are based on established standards, the third-party registration approach allows organizations to do the following:

1. Take advantage of tailoring health and safety quality management systems that reflect both the firm's marginal abatement cost functions and its employee's social welfare functions.

2. Take advantage of economy-of-scale savings based on preexisting health and safety quality management systems.

Third-party registration is a quasi-market-based/private-regulation strategy for compliance, which thereby creates flexibility and incentives. While the market-based strategy is sound, there is the potential that all stakeholder interests may not be satisfied. Employee representation in a third-party registration policy is crucial. If properly crafted with the inclusion of employee participation and consideration of welfare functions, the values of both efficiency and equity can be fulfilled.

The American Industrial Hygiene Association OHSMS Guidance Document

In response to the interest and success of ISO 9000 and its quality-system approach, the American Industrial Hygiene Association (AIHA) has developed and is issuing OHSMS guidance documents to assist employers and employees in improving safe working conditions. It is AIHA's intention that the OHSMS documents may be used by practicing health and safety professionals in the United States and elsewhere as a basis for designing, implementing, and evaluating OHSMSs that may be established by organizations.

The AIHA document is compatible with the ISO 9000 series standards since ISO 9001:1994 was used as a template for its structure. The AIHA system is not meant to serve as either a U.S. national standard or as an international consensus standard; however, it may be helpful in the consensus process. The main body of the AIHA OHSMS is contained in the quality systems requirements of section 4.0. There are a total of 20 clauses, a listing of which is shown in Table 18–1.[42]

The AIHA document specifies the basic elements of an OHSMS for organizations wishing to implement a deliberate, documented approach to anticipation, recognition, evaluation, prevention, and control of OHS hazards. The document does not state specific technical requirements, nor does it provide a prescriptive implementation regimen.[43]

CONCLUSION

The ISO management-systems model presents a novel approach to meeting OHS goals. Some believe that in a broader context, ISO 14000 and an ISO OHSMS may provide the necessary bridge between competing interests and paradigms in trade, environmental protection, and sustainable development. The ISO approach appears to offer an instrument through which negative externalities can be internalized by a system of modified market incentives; namely, by tying environmental, health, and safety performance to market participation and procurement language.

The OHSMS approach can lead to the most significant paradigm shift in domestic and international OHS since the inception of federal OSHA and the formation of the International Labor Organization. Further, initial analysis indicates that this approach can reduce occupational illness and injury while improving economic efficiency, variables traditionally considered to be inversely correlated.[44]

TABLE 18-1

AIHA Quality System Requirements

4.1	Occupational Health and Safety Management Responsibility
4.2	OHS Management Systems
4.3	OHS Compliance and Conformity Review
4.4	OHS Design Control
4.5	OHS Document and Data Control
4.6	Purchasing
4.7	OHS Communication Systems
4.8	OHS Hazard Identification and Traceability
4.9	Process Control for OHS
4.10	OHS Inspection and Evaluation
4.11	Control of OHS Inspection, Measuring and Test Equipment
4.12	OHS Inspection and Evaluation Status
4.13	Control of Nonconforming Process or Device
4.14	OHS Corrective and Preventive Action
4.15	Handling, Storage and Packaging of Hazardous Materials
4.16	Control of OHS Records
4.17	Internal OHS Management Systems Audit
4.18	OHS Training
4.19	Operations and Maintenance Services
4.20	Statistical Techniques

If an effective OHSMS standard or policy is to be formulated and implemented, active debate is necessary. While the OHSMS approach does not represent a cure-all for OHS problems, many believe that this approach would establish structures and procedures that could overcome the inherent limitations of the traditional command-and-control approach and replace it with an inherently inclusive, flexible, and self-correcting systems model that would extend the range of what is possible.

BIOGRAPHIES

Charles Redinger, CIH, MPA, and Steven Levine, CIH, PhD

Charles Redinger is a University of Michigan doctoral student who is conducting research in public policy issues related to occupational health and safety management systems. He has a master's degree in public policy from the University of Colorado; is a member of the Public Policy honor society, *Phi Alpha Alpha,* and is a Kemper Fellow in Public Health. He is the coeditor of the book *New Frontiers in Occupational Health: A Management Systems Approach and the ISO Model.* He also is a contributor to the American Industrial Hygiene Association's *Occupational Health and Safety Management System.*

As a cofounder and officer of a national consulting firm, he has over 12 years of industrial hygiene and environmental consulting experience in both the public and private sectors. He served for two years on the governor of California's Asbestos Task Force and is currently assisting the Federal OSHA in the analysis of several policy approaches related to occupational health and safety management systems. He is certified by the ABIH in Comprehensive Practice, and is a Registered Environmental Assessor in the State of California.

Steven Levine began his career in industry, where he worked for eight years. He worked for Stauffer Chemical Company, Ford Motor Company, and Oil and Hazardous Materials (OHM) Company. He has taught at the University of Michigan for thirteen years and currently is Professor of Occupational and Environmental Health. In addition to his numerous publications, he is the coeditor of the book, *New Frontiers in Occupational Health: A Management Systems Approach and the ISO Model.* He too is a major contributor to the American Industrial Hygiene Association's *Occupational Health and Safety Management System.*

Dr. Levine is a member of the ISO 9000 and 14000 Advisory Councils of a nonprofit company, NSFI; a member of the U.S. Technical Advisory Group for ISO TC 207; a member of the AIHA-ACGIH-AAIH-ABIH Unification Task force; and the Director of the University of Michigan WHO Collaborating Center for Occupational Health. He has been honored with the AIHA-ACGIH "Drum Buster" Award, and the AIHA John White Award. He is certified by the ABIH in both Comprehensive and Chemical Practice; and, by the IRCA against the ISO 10001.2 requirements.

NOTES

1. David Dyjack and Steven Levine: "Critical Features of an ISO 9001/14001 Harmonized Health and Safety Assessment Instrument." In *New Frontiers in Occupational Health and Safety: A Management Systems Approach and the ISO Model,* ed. Charles Redinger and Steven Levine (Fairfax, Virginia: American Industrial Hygiene Association, 1966), p. 128.

2. Raychem: "Raychem EHS Standard." Raychem Corporation, Menlo Park, CA 94015-1164, 1995.

3. *American Industrial Hygiene Conference and Exhibition,* Kansas City, MO, June, 1995.

4. C. Bell: "Managing for Business Advantage: Optimizing Health and Safety Performance at Tenneco," Paper presented at the Tenneco Risk Management Conference, Houston, Texas, November, 1994.

5. Charles Redinger, David Dyjack, and Steven Levine: *New Frontiers in Occupational Health and Safety: A Management Systems Approach and the ISO Model,* ed. Charles Redinger and Steven Levine (Fairfax, Virginia: American Industrial Hygiene Association, 1966), p. 1.

6. Ibid.

7. Charles Redinger: "A Paradigm Shift at OSHA: ISO-Harmonized Third-Party Registration of Occupational Health and Safety Programs." In *New Frontiers in Occupational Health and Safety: A Management Systems Approach and the ISO Model,* ed. Charles Redinger and Steven Levine (Fairfax: Virginia: American Industrial Hygiene Association, 1966), p. 35.

8. Workshop on International Standardization of Occupational Health and Safety Management Systems. American National Standards Institute, Rosemont, Illinois, May 7–8, 1996.

9. Voluntary Environmental Self-Policing and Self-Disclosure Interim Policy Statement, April 3, 1995, *Federal Register,* 60:63, p. 16877.

10. Charles Redinger: "A Paradigm Shift at OSHA: ISO-Harmonized Third-Party Registration of Occupational Health and Safety Programs." In *New Frontiers in Occupational Health and Safety: A Management Systems Approach and the ISO Model,* ed. Charles Redinger and Steven Levine (Fairfax, Virginia: American Industrial Hygiene Association, 1996), p. 68.

11. *National Performance Review Commission* (Washington, D.C.: Government Printing Office, September 7, 1993), pp. 6–7.

12. Charles Redinger: "A Paradigm Shift at OSHA: ISO-Harmonized Third Party Registration of Occupational Health and Safety Programs." In *New Frontiers in Occupational Health and Safety: A Management Systems Approach and the ISO Model,* ed. Charles Redinger and Steven Levine (Fairfax, Virginia: American Industrial Hygiene Association, 1996), p. 36.

13. Ibid.

14. Occupational Safety and Health Administration; *The New OSHA - Reinventing Worker Safety and Health.* (Washington, D.C.: Government Printing Office, May 16, 1995.)

15. Theodore J. Lowi: *The End of Liberalism: The Second Republic of the United States, Second Edition.* (New York: W.W. Norton & Company, 1979.)

16. Charles Redinger: "A Paradigm Shift at OSHA: ISO-Harmonized Third Party Registration of Occupational Health and Safety Programs." In *New Frontiers in Occupational Health and Safety: A Management Systems Approach and the ISO Model,* ed. Charles Redinger and Steven Levine (Fairfax, Virginia: American Industrial Hygiene Association, 1996), p. 56.

17. Steven Kelman: "Occupational Safety and Health Administration." *The Politics of Regulation,* ed. James Q. Wilson. (New York: Basic Books, Inc. 1980), p. 264.

18. Occupational Safety and Health Administration: *The New OSHA - Reinventing Worker Safety and Health.* (Washington, D.C.: Governing Printing Office, May 16, 1995.)

19. American National Standards Institute. *An Outline of Issues: International Standardization of Occupational Health and Safety Management Systems.* (New York: ANSI, March 1996). (Prepared for the Workshop on International Standardization of Occupational Health and Safety Management Systems. American National Standards Institute, Rosemont, Illinois, May 7–8, 1996.)

20. J. Dear: Keynote Address, American Industrial Hygiene Conference and Exhibition, Anaheim, California, May 26, 1994.

21. *National Performance Review Commission.* (Washington, D.C.: Government Printing Office, September 7, 1996.), p. 62.

22. Occupational Safety and Health Administration; *The New OSHA - Reinventing Worker Safety and Health.* (Washington, D.C.: Government Printing Office, May 16, 1995.), p. 8.

23. Anonymous, "Other ISO Rules en Route," *Environment Today,* 6(7), 1995, p. 19.

24. David Dyjack and Steven Levine: "Critical Features of an ISO 9001/14001 Harmonized Health and Safety Assessment Instrument." In *New Frontiers in Occupational Health and Safety: A Management Systems Approach and the ISO Model,* ed. Charles Redinger and Steven Levine (Fairfax, Virginia: American Industrial Hygiene Association, 1966), p. 133.

25. A. J. Liebowitz, ed.: *Industrial Hygiene Auditing - A Manual for Practice.* The American Industrial Hygiene Association, 1994, pp. 6–7.

26. David Dyjack and Steven Levine: "Critical Features of an ISO 9001/14001 Harmonized Health and Safety Assessment Instrument." In *New Frontiers in Occupational Health and Safety: A Management Systems Approach and the ISO Model,* ed. Charles Redinger and Steven Levine (Fairfax, Virginia: American Industrial Hygiene Association, 1966), p. 134–35.

27. International Organization for Standardization. *Unofficial ISO Draft International Standard 14001.* ISO Technical Committee 207, June 26, 1995, Geneva, Switzerland.

28. David Dyjack and Steven Levine: "Critical Features of an ISO 9001/14001 Harmonized Health and Safety Assessment Instrument." In *New Frontiers in Occupational Health and Safety: A Management Systems Approach and the ISO Model,* ed. Charles Redinger and Steven Levine (Fairfax, Virginia: American Industrial Hygiene Association, 1966), p. 137.

29. "Voluntary Protection Programs to Supplement Enforcement and to Provide Safe and Healthful Working Conditions Changes," *Federal Register,* 7/12/88, 53:133, pages, 26339–26348.

30. David Dyjack and Steven Levine: "Critical Features of an ISO 9001/14001 Harmonized Health and Safety Assessment Instrument." In *New Frontiers in Occupational Health and Safety: A Management Systems Approach and the ISO Model,* ed. Charles Redinger and Steven Levine (Fairfax, Virginia: American Industrial Hygiene Association, 1966), p. 138.

31. David Dyjack and Steven Levine: "Critical Features of an ISO 9001/14001 Harmonized Health and Safety Assessment Instrument." In *New Frontiers in Occupational Health and Safety: A Management Systems Approach and the ISO Model,* ed. Charles Redinger and Steven Levine (Fairfax, Virginia: American Industrial Hygiene Association, 1966), p. 139.

32. B. Wenmonth: "Quality Systems and Environmental Management," *Environmental Health Review* 23(2), (Australia), 1994, pp. 41–54.

33. David Dyjack and Steven Levine: "Critical Features of an ISO 9001/14001 Harmonized Health and Safety Assessment Instrument." In *New Frontiers in Occupational Health and Safety: A Management Systems Approach and the ISO Model,* ed. Charles Redinger and Steven Levine (Fairfax, Virginia: American Industrial Hygiene Association, 1966), p. 141.

34. U.S. Congress: *House Safety and Health Improvement and Regulatory Reform Act of 1995* (H.R. 1834). (Washington D.C.: U.S. Government Printing Office, June 14, 1995), pp. 20–22.

35. 29 USCA § 651(b) (9).

36. Theodore J. Lowi: *The End of Liberalism: The Second Republic of the United States, Second Edition.* (New York: W.W. Norton & Company, 1979).

37. Robert Gilpin: *The Political Economy of International Relations* (Princeton: Princeton University Press, 1987.)

38. *BNA Occupational Safety & Health Reporter,* 6/1/94; The Bureau of National Affairs, 1231 25th Street, N.W., Washington, D.C. 20037, p. 3.

39. *BNA Occupational Safety & Health Reporter,* 7/27/94; The Bureau of National Affairs, 1231 25th Street, N.W., Washington, D.C. 20037, p. 421.

40. *BNA Occupational Safety & Health Reporter,* 7/27/94; The Bureau of National Affairs, 1231 25th Street, N.W., Washington, D.C. 20037, p. 404.

41. Occupational Health and Safety Management System (OHSMS) Guidance Document. (Fairfax, Virginia: American Industrial Hygiene Association, May 1996.)

42. Ibid.

43. David Dyjack and Steven Levine: "Critical Features of an ISO 9001/14001 Harmonized Health and Safety Assessment Instrument." In *New Frontiers in Occupational Health and Safety: A Management Systems Approach and the ISO Model,* ed. Charles Redinger and Steven Levine (Fairfax, Virginia: American Industrial Hygiene Association, 1966), p. iii.

PART FOUR

ISO 14001 Registration

CHAPTER 19

Overview of Conformity Assessment

Tom Tibor and Ira Feldman

INTRODUCTION

Although it is suitable for self-declaration and second-party use, the ISO 14001 specification standard was drafted in anticipation of its use in third-party registration (certification). To a large extent, the acceptance of ISO 14001 worldwide will depend on the credibility of the framework for conformity assessment. Conformity assessment refers to all activities that are intended to ensure the conformity of products and/or processes to standards. These activities can include testing, inspection, certification, registration, and other activities.

This chapter addresses some important conformity assessment issues, including the following:

- Who ensures the competency of ISO 14001 registrars; that is, who accredits registrars?
- What criteria are used in the accreditation process?
- Who ensures the competence of ISO 14001 auditors and the consistent interpretation of ISO 14001 standards?
- Under what conditions will ISO 14001 certificates be recognized and accepted worldwide?

The registration process itself is described in the next chapter.

It is important to note that ISO's work is confined to the development and publication of international standards. It has no direct responsibility for conformity assessment. The structure of conformity assessment is developed by national testing and certification bodies, by accreditation bodies set up specifically to ensure the credibility and effectiveness of third-party registration, and by governmental bodies that recognize the competence of accreditors.

REGISTRAR ACCREDITATION

The credibility of the ISO 14000 process will depend to a large extent on the competence of the ISO 14001 registrar (certifying body). Who ensures the competence of registrars, and according to what criteria? This is usually determined by recognized accreditation organizations.

Figure 19–1 illustrates the registration/accreditation/recognition hierarchy. The companies are at the bottom of the hierarchy. Their EMS systems are audited by the registrars, who are at the next level. The registrars' competence is assured by accreditors. The competence of the accreditors, in turn, is recognized by governmental or quasi-governmental authorities.

What is Accreditation?

According to ISO/IEC Guide 2, accreditation is the "procedure by which an authoritative body formally recognizes that a body or person is competent to carry out specific tasks." Accreditation is the initial evaluation and periodic monitoring of a registrar's competence, performed by an accreditation body. Accreditation bodies are either already in operation in most countries or being put into place. In some countries, the accrediting body is a governmental organization and in others (including the United States) it will be a nongovernmental organization. A few well-known accreditation organizations include the United Kingdom Accreditation Service (UKAS) and the Dutch Council for Accreditation (RvA) in The Netherlands. In Canada, the Standards Council of Canada is working on an accreditation program for registrars, EMS auditors, and training course providers. Likewise, in the United States, two organizations, RAB and the American National Standards Institute (ANSI), are in the process of developing accreditation systems (see Box 19–1).

FIGURE   19–1

The Registration/Accreditation/Recognition Hierarchy

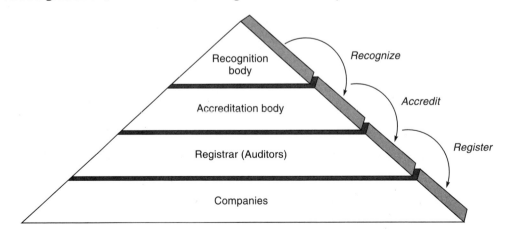

Accreditation Scope

Registrars are accredited to conduct third-party audits in selected industries; that is, they are accredited to audit within a scope of industrial classifications. An organization that selects a registrar to perform a third-party audit of its EMS must be certain that the registrar is accredited and competent to perform audits in that organization's industry sector. The registrar's scope is determined by reference to some classification system. The United States for instance, uses the Standard Industrial Classification (SIC) Codes. In Europe, a similar system of codes, Nomenclature Generale des Activites Economiques Dan les Communautes Europeenes (NACE), is used to define scope.

BOX 19–1

U.S. ACCREDITATION SYSTEM

As of this writing, the Registrar Accreditation Board (RAB) and the American National Standards Institute (ANSI) are close to agreement on a joint program to accredit registrars, auditor certifiers, and auditor training course providers. The ANSI program is known as the Environmental Management Systems National Accreditation Program (NAP). Earlier, the RAB and ANSI had embarked on separate plans to create a U.S. accreditation system.

ANSI has established an Environmental Systems Council (ESC) to oversee the formation of its accreditation program and to serve as a mechanism for stakeholder input. The ESC includes representatives from industry, federal and state governments, registrars, the auditor and auditor training professions, and nongovernmental organizations.

The RAB has also launched a pilot EMS registrar accreditation program. Designed to meet the needs of U.S. industry in obtaining ISO 14001 registration, the pilot program will culminate in the accreditation of up to five EMS registrars. The pilot program will include both an office audit at the registrar's facilities and a witnessing of the registrar's audit of a client organization.

Auditor Certification

Currently there is not a comprehensive auditor accreditation or certification scheme in the United States, although there are various unaccredited private schemes. Professional organizations offer certifications relevant to environmental auditors, including the Institute of Professional Environmental Practice's Qualified Environmental Auditor or Qualified Environmental Professional credential.

The U.S. ISO 14001 accreditation program, when it is fully developed, may form the foundation for a national auditor accreditation scheme. Such a scheme would include the certification of auditors and training courses, and the development of criteria for auditor certification and course accreditation.

Accreditation Criteria

Accreditation bodies use established criteria against which to evaluate the competence of registrars (certifiers). For example, quality system registrars are evaluated against the requirements of the EN 45000 series of standards, developed by CEN/CENELEC. Particularly relevant is *EN 45012, General Criteria for Certification Bodies Operating Quality System Certification,* which sets out key criteria for registrars. Most accreditation bodies use EN 45012 to evaluate the competence of quality systems registrars.

This standard is being adapted for use in the ISO 14000 context. Among other countries, the United Kingdom, The Netherlands, and the United States are developing draft accreditation criteria for registrars conducting environmental management system audits (see chapter appendix).

Other guidance for the accreditation of registrars is contained in CASCO guides. CASCO is ISO's Committee on Conformity Assessment. It has developed several guidance documents that are adopted by organizations for use in accreditation and certification. Two examples of such guides are *ISO/IEC Guide 48, Guidelines for a third-party assessment and registration of a supplier's quality system* and *ISO/IEC Guide 62, General requirements for bodies operating assessment and certification/ registration of quality systems* (See Box 19–2 for other relevant CASCO guides).

Recognition of the Accreditation Body

If accreditors ensure the competence of registrars and registration auditors, who recognizes the competence of the accreditors? In most countries, this is the task of government or quasi-governmental authorities. In the United States, the National Institute of Standards and Technology (NIST) has recognized RAB as the official accreditation body for ISO 9000 registrars. In the future, NIST may also recognize the ISO 14001 registrar accreditation body. Both UKAS in the United Kingdom and Raad voor Accreditatie (RvA) in The Netherlands have similar agreements with their respective governments.

Harmonizing Accreditation Schemes

In 1991, European accreditation bodies established the European Accreditation of Certification (EAC). EAC's goal is to develop consistency in the accreditation of environmental management system certification. To this end, it has developed harmonized interpretation guides to relevant standards in the EN 45000 series, including EN 45011 for product certification, EN 45012 for quality system certification, and EN 45013 for certification of personnel. EAC also operates a peer review system to ensure that the accreditation process works effectively. The ultimate goal is consistent, high-quality application of accreditation criteria among all accreditation bodies. This should lead to mutual recognition of certification results.

B O X   19–2

CASCO AND CASCO GUIDES

CASCO is the conformity assessment committee of ISO. Its goals include the following:

- Study means of assessing the conformity of products, processes, services, and quality systems to appropriate standards or other technical specifications.

- Prepare international guides relating to the testing, inspection, and certification of products, processes, and services and to the assessment of quality systems, testing laboratories, inspection bodies, certification bodies, and their operation and acceptance.

- Promote mutual recognition and acceptance of national and regional conformity assessment systems and the appropriate use of international standards for testing, inspection, certification, assessment, and related purposes.

CASCO guides are developed by working groups of experts from around the world using a consensus process. These guides serve as a basis for national practices. They are used by suppliers, conformity assessment bodies, accreditors, approval bodies, and trade policy makers. CASCO guide usage should increase since all members of the new World Trade Organization must adhere to the chapter on Technical Barriers to Trade. That chapter of the GATT agreement specifically cites the use of international guides for conformity assessment.

CASCO's Working Group 8 has revised existing guides relevant to the accreditation of certification bodies. These include the following:

- ISO/CASCO Guide 61 *General requirements for assessment and accreditation of certification/registration bodies.*

- ISO/CASCO Guide 62 *General requirements for bodies operating assessments and the certification/registration of quality systems.*

- ISO/CASCO 228 (rev 2) *General requirements for bodies operating product certification systems.*

Along with the EN 45000 standards, these CASCO guides will provide international guidelines for the certification of EMSs and the accreditation of EMS registrars and EMAS verifiers.

RECOGNITION OF THE ISO 14001 CERTIFICATE

An accredited and competent registrar should conduct a professional audit and issue a credible ISO 14001 registration certificate. Naturally, the organization that earns the ISO 14001 certificate expects that it will be recognized and accepted worldwide in those areas where the company does business. However, this is not automatically the case.

ISO/IEC Guide 2 defines recognition as "an agreement that is based on the acceptance by one party of results, presented by another party, from the implementation of one or more designated functional elements of a conformity assessment system."

At the company level, if a company's customers recognize its ISO 14001 certificate, that may be sufficient, no matter which registrar awarded the certificate or even if the registrar is accredited. The marketplace ultimately determines the acceptability of a certificate.

At the accreditation body level, accreditation bodies need not automatically accept the certificates awarded by each other's accredited registrars. That is, Accreditor A that accredits Registrar A need not accept the certificates awarded by Registrar B who, in turn, is accredited by Accreditor B. However, many organizations are working to develop agreements that ensure the mutual recognition of ISO 9001 and ISO 14001 certificates worldwide.

The International Accreditation Forum (IAF), for example, was formed in 1993 from representatives of various international standards bodies and registrars to work toward a system where accreditations are recognized throughout the world.

There is also a proposal for an international system of recognition, the Quality System Assessment Recognition (QSAR), that would lead to worldwide recognition of the ISO 9001 registration certificate. This system, now under development, is based on the goal of having a single ISO 9001 registration certificate that is recognized and accepted anywhere in the world, regardless of the location of either client or registration body. The QSAR concept may be expanded to include ISO 14001.

AUDITOR CERTIFICATION

A final major issue is the competence and professionalism of ISO 14001 auditors. Who will certify their competence? According to what standards? What about recognition of certified auditors? Certified ISO 14001 auditors want their credentials recognized so that they can perform EMS audits that are accepted worldwide.

Consistent interpretation of the standard will be another big challenge. How can customers be confident that auditors are consistently interpreting and applying the ISO 14000 standards? There are many concepts in the standards that are open to interpretation, such as environmental aspects and continual improvement.

In the ISO 9001 context, the ISO 10011 auditing standards, *Guidelines for auditing quality systems,* have been accepted by most registrars and accreditation bodies to evaluate the work of ISO 9001 auditors. Similarly, the ISO 14010-12 auditing standards should be adopted worldwide to assist in the performance of consistent and competent audits in the EMS area.

In addition, auditors are certified in many programs worldwide. Two of these in the quality area include the Institute for Quality Assurance's (IQA) National Registration Scheme for Assessors of Quality Systems in the United Kingdom and the RAB's Certification Program for Auditors of Quality Systems in the United States.

Quality management system auditors are registered with the United Kingdom's Institute of Quality Assurance/International Register of Certificated Auditors. IQA/IRCA has published environmental management system qualification criteria for U.K. auditors. Auditors certified by IQA/IRCA will be trained to audit companies to ISO 9001, BS 7750, ISO 14001, and EMAS.

International Auditor Training and Certification Association

The International Auditor Training and Certification Association (IATCA) was formed in 1993 by 13 national auditor certification and auditing course accreditation programs. Its goal is to develop an international, harmonized set of auditor qualification criteria and criteria for auditing training courses. Variations among countries regarding auditor certification criteria mean multiple certifications for auditors who operate in several countries. Although auditor certification for ISO 14001 is not yet on IATCA's agenda, it may fall under the IATCA agreement in a few years.

Challenges for EMS Auditors

UKAS began to accredit BS 7750 registration/certification bodies in March 1995 by accrediting the first eight registrars. In January 1995, UKAS published *The Environmental Accreditation Criteria*. These criteria are based on the requirements of EN 45012. As part of the development process, UKAS assessed more than 40 certification bodies. This experience may shed some light on the challenges faced by registration auditors.[1]

Process, Not Performance

A familiar issue by now is the degree to which auditors assess the management process rather than the environmental performance output. UKAS's criteria does not recommend that the assessment or judgment of performance be the basis for certification.[2]

Yet commentators imply that process cannot be easily separated from performance and that effective ISO 14001 auditors, in addition to their basic understanding of management elements, will need a technical understanding of environmental performance issues, specialized environmental knowledge and experience, and the ability to evaluate environmental aspects and impacts.

Auditors will need to understand issues such as the nature of the organization's regulatory compliance, its performance measuring systems, its significant environmental impacts, and other aspects of environmental performance.

The implication is that ISO 14001 auditors, more so than ISO 9001 auditors, may not need to judge environmental performance but may have to go beyond ensuring that basic management elements, such as policies, manuals, and procedures, are in place.[3]

Key Areas

The UKAS criteria point out some key areas of the EMS that both the organization and auditors should focus on. These include the following:

- Has the organization identified and evaluated environmental aspects in a systematic way?
- Have objectives and targets been set in such a way that they can be compared to actual performance?
- Is environmental performance being monitored and reported appropriately for the objectives and targets?
- Are audits focusing on the environmental management system?
- Is there evidence of corrective action and management system improvement resulting from audit information?

Assessing Regulatory Compliance

If a site is not in compliance with regulations, will it achieve certification? Since few sites are completely in compliance, the question that experts have posed is the following: What level of noncompliance will auditors accept? A major violation? Several small violations? One opinion is that as long as a site has an EMS in place that allows it to comply within a reasonable time frame and to correct violations, it should meet the standard.[4]

Also, if the auditor discovers a violation, is he or she responsible for reporting it to management? If not, what is the auditor's legal liability, if any? If so, what type of violation should be reported? Again, these questions will take experience to fully resolve, including the nature and extent of an auditor's legal responsibilities.

Generally, experts agree that violations should be reported to management but not to anyone else. This is called for in the ISO 14010-14011 standards. Once the auditor reports the violation, it becomes management's responsibility to report the violations to the appropriate regulatory agency.

CONCLUSION

Even the brief discussion in this chapter is evidence that conformity assessment issues are complex. The success of the ISO 14000 movement and confidence in the usefulness of the ISO 14000 certificate will depend on consistent and credible conformity assessment procedures. Registrars working with EMS standards such as BS 7750 and ISO 14001 are gathering experience that will help resolve the conformity assessment issues.

In addition, CASCO and many other groups are hard at work to create the mechanisms that will support the successful implementation of ISO 14001 worldwide.

APPENDIX

RAB'S CRITERIA FOR ACCREDITATION OF REGISTRARS

As discussed in this chapter, several countries have developed or are in the process of developing criteria for the accreditation of EMS registrars/certifiers. The EAC in Europe is working on final criteria, largely adapted from EN 45012. This appendix describes some key aspects of the Registrar Accreditation Board's draft criteria for accreditation of registrars for environmental management systems.[5]

The draft document describes how a registrar must organize and operate to achieve and maintain EMS accreditation by RAB. The criteria are designed to be consistent with existing RAB accreditation criteria for registrars of quality systems.

To facilitate the harmonization of registration activities among different countries, these criteria embody the requirements of the standard *CEN/CENELEC EN 45012, General criteria for certification bodies operating quality system certification,* as modified in the *Draft EAC Guidelines for accreditation of certification bodies for environmental management systems, revision 2.* Consistent accreditation worldwide for EMS registrars/certifiers will provide stakeholders with confidence that registrars are consistently and credibly auditing the ISO 14001 standard.

Key Definitions

Site

A site, according to the RAB draft criteria is defined as "all land on which the activities under the control of a company at a given location are carried out, including any connected or associated storage of raw materials, byproducts, intermediate products, end products and waste material, and any equipment or infrastructure involved in the activities, whether or not fixed. Where applicable, the definition of a site shall correspond to definitions specified in legal requirements."

Major Nonconformity

A major nonconformity, as discovered by an auditor, is defined as any of the following:

- One or more elements of ISO 14001 have not been addressed.
- One or more elements of ISO 14001 have not been implemented.
- Several elements of ISO 14001 show similar nonconformances in documentation and/or implementation.
- Significant environmental aspects are consistently not taken into account.

- Noncompliances with legal requirements that have been identified by the organization have not appropriately been addressed.

Registration

Registration is action by a third party (registrar) that demonstrates confidence that an organization's EMS conforms to a specific standard or other normative document.

EMS Considerations

The draft criteria emphasize that the scope of an EMS is broader than a quality system, since it encompasses, among other things, environmental aspects, commitment to compliance with legislation, and commitment to continual improvement. Thus, "a much broader responsibility is placed on registrars. Registrars must consider the broader aspects of EMS when performing audits of the system. Environmental management system registration is separate from, and is not to be considered as an extension of, quality system registration." The criteria emphasize that the EMS focuses on the existence and implementation of an appropriate management system; *the EMS registration process does not evaluate an organization's degree of compliance with legislation and regulations.*" [Emphasis added.]

ISO 14001/ISO 9001 Registrations

The draft criteria acknowledge the needs of those organizations already registered to one of the ISO 9001 standards and their desire for a single, integrated system. The criteria expect registrars to take into account the common aspects of an organization's management system, "considering the size of the organization, the types of activities and products, the organization's culture, and the effectiveness of interfaces between the management systems." When the EMS shares elements common to other management systems, the registrar is expected "to ensure that there is compatibility between the management systems with regard to the shared elements." The organization's EMS documentation should describe the EMS and make clear its relationship to any other management systems in operation at the site.

Small Organizations

The draft criteria acknowledge that small organizations may operate differently from large organizations, typically requiring fewer procedures and instructions and personnel with more multidisciplinary responsibilities. Registrars are expected to take these factors into consideration when planning audits and selecting audit teams.

Scope of Registration

The registrar grants a certificate applicable to activities that take place at a site (as defined above). The registrar ensures that the scope of registration applies to the entire site and all environmental aspects of that site. It emphasizes that the definition of the site should be "consistent with any environmental permits or licensing documents for the location."

The criteria gives guidance for the following types of situations:

Separate Organization-Shared Site   If the organization seeking registration shares the location with another organization, the registering organization should manage the interfaces between it and the other organization(s) whose "activities are relevant to the significant environmental aspects in question."

Similar Activities at Multiple Sites   An organization can operate several sites under the same EMS. In this case, the registrar can issue the registration document to cover all sites, provided that the registrar has audited the sites "by way of sample" and has taken into account "significant environmental aspects which may vary from site to site" and the "effectiveness of the organization's internal audit system."

The internal audit system must audit all sites within a three-year period.

If the number of sites is so large that the three-year period is impractical, "registration may be granted, subject to agreement with RAB, on the basis of a smaller sample and corresponding greater demonstration of the competence of the organization's internal audit system."

Services   The criteria acknowledge that for services, a physical site is not the most appropriate unit for registration. In this case, operating units may be registered. In such cases, however, "the interfaces with other activities that are relevant to significant environmental aspects of the operating unit subject to registration should be managed as part of the EMS."

Registration of One Activity within a Larger Organization   The criteria also recognize the situation where different operating units or divisions of an organization operate at the same site, but independently of each other. Registrars can register the individual operating unit if the following conditions are fulfilled:

- The operating units have separate managers, reporting to different senior executives, "responsible for managing the activities which cause or have the potential to cause significant environmental impact."
- Managers of the operating unit have the authority to set their own objectives and targets and sufficient authority to allocate resources to achieve those objectives "independently of other operating units at the same location."
- Each EMS must address all interfaces with environmentally relevant activities at the same location. This applies "in particular to shared or common facilities giving rise to significant environmental impacts."
- Where applicable, the operating unit has its own operating facilities with a separate environmental permit(s).

Accreditation Requirements for Registrars

The draft criteria detail a lengthy list of requirements that registrars must meet to become accredited. Several of the key requirements of particular interest to organizations considering ISO 14001 registration are summarized below.

Competent Auditors

The registrar must employ a sufficient number of personnel with the necessary education, training, and environmental knowledge to perform the audits. The audit team chosen should have skills and understanding in the following areas:

- Environmental science and technology.
- Technical and environmental aspects of facility operations.
- Relevant requirements of environmental laws, regulations, and related documents.
- Environmental management systems and standards.
- Audit procedures, processes, and techniques.

Audits Performed According to ISO 14010-12 Standards

Auditors will perform according to the ISO auditing standards. In certain cases, the audit team can be supplemented with either special training or the use of technical experts. When work is subcontracted to an external body, the registrar remains fully accountable and must ensure that the subcontractors meet the applicable requirements in the criteria.

Registration and Surveillance Procedures and Operations

The registrar shall require the organization seeking registration to have a documented and operational EMS. In practice, this means that prior to the initial audit:

- The EMS has been operational for a minimum of three months.
- The internal audit system is fully operational and can be shown to be effective.
- At least one management review has been conducted.

Combined Audits

The criteria takes into account combined ISO 9000/ISO 14000 audits. The following conditions are mentioned:

- The quality of the audit must not be adversely affected by combining the audits.

- The organization's EMS documentation should describe the EMS and make clear the relationship to any other management system that is in operation at the site(s) or that influences the operations at the site(s).
- The documentation for the EMS can be combined with documentation for other management systems as long as the EMS can be clearly identified, together with the appropriate interfaces to other systems.

Issuing the Registration Document

The criteria states that to receive the registration certificate, the organization must meet the following conditions:

- Address all identified nonconformities and eliminate all major nonconformities.
- Provide confidence to the registrar that compliance with regulatory requirements is effective.
- Incorporate continuous improvement into the EMS and adhere to it.
- Make staff aware of the organization's environmental effects objectives and the EMS.
- Provide appropriate training for key staff.

Surveillance Audits

Registrars are required to perform surveillance audits of the registered facility no less than annually and to conduct a full re-audit every three years. If the organization modifies its EMS, it must notify the registrar. Surveillance and/or audits' schedules may be modified as a consequence of changes to the EMS.

Confidentiality

The registrar must be able to ensure confidentiality of the information obtained in the course of its registration activities. In situations where the law requires information to be disclosed to a third party, the registrar must inform the organization of the information provided, as permitted by law.

Use of the Registration Mark

The organization cannot use its ISO 14001 certification mark on a product or in a way that may be interpreted as denoting product conformity. The certification mark refers to registration of an environmental management system, not of any product or process.

Conflict of Interest

The registrar is prohibited from engaging in activities that constitute a conflict of interest. A key such activity is consulting. The criteria emphasize that a registrar, or a related body, shall not offer or provide the following:

- The services that it registers others to perform.
- Consulting services to obtain or maintain registration.
- Services to design, implement, or maintain environmental management systems.

NOTES

1. The RvA in The Netherlands has also accredited registration organizations to offer BS 7750 registrations. Both RvA and UKAS are allowed to accredit non-U.K. firms that offer BS 7750 certifications. RvA and UKAS are working toward mutual recognition of their certificates. UKAS is also working with its European counterparts in the European Accreditation of Certification (EAC) to establish a consistent basis for the accreditation of EMAS verifiers on the basis of BS 7750 and ISO 14001.

2. This discussion is based in part on Martin Houldin, *Environmental Management and Conformity Assessment—The BS 7750 Experience.* Paper presented at ISO/CASCO Conformity assessment for environmental management workshop, June 12–13, 1995, Geneva, Switzerland.

3. Ronald McLean, *Paper from Respondent to the BS 7750 Experience.* Paper presented at ISO/CASCO Conformity assessment for environmental management workshop, June 12–13, 1995, Geneva, Switzerland.

4. Ibid.

5. Registrar Accreditation Board *Criteria for Accreditation of Registrars for Environmental Management Systems Draft 1 1996-02-15.*

CHAPTER 20

The ISO 14001 Registration Process

Antonio Guerra

INTRODUCTION

This chapter describes the different aspects of ISO 14001 registration. Of particular interest are the steps in the registration process, auditor competencies, assessment timing, and costs of registration.

EMS audits can be performed internally, for internal purposes. Companies can also use the results of such audits to self-declare compliance to ISO 14001 (first-party). A company can be audited by another company, such as a customer, as part of a contractual arrangement (second-party). Third-party registration is the assessment of an EMS by independent auditors associated with an organization qualified to perform EMS audits. This organization is referred to as a registrar or registration (certification) body.

THE REGISTRATION PROCESS

The registration process generally consists of the following five basic steps, regardless of which registrar is selected:

1. Application.

2. Initial assessment/document review.

3. Certification assessment.

4. Registration.

5. Surveillance.

During each phase of the registration process, the auditor(s) must meet certain qualifications and competencies to properly conduct an environmental management system assessment or make a certification decision. The time required to implement an ISO 14001 EMS is a function of the organization's resources, while the time required for registration is a function of the registrar's schedule availability. The overall cost of registering to ISO 14001 is the cumulative cost for implementation and third-party registration.

Details of these aspects and what to expect will be discussed below, in addition to comments from the registrar's perspective and some practical guidance.

Application

To begin the registration process, most registrars require a completed application, sometimes called a *contract*. The application should cover the rights and obligations of the client and the registrar. It should contain such client rights as confidentiality, the right to appeal and complain, and instructions for the use of the registration certificate and associated marks. It should contain such registrar rights as access to facilities and necessary information, as well as liability issues. Clients should also check on the conditions for terminating the application, should it become necessary.

Because protection and improvement of the environment goes beyond the products/services of an organization, the organization should assure itself that the registrar fully understands the extent of the operation to be certified and that the certification is within the registrar's scope of accreditation.

Defining the Scope of Certification

The organization's scope of certification should apply to a complete site and include all environmental aspects of relevance to the industrial activities/services at the site. (The definition of *site* is consistent with that under the national or local license/permit regimes.) Therefore, the registrar's scope should reference the organization's activities and related environmental effects on air, water, land, and so on.

The scope may be extended from a site to a division or the entire company. Small companies (less than 50 people) should request a certification body to consider their individual needs throughout the contract-review process. For large companies with centralized functions such as purchasing or design that elect to use more than one registrar, it is crucial to determine each registrar's policy relative to acceptance of the registration by another registrar.

Whether or not the registration of centralized functions that form part of a specific site registration is accepted can greatly impact the overall time and cost of registration. In all cases, the registrar should be willing to work with the organization to define the extent of certification and how it will be achieved. This contract review extends into the initial assessment, as described below.

INITIAL ASSESSMENT/DOCUMENT REVIEW

Once the application is completed, with basic information on the company's size, scope of operations, environmental effects, and desired time frame for registration, the registrar schedules an initial assessment.

Initial Assessment

Most registrars recommend conducting an on-site initial assessment; some may require it. The initial assessment is an extension of the contract review process. It is intended to gain an understanding of the existing state of preparedness of the EMS for a certification assessment. The registrar will evaluate the EMS with respect to such topics as the following:

- Environmental effects and regulatory regulations.

- Continuous improvement of environmental performance.

- Adequate objective evidence of implementation.

- Proper implementation of internal EMS audits.

The auditors will be looking for documentation that describes the EMS and appropriate implementation so that it can be compared to the corresponding ISO 14001 element to determine compliance.

The audit team will then give the client feedback on the readiness of the EMS for a certification assessment and the potential timing. The feedback should be constructive and assist with the remainder of the certification process without jeopardizing a conflict of interest. Registrars are prohibited from consulting with the client company during an initial assessment.

The registrar may properly evaluate the state of the supplier's EMS and documentation, and indicate the requirements for each ISO 14001 element. However, the registrar is not to provide substantive advice and guidance to the company. An effective initial assessment may uncover areas for which the company might then enlist the aid of an independent consultant. It is not appropriate that such aid be provided by the registrar, since this constitutes a conflict of interest. However, the organization should not overlook the wealth of experience captured in ISO 14004, ISO 14001 Annex A, ISO 14010, ISO 14011/1, ISO 14012, BS 7750 Annexes A and B, and other references, to design a practical and effective EMS.

The auditors will also use the information to prepare the appropriate resources and audit plan for the certification assessment. An initial assessment could result in a smaller audit team and a shorter audit, and thereby reduce the overall cost of the registration process. An aggressive response to the initial assessment will increase an organization's chance of passing the certification assessment on the first attempt.

Document Review

The organization can expect the registrar to request documents similar to those listed below during the initial assessment, if not before:

- The environmental management system manual.
- Description of on-site processes.
- Analysis of environmental effects.
- A continuous improvement plan.
- Applicable regulations and agreements.
- Most important license requirements.
- List of breaches of legislation and regulations.
- Summary of correspondence with licensing authorities.
- Internal environmental management system audit reports.
- Management review minutes.

CERTIFICATION ASSESSMENT

Preparation

After the initial assessment and appropriate planning by the organization and registrar, a certification assessment is conducted. The duration of the assessment will be highly dependent on the processes, size, complexity, and relevant environmental effects of the operations to be registered. An organization should expect a typical certification assessment to require two or three auditors to spend three to five days at a facility. The client should not hesitate to challenge or question an audit that appears overly short or long.

In preparation for the certification assessment, the organization should modify, as appropriate, any documentation based on the results of the initial assessment. The EMS manual does not have to be documented separately from other management systems but should clearly show the relationship to other management systems in operation. The manual should reference where significant environmental effects are covered by other management systems, such as safety.

When an organization identifies its environmental aspects, it should make sure that it has considered its significant environmental effects and has addressed them by taking into consideration both internal and external activities. The organization should consider the best available technology when addressing environmental effects, but postponement of implementation should be acceptable as long as it is justified.

The documented EMS should be implemented for a minimum of three months prior to the certification audit to acquire sufficient evidence of proper implementation and effectiveness. The organization should consider performing activities such as the following:

- Conducting awareness training.
- Implementing of internal EMS audits.
- Conducting a management review.

The organization should be diligent in implementing corrective action procedures in response to regulatory violations. This includes proper notification of authorities when required. It should maintain a record of noncompliance incidents and the remedial actions taken to correct and prevent recurrence.

Implementation

The audit of an EMS should not be an extension of a quality management system audit. The certification assessment should focus on the EMS but may be combined with a quality or safety management system audit if it does not jeopardize the quality of the audit due to time restraints.

The EMS differs from the quality management system in that the organization sets the performance criteria while, in a quality system, the customer sets the specifications. This places a broader burden on the certification body to assess the performance criteria, compliance to the criteria, continual improvement of the system, and the effectiveness of the system.

Expect the registrar to conduct the audit as defined by ISO 10011 and ISO 14011/1. The auditors will hold an introductory meeting with company management, request escorts to assist them during the audit, and hold a closing meeting to communicate any deficiencies that were discovered.

During the assessment, the auditors will interview all levels of personnel to determine whether the EMS has been fully implemented within the company, as documented in the environmental management manual and supporting procedures.

The organization should be able to demonstrate that the EMS is designed to address applicable environmental effects and to comply with legislative and regulatory requirements, and that continuous improvement is the cornerstone for the environmental management system.

Most registrars conduct a daily review of their findings with the client to keep them apprised of deficiencies or findings that will be documented. Any breach of regulatory compliance observed during the audit should be reported to the site's management immediately. This allows the client an opportunity to respond to the stated deficiency. In most cases however, all detected deficiencies, even if rectified in the course of the audit, will be recorded in the report.

The audit team's report will be left with the organization at the conclusion of the assessment, as appropriate. The report should address the implementation and effectiveness of the EMS in achieving objectives and targets, any nonconformances, and opportunities for improvement. The audit team's recommendation regarding registration will also be addressed. The client should verify whether the audit teams' recommendation is binding or if further internal review and disposition are required by the registrar.

REGISTRATION DECISIONS

The audit team may recommend that the organization be approved, conditionally/ provisionally approved, or disapproved. The registrar will have a system in place to independently assess the audit results and support or modify the lead auditor's recommendation. The certification decisions are ultimately based on the following.

Approval

An organization can expect to become registered if it has documented and implemented all the elements of ISO 14001 and if only minor (isolated) deficiencies are detected during the certification assessment. For the registrar to grant approval, he or she must be confident that the EMS is designed to comply with legislative and regulatory requirements and that commitment to environmental continuous improvement is prevalent in the organization.

Conditional or Provisional Approval

A company will probably be either conditionally or provisionally approved if:

- It has addressed all of elements of the standard but perhaps not fully documented or implemented them.
- A number of deficiencies detected in a particular area show a negative systemic trend.

Conditional approval requires the organization to respond to any deficiencies noted during the time frame defined by the registrar. The registrar, upon evaluating the organization's corrective action, may elect to perform an on-site reevaluation or accept the corrective action in writing and review the implementation in conjunction with subsequent surveillance visits.

The organization can expect the auditor to return to complete an audit. That is, if the nonconformance was complete lack of implementation and the element could not be audited, the auditor will probably want to return to finish the verification of implementation.

Disapproval

Some registrars may recommend disapproval. A disapproval typically occurs when a company's system is neither very well documented nor implemented. The registrar may also recommend disapproval if the audit team concludes that the management system is not effective in complying with regulatory and legislative requirements and/or that continuous improvement measures are not effective.

This situation will definitely require a comprehensive reevaluation by the registrar prior to issuing registration.

BOX 20-1

USE OF THE CERTIFICATE

The ISO 14001 registration certificate can be used in marketing and advertising. It is not a product certification nor an environmental label and therefore cannot be displayed on a product or its packaging. ISO has published rules regarding the proper use of registration certificates in the quality field. It is expected that these rules will apply to ISO 14001 certificates.

Registration

Once an organization is registered, the organization's site receives a certificate for a defined scope. The organization is listed in a register or directory published by the registrar or another organization. The organization should also expect to receive rules for use of the certificate and associated accreditation marks at this time. The client should be aware of the registrar's policy for publishing registrations, including actions taken when registration is suspended or withdrawn.

SURVEILLANCE

It is important for an organization pursuing registration to understand the duration and/or validity of its registration. Some registrars offer registrations that are valid indefinitely, while others offer registrations for a specific time, such as three years. Both require periodic evaluation—surveillance audits—to verify that the operator continues to comply with the criteria of the standard and the company policy.

Most registrars conduct surveillance audits every six months, though annual surveillance audits may be available to better suit the needs of small organizations. Those organizations whose registration expires may require a complete reassessment at the end of the registration period or an assessment that is somewhere between a surveillance audit and a complete reassessment.

If an organization requests annual surveillance audits, it can probably expect a mandatory reassessment at the end of the certification period. For registrations that do not have an expiration, the organization can expect every clause of the standard to be covered across the three-year period. During the surveillance audits, the registrar will follow up on nonconformances from previous audits and may choose to evaluate some topics during every visit (i.e., system audits, corrective and preventive action, management programs, continuous improvement, and regulatory compliance).

In both cases, a reevaluation of the overall effectiveness of the environmental management system can be expected periodically. These surveillance audits of the EMS may be combined with surveillance audits of quality management systems or

B O X   20–2

KEY REGISTRATION AUDITING ISSUES

The following discusses some key registration auditing issues. The viewpoints expressed here result from a variety of sources: conversations with several registrars and auditors, and documents such as draft accreditation criteria. In some cases, they are speculative. Since the registration process for ISO 14001 is in its earliest stages, these issues will be clarified as the process proceeds.

Exposure to Performance Data

A key issue is the extent of an auditor's exposure to performance data. That is, to what extent will the third-party auditor review performance or compliance data to determine conformance with ISO 14001 requirements? Information from several sources indicates that a registrar may sample performance-related data to evaluate the effects of the management system. To confirm conformance to ISO 14001 requirements, especially those related to environmental aspects and impacts, legal requirements, and objectives and targets, some sampling of performance data may be necessary. According to one point of view, ISO 14001 requires knowledge of performance measures. According to this view, EMS auditors will look at performance data to assess whether the EMS is working to achieve the organization's objectives and goals, and to assess whether the EMS has improved overall.

Checking for Regulatory Compliance

Will the auditor determine whether the organization actually complies with regulations or simply confirm that the EMS has a system in place that is committed to compliance. That is:

- Does the EMS identify legal requirements?
- Does it have a policy committed to compliance and to objectives and targets that are based partly on legal requirements?

If the audit is confined to checking for the existence of a system, not to checking whether the system is actually achieving compliance or working toward that goal, how will stakeholders be fully confident that an ISO 14001-registered organization actually complies with legal requirements? The common interpretation of ISO 14001 and the registration-auditing process is that it will not include actual compliance auditing. According to some registrars, however, actual regulatory compliance may be checked randomly to confirm the appropriate implementation of procedures to ensure regulatory compliance.

Legal Obligation to Report Regulatory Violations

The following are questions of concern to most organizations:

- What happens if the auditor finds a regulatory violation during the course of the audit?
- What happens if the auditor reports the regulatory violation to the company's management and it is not corrected? Will the company be assumed to have an ineffective EMS?
- If the certification has been granted and a surveillance audit discovers several violations, either the same or others, will the certification be withdrawn?

The general understanding is that the auditor is responsible for reporting the violation to the organization; then it is up to the organization to report the violation to the appropriate regulatory body. According to legal experts, the registrar's auditors have no legal duty to report or contact legal authorities. The duty of the auditor ends with telling the client that the client may have a legal duty or some other duty to report the violation to authorities. In fact, the draft ISO 14010 auditing principles standard includes a statement that it may be a violation of due professional care for the auditors to report regulatory violations to bodies other than the client.

Would a regulatory violation prevent the organization from achieving ISO 14001 registration? According to several registrars, if the violation or deviation is caused by a system failure, such as insufficient implementation of a procedure, the registration will be withheld until appropriate corrective measures are applied. If corrective measures correct the problem or if the violation or deviation is already acknowledged in the EMS and suitable corrective measures are applicable, the registration may continue and the certificate may be awarded.

Making Findings of Audits Public

Under what circumstances, if any, could findings of EMS registration audits be made public? The answer from the registrar's point of view is that no findings will be made public by the registrar. The registrar's auditors report to the company's management, not to outside parties. Nor is the organization required to make audit findings public. The only exception is in the EMAS context, where the company should describe the results of environmental audits in its required environmental statement.

—*The Editors*

safety management systems if in place and part of the scope. The organization should clearly understand the registrar's policy relative to surveillance of registration.

During the interval between surveillance visits, the company should focus on continual improvement and ensure that its registered EMS remains effective so that the surveillance audits will merely confirm the fact. The environmental management audits, corrective and preventive action (required by ISO 14001, Clause 4.5), and their review by management (required by ISO 14001, Clause 4.6) are mechanisms to aid in this process.

Rigorous documentation and deployment of an existing EMS should not stifle continual improvement. If the company identifies an improvement that requires a modification in the EMS, the company should feel free to make it, so long as the change is specifically documented.

An organization should always inform its registrar of such changes since some require notification of only major changes to the environmental management system while others require notification of all changes. The organization can expect the surveillance duration to change if major modifications to the organization's EMS affect the scope of certification. The registrar's policy in this area can have a profound impact on registration maintenance and cost.

AUDITOR COMPETENCY

The competence that an audit team will need to conduct an EMS audit is subjective. Some experts view the audit as strictly a management system audit, which any auditor proficient in management systems auditing should be able to execute effectively. Others expect the auditor(s) to have appropriate environmental experience. The environmental auditing requirements established by ISO for internal and external EMS auditors are documented in ISO 14012 (see also ISO 10011 Part 2). These are the minimal requirements for which an accreditation body will hold the registrar responsible.

The environmental competence may be in the audit team and not necessarily in an individual auditor. When special environmental or sector needs become evident during the contract review process, the registrar may contract nonauditing technical experts to join the audit team.

The competencies that an EMS auditor should have include an understanding of the certification process, and the ability to verify compliance with the ISO 14001 standard and to test the effectiveness of the EMS.

For an auditor to gain these abilities, a level of skill, training, experience, education, and personal attributes is required. The environmental auditor(s) should have background knowledge in environmental science, technology, aspects, effects, laws, and regulation, as well as management systems auditing experience. An understanding of the ISO 14001 standard and its intent is critical to the success of the EMS audit. The work experience for environmental auditors is expected to be four years, minimum.

Personal attributes play an important role in the conduct of an environmental management system audit. A competent auditor will have good interpersonal skills and will clearly express the concepts and ideas associated with the questioning process.

The auditor should be well organized and sensitive to the environment in which the audit is conducted. Of particular importance to an organization is the auditor's ability to maintain independence and objectivity and to use sound judgment to arrive at conclusions and a final recommendation for certification.

For uniformity and consistency, the registrars' environmental auditors can expect to be registered with the accreditation bodies and with auditor registration firms such as Environmental Auditors Registration Association (EARA). An organization should always verify the competence of the audit team and reject auditors with cause, as appropriate.

TIME AND COST OF REGISTRATION

The time required to implement an ISO 14001 EMS depends on the organization's current status (i.e., whether the organization is ISO 9000 registered, the extent to which an organization is complying with regulatory requirements), its commitment to the implementation of the system, and the resources it is willing to expend. A good time frame, if a company is starting with no system or a poorly documented system, is 18–24 months. However, a company that has gained experience by certifying a quality system to ISO 9000 can expect to cut this time in half.

The time required for actual registration depends on the preparedness of the company as detected during the initial assessment. Registrar lead times will become increasingly critical as the demand for registration of environmental management systems increases. It is important, prior to choosing a registrar, to determine the resources of that registrar and whether she or he can meet the organization's needs for registration. Current registrar lead times for ISO 9000 range from one month to over a year. The duration of an EMS audit is expected to increase by approximately 40–50 percent with respect to ISO 9000 audits, based on the issues identified earlier.

The first and largest cost associated with registration is the development and implementation of the EMS. An organization may elect to use internal resources to implement the EMS, to rely on the services of an outside consultant, or to combine both approaches.

Based on ISO 9000 costs, an organization can expect the development and implementation cost to be approximately 90 percent of the total cost of registration. In an ISO 9000 survey conducted by Deloitte Touche and Quality Systems Update ISO 9000 Information Service, internal implementation costs among respondents ranged from less than $100,000 to over $600,000. The average cost reported was $245,200.[1]

The remaining 10 percent of the cost will be for the registrar's services. When selecting a registrar, organizations should assess actual costs of the registration process by becoming familiar with all the detailed costs associated with the registration process.

The company should ensure that it has obtained cost estimates for the following major services in the registration process:

- Application.
- The initial assessment and document review.
- The certification assessment.

- Any costs associated with issuing the registration and writing the report.
- Surveillance visits.

An organization should be aware that some registrars require application fees, listing fees, and registration fees in addition to those prices normally quoted for the above activities. An organization must ask about all fees to determine the full cost of the registration.

As previously mentioned, an organization should know how long the registration is valid, as well as any reassessment or partial reassessment costs that may be required in the future.

CONCLUSION

Throughout the registration process, an organization should remember that they are clients of the registrar; they should have no apprehension or concern about retribution if a complaint is necessary. The client should feel comfortable openly discussing issues, such as cost, scheduling, and the qualifications of audit team members, with the registrar. In all cases, although the registrar cannot act as a consultant, he or she should be willing to guide the client through the registration process.

The registrar on the other hand must operate ethically and in accordance with the requirements of his or her accreditors. The registrar should actively seek customer feedback in order to continuously improve the environmental systems registration program.

BIOGRAPHY

Antonio Guerra, PE

Antonio Guerra is the Environmental Program Manager for ABS Quality Evaluations, Inc. where he designed the environmental audit protocols for ISO 14001 certification. He holds a bachelor of science degree in natural gas engineering and has 14 years of experience in quality, environment, and safety programs. He is a licensed Professional Engineer, has been certified by ASQC as a Quality Engineer and Quality Auditor, and is qualified as a registered lead assessor to conduct quality (ISO 9000 and QS-9000), environmental (ISO 14000) and Process Safety (OSHA CFR 1910.119) audits.

NOTE

1. Deloitte Touche Tohmatsu International and Quality Systems Update. *ISO 9000 Survey* (Fairfax, Virginia: CEEM Information Services, September 1993).

PART FIVE

Regulatory and Enforcement Issues

CHAPTER 21

ISO 14000: A Regulatory View

Mary C. McKiel

INTRODUCTION

In 1905, when Albert Einstein published his general theory of relativity, the era of classical physics ended. In a giant leap of intellect and insight, Einstein stood outside traditional constrictions of Newtonian physics and repostulated the way the world works. The physical world did not suddenly change in 1905, but humankind's understanding of it did. Today, changes in the global community are challenging other traditional points of view about environmental, health and safety issues, economic growth, and international trade. In the United States, as elsewhere, government and the private sector are mutually exploring ways to make environmental regulatory schemes more efficient without lessening protection. At the same time, there is a need to increase productivity. Old platforms are giving way to new approaches.

The ISO 14000 series of environmental management standards are part of the new world platform. ISO is a private sector, nonregulatory standards developer. ISO 14000 management standards deal with a public issue, the environment. How do regulatory agencies such as the U.S. EPA view this private-public overlap? How will the standards play out in agency policy and programs? Many believe that EPA holds an important key to the success of ISO 14000 use in the United States. How critical is the EPA role?

To understand EPA's view of ISO 14000, it will be important to outline EPA's internal process for following ISO 14000, the role of agency representatives in the U.S. Technical Advisory Group (TAG) to the ISO Technical Committee 207 responsible for the ISO 14000 standards, and critical issues for EPA in the development and use of the standard, including conformity assessment.

Conversely, how does the private sector in the United States view EPA's role? EPA and private industry view each other cautiously. This chapter will touch on some of the private sector's expectations and fears regarding EPA's willingness to explore new points of view regarding environmental regulation.

THE NEW ENVIRONMENTAL FRAMEWORK

Environmental burdens result from human interaction with the physical world. Assumptions that the earth is an inexhaustible resource and a bottomless receptacle have already proven disastrously incorrect. Equally incorrect are assumptions that ignore local impacts from global problems. Governments as well as industry have been culpable over the past decades for these assumptions, and both sectors are in the process of correcting their vision.

A new point of view is beginning to take shape in environmental management and regulation. Productivity and economic gain at the expense of environmental protection is no longer accepted as the status quo. Theories and practices of sustainable development and renewable resource use are gaining acceptance.

Looking at environmental protection and business from a different viewpoint, however, requires new tools. ISO 14000 is one of these new tools. Specifically, the ISO 14001 specification standard can help organizations move into sync with the more comprehensive and complex point of view regarding environmental management.

ISO 14000 is useful because it is compatible with other environmental tools. Environmental cost accounting and environmental auditing are two tools that can be integrated into an ISO 14001-based management system. The ISO 14000 standards are broad enough to encompass existing expertise in all management and functional systems. They are targeted enough to shape an environmental direction that can last beyond management changeovers, stock market variations, upsizing, and downsizing.

New Framework for Government

The Clinton Administration has stressed government reinvention and regulatory reform. Reinvention of all aspects of government from procurement to regulatory activities is occurring through projects such as the National Performance Review Program. The Administration rightly believes that streamlining is needed. Budgetary reforms and deficit-reduction strategies will contribute to making all federal agencies more efficient. The fact of life for federal agencies in today's climate—executive or legislative—is that there are going to be fewer people, fewer programs, and fewer dollars.

Reform means more than reduction. Partnership between the public and private sectors is one of the most significant characteristics of the process. The idea is to leverage resources and expertise so that government and industry are not working at odds with each other, particularly when they share common interests and goals. Environmental protection is an area where much care has to be exercised in developing partnership approaches but where success is defined by better places to work, live, play, and learn.

EPA's New Ethic

EPA's administrator has championed the need for doing things "cleaner, cheaper, smarter." This includes the way the Agency carries out its enforcement and compliance activities. Pollution prevention is the central ethic of the Agency, and the EPA's administrator intends that this ethic guide the Agency's rule making, enforcement, and technical assistance. All Agency programs are working to achieve multimedia and cross-media benefits.

A focus on prevention does not mean the Agency is moving away from command and control. Enforcement and compliance are a huge part of the Agency's mission. In the mid-1960s, the Cuyahoga River was aflame as a result of toxic releases, and lives were lost in Massachusetts as a result of contaminated ground water. Since then, these and many of the nation's largest environmental problems have been virtually eliminated. Command and control has not been a failure; it has been a spectacular success.

But the success, at times, has been very costly. In fact, the cost has been devastating to some. Many believe that the best remedies do not always have to come at overburdensome costs. Cleaner, cheaper, and smarter are bound together like three legs of a tripod. "Cleaner" means that a holistic, prevention-oriented system can and will have better results than a combination of unintegrated single-source regulations.

"Cheaper" means that there needs to be room for technological innovation and cost-effective systems for preventing, treating, and disposing of emissions and wastes. The cost of doing things right the first time needs to be less than the cost of cleaning up or paying up.

"Smarter" means total quality management of environmental responsibilities, whether inside the government or in the private sector. One of the strongest arguments for moving toward a prevention-oriented regulatory system is that multimedia problems require a hierarchical approach. Everything cannot be solved simultaneously. Prevention methods do not necessarily cost less to implement, but the costs are spread over a range of solutions instead of concentrated on one area to the neglect of others.

There are many problems left to tackle, but regulatory fixes may not be the only solution. Command and control is being reshaped to be:

- More effective in the face of reduced resources.
- More flexible to accommodate the changing needs of the nation and the environment.

The variables available within the regulatory structure itself include the way regulations are written, the type and degree of technical assistance, the way regulations are enforced, and the type and degree of compliance assistance. The ISO 14001 environmental management system standard may provide a set of voluntary parameters within which the EPA and private industry along with the public can explore ways to better use these available variables.

EPA is also exploring benefits and incentives to be gained from voluntary or nonregulatory projects, such as environmental excellence programs, design for the environment, the Common Sense Initiative, and others. It faces several obstacles, however, in moving toward a more flexible but effective regulatory system. These include conflicting statutory requirements and inexperience in applying prosecutorial flexibility. It also includes performance measurement systems that reward the imposition of fines but lack an alternate system to reward fines avoided through successful compliance and prevention assistance. State and federal regulators are currently implementing a wide variety of internal and external pilot programs for addressing each of these obstacles and moving prevention closer to the fore.

EPA AND ISO 14000 CONVERGENCE

The ISO 14000 series of environmental management standards is an almost predictable development given economic and trade developments associated with global environmental concerns. Equally predictable is the U.S. EPA's role as an active participant in the development of the ISO 14000 standards. The environment is a public sector issue even when couched in private sector management standards, and the Agency's stakeholders can rightly expect that the EPA would sit at the ISO table along with industry, environmental groups, and others.

EPA participation in the U.S. TAG to TC 207 makes sense in today's political and budgetary climate. The Administration has a keen interest in leveraging constructive partnerships between the regulators and the private sector. The focus in today's regulatory world is on pollution prevention and relieving multimedia stressors. An environmental management framework voluntarily used by the private sector and by government facilities sets a stage on which the goals of the Administration, business and industry, and the public converge.

The EPA Standards Network

Members of the U.S. EPA have participated in the development of ISO 14000 since ISO formed the Strategic Advisory Group on the Environment (SAGE) in 1991. The American National Standards Institute (ANSI) is the official U.S. member body to ISO. EPA is a member of ANSI along with 30 other federal and state government agencies, including the Department of Energy, the Food and Drug Administration, the Department of Commerce, and the Department of Defense.

In 1993, the EPA formed the EPA Standards Network ("Network") to coordinate and plan Agency involvement in the U.S. input to ISO. The Network consists of representatives from offices throughout the EPA and is organized parallel to the structure of the U.S. TAG to TC 207. The Network director, or coordinator, represents the entire Agency on the full U.S. TAG. Each sub-Tag group—environmental management systems, ecolabeling, auditing, life-cycle assessment and environmental performance evaluation—also has representation from a member of the EPA Network. Network members are voting participants in the U.S. TAG, with full rights and responsibilities accorded all other TAG members.

The EPA Network serves as the focal point for developing Agency input to the ISO 14000 development process. Network members coordinate throughout EPA central and regional offices on critical issues arising in the TAG and sub-Tag work. As an ongoing coordination vehicle, the Network is somewhat unique in the Agency. Like voluntary programs, such as the Common Sense Initiative, the Network cuts across, as well as up and down, Agency lines. Unlike Agency-run voluntary programs, the Network acts as a bridge between the Agency and a private-sector-driven initiative. Participation in the U.S. TAG is a major EPA involvement where the Agency ultimately has influence and presence but not control. It is important to note that the first vice chairmanship of the 500-member private sector U.S. TAG is an EPA representative.

The Agency's executive leadership, from the administrator through various assistant administrators, has provided resource support in the form of personnel, time and, where appropriate, budget for travel. The assistant administrator for the Office of Prevention, Pesticides, and Toxic Substances (OPPTS) has overall leadership for the network and for the development of EPA policy concerning the use of voluntary standards.

EPA Policies Regarding ISO 14000

EPA has not issued any Agency policy on the ISO 14000 standards, nor is it apt to do so in the short term. Collectively, the responses and inputs of the Agency to the U.S. TAG form the body of written positions that have been taken. These do not constitute EPA policy in the same sense as Agency policy, for example, regarding the presence of lead in drinking water.

The coordinated inputs and responses, however, provide a good picture of how Agency offices view the content of specific ISO 14000 standards. In some areas, including life-cycle assessment, EPA has had pioneers in the field. Recognized worldwide for its leadership in LCA methodology development, the Agency has contributed significantly to the international reference material from which the ISO 14000 standards on LCA are being developed.

The Role of ISO 14000 in Environmental Excellence Programs

ISO 14000 will play a role in voluntary programs developed by the EPA. The Agency has initiated a variety of programs that seek to recognize and reward business leaders who initiate proactive programs. These include not only the following programs, but also the EPA Wastewise, Green Lights, and 33/50 programs.

Project XL

Sponsored by President Clinton, Project XL is applicable to EPA and to other regulatory Agencies such as the Department of Energy. Project XL encourages the private sector to achieve environmental performance in ways that are better, less costly, and more effective than can be achieved through the existing regulatory regime.

Organizations or companies submit project plans and identify specific regulatory and environmental performance goals that they will meet. The plans also identify the regulatory flexibility needed to achieve results. Once the projects are mutually agreed upon by government and industry, applicants have up to three years to achieve their planned goals. The idea is to let innovation and cooperation result in a level of environmental improvement that could not be achieved through the existing regulatory structure alone.

One of the currently accepted XL Projects, submitted by AT&T Microelectronics, (now called LUCENT Technologies),[1] uses for its basis the ISO 14001 standard. Putting ISO 14001 into place in specified facilities, LUCENT plans to use ISO 14001 implementation as the vehicle for discovering and correcting environmental problems that it might not otherwise find. Water permits under the National Pollutant Discharge Elimination Program (NPDES) are the specific target for the proposal. AT&T is looking for a quicker, less burdensome response from EPA based on proven reliability of the ISO 14001 system. In return, Federal EPA and the appropriate state agencies will in effect build a regulatory bubble around the XL facilities and will work closely in a monitoring and technical assistance mode to help AT&T achieve the improvements.

There are many details to work out between the regulators and their counsel and AT&T and its counsel, but the project is a unique one for testing the utility of the standard. In addition, the project will also determine ways in which the existing regulatory structure might otherwise aid or impede environmental improvement.

The Common Sense Initiative (CSI)

CSI is also aimed at identifying ways to make environmental protection cleaner, cheaper, and smarter. The difference between CSI and other programs is that CSI is done on a sectorwide level rather than a companywide or facilitywide basis.

Here, the Agency is asking the following question: If an entire industry (currently about six major industry sectors are participants in the CSI program) identifies all the regulations and requirements applicable to it, is there a more holistic, less expensive, and more effective approach to compliance than the sum of the collective environmental regulatory parts?

ISO 14000 may play a useful role in the CSI. The environmental management system described in ISO 14001 is designed for organizational or facility implementation. That's not to say that all the representatives in the auto sector, for example, who are part of the CSI project, could agree to individually implement ISO 14001 in their own facilities.

Some adjustments would have to be made, however, to gain meaningful common data. The standard requires identification of significant environmental aspects and goals and objectives that are consistent with those aspects. Participating companies would have to agree on some common goals and objectives and on common elements in the measuring, training, auditing, and feedback systems.

Companies, even in the same industry sector, differ widely as to resources, existing management systems, compliance history, environmental expertise, and so on.

ISO 14001 is intentionally designed to be uniquely applicable to anyone using the standard. It is not intended to act as the basis for comparing companies, organizations, or even facilities within an organization. Still, CSI may find ways to use ISO 14001 certification as a benchmark for an organization's ability to systematically and reliably perform, given whatever agreements the industry and the Agency come to under this project.

The ISO 14000 standards for life-cycle assessment (LCA) and for environmental performance evaluation (EPE) may be more immediately useful to the CSI program. LCA and EPE apply to products rather than to management systems and could be the foundations for assessing the effectiveness of CSI goals, particularly that of designated regulatory flexibility.

Environmental Leadership Program (ELP)

ELP is a pilot project that was launched in March 1995. The basic concept is to encourage companies to go beyond compliance by testing innovative management techniques such as environmental auditing, prevention technologies, and management system programs. Another purpose of the programs is to test criteria for auditing and for certification of voluntary compliance programs to standards such as ISO 14000.

EPA and Voluntary Standards

The EPA's involvement with international voluntary standards such as ISO 14000 is in keeping with U.S. government policy. This policy is described in OMB Circular A-119, "Federal Participation in the Development and Use of Non-Government Standards," revised in 1995. The terms *non-government* and *voluntary* are defined by the circular and fundamentally refer to standards that are developed through a private sector process, not through a government process such as the regulatory process. The term *voluntary*, however, does not mean that conformance to such a standard is optional when the standard is incorporated into a contract or trade agreement or any other legal vehicle.

The OMB circular was first published in the late 1970s and has two basic messages for the federal government, regardless of department, agency, or mission. First, agencies must prefer the use of voluntary standards where those standards meet the requirements of the agency for the intended use. Second, where no voluntary standards meet the needs of the agency, agencies are to preferentially develop such standards by working within the voluntary process. That is, federal employees are supposed to join and participate in voluntary standards development organizations and committees.[2]

The circular is in keeping with the trend of the federal government toward more reliance on the private sector for products and services. An important addition to the revised circular is the specific reference to the use of international standards developed through internationally recognized bodies such as the International Organization for Standardization (ISO).

EPA is responsible under the circular for some specific actions:

- Setting up an internal mechanism for tracking activities covered by the circular, educating employees in the provisions of the circular, and providing specific policies and procedures for agency employee participation in the voluntary standards process.

- Reporting annually to the Secretary of Commerce on Agency activities under the circular, including how many EPA standards have been replaced by voluntary standards and how many EPA employees are official participants in voluntary standards activities.

In 1995, EPA for the first time in its history designated an EPA standards executive responsible for carrying out the provisions of the circular. Previously, EPA did not have a formal vehicle for implementing the circular although individual Agency experts worked with standards-developing organizations. Standards executives from all federal agencies coordinate with one another through the Interagency Committee on Standards Policy (ICSP), chaired by the National Institute for Standards and Technology of the Department of Commerce.

The Role of International Trade Agreements

The World Trade Organization, or WTO, born in 1994 from the Uruguay round of the General Agreement on Trade and Tariffs, similarly sets preferences for the use of international voluntary standards. One significant action of the Uruguay round was to integrate the previously separate Standards Code into the body of the WTO. The Standards Code generally does not distinguish in application between regulatory and nonregulatory uses of international standards.[3] This can have a huge impact on U.S. regulatory bodies, including the U.S. EPA.

Basically, the U.S. government is responsible for adhering to the WTO. As the federal agency responsible for environmental protection policies and regulations, EPA is primarily responsible for ensuring that federal environmental standards, including technology and testing standards, are consistent with the WTO. Exceptions, justifications, and other legal flexibility notwithstanding, the Agency now has to educate its rulemakers on the disciplines of the WTO. The aim is to avoid creating unnecessarily discriminatory technical standards in instances where existing international voluntary standards might be used. In cases involving standards other than plant and food safety, the burden of proof is on the Agency.

Trade rules of the North American Free Trade Agreement (NAFTA) are essentially the same, with some important differences that make NAFTA more environmentally friendly than the WTO.

ISO 14001 AND THIRD-PARTY CERTIFICATION

Conforming an organization to the requirements of ISO 14001 is one thing; certifying that the job has been done properly and in accordance with the standard is quite another.

Still another issue is: What does certification really mean to business, to trade partners, to communities, and to regulators?

The Credibility of Third-Party Certification

EPA and State Agencies have expressed both optimism and concerns about the use of third-party, private-sector certification to ISO 14001. Both federal and state regulators are quick to understand the potential for resource savings associated with reliance on third-party verification. The agencies would not give up any existing rights to secure information or to conduct inspections but might comfortably choose to use EMS certification as the basis for scheduling fewer visits or for accelerating the granting of discharge permits. The solid foundation for this must be an accredited third-party system that is standardized and regularly maintained.

The Department of Environmental Protection offices in Pennsylvania, California, Florida, Texas, and other states are already turning to ISO 14001 as a way to help diminish the growing pressures of reduced government environmental resources. Pennsylvania is exploring ways to begin assisting the private sector in adopting and using ISO 14001. Over 20 states have issued self-audit privileges under a variety of conditions. In each case, however, credit is given to organizations that can demonstrate the ability to achieve and maintain compliance through a systematic management scheme.

ANSI is setting up a national accreditation system for accrediting qualified registrars (certifiers), auditor certification bodies, and providers of auditor training courses. The combination of these activities forms a chain of checks and balances, policies and procedures, and qualification requirements that are the backbone of third-party certification. If the system is robust enough, regulators and communities may gain confidence in the ability of private sector systems to achieve a level of self-policing.

Disclosure is a Critical Factor

EPA and its stakeholders are participating in the ANSI process. Active involvement of nongovernment organizations (NGOs), environmental groups, and community groups is a key concern to EPA. The Agency believes that public confidence in third-party certification, even when the certification is tied to a credible national accreditation system, will hinge on the integrity and openness of the system. Involving a broad range of interested parties right from the beginning will help ensure the viability and acceptance of the system.

International Recognition

Ideally, the U.S. system for ISO 14001 accreditation will be recognized or accepted by other countries and will, in turn, recognize and accept foreign systems. (This has happened in the ISO 9000 context.) Great Britain, Sweden, The Netherlands and other countries have national accreditation systems. Many countries are hard at work developing their own systems.

Mutual recognition of accreditation among countries is not easily accomplished, but organizations involved in international trade are at a disadvantage when they have to obtain product or services certifications from multiple accreditation systems.

If there is not a single, well-polished U.S. accreditation system in place, more and more U.S. organizations will turn to registrars who are accredited by UKAS and other foreign accreditation bodies. The difficulty with this scenario from the EPA perspective is the lack of U.S. stakeholder input to the process.

From the industry perspective, if U.S. government buy-in to the applicability and usefulness of the ISO 14001 standard is desired, then reliance on a foreign accreditor weakens the chance that the Agency will accept third-party certification.

CRITICAL ISSUES FOR THE EPA

EPA considers the following to be critical issues if ISO 14001 is to become a true tool for improving environmental performance and gaining acceptance among Agency stakeholders. There is no question that the top two issues are openness, both in the standards development process and the conformity assessment structure, and disclosure of information to communities.

Accessibility and Openness

From the onset of EPA's participation in the development of the ISO 14000 standards, the Agency has gone on record with concerns for the openness and transparency of the process. The belief is that standards so widely used should not be dominated by any single interest group. The U.S. national input to the development of the standards, through ANSI, should actively encourage participation by environmental groups, communities, government agencies, and all interested parties. In this way, stakeholder groups can have not only input but also ownership of the standards, can understand their applicability and use, and recognize their limitations.

To this end, EPA awarded $450,000 in Environmental Technology Initiative grants to ANSI for outreach to small and medium-size enterprises, environmental groups, and states. Since 1995, ANSI has conducted workshops and seminars around the United States, helping to educate these stakeholder groups about the ISO 14000 process.

The National Wildlife Federation, the Environmental Law Institute, and other environmental groups are forming their own outreach and educational vehicles. Environmental groups have been reticent about participating in the U.S. TAG. The World Wildlife Federation and the United Nations Environmental Program are two organizations that are active environmental liaison members of TC 207.

The standards development process is demanding and time-consuming. It is ongoing because revision of all standards is required at three- to five-year intervals. Environmental groups and communities typically do not focus resources toward standards processes, partially because the visible payback can be very long term. Nevertheless, the complete paradigm shift implied by the acceptance of ISO 14001 will not occur without the help and input of these groups.

Environmental Performance

Although not a performance standard, the EMS requirements set the stage for companies to implement a process that should ultimately result in improved performance. The question is whether this will happen.

The ISO 14001 standard requires that organizations set management goals and objectives that are consistent with the significant environmental aspects of the organization. These goals and objectives and the systems set in place to accomplish them have to demonstrate an organization's commitment to compliance, to the prevention of pollution, and to continuous improvement of the system.

Industry and government have the opportunity to develop measurement tools and methods that demonstrate environmental improvement as well as management system improvement. Over time, the American public will not tolerate reduced environmental performance when technology is available to achieve positive growth—growth that is a function of productivity and cost benefits combined with environmental improvements. Results may not show up until several years into an EMS, but it is not too early to begin designing more sophisticated and integrated measurement tools.

Most companies claim that compliance with regulations and improved environmental performance are not the same thing. One-size-fits-all regulations that prescribe not only what to do but how to do it can impede technical improvements that would otherwise lead to improving the environment.

This is true not only throughout industry as a whole but also within the environmental technology community. One message from the December 1995 meeting on environmental technology held by the White House, was that the current regulatory structure is a significant impediment to developing a strong U.S. position in the global environmental technology market.

Compliance Assurance

EPA lobbied to include language regarding compliance with law and regulations in the ISO 14001 standard. Obviously, one benefit of the standard should be improved compliance with regulatory and statutory requirements. This may result in freeing up EPA resources to shift toward truly "bad actors," with assurance that ISO 14001-certified companies are following requirements. Other benefits are:

- The ability to allocate scarce resources to compliance assistance for small and medium-size enterprises.
- The opportunity to study application of environmental management systems in a wide range of companies, industries, and settings.

Issues Related to Small and Medium-Size Enterprises (SMEs)

Small and medium-size enterprises (SMEs) are concerned about their ability to make use of a third-party certification system. Certification can be costly.[4] It is true that organizations can (and many probably will, initially) choose to set up an environmental management system using ISO 14001 without choosing to become registered.

What will be the effect on SMEs if EPA and state agencies link a regulatory advantage such as reduced monitoring and inspections to certification? SMEs and others worry that they will be unable to take advantage of the flexibility.

The picture as painted is somewhat misleading. To date, the Agency has not offered any flexibility associated directly with ISO 14001. The Agency has issued a revised audit policy and self-policing policy (see Chapter 22). Both of these have elements recognizing compliance management systems, or CMSs, but not environmental management systems in the ISO 14001 mode. Compliance management is different and less comprehensive than an ISO 14001 EMS. By definition, compliance depends upon laws and regulations to provide benchmarks of performance. ISO 14001 is a template for *all* the environmentally related activities of an organization, not just those currently mandated by law.

EPA has not yet made any necessary links between a CMS and an EMS. In time, the two may become one, but for now certification to ISO 14001 is not viewed by the Agency as certification to compliance.

Small businesses have the same opportunity to take advantage of EPA's flexibility as do larger organizations. Certification to ISO 14001 will be regularly revisited as a means of improving the EMS, while vehicles such as consent decrees or, where no violations exist, self-declarations under Title 18 (invoking prosecution for false statement of conformance) are more applicable to a CMS.

ISO 14001 Is a Market-Driven Standard

Regarding market advantages to SMEs for ISO 14001 certification, the issue of resources is very real. Resources for registration may not be proportional to the size of the organization, and larger organizations may simply be better equipped to absorb the increments of expenditures. Self-declaration to ISO 14001 is an attractive option for a variety of reasons, including the fact that third-party certification may not be required in a supplier-to-supplier relationship. Not only SMEs but multinational organizations may prefer to self-declare conformance to ISO 14001 based on the needs of their customers. Where international recognition of conformance is a market advantage or a necessity, third-party certification will be available and used.

The downside of self-declaration is the potentially significant variability in interpretations. Accredited training courses for auditors will be available, and organizations may hire certified auditors to evaluate an EMS system without necessarily applying for registration. In the practical world, most companies that have gone through the rigorous process of setting up an EMS and being audited by an accredited auditor will choose to become registered. Registration is a public announcement of conformance to ISO 14001 and can be used as a market tool although not applied to products.

WHAT THE PRIVATE SECTOR IS LOOKING FOR

Many in the private sector would like confirmation that regulators are *not* going to adopt ISO 14000 into regulatory rulemaking. Adoption of voluntary standards into regulation and even law is hardly without precedent.[5] Technical product standards and testing standards are sometimes even developed by standards organizations with the expectation that the result will become part of a government requirement. In EPA's case, there is no legal mandate for environmental management as there is for protection of air and water. While the environment is a public issue, management systems are not. EPA can be expected to find ways to adapt the private sector's experience with all of the ISO 14000 standards to new ways of achieving Agency goals through partnership and voluntary programs. Specific ideas of how Federal and state EPA agencies might recognize organizations that conform to the ISO 14001 standards include the following:

- Reduction of penalties and recognition of due diligence in compliance with regulations.
- Special public recognition.
- Fewer routine inspections in exchange for EMS implementation.
- Faster permitting procedures.
- Less frequent inspections and regulatory audits.
- Adoption of ISO 14000 by companies in place of compliance penalties in consent decree negotiations.
- Reduced or streamlined reporting and monitoring burdens and less paperwork.

Many of these ideas are consistent with trends in government. As organizations and regulators develop a history of using ISO 14001, refinements can be made to regulatory flexibility. Trust takes time to build. Current federal and state pilot projects will help ease government and industry into new perspectives on the role of self-policing, third-party certification and beyond-compliance reliability.

CONCLUSION

Forces in government, industry, and trade are shaping a new platform on which to stand and view humankind's environmental responsibilities and opportunities. The trend is unquestionably toward achieving global perspectives and working out global solutions within local jurisdictions. Integration of environmental protection into activities is emerging as the cleaner and smarter way to do everything from regulatory rulemaking to manufacturing. The "cheaper" part will come by combining regulatory refinements with systematic environmental management. Getting everyone from top management down to understand both operational and environmental responsibility will eventually result in greater transparency between the two. Markets, global and national, are already beginning to call for commercial environmental technologies to bolster productivity.

A constant in all of this is the role of the public. Leave it to the constitutional judges to explain the intricacies of the American legal system. It is still a fact that the laws of the land and public policy ought to reflect public concerns. To that end, community involvement is essential to both the development of regulatory require-ments and the understanding of environmental burdens and controls over them.

Regarding the regulatory system, is the public getting the protection it is paying for? If not, is the solution more enforcement or smarter enforcement? More regulations or smarter regulations? Considering the essentially bottom-line interests of industry, can communities trust the information they receive, if any, from the private sector on how well an organization or facility is dealing with its environmental responsibilities? In the old way of looking at things, this would be a stalemate situation, but viewed from a new, integrated perspective these questions frame opportunities for cooperation and partnerships.

Once, when questioned about the relationship between his theories and his faith, Einstein replied: "God does not play dice with the Universe." In other words, the new platform of relativity worked because it was closer to reality. The new platform of sustainable development—productivity and environmental protection—is also closer to reality. ISO 14001 offers one way for government, industry, and the public to shape that reality.

BIOGRAPHY

Mary C. McKiel, PhD

Mary McKiel is the director of the EPA Standards Network and works in the Office of Prevention, Pesticides and Toxic Substances at the EPA. As network director, she manages the EPA's first cross-office program for voluntary standards and coordinates EPA's nationwide participation in the U.S. Technical Advisory Group (TAG) for the development of the ISO 14000 Environmental Management Standards. In 1995, Ms. McKiel was elected Vice Chair of the U.S. TAG to TC 207. She also serves as the Vice Chair of the EMS Council for Accreditation of U.S. Registrars for ISO 14000 certification programs and is a member of the Steering Committee for the EPA Trade and Environment Task Force. Previously, Ms. McKiel served in the Federal Supply Service of the General Services Administration as specification manager for paper products. She served at GSA until 1993 in managerial and executive positions including Chief of Engineering and Standards Policy, Director of Quality Standards, and the first Director of the GSA Environmental Planning Program.

REFERENCES

Born, Max. *Einstein's Theory of Relativity.* New York: Dover, 1962 (revised edition).

Brown, Lester, ed. *State of the World.* Worldwatch Institute Report. New York: W.W. Norton, 1995.

Durnil, Gordon K. *The Making of a Conservative Environmentalist.* Bloomington: Indiana University Press, 1995.

Gore, Albert. *Earth in the Balance.* Boston: Houghton Mifflin, 1992.

Green Ledgers (EPA sponsored publication).

Harr, Jonathan. *A Civil Action.* New York: Random House, 1995.

Mitchell, George J. *World on Fire.* New York: Charles Scribner's Sons, 1991.

NOTES

1. LUCENT Technologies is an independent company but still part of AT&T.

2. For more information on U.S. national voluntary standards developers, contact the American National Standards Institute, 11 W. 42nd Street, New York, NY 10036.

3. The WTO structure is complex and does make distinctions, particularly in sections on sanitary and phytosanitary applications, that are pertinent to any government's need or ability to use international voluntary standards. The sovereign right of a country to establish its own levels of protection is carefully preserved, and the preference for use of voluntary standards does not alter this right.

4. One example of costs associated with certification involves one of the largest multinational telecommunications corporations. Drawing from their experience with the ISO 9000 quality management standards, they estimate that 80 percent of the cost associated with the standards is internal, while only 20 percent is due to the actual cost of paying for certification.

5. One of the most famous examples is the adoption into law of voluntary standards for fasteners developed by the American Society of Mechanical Engineers.

CHAPTER 22

A Regulatory Enforcement Perspective of ISO 14001

Brian Riedel[1]

INTRODUCTION

The government and the public have an interest in protecting human health and the environment. Congress and EPA have devised innumerable inflexible standards for regulatory compliance. Most recently, President Clinton's Council on Sustainable Development (PCSD) issued a report that calls for environmental regulations that specify performance standards to protect the public and the environment—but without mandating the means of compliance. The aim is to provide regulated entities the flexibility to find the most cost-efficient way to achieve environmental goals. The report continues: "But this flexibility must be coupled with accountability and enforcement to insure that public health and the environment are safeguarded."

Voluntary industry standards such as ISO 14001 are consistent with the PCSD recommendations and provide a significant opportunity to improve environmental performance above current regulatory levels. However, several missing elements of the ISO 14001 standard—accountability, for example—make it inappropriate as a wholesale replacement for the U.S. regulatory regime.

This chapter will briefly explore the potential advantages an organization may enjoy with respect to improving its environmental enforcement. The chapter will then analyze the potential role of ISO 14001 with respect to various regulatory benefits, including penalty mitigation and reduced regulatory responsibilities. As part of this analysis, the chapter will explore some of the characteristics of the ISO 14001 standard and how certain modifications can make the industry standard more palatable from a regulatory standpoint.

LIFTING AND LEVELING ENVIRONMENTAL PERFORMANCE

ISO 14001 has the potential to significantly "lift and level" an organization's environmental performance above and beyond compliance levels. ISO 14001 sets forth a "plan, do, check, act" approach to identifying impacts, setting goals, establishing procedures, measuring and reviewing results, and improving the process. This systematic approach to environmental management, theoretically, is focused, effective, and efficient. A strong commitment to implementation of the ISO 14001 standard has enormous potential to lift and level environmental performance.

First, ISO 14001 provides the framework for implementing a potentially lofty set of environmental performance goals—zero release, for example—that go beyond performance levels dictated by regulations. However, the caliber, or quality, of an organization's environmental performance under ISO 14001 will depend on a myriad of factors, including the objectives an organization sets for itself and its level of commitment to regulatory compliance, prevention of pollution, and continual improvement.

Second, ISO 14001 addresses an extremely broad scope of activities that may affect the environment. ISO 14001 operates on a holistic multimedia basis, which more accurately reflects the impacts of human activity on the environment and the dynamics of environmental ecosystems than does a media-by-media approach.

Often, existing regulations simply transfer pollutants from one media to another, with little or no net decrease in pollutants released, or harm or risk to public health and the environment. ISO 14001's multimedia and unlimited horizon is conducive for development, implementation, and experimentation with new pollution prevention concepts and practices.

In addition, the ISO 14001 standard addresses *all* "significant environmental aspects and impacts," not just those that are regulated. This identification and control of a more expansive set of environmental impacts may result in the reduction of substantial unregulated risks. Moreover, an organization must identify all significant aspects and impacts resulting from its "products and services" in addition to its "activities."

Third, ISO 14001 implementation should result in a positive culture change in the organization with more employees being in a position to identify and respond to regulated and unregulated problems. Environmental responsibility will rest with all employees, not just an individual or group of environmental engineers or coordinators.

All employees "whose work may create a significant impact upon the environment" must be made aware of the significant environmental impacts of their work activities, the environmental benefits of improved personal performance, and their roles with respect to conformance with policies, procedures, and EMS requirements.

This training should result in the dispersion of environmental awareness and responsibility throughout the entire organization. Many employees want to do the right thing with respect to the environment—the ISO 14001 standard provides a framework in which to do this. (Note that an EMS must have time to mature, and policies and procedures must become inculcated in the workforce before improved environmental performance can be expected.)

All of these characteristics of the ISO 14001 standard tend to improve, or lift, environmental performance. They also level performance by managing activities across all media and treating similar incidences in the same appropriate manner every time.

OPERATION OF ISO 14001 IN THE REGULATORY CONTEXT

Should EPA encourage ISO 14001 registration by providing regulatory incentives, such as reduced enforcement response (penalties), reduced monitoring and reporting, fewer inspections, streamlined permitting, and so on? Applicants to several EPA initiatives such as Project XL have urged EPA to do so. The answer to this question requires an exploration of the relationship between ISO 14001 and regulatory compliance.

Regulatory Compliance

Whether an organization (ISO 14001-registered or not) is in regulatory compliance depends on many factors, including the nature of its business, its regulatory responsibilities, and its level of commitment to compliance-related objectives in light of the many other business decisions it faces.

ISO 14001 was designed to offer a flexible means of structuring environmental management. This flexibility allows organizations to set their own objectives and determine the appropriate level of resources needed to carry them out, based on a variety of considerations. Consistent with this flexible approach to environmental management, ISO 14001 states that an organization must "consider" legal and other requirements in establishing its objectives and must make a "commitment" to regulatory compliance. The ISO 14001 standard does not prescribe what level of priority or commitment should be accorded compliance-related goals.

ISO 14001 registration does not guarantee any specific level of environmental performance, including regulatory compliance. Since a high level of environmental performance is the desired behavior, and ISO 14001 is a means to those ends, ISO 14001 registration should not be the sole basis for providing regulatory benefits.

While ISO 14001 registration will not provide a "talisman for compliance," the ISO framework nonetheless should better position organizations to meet or exceed regulatory requirements. An organization is more likely to detect and correct violations if it has a workable system for doing so. In light of ISO 14001's requirements for monitoring, measuring, and reviewing, ISO 14001-registered organizations should be in a position to generally prevent environmental violations from becoming serious, for example, catastrophic environmental disasters such as major spills.

A regulatory structure that can incorporate ISO 14001 registration while assuring protection of human health and the environment can greatly relieve the government's strained resources devoted to inspecting facilities, reviewing reporting data, processing permits, and engaging in enforcement action. However, before ISO 14001 can serve as the foundation for a "systems-based regulatory alternative," important issues—such as measurement and disclosure of environmental performance—must be addressed.

The discussion of regulatory benefits for ISO 14001-registered organizations will begin with the end of the regulatory process—after a violation has occurred—because this set of potential regulatory benefits is the most well-defined under existing enforcement policies.

Enforcement Response and Penalty Mitigation

Would an organization be eligible for reduced enforcement response by virtue of its ISO 14001 registration? In one respect, violations committed by an ISO 14001-registered organization may be symptoms of an EMS that has been ineffective in preventing violations. However, no EMS will prevent all noncompliance, particularly EMSs for sophisticated operations and/or highly regulated activities.

Regulators have recognized the value of a "systems approach" to managing environmental requirements and have fashioned enforcement policies to encourage the adoption and implementation of systems to prevent, detect, disclose, and correct environmental violations.

EPA Criminal Investigative Discretion

In determining whether a matter is worthy of criminal investigation, a 1994 EPA memorandum on criminal investigative discretion[2] states that EPA will consider the following:

- Actual and threatened harm to human health or the environment.
- Culpable conduct, which may be indicated by, for example, evidence of criminal intent or an organization's compliance history.

With respect to determining corporate culpability, the memorandum states:

> [A] violation that is voluntarily revealed and fully and promptly remedied as part of a corporation's systematic and comprehensive self-evaluation program generally will not be a candidate for the expenditure of scarce criminal investigative resources.

Criminal Prosecutorial Discretion

A 1991 Department of Justice (DOJ) memorandum sets forth the factors it will consider in determining whether to prosecute an environmental violation involving significant voluntary compliance or disclosure efforts.[3] These factors include voluntary disclosure, cooperation, preventive measures and compliance programs, pervasiveness of noncompliance, internal disciplinary action, and subsequent compliance efforts. With respect to preventive measures and compliance programs, the DOJ policy identifies numerous factors, including the existence of a compliance management system (CMS) and commitment to regulatory compliance.[4]

Corporate Criminal Sentencing Guidelines

Finally, the 1991 U.S. Sentencing Commission guidance states that the existence of "an effective program to prevent and detect violations of law" will provide the basis for substantial reductions in criminal sentences for convicted corporations.[5] The guidelines state, "The hallmark of an effective program to prevent and detect violations of law is that the organization exercised due diligence in seeking to prevent and detect criminal conduct by its employees and other agents." In defining "due diligence," the Sentencing Commission set forth what has become the generally accepted core components of a CMS. These include the following:

- The development of standards and procedures to prevent noncompliant behavior.
- Allocation of responsibility to oversee conformance to these standards and procedures.
- Training to communicate the standards, procedures, and roles.
- Use of appropriate disciplinary mechanisms to encourage consistent enforcement of the standards.
- The execution of steps such as monitoring and auditing systems to implement the standards.
- Steps to correct the noncompliance and prevent future noncompliance.[6]

These three guidelines, especially the Sentencing Guidelines, have had an enormous impact in encouraging the development and implementation of CMSs in the United States.

EPA Audit and Self-Policing Policies

EPA's 1986 auditing policy[7] strongly encourages organizations to use environmental auditing to help achieve and maintain regulatory compliance. Toward that end, the 1986 policy sets forth the basic elements of effective environmental auditing programs.

On December 22, 1995, EPA announced *Incentives for Self-Policing: Discovery, Disclosure, Correction and Prevention of Violations Final Policy Statement* (final self-policing policy). Under the new policy, the agency will greatly reduce civil penalties and limit liability for criminal prosecution for regulated entities that meet the policy's conditions for discovery, disclosure, and correction.

Specifically, EPA will not seek gravity-based civil penalties[8] for violations that are discovered through a Compliance Management System (CMS) or an environmental audit[9] and that are promptly disclosed and expeditiously corrected, provided other important conditions or safeguards are met. These safeguards require entities to take steps to prevent recurrence of the violation and to remediate any harm caused by the violation. The policy does not apply to violations that result in serious actual harm or may present an imminent and substantial endangerment to human health or the environment. Repeat violations are not eligible for relief under the policy. The policy does not apply to individual criminal acts or corporate criminal acts arising from conscious disregard or willful blindness to violations. Finally, EPA retains its discretion to collect any economic benefit gained from noncompliance in order to preserve a "level playing field" for entities that invest in timely compliance.[10]

With respect to discovery through a CMS, the policy states that the violation must have been discovered through an "objective, documented, systematic procedure or practice reflecting the regulated entity's due diligence in preventing, detecting, and correcting violations." "Due diligence" is defined in terms of criteria based on the 1991 Sentencing Guidelines which are generally recognized as the fundamental elements of a sound CMS including the following:

- The development of compliance policies, standards, and procedures to meet regulatory requirements.

- Allocation of responsibility to oversee conformance with these policies, standards, and procedures.

- Mechanisms, including monitoring and auditing of compliance and the CMS, to assure the policies, standards, and procedures are being carried out.

- Training to communicate the standards and procedures.

- Incentives for managers and employees to perform in accordance with the compliance policies, standards, and procedures, including consistent enforcement through appropriate disciplinary mechanisms.

- Procedures for the prompt and appropriate correction of violations, including program modifications needed to prevent future violations.

In addition to full mitigation of gravity-based penalties for satisfaction of all of these conditions, EPA will generally not recommend criminal prosecution against the organization if the violation results from the unauthorized criminal conduct of an employee. Finally, where the violation is not discovered through a CMS or an audit, but where all the other conditions are met, EPA will reduce gravity-based penalties by 75 percent.[11]

Policy Analysis

Criminal Enforcement Policy Documents

The fact that a violator has a sound EMS (ISO 14001-certified/registered or not) will be one of the many factors a criminal investigator, prosecutor, or judge will consider in applying the appropriate criminal policy documents.

But in order to obtain maximum benefit under these policies, a violator must actually accomplish many of the tasks for which the ISO 14001 EMS has established procedures. One example is correction of the violation. The ISO EMS standard requires organizations to "establish and maintain procedures . . . for initiating and completing corrective and preventive action." All three policy documents indicate that prompt correction of the violation is a very important factor.

Prompt disclosure of the violation is also another important factor considered under the policy documents. Disclosure is not a featured component of the ISO 14001 EMS standard.

Other examples are as follows: ISO 14001 requires that an organization consider regulatory requirements in setting its objectives and targets, have a procedure for tracking conformance with those objectives and targets, and have a management review that addresses the possible need to change the EMS.

In contrast, factors in the DOJ memorandum include whether "environmental compliance was a standard by which employee and corporate departmental performance was judged," and whether "the [EMS/compliance] auditor's recommendations [were] implemented in a timely fashion."

Practically speaking, an organization that vigorously implements a sound EMS is not likely to be the subject of a criminal investigation or to be criminally prosecuted or convicted. The requisite level of intent for criminal liability under most environmental statutes—knowing or intentional—involves behavior that is antithetical to behavior required to effectively implement an EMS.

In addition, the systematic management of environmental activity, commitment to compliance, procedures for emergency preparedness and response, and procedures for employee accountability, among other things, would tend to prevent a violation from resulting in serious harm, a factor under the three policy documents.

Final Self-Policing Policy

The prerequisite conditions for significant reductions in civil penalties and for other relief under the final self-policing policy are consistent with many of the factors featured in the criminal policy documents. The conditions in the final self-policing policy represent safeguards to deter irresponsible behavior and protect health and the environment.

ISO 14001 registration does not assure EPA and the public that these important safeguards will be met. For example, ISO 14001 registration does not mean that an organization's violations will not result in serious harm or imminent and substantial endangerment to the public or the environment. Nor does ISO 14001 registration confirm that an organization promptly discloses, expeditiously corrects, or remediates harm caused by the violation. Nor does ISO 14001 registration guarantee that the organization takes measures to prevent recurrence of the violation or that the same violation had not occurred many times recently. EPA has determined that it would be inappropriate to provide significant penalty mitigation or a criminal safe harbor unless those safeguards are met.

EPA's enforcement response toward ISO 14001-registered organizations will likely be consistent with existing enforcement response policies. Specifically, full mitigation of gravity-based civil penalties will likely require an organization to meet the conditions or safeguards in the final self-policing policy. Moreover, consistent with the self-policing policy, complete penalty amnesty—including waiver of significant economic benefit gained from noncompliance—will probably not be available. Finally, it is highly unlikely that EPA would refrain from pursuing injunctive relief by virtue of the fact that the threat at issue involves an ISO 14001-registered organization.[12]

Advantages of ISO 14001 Registration with Respect to Final Self-Policing Policy

Nonetheless, ISO 14001-registered organizations may have substantial advantages over nonregistered organizations with respect to application of EPA's final self-policing policy.

First, ISO-registered companies may be more likely to satisfy the condition involving discovery of the violation through a system reflecting due diligence or a CMS. The due diligence or CMS criteria in the final self-policing policy are very similar to the requirements in the ISO 14001 standard because they both incorporate the same "plan, do, check, act" formula. The ISO 14001 EMS is much broader than a CMS and should subsume the generally accepted elements of a compliance management or compliance assurance system.

However, there are important differences between the due-diligence criteria and ISO 14001. Most significantly, the due-diligence criteria focus on compliance with regulatory requirements, whereas the ISO 14001 standard focuses on selected "objectives and targets," which may include regulatory compliance. In addition, the due-diligence criteria require "appropriate incentives" (including disciplinary mechanisms) to encourage performance in accordance with compliance policies, standards, and procedures. In contrast, ISO 14001 merely requires training on the "potential consequences of departing from specific operating procedures," without stating what those consequences might be.

Note that whether an ISO 14001-registered organization meets the due-diligence criteria also rests upon the integrity and credibility of the program and process for accrediting registrars and auditor certifiers, approving training providers, and certifying auditors and registering companies.[13]

Second, as discussed above, another advantage is that a mature and effective ISO 14001 EMS should make it less likely that violations will occur in the first place; where they do, procedures should be in place to promptly correct the violation and take appropriate action to remediate the harm.

Third, violations that do occur should not rise to the level of actual serious harm or imminent and substantial endangerment.

Fourth, the mandate for continuous improvement of the EMS and management review sets forth the processes by which an organization can meet the self-policing policy condition to agree to take steps to prevent recurrence of the violation. Finally, these same "continuous improvement" processes should make it unlikely that the violation at hand was a "repeat violation" as defined under the final audit policy.

The remaining conditions for penalty mitigation under the final audit policy are "full and prompt disclosure" and "cooperation," both of which are not addressed in the ISO 14001 EMS standard. (Many of the legal issues related to disclosure are considered in Chapter 10.)

In developing the self-policing policy, EPA considered several options for providing the certainty of enforcement response that industry desired and for encouraging environmental auditing and the adoption of management systems. These options included the (adopted) enforcement policy approach, voluntary industry standards for EMS (such as ISO 14001) as an alternative to the current regulatory regime, and mandatory auditing or management programs. The latter option was not politically or administratively feasible. With respect to the second option, the environmental performance flowing from the operation of an EMS pursuant to voluntary standards was not—and is not—fully understood. In addition, as discussed below, there were several problems regarding the accountability issue.

FACTORS IN DETERMINING THE EXTENT TO WHICH REGULATORY BENEFITS ARE APPROPRIATE INCENTIVES FOR ISO 14001 REGISTRATION

Since ISO Registration Does Not Guarantee Any Specific Level of Environmental Performance, Regulatory Benefits Should Not Be Provided by Virtue of ISO Registration Alone

In determining the extent to which regulatory benefits are appropriate for ISO-registered organizations, the central question is whether ISO registration will be a reliable indicator of a minimum level of environmental performance. Given the agency's mission to protect human health and the environment, this minimum level of performance must yield at least the level of protection provided under the current regulatory structure.

While ISO 14001 can be a highly effective tool for improving environmental performance within and beyond the sphere of regulated activity, it does not guarantee any particular level of environmental performance, such as compliance with regulatory requirements. Like ISO 9000 quality-management standards, ISO 14001 registration will not result in an output of any predetermined quality. Given this fact, regulators will probably not be willing to provide any significant regulatory benefits for ISO 14001 registration in and of itself.

The ISO EMS standard can be likened to a tapestry board, which may be used to weave either a splendid or a shoddy tapestry, depending on the quality of the threads used and the artisanship of the weaver. A customer would not be likely to order a tapestry simply on the basis of information about the tapestry board without having knowledge of the weaver's skill or the quality of tapestries woven in the past.

ISO Registration Combined with a History of Compliance or Superior Performance Would Make Companies Likely Candidates for Additional Regulatory Benefits

If a history of good performance is combined with an objective certification of sound environmental management, regulators would be much more likely to provide meaningful regulatory benefits. Regulators may be willing to provide additional regulatory benefits to ISO 14001-registered organizations if the results of the ISO 14001 system have yielded a significant history of compliance or a history of superior performance. Superior performance might be achieved through the implementation of pollution prevention practices.

In other words, if the same weaver using the same tapestry board has woven many high-quality tapestries in the past, it is likely that the weaver will weave high-quality tapestries in the future.

EPA is evaluating proposals to provide regulatory benefits to organizations—both ISO 14001-registered and not—that have a history of compliance or a history of superior performance levels above compliance.[14] EPA is exploring the extent to which ISO 14001 registration might entitle organizations with a history of compliance or superior performance to additional regulatory benefits.

Regulatory Recognition of ISO 14001-Registered Organizations Would Require Accountability for and Disclosure of Environmental Performance

Without disclosure of environmental performance, the public and government will not know whether an organization is operating in a manner consistent with the environmental goals society has set for itself.

The external communication requirements of the ISO 14001 EMS standard are weak in this regard: "The organization shall consider processes for external communication on its significant environmental aspects and record its decision," shall establish and maintain procedures for responding to communications from external interested parties, and must make its environmental policy publicly available.

Countries or blocs may integrate their own disclosure schemes in conjunction with the ISO 14001 standard. For example, the Eco-Management and Auditing Scheme (EMAS) requires companies to prepare and publish a validated, site-specific environmental statement that sets forth the significant environmental issues and data on performance. In addition, the company must publish its policies and programs and a description of its EMS system.

If regulatory benefits are provided for ISO 14001 registration, and such benefits rely upon an organization's environmental performance, there must be a means of verifying the performance. This must involve some degree of disclosure to the government or the public in order to ensure that the public and environment are being adequately protected.

There is greater and greater pressure for companies to provide communities with performance information and to consider the perspectives of community stakeholders in making decisions that affect these stakeholders. As a condition of providing regulatory benefits for ISO 14001-registered organizations, the government will probably require disclosure to and involvement of local communities.

Incentives for increased levels of performance may be provided through public and market pressures, which in turn require dissemination of information about an organization's environmental performance. Examples include public pressure in response to information voluntarily or involuntarily provided by the organization through the government and/or press. In addition, there are a myriad of market incentives that exert themselves through preference toward suppliers, reduced insurance premiums, and other risk-based benefits manifested through financial, lender, and investment markets. In general, there is greater pressure—public and market—toward greater disclosure of environmental performance.

Development of Performance Measures for ISO 14001-Registered Organizations Would Promote Regulatory Reliance on ISO 14001 Registration

The primary value of ISO 14001 from a regulatory standpoint will be its effect on improving environmental performance. An ISO 14001-registered organization will utilize many performance measures that are designed to serve its needs according to its selected objectives. Improvement of the EMS and environmental performance requires monitoring and measurement of performance.

Since the EMS addresses the significant environmental impacts of its activities, services, and products across all media, many of these performance measures must be multimedia-based. In addition, many of these performance measures may not directly relate to current regulatory measures of compliance, yet they are still valuable in characterizing the organization's impact on the environment. For example, the amount of a raw material—water, for example—utilized per unit of production is not a measurement employed in the current regulatory system, but it is nonetheless useful information from the perspective of developing mechanisms for addressing problems involving depletion of natural resources, sustainable development, and decertification.

Thus, the challenge is to develop measures of environmental performance that are consistent or fungible with measures of performance utilized within an ISO-certified/registered EMS. This requires a definition of "environmental performance" that captures activity beyond the range of regulated activity.

The work of ISO/TC 207 SC4—Environmental Performance Evaluation (EPE)—should provide some insight into development of useful measures of performance. EPE will be utilized to help organizations measure their performance vis-á-vis their selected objectives and targets.[15] One component of this task is to identify environmental performance indicators (EPIs), which are specific measures of environmental performance.[16] EPIs can reflect the total amount of toxics released, can be information scaled to another parameter such as production, or can be characterized in other ways.[17] Some of the information that is currently required for regulatory compliance purposes, such as toxic release data and emissions and discharge monitoring data, could be utilized.

In addition, activities relating to assessment of the life cycle of a product or service could prove very useful in developing performance measures as well. The ISO Subcommittee on Life Cycle Analysis (SC5) could provide valuable input.

As noted above, the levels of performance flowing from any EMS in an "ISO regulatory scheme" must, at a minimum, be adequate to protect the public and the environment. It is therefore important to develop performance measures that are capable of being utilized in setting standards for protecting the health and the environment. Such standards should be flexible and multimedia-based wherever possible. For example, a flexible multimedia approach may be taken in setting overall permit limits with respect to a pollutant or class of pollutants for an entire facility, group of facilities, or even an entire industry sector or geographical region. Sector-based standards, including those that rely on relative EPIs involving materials used or waste generated per unit of product, have particular promise. Facilities should have sufficient flexibility to develop and utilize the method of controlling or reducing pollutants that makes the most sense from their perspective; governments should not prescribe the technology that must be utilized.

SPECIFIC REGULATORY BENEFITS FOR ISO 14001-REGISTERED ORGANIZATIONS

Reduced Reporting and Monitoring Requirements

Self-monitoring and self-reporting requirements have been an essential part of determining whether applicable permit limits are being met. It is unlikely that EPA would reduce the amount of substantive information that an ISO 14001-registered organization must report by virtue of its ISO registration. However, if an ISO 14001-registered organization can demonstrate significant compliance history or superior performance, less information would need to be reported or reported as frequently to verify its performance.

With respect to organizations that achieve "superior" environmental performance, an alternative model could be developed that involves identification of performance measures that can be utilized to determine whether the public and environment are being adequately protected. Consistent with the ISO EMS standards, these performance measures should be multimedia and flexible. Organizations still must report a certain level of information, but reporting could be much less burdensome and more easily integrated into its own management system.

Consolidated Reporting and Monitoring Requirements

Under the ISO EMS standard, the identification of significant environmental aspects and impacts, development of objectives, and the measurement of key characteristics of operations and activities all have a multimedia focus. From the perspective of an ISO 14001-registered organization, regulatory requirements for monitoring, reporting, and recordkeeping should (optimally) be consistent with ISO's multimedia focus. From a regulatory perspective, a multimedia characterization of impacts on the environment is generally more accurate than a media-specific focus. In addition, multimedia regulation generally provides more effective controls over environmental effects than media-specific controls.

The implementation of ISO EMS standards presents the regulated community and regulators with an opportunity to streamline information submissions. Consolidation and simplification of reporting, monitoring, and recordkeeping requirements are already occurring under the auspices of EPA's "one-stop reporting" initiative.

Information Required for Permitting; Streamlined Permitting

Flexibility regarding permitting procedures may be possible for ISO-14001-registered organizations where environmental performance is measured, meets a minimum level of protection for the public and the environment, and is disclosed. Much of the information required for permit applications will already be collected through operation of the ISO EMS information-collection functions. EPA may require permit application information in a form that is consistent with information generated through its EMS. This recharacterization of information may also eliminate much of the process associated with modifying a specific permit. As discussed, permit standards should be flexible (at least facilitywide) and multimedia focused.

Reduced Inspections

Given the substantial resources that are expended by government and industry in preparing for and conducting EPA compliance inspections and the perceived environmental benefits associated with ISO registration, it has been suggested that ISO-registered organizations might be subject to fewer EPA inspections and/or inspections that are narrower in scope.

Whether a facility or group of facilities within an industry sector are inspected depends upon a myriad of factors, including the toxic release inventory (TRI) data with toxicological weights, demographic information, compliance history, and productivity of the facility.[18]

As discussed above, ISO 14001 registration does not guarantee any set level of environmental performance. However, conformance with ISO 14001 has a great potential to improve environmental performance, both in preventing serious violations and ultimately decreasing the number of violations overall. A demonstrated direct correlation between ISO-14001-registered organizations and significantly higher rates of compliance would be valuable information to EPA for purposes of targeting inspections. This may be a potential area for a sector-based pilot project.

Nonetheless, compliance rates and seriousness of violations would not address factors relating to demographic factors and exposure of substances to humans or the environment. For example, an ISO-14001-registered organization with a facility that handles hazardous waste in a heavily populated area may be inspected regardless of a facility's performance history.

CONCLUSION

The above analysis of the possible impact of ISO 14001 on regulatory enforcement and compliance is contingent upon a credible ISO 14001 registration mechanism. The credibility of ISO EMS registration depends on the credibility of the entire program for accrediting registrars and certifiers and for approving training providers and programs. EPA has indicated that a credible accreditation program should include a single dedicated body with environmental expertise and an open and inclusive process for developing criteria and accrediting qualified entities. (A discussion of the conformity assessment process and related issues appear in Chapter 19.)

EPA Voluntary Programs

Many EPA programs and projects involve EMSs generally or ISO 14001 specifically. Project XL involves the granting of regulatory flexibility in exchange for a commitment by a regulated entity to achieve better environmental results than would have been attained through full compliance with regulations. EPA and the following companies are negotiating XL projects that specifically involve EMSs or ISO 14001: AT&T-Lucent Technologies, Intel, 3M, Anheuser-Busch, and Weyerhauser.

In response to the Administration's interim goal of reducing reporting and monitoring by at least 25 percent, the Office of Water has developed the Interim Guidance for Performance-Based Reduction of NPDES Permit Monitoring Frequencies, dated April 19, 1996. Under the guidance, EPA will significantly reduce monitoring and reporting burdens based on superior compliance history and superior control performance history. Through the AT&T-Lucent Technologies XL project, EPA is also exploring possible incentives for facilities that implement EMSs.

The Environmental Leadership Project (ELP) recognizes facilities that have shown leadership and innovation in complying with environmental requirements. Most of the twelve ELP pilot projects involve the development and use of EMSs. The criteria for entry into the full-scale ELP are being developed through groups that focus on the following areas: incentives, an ELP EMS framework, compliance auditing and self certification, mentoring, and community outreach and employee involvement.

EPA Region 1's ELP "Startrack" program involves third-party certification/ verification of a company's environmental performance focusing on EMSs, compliance audit programs and pollution prevention programs, in exchange for benefits such as fewer inspections, reduced reporting, expedited permitting, and reduced penalties.

EPA Region 9's "Merit Partnership Program" may involve demonstration projects for strengthened ISO 14001 standards that include compliance auditing, pollution prevention auditing and practices, community participation, and mentoring. These demonstration projects may also involve the development of new forms of insurance coverage to foster greater use of EMSs.

The Federal Facility Enforcement Office developed the Environmental Management Review (EMR) Interim Policy for Federal Facilities, dated May 30, 1996, which involves EPA evaluations of programs and management systems of federal facilities to determine the extent to which facilities have developed specific environmental protection programs and plans.

EPA's Sustainable Industry Project (SIP), led by the Office of Policy, Planning, and Evaluation, is designed to improve the efficiency of environmental activities in order to facilitate the international competitiveness of U.S. companies. The SIP Best

Management Practices (BMP) work group is developing a project with Union Carbide involving ISO 14001.

Finally, EPA and NSF International are funding a demonstration project in which eighteen organizations (about half of which are small and medium-size) are piloting ISO 14001 EMS assessment and implementation. Part of this project will involve the development of an EMS implementation guide for small and medium-size organizations.

EPA is in the preliminary stages of determining what role EMSs and ISO 14001 may play in each of these initiatives. EPA has indicated that it looks forward to working with the states, regulated entities, public interest groups, and other important stakeholders in exploring this exciting area.

BIOGRAPHY

Brian P. Riedel, Esq.

Brian P. Riedel is Counsel for the U.S. Environmental Protective Agency's Office of Planning and Policy Analysis (OPPA) which serves the Assistant Administrator for Enforcement and Compliance Assurance (OECA). Mr. Riedel is the Chair of the OECA ISO 14001/EMS Task Group, a group of federal and state officials responsible for making recommendations on enforcement and compliance matters associated with the ISO 14001 standards and environmental management systems. He is a member of the U.S. Technical Advisory Group (TAG) to ISO Technical Committee 207 on environmental management.

In addition, Mr. Riedel is coauthor of EPA's interim and final Audit/Self-Policing Policies. He is Vice Chair of the Audit Policy Quick Response Team responsible for making recommendations on nationally significant issues and cases involving application of the interim and final policies. Before moving to EPA in 1993, Mr. Riedel practiced environmental law for three years with the Washington, D.C. law firm of Newman & Holtzinger. He received his law degree from the University of Wisconsin and A.B. from the University of Michigan.

NOTES

1. This chapter reflects the views of the author and not necessarily those of the U.S. Environmental Protection Agency (EPA) or any other governmental entity.
2. Memorandum from Earl E. Devaney, Director, EPA Office of Criminal Enforcement, regarding *The Exercise of Investigative Discretion,* January 12, 1994.
3. U.S. Department of Justice, *Factors in Decisions on Criminal Prosecutions for Environmental Violations in the Context of Significant Voluntary Compliance or Disclosure Efforts by the Violator,* July 1, 1991.
4. The DOJ policy states:

   The attorney for the Department should consider the existence and scope of any regularized, intensive, and comprehensive environmental compliance program. . . . Compliance programs may vary but the following questions should be asked in evaluating any program: Was there a strong institutional policy to comply with all environmental requirements? Had safeguards beyond those required by existing law been developed and implemented to prevent noncompliance from occurring? Were there regular procedures, including internal or external compliance and management audits, to evaluate, detect and prevent, and remedy circumstances like those that led to the noncompliance? Were there procedures and safeguards to ensure the integrity of any audit conducted? Did the audit evaluate all sources of pollution (*i.e.,* all media), including the possibility of cross-media transfers of pollutants? Were the auditor's recommendations implemented in a timely fashion? Were adequate resources committed to the auditing program and to implementing its recommendations? Was environmental compliance a standard by which employee and corporate departmental performance was judged?

5. *United States Sentencing Commission Guidelines Manual.* Chapter 8: Sentencing of Organizations, Part A—General Application Principles (effective November 1, 1991).

6. The Sentencing Guidelines state: "Due diligence requires at a minimum that the organization must have taken the following types of steps:

(1) The organization must have established compliance standards and procedures to be followed by its employees and other agents that are reasonably capable of reducing the prospect of criminal conduct.

(2) Specific individual(s) within high-level personnel of the organization must have been assigned overall responsibility to oversee compliance with such standards and procedures.

(3) The organization must have used due care not to delegate substantial discretionary authority to individuals whom the organization knew, or should have known through the exercise of due diligence, had a propensity to engage in illegal activities.

(4) The organization must have taken steps to communicate effectively its standards and procedures to all employees and other agents, *e.g.,* by requiring participation in training programs or by disseminating publications that explain in a practical manner what is required.

(5) The organization must have taken reasonable steps to achieve compliance with its standards, *e.g.,* by utilizing monitoring and auditing systems reasonably designed to detect criminal conduct by its employees and other agents and by having in place and publicizing a reporting system whereby employees and other agents could report criminal conduct by others within the organization without fear of retribution.

(6) The standards must have been consistently enforced through appropriate disciplinary mechanisms, including, as appropriate, discipline of individuals responsible for the failure to detect an offense. Adequate discipline of individuals responsible for an offense is a necessary component of enforcement; however, the form of discipline that will be appropriate will be case specific.

(7) After an offense has been detected, the organization must have taken all reasonable steps to respond appropriately to the offense and to prevent further similar offenses—including any necessary modifications to its program to prevent and detect violations of law."

7. Environmental Auditing Policy Statement, July 9, 1986 (51 FR 25004).

8. The "gravity" component of a penalty represents the "seriousness" or "punitive" portion of penalties. The other major part of a penalty, the economic-benefit component, represents the economic advantage that a violator gains through its noncompliance.

9. An environmental audit has the definition given to it under EPA's 1986 auditing policy: "a systematic, documented, periodic and objective review by regulated entities of facility operations and practices related to meeting environmental requirements."

10. Under the final self-policing policy, EPA may waive the entire penalty for violations which, in EPA's opinion, do not merit any penalty due to the insignificant amount of any economic benefit.

    Under some environmental statutes, EPA is required to consider the economic benefit a violator gains from noncompliance is assessing penalties. See, for example, CWA §309(g), CAA §113(e), and SDWA §1423(c). EPA's long-standing policy has been to collect significant economic benefit gained from noncompliance. See *A Framework for Statute-Specific Approaches to [Civil] Penalty Assessments, EPA General Enforcement Policy GM-22,* February 16, 1984; see also the approximately 24 EPA media and program-specific penalty and enforcement response policies. The reason for collecting economic benefit is to preserve a level playing field for entities that make the timely investment in compliance. Recovery of economic benefit can be likened to the IRS requirement of paying interest or fees on taxes paid late.

11. For a more detailed discussion of EPA's final self-policing policy, see this author's chapter in *The Environmental Audits Book,* 7th Edition, Government Institutes, 1995.

12. Note that the minimum conditions of the self-policing policy—disclosure, correction, no repeat violations, no criminal acts, no serious actual or threat of harm, recovery of economic benefit, and so on—are also part of the enforcement response agreed to by EPA and Environmental Leadership Program pilot participants in exchange for no enforcement action if violations are corrected within 90 days.

13. See also discussions of the ISO 14001 conformity assessment process in Chapter 19.

14. See, for example, the draft document describing the NPDES program of performance-based reporting and monitoring, June 14, 1995.

15. The ISO 14031 working draft "Evaluation of the environmental performance of the management system and its relationship to the environment" defines EPE as a process to "measure, analyze, assess, and describe an organization's environmental performance against agreed criteria for appropriate management purposes."

16. The SC4 working draft defines EPI as a "specific description of [environmental performance] within an evaluation area."

17. The working draft provides the following examples of ways to characterize EPIs:

    - Absolute (e.g., total emissions of SO_2).
    - Relative (e.g., SO_2 emissions per ton of primary product).
    - Indexes (baseline year at 100 percent or weighing of equivalents to consolidate data, e.g., total greenhouse gas releases expressed as CO_2).
    - Aggregated (combining from various sites or assigning data to a category of environmental effect; for example, SO_2 emissions aggregated from 20 plants or amount of hazardous waste generated per site).
    - Weighted (weighing of noncomparable effects; involves making value judgments).

18. Final FY 96/97 OECA Memorandum of Agreement Guidance, June 22, 1995.

CHAPTER 23

U.S. Sentencing Guidelines and ISO 14000: A Basis for an Alternative Environmental Compliance Pathway in the United States

Lawrence P. Raymond

INTRODUCTION

ISO 14001 promises to create, for the first time, international consistency in the fundamental structure and management of environmental affairs within organizations. The move toward ISO 14001 adoptions creates opportunities for greater self-control over operations and performance, away from the command-and-control policies of the 70s and 80s. It can also lead to economic improvements, as operating efficiencies reduce waste, increase product output and revenues, and reduce costs of waste management.

The promise of better environmental performance, however, is not a specific requirement of ISO 14001. ISO 14001 requires continuous improvement of the environmental *management* system and a commitment to compliance; actual improvements in environmental performance are *anticipated* results. Anticipated results, however, are not likely to gain ISO 14001 the acceptance and approval of public environmental regulators or private environmental interest groups.

Many of the elements of U.S. environmental policy are embodied in the ISO 14001 EMS standard. Adopting ISO 14001 in the United States will not eliminate the requirements set forth in existing environmental law. The public's sensitivity to environmental problems is increasing, and the public remains suspicious of industry's commitment to environmental improvement. Governments are responding to public concerns by setting standards and guidelines for levels of environmental performance.

Successfully implementing ISO 14001 requires incorporating processes designed to lessen environmental exploitation, improve natural resource management, and achieve long-term environmental quality into the basics of daily business. Although these are stated objectives of the ISO 14000 initiative, the ISO 14001 EMS standard does not detail how to achieve them. It is by design a general standard. Even though the Annex to ISO 14001 and the ISO 14004 guidance standard provide significant clarification regarding implementation, the standard does not chart a pathway for the regulated community in the United States but instead presents a new challenge, not just in the United States, but in all nations with strong environmental regulatory programs.

Minimizing Environmental Liability and ISO 14001

The challenge is this: How can organizations minimize environmental liability through compliance within the context of an ISO 14001 program? Will the move to ISO 14000 increase the burdens on industry for environmental compliance? Will the adoption of the ISO 14000 series lead to the regulated community serving two masters—those of command-and-control compliance and those of ISO 14001?

ISO 14001 clearly requires an organization's environmental policy to include commitments to compliance and to continuous improvement of the management system. These must be reflected in its objectives, targets, and demonstrated performance. Will organizations need to add new layers to existing environmental management programs to achieve these policy goals? And what exactly does compliance mean under the new set of ISO 14001 obligations?

The marketplace, the public, governments, investors, and other stakeholders are demanding better environmental performance from companies. The regulated community must now respond. Experience, understanding, and knowledge specific to corporate and institutional needs, as well as a broad vision for ISO 14000 structure and linkage globally, will be required to realize the full potential of the ISO 14000 movement.

In the United States, the challenges include getting traditional systems to accept and adapt to change, the costs of creating change, and risking fixing something that doesn't appear to be broken. The challenge also is understanding just what expectations government has with respect to these changes. How does government expect companies to demonstrate environmental responsibility? How can this be achieved cost-effectively? How will government and the regulated community deal with alternative pathways to environmental compliance and environmental improvement?

Compliance Expectations

Environmental management has been transformed in the 1990s. It began with the Pollution Prevention Act of 1990 (PPA), which changed U.S. environmental policy. No longer does the United States emphasize waste management as its principal strategy for controlling pollution. Emphasis now includes controlling the amount of waste industrial activities create, reviewing current practices with an eye to improving efficiencies in use, and conversion of raw materials into useful product. The Act calls for a multimedia approach, dealing collectively with all contaminants, pollutants, emissions, and solid wastes in and on water, air, and land. The law further directs that efforts focus on reducing waste at its source (termed *source reduction*) through cost-effective changes in production, operation, and raw material use. This has changed the nature of environmental compliance. Given that compliance is achieved by proving conformance with the policies, statutes, regulations, and directives of government, the PPA changed the rules. Compliance means operating with sensitivity to the surrounding environment, to neighbors, and to long-term effects. It demands higher levels of performance, system boundaries that include energy efficiency, the production of less harmful substances, expanded recycling and material recoveries, and natural resource conservation. Such considerations are now expected in the engineering of plants and supporting facilities, as well as in the examination of management practices.

Despite the evolution in environmental management, government has not been fast in providing an explicit, integrated definition of *environmental compliance.* Guidance has been mostly through program initiatives and federal facility examples. For example, the EPA Leadership Program focuses on the accountability of corporate leadership and an expectation for manufacturing facility plans to include broad risk-reduction goals. It also stipulates measures for public accountability, source reduction, integration of environmental issues into sound business practices, involvement of employees in environmental decision making, and a commitment to comprehensive self-auditing and compliance programs.

Similarly, Executive Order 12856, issued in August 1993, directed all federal facilities to comply with right-to-know laws and pollution-prevention requirements. These requirements extend to the development of written plans, developed with public involvement, that contain policy statements, designate responsibilities, and provide for implementation and continued performance evaluation of pollution-control measures. Other federal programs, such as the Common Sense Initiative, the Merit Program, and the Star Track Program, can be viewed as initial pilot tests of alternative compliance pathways for environmentally responsible organizations.

Perhaps the single, most complete statement of compliance expectations offered by government has come from the federal courts. The U.S. Sentencing Commission's proposed guidelines for federal environmental crimes were published in the Federal Register on December 16, 1993.[1] These guidelines were incorporated as a new chapter in the U.S. Sentencing Commission Guidelines Manual in 1994 but were not officially adopted.

The proposed guidelines for organizational offenses reflect the combined considerations of representatives of the U.S. Department of Justice, the Environmental Protection Agency, and private practice ad hoc groups. Thus, they are the best available consensus to the discretion the agencies and courts are likely to use in making enforcement as well as penalty decisions regarding environmental compliance. Taken in context with agency programs and guidance, they are instructive regarding the content and coverage of a responsible environmental management program.

Interpretations and judgments in this chapter suggest a structure and process for environmental programs that incorporate the elements of both ISO 14001 and the Sentencing Guidelines for Environmental Crimes. The intent is to provide a foundation for corporate environmental programs that give decision makers in the regulated community a reasonable assurance of environmental compliance while reducing individual and corporate exposure to civil and criminal liability.

U.S. SENTENCING COMMISSION GUIDELINES

The following is the formula established by the U.S. Sentencing Commission for setting sentences:

$$BF + AF - MF = Sentence$$

Where: BF = Base Fine

AF = Aggravating Factors

MF = Mitigating Factors

The Base Fine is the greater of:

1. The economic gain plus costs directly attributable to the offense.

2. A percentage of the maximum statutory fine that could be imposed for the offenses of conviction.

The setting of the base fine does not group environmental offenses; instead, it requires the court to consider the aggregate economic gain and environmental costs from each offense of conviction. Base fines as a percentage of the maximum statutory fine are given in Table 23–1, according to offense type. This table should not be taken as inclusive; numerous other factors (e.g., natural resource damages; civil and administrative charges; endangered species, protected habitat) can modify the fines.

TABLE 23–1

Base Fine Table

Offense Type	Percentage of Maximum Statutory Fine
(a) An offense involving knowing endangerment (under RCRA, CWA, or CAA)	90–100%
(b) An offense involving unlawful handling of a hazardous substance or other environmental pollutant resulting in an actual release, discharge, disposal, or emission into the environment	60–90
(c) An offense involving unlawful handling of a hazardous substance or other environmental pollutant, creating a material threat of actual release, discharge, disposal, or emission into the environment	40–70
(d) An offense involving knowing falsification; knowing concealment or destruction; knowing omission or tampering	30–50
(e) Other offenses involving unlawful handling of a hazardous substance or other environmental pollutant not resulting in an actual or threatened release, discharge, disposal, or emission into the environment	15–30
(f) Wildlife offense	(not yet established)

Table 23–2 identifies and defines aggravating factors. It suggests that enforcement will focus more on persons, qualified by reason of their responsibilities or position within their organization and industry, who commit an act that could be expected to cause personal injury, property damage, or other violation of permit terms and conditions. This might be interpreted to mean that the U.S. government expects persons who own and operate a business to have a reasonable understanding of how its operations might affect the health and well-being of those around it. Management is responsible for ensuring that pollutants are characterized at each facility and operation, that controls and procedures governing discharges are identified, and that installed controls are fulfilling their function.

Table 23–3 identifies and defines mitigating factors. These offer the potential for liability protection. Penalties are reduced and potentially eliminated in cases where

T A B L E   23–2

Aggravating Factors in Sentencing

Factor	Definition/Explanation
(a) Management Involvement	One or more members of the "substantial authority personnel" of the organization participated in, condoned, solicited, or concealed the criminal conduct, or recklessly tolerated conditions that created or perpetuated a significant risk that criminal behavior of the same general type or kind would occur or continue.
(b) Scienter	Employees or agents of the organization knowingly engaged in conduct that violated the law under circumstances that evidenced at least a reckless indifference to legal requirements.
(c) Prior criminal compliance history	The organization has been convicted of a state or federal environmental crime within the last five years. Greater factor if the prior adjudication was for similar conduct.
(d) Prior civil compliance history	The number, severity, or pattern of the organization's prior civil or administrative adjudications within the past five years, when considered in light of the size, scope, and character of the organization and its operations, reveals a disregard by the organization of its environmental regulatory responsibilities.
(e) Concealment	An employee or agent of the organization sought to conceal the violation or to obstruct administrative, civil, or criminal investigation of the violation by knowingly furnishing inaccurate material information or omitting material information.
(f) Absence of compliance program or other organized effort	The organization either had no program or other organized effort to achieve and maintain compliance with environmental requirements, or it had such a program in form only and had substantially failed to implement it.

the organization can demonstrate that, prior to the offense, it had committed the resources and the management processes (reasonably determined to be sufficient, given the size and nature of the business) to achieve and maintain compliance with environmental requirements, including detection of criminal conduct by its employees or agents.

Key to full mitigation of fines and penalties is a clear demonstration of an organization's commitment to environmental compliance. Accomplishing this is possible only when an organization knows exactly what performance is expected. Table 23–4 identifies the specific criteria the Working Group of the Sentencing Commission considered important when evaluating an organization's commitment to environmental compliance. It communicates what federal enforcement agencies are likely to search for when investigating the adequacy of an environmental management program in the context of the resolution of a criminal matter. As a result, these criteria help define compliance and provide a basis for negotiating and structuring program defense with regulators. The impact of the draft guidelines, however, will be felt more broadly in civil enforcement actions.

When achieved using standard engineering and scientific principles and in good faith, corporate environmental compliance management systems are being viewed by the U.S. EPA, U.S. Department of Justice (DOJ), and U.S. judiciary as evidence of a willingness to comply with the intent of the environmental law. This commitment to enhance EMSs translates directly to reduced liability exposure.

T A B L E   23–3

Mitigating Factors in Sentencing

Factor	Definition/Explanation
(a) Commitment to environmental compliance	The organization demonstrates that, prior to the offense, it had committed the resources and the management processes that were reasonably determined to be sufficient, given its size and the nature of its business, to achieve and maintain compliance with environmental requirements, including detection of criminal conduct by its employees or agents. Specific factors evidencing a commitment to environmental compliance are given in Table 23–4.
(b) Cooperation and self-reporting	The organization (a) prior to imminent threat of disclosure or government investigation and (b) within a reasonable prompt time after becoming aware of the offense, reported the offense to appropriate government authorities, fully cooperated in the investigation, clearly demonstrated recognition of its responsibility, and took all reasonable steps to assess responsibility within the organization and prevent recurrence.
(c) Lack of scienter	The criminal conduct was the result of negligent errors or omissions or was imposed on the basis of strict liability or collective knowledge; no corporate employee or agent acted with a level of intent at least equal to that of reckless indifference.
(d) Remedial assistance	The organization takes prompt action to provide assistance (in addition to any legally required restitution or remediation) to the victims of its crime to mitigate their losses.

T A B L E   23–4

Elements of Environmental Compliance

Element	Definition/Explanation
(a) Line management attention to compliance	Line managers, including executive and operating officers at all levels, direct their day-to-day attention to measuring, maintaining, and improving the organization's compliance with environmental laws and regulations. They use routine management mechanisms (e.g., objective setting, progress reports, operating performance reviews, departmental meetings) and routinely review environmental monitoring and auditing reports, direct the resolution of identified compliance issues, and ensure application of the resources and mechanisms necessary to carry out a substantial commitment.
(b) Integration of environmental policies, standards, and procedures	The organization has adopted, and communicated to its employees and agents, policies, standards, and procedures necessary to achieve environmental compliance, including a requirement that employees report any suspected violation to appropriate officials within the organization, and that a record will be kept by the organization of any such reports. To the maximum extent possible, given the nature of its business, the organization has analyzed and designed the work functions (e.g., through standard operating procedures) assigned to its employees and agents so that compliance will be achieved, verified, and documented in the course of performing the routine work of the organization.
(c) Auditing, monitoring, reporting, and tracking systems	The organization has designed and implemented, with sufficient authority, personnel, and other resources, the systems and programs necessary for the following:

1. Frequent auditing and inspection of its principal operations and all pollution-control facilities to assess, in detail, their compliance with all applicable environmental requirements and the organization's internal policies, standards, and procedures, as well as internal investigations and implementation of appropriate follow-up countermeasures with respect to all significant incidents of noncompliance.

2. Continuous on-site monitoring, by specifically trained compliance personnel and by other means, of key operations and pollution-control facilities that are either subject to significant environmental regulation, or where the nature or history of such operations or facilities suggests a significant potential for noncompliance.

3. Internal reporting, without fear of retribution, of potential noncompliance to those responsible for investigating and correcting such incidents.

4. Tracking the status of responses to identified compliance issues to enable expeditious, effective, and documented resolution of environmental compliance issues by line management.

5. Redundant, independent checks on the status of compliance, particularly in those operations, facilities, or processes where the organization reasonably believes such potential exists.

(Continued)

T A B L E   23–4 *(Concluded)*

Element	Definition/Explanation
(d) Regulatory expertise, training, and evaluation	The organization has developed and implemented, consistent with the size and nature of its business, systems or programs that are adequate to: **1.** Maintain up-to-date, sufficiently detailed understanding of all applicable environmental requirements by those employees and agents whose responsibilities require such knowledge. **2.** Train, evaluate, and document the training and evaluation of all employees and agents of the organization, both upon entry into the organization and on a refresher basis, as to the applicable environmental requirements, policies, standards, and procedures necessary to carry out their responsibilities in compliance with those requirements, policies, and standards. **3.** Evaluate employees and agents sufficiently to avoid delegating significant discretionary authority or unsupervised responsibility to persons with a propensity to engage in illegal activities.
(e) Incentives for compliance	The organization has implemented a system of incentives, appropriate to its size and the nature of its business, to provide rewards and recognition to employees and agents for their contributions to environmental excellence.
(f) Disciplinary procedures	In response to infractions, the organization has consistently and visibly enforced the organization's environmental policies, standards, and procedures through appropriate disciplinary mechanisms, including, as appropriate, termination, demotion, suspension, reassignment, retraining, probation, and reporting individuals' conduct to law enforcement authorities.
(g) Continuing evaluation and improvement	The organization has implemented a process for measuring the status and trends of its effort to achieve environmental excellence, for making improvements or adjustment in response to those measures, and to any incidents of noncompliance.

ENVIRONMENTAL MANAGEMENT SYSTEMS

Environmental management systems (EMS) need to address management, operating, and liability issues associated with the creation, reuse/recycle, treatment, transportation, and disposal of wastes from industrial activity. The EMS focuses attention on energy and material conversion efficiencies, costs, revenues, impacts of material usage and waste on the environment, and risk to the company and surroundings. A general structure for an environmental management system (EMS) is illustrated in Figure 23–1. Its principal elements are similar to those described in ISO 14001 and include the following:

FIGURE 23–1

Generalized Environmental Management System

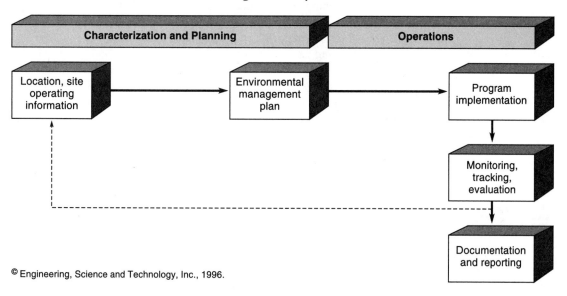

© Engineering, Science and Technology, Inc., 1996.

- A plan that clearly identifies environmental goals; calls for opportunity assessments at facilities to establish a benchmark of chemical usage and to determine where efforts should be directed; identifies environmental problems and priorities; generates and selects solutions based on feasibility and economics; and sets priorities for implementation, including prioritizing, scheduling, and budgeting.

- An implementation strategy that includes the design and installation of pollution-control equipment, and the preparation and implementation of training and operating procedures.

- A performance monitoring and tracking system that includes product quality comparisons, cost analyses, and evaluations of worker acceptance.

- A recording and documentation system.

- A systematic mechanism and procedure for updating and improving the plan and program.

The system is an ongoing process, completed only when all objectives are met and maintained.

Planning includes a systematic and functional analysis of waste generated within operating facilities. It focuses on identification of costs associated with materials usage. Figure 23–2 illustrates the life-cycle analysis and identification of costs associated with materials usage. This approach ensures efficient use of capital resources and realistic assessments of cost savings for alternative chemicals, materials, processes, or procedures. Projects that pass the life-cycle cost-analysis criteria are prioritized according to risk and regulatory requirements. A "post implementation" cost analysis of installed projects is completed to verify cost-effectiveness and to provide insight regarding improved methods for performing future projects.

This type of planning permits considerable freedom and flexibility for tailoring controls, procedures, policies, and performance goals to meet the needs and limitations of individual situations. Integrated approaches examine and prioritize actions based on assessment of risks to human health and the environment, resource conservation, and waste management costs. The ability to integrate environmental regulations and scientific principles into the design and engineering of facilities and facility operations is key to plan success.

FIGURE 23–2

Material Life-Cycle Analysis

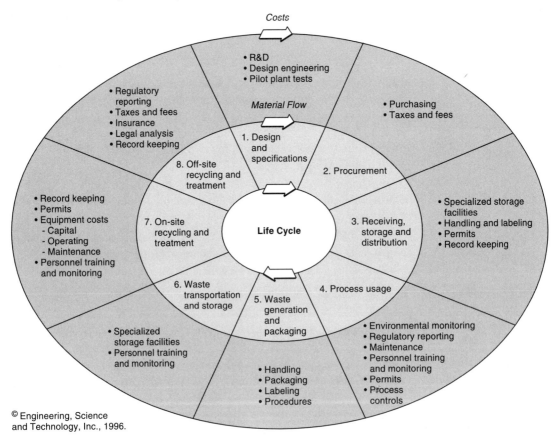

© Engineering, Science
and Technology, Inc., 1996.

Preparing Environmental Management Plans

Figure 23–3 illustrates the tasks and activities required for an environmental management program that is consistent with the Sentencing Commission guidelines for environmental compliance.

FIGURE 23–3

Environmental Management Program

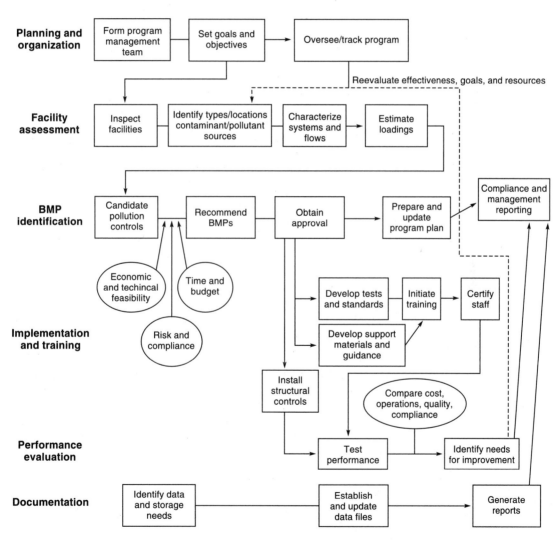

© Engineering, Science and Technology, Inc., 1996.

Planning and Organization

This task includes establishing a team of corporate individuals who are responsible and accountable for developing and managing the program. It includes setting the environmental policies, standards, and procedures for the organization. The team builds, oversees, tracks and controls program provisions. The team should represent the principal operating activities of the firm, particularly those responsible for the following:

- Materials ordering.
- Inventory control.
- Facilities maintenance.
- Engineering and operations.
- Manufacturing.
- Product packaging, shipping, and distribution.
- Quality control.

Goals and objectives for the program should be established by those with ultimate authority over the policies and direction of the company. They should set measurable corporate environmental standards. These standards should demonstrate line management attention to compliance that includes the following:

- Integration of environmental policies, standards, and procedures.
- An established auditing, monitoring, reporting, and tracking system.
- An appropriate regulatory capability.
- Established incentives for compliance.
- A consistent and visible disciplinary policy enforceable throughout the organization.
- A commitment to continued performance evaluation and improvement.

Facility Assessment

Facility assessment begins with the inspection of facilities, identification of the types and locations of pollutant sources, characterization of systems and flows, and estimatation of expected pollutant loadings. This is key to the process, central to the measurement and monitoring of program performance, and fundamental to the selection, modification. and improvement of *best management practices* (BMPs) for pollutant management and control.

Persons or teams who perform this function must be qualified; familiar with the facility and its operations; cognizant of environmental regulations, environmental science, and environmental engineering; and knowledgeable regarding field sampling and chemical protocols for sample analysis. Structure and reporting within the organization must ensure the integrity of the team and its ability to report internally without fear of retribution.

Best Management Practice Identification

BMP identification involves the selection of practices, procedures, and controls appropriate for managing pollutants and other environmental features at the facility. The focus should be on improvements in housekeeping, maintenance, training or inventory control, process or procedure modifications, substitution of raw materials, equipment or technology modifications, and reformulation or redesign of products and facilities. Pollution controls should be selected following a feasibility evaluation process that uses technical, regulatory, and economic criteria.

Estimates should be made to examine potential changes in regulatory status, environmental risks and risks to human health, and requirements that apply to the technology. Life-cycle analyses and cost estimates are then developed. Integrating these data leads to project definition (Best Management Practices) and optimization. Projects are rank-ordered, and budgets and schedules for their implementation are developed.

The output of the process is a list of pollution control projects that require attention, along with recommendations for prioritization. This list is provided to the line management responsible for measuring, maintaining, and improving the organization's compliance with environmental laws and regulations.

Detailed analyses are not required to be fully completed before the initial plan can be considered complete. All identified problems, however, should be prioritized and scheduled for analysis in an objective, good-faith effort, and this information should be included in the plan.

Budget and regulatory issues relate to the size and nature of the business, current liability condition, prior compliance history, public perception and image, and the funds available to the program. These and other issues may lead to business decisions regarding the implementation and scheduling of BMPs selected for installation. Decisions are made by line managers, appropriate executive officers, or those otherwise delegated these responsibilities in writing. Approval of BMPs for installation initiates implementation and training.

Implementation and Training

This stage of the process is conducted in a manner to ensure that BMP installation is undertaken and evaluated by appropriate personnel. These personnel must be properly trained and have the resources necessary to carry out the job. Complex installations are handled as projects, with a project team developed to undertake all required actions. The program management team, the focal point for all pollution-control activities within the program, designates the project team coordinator to guide each project to completion. Project implementation typically includes design, installation of pollution-control equipment, and preparation and implementation of training and operating procedures.

Persons responsible for and affected by the program need to be trained to understand its objectives and process, its operating procedures and standards, and the internal policies applicable to their roles and functions. At least four distinct functions exist:

1. **Engineering.** Engineering includes the design, management, and tracking of the process or procedure being installed to ensure that it operates according to design, that installation occurs on time and within budget, and that installed and operating costs meet expectations.

2. **Independent performance evaluation.** This includes monitoring and tracking the process during installation and operation to determine if environmental objectives are met, to verify that the process operates according to quality expectations, and to identify additional needs for process improvement.

3. **Quality assurance.** This includes data-management procedures (data generation, processing, and storage) for technical data (field, laboratory and engineering analyses) and the documentation of data quality and controls.

4. **Independent environmental compliance audits.** Audits determine facility compliance with all applicable environmental requirements and the organization's internal policies, standards, and procedures, as well as personnel training programs to ensure continued compliance.

Each facility must ensure that these capabilities are available and appropriate to their program. Facilities that have proven most successful in dealing with environmental concerns have developed plans for program monitoring, project assessments, data management, compliance auditing, and employee training well in advance of their actual performance.

Training entails the development of standard operating procedures, performance standards, reporting and documentation standards, production of manuals and guidance material, and the like. Tests of personnel proficiency should be developed and qualification standards established. Regulations require that inspections and tests of BMP performance be conducted by personnel qualified to perform this work. To be qualified, inspection personnel should be trained and capable of making the kinds of inspections, measures, and evaluations that assure BMPs are working properly. Line management and executive officers ultimately are responsible for these certifications as well as for providing the full set of resources necessary to perform all work in good faith.

Auditing personnel should be given explicit audit program objectives, scope, resources, and frequency schedules. Auditors should be provided with all corporate policies, permits, and federal, state, and local regulations pertinent to the facility. They should use checklists or protocols that address specific features included in the audit. Explicit written audit procedures for planning audits, establishing audit scope, examining and evaluating audit findings, communicating audit results, and following up should be developed and provided to auditors for training. If necessary, they should receive periodic refresher training courses.

Performance Evaluation

Performance evaluation examines the effectiveness of control measures needed to achieve program objectives and provides the feedback necessary to identify needs for program and project improvement. Pollution-control approaches that prove technically sound and economically feasible become permanent parts of the facility. Approaches that require improvement are identified, documented, and added to the plan for continued improvement.

Inspections of BMP performance are required for all pollution-control projects. Standard procedures and forms for documenting results should be developed and used to inform the project team, measure performance, develop maintenance requirements, and show the need for BMP improvement.

Documentation

Documentation is the process of recording and demonstrating program events, changes and adjustments, and the quality of the program. Documentation includes the following:

- The environmental management plan and its updates.
- Inspection and quality control records.
- Data and evaluations demonstrating changes in pollutant/contaminant loadings over the course of the program.
- Audit materials and findings.
- Other materials that demonstrate environmental compliance.

Very large amounts of multipurpose data need to be managed, organized, and used to track material and mass balances of processes or procedures judged important to source reduction and potential material release.

CONCLUSIONS

The EMS process described in this chapter combines the essence of ISO 14001 with the performance requirements the federal courts have specified are important in their considerations of fines and penalties. Draft U.S. Sentencing Guidelines for organizational offenses suggest that internal reviews of operations are required to determine what works and what doesn't, both with respect to existing systems and new projects. As more regulations focus on performance, industry must find its own solutions to the environmental problems confronting them. To do this, organizations need to try new approaches, install new technologies, and monitor their activities more closely to establish performance and cost levels. Success will be achieved by organizations that establish environmental management systems that maximize efficiency while minimizing environmental compliance cost and liability exposure.

Environmental management plans, prepared and conducted as a program and implemented in good faith, provide a solid foundation for environmental compliance that is compatible with the expectations of the U.S. Sentencing Commission as well as other agency guidance. Incorporating these measures does not guarantee that liabilities will disappear. Their use, however, will reduce the potential for agency investigations and reduce individual and corporate exposure to prosecution.

BIOGRAPHY

Lawrence P. Raymond, PhD

Lawrence P. Raymond is a professional environmental manager who has worked extensively in industry, government, and environmental consulting since 1964. He received undergraduate and master's training in marine biology at San Diego State College (University), his doctoral degree through the Biology Board of Studies at the University of California, Santa Cruz, and an M.B.A. through the executive program at the University of Colorado.

His professional career evolved with the emergence of environmental and marine science as a business discipline. He founded the Environmental Planning and Analysis Division of the Oceanic Instute in Hawaii where he was instrumental in establishing early environmental planning policy (NEPA, CEQ, CZM, CWA), dealing principally with transportation systems and resort development in the South Pacific. He founded and managed the Aquatic Species Program, and later took on overall responsibility for the nontraditional biomass energy technology programs conducted by the Solar Energy Research Institute for the U.S. Department of Energy. He continued the development and commercialization of these emerging technologies as the CEO and Chairman of International Bio-Resources, Inc.

For the last six years, Mr. Raymond has been active in environmental consulting, dealing principally with natural resource management, pollution prevention, information management, and the development of environmental management systems. He is a participating member of the U.S. TAG to ISO/TC 207, a member of its Legal Issues Forum, and active in the development of environmental performance evaluation standards under Sub-TAG 4.

REFERENCES

Environmental Protection Agency. *Environmental Leadership Program: Notice of Intention to Develop an Environmental Leadership Program and Request for Comments.* Federal Register 58:10; 4802–4814, Friday, January 15, 1993.

Federal Compliance with Right-to-Know Laws and Pollution Prevention Requirements. Executive Order 12856 of August 3, 1993. Federal Register 58:150; 41981–41987, Friday, August 6, 1993.

ISO/TC 207/SC 1. *ISO 14001 Environmental management systems—Specification with guidance for use,* 1996.

Tibor, T. and I. Feldman. *ISO 14000: A Guide to the New Environmental Management Standards.* Chicago: Irwin Professional Publishing, 1996.

U.S. Sentencing Commission, Advisory Working Group on Environmental Sanctions. *Working Draft Recommendations. Memorandum to Interested Members of the Public.* Washington, DC: U.S. Sentencing Commission, 2002–8002, March 5, 1993.

Wynne, B. J. and C. G. Rogers. "How Effective is Your Audit Program?" Institute for Corporate Environmental Management, Implementation Management III. University of Houston Center for Executive Development, University of Houston, November 9, 1993.

NOTE

1. 58 Fed. Reg. 65764, December 16, 1993.

PART SIX

Other ISO 14000 Tools

CHAPTER 24

Environmental Labeling

Ahmad Husseini

INTRODUCTION

The last decade will probably be known for the power of consumers to get as much information as possible about the products they buy. Consumers started to ask how and why particular products are "environmentally preferable" to others. Manufacturers were faced with a strong demand to provide information on their products and packaging. This race to supply data became so fierce that labels started to appear on products, packages, and virtually everything.

This confused consumers even more than before. Governments got involved, both on the federal and regional levels to protect consumers from "mislabeling and misadvertising."

Eco-labeling programs entered the picture by initiating processes that would advise consumers as to which products constituted a preferable environmental choice. The confusion prevailed, and worse still, it started to affect free trade of goods and services. Organizations raised concerns that exports and imports were being unfairly discriminated against through the effects of local and regional environmental labels.

Many of the emerging environmental labels worldwide were being understood differently by consumers. This issue raised the interest of trade proponents and, through the recommendation of an ad hoc advisory group, ISO was encouraged to develop standards in the field of environmental labeling.

Environmental labels were to be accurate, verifiable, and not misleading. This would prevent unwarranted claims; reduce marketplace confusion, restrictions, and barriers to international trade; and, most importantly, increase the potential for market forces to stimulate environmental improvement in product delivery. These labels would also better enable purchasers to make informed choices when buying goods and services.

What is Environmental Labeling?

Environmental labeling is any environmental declaration that describes or implies by whatever means the effects of the life cycle of a product or service on the environment. It may take the form of statements, symbols, or graphics on product or packaging, literature, technical bulletins, advertising, publicity and so on.

Environmental labeling can be divided into three types. Third-party certified "eco-labels" are known as *Type I.* These are granted by practitioner seal programs (either government-sponsored or privately operated). In general, seal programs require that a manufacturer meet a "threshold" to receive the seal or eco-logo of that program.

Type II labels, on the other hand, are known as self-declaration environmental claims. Manufacturers may place these labels on their products, without third-party verification, provided they follow specific requirements set forth in the developing ISO 14021 standard. (Remember, however, that SC3 labeling standards are presently for guidance only.) Type III labels convey quantitative information that derives from life-cycle inventory data.

The Influence of World Politics and International Trade on Environmental Labeling

As with all other international activities, the development of standards for environmental labeling is subject to pressures from various stakeholders. The basic perceptions and approaches to labeling differ among countries and regions. These differences are more prominent between North America and Europe. North Americans tend to give more flexibility to manufacturers to self-regulate their actions, provided the self-regulation meets the overall goals set by the governments. Europeans tend towards more prescriptive requirements.

To add to the complexity of the equation, various stakeholders want to influence the process as well. Consumers want honest, clear labels. Environmentalists want labels that lead to the protection of the environment. Developing countries want labels that are achievable, meaning the labels should have requirements and specifications that can be met, so that they can maintain or increase their exports to industrialized countries. Finally, large corporations want labels that will be internationally applied.

On the positive side, countries are preparing to adopt and live with the new ISO environmental standards. For example, Canada, which is one of the first countries in the world to have both environmental labeling regulatory guidelines and national standards, has indicated very clearly that it will be the first to consider adopting the new environmental labeling standards once they are published.

Eco-labeling practitioner programs (Type I) have been multiplying rapidly. Some have been successful and may be considered financially viable. Others still require financial support from government. This support, however, comes with a price. Government policy and politics play a role in the direction these programs normally have to take.

Another factor complicating the issue is that governments all over the world are "rationalizing" their expenses and cutting down on "unessential" costs. Eventually, support for eco-labeling programs may fall prey to cost-rationalizing policies. Unless these programs modify their terms of reference and look for more cost-effective means, many will fade away in the coming years.

Issues That Affect the Development of the Environmental Labeling Standards.

The first issue relates to environmental improvement, or what is known as *continuous improvement.* Some delegates, led by the United States, believe that outlining environmental improvement as an *objective* may cause problems for industry if industry is challenged at some stage to prove that they are achieving continuous environmental improvement. Other delegates, who do not agree with the American vision, suggest that if environmental improvement (and the minimization of environmental impacts) is not going to be in the objective statement, there isn't much point in developing all these standards.

The second issue relates to international trade and nontariff trade barriers. Some countries with very strong Type I programs do not particularly subscribe to prescriptive language that would restrict their freedom in setting criteria for their Type I guidelines.

ISO ENVIRONMENTAL LABELING STANDARDS

ISO developed environmental labeling standards, in general, to harmonize national and regional standards worldwide to meet five main benefits. These benefits may vary as to their importance, depending on the party and stakeholder concerned. However, they may be summarized as follows:

1. Reduce consumer/purchaser confusion. The proliferation of environmental claims and labels in the marketplace has contributed to a general consumer mistrust of all labels. Consumers and purchasers facing inaccurate and deceptive claims have longed for a system they can trust and rely on. ISO developed environmental labeling standards as a first step in reducing this confusion.

2. Improve environmental performance. An essential goal of environmental standards has been to contribute to the reduction in the environmental burdens associated with the impacts of the life cycle, including the manufacturing, use, and disposal of a product or packaging. Whether this is achievable through improving the systems or the process, however, is still under debate.

3. Enhance international trade. Labels have always been a major concern for exporters and importers. As the world moves closer toward open borders and free trade, the World Trade Organization (WTO) is interested in ensuring that environmental labels do not act as nontariff trade barriers. ISO-developed environmental labeling standards would be a first step in limiting the negative trade effects of regional labeling.

4. Strengthen voluntary "self-regulating" standardization versus regulation. As governments all over the world try to cut down on expenses through downsizing, there appears to be more emphasis on self-regulation through voluntary standardization. This trend is accelerating, particularly because manufacturers realize that consumer purchasing power is just as effective as regulation in the field of environmental labeling. The bad players will eventually be "marked," and market forces will prevail. Governments will still be able to oversee the functioning of the voluntary system.

5. Allow consumers/purchasers to make informed choices. Consumers today are asking for more information about the products they buy. If the information, in the form of labels or otherwise, is accurate and nondeceptive, consumer confidence will increase. ISO environmental labeling standards will be one of the vehicles that will assist consumers in making better choices.

Advantages of ISO Environmental Labeling Standards

ISO standards are voluntary. It is generally understood that if a user chooses to adopt them, they should be implemented as a whole, that is, users may not pick and choose the elements they like and leave out the elements they do not. In general these standards, once adopted, tend to appeal to the marketplace and generate enough impetus to establish a level playing field for all.

Environmental labeling standards assist in the harmonization of practitioner Type I programs around the world. Other environmental labeling standards work towards reducing trade barriers and encourage manufacturers to use accurate, verifiable, and nondeceptive claims.

Scope of Subcommittee 3

SC3's scope covers standardization in the field of environmental labeling. It includes Type I third-party certification practitioner seal programs, Type III programs, and first-party practices (self-declaration environmental claims). It also covers advertising, environmental statements, and reports. At present, SC3 has three Working Groups (WGS):

- **WG1—Guiding Principles of Environmental Labeling Practitioner Programs and Systems.** WG1 is developing two standards, ISO 14024 (for Type I labeling) and ISO 14025 (for Type III labeling) (see Box 24–1).

- **WG2—Self-Declaration Environmental Claims—Type II Labeling.** WG2 is working on three standards for self-declaration environmental claims: terms and definitions, symbols, and testing and verification methods.

- **WG3—Basic Principles of All Environmental Labeling.** WG3 has developed a general principles standard that applies to all environmental labeling and claims.

WG1 Type I Labeling

WG1's standard, *ISO 14024—Environmental labels and declarations—Environmental labeling Type I—Guiding principles and procedures,* is undergoing revision. The draft standard contains guiding principles and procedures for multiple criteria-based, practitioner-operated, environmental labeling programs. The standard applies to all labeling programs worldwide. It establishes basic principles that these, and later, programs may

BOX 24-1

STANDARDS BEING DEVELOPED BY SC3

The following standards are in development by the three work groups of SC3:

- ISO 14020—Basic principles of all environmental labels and declarations.
- ISO 14021—Environmental labeling—Self-declaration environmental claims—Terms and definitions.
- ISO 14022—Environmental labeling—Self-declaration environmental claims—Environmental labeling symbols.
- ISO 14023—Environmental labeling—Self-declaration environmental claims—Testing and verification methodologies.
- ISO 14024—Environmental labels and declarations—Environmental labeling Type I—Guiding principles and procedures.
- ISO 14025—Environmental labels and declarations—Environmental labeling Type III—Guiding principles and procedures (Title not yet confirmed).

decide to use to enhance their schemes. Type I labeling addresses multiple criteria based on the environmental impacts associated with the product. In simple terms, it is built on going beyond a single environmental attribute.

It sets principles based on life-cycle considerations, compliance with regulations, transparency, consultation, and functional characteristics. It also describes procedures for the selection of product categories including selection matrices, and qualitative and quantitative indices. It addresses certification procedures, licensing, the assessment of compliance and conformity, monitoring, and final granting of the label (program seal).

As suggested earlier, one of the major issues in the development of this ISO 14024 standard is linked to restrictions to international trade posed by Type I programs. Clause 5.9, which reads as follows—"Environmental labeling programs shall not create unnecessary trade restrictive effects"—was developed to address these concerns. Some free-trade advocates still consider it a weak clause.

Another issue of concern relates to the timing of development. The standard is being developed at the time when many of the practitioner programs have already established their terms of reference and work plans. They appear to be reluctant to change what already exists. The result is a standard that meets the lowest common denominator.

WG1 Type III Labeling

In December 1995, SC3 agreed to revitalize Type III labeling. It agreed to assign responsibility to developing a standard to WG1, recommending that the task leader for Type III be from Sweden.

So what is Type III labeling? It is a quantitative information label that is based on life-cycle inventory data. The label outlines the environmental loadings associated with the various stages of the life cycle of the product (or packaging). The concept, being scientifically based, gives the consumer a satisfactory feeling as it relays more comprehensive information.

Although the concept of Type III labeling is valid, its execution is challenging. Life-cycle assessment (LCA) is still an emerging science. SC5 is heavily involved in the development of LCA standards. Life-cycle impact assessment, which is a part of LCA that is still in its infancy, and most of the studies indicate that it will be a long time before LCA will be used credibly for external comparison of products. This is exactly what Type III labeling wants to achieve.

Life-cycle inventory databases are just starting to be developed both nationwide and internationally. Type III labeling would require LCA data. How fast this data will be available is anybody's guess. Another factor associated with Type III labeling is the issue of consumer confusion. How will an ordinary consumer differentiate between a product that uses more energy in its production and another that has been manufactured with a process that emits SO_2, or another that consumes more water in its use cycle? Even experts in the field of life-cycle impact assessment cannot answer that question without an element of subjectivity.

Sweden, as the task force leader, will have to work with international experts to develop this Type III labeling standard in a manner that would be credible and acceptable to consumers, industry, and international trade. Three to five years development work will probably be needed before we see a Type III standard.

WG2—Self-Declaration Environmental Claims

Self-declaration environmental claims are those made, without independent third-party certification, by manufacturers, importers, distributors, retailers, or anyone else likely to benefit from such claims. These may take the form of statements, symbols, or graphics on products or packaging. They may also be in the form of product literature, technical bulletins, advertising, publicity, or telemarketing.

These claims normally address an environmental aspect of a product, packaging, or the like. Terms and definitions such as *recyclable, biodegradable, recovered energy,* and *water conserving* are all self-declaration environmental claims.

The *ISO 14021—Environmental labeling—Self-declaration environmental claims—Terms and definitions* standard addresses terms and definitions used in making claims. ISO 14021 has two major sections: "General Guidelines," which are applicable to all such claims, and "Specific Terms," which covers the most commonly used terms such as *recyclable, recycled content,* and so on."

While this standard (discussed below) sets guidelines for the use of terms and definitions, a second standard, *ISO 14022—Environmental labeling—Self-declaration environmental claims—Environmental labeling symbols,* addresses the most common symbols that correspond to the terms and definitions, such as the familiar Möbius loop (see Figure 24–1).

Möbius Loop

A third standard, *ISO 14023—Environmental labeling—Self-declaration environmental claims—Testing and verification methodologies,* describes testing and verification methodologies. These may be used to prove and verify that self-declaration environmental claims are duly implemented and meet the general requirements such as being nondeceptive, clear, accurate, and so on. The draft standard includes general principles common to specific environmental claims and provisions inherent to such claims.

WG3-Basic Principles of All Environmental Labeling

WG3 was created at the first meeting of ISO/TC 207 in Toronto (June 1993). The intent was to develop general guidelines that would apply to all types of labeling, not only Types I, II, and III. This intent is one reason WG3 is finding the challenge of developing principles general enough to apply to all environmental labeling so difficult.

WG3 is developing *ISO 14020—Basic principles of all environmental labels and declarations* (discussed below).

DESCRIPTION OF WG3 LABELING STANDARDS

Environmental Labels and Declarations—ISO 14020 General Principles of All Environmental Labels and Declarations

As suggested earlier, ISO 14020, developed by WG3, is being prepared to create a foundation for environmental labels and claims. By putting together a set of principles, this draft standard aims to create an umbrella that all environmental labeling standardization activities have to meet. That is why this draft is both powerful and problematic. Most of the basic principles included in the draft would be applicable to the other ISO 14020 series. However, there still may be a situation whereby one or more of the principles would not be readily acceptable for a particular type of labeling (I, II, III, or others in the future).

Below is a summary of the ISO 14020 draft.

Introduction

The Introduction outlines the overall goal of the ISO 14000 series of standards: an effort to lessen the stress placed on the environment. This is achieved by using a system of continual environmental improvement. It emphasizes that such stress on the environment normally occurs during the life cycle of a particular product (packaging or service), during its production, use, or disposal phases. It further indicates that environmental labeling standards are complementary to the EMS standards. It recognizes the strength of the labeling standards as outlined earlier in this chapter.

Major Definitions

The draft defines the following three major terms:

- **Environmental label/declaration.** A claim indicating the environmental attributes of a product or service that may take the form of statements, symbols, or graphics on a product or package label, literature, technical bulletins, advertising, publicity, and so on.
- **Purchaser.** Anyone in a product or service supply chain who buys the product or service from a seller.
- **Life cycle.** Refers to consecutive and interlinked stages of a product or service system, from the extraction of natural resources to the final disposition.

Summary of Key Principles in ISO 14020

These principles have undergone various revisions and may be revised further. The trend in the revisions appears directed toward giving the principles more strength. This is apparent through the use of words such as *shall* instead of *should*.

1. Environmental labels/declarations shall be accurate, verifiable, relevant, and nondeceptive. This principle outlines the need to reach consumers and purchasers to give them reliable, verifiable information. Requesting that the information be relevant is an assurance that only nontrivial environmental attributes will be claimed. This information should be clear enough to not suggest specific environmental attributes that do not exist, thus misleading the consumer into purchasing the product.

2. Information on the environmental attributes of products and services relevant to an environmental label/declaration shall be available to purchasers from the party making the environmental label/declaration. This is an important addition to the draft standard. It establishes the right of purchasers to know. They need accurate information to make an informed choice. This also puts the responsibility on the parties making the claim to research the information and ensure its credibility. It also has to be reasonably understandable by the general purchasing population.

3. Environmental labels/declarations shall be based on scientific methodology that is sufficiently thorough and comprehensive to support the claim and that produces results that are accurate and reproducible. This principle is very important since it outlines the basis by which claims and labels may be made. Scientific methodology includes life-cycle considerations, databases, risk assessment, and full cost accounting. Reproducibility of these methods is in line with all scientifically based tests. It also ensures verification.

4. Information concerning the procedure and methodology used to support environmental labels/declarations shall be available and provided upon request to all interested parties. This principle ensures that unsubstantiated claims and half-truths are not presented. Information available must include underlying principles, assumptions, and boundary conditions. This principle is also in line with other ISO 14000 standards.

5. The development of environmental labels/declarations should, wherever appropriate, take into consideration the life cycle of the product or service. Again, this principle emphasizes life-cycle considerations, particularly identifying the potential of a particular life-cycle impact to increase while another is decreased.

6. Any administrative requirements or information demands related to environmental labels/declarations shall be limited to those necessary to establish conformance with applicable criteria and/or standards of the labels/declarations. This principle addresses the requirement of relevancy of the claims to the environmental attributes. It also emphasizes that the involvement of companies, large or small, should not be hindered by unreasonable costs, administrative complexities and requirements, or demands.

7. Procedures and criteria for environmental labels/declarations shall not create unfair trade restrictions nor discriminate in the treatment of domestic and foreign products and services. This is the principle that has been so difficult to develop. It is meant to be in line with the activities of GATT and the new WTO. The issue is still being debated at the work group, subcommittee, and full TC 207 level. It is important that labeling standards should not "permit" the creation of nontariff trade barriers through specific requirements that discriminate against imported foreign products.

The problem becomes more serious as some environmental groups indicate, understandably, a preference for the protection of the environment in lieu of conformance to freer trade. Since ISO standards are developed by consensus, SC3 hopes to develop a final text for this principle that is both in line with the WTO international agreements and gives allowance to environmental concerns.

ISO 14024 Environmental Labels and Declarations—Environmental Labeling Type I—Guiding Principles and Procedures

The ISO 14024 draft contains guiding principles for selecting product categories, setting product environmental criteria and product performance characteristics and certification, for multiple criteria-based, practitioner-operated, environmental labeling seal programs.

"Multiple criteria" is emphasized here; single criteria environmental claims do not normally create an overall environmental benefit since life-cycle considerations are not included.

Introduction

The introduction explains that the label (seal) of Type I labeling schemes identifies products that have been selected as "a preferred environmental choice" within a particular product category. It also states that Type I labeling programs are voluntary, can be operated by public or private agencies, and may be national, regional, or international. Certification (or awarding of the label) is different from certification of conformity to ISO standards.

Objective

The objective states clearly that the overall goal of Type I labeling is to contribute to a reduction in the environmental burdens and impacts associated with products. This is achieved by identifying those products that claim an overall environmental preference. The point is that the seal is still a claim of overall environmental preference, not a ruling of overall environmental performance.

Major Definitions

- **Type I environmental labeling program.** A voluntary, multiple criteria-based, practitioner program that awards labels claiming the overall environmental preference of a product within a particular category based on life-cycle considerations.

- **Product.** Any good or service (includes packaging).

- **Product category.** A group of products that have equivalent functions. (Water-based paint would be considered as a category.)

- **Product function characteristics.** Environmental requirements that the product shall meet to be awarded an environmental label.

- **Practitioner.** A third-party body (government or private agencies included) that operates an environmental labeling program.

Key Guiding Principles

The standard emphasizes several guiding principles:

- The program should be voluntary in nature and implementation.
- It should assess only those products that are in compliance with regulations.

Life-cycle considerations apply to extraction of resources, manufacturing, distribution, use, and disposal. Considerations will be assessed relevant to cross-media environmental indicators. Departure from this comprehensive approach must be clearly stated and justified.

Selectivity is an important principle. Product environmental criteria must be established to "differentiate" leading products from others in product categories. This will be based on a significant difference in total environmental impact achieved through compliance.

It is understood and taken into account that assessment methodologies may vary in level of precision and accuracy in evaluating those products that satisfy the criteria. Arbitrary cut-off levels should not be established, that is, levels designed to exclude a predetermined percentage of products from qualifying for the level.

In other words, a threshold set to accept 20 percent of the top performers may be challenged. In practice, it is difficult to comply with this requirement. Threshold levels are normally set through political and subjective decisions based on background information. Hopefully, this requirement will influence existing programs to use technical and scientific rather than political decision making.

Product environmental criteria are based on life-cycle considerations set to attainable levels (not targets) within a predetermined period. They shall be reviewed at the end of that period.

Products should meet their intended purpose (performance). This is achieved through meeting international and regional standards.

The process should also be transparent, and consultation with stakeholders is a requirement. Transparency includes the selection and award procedures, the certification, the periodic review requirements, the funding sources, the testing and verification methods, and compliance verification.

The programs must not create unnecessary trade restrictive requirements. It shall be open to all potential parties that wish to apply. The program criteria selection must be based on scientific methodologies. Conflicts of interest shall be avoided. Fees should be reasonable and based on program costs. Confidentiality of information from applicants must be ensured.

Procedures for Establishing Program Requirements

The selection of product categories and the development of product environmental criteria is an iterative process that needs to be reassessed and revisited. Stakeholders should be consulted and new technological and scientific methodologies included.

The selection of product categories is based on an initial review, consultation with stakeholders, market surveys, assessment of environmental performance of products, the need for environmental improvement within that product category, feasibility of product categories and the equivalence of performance, their functional characteristics, the availability of data (including life-cycle consideration data), and the current national and international regulatory agreements.

Once the proposal for a product category is submitted, the selection of product environmental criteria begins. Life-cycle considerations, based on scientific methodologies, are included in an assessment matrix. This comprises the "stages in the life cycle" (which includes extraction of resources, manufacturing, use, and disposal) and the corresponding environmental loadings (inputs and outputs). These include energy (renewable and nonrenewable), resources (renewable and nonrenewable), and emissions to water, air, and soil.

Relevant local, regional, and global issues should be also taken into account.

The toughest challenge is the identification of the relevant areas for reduction of environmental burdens. This is done through the use of qualitative and quantitative indices, including weighting factors. The use of such weighting factors must be clearly justified.

The practitioner then determines the best criteria and assigns values to them. Minimum values and threshold levels are set. A scale point system may be used. Test methods are then determined and outlined. The selection of product functional characteristics is set. This includes performance levels. Since the process is transparent, reporting is an important element. Modifications to the process should be clear and carried out with stakeholder consultations.

The Certification Process

Compliance with the general rules and the technical specific requirements (product environmental criteria and function characteristics) must be met. Supporting documentations are required with each application.

The practitioner should also make the necessary documentation available to the applicant, outlining the basic elements of the program and the methods by which the assessment is to be made. Upon granting of the label seal, the program shall monitor the marketplace and assess any deviations from the requirements. The licensee should also report any such deviations.

ISO 14021 Environmental Labeling—Self-Declaration Environmental Claims—Terms and Definitions—Type II Labeling

ISO 14021 addresses Type II labeling. Self-declaration environmental claims (SDEC) may be made by manufacturers, importers, retailers, or anyone else likely to benefit from such claims. Claims can take the forms of statements, symbols, product literature, advertising, telemarketing, and so on. ISO 14021 is the first in a series of three standards. ISO 14021 covers terms and definitions, ISO 14022 covers symbols, and ISO 14023 covers testing and verifications.

Scope

The scope section of ISO 14024 emphasizes that the standard establishes "general" guidelines regarding claims in relation to the supply of products and services. It also defines and sets rules for the use of specific terms. The scope emphasizes that the standard does not override legally required information supplied through labels or claims. It also states that the issue of sustainability is complex, and therefore a claim denoting it is not appropriate at this time.

Objective

The objective statement suggests that the objective of ISO 14021 is to contribute to a reduction in the environmental burdens and impacts associated with the consumption of products and services. Anticipated benefits comprise accurate, verifiable, nondeceptive environmental claims, the stimulation of environmental improvement through market forces potential, prevention of unwarranted claims, reduction of marketplace confusion, reduction of barriers to international trade, and providing consumers with better informed purchasing choices.

Major Definitions

- **Environmental claim.** Any environmental declaration that describes or implies, by whatever means, the effects that the raw material extraction, production, distribution, use, or disposal of a product or service has on the environment. This applies to effects that are local, regional, or global, and to the environment that an individual lives in, affects, or is affected by.

- **Self-declaration environmental claim (SDEC).** An environmental claim that is made, without independent third-party certification, by manufacturers, importers, distributors, retailers or anyone else likely to benefit from such a claim.

- **Package/packaging.** A material or item that is used to protect or contain a product during transportation, storage, or marketing. A package can also be a material or item that is physically attached to, or included with, a product or its container for the purpose of marketing the product or communicating information about the product.

- **Qualified environmental claim.** An environmental claim that is accompanied by a statement that describes the limits of the claim.

Some Elements in the General Guidelines for Terms and Definitions in SDEC

In addition to referencing that they meet the elements of ISO 14020, SDECs are expected to be:

- Accurate.
- Nondeceptive.
- Substantiated.
- Verifiable.
- Relevant.
- Used only in an appropriate context or setting.
- Specific and clear as to what particular environmental attribute the claim relates to.
- Unlikely to result in misinterpretation.
- Meaningful in relation to the overall environmental impact of the product or service during its life cycle.
- Presented in a manner that clearly indicates that the environmental claim and explanatory statement be read together.
- Not presented in a manner that implies that the claim is endorsed or certified by an independent third-party organization when it has not been.

SDECs must specify the environmental improvement or attribute of the product or service. They must not, either directly or by implication, suggest an environmental improvement that does not exist, nor shall they exaggerate the environmental benefit of an attribute or of the product or service to which the claim refers. Unqualified environmental claims should be made only if they are valid in all foreseeable circumstances with no qualifications.

Any SDEC that involves a comparative assertion of environmental superiority (this term is used in life-cycle assessment studies comparing one product to another and suggesting its overall environmental superiority) based on improvement shall be specific, valid, and make clear the basis for the comparison.

In particular, the SDEC must be relevant in terms of how recently any improvement was made. If comparisons are made, they should be in accordance to a published standard or recognized test method and/or comparable products or services serving similar functions, supplied by the same or another producer.

SDECs must not be presented in a manner that might lead purchasers to believe that the claim is based on a recent product or process modification if this is untrue. SDECs should also be relevant to the life cycle of the product. SDECs must clarify to the purchaser whether the claim applies to the product or packaging.

SDECs should not be made if the claim is based on the absence of an ingredient that was never there in the first place. In other words, if a cleaner never had ozone-depleting substances, such as CFCs, the manufacturer should not make a claim for marketing purposes only. SDECs must also be relevant to the geographic area in which the corresponding benefit occurs.

This issue has been the source of debate in WG2. Exporting countries raised concerns that it would be not practical for them to claim specific SDECs if these do not occur in their exporting country. For example, locally produced products that conserve water in their manufacture in a country where water is scarce may be able to put a SDEC on their products, while foreign products that do not conserve water in their manufacture in a country where water is abundant may not make that claim.

Finally, SDECs should only be made for actual benefits, not potential ones.

Verification of SDECs

Though ISO 14021 references ISO 14023 for testing and verification of SDECs, it states that verification methodologies shall be reproducible, repeatable, and scientifically sound.

BOX 24–2

SOME SPECIFIC TERMS IN THE ISO 14021 DRAFT

The following are specific terms defined in ISO 14021. Note that the word *qualification* in the following terms means the conditions under which the claim *can* be used. That is, it is an explanatory statement that describes the limits of the claim.

In general, claims such as "environmentally friendly, safe, beneficial," and so on, are not permitted.

Recyclable

A characteristic of a product, packaging, or component thereof that can be diverted from the waste stream through available processes and programs and can be collected, processed, and returned to use in the form of raw materials or products.

Qualifications (conditions) for the use of the term *recyclable*. A *qualified* claim of recyclability has to be used if collection or drop-off facilities for recycling the product or packaging are not *conveniently* available to a reasonable portion of the population where the product is sold. If such facilities are not conveniently available to a reasonable portion of the population, *explanatory statements* have to be made to convey the limited availability of collection facilities. Explanatory statements that do not convey the limited availability of collection facilities, with phrases such as "Recyclable where facilities exist," are not adequate . Where only the package, or only an identifiable component of the product or package, is recyclable, the claim must specifically identify what is recyclable. Where the claim appears on the package but refers only to the product, the claim shall specifically identify what is recyclable.

(Continued)

B O X   24–2 *(Continued)*

Recycled content/material

This refers to the proportion, by mass, of recycled material in a product or package. Recycled material is that which would have otherwise been disposed of as waste but has instead been collected and reclaimed as a material input, in lieu of new primary material, in the manufacture of products. Only postconsumer and preconsumer recycled materials may be considered as recycled content.

Preconsumer material. That which is diverted from the waste stream during a manufacturing process. Excluded is reutilization of materials such as rework, regrind, or scrap generated in a process and capable of being reclaimed within the same process that generated it.

Postconsumer material. That material which is generated by commercial, industrial, and institutional facilities, or households, which can no longer be used for its intended purpose. This includes returns of material from the distribution chain.

Qualification (conditions) for the use of the term *recycled content.* If the claim applies to both the product and its package, the percentage recycled content for each shall be specified independently.

Reduced resource use

A reduction in the amount of material, energy, or water used to produce or distribute a product or package or specified component thereof.

Qualification (conditions) for the use of the term *reduced use.* No unqualified reduced resource use claims shall be made. As "reduced resource use" is a comparative claim, life-cycle considerations for comparative assertions shall be met.

Recovered energy

Energy recovered from material that would have been disposed of as waste but has instead been collected and converted through specific processes and is used to produce products or services.

Reducing solid waste

Reduction in the quantity of material (mass) entering the solid waste stream due to a change in the product, process, or packaging.

Qualification (conditions) for the use of the term *solid waste reduction.* No unqualified claims regarding waste reduction shall be made. Calculations of process waste reduction must not include in-process reutilization of materials such as rework, reground, or scrap materials generated within the plant and capable of being reused within the process that generated them.

Energy-efficient/energy-conserving/energy-saving

Reduced energy consumption associated with the use of a product compared with functionally equivalent products that perform the same task.

Qualifications (conditions) for the use of the term *energy-efficient/energy-conserving/energy-saving*. No unqualified claims regarding energy reduction must be made. Energy-efficient/energy-conserving/energy-saving are comparative claims.

Water-efficient/water-conserving/water-saving

Reduced water consumption associated with the use of a product compared with functionally equivalent products or processes providing a generally equivalent service.

Qualification (conditions) for the use of the term *water-efficient/water-conserving/water-saving.* No unqualified claims regarding water efficiency/reduction must be made unless a performance test method is identified. Water-efficient/water-conserving/water-saving are comparative claims.

Extended life product

A product designed to provide prolonged use, based on either improved durability or an upgradability feature, that results in reduced resource use or reduced waste.

Qualifications (conditions) for the use of the term *extended life product.* No unqualified claim of extended life must be made. Extended life product is a comparative claim. A claim of extended life for a product should be based on overall life-cycle environmental considerations. Other conditions apply.

Reusable/Refillable

Reusable. A characteristic of an item that has been conceived and designed to accomplish within its life cycle a certain number of trips or rotations for the same purpose for which it was conceived.

Refillable. A characteristic of an item that can be filled with the same or similar product more than once, in its original form, and without additional processing except for specified requirements such as cleaning and washing.

Qualifications (conditions) for the use of the terms *reusable/refillable.* No product or package must be claimed to be reusable or refillable unless the item can be reused/refilled for its original purpose. Similar conditions to *recyclable* apply.

(Continued)

BOX 24-2 *(Concluded)*

Designed for disassembly

A characteristic of a product's design that enables the product to be taken apart at the end of its useful life and the parts reused or recycled.

Qualification (conditions) for the use of the term *designed for disassembly.* All claims that a product is designed for disassembly must be clearly qualified so that the claim specifies whether the disassembly is to be done by the purchaser or whether it is to be returned for disassembly by specialists. The claim shall also identify the environmental benefits of disassembling the product. Other conditions apply.

Compostable

A product, package, or element thereof is compostable if, through an available, managed composting procedure, biodegradation occurs and the material is converted into a relatively homogenous and stable humus-like substance.

Qualifications (conditions) for the use of the term *compostable.* A compostability claim must not be made for a product or package or a component of a product or package that negatively affects the overall value of the compost as a soil amendment. Likewise, if it releases substances uncharacteristic of the process in concentrations toxic to humans or the environment at any point during decomposition or subsequent use. Other conditions similar to those for *Recyclable* apply.

Degradable/biodegradable/photodegradable

A characteristic of a product or packaging that allows it to break down so that the resulting materials can be easily assimilated into the environment. Degradability is a function of susceptibility to changes in chemical structure that result in molecular weight reduction. Consequent changes in physical/mechanical properties lead to the disintegration of the product/material. For purposes of the following qualifications, unless otherwise qualified, the term *degradable* refers to all types of degradability.

Qualifications (conditions) for the use of the term *degradable/biodegradable/ photodegradable.* Claims of degradability must only be made in relation to a specific test method, end point, and period of time to reach the end point. They must be relevant to the circumstances in which the product or package is likely to be disposed.

Environmental Labeling—Self-Declaration Environmental Claims—Symbols

ISO 14022 complements ISO 14021 on Type II Labeling. Self-declaration environmental symbols may also be used by manufacturers, importers, retailers, or anyone else likely to benefit from such a claim.

Since the draft standard complements the terms and definitions standard ISO 14021, it has adopted the same text in the introductory clauses, such as the introduction, objective, definitions, and general guidelines. These sections will not be repeated in the following summary. WG2 has briefly discussed combining ISO 14021 and ISO 14022. No decision has been made regarding this issue.

Definitions

- **Environmental symbol.** Any symbol in the public domain that conveys or implies or is likely to be interpreted as making an environmental claim.
- **Qualified environmental symbol.** An environmental symbol that is accompanied by an explanatory statement. For example, the **portrayal of natural objects** (such as trees or animals) that are likely to be interpreted as making an environmental symbol shall not be used unless the requirements of ISO 14020 and ISO 14021 are met.

Accompanying Text

Environmental symbols for self-declaration environmental claims shall be accompanied by explanatory text if the symbol alone is likely to result in misinterpretation.

Nonenvironmental Claims

Text, numbers, or symbols can be used in addition to environmental symbols to communicate information such as material identification, disposal instructions, or hazard warnings.

Text, numbers, or symbols used for nonenvironmental claim purposes should:

- Not be used in a manner that is likely to be misconstrued as making an environmental claim. For example, text, numbers, or symbols used for material identification should not imply recyclability.
- Not be modified to relate the symbol to a specific brand, company, or corporate position.
- Not be used on a product or service to express conformance to an environmental management system.
- Be simple, easily reproducible, and capable of being positioned and sized to suit the product range to which the symbol is likely to be applied.

Environmental symbols for one type of environmental claim should be unique and easily distinguishable from other symbols, including symbols for other environmental claims.

Explanatory text accompanying a symbol shall be governed by the general principles and the applicable specific requirements in ISO 14021.

Specific Symbols

Möbius Loop Symbol (Chasing Arrows)

The Möbius loop is a graphical symbol in the shape of three chasing arrows forming a triangle. The draft standard includes the following guidance about the use of the Möbius loop.

Subject to the design constraint prescribed in the ISO 7000 standard, the Möbius loop:

- May be used in outline form, in reverse print, or as a solid symbol. There should however, be enough contrast so that the symbol is clear and distinguishable.
- May be used to convey information regarding either recyclability or recycled content. Its use is limited exclusively to information regarding recyclability or recycled content. It shall not be used in any other environmental context.
- Shall always be accompanied by explanatory text to ensure that the consumer, purchaser, or user is not misled. The explanatory text's purpose is to inform the consumer, purchaser, or user whether the symbol represents recyclability or recycled content. The text shall be immediately adjacent to, normally below, the symbol.
- When a recyclable or recycled content claim is made, the use of a symbol is optional. If a symbol is used, it shall conform to all of the requirements of the standard.
- May apply to the product or to the package. Whether it applies to the product or package should be made clear to the purchaser.
- Design shall meet the graphic requirements of ISO 7000-1135. If the Möbius loop is used, the requirements of ISO 14020 and ISO 14021 shall be met.
- May have additional accompanying text identifying material type.
- Used as a recycled content symbol, shall include the percentage recycled content within the loop.

CONCLUSION

As international trade becomes an important factor in the planning, research, and development of new products, considerations of environmental labeling get more weight than traditional factors such as quality, cost, and performance. This, coupled with the very strong pressures from consumers and environmental groups requesting more information about the life cycle of products, makes the issue of environmental labeling a major consideration. Moreover, the growing strength of ISO 9000 certification around the world will also be paralleled with ISO 14001 registration for environmental management systems. This in itself will spur interest in the environmental labeling standards. Finally, as governments all over the world rationalize and downsize, voluntary standards such as the ISO environmental labeling standards will be ideal as replacements for government guidelines and, in some countries, regulations.

BIOGRAPHY

Ahmad Husseini, PE

Admad Husseini is a Mechanical Engineer by training, with 30 year's experience in various fields of engineering, including environmental and utility engineering, design, construction, maintenance, water treatment, oil and gas, and production management. He also managed CSA's contract to develop guidelines for the federal gov-ernment's Eco-labeling program—"Environmental Choice" (ECP) for four years.

At present, Mr. Husseini is managing the national environmental program at CSA. This program includes Life Cycle Assessment (LCA), Canadian Raw Materials Database for LCA, Life Cycle Review, Environmental Labelling, Design for the Environment, Environmental Impact of Pulp and Paper, Sustainable Forest Management, Environmentally Responsible Procurement, Environmental Risk Assessment, and Environmental Site Assessment and Environmental Auditing. In addition, he manages Working Group #2 (on Self-Declaration Environmental Claims), under the Environmental Labelling Subcommittee (SC3) within ISO TC/207, and is secretary to SC1/WG1 on ISO 14004 Environmental Management Systems standard. Mr. Husseini is a Canadian expert in the fields of *LCA (ISO 14040), EL (ISO 14021/2/3) and Environmental Aspects in Product Standards (ISO 14040)*. He also assists the Secretary of ISO/TC 207 in all functions relating to the development of the ISO 14000 series of standards.

Mr. Husseini has written various papers on Life Cycle Assessment, Packaging, ISO activities, Green Procurement, Environmental Labelling and Design for the Environment. He also makes many presentations relating to the Environmental subjects. He is a member of PEO, ASTM, ASME, SETAC, and CSPE.

Ahmad Husseini, PE
Manager, Environmental Program/Standards Division
Canadian Standards Division
178 Rexdale Boulevard
Etobicoke, Ontario
Canada M9W-1R3

CHAPTER 25

ISO 14000 Labeling Standards— Legal and Practical Issues

Jake M. Holdreith

INTRODUCTION

The increasing popularity of environmental labeling and advertising since the mid-1980s has raised a number of difficult problems for consumers, product manufacturers and distributors, and the governmental entities that regulate them. While laws and industry codes of practice have long attempted to bring order to the advertising and labeling of products, environmental labels and claims raise at least two problems that deserve special attention. First, consumers have a very specialized (and not necessarily realistic) set of expectations with respect to the environmental attributes of products. Second, scientific opinions regarding environmental attributes of products is often uncertain and conflicting. Moreover, both consumer expectations and scientific opinions regarding the environment are in a period of rapid change.

A nonexhaustive list of some of the most prominent challenges to environmental marketing claims includes the following:

1. Consumers expect producers to reduce the burden on the environment while maintaining or improving the performance and the cost of products.

2. Advertising regulators, consumers, and competitors demand substantiation (proof) of environmental claims. Regulators and markets view claims that cannot be proved scientifically with increasing skepticism and hostility.

3. Globalization of the economy subjects products and advertising to scrutiny under a variety of potentially different standards. These include differing national laws as well as differing sets of consumer expectations and environmental priorities.

4. The developing world has voiced opposition to environmental preferences that may bias markets in favor of producers in developed countries.

5. Pushed to ever-stricter standards and ever more subtle inquiries, science has proved inconclusive on a variety of environmental questions. This makes it difficult to substantiate some environmental claims.

6. A substantial level of skepticism and confusion exists in the market regarding environmental attributes of products. This skepticism and confusion can be attributed to a variety of causes, including "green hype," perpetuated during the initial boom of environmental advertising; conflict in scientific opinions; the absence of an agreed-on method for comparison between products; and the inflation of consumer expectations regarding what improvements to products are possible.

Governments, private organizations, and individual market participants have recently attempted to address some of these challenges by adopting regulations or standards specific to environmental labeling, of which the developing ISO 14020-25 labeling guidelines are an example.

For example, the United States Federal Trade Commission (FTC), which is the agency generally responsible for the regulation of advertising and labeling in the United States, has developed a set of guidelines intended to help industry determine which environmental claims are permissible and to educate consumers as to the correct interpretation of environmental claims. *FTC Guides for the Use of Environmental Marketing Claims* has helped stabilize environmental advertising and label practice.[1]

A number of states, as well as other developed countries, have created similar guidelines. In addition, governments and private organizations have created programs that examine products and certify those that pass scrutiny of the certifier as environmentally preferable, such as the EU eco-label.[2]

The ISO 14020-25 series of environmental labeling guidelines are an attempt to distill the lessons learned from the various practices of organizations, governments, markets, and individuals into a coherent and fair set of common principles that may guide future environmental advertising and labeling practice. They hold the promise of offering industry a clear set of rules that offer a level playing field and limit disputes regarding which claims are fair. They offer consumers a common language that may make environmental claims clearer and more meaningful. In particular, ISO 14020 (basic principles), ISO 14021 (self-declaration terms and definitions), and ISO 14022 (symbols), provide guidance on "self-declaration" claims—the type usually made in labels and advertisements. These self-declaration claims are the main focus of this chapter.

A major challenge faced by the ISO 14020-25 labeling guidelines, especially in the United States where legal regulation of advertising is pervasive, is to provide a practical framework for producers, distributors, regulators, and consumers to use environmental claims in ways that are also consistent with the requirements of law. To the extent ISO 14020-25 can provide such practical guidance, the guidelines will be valuable indeed. Most relevant to the United States practitioner, then, are the guides for self-declaration environmental claims, which attempt to provide a practical framework that will be valid around the globe and consistent with the practice that is now prevalent in the United States.

U.S. LEGAL STANDARDS CURRENTLY APPLIED TO ENVIRONMENTAL ADVERTISING AND LABELING

Since at least the 1970s, the U.S. FTC has applied general rules requiring truth in advertising to regulate environmental labeling and advertising. In its first enforcement efforts, FTC simply applied directly its general prohibitions on deceptive or unfair advertising and its requirement for advertising substantiation. The basic rules imposed by these principles are that advertising and labels must be (1) true, (2) not misleading, and (3) substantiated.

In 1992, in an effort to bring more specificity and certainty to advertisers and to consumers, FTC published its guidelines for environmental marketing claims. The FTC guidelines discuss four general principles for environmental claims. Because the ISO 14020-25 environmental labeling guidelines are intended to be consistent with the FTC guidelines, the four principles are similar to principles contained in the ISO 14020 guidelines. The four FTC principles are as follows:

1. Claims should include qualifications and disclosures that are sufficiently clear and prominent to prevent deception.

2. Claims should make clear whether they apply to the product, the package, or only a component of either.

3. Claims should not overstate an environmental attribute or benefit.

4. Comparative claims should be presented in a manner that makes the basis for comparison clear.

In addition, like the ISO 14020-25 guidelines, the FTC guides contain specific definitions and guidelines for eight specific types of environmental claims also defined in ISO 14021. These are as follows:

1. General and environmental benefit claims.

2. Degradable/biodegradable/photodegradable.

3. Compostable.

4. Recyclable.

5. Recycled content.

6. Source reduction.

7. Refillable.

8. Ozone safe or ozone friendly.

In the United States, use of these terms must be consistent with FTC's definitions.

The fundamental principle of the FTC guides is to enforce the requirement of the Federal Trade Commission Act that "unfair methods of competition in or affecting commerce, and unfair or deceptive acts or practices in or affecting commerce are . . . unlawful." A summary of the three basic elements of this prohibition against deception and unfairness follows.

Prohibition on Deception

There is a detailed and complicated body of law that attempts to define exactly when an advertising practice is deceptive, but the concept is deliberately somewhat vague to allow FTC to prosecute the infinite variety of novel approaches that deceptive marketers may invent. Unfortunately, this places the risk that a new practice may be deemed "deceptive" on the person making a new type of advertising claim. FTC has attempted to summarize the basic principles of deception as follows:

1. Deception is a representation, omission, or practice that is likely to mislead the consumer.

2. The representation must be likely to mislead from the perspective of a consumer acting reasonably in the circumstances.

3. The representation, omission, or practice must be "material."

Generally, the determining factor is whether an advertising claim would lead a reasonable consumer to believe something that is untrue about the product. Generally, claims are considered material if they involve health or safety, the central characteristics of the product or service, or if the information would lead the consumer to change his or her decision about purchasing the product. FTC has indicated that it believes environmental claims are usually material.

Prohibition on Unfairness

Unfairness is even less well defined than *deception*. FTC uses the prohibition on unfairness to challenge practices that do not necessarily involve advertising or labeling claims but that otherwise unfairly and substantially injure consumers.

Unfairness has not been widely used in the area of environmental labeling and advertising. An example might be a practice under which a product is represented to be refillable or returnable when the ability of the consumer to actually refill or return the product is so limited that it frustrates the consumer's expectation.

Advertising Substantiation

The basic rule for advertising substantiation is that an advertiser must have a reasonable basis for an advertising or labeling claim before it is disseminated. When an advertisement or label expressly claims a level of substantiation (for example, "tests prove . . ."), the advertiser must have at least the level of substantiation claimed (e.g., test results). Where there is no express level of support claimed, the advertiser must have at least a reasonable basis for the claims.

FTC has summarized these requirements as applied to environmental attributes as follows:

[A]ny party making an express or implied claim that represents an objective assertion about the environmental attribute of a product or package must, at the time the claim is made, possess and rely upon a reasonable basis substantiating the claim. A reasonable basis consists of competent and reliable evidence. In the context of environmental marketing claims, such substantiation will often require such competent and reliable scientific evidence. For any test, analysis, research, study or other evidence to be 'competent and reliable' for purposes of these guides, it must be conducted and evaluated in an objective manner by persons qualified to do so, using procedures generally accepted in the profession to yield accurate and reliable results.[3]

State Regulation of Advertising Claims

Many states enforce truth-in-advertising laws similar to those of the federal government. Some states have passed very specific laws regulating environmental claims and labeling. In general, state laws are formulated according to the same principles as the FTC act discussed above. There are, however, some local and regional variations on the definitions and principles set forth in FTC's environmental marketing guides.[4]

Enforcement

The risks of making an improper environmental claim are significant. In the United States, a violation of advertising regulations can result in an investigation and prosecution by FTC. FTC has the power to order an advertiser to cease and desist making the claim or offering the product for sale, and to impose large fines. In addition, competitors and consumers can bring suit challenging deceptive advertising. During the first three years after FTC's environmental guides were published, FTC entered into 22 consent orders, settling claims alleging false and/or unsubstantiated environmental claims.

An equally troubling problem for advertisers has been the risk that environmental claims may backfire. Several prominent environmental advertising campaigns have resulted in sustained attacks by public interest groups challenging the accuracy of the claims, and several unfortunate campaigns have been openly ridiculed. For example, one newspaper ran an ongoing critique of a plastic bag manufacturer's claim of photodegradability. The paper featured a monthly photograph of one of the plastic bags that had been nailed to a telephone pole outside the reporter's house, showing that no degradation had occurred. The series ran for many months. Many other examples of this backfire risk have been publicized.

In short, practical guidance from the ISO 14020-25 guidelines that will reduce the risks of legal action or negative publicity can be a valuable tool to reduce the risks of enforcement and negative publicity.

Legal Status of ISO 14020-25 Labeling Guidelines

The ISO 14020-25 series of guidance standards are not legal standards or requirements. ISO deliberately constructs its procedures to harmonize existing industry practices rather than to create new norms or requirements. The committees drafting the ISO

14000 series of environmental management standards have been particularly concerned about avoiding creating legal standards in view of the very high stakes of United States environmental litigation. The U.S. sub-Tag has even specifically examined whether certain proposed language in some of the standards might be advanced as the basis for U.S. litigation in the future and has insisted on language that is less likely to do so. Accordingly, a fundamental premise of the ISO 14000 standards is that they are not law.

The ISO standards recognize that they deal with practices that are the subject of legal requirements and in fact specifically call the practitioner's attention to legal requirements of the various countries and regions in which practitioners may be active. Accordingly, although the ISO 14000 standards are not law, they typically require, or at least assume, that a practitioner is in compliance with applicable government regulations. A deviation from the ISO 14020-25 guidelines is not intended, however, to be punishable as a violation of law.

While the ISO 14020-25 standards are not intended to create legal requirements or to be used as a sword in litigation, one potential benefit of the standards is to provide industry with a potential safe harbor from legal challenges to advertising and labeling claims. That is, it may be possible under certain circumstances to use the ISO 14020-25 guides as a shield in litigation. Because they lack status as law, the ISO 14000 labeling guides cannot directly provide such a shield. An organization in compliance with the guides will not automatically be deemed to be in compliance with the law. There are, however, helpful developments that may make the guides useful as a compliance tool.

The most important development in this regard is the participation of FTC representatives in development of the ISO 14020-25 standards. An attorney advisor to FTC is a member of the U.S. sub-Tag, and has participated actively in the development of labeling standards. This is not intended to bind FTC to honor the ISO 14020-25 guidelines, but it indicates that individuals within FTC believe the guidelines are relevant and important. An FTC representative has expressed her personal view that in general the ISO 14020-25 labeling standards "tend to be a little more demanding than" the FTC guides for environmental claims, and that "if someone followed all of the [ISO 14020 labeling] standards, [he or she] most likely would be in compliance with [FTC's] guides as well."

The comments of the FTC representative are consistent with FTC policies that take into account (but do not strictly follow) industry guidelines. In one of its most important pieces of guidance, FTC has recognized that industry self-regulation is important, although not binding on FTC:

> The Commission traditionally has enjoyed a close working relationship with self-regulation groups and government agencies whose regulatory policies have some bearing on our law enforcement initiatives. The Commission will not necessarily defer, however, to a finding by a self-regulation group. An imprimatur from a self-regulation group will not automatically shield a firm from Commission prosecution and an unfavorable determination will not mean the Commission will automatically take

issue, or find liability if it does. Rather the Commission will make its judgment independently, evaluating each case on its merits. We intend to continue our useful relationships with self-regulation groups, and to rely on the expertise and findings of other government agencies in our proceedings to the greatest extent possible.[5]

At the same time, FTC's internal policy for prosecution of alleged violations indicates that FTC is particularly likely to take action when "a violation is so evident to other industry members that, if [FTC] does not act, [its] credibility and deterrence might be adversely affected. . . ." This suggests that a clear and highly visible violation of the ISO 14020-25 guides, which is readily apparent to other users of the guides, might be a target for FTC prosecution.

The U.S. sub-TAG has explicitly requested that FTC consider "harmonizing" the FTC environmental marketing guides with the ISO 14020-25 environmental labeling guidelines. It is likely that FTC will explicitly acknowledge the ISO 14020-25 guidelines as a relevant factor for consideration, although it is unlikely that FTC will commit to a position that a violation of the guides would necessarily be a violation of law or that compliance with the guides would necessarily be compliance with law.

SPECIFIC LEGAL AND PRACTICAL ISSUES RAISED BY THE ISO 14020-25 GUIDANCE STANDARDS

The practical and legal significance of the ISO 14020-25 guidance standards will necessarily develop as the standards come into popular use and will depend on the level of acceptance obtained by the guidelines. Following are some major legal and practical effects the standards are likely to have.

Level Playing Field/Stricter Standard

A major goal of the ISO 14020-25 labeling standards is to prevent unjustified environmental advertising claims from publication in the marketplace. The restriction of unjustified claims would have a number of beneficial effects including the following:

1. A reduction in marketplace confusion and a corresponding increase in consumer trust in environmental claims.

2. A reduction of unfair competitive advantage for exaggerated claims.

3. Increased potential for market forces to stimulate environmental improvements.

A presupposition of the goals outlined above is that unwarranted and untrustworthy claims are currently being made and that the standards will be more restrictive than current standards in order to accomplish the proposed reduction. As discussed below, the standards include presumptions against comparative claims based on life-cycle analysis and against claims of sustainability. It is not clear that such claims are improper under current U.S. law and current U.S. advertising practice.

The consequence of this more restrictive interpretation of the ISO labeling standards would be a limitation on the ability to make environmental claims. Accordingly, claims might be more difficult to substantiate, and fewer claims may be made. The hope is that claims that are made will be more reliable, more accurate, and better verifiable.

This restrictive interpretation of the guides has been challenged as being biased in favor of larger and more sophisticated organizations, particularly those in the developed world, which are better able to meet stricter standards. Although the international trade debate is one aspect of this challenge, smaller organizations in the developed world have also voiced concerns that they will be excluded from making environmental claims that only larger organizations will be able to make. Small businesses fear that the guidelines will exclude them entirely from some types of environmental labeling and advertising claims. This concern is implicated, for example, to the extent that sophisticated and expensive research may be required to substantiate a claim.

While there is some basis for the fears of a more restrictive standard, this argument is subject to at least two important qualifications. The first is that ISO 14020-25 are voluntary standards. There is no legal prohibition on publication of a claim or label that arguably may not comply with the ISO 14020-25 guidelines. Accordingly, if organizations believe their claims are potentially inconsistent with the ISO 14020-25 guidelines, but that the claims are nevertheless proper under U.S. law, they may continue to make those claims.

A second qualification to the fear of a restrictive interpretation of the guidelines is that there appears to be a consensus among regulators and industry that the guidelines do no more than provide practical standards to assist in the development of fair and accurate claims. That is, there is a strong argument that the standards do not impose stricter standards than those imposed by law but merely provide practical guidance on how existing legal requirements apply in the context of environmental labels and claims. The only restrictive effect the guidelines could have under this interpretation is to prevent publication of claims that are currently inconsistent with law but are not prosecuted because the legal standard is not clear.

Small businesses concerned about the legality of their claims should keep in mind that from the perspective of the United States Federal Trade Commission, a restrictive interpretation of the ISO standards that is more limiting than federal law is not binding on FTC. One way in which the more restrictive interpretation of the ISO 14000 guides nevertheless may be imposed on the market within the United States, however, is through private litigation by competitors, consumers, and public interest groups.

This avenue has proved effective in the past to challenge environmental marketing claims, and private litigants may have an interest in advancing restrictive interpretations of the guidelines. While the ISO 14020 labeling guidelines would not be binding on a court or determinative on the outcome of a lawsuit, courts can and do consider industry standards in determining whether conduct is consistent with law.

Clarification of Terms

The vagueness of some common environmental claims has presented a risk to conservative advertisers. For them, vague terms represent a risk because they are more easily misinterpreted by consumers than terms with a more definite meaning. FTC takes the position that when a term is subject to a number of reasonable interpretations, the claim is improper if any reasonable interpretation leads the consumer to a false conclusion about the product. Accordingly, conservative and responsible environmental advertisers generally welcome measures that will bring greater definition to terms and more certainty in the market as to the proper interpretation of environmental claims.

The ISO 14020-25 labeling guidelines are useful in this connection because they define a larger number of terms than the existing FTC guidelines. The FTC guidelines define only eight terms, as discussed above. In addition to those terms defined by FTC, the ISO 14021 standard on self-declaration claims defines the terms *reduced resource use, recovered energy, solid waste reduction, energy efficient, water efficient, extended life product,* and *designed for disassembly.* Additional terms may eventually be defined under the ISO 14020-25 guidelines.

By their own force, the guidelines provide industry with a consensus view on the meanings of these additional terms. This does not, by itself, automatically introduce clarity into the market because consumers will not necessarily be familiar with the ISO 14020-25 guidelines. It is likely, however, that increasing use of these claims under standardized definitions will ultimately introduce clarity and definition to the market and to consumers. FTC has concluded, for example, that its environmental marketing guides have had this beneficial effect. This clarity in the marketplace should reduce the risk that consumers will misunderstand some claims that use defined terms.

Level of Substantiation

At present, the FTC guides require that an advertiser have a reasonable basis to believe its claims are true. The specific legal requirements for substantiation are not well defined, but include requirements that the information relied on be generally relied on by experts in the field. While helpful, the FTC guides leave some ambiguity as to when substantiation is adequate.

The ISO 14020-25 guidelines attempt to be more specific regarding the nature and quality of the substantiation required for environmental claims. Accordingly, the standards require that claims be verified by methodologies that are reproducible and scientifically sound. A specific standard under development, ISO 14023, addresses testing and verification methodologies to provide guidance on specific methods that are acceptable.

Like other aspects of the ISO 14000 standards, this more specific (and perhaps more restrictive) standard for verification is helpful to the advertiser who has the resources to comply with the standard. They do not provide a guarantee of compliance with law but some will argue that they do supply a relevant guideline, and this view may eventually be accepted. At the same time, smaller organizations may argue that the verification requirements under the ISO 14020-25 guidelines are stricter than law and are not legally required in order for a claim to be proper under law.

Interestingly, FTC explicitly considers, when deciding whether to challenge an environmental claim, whether a substantiation requirement proposed by FTC will make it extremely difficult as a practical matter to make the type of claim and whether such a result is reasonable. Accordingly, FTC may refrain from arguing that some claims have improper substantiation when a higher level of substantiation would be difficult or impossible, the claim is accurate under the lesser kind of substantiation, and the other requirements of the FTC act are met.

Representation of Compliance with ISO 14020-25 Standards

The ISO 14020-25 standards do not explicitly contemplate that an advertiser or labeler will claim that its advertising claims are consistent with the ISO 14020-25 labeling guidelines. Naturally, such a claim is possible.

An interesting question is whether the mere attempt to make an environmental claim that is consistent with the ISO 14020-25 guidelines could be deemed to contain an implicit claim that the advertiser has complied with all of the ISO 14020-25 guidelines. While it seems unlikely that a reasonable consumer would reach such a conclusion absent some express declaration of compliance with ISO 14020-25 guidelines, an advertiser who expressly represents compliance with the ISO 14020-25 guidelines could be required to verify compliance with each of the guidelines.

A portion of the ISO 14020-25 labeling guidelines that has caused particular concern in this connection is proposed language that indicates that one of the objectives of the guidelines is environmental improvement. The concern is that an advertiser might be accused of failing to comply with the ISO guides based on an inability to show that a product in fact achieved some sort of vague or general environmental improvement. This type of argument seems an unfair and poorly founded interpretation of the guidelines. In particular, reading such a requirement into the guidelines is contrary to the ISO guidelines' specific prohibition of vague or general environmental benefit claims.

Comparative Claims

The ISO 14020-25 environmental labeling guides are slightly more strict with respect to comparative claims than the FTC guides, or at least more specific. The FTC guides generally require that in addition to meeting the requirements for all environmental claims, comparative claims must make the basis for the comparison clear. The ISO 14020-25 guidelines add that a comparative claim must be based on a published standard or recognized test method and/or that the comparison must involve comparable products or services serving similar functions. While such a requirement can be read into the FTC guides, it is not expressed.

This requirement is intended to ensure that comparisons are made of apples to apples. The ISO 14020 guidelines express a preference for published, recognized test methodologies that are not expressly required in the FTC guides. While such test methodologies are not strictly required by the ISO 14020 guidelines, a conservative advertiser will attempt to use one for comparative claims.

Perhaps the most significant restriction on comparative claims under the ISO 14020-25 labeling standards is a concern that life-cycle assessment (LCA) is not sufficiently developed to allow comparisons between competing products or materials in advertising claims that purport to be based on LCA. FTC declined to take a position on the propriety of life-cycle assessment in its guides, based on the lack of adequate information on which to determine whether comparative life-cycle claims are appropriate. The work of TC 207 on standards for life-cycle assessments has led to a widespread belief that the parameters of life-cycle assessment are not sufficiently developed to allow fair comparisons among products.

Standardization

An intended effect of the ISO 14020-25 labeling standards is harmonization of world-wide standards to allow distribution of a product around the world using a uniform claim and label. The ISO 14020-25 labeling standards cannot, of course, solve the problem of differing languages, which currently means that manufacturers are often required to use different advertising and labels in different markets around the world for business reasons, without regard to law. Efforts to create a global standard for environmental labeling symbols (such as the Möbius loop and EU efforts to develop new "reuse" and "recycle" symbols) are aimed at solving precisely this problem.

Governments are not required to adopt or follow the ISO 14020-25 standards, and accordingly the effectiveness of the guidelines' standardizing purpose depends on the degree to which governments voluntarily accept the standards. Within the United States, the federal government and many of the states have indicated their understanding of the problem posed by a multiplicity of differing requirements and have shown some willingness to adopt relatively uniform standards. As noted above, the U.S. sub-Tag has asked FTC to harmonize the FTC guides with the ISO 14020-25 guidelines. It remains to be seen how well the ISO 14020 guidelines achieve this harmonizing purpose following their implementation.

An important, and developing, issue is how the ISO 14020-23 labeling guidelines will fit into global trade agreements and regulation. There is hope that the guidelines will facilitate trade by standardizing many practices related to environmental issues. At the same time, there is concern that the standards will impose trade barriers to the extent they imply environmental performance requirements that are difficult to meet for producers in some parts of the world. Some have questioned whether portions of the guidelines are contrary to the Technical Barriers to Trade Agreement. Based on these concerns, it is not yet clear how the existence of an international standard will affect the ability of national governments to impose differing standards on producers, on the one hand, and the ability of distributors to resist differing national standards on the other hand.

CONCLUSION

The primary purpose of the ISO 14020-25 labeling guidelines is to provide uniform, practical guidance on how to properly make environmental claims. As a voluntary standard, the guidelines do not have the force of law, although national and regional governing bodies may choose to honor or adopt the standards.

At present, compliance with the standards provides industry with a practical and uniform method for making claims that is generally consistent with legal requirements in the United States and many other countries. Compliance with the standards does not guarantee compliance with law but is a substantial step towards compliance. As use of the ISO 14000 standards becomes widespread, they may well provide a permanent consensus standard that will also satisfy the requirements of law in most or all markets.

BIOGRAPHY

Jake M. Holdreith, Esq.

Jake M. Holdreith is an attorney with Oppenheimer Wolff & Donnelly in Minneapolis, Minnesota. He is a member of the U.S. sub-TAG to TC 207. He is coauthor of *The Handbook of Environmentally Conscious Manufacturing* (Irwin 1995). Mr. Holdreith focuses his law practice on environmental compliance, counseling, and management.

Jake M. Holdreith
Oppenheimer Wolff & Donnelly
3400 Plaza VII bldg.
45 South Seventh Street
Minneapolis, Minnesota 55402
Phone: (612) 344–9316
Facsimile: (612) 344–9376

NOTES

1. 16 Code of Federal Regulations § 260 (1995).
2. For more discussion of market challenges and legal regulation of environmental advertising claims, see Cattanach, Holdreith, Reinke and Sibik, *The Handbook of Environmentally Conscious Manufacturing: From Design & Production to Labeling & Recycling,* Chapters 7–10 (Chicago: Irwin, 1995).
3. 16 Code of Federal Regulations § 260 (FTC Guides), Subsection E.
4. For a discussion of state and regional regulations, see Cattanach et al., ibid. Chapter 8.
5. FTC statement on advertising substantiation, 48 Federal Register 10471 (March 11, 1983).

CHAPTER 26

A Practical View of Life-Cycle Assessment

Will Gibson

INTRODUCTION

In the manufacturing world, it is well ingrained that no design gets far without budget projections, flow charts, parts inventories, and so on, that reveal the economic significance of the project. There has been little or no familiarity with an analogous set of accounts that links the designs to the health of ecosystems.

Life-cycle assessment (LCA) is such an accounting tool. It represents a "cradle to grave" accounting for products, processes, and services. It recognizes that all life-cycle stages, such as acquisition of raw materials, transportation, manufacturing, distribution, use/reuse, and final disposal have environmental and economic impacts.

There is an urgent need to drastically reduce current and projected rates of resource depletion, waste generation, and environmental degradation because of the effect these processes have on the ecosystem. The earth's balance is dependent upon a complex interconnected network of processes that include biogeochemical cycling, metabolic degradation of toxins, temperature and light modulation by the atmosphere, and many other processes.

It is a zone of tolerance likely to be so small that any significant changes will have dire consequences for the biological organisms that are part of the balance. Since we have only a sample size of one planet, the scientific method fails to elucidate with measured certainty how near we are to those limits.

Both sectors, public and private, are rapidly converging to address these problems proactively—locally and globally. Life-cycle assessment is quickly becoming a valuable component of product and service management efforts that aim to reduce negative environmental effects. It is a vital tool for strategic planning and marketing and is changing the way product and service systems are planned and implemented.

Historical Development of LCA

LCA has been used occasionally in the past to promote the "environmental superiority" of products or packaging systems. But LCA lacks the robustness necessary to support overall superiority claims, and this misuse has brought a fair amount of cynicism and disrepute to the process. Despite this turmoil, however, the concept of reducing the environmental burdens that are associated with a product throughout its life cycle has survived and flourished.

Early LCA efforts were life-cycle inventory studies that emerged in the 1970s. These were systems-oriented engineering studies that evaluated material and energy flow in manufacturing systems. The life-cycle inventory model was gradually extended to encompass solid waste releases and emissions to air and water. By the late 1980s, a variety of life-cycle inventory models were in operation around the world.

Expanding interest in this methodology coincided with an increased interest in developing LCA into an environmental impact assessment tool. Progress on this front emerged from Society of Environmental Toxicology and Chemistry (SETAC) workshops in 1990 and 1992. Today, there is intense research and discussion directed at formulating LCA procedures that will allow valid decision making based on environmental impacts in product systems management.

Uses of LCA

Given its early beginnings as a mass and energy inventory, LCA is adept at identifying material, energy source, and process substitutions that increase efficiency and reduce end-of-pipe waste problems. The consequent act of optimizing resource inputs and reducing waste outputs makes both economic and environmental sense.

LCA is also being used to address environmental problems that are more global and diffuse. A prime example is its application in reducing the pollution that follows the product "through the factory gate." For many products, the most significant environmental burdens are those linked to the product-use phase.

LCA is a the primary tool that a manufacturer can use to identify and subsequently reduce product-use impacts. To the extent that retail consumers continue a trend toward using "environmental friendliness" in purchase-preference criteria, LCA becomes an integral part of a market-incentive approach to natural resource conservation.

This market-incentive approach to environmental improvement also functions at the manufacturing supply-chain level. An LCA would likely be prepared by a raw material or component part supplier for a customer who is concerned with the overall environmental profile of the product, incorporating the supplier's materials that the customer eventually markets. Whether end-point consumer or supply-chain customer, there is a trend for environmental performance to loom large in the suite of purchasing criteria that already normally includes cost and quality.

LCA represents a progression beyond single-issue environmental attributes of a product system—such as it uses less water, it has "x" percent recycled content, it consumes "x" percent less energy. LCA results reflect a much broader profile of environmental performance. Often no clear distinctions of overall environmental superiority can be made. Nonetheless, getting a clear picture of the trade-offs to be made within a system results in better decision making.

LCA can be used to guide private-sector management and designers in doing the following:

- Identifying processes, materials, or ingredients within a given product system that are major contributors to resource depletion, waste-stream impacts, or other environmental impacts. (Identifying these at the beginning of the design phase when it may be easiest to avoid adverse environmental impacts is economically wise.)

- Comparing options of different processes, materials used, or material sources in a product system to minimize environmental impacts.

- Comparing functionally equivalent products with regard to environmental impacts.

- Gathering information relative to customer environmental concerns.

Public sector uses of LCA include the following:

- Helping to develop long-term policy regarding overall material use, resource conservation, and reduction of environmental impacts and risks posed by materials and processes throughout the product life cycle.

- Evaluating resource effects associated with source reduction and alternative waste management techniques.

- Providing information to the public about the resource characteristics of products and materials.

- Supplying information needed for legislation or regulatory policy that governs uses of product materials.

- Helping to evaluate and differentiate among products for eco-labeling programs.

- Defining criteria for eco-labeling.

- Identifying research needs.

As protecting the ecological balance of the planet convincingly emerges as a common goal, the divide between public and private sector narrows to nothing. Previously, it was the purview of government regulatory agencies to administer policies that maintained that balance in the interest of the common good. But current conditions find designers and managers thoughtfully planning not only the reduction of upstream resources but also the lessening of downstream impacts. LCA is part of a movement away from more government regulation and toward more voluntary environmental protection.

Benefits of LCA

There are significant tangible benefits to a company or organization that adds LCA to its accounting and analysis structure. LCA is adept at detecting resource inefficiencies and major sources of waste generation in a system. It is effective at planning and prioritizing reductions in these areas. Amidst a climate of rapidly changing environmental management challenges, LCA can be a welcome support to the very complex decision-making process associated with meeting these challenges.

LCA is increasingly playing a role in company marketing strategies. It forms the basis upon which companies communicate to their customers, vis-á-vis competitors, the environmental efficiency of their products.

An unexplored benefit of LCA is its role in bringing together heretofore separate disciplines within a company—the result being that companies discover new and better ways of doing business.

Yet another benefit involves avoiding the trade and market-share implications of not taking a life-cycle approach. National and international standards that are rapidly coming into use favor the adoption of life-cycle management tools such as LCA. Increasingly, downstream customers and consumers are requiring suppliers to show commitment to improved environmental performance.

ROLE OF LCA IN THE ENVIRONMENTAL MANAGEMENT SYSTEM CONTEXT

The ISO 14000 series is the most ambitious international effort ever undertaken to guide global business toward more responsible environmental practices. Key principles of the EMS standards (ISO 14001 and ISO 14004) include:

- Encouragement of environmental planning throughout the product or process life cycle.
- Emphasis on prevention rather than corrective action.

LCA provides the basis for implementing these principles. It is the only assessment methodology being formally standardized by ISO's TC 207. LCA puts the flesh on the bones of the ISO 14000 skeleton by helping to identify the environmental aspects of an organization's activities, products, and services and to subsequently evaluate their impact.

LCA Framework

In principle, LCA is a technique for assessing all environmental aspects and potential impacts associated with a product or service system over its entire life, from "earth to earth." This includes extracting raw resources, processing them into materials and fuels, manufacturing a product, using and maintaining the product, and disposing of the product.

In practice, LCAs must be practical and economical studies. They attempt to closely approximate models of a technical system and its environmental impacts but will never claim to provide an absolute representation of all environmental interactions.

According to the framework that is in the process of being standardized by ISO TC 207's Subcommittee 5 on life-cycle assessment, there are four phases of an LCA:

1. Goal definition and scoping.

2. Inventory analysis.

3. Impact assessment.

4. Interpretation.

A brief description of each of these phases is given below.

Goal Definition and Scoping

Goal   It is necessary to begin an LCA study with a clearly defined goal—or, in scientific terms, an appropriate hypothesis. The goal definition element identifies the purpose of the study, the nature of the comparison, the intended application, and the intended audience. Most, if not all, LCAs involve a comparison of different ways of achieving a particular function.

That is, most LCAs address the question: Are different products, processes, or materials significantly different from one another with respect to environmental burdens and, if so, which has less of an environmental burden? Even if the study is only exploratory or is meant to identify a baseline, the information gains its relevance from the subsequent process of comparison.

LCA studies can differ greatly in terms of depth and breadth. An LCA that meets the goal of informing a small team of designers within a company as to the appropriate choice of input materials will look quite different from one that is providing an environmental performance profile to customers or government agencies.

Scope   The scope delineates the means of reaching the goal. It represents the intended reproducible methods that will eventually support or refute the initial hypothesis (or will provide a valid baseline from which subsequent comparisons can be made).

In current practice, LCAs are individual, case-dependent studies with very few generally applicable methods. A number of basic decisions are made in the scoping phase to adapt the study to the goal. It is important to state as part of the scope the assumptions being used and the limitations that are known. The scope should also include the types and quality of data required.

For the sake of validity, normal scientific practice dictates that a scope—for example, assumptions, type of investigation, statistical considerations, and methods of interpreting results—be developed at the beginning of a study and then be left unaltered. That is likely a desirable point toward which the development of LCA science can head. In current LCA practice, however, midstudy scope alterations and adjustments have been justifiable on the grounds of improving significance.

If midstudy goal and scope changes are something of the norm, it might be advisable to have an initial goal and scope that is implicitly tentative. If the data requirements of the initial goal are unrealistic (or, much less likely, allow an even broader or more precise comparison), the goal and scope can be brought into alignment with existing conditions.

Regardless of approach, transparent reporting is necessary to avoid studies that become compromised by manipulations that consciously or unconsciously introduce bias into the results. If an initial goal and scope is changed, it is important to explain in the final report the reason for these revisions.

If there is to be a critical review or validation by a reference panel, the form of these should be determined in the initial scope.

System Function   The results of an LCA are entirely dependent on how the system function and functional unit are defined. Any product or service aims to provide the user with a specific function. It is the function, not the product, that is the interest of LCA. LCAs are only meaningful when their explicit or implicit comparison involves alternative systems that fulfill reasonably the same function. A proper definition of the function under study is of key concern.

Functional Unit   From the defined system function, it has been the norm to choose a functional unit that is relevant to the product user and is objectively measurable. It should take into consideration performance quality standards such as efficiency and durability. An example of a functional unit for beverage containers might be the volume of beverage delivered to the consumer by single servings. The functional unit for a paint might be the unit surface area protected for a defined period of time.

Another factor to consider is having a functional unit that is large enough to appear on a resolution scale of measurable environmental impacts. Such units may be much larger than those that have been used in LCA studies previously. (Refer to discussion of functional units in "LCA Obstacles and Impediments," below.)

System Boundaries   Setting system boundaries is the other critical step that occurs early in the study. There are various levels and types of boundary setting associated with inventory analysis and impact assessment. Some of the obvious issues involve spatial scale, temporal scale, biosphere–technosphere interface, and definition of the discrete "cradle" (starting) point.

Conceptualizing the boundaries and setting the decision rules for cutting off the cradle should be explicit in the scope of the study. Though LCAs in theory encompass the entire life cycle, in practice it is not possible to follow every little flow back to its cradle. An objective procedure must be in place to decide at what point small upstream flows are insignificant to the goal of the study.

Allocation   There are often processes within a product system that result in more than one useable output. Even though these secondary products are not directly of interest to a particular study, their production contributes to environmental burdens.

Allocation is the technique of partitioning these burdens between co-products. It is a decision-rule activity that defines how secondary products in the system are treated when they leave the system.

Inventory Analysis

This phase of the study involves actually compiling and quantifying the inputs and outputs of a product system that will have potential environmental impacts, including releases to air, water, and land, and the depletion or disruption of natural resources.

The results of an inventory analysis form the basis for the next phase of the study: impact assessment. The inventory analysis is highly dependent on the system boundaries and functional unit that were chosen in the goal and scoping phase.

Interpretations may sometimes be drawn from these inventory results. In addition to forming the basis for impact assessment, the inventory analysis alone can be valuable for establishing a baseline of information on a system's resource requirements and environmental releases, and planning for reductions. Using a less-is-better criterion, inventory analysis can be a factor in choosing between product systems that have significantly different inputs and outputs.

The inventory analysis process is usually a complex and iterative one. Often, the process of compiling and categorizing data exposes new data requirements and new scope limitations. Since LCA is a relatively new type of accounting system, there are voids and shortcomings with respect to data that is both suitable and reasonably accessible. Monitoring protocols and data libraries tailored to the needs of LCA are mostly in their infancy. It seems inevitable that as LCA becomes a more widespread practice, the process of acquiring appropriate data will become less formidable.

Impact Assessment

The purpose of the impact assessment phase of LCA is to analyze the inventory results in relation to potential environmental impacts. An impact is defined here as that which causes a significant change in natural or human systems.

Impact assessment attempts to accomplish that which inventory analysis legitimately cannot. It is an attempt to reliably determine whether two different inventory profiles (for two different product systems) are significantly different from one another; that is, whether different calculated quantities will reasonably translate into different environmental effects. In a baseline study, the goal might be to calculate potential impacts of a single product system from which alternative product systems would subsequently be compared.

There is currently no consensus in the scientific community on which methods provide the most meaningful result. Efforts are underway to test and evaluate various impact-assessment methods as they are being developed.

Both the SETAC impact assessment framework and the Nordic Guidelines divide the impact assessment process into three subcomponents: classification, characterization, and valuation.

Classification   The first step, classification, is qualitative, in which the various inputs and outputs of the product system are assigned to different impact categories based on the expected type of impacts on the environmental. The impacts that are assessed normally fall into three broad categories: human health, ecological health, and resource use. These categories are interconnected to various degrees; however, for purposes of analysis they are viewed as discrete.

A more detailed list of commonly used categories, from the Nordic Guidelines, includes the following:

- Resources—Energy and materials.
- Resources—Water.
- Resources—Land.
- Human health—Toxicological impacts (excluding work environment).
- Human health—Non-toxicological impacts (excluding work environment).
- Human health impacts in work environment.
- Global warming.
- Depletion of stratospheric ozone.
- Acidification.
- Eutrophication.
- Photo-oxidant formation.
- Ecotoxicological impacts.
- Habitat alternations and impacts of biological diversity.
- Inflows that are not traced back to the system boundary between the technical system and nature.
- Outflows that are not followed to the system boundary between the technical system and nature.

Characterization   Characterization is a largely quantitative step that analyzes by category the relative contribution of the multiple inputs or outputs, which were quantified by inventory analysis, to a potential impact. Characterization attempts to aggregate within an impact category based on devised equivalency factors. These factors should be scientifically supportable and clear to all relevant parties.

Valuation   Valuation is a subjective exercise that attempts to rank and to compare the relative importance of different individual impact categories for a given product system.

Interpretation

An interpretation phase could, and probably should, follow the result in each or all of the LCA phases—inventory analysis, classification, characterization, or valuation—depending on the goal and scope of the study.

LCA interpretation in the sense of that which follows or is closely tied to LCA valuation involves weighing different types of environmental impacts against each other as the basis for subsequent decision making. This cannot be done without introducing political or social values. Depending on the underlying value system, the interpretation is usually a different result. Ethical product system choice at the design phase or at the consumer level cannot be based solely on quantitative criteria.

Numerous methodologies (checklists, matrices, flow diagrams, overlays, etc.) have been developed for predicting effects, interpreting impacts, and communicating results. General approaches to impact-assessment interpretation include the systems approach, futures paradigm, integrated approach, adaptive assessment, holistic approach, and comprehensive approach.

A number of quantitative valuation systems are being used (e.g., EPS system, Tellus Method, Ecoscarcity, etc.) that are of an interpretive nature. None of these systems or methodologies have reached a state of development that would make them a normative standard.

LCA OBSTACLES AND IMPEDIMENTS

LCA is a developing methodology that promises to bring great improvements in the way industries account for and subsequently reduce adverse environmental impacts. But there are significant obstacles as well.

Relating Input/Output Data to Environmental Impacts

Life-cycle inventory methods have been used in practice for at least two decades and are fairly effective at identifying resource waste and inefficiency. Using a less-is-better approach, they are appropriate for guiding the selection of options for design and improvement. What is problematic is objectively relating these inventory input and output data to actual, or even potential, environmental impacts. If, for example office chair A has a better overall profile of environmental aspects than office chair B—that is, it depletes less resources, uses less energy, produces less of the entire suite of air and water pollutants, and creates less solid waste—one can be quite certain that office chair A has more value than office chair B on an environmental-impact-avoidance scale.

But this is rarely the case. There are nearly always trade-offs, and this introduces the dilemma of valuing one type of impact over another, for example, water pollution over air pollution, human toxicity pollutants over acid rain precursors, nonrenewable resource depletion over habitat destruction. The list of potential trade-offs is nearly inexhaustible.

Aggregation of Data

Another problem associated with current LCA approaches involves the practice of aggregating mass and energy input/output data. The subsequent loss of spatial, temporal, and threshold-level resolution results in crude representations of the way the system interacts with the environment.

The less resolution one has in the product system models, the less certain the estimate of detecting differences between them. Adding up all the point-source emissions for a given pollutant, say, volatile organic compounds (VOCs), will have an uncertain relationship to individual point-source emissions, the effects of which depend on such factors as season, rate, geographic location, biological thresholds, and so on.

The current practice of attempting to relate environmental impacts to a single retail unit may be unrealistic. Given the complexity and uncertainty involved in LCA, the resolution needed to measure environmental impact differences at this minute level may not be practical or possible.

Objectively Defining System Boundaries

Other potential pitfalls lie in objectively defining system boundaries. Since all processes are in some way connected, there is an arbitrary element to portraying the system as a discrete item of study. For example, unlike mineral resources, raw materials derived from biological systems have no distinct upstream boundary. At what point does a tree enter the industrial system? Perhaps when it is harvested from the earth, but what about planting, chemical inputs, ditching, or thinning?

What about the challenge of accounting for the effects on flora, on fauna, on hydrology? One begins to glimpse in this limitation a gap that exists between tools, such as LCA, that may be adept at addressing technological sustainability, and other approaches, such as ecological design and engineering, that are developing to address ecological sustainability.

The subjective nature of comparing the relative importance of different impact categories, the lack of appropriate resolution, and functional unit and boundary definition problems are some major factors responsible for making comparison between product systems a difficult, uncertain process. These same obstacles have impeded efforts to standardize LCA practice. Lack of standardization in turn impedes wholesale adoption of the practice by potential users.

Practical Considerations

These are theoretical considerations. On a pragmatic level, LCAs are expensive studies, with costs that range from $15,000 to $500,000 per product system and beyond. Therefore, the burden of performance on the benefit side of the equation can be acute. The time needed to perform an LCA, perhaps a year or more, can be another impediment. This would be especially critical in industry sectors that must respond to the market with rapid product design changes.

SOFTWARE MODEL AND DATABASE DEVELOPMENT

If a company or organization decides that LCA would be a helpful tool, how do they get started? One strategy is to begin the commitment to LCA with a small pilot study.

Such studies can result in tangible evidence regarding the usefulness of the LCA approach. This, in turn, can foster greater commitment to life-cycle thinking within the organization.

Full LCAs are generally complex and costly studies that require modeling and environmental assessment expertise. Most companies or organizations will look to outside consulting firms for such expertise. This may take the form of contracting out the entire assessment with proportionately minimal in-house staff time devoted to the project. Or it might entail the licensure of software and databases for use by largely in-house experts.

There are several large consulting firms in the United States and abroad that have developed proprietary software models for conducting LCAs. The model and the database are commonly a combined product that is available for license by the customer. Since much of the early work in LCA occurred in Europe, many of the databases rely on data that is more specific to that region than others.

To date, there are more LCA practitioners in Europe than in North America. Historically, there has also been more openness among European industries to make environmental data available; consequently, the access to public databases relevant to LCA has been better.

The following are some of the organizations that are involved in developing databases, computer software, and expert systems:

- Center for Economics and Business Administration, University of Basel.
- Ciba Geigy.
- Ecobilan.
- European Design Center ("Simapro" software), Franklin Associates ("Ecomanager"), Institute for Polymer Science and Polymer Testing, University of Stuttgart.
- Johnson & Johnson ("Packtrack").
- Migros ("Oekobase").
- Product Life Institute, Geneva.
- Ottman Consulting ("Getting to Zero Process").
- Research Triangle Institute ("E-cycle").
- Sandia National Laboratory—General Motors ("Intelligent Materials Selection System").
- University of Tennessee—Saturn-USEPA Life-Cycle Design for the Automobile—United States Automobile Materials Partnership Life-Cycle Inventory.
- Volvo Car Corporation—Federation of Swedish Industries—Swedish Environmental Research Institute ("EPS").

U.S. government funds are supporting the development LCA software tools that may become available in the public domain. The U.S. Department of Energy is supporting this effort, which Battelle Northwest Laboratory is orchestrating. Several large industry groups and government agencies are participating in the development of this database.

Similar efforts are underway in Canada. Environment Canada, raw materials industries, and the Canadian Standards Association are developing a raw materials database to quantify all energy and raw material inputs and environmental releases for raw materials acquisition and primary processing.

Companies in some sectors, such as electronics and computers, may need to be more aggressive than other companies because of a precedent for companies in that sector to address environmental issues at an early stage of product development.

LCA IN THE CONTEXT OF INDUSTRIAL ECOLOGY

With many years of ever-increasing environmental regulation, industries have become quite focused on controlling pollution outputs from individual facilities without regard to linkages to other stages of the product life cycle. But as they move toward the design of whole product systems, including material uses, product attributes, recycling, and disposal schemes, they find they cannot solve the underlying pollution problems by focusing on the individual actors in the system.

Life-cycle management is the cooperative effort by persons at different stages of the life cycle of a product to redesign product systems to reduce their overall environmental impacts. It is the movement of normal industrial management practice away from *linear mechanistic thinking* and toward *holistic systems thinking*. It is an expansion of perspective from cradle-to-gate, to cradle to grave, and eventually, cradle to cradle. LCA is the primary scientific methodology that underlies the concept of life-cycle management.

The concept of envisioning industrial systems as analogous to natural systems has been termed *industrial ecology.* LCA, in its current usage, is analogous to what in ecological science is called *autoecology*, the study of a single species (or specific product system) in relation to its environment. What will develop from it is an industrial counterpart to *synecology*, the study of how manufacturing processes fit together into a viable community, wherein almost nothing is wasted.

Historically, the path of human progress must have diverged, even if just temporarily, from the earth's health maintenance trajectory. Compared to anything the planet has experienced before, the modern industrial society has consumed gross amounts of resources and created absurd amounts of waste.

Many experts reason that the sum total of the various repercussions—renewable resource exhaustion and dispersion, ecosystem destruction, pollutant-induced stratospheric ozone depletion, biogeochemical cycle disruption, and toxic bioaccumulation—has quite certainly sent the earth's physical and biological systems on a trajectory of disintegration.

Increasingly, levels of environmental protection in western industrial countries through legislation, administrative controls, industrial commitments, and nongovernmental organization pressure have represented a step toward sensibly lessening rates of environmental degradation.

Initially, improvements in developed countries may have been offset by worsening impacts in newly industrialized countries. But these countries subsequently adopted environmental regulation to control further degradation of the environment.

The historical record will likely show that regulatory limits were an evolutionary step that slowed the divergence of human progress and environmental health. It will likely show that this phase was in turn followed by a global industrial system that voluntarily accounted for environmental burdens: the intent was to efficiently reduce them.

Life-cycle thinking will certainly figure significantly in the history of this latter phase. LCA will most likely be a necessary interim accounting tool that stands as a bridge spanning two periods:

- A period when ecological burdens were nowhere to be found on the balance sheet.
- A time when ecological burdens are insignificant, because the industrial system, like the natural system, cyclically metabolizes outputs.

As we approach the reconvergence of human progress and health of the larger environment, all materials literally become resources—that which rises again. All processes will be resources as their by-products provide the primary material for a subsequent process in a continuous regenerative loop.

BIOGRAPHY

William Gibson, PhD, Senior Environmental Scientist

William Gibson, head of Cummins & Barnard's (C&B) environmental management consulting team, has a unique wealth of experience in merging economic development with natural resource preservation/rehabilitation. He has over twenty years of experience in environmental science and ecological engineering, including environmental impact assessment, environmental site assessment, energy conservation analysis, water quality management, and sustainable forestry and agriculture. Since 1994, Dr. Gibson has been an active delegate and expert of the U.S. Technical Advisory Group of ISO 14000, working especially with Life-Cycle Assessment (SC 5 of TC 2207). He has been instrumental in developing and presenting training in life-cycle management.

The group that Dr. Gibson oversees at C&B is active in instituting market-based natural resource conservation systems. They specialize in performing life-cycle assessments and total cost accounting studies, implementing wetland mitigation banks, setting up and brokering air and water quality credit trading systems, and appraising ecological and economic real estate values so as to maximize conservation easement tax benefits.

He also conducts a number of other projects involving ecosystem management, stormwater and wastewater treatment of wetlands, biomanipulation for surface water clean-up, and pollution management/prevention. Dr. Gibson serves as an adjunct faculty member at The University of Michigan, and is on the board of several nonprofit environmental science organizations and advisory bodies.

Dr. Gibson has published numerous articles and papers concerning the structure and function of ecological systems, impact assessment, resource allocation/conservation, and life-cycle assessment.

His education includes: Ph.D., community ecology, Michigan Technological University, 1991; master of science, plant ecology, Michigan Technological University, 1980; bachelor of science, botany, University of Michigan, 1975; engineering coursework, General Motors Institute, 1970–1972.

APPENDIX

SC5's LCA Work—Status of Standards

The overall scope of SC5 is standardization in the field of life-cycle assessment as a tool for environmental management of product and service systems. Among the goals of SC5 are to develop useful and flexible LCA tools that describe a consistent methodology and create a common understanding of LCA. Another goal is to provide methods for reporting LCA studies in a responsible, transparent, and consistent manner. As with all draft standards in the ISO 14000 series, except ISO 14001, the LCA draft standards provide guidance; they do not contain specifications for registration or certification purposes.

Principles and Framework—ISO 14040

WG1's standard, *ISO 14040 Environmental management—Life cycle assessment—Principles and guidelines,* defines life-cycle assessment as a "compilation and evaluation, according to a systematic set of procedures, of the inputs and outputs and the potential environmental impacts of a product system throughout its life cycle." The standard describes the basic principles and framework for LCA and posits a four-phase model, based largely but not completely on the model developed by the Society of Environmental Toxicology and Chemistry (SETAC).

The first phase is goal and scope definition, which involves clearly defining the purpose of the LCA study and delineating a scope consistent with that purpose. This involves, among other things, specifying the functions of the system under study, drawing system boundaries, and setting requirements for data quality.

The second phase is the life-cycle inventory, which involves "compilation and quantification of relevant inputs and outputs for a given product system throughout its life cycle." Inputs include energy and raw materials. Outputs include water effluents, airborne emissions, solid waste, and other environmental releases.

The third phase, life cycle impact assessment, aims "at understanding and evaluating the magnitude of the potential environmental impacts of a product system" using the results of the life cycle inventory analysis.

In the SETAC model, the next phase is life-cycle improvement assessment, which evaluates the results of the impact assessment process to look for opportunities for environmental improvement. ISO 14040 has characterized this phase instead as life-cycle interpretation, "the phase of LCA in which a synthesis is drawn from the findings of the inventory analysis and the impact assessment or, in the case of life-cycle inventory studies, from the findings of the inventory analysis only, in line with the defined goal and scope."

The ISO 14040 standard recognizes that the complete model has been rarely used in its entirety and that the phases are not linear steps but interrelated. In fact, most LCA studies haven't gone beyond the life-cycle inventory phase of quantifying re-source and energy use and releases. The standard recognizes the value of streamlined studies, which minimize the scope and boundaries of the LCA or exclude certain types of data.

Inventory Analysis—ISO 14041

ISO 14041 Environmental management—Life cycle assessment—Inventory analysis describes in more detail the first two phases of LCA: goal and scope definition and life-cycle inventory analysis (LCI). The standard covers the following areas:

- How to formulate the goal and scope of the LCA study.
- How to define and model the systems to be analyzed.
- How to collect and prepare data for impact assessment.
- How to verify and evaluate the reliability of the results obtained.
- How to interpret and use the results of an LCI analysis.
- How to report the results of an LCI analysis.

The standard contains three informative annexes: an example of a data collection sheet, a checklist of critical aspects of an LCA, and examples of different allocation procedures.

Impact Assessment—ISO 14042

WG4 has developed a working document entitled "The Basic Life-Cycle Assessment Process," which reads more like a discussion report than a standard. It reviews existing LCA methods and discusses the shortcomings of current LCA practices. The document points out that the SETAC-based framework "has resulted in considerable confusion in the development of standards, and has been applied in actual practice." The document gives an example of packaging studies conducted strictly as inventory exercises that were used as the basis of major policy decisions, despite the fact that no effort was made in the studies to link the mass and energy findings of the inventory study to environmental effects. The impact assessment phase itself has been discussed only conceptually, with limited actual practice on which to base a standard.

The document describes various problems with impact assessment. For example, one problem is that a heavy emphasis on the inventory phase results in a huge collection of data that, for a number of reasons, may be of little or no use. The data is difficult to prioritize. Another problem is defining environmental impacts. Impacts are elusive when multiple products result from a single process. Some impacts, especially downstream ones such as natural resource depletion or global warming, are difficult if not impossible to quantify.

The document goes on to outline a basic LCA impact-assessment process designed to ensure that the information collected and analyzed in an LCA study is environmentally relevant and accurate. The draft points out that the type of impact assessment and level of detail needed will depend on the specific goals of an LCA and that a single methodology will almost certainly not be appropriate for all users and studies.

Life-Cycle Interpretation—ISO 14043

The work of WG5 focuses on the interpretation of LCA results. Based on the meetings in Vancouver in November 1995, WG5's scope is to "prepare a generic systematic procedure for interpreting information provided by inventory analysis and/or impact assessment of a system . . ." Among its tasks are to study different applications of LCA to identify approaches to interpretation. Four key applications identified by WG5 include product development/improvement, strategic planning, marketing (e.g., environmental labeling), and public policymaking.

Most members of SC5 agree that the conclusions drawn from an LCA study should be limited to addressing the findings and outcomes of the study but that subsequent application of the results and the decisions made are completely outside the scope of the LCA study and the LCA standards. These decisions bring other factors into play, including economic and social aspects.

The draft document describes an interpretation process that includes four steps. Step 1 is synthesis. Synthesis is the process of aggregating information from the inventory analysis and/or impact assessment, consistent with the goal and scope definitions of the study. Step 2 is reviewing the results and comparing them, in terms of their consistency and relevance, to the goal and scope definitions. Steps 3 and 4 are to develop conclusions and recommendations. These encompass observations, answers to questions, judgments and opinions, and so on.

CHAPTER 27

Environmental Cost Accounting: An Ideal Management Tool

David W. Vogel

WHAT IS ENVIRONMENTAL COST ACCOUNTING (ECA)?

Environmental cost accounting has been defined as "the addition of environmental cost information into existing cost accounting procedures and/or recognizing embedded environmental costs and allocating them to appropriate products or processes."[1] The task of defining and quantifying environmental costs falls within the realm of management accounting, whose purpose is to develop information useful to management in making business decisions. These business decisions include primarily capital investment decisions, determining profitability of products and other performance decisions, and planning decisions.

The determination of a cost as an "environmental cost" is subjective and depends on how management intends to use the information. Most managers would agree, however, that the costs of complying with environmental laws and regulations are environmental costs. Further, they would agree that noncompliance penalties, environmental remediation, and pollution prevention are environmental costs.

BENEFITS OF ECA

The primary benefit of environmental cost accounting is in obtaining a better understanding of the total costs of protecting the environment so that an organization can make more informed business decisions.

Perhaps the most useful management accounting tool for beginning to understand the total environmental costs for a product, product line, plant, division, or the total firm is "activity-based costing." This tool is a means to identify all environmental costs within an organization irrespective of where they are incurred within that organization and to better assign those costs to the products that caused the costs to be incurred.

BOX 27-1

ISO 14001 AND ENVIRONMENTAL COST ACCOUNTING

The ISO 14001 standard does not prescribe the use of environmental cost accounting. The standard mentions that when establishing objectives, an organization "shall consider financial, operational, and business requirements." The Annex to ISO 14001 emphasizes that this does not imply that ISO 14001 requires the use of environmental cost accounting methods to track the costs and benefits of environmental performance, such as the costs and benefits of pollution control, waste management, and other activities. The organization, however, is free to use these techniques if it finds them useful.

This results in the identification of many so-called "hidden costs" that are buried in overhead accounts and allocated in a rather arbitrary manner (e.g., as a percentage of worker hours, machine hours, or sales).

For example, the costs of the legal department in negotiating Superfund remediation liabilities or creating directives for complying with new environmental regulations may be buried in administrative overhead and allocated to businesses based on sales. Activity-based costing would uncover the cost of each activity and provide the means to allocate the costs to each business that was responsible for incurring the cost. Other examples might include the costs of toxicological testing and other costs incurred in the preparation of product safety data sheets or the costs incurred in preparing and filing various environmental compliance reports with appropriate regulatory agencies.

Activity-based costing can best be illustrated by Figure 27–1, which shows the difference between traditional cost accounting and activity-based costing. In summary, it shows that costs associated with identified activities are allocated to products based on the linkage between those activities and the products—not on more arbitrary allocations, as under traditional methods.

The case study presented at the end of this chapter will illustrate these concepts in more detail and will enhance the reader's understanding of activity-based costing. Another significant benefit is the ability to better assign pollution control and waste treatment costs to individual products or product lines based on the source contribution of each of those products or product lines. Situations exist where no efforts were made to determine how much wastewater was generated by individual chemical processes; the wastewater treatment costs were considered a plant overhead cost and allocated to all processes without regard to the source contribution of each. Accordingly, the product costs did not reflect accurate shares of an environmental cost.

Environmental cost accounting also enables a firm to identify and better assign costs related to human health impacts of operations. Such health-impact costs can often be overlooked as environmental costs since some might consider them to be safety or

FIGURE 27–1

Comparison of Traditional Cost Allocations to ABC Allocations

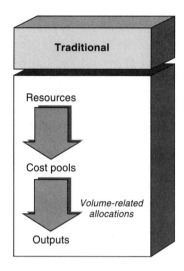
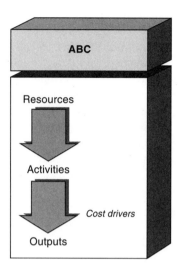

occupational-type costs. The costs associated with protecting human health from the effects of toxic chemicals have sometimes been overlooked and have not been accurately reflected in product costs.

Another benefit is that environmental cost accounting facilitates and improves the economic evaluation of alternative materials, technologies, production processes, and delivery processes. This can be accomplished using life-cycle assessment, which identifies the environmental consequences of a process through its entire life cycle: raw materials acquisition, manufacturing, consumer use/reuse/maintenance, and recycling/waste management. While life-cycle assessment focuses on environmental impacts only, one can add a monetary or financial dimension to this assessment by estimating a cost for each impact.

LIFE-CYCLE COST ASSESSMENT

This latter tool is referred to as *life-cycle cost assessment.* The identification and quantification of environmental costs associated with alternative raw materials and process changes (including new technology) is essential to making informed business decisions based on sound environmental principles and on true manufacturing costs, as well as true environmental costs over the long term. Consider the case of an organization that has the opportunity to substitute a higher-cost raw material for the lower-cost one currently being used. The current manufacturing process must be modified to accept the alternative raw material, resulting in higher operating costs. These costs must be weighed against the benefits of less waste and lower disposal costs.

Finally, environmental cost accounting facilitates the determination of the economic impacts of future regulations and changes in consumer preferences. Similar to the analysis of raw material substitution described above, the analysis of the effect on capital spending and/or operating expenses related to more stringent regulatory requirements (e.g., reducing air emissions) can contribute to improved business decisions. Likewise, the changes in packaging or chemical content of a product desired by customers results in the interplay of cost and revenue changes that can be analyzed and used to make more informed business decisions.

To generalize the benefits cited above, one can say that environmental cost accounting provides more comprehensive environmental cost information that improves allocation of such costs to individual product lines. Accordingly, managers can be more certain about their real product costs. This same information applied to the future improves the forecasting of cash flows, costs, and earnings. As such, the quality of capital budgeting and business plans is improved, as is the company's competitive position.

These benefits are significant and place environmental cost accounting "where the rubber meets the road" for the foreseeable future. Indeed, some observers would say that success in this endeavor is critical to business success in a world that is increasingly environmentally conscious and globally competitive.

ENVIRONMENTAL COST ACCOUNTING AS A BUSINESS INTEGRATION TOOL

An additional utility of environmental cost accounting relates to its growing acceptance as the measurement tool for compliance management systems and environmental management systems—cornerstones of environmental performance expected in the world community.

In most firms, environmental, health and safety (EH&S) activities are performed at corporate, division, and plant levels by individuals in diverse functional organizations within the firm. For the most part, these activities result in costs that must be borne by products, divisions, and the corporation. As such, alignment of these activities (and associated costs) within the corporation is often problematic since the activities create costs that reduce the earnings that line managers are responsible for but that are perceived as being generated by nonline organizations. What is needed to properly align environmental activities and performance with the other activities and performances of the firm (especially earnings and cash flow) is a total business approach that incorporates environmental performance.

Environmental cost accounting provides the means to transform seemingly uncoordinated EH&S activities into an integrated component of a business plan—and one that is based on reliable environmental costs.

From an organizational perspective, more progressive organizations are implementing a matrix organizational structure that includes the major functions responsible for manufacturing costs. One organization in particular has a manufacturing committee comprised of the directors of manufacturing for each major product line—engineering, corporate EH&S, and environmental directors for each major product line. Appropriate staff functions attend meetings to ensure completeness and to provided expertise as needed (e.g., legal environmental law experts, accounting, and public affairs). To complete the business system, the members of the manufacturing committee participate in the development of the business plan for their respective businesses. In this way, environmental performance is built into manufacturing costs and thus into the individual business plans. Further, environmental performance (including waste reduction) is incorporated into business unit performance metrics by corporate management.

This combination of organizational structure and business performance metrics contributes to proper alignment of environmental activities. Since cost reduction and competitiveness are essential to business survival, managers are continuously forced to examine product design, process technology, engineering standards for building new plants, and business delivery.

ENVIRONMENTAL COST ACCOUNTING AS AN INDISPENSABLE REPORTING TOOL

Organizations that have identified their environmental costs and built this information into their existing management accounting system or have established a separate information system to collect this data have a resource that goes beyond providing management with improved environmental cost information. This latter benefit is sufficient reason to adopt environmental cost accounting, but there is an additional benefit.

As society demands additional accountability from management on its environmental performance, any internal system that assists management in demonstrating its performance will be of value, provided it is sufficiently reliable.

Already on the horizon are at least two examples of external accountability. The first, "green accounting," has been proposed in Europe and would make management account for the use of resources consumed in production and the damage to the environment associated with its processes. The thrust of this concept is on quantifying the cost to society of using natural resources or of damaging the environment and goes beyond the actual costs incurred in manufacturing products. An environmental cost system, however, could be useful in studying alternative raw materials, waste disposal technologies, and processes that will permit management to explain its decisions.

Another proposal, originating in the United States, would require petroleum companies to be liable for restoration of environmental damages associated with both on-shore and off-shore environmental incidents. This proposal is referred to as Natural Resource Damage Assessments. The availability of an environmental cost-accounting system by petroleum companies would assist them in quantifying the cost of restoration, as the majority of the cost elements would probably be in such a system.

THE LONG-TERM PAYOFF: REMAINING COMPETITIVE AND BECOMING ENVIRONMENTALLY RESPONSIBLE SIMULTANEOUSLY

A properly designed environmental cost-accounting system provides management with the information needed to make more informed business decisions in a society that demands better environmental stewardship and seeks sustainable development. These increasing demands require resources and involve trade-offs. Environmental cost accounting assists in the identification of relevant costs and their quantification in the present and the future—that is, in the short term and in the long term.

Since the firm must remain viable and earn sufficient profits to pay for higher standards of environmental stewardship, management must make sound business decisions about its product lines and ensure that it maintains a stable of products (product mix) that generates sufficient earnings over the long term to pay for required environmental excellence. Thus, maintaining sufficient cash flows is critical to successful management. Whether the cash is generated by cost savings or by additional revenues, management will be assisted by the information emanating from a properly designed environmental cost-accounting system.

CASE STUDY

IMPROVED PRODUCT COSTS OBTAINED BY APPLICATION OF ACTIVITY-BASED COSTING TO ENVIRONMENTAL ACTIVITIES

The case study situation is as follows:

- A chemical plant manufactures two products, product A and product B, in equal quantities.
- Manufacturing costs other than overhead costs are assigned directly to product A and product B.
- Overhaul costs consist primarily of environmental costs that can be categorized as compliance costs (e.g., permitting and reporting), prevention costs (e.g., air emission control), and waste disposal costs (e.g., on-site and off-site treatment).
- Traditional overhead allocation method has been based on production quantities.
- Activity-based costing techniques have been employed to identify environmental activities and relate them and related costs to products A and B in a more precise manner.

Traditional Costing

Figure 27–2 illustrates the traditional allocation of environmental costs to products A and B.

FIGURE 27–2

Visual Demonstration of Improved Cost Allocation

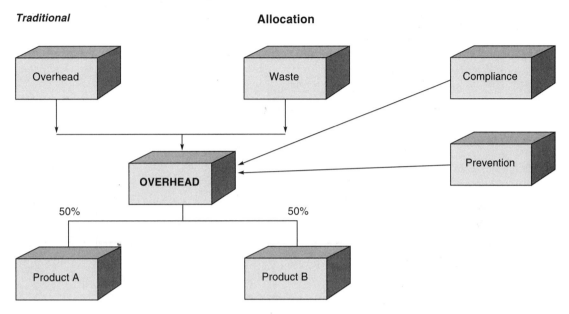

The actual costs for each component of environmental activity have been calculated as follows:

Compliance	$ 100,000
Prevention	300,000
Waste disposal	600,000
Total:	$1,000,000

Environmental Costs

Since each product is produced in equal quantities and no efforts have been made to more accurately trace environmental costs to each product, product A is allocated $500,000 and product B $500,000.

Activity-Based Costing

By carefully reviewing process flows and determining quantities of waste produced from each product's process as well as interviewing production and environmental staff, we are able to implement activity-based costing—that is, to identify all activities related to protecting the environment, accumulate the costs pertaining to those activities, and then to better relate those costs to the products.

From the statement above, one can reasonably infer that the costs of each activity (using the general activities: compliance, prevention, and waste disposal) may be increased over levels identified in the traditional model. Interviews and detailed reviews of plant records are likely to identify additional subactivities and "hidden costs" (e.g., laboratory analysis, computer costs, clerical effort, etc.). However, for this example, assume that ABC resulted in the same dollar costs for each activity since we want to demonstrate the impact of an improved product cost allocation. To do this, look at each activity in more detail, as follows:

First, the review of compliance activities revealed that 75 percent of the costs related to permitting and reporting pertained to product A and only 25 percent to product B.

Second, in the area of prevention, it was determined that 40 percent of the costs related to operating and maintaining air filters related to product A and 60 percent to product B.

Third, the review of waste disposal activities showed that the vast majority of the costs for on-site and off-site treatment were related to product A—80 percent versus only 20 percent for product B. This determination was based on the kinds of wastes generated by each process, the quantities of wastes resulting from each process, and the waste treatment/disposal.

These more specific allocations are summarized in Figure 27–3 and can be compared to the traditional allocations in Figure 27–1.

FIGURE 27–3

Visual Demonstration of Improved Cost Allocation

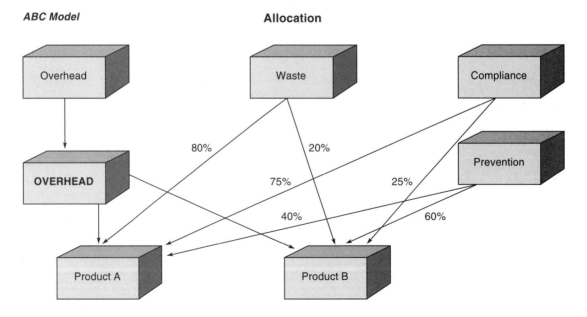

TABLE 27-1

Comparison of Product Costs under Traditional and ABC Techniques

	Traditional		Activity-Based Costing	
	Product A	*Product B*	*Product A*	*Product B*
Compliance	$ 50,000	$ 50,000	$ 75,000	$ 25,000
Prevention	$150,000	$150,000	$120,000	$180,000
Waste Disposal	$300,000	$300,000	$480,000	$120,000
Total	$500,000	$500,000	$675,000	$325,000

Comparison of Environmental Costs Allocated to Products A and B

Table 27–1 presents product costs related to environmental activities for product A and product B under both traditional and ABC techniques:

As Table 27–1 shows, product A was allocated an additional $175,000 of environmental costs, while product B's allocation was correspondingly decreased. Thus, the profitability of product A is decreased, while product B's is increased. This observation affects the financial performance evaluation of the products internally and externally as well as strategic planning, including capital budgeting decisions. Indeed, the future of product A may be called into question.

Of course, this analysis provides management with better cost information and points them to waste-minimization efforts, especially for product A. Raw material changes, process changes, and new disposal technologies must all be looked at as possible options to reduce waste disposal costs. Failure to examine these options and make prudent decisions could result in a noncompetitive product.

BIOGRAPHY

David W. Vogel

David W. Vogel is director of environmental cost accounting at The Gauntlett Group. He has 27 years' experience in financial accounting and has been a leader for the past five years in Environmental Cost Accounting. He has developed and applied tools to solve financial and environmental issues relevant to product lines, facilities, disposal sites, and financial reporting issues. Mr. Vogel has conducted Environmental Cost Accounting studies at numerous large multi-product plants with the purpose of defining, identifying, and measuring environmental costs and assigning these costs to individual product lines. Mr. Vogel has identified alternative methodologies to allocate "orphan site" costs (i.e., those related to inactive plants, discontinued operations and

Superfund sites) to individual businesses and/or corporate accounts. Mr. Vogel is a specialist in environmental regulations, environmental control technologies and remediation. He combines his accounting knowledge and environmental knowledge to develop appropriate solutions.

NOTE

1. The term is defined in a June 1995 publication of the United States Environmental Protection Agency entitled *An Introduction to Environmental Accounting as a Business Management Tool: Key Concepts and Terms* (EPA 742-R-95-001).

PART SEVEN

ISO 14000 in Perspective

CHAPTER 28

Waste Reduction: The Cost-Effective Approach to ISO 14000 Compliance

Burt Hamner

INTRODUCTION

One of the most significant environmental issues facing industry today is responding to the challenge of the new ISO 14001 environmental management systems (EMS) standard. An organization's environmental stakeholders, which may include customers, government, communities, public interest groups, and others, may ask an organization to obtain ISO 14001 certification to demonstrate that the organization is managing its environmental responsibilities in an organized and serious fashion. Developing an EMS that meets the ISO 14001 requirements will be a significant undertaking for any organization. Obtaining ISO certification of the EMS will require additional efforts, especially if an outside certifying body is to audit the EMS and verify that it meets the ISO 14001 requirements.

The ISO 14001 EMS standard only specifies the structure of the EMS. It is up to the organization that seeks compliance with the standard to determine what the content of the structure will be. In other words, the organization has to decide what it wants to do regarding the environment.

ISO 14001 specifies that the EMS must include a commitment to compliance with applicable regulations. For companies that take a minimum approach, having an ISO-certified EMS is a complex and costly way to ensure and prove that compliance is maintained. A minimum approach does not save organizations money except perhaps in the avoidance of penalties for noncompliance and reduced risks from noncompliance. For companies that go beyond a compliance, an ISO EMS can be a cost-saving system that systematically eliminates production inefficiencies and environmental risks throughout the product life cycle, from natural resources to suppliers to customers and product disposal. For companies that want to reduce environmental costs and risks, waste reduction is one of the most important operational goals that an EMS can achieve.

Generic Approach to EMS

The ISO 14001 EMS standard is intended to be applicable to any organization of any size, anywhere. Accordingly, it provides a very general structure for an EMS. It does not require that an organization implement any particular environmental management strategy. It only requires that organizations have a commitment to compliance, continual improvement, and pollution prevention. *Commitment* is not defined in the ISO 14001 standard, but it is expected that an organization that makes a policy commitment will be able to demonstrate to interested parties that the commitment is in fact implemented. This will be a necessary condition for achieving ISO certification of an EMS.

Variation in the Perceived Quality of EMS

Because the EMS standard is very general, organizations will develop and implement EMSs that are focused on subjects in which the organizations have a particular interest. Thus, one company, which is a retailer of clothes and which does no manufacturing, may have an EMS that is largely focused on the environmental behavior of its suppliers. Another company, which makes a product that is dangerous if used improperly, may have an EMS focused on designing a more environmentally friendly product and on recovery and recycling of the product. For outsiders, this means that one ISO EMS cannot be compared to another ISO EMS, except that both meet the structural requirements of ISO 14001 and that the certifying body has determined that the policy, objectives, and targets of the EMS are in fact met. To answer the question as to whether the company is environmentally responsible regarding various topics, the observer needs to know exactly what the company's EMS is trying to accomplish. The fact that the EMS is certified does not mean that the company is achieving any particular environmental accomplishments.

ISO 14001 requires a commitment to compliance with applicable laws and regulations. These will differ widely from country to country. Accordingly, organizations in countries with few environmental regulations may be able to meet the compliance commitment with relatively little effort. In countries with no laws regarding the disposal of toxic waste, for example, an organization's EMS does not have to address this subject.

In summary, ISO 14001 certification does not enable an outside party to determine if one organization is more "eco-friendly" than another or if an organization is making significant progress towards being more eco-friendly. Organizations that want to convince stakeholders they are eco-friendly will need to provide information about what exactly their EMS is doing, not just provide evidence that their EMS is certified to ISO standards.

Potential Reaction from Public Interest Groups

There are some indications that public interest groups are beginning to take a hostile attitude towards ISO 14001 because certification to the standard does not enable stakeholders to determine whether an organization is really eco-friendly. In Europe, a major public interest group has characterized the ISO 14001 effort as an attempt to weaken European environmental management standards that are already in place. There appears to be a possibility that some environmental advocates will view ISO 14001 certification as a smokescreen, used by organizations that are not really interested in environmental improvement but that are simply making sure their environmental affairs are under control. The next few years will be a watershed in the acceptance of ISO 14001 certification.

Strategic Approach to ISO 14000

Companies that are concerned about their environmental reputations, costs, and risks need to take a strategic approach to ISO 14001 certification that reflects both the uncertainty about its political and social acceptance, and the reality that an ISO EMS only accomplishes what the company decides it wants to accomplish. In particular, companies need to recognize that stakeholders who are actively concerned about environmental performance will probably want to know the details of the EMS, including specific objectives and targets.

Developing an ISO EMS is a complex and costly project for organizations. A great deal of documentation and systems integration is needed. Determining just what the EMS is supposed to accomplish takes substantial data collection, discussion, and negotiation. If the objective of the EMS is to demonstrate that the company is committed to compliance with applicable regulations, the EMS is not likely to reduce the company's operating costs (although it may reduce the potential for noncompliance penalties and other liabilities). However, if the EMS is focused on eliminating waste and pollution at its source, the EMS becomes an efficiency system that can reduce operating costs significantly.

The recommended strategy for companies interested in eventual ISO 14001 certification is based on the quality of the ISO EMS standard, its potential politics, and the real economics of environmental management. Organizations, especially companies with international markets, should do the following:

1. Seriously study and adopt the framework of EMS that is outlined in ISO 14001. This framework was developed by many experienced environmental managers in many countries and provides a sound basis for organizing an EMS.

2. Establish objectives and targets for the EMS that will result in elimination of waste and consequent pollution at the source, meaning at the process or production unit level.

3. Begin implementing the EMS immediately and have a plan to implement the full EMS within a time frame of not more than two years.

4. Prepare a public report on corporate environmental performance that reflects both real and perceived environmental concern, includes real operational data, and describes realistic objectives and targets for achieving meaningful environmental results. This report may be more important to top management than to anyone else because it will identify major strategic issues for the company. Make sure the report is as honest and

objective as possible. If real problems about performance are identified by the draft report, implement targeted strategies to fix the problems and describe the strategies in the final report.

5. Communicate with all environmental stakeholders, and use the corporate environmental report to begin a dialogue with them regarding their concerns and expectations about corporate environmental performance. Stakeholders want to see what is actually being done, not a description of a management system. Environmental activists in particular want to see results, not procedures.

6. Carefully observe the ISO 14001 process using all available information sources. In Europe, environmental activists are attacking the ISO standard as being weaker than existing European standards. On the other hand, many U.S. organizations believe that the ISO EMS standard will help companies achieve meaningful organizational improvements, beyond the technical solutions for specific environmental problems.

7. Using information from environmental stakeholders and from internal sources, make a cost-benefit decision regarding whether ISO certification will be necessary. It may be that a solid environmental report identifying real progress towards meaningful goals will satisfy most stakeholders, without the cost and complexity of an ISO-certified EMS. On the other hand, stakeholder pressure or the need for tight internal controls may make an ISO-certified system either a marketing or a management imperative.

8. Do not attempt certification for at least a year after the ISO EMS standard is finalized. There is a real possibility that environmental interest group politics will denigrate the ISO 14001 label, and companies that really want to do better will be lumped together in the public eye with companies that are gross polluters and that have obtained ISO certification as a public relations device. The way for a concerned company to distinguish itself is to implement meaningful pollution-prevention and waste-reduction strategies and to report real facts and results to stakeholders, within a framework that is guided by the ISO EMS standard.

WASTE-REDUCTION STRATEGIES WITHIN AN ISO 14000 FRAMEWORK

Although ISO 14001 includes pollution-control and treatment within its definition of *pollution prevention,* environmental management experts commonly agree that waste reduction and pollution prevention denote reducing the generation of pollution at the production unit source, through means such as more efficient equipment, housekeeping, maintenance, training, and process control, and by eliminating the use of toxic input materials. (See Table 28–1.) When organizations regard pollution as wasted resources and defective production, they can realize production cost savings and improved efficiency by eliminating the waste.

T A B L E   28-1

Pollution-Prevention Hierarchy

**Source Reduction:
Don't Buy It**

End product redesign

Hazardous chemical
substitution

Hazardous chemical
modification

Purchasing and
inventory control

Best management
practices and good
housekeeping

Water conservation

Waste Reduction: Don't Waste It

Benchmarking

Employee training

Maintenance

Process control

Process modification

Equipment modification

Recycling: Don't Throw It Away

Closed-loop recycling

Waste segregation

Reuse wastes

Reclaim wastes

Treatment: Turn Wastes into Resources

Convert wastes into new products

Find outside users for wastes

There are many different ways to achieve waste reduction in an organization. The ISO 14001 EMS standard includes a number of elements where waste-reduction strategies are appropriate and can add value.

Environmental Policy Considerations

ISO 14001 requires a written environmental policy that includes a commitment to pollution prevention. ISO 14001 defines pollution prevention as "use of practices, materials or products that avoid, reduce or control pollution, which may include recycling, treatment, process changes, control mechanisms, efficient use of resources and materials substitution."

Most managers realize that controlling and treating pollution is an expense, not an investment. If an organization wants to realize significant cost savings from an EMS, its environmental policy needs to clearly state that the top priority of the EMS is to prevent the generation of waste and pollution in the first place, thereby eliminating the costs of pollution control and treatment and also improving production efficiency. The objectives and targets to achieve this goal are described in the planning section of the EMS.

Environmental Aspects

ISO 14001 defines *environmental aspects* as "elements of an organization's activities, products or services which can interact with the environment." ISO 14001 requires that organizations have a procedure to identify their environmental aspects that can have a significant impact on the environment and to consider these impacts in setting objectives and targets for the EMS.

For waste reduction to be successful, it is very important that the identification of environmental aspects includes a definition of the source that creates the concern. For example, "waste water containing toxic chemicals" may be a significant environmental aspect of operations. But this alone does not help the EMS focus on the source of the problem. For a true waste-reduction focus, the aspect should be defined as "waste water from production unit(s) XXX" or a similar, process-oriented definition. Establishing which production units are truly responsible for the existence of a significant environmental aspect of operations is the first step in an EMS that is designed to prevent pollution.

Objectives and Targets

ISO 14001 requires that organizations establish environmental objectives and targets at each relevant function and level within the organization. For waste reduction, the relevant function and level is the production unit. General objectives and targets should be broken down into production unit targets for those units that are responsible for creating significant environmental concerns. For example, a factory objective and target may be "to reduce the use of water by 20 percent in two years." At the production-unit level, the objective and target may be "to reduce the use of water at production unit #4 by 30 percent in one year." The combination of production unit targets enables the factory to meet its overall targets. By focusing on the production unit targets, the EMS treats pollution as a production issue and does not become overly focused on pollution control and treatment.

Structure and Responsibility

When the EMS is focused on pollution control and treatment, the responsibility for implementing it falls solely on the environmental department. When the EMS is designed to treat pollution as a production inefficiency problem, it becomes the responsibility of everyone in the organization. Environmental and waste-reduction responsibilities should be part of all job descriptions and, most importantly, included in job-performance evaluations. People do what they get measured for. If meeting the waste-reduction objectives and targets is a factor in individual performance measurement, people will work to meet the targets. It is very important for top management to understand that pollution-control engineers are not responsible for the generation of waste. This is the responsibility of the production staff and engineers, and they need to be evaluated on their performance in this area.

Training

Training is fundamental to the success of an EMS focused on waste reduction. Production employees and all who support them, including purchasing, engineering, maintenance, shipping, and others, need to understand the many tools they have available to prevent waste from being generated.

ISO requires that training include the potential environmental impacts of work activities, roles, and responsibilities as well as the benefits of improvement. To stimulate waste reduction, training should also include measurement and allocation of the true costs of waste. Waste costs much more than is usually recognized. Costs include lost raw materials, replacement materials, excess capacity needed to accommodate inefficiency, waste collection and handling, land for treatment equipment, equipment, treatment chemicals, energy, and much more. By training all employees to be aware of the actual costs of the waste they generate and by training them to control those costs, the EMS becomes a significant tool for productivity improvement. (Table 28–1 suggests key topics for employee training. Topics higher up the list are more important than those below, as these enable the prevention of pollution earlier in the production process.)

Operational Control

ISO 14001 requires that the EMS include specific environmental criteria in the operations and activities that have significant environmental aspects. This is a relatively generic requirement, but there are three specific areas where an EMS can play a major role in significantly reducing waste: cost management, managing suppliers, and monitoring and measurement.

Cost Management

As described earlier, pollution and waste cost most organizations much more than they realize. Identifying the true total cost of waste is fundamental for long-term success in waste reduction. After all, it is not possible to know how much you can save by waste reduction if you don't know how much you are spending on waste now. Once true costs are known, they should be allocated back to the production units that are responsible for generating them. If the cost of waste is considered overhead, the units that produce the least waste carry an extra and unfair burden, and the units that generate the most waste get off without paying their fair share for waste management. This tends to subsidize the most wasteful processes and penalize the least wasteful. When supervisors are charged directly for their unit's waste, they begin minimizing the costs by reducing the waste generated. The EMS should therefore include accounting and financial functions as well as production and waste-management functions.

Managing Suppliers

ISO requires that the EMS include procedures to manage goods and services and suppliers and contractors used by the organization. Managing suppliers is a key element in waste reduction. The basic premise of waste reduction is if you don't buy it, it can't become waste. Organizations can work with their suppliers to substitute non-toxic materials for toxic ones, reduce incoming packaging, and return packaging to suppliers. Suppliers can also be directed to supply the organization with more environmentally friendly materials and to show the buyer that the supplier has its own EMS focused on waste reduction. This strategy leads to cost savings for the organization and improved reliability of suppliers who are reducing their own environmental costs and risks.

Monitoring and Measurement

ISO 14001 requires organizations to measure and monitor on a regular basis the key characteristics of operations that can have significant environmental impacts. In most companies, this takes the form of measuring pollution discharges to ensure they are within limits set by the government. But this approach does not help the companies prevent pollution from generation. To promote waste reduction, wastes should be monitored and measured at the process level so the operators can see exactly what is wasted and the EMS can focus on the production units that are generating the wastes with the highest costs and the greatest potential impacts. The measurements can be used to allocate waste costs back to the production units in support of the EMS cost-management elements.

Auditing

ISO 14001 requires that organizations have a procedure to audit their EMS. This is a systems audit only. To identify opportunities for waste reduction, the EMS should also include regular process waste-reduction audits. These audits examine the production processes to determine how much and what kind of waste is generated, how much the waste costs the organization, and what happens to the waste. The information gathered is used to update the EMS and set new objectives and targets as necessary.

ISO 14001 requires continual improvement of the EMS. If organizations want continual improvement to mean saving more money, the waste reduction audits are the tools that will identify cost-saving opportunities on an ongoing basis.

CONCLUSION

It is up to each organization to determine exactly what it expects its ISO 14001 EMS to do. Some organizations will only be interested in the "seal of approval" for its EMS so it can satisfy stakeholders that the organization is effectively managing its environmental affairs. Other organizations will want to make sure that the significant investment in an ISO 14001-compliant EMS has a good payback. These organizations will want to ensure that the EMS is designed as a production-efficiency and waste-reduction system that results in reducing environmental costs and risks. Within the ISO 14001 framework, there are a number of opportunities to implement waste-reduction strategies that can achieve these goals. But top management has to make the decision to do it.

ISO 14001 certification may become a necessity for some businesses in some markets. It is not likely, however, to be necessary for the majority of businesses. Certification may also prove to be a politically sensitive issue if companies in countries with few or o environmental protection laws become certified, or if a certified company has a major environmental disaster that radical environmental groups use to discredit the ISO 14001 standard. As the generic nature of ISO 14001 becomes more widely recognized, stakeholders with a serious concern about an organization's environmental performance are likely to ask for the intimate details of the EMS, especially the specific objectives and targets that the organization set, and the organizations' progress in meeting those targets. If the objectives and targets are found to be wanting, the fact that the EMS is certified will not be very convincing to stakeholders who want environmental protection.

Companies can get the best out of ISO 14001 by implementing an EMS that follows the ISO 14001 structure and that focuses on real waste reduction, environmentally friendly product design, use of environmentally responsible suppliers, and solid documentation of actual results obtained. By providing a corporate environmental report that describes the EMS and provides solid data on accomplishments, stakeholders can be satisfied that the organization is in fact protecting the environment to the fullest extent feasible, and top management can be sure that their EMS system is a tool for long-term productivity improvement and increased market share.

BIOGRAPHY

Burton Hamner

Burton Hamner is an Environmental Management and Pollution Prevention Specialist for Louis Berger International, Inc., one of the world's largest international transportation and environmental planning consultancies. He works as the Corporate Programs Manager for the ASEAN Environmental Improvement Project (EIP). Mr. Hamner's responsibilities include industrial environmental training, corporate consultation, factory opportunity assessments, clean technology transfer, information resource development, government and NGO program design, and academic curriculum development. He has produced several highly successful pollution prevention training courses, attended by over 800 industry managers in Southeast Asia. He also advises several of the Philippines' largest corporations on environmental management. Mr. Hamner designed and directs the Centers for Industrial Technology and Environmental Management established by EIP in Singapore, Manila and Jakarta. He is a part-time faculty member at the Asian Institute of Management, Operations Management area.

Before joining EIP, Burton Hamner was the Pollution Prevention Manager for a U.S. consulting company, providing pollution prevention training in Asia and helping U.S. companies develop pollution prevention plans. He spent three years as an environmental planner with the Washington Department of Ecology, where he supervised over 100 companies preparing and implementing five-year Pollution Prevention Plans in compliance with state regulations. Mr. Hamner is a recognized expert on ISO 14001, environmental management accounting and financial analysis, and on clean technology information sources. He has published papers in academic, technical and popular journals, and given hundreds of presentations on pollution prevention and corporate environmental management strategies. His degrees include business administration (MBA, University of Washington), marine environmental policy (MMA, University of Washington), the history of science (BA *cum laude,* Harvard University), and many certified environmental and management training courses.

Burton Hamner
Louis Berger International, Inc.
12/F Sagittarius Building, HV dela Costa St
Salcedo Village, 1227 Makati, Philippines
phone 632-816-6576
fax 632-818-6470
e-mail asean2@mozcom.com

Environmental Management System Trends in Asia: Implications for ISO 14000 Implementation

David Nelson

INTRODUCTION

Any discussion of environmental management in Asia should start with a simple question: What and where is Asia? Most of us are familiar with China, Hong Kong and Taiwan (sometimes called "Greater China"), Japan, and the Association of Southeast Asian Nations (Asean) countries of Thailand, Malaysia, Indonesia, Philippines, Singapore, Brunei, and now Vietnam. Other Asian countries are, of course, the Koreas, Myanmar (Burma), Laos, and Cambodia. India, Pakistan, and Bangladesh are also often considered part of Asia but are sometimes relegated to their own region. Finally and importantly, the Russian Far East (RFE) is geographically and to some extent culturally part of Asia. While some writers call Australia and New Zealand Asian countries, this chapter will not include them as such.

Asia is the most rapidly industrializing region of the world and home to the fastest-growing economies, megacities, and middle classes. The double-digit growth experienced by many Asian countries in recent years has also generated spectacular environmental problems. The air pollution of Bangkok, Taipei, and Jakarta is infamous, as are their traffic jams, both of which are getting worse.

According to the World Bank, air pollution in many large Chinese cities is a recognized leading cause of death. Most Asian megacities lack adequate sewage treatment facilities; hazardous waste, despite regulations prohibiting it, is discharged into the ground, into the rivers, and into the ocean. The rate of tropical deforestation in the region rivals South American clear-cutting. Extremely poor water quality, including groundwater, in many parts of Asia is a leading cause of exposure to enteric diseases and, increasingly, toxic chemicals. The region continues to industrialize in the face of a grossly underdeveloped environmental infrastructure.

In spite of these daunting problems, the situation may be slowly improving. A growing and better-educated middle class, financially powerful and increasingly empowered politically, has begun to demand of their governments and industries a more aggressive environmental agenda. Numerous other driving forces such as international trade agreements are also, in their own way, adding to this change. This is met in turn with growing interest in environmental protection strategies, including ISO 14000 management system standards.

No discussion of environmental management system trends in Asia should begin without recognizing that considerable differences in culture, communication styles, and business structures affect the implementation of such systems in extremely important ways. Richard Halloran, writing in the Spring 1996 issue of *Foreign Policy* ("The Rising East"), says:

> Westerners tend to be logical and analytical; Asians are more intuitive and sometimes more emotional. Westerners assert rights, Asians respond to obligations. In the West, the individual takes priority, in Asia, the community. Westerners, especially Americans, are governed by law and contract, Asians by custom and personal relations. In the West, decisions are made by voting; Asians decide by consensus.

Halloran's succinct summary has enormous implications for implementation of EMSs in Asia.

Those interested in environmental management systems in Asia will not only need to understand these differences but to embrace them. Key Asian environmental players are serious about and resigned to the inevitable regional and global implementation of ISO 14001 but are concerned that it is mostly a western environmental, and possibly trade-barrier, agenda.

How then, will ISO 14001 be implemented in Asia within its diverse cultural context? How will the developing economies and environmental policies of Asia interact with the West? Will ISO 14001 increase or decrease trade tensions? What does the West have to learn from Asian-style communication and consensus-building mechanisms, and does this have implications for more successful implementation of ISO 14001 within western corporate cultures? This brief chapter looks at regulatory and nonregulatory environmental change in Asia and concludes by suggesting how environmental management systems, in particular, ISO 14001, are being adopted throughout the region.

DRIVING FORCES FOR IMPLEMENTATION OF ENVIRONMENTAL MANAGEMENT SYSTEMS IN ASIA

Each region of the world is addressing, at various levels of sophistication, implementation of environmental management systems, depending on economic, cultural, and legal conditions. Europe, lacking the heavy enforcement regimes of the United States, has developed alternative EMS standards and regulations, such as BS7750 and the European Eco-Audit and Management Scheme (EMAS). Developing countries, however, have little history with such Western designs but must necessarily grapple with the coming of ISO 14000. This section looks at some of the reasons for environmental change in Asia and suggests ways in which it may affect the implementation of environmental management systems.

An Increase in Environmental Regulations

In the last decade, most Asian countries have seen a dramatic increase in the volume, sophistication, and scope of environmental regulations, especially in ASEAN. Various reasons account for this, including the agendas of multilateral lending and insurance institutions; trade agreements, especially those with environmental sanctions; pressure from the West; and an internal demand for a cleaner and better protected environment. With the coming of ISO 14001, an increasing number of Asian countries are coming to grips with the potential trade implications of the standards, and environmental regulatory agencies are acting accordingly, viewing their own agendas as necessarily complementing those of ISO.

It is tempting to believe, therefore, that Asia may be heading toward a command-and-control system of environmental regulations, including U.S.-style enforcement. But this is simply not the case.

While most Asian countries clearly have tougher enforcement, it is not true that they are adopting wholesale U.S.-style litigious systems. At the same time that environmental regulations are proliferating in Asian countries, alternative systems of dispute resolutions are being used. These are, of course, deeply rooted in the diverse cultures of the region and are mostly consensus-based systems.

Such mechanisms involve much more reconciliation on the part of regulatory agencies, the private sector and the public through formal and informal meetings, negotiations, and nonlegal mediation. Often, mutually agreed upon third parties carry these messages between stakeholders until a satisfactory result is obtained.

Thus, while their regulatory programs become increasingly sophisticated, frequently overseen by Western-educated doctorate engineers and scientists, stakeholders in Asia will continue to rely on their cultural perspective in the implementation of EMS programs. It is also accurate to report, however, that the courts are increasingly involved with environmental matters. This trend, though, still bears the cultural hallmark of Asian-style methods of communication and dispute resolution.

Increase in Public "Right-to-Know" Issues

It is conventional wisdom that in many parts of the world the public is demanding the "right-to-know" (RTK). This is not necessarily an environmental agenda, although it is fueled by and related to it. Massive environmental protests directly led to the overthrow of central European governments. Extensive studies of environmental pollution in central and eastern Europe, formerly state secrets before 1989, are now common knowledge, extracted from government files by an angry and demanding newly empowered citizenry. Bhopal arguably did more to sensitize Asians to the potential negative effects of toxic chemicals than it did Americans. This is because of Asia's close proximity to India as well as the similarities between India and Asian countries with regard to the potential of chemical exposures to large numbers of people.

This increase in the so-called RTK movement has clear empowerment in new enactment of U.S.-style Freedom of Information Act (FOIA) legislation in many Asian countries. This is true even in several Chinese provinces where a common citizen may now obtain records of environmental complaints lodged with the local agency.

Additional fuel for the environmental RTK movement is found in language in the Rio Declaration of 1992, signed by more than 175 countries. Principle 10 argues that individuals at the nation-state level have the "right" to environmental information. The principle also requires nations to provide "judicial and administrative" procedures that must include opportunities for rectification and relief. Westerners engaging Asian environmental officials are often surprised to find that the agencies take seriously the principles laid down in the Rio Declaration.

The Asian press also plays an important role in increasing public awareness of environmental problems, despite the fact that much of the press in Asia is controlled and censored. It is almost impossible to read a single issue of any major Asian newspaper without finding at least one critical article on the environment. Often, the article cries for more enforcement of regulations, an empowered citizenry, and stiffer penalties.

Increase in Regulatory Agendas of the West

The United States, certain European countries, Canada, and Australia heavily influence Asian regulatory agendas. This comes about through a variety of mechanisms, including formal regulatory training programs such as the United States Environmental Training Institute (USETI) and the international division of the Environmental Protection Agency. Additionally, the U.S. Securities and Exchange Commission's (SEC) requirement to disclose environmental liabilities of publicly held corporations to their shareholders, including foreign environmental liabilities, has the arguable if unintended effect of extraterritoriality application of a U.S. environmental agenda. An Asian's view of U.S.-style environmental protection is, not surprisingly, one of heavy-handed enforcement, retroactive liability, and extreme financial penalties.

Canada, long active in international standard setting through the Canadian Standards Association (CSA), is a major player in Asian environmental regulatory and EMS affairs. Canada has an advanced program for environmental auditor certification, much further along than any program in the United States. Through Canada's international aid agency (Canadian International Development Agency), it regularly counsels Asian countries on regulatory and EMS program development.

Increase in "Formal" Environmental-Auditing Requirements

Environmental auditing, exclusively an export of the West, is increasingly used by sophisticated Asian industry as a management tool and by government agencies, most typically in enforcement and consent agreements. In fact, it is increasingly used entirely in lieu of a financial penalty. This is a very Asian approach. Mutually rewarding and consensus-based, it provides the opportunity for corrective action by a company at the same time the government is involved, but not involved directly. Unlike in the West, the trend in Asia is to not make enforcement-related environmental audits available to the public. However, it is important to note that the public is increasingly demanding that they do so, supporting the environmental RTK movement discussed earlier.

The Indonesian environmental auditing program, a world-class document at least on paper and increasingly in application, was essentially developed by European aid programs. Singapore has an auditing requirement, and Malaysia and Thailand are considering it. China has an "audit agenda" (i.e., enforcement) targeted at American and European multinationals. Considerable confusion exists in Asia, however, with regard to the difference between environmental impact assessments (EIAs) and auditing; they are often incorrectly seen as the same thing. Numerous training programs currently underway in Asia are bound to correct this misconception.

Multi- and Bilateral Development Agencies

The World Bank, the Asian Development Bank, and the European Bank for Reconstruction and Development are considered multilateral development banks (MDBs); they lend to or insure government and private-sector projects. Many developed countries, such as the United States, Canada, Australia, the United Kingdom, Germany, and Japan have bilateral development agencies, lending to or insuring only their own companies. Since 1980, most major MDBs have developed environmental policies. The bilaterals have more recently developed or are in the process of developing environmental policies, all of which affect business deals by becoming incorporated as loan covenants, the breach of which may result in cancellation of loans and insurance coverage.

The U.S. government agency Overseas Private Investment Corporation (OPIC) is very active in many Asian countries and has a substantially developed environmental policy, virtually required by Congress through the Foreign Assistance Act. Similarly, Canada's Export Development Corporation (EDC) and Australia's Export Finance and Insurance Corporation (EFIC) are active in Asia and have environmental covenants in their loans, loan guarantees, and political risk insurance policies.

Most, if not all, multi- and bilateral development agencies have recently expressed an interest in environmental auditing systems as well as ISO 14000. The World Bank has recently undergone extensive internal training on ISO 14000 and has issued a paper on its views encouraging environmental auditing as an enhancement to a management system. It is too early in the process to predict whether ISO 14001 certification or implementation will become a condition of doing business with the MDBs; however, there is a great deal of speculation that it will. It is arguably much more cost-effective for them to do so rather than spend their limited resources on conducting ongoing monitoring of each company and project in far reaches of the globe.

Rio Declaration on the Environment and Development

The largest gathering ever of heads of state met in Brazil in 1992 to agree on and draft a "blueprint for sustainable development." The so-called Rio Declaration is influencing Asia, despite the conference's failures. It is difficult to meet with any high-ranking Asian environmental official without raising the subject of Rio.

Why is this the case? Why is the Rio Declaration not having the same effect in the United States where the declaration is seen by many environmentalists as a vague, underfunded promise without substance or effect? The declaration calls for the development of the "polluter-pays" principle, already adopted in the United States. While U.S. citizens are familiar with this concept,it is in fact a new concept in many parts of the world. It is tempting therefore, and in fact irresistible in developing countries, to "blame it on Rio" when adopting such a system.

Importantly, the declaration also calls for the development of environmental RTK laws, as mentioned previously, as well as an overall increase in environmental programs. Finally, the declaration calls for the adoption of "transparency" in the public process; while related to RTK laws, there is an important distinction. While mere access to environmental information is important, it is also crucial to allow organized, public input—through, for example, public hearings—on projects that may impact the environment.

International Trade Agreements, Conventions, and Protocol

More than 120 international environmental agreements have been passed, most after 1979. Seventeen of these agreements, such as the North American Free Trade Agreement (NAFTA) and the Convention on International Trade in Endangered Species (CITIES), have trade sanctions for violations.

The World Trade Organization (WTO) has resurrected long quiescent environmental dispute-resolution committees under the former GATT, and they are extremely active in hearings regarding environment–trade conflicts. In fact, the first ruling ever by the new WTO at the beginning of 1996 was in *favor* of a complaint brought against the United States by Venezuela and Brazil, arguing that EPA regulations (Clean Air Act) on gasoline standards discriminate against foreign producers. Many predict a huge increase of environment-trade conflicts in the near future, as nontariff barriers continue to be reduced worldwide, only to be replaced with another form of competitive advantage disagreements, that is, environmental trade barriers (ETBs).

NAFTA-like agreements are likely to be the wave of future trade agreements; however, in Asia, the environmental side agreements were troubling. Issues of sovereignty, effective extraterritoriality application of one country's environmental agenda onto another, and enforcement are some of the issues of concern. The recent Asia-Pacific Economic Cooperation (APEC) meeting, concerned that the West has an agenda with harmonization of international environmental, health, and safety standards, suggested that these issues "were not part of" the negotiations.

Environmental Management Systems of Multinationals

Multinational corporations (MNCs), sometimes called "transnationals," typically have corporate-based EMS systems, the implementation of which varies, especially in developing countries. Companies choose from a menu of possibilities, such as compliance with corporate policy, U.S. EPA standards, World Bank standards, host-country regulations, or even a combination of these. Most companies require local plants, at least theoretically, to be in compliance with local regulations. Problems arise when a large MNC, corporately based in a developed country, locates a plant in a developing country without substantive environmental programs or infrastructures.

ISO 9000 has long been accepted in Asian countries. In 1993, more Asian facilities were certified than U.S. facilities. While the vast majority of these facilities were owned by western companies, they were and continue to be managed by Asians. And while United States' industries have "caught up" with ISO 9000 implementation in this country, ISO 9000 remains an important initiative of its own accord in Asia where it is difficult to read a newspaper without seeing an advertisement from an Asian-based company touting its recent certification.

Numerous training workshops on ISO 9000 have been conducted, sometimes by U.S. manufacturers as members of their local American Chambers of Commerce (AMCHAMs) and by European counterparts. This has the effect, of course, of transferring the management systems of U.S. companies into the business structures of Asian economies.

An increasing number of facilities in Asia, owned by Europeans but managed by Asians, are certifying to the European Eco-Audit and Management Scheme (EMAS). Similarly, the BS 7750 EMS standard is seen by a seemingly growing number of Asian companies as the flagship EMS standard, although this standard is also sometimes applied to the facility by a European parent company. Nevertheless, this has once again the effect of transferring western views of environmental management systems.

MNCs typically have sophisticated personnel responsible for implementation of EMS systems in their foreign plants. These professionals, whether expatriates or locals, often have extensive corporate training; some have spent considerable time, often years, at the parent company, enhancing their technical and managerial skills. These people, upon returning to their homeland, frequently interact with in-country environmental regulatory personnel, once again influencing local governments, business sectors, and economies. Many Asian environmental regulatory officials received their ISO 9000 and ISO 14000 training by attending western industry-sponsored workshops.

Environmental Nongovernmental Organizations (NGOs)

Asian NGOs, now numbering in the thousands, are increasing in numbers, influence, and success. While people are still imprisoned in several Asian countries for environmental activism, virtually all countries are seeing a rise in NGO activity, even China. They equally pressure MNCs and governments, and they do so with a combination of changing legal systems, political pressure, and international networking, increasingly via the Internet. Several Asian NGOs regularly access, via personal computers, the U.S. EPA enforcement database to embarrass, during public hearings and via press releases, violation-plagued companies desiring to locate or expand their operations in Asia.

Another form of grassroots environmental protest clearly on the rise throughout Asia, technically not organized NGO activity but nonetheless effective, is "eco-vigilantism." This term applies to the practice of local citizenry shutting down polluting plants, often by destroying or otherwise disabling important facility infrastructures such as power lines or access roads. This is most often performed by groups frustrated by lax or corrupt regulatory enforcement and is targeted at local plants as well as polluting MNCs. Several MNCs in Asia have recently reported that local citizens have demanded ISO 14000 certification of their facilities.

INTEGRATION AND SUMMARY

This chapter has briefly reviewed the diversity of environmental agendas and forces currently underway in Asia. An increase in regulations and enforcement, expanded access to public files, auditing and environmental labeling requirements outside of ISO 14000, influence by trade and other international agreements, policies of multilateral development banks, and an increasingly empowered NGO community, along with the pressures of ISO 14000 itself, all add up to unquestionable environmental change in Asia. Any company operating in Asia, regardless of the origin of ownership and management, will need to understand, respond to, and integrate these often disparate environmental issues within their corporate cultures.

This need is, of course, met by the implementation of an environmental management system, best exemplified by ISO 14001. If properly executed, it will respond to most, but perhaps not all, of these factors. True, environment–trade conflicts are exceedingly complex and are mostly outside the realm of the day-to-day operations of a manufacturing facility. Nevertheless, as larger industries that play on the world stage are, as an industrial sector, dragged into the environment–trade fray, they will benefit collectively and individually by implementation of EMS programs.

The Asian companies that will suffer most are the small and medium enterprises (SMEs), currently comprising an enormous sector in and of itself and providing huge numbers of jobs but typically lacking the resources for even a minimal attempt at environmental accountability. Larger industries in Asia, whether owned and operated by locals or foreigners, will benefit by providing EMS resources to smaller companies at the early stages of ISO 14000 developments. The vendor-supplier-customer-client loop is brought close together, a requirement of ISO 14000 EMS systems anyway, and such a process cannot but help overall implementation of ISO 14000 in the region.

Important differences between the West and Asia still remain with regard to the perception and expectation of ISO 14001. U.S. companies considering ISO 14001 are preoccupied with trying to predict whether the documentation required by the process will result in files papered with "smoking guns," potential fodder for government or third-party lawsuits. Many Europeans are engrossed with the notion that ISO 14001 is not as robust a standard as BSI 7750 or EMAS. Asian companies, on the other hand, are seriously looking at the potential trade ramifications as well as the implications of ISO 14001 implementation in countries with little or no environmental infrastructure. Asian companies wonder: Isn't ISO 14001 *really* a western agenda that stands to become part of the environmental corporate culture in places largely unprepared in some ways to implement it?

What is currently different with regard to implementation of ISO 14001 in Asia? The following suggest some, but not all, ideas on this subject:

1. There is much more NGO involvement in Asia with regard to ISO 14000. For example, the sophisticated and well-funded Thailand Environment Institute (TEI) is a major player not only in its own country but regionally.

2. There is much more concern regarding the potential trade impacts of ISO 14000. This is openly discussed in training sessions as a "first question," unlike similar activities in the United States where queries are more typically oriented towards specific implementation of the standards.

3. In the West, ISO 14000 is "homegrown," that is, from European countries with enormous interest and by numerous stakeholders in the United States. In Asia, however, a variety of "menus" exist from which to choose: ISO 14000 policies of foreign companies, foreign AID programs, and Asian ISO 14000 programs. Similarly, much of Asia's ISO 14000 initiative comes from large western MNCs. The reverse is not true; that is, major ISO 14000 initiatives in the United States and Europe are not coming from Asian-owned companies.

4. ISO 14000 will be implemented in a region not accustomed to litigious societies.

5. By far, only big companies in Asia have shown some interest in ISO 14000, unlike the West where interest is beginning to trickle down to SMEs.

6. ISO 14000 will be implemented in a region of the world with a dearth of environmental infrastructure but greatly expanding energy and general infrastructure needs.

7. ISO 14000 will be implemented in a region of the world with dramatically changing environmental laws, regulations, policies, and legal systems. In the West, our similar environmental systems evolved relatively slowly, hand-in-hand with growth in scientific and technological understanding of environmental problems.

8. ISO 14000 is being implemented in a region where diverse cultures exist, each with its own type of economics, legal systems, business climate, and language. Yet these countries regularly and increasingly trade across borders, and their environmental management practices are sure to interact as never before.

9. ISO 14000 is being implemented in a region where environmental problems are extremely severe. It will also be implemented in a region where these problems are often expected, too simply in most cases, to be solved simply by the application of a "technological black box." Only recently has Asia looked to larger EMS, "holistic," U.S. NEPA-like paradigms of environmental problem solving.

10. ISO 14000 is being implemented in a region where publicly-held companies do not as yet have U.S. SEC-type environmental disclosures.

11. ISO 14000 is being implemented in a region where large companies interact with countless SMEs, most of which do not have the resources to implement *any* kind of environmental protection programs, let alone an EMS.

12. ISO 14000 will be implemented in a region where many governments shield companies from NGO activity. This is especially interesting where governments are partial owners in projects, particularly in the large extractive industries such as mining, forestry, and petroleum.

Many of these points will become, in the near future, environmental trade barrier issues. Many people, in developed and undeveloped countries alike, incorrectly believe that ISO 14000 will put an immediate system of accountability onto companies in developing countries and that this will lead to immediate improvement in environmental conditions. This simply will not happen, or at least not to the extent that they may wish. Additionally, other Asian companies following ISO 14000 incorrectly believe they cannot get certified if they do not have access to appropriate environmental infrastructure. This misconception is widespread in Asia. Still others believe that ISO 14000 may only be a western "paper game," played in the same manner that they achieved ISO 9000 certification. While many companies in the region worked hard to obtain their certification, as did their western counterparts, it is simply naive to think that graft and corruption have not penetrated ISO 9000 certification in Asia. This is certainly not to say that this problem is Asia-specific—it most certainly has happened elsewhere—but well-known cases in certain Asian countries are standouts. There is no reason to believe that ISO 14000 certification will not meet, in some cases, the same fate. In order for this particular issue to not become an environmental–trade conflict, it will have to be monitored carefully.

Finally, Asia is an exceedingly beautiful and culturally rich region of the world, home to half the world's population, and stands to, by the turn of the century, forever alter the balance of global power. The West, much younger than the East, still needs to learn that Asia has much to teach us if we would listen. For this and other reasons, it is extremely worthwhile to consider how the West may benefit from understanding and incorporating Asian-style communication and consensus-building into its EMS systems. After all, isn't an effective EMS built upon internal "buy-in," consensus building within the corporate culture, with sanctification from the top? This process sounds fairly Asian to this writer.

BIOGRAPHY

David Nelson

David Nelson is the founder, president, and CEO of Salt Lake City-based EnviroSearch International, an environmental consulting firm providing services to the private and municipal sectors as well as foreign governments. His work for private and public clients focuses on national and international aspects of environmental auditing, environmental management systems, complex international environmental litigation and international regulatory developments and environmental policies.

Mr. Nelson also sits on numerous committees and Boards of Directors of domestic and international organizations dealing with environmental issues such as hazardous waste, mining, environmental auditing, ISO 14000, and regulatory policy development. He has traveled extensively on business throughout Mexico, Central Europe, and most Asian countries including Vietnam and China and has consulted to many Asian governments and private companies on environmental policy development. He writes, speaks frequently, and conducts training courses on environmental issues related to international regulatory affairs, trade and environment conflicts including environmental trade barriers, environmental auditing, and broad-based issues related to hazardous waste. In late 1994, he completed a six-week, 30-city, six-Asian-nation environmental speaking assignment for the U.S. Information Agency.

As an Assistant Professor at the University of Utah, College of Medicine, Mr. Nelson teaches graduate classes to medical professionals on toxicological aspects of hazardous waste. He is currently writing a book on international environmental auditing.

CHAPTER 30

ISO 14000: Evolution, Scope, and Limitations

Jennifer Nash[1]

INTRODUCTION

Many firms are looking to ISO 14000 implementation and certification as a way to strengthen environmental performance and demonstrate their commitment to environmental excellence. What kinds of changes will ISO 14000 implementation bring about? One way to understand what ISO 14000 will change—and what it may not—is through a comparison of its requirements with those of other environmental management standards. This chapter compares ISO 14001[2] with two other environmental management standards: British Standard 7750 and the European Union's Eco-Management and Auditing Scheme regulation, or EMAS.

It also examines critical differences between ISO 14001 and three codes of environmental management developed by business and environmental groups: the U.S. Responsible Care® initiative, the CERES principles, and the Keidanren Global Environmental Charter.

Practices ISO 14001 Does Not Require

As firms consider what ISO 14001 has to offer, they should be aware of the environmental practices it does not require. While the British and European standards require firms to make measurable improvements in their environmental performance, ISO 14001 requires firms to improve only their environmental management systems. ISO 14001 does not require firms to interact with outside stakeholders, nor does it require disclosure of environmental activities to the public. It does not require that firms take a role in strengthening the environmental performance of their suppliers or distributors. It says very little about protection of the biosphere or sustainable use of resources. These areas, the focus of public concern in many developed countries, are more thoroughly addressed by the other standards and codes discussed here.

Impact of ISO 14001

Some predict that ISO 14001's impact on business will be "revolutionary."[3] ISO 14001 requires firms to assess environmental impacts, train workers about their environmental responsibilities, audit environmental management systems to ensure they comply with firm environmental policies, and document audit findings. ISO 14001 will not necessarily steer firms in the direction of environmentally sustainable practices, however. Firms with an interest in pursuing sustainable development may choose to adopt one of the other codes discussed in this chapter as an alternative, or in addition, to ISO 14001 implementation.

COMPARISON OF ISO 14001 AND BS 7750

ISO 14001 and BS 7750 have much in common.[4] The standards share the following:

• A common purpose: "ensuring and demonstrating compliance with stated environmental policies and objectives." Neither standard establishes absolute requirements for environmental performance beyond compliance with environmental laws and regulations. Instead, the standards require firms to establish and meet environmental goals they set for themselves.

• Virtually identical requirements in many areas. Both standards require participating firms to develop environmental management systems, establish environmental objectives and targets, keep track of environmental regulatory requirements, train employees about their environmental responsibilities, implement measurement systems, and periodically self-audit to ensure they are in compliance with their environmental policies. An important component of both standards is the option that firms hire third-party contractors to certify that their management systems comply with the standard.

Three Critical Differences

Beyond these similarities, however, ISO 14001 and BS 7750 differ in important respects. Generally, BS 7750 is more specific and comprehensive in its requirements. Three critical differences stand out.

Definition of Continuous Improvement

A key difference is the requirement for continuous improvement. BS 7750 requires improvement in a firm's actual environmental performance. Firms that adopt this standard must progressively reduce waste, emissions, accidents, and other environmental impacts. ISO 14001, however, limits the required improvement to the management system. ISO 14001-participating firms will be required to continuously improve systems for establishing goals, assessing impacts, auditing performance, and training workers. Such improvements may or may not reduce a firm's impact on the environment.

In addition, the British standard defines an expected level of environmental performance, stating that environmental impacts should not exceed those "corresponding to economically viable best available technology." ISO, in contrast, requires only that a firm's environmental management system "encourage . . . consider[ation] of best available technology where appropriate and where economically viable." BS 7750 ties firm performance to best available technology; ISO 14001 only requires consideration of such technology. Table 30–1 summarizes the requirements for continuous improvement embodied in six major codes of environmental management.

Authority of Environmental Managers

Under the British standard, managers are given specific authority. The standard stipulates that these managers must have access to sufficient resources for implementing BS 7750, as well as authority to "initiate action to ensure compliance," "provide

T A B L E   30–1

Comparison of Requirement for Continuous Improvement in Selected Standards and Codes

ISO 14001	BS 7750	EMAS
Company environmental policy must "include . . . a commitment to continual improvement" of the environmental management system.	Company environmental policy must commit to continual improvement of environmental performance, which will be quantified, if practicable, in the environmental goals and targets.	Company must commit to "reasonable continuous improvement of environmental performance, . . . reducing environmental impacts to levels not exceeding those [of] economically viable application of best available technology."
Responsible Care	**CERES**	**Keidanren Charter**
Continuous improvement required explicitly in pollution prevention and product stewardship codes.	Company must "update . . . practices constantly in light of advances in technology and new understandings in . . . environmental science." It must "make continual progress toward eliminating the release of any substances that may cause environmental damage."	Not addressed.

solutions," and "control" a firm's activities until environmental problems have been corrected. The corresponding section of the ISO standard stipulates only that responsibility and authority are defined and communicated within a firm and that resources are provided for "implementation and control" of the environmental management system. The difference in the use of the word *control* is significant. The British standard refers to a manager's responsibility to control the firm in the case of an environmental deficiency. ISO 14001 limits a manager's control to the environmental management system.

What happens when a firm fails to comply with its stated environmental policy? The British standard prescribes procedures firms must take to investigate and correct violations, including determining the cause, drawing up a plan of action, and undertaking "preventive actions." ISO 14001 requires only that firms establish procedures for handling noncompliance. It does not stipulate what these procedures should involve.

Scope of Environmental Impacts That Must Be Addressed

Both standards require firms to assess their impact upon the environment. Both call upon firms to identify environmental effects of activities, products, and services. The British standard, however, specifically enumerates impacts companies should consider, including emissions into air and water, natural resources used, as well as impacts on ecosystems. ISO 14001 requires firms to identify environmental effects of activities, products, and services but limits these to effects a company "can control" and over which it has an influence. Natural resources consumption and impacts on ecosystems are not mentioned in the standard but are included in the optional "guidance" document that accompanies it.

COMPARISON OF ISO 14001 AND EMAS

As international teams worked to develop the ISO 14001 standard, the European Commission was simultaneously drafting its own environmental management standardization, known as the Eco-Management and Audit Scheme (EMAS).[5] Discussions about EMAS began in 1990 and resulted in development of a working document in the fall of that year.[6] Like ISO 14001, EMAS was modeled closely on BS 7750. Unlike ISO 14001, however, the European standard maintained the critical features deleted from the ISO draft. Participating firms must commit to continuous improvement of environmental performance. They must strive to reduce impacts to "levels not exceeding those corresponding to economically viable application of best available technology." EMAS firms must compile a register of environmental effects, including controlled and uncontrolled releases, natural resource use, and impacts from past, current, and planned activities.

In one respect, EMAS goes beyond the requirements of even the British standard. A central feature of EMAS is its requirement for companies to publish statements of their "significant" environmental impacts after validation by third-party auditors. BS 7750 and ISO 14001 say very little about public participation in firm environmental activities. The only information that firms registered with ISO 14001 or BS 7750 must disclose is their environmental policies. EMAS requires firms to publicly disclose pollutant emissions, waste generation, and consumption of raw materials, including energy and water, as well as other factors.

The European Commission's rationale for EMAS can be understood in the larger context of European Union environmental law. The commission often has difficulty inducing member states to adopt strong environmental laws and faces even greater obstacles in consistent enforcement of such laws:

> [E]nforcement powers are confined to cumbersome, time-consuming actions before the Court of Justice against member states for failure to implement [European Union environmental] . . . law. Such cases are necessarily reserved for the most flagrant instances of national delinquency.[7]

EMAS harnesses public participation as a means to circumvent these difficulties. The commission hoped that members of the public, armed with information about company environmental performance, would pressure firms to reduce their impacts and comply with the law.

OTHER MAJOR CODES OF ENVIRONMENTAL MANAGEMENT PRACTICE

BS 7750, ISO 14001, and EMAS have been developed in the 1990s. Prior to this time, in the late 1980s, industry and environmental groups in the United States and elsewhere were developing their own codes of environmental management practice. Three such codes, the U.S. Responsible Care initiative, the CERES principles, and the Keidanren Global Environmental Charter, are discussed in this section. Unlike the national and international standards already described, these initiatives were developed privately, without the participation of quasi-governmental standards organizations. However, these codes have important features in common with the standards—in particular, a strong focus on development, implementation, and auditing of environmental management systems.

Both Responsible Care and CERES require participating firms to commit to the principles and activities they recommend. The Keidanren Charter is a set of guidelines; the management practices it contains are recommendations, not requirements. These three codes of environmental management practice represent just a few of the dozens of codes that have emerged in the past decade. They are among the most significant, in terms of the number of firms that have signed on to participate and their influence on business practice.

Responsible Care

Responsible Care was launched by the U.S. chemical industry in 1987. Its impetus was an accidental chemical release at a Union Carbide chemical plant in Bhopal, India, that killed more than 2,000 people. Many executives in the chemical industry feared that if they did not take action immediately to demonstrate their responsibility and concern, they would soon be subject to a new round of stringent safety and environmental regulations. Public opinion polls showed that less than one-quarter of the public held a positive view of the industry.[8]

The Canadian Chemical Producers Association had developed the Responsible Care concept in 1984. The U.S. Chemical Manufacturers Association (CMA) learned of the concept from CMA members with Canadian operations. In 1988, the U.S. CMA board adopted the Responsible Care initiative as a requirement for membership in the association. Today, more than 90 percent of basic chemicals produced in the United States and Canada are manufactured by companies that have signed on to Responsible Care.

Under Responsible Care, the chief executive officer of each CMA member-company must sign a statement of guiding principles and make good faith efforts to implement six codes of management practices.[9] The six codes include over 100 practices that firms must put into place and continuously improve. Codes address how companies operate their manufacturing processes, distribute their products, and interact with suppliers and customers. They require firms to reduce their releases to air, water, and land. In addition, Responsible Care codes stipulate that firms adopt a policy of openness with the public, especially facility neighbors and employees, and work conscientiously to protect health and safety.

Responsible Care does not prescribe absolute or quantitative standards. Rather, companies are expected to define for themselves precisely what Responsible Care practices would consist of in their firms. Each code begins with a section on "management leadership," which stipulates that senior management must demonstrate a "clear commitment" to the codes through "policy, communications and resources." Inventory of existing practices, education of employees, and dialogue with community members are elements of most of the codes. Since 1990, companies must annually self-assess their progress toward code implementation and submit their findings, signed by the firm's chief executive officer, to CMA. In addition, member companies are now required to submit a timetable for the implementation of each code to the CMA. CMA expects its members to have achieved full implementation of all of the initiative's requirements by the end of the century.

CERES Principles

The Coalition for Environmentally Responsible Economies (CERES) was formed in 1989 to foster two goals: to provide consistent and comparable information to investors on corporate environmental performance and to lower trust barriers between corporations and the public. CERES began informally when a group of social investment professionals, concerned that they lacked information necessary to evaluate the environmental performance of companies, began meeting with environmental professionals to close this gap. On March 24, 1989, the Exxon Valdez oil tanker ran aground off Prince William Sound in Alaska. The massive oil spill and resulting public alarm served as a catalyst for group leaders to formalize the coalition and go public.

The first order of business of the new coalition was to develop a set of environmental principles. Coalition members drafted 10 principles with the hope that they would help to prevent environmental damage like that of the Valdez accident. In the principles' introduction, the drafters' beliefs are stated explicitly. These principles call upon firms to become "stewards of the environment," to pledge "not [to] compromise . . . future generations," and "make consistent, measurable progress."

The first six of the principles require endorsers to commit to sustainable use of natural resources, waste reduction, wise use of energy, and the marketing of safe products. The last four principles go further. Number seven says that after causing any damage to the environment, companies will "promptly and responsibly correct conditions . . . [and] restore the environment." Number eight promises to disclose any potential environmental, health, or safety hazards. Number nine in the original version promised to appoint someone representing environmental interests to the company's board of directors. This was later amended to require companies to include environmental concerns in their consideration of directors. The tenth and final principle promises an annual public audit of a company's progress toward implementing the principles and public disclosure of the results. To fulfill this requirement, firms must complete and make public a "CERES report," containing detailed information on corporate environmental practices.[10]

Most of the companies that have endorsed the CERES principles are small firms. More than 80 small firms have now signed on to the principles. In addition, six large firms have become endorsers: Sun Company, General Motors, H.B. Fuller, Polaroid Corporation, Arizona Public Service Company, and Bethlehem Steel.

Keidanren Global Environmental Charter

Keidanren is a private nonprofit organization that represents virtually all business sectors in Japan. As of July of 1995, 969 corporations were members, including Japanese companies and foreign businesses operating in Japan. Keidanren announced its Global Environmental Charter in April of 1991. The organization had announced earlier that year environmental measures as one of the five "pillars" of the Keidanren's "Action Guidelines." The charter represented a step toward implementation of this portion of the guidelines.[11] Its release coincided with worldwide preparations for the 1992 U.N. Conference on Environment and Development in Brazil. The charter received substantial coverage in the Japanese news media and was supported by the Diet (Japanese Parliament). While the charter is a set of guidelines, and implementation is not specifically required of members, a May 1992 Keidanren survey suggested that a large percentage of the organization's members have adopted the charter as corporate policy.[12]

The charter consists of a preamble followed by 24 points covering 11 areas of concern. Under the section "General management policies," the direction of corporate environmental policy is established for member firms. Companies must protect the global environment and ecosystems, conserve resources, and ensure the soundness of products.

The Charter requires firms to adopt environmental management systems similar to those called for under ISO 14001. Companies must establish "environmental regulations," or policies, and ensure, through an internal inspection at least once a year, that the regulations are adhered to. The charter stipulates that companies set environmental goals that reduce their "load" on the environment. Firms are to take measures to conserve energy and resources "even when environmental problems have not been fully elucidated by science."

Unlike Responsible Care or the CERES principles, the Keidanren Charter specifically addresses the conduct of a firm's overseas operations in a separate "ten points" guideline. These points are considerably less far-reaching than the charter itself. For example, on the subject of environmental assessment, companies are urged to study impacts before starting overseas operations, and after start-up to "try to collect data, and if necessary, conduct an assessment."

ISO 14001 AND SUSTAINABILITY

It is now possible to compare the requirements embodied in the six environmental management standards and codes in terms of their potential to promote practices that are environmentally sustainable. ISO 14001 makes only passing reference to the subject of sustainability. The word *sustainability* appears only once in the standard—in the introduction, where it is mentioned as a public concern. In contrast, sustainability features strongly in both the CERES principles and the Keidanren Global Environment Charter. CERES requires participating companies to pledge that their activities will not "compromise the ability of future generations to sustain themselves." The Keidanren Charter requires that firms "contribute to the establishment of a new economic system for realizing an environmentally protective society leading to . . . sustainable development."

Management theorists predict that sustainability will likely grow as a concern for companies in the coming decade.[13] Companies that have developed environmentally sustainable business practices will enjoy a competitive advantage and be positioned to respond quickly and efficiently to increasingly stringent government regulations. But the path to becoming an environmentally sustainable company is long and arduous. At a minimum, an environmentally sustainable firm must do the following:

- Systematically increase awareness of environmental impacts on ecosystems and natural resource consumption among workers at all levels of the firm.

- Adopt strategies that will lead to new products, processes, and technologies with substantially reduced environmental impacts.

- Accept responsibility for the environmental impacts of products throughout their life cycles—from extraction of the materials necessary for manufacture, to production, transport, use, and disposal.

- Train workers to contribute to environmental improvements, and measure and reward workers' contributions.

- Foster communication and dialogue with communities and outside stakeholders, especially those whose values may differ from company managers.

The requirements that each of the standards and codes places on companies to address these activities are discussed below.

Raising Awareness

Each of the codes, to varying degrees, requires firms to identify the environmental "aspects" of their activities. Several of the Responsible Care codes require participating firms to identify environmental risks associated with their processes. Responsible Care's pollution prevention code, in particular, requires a quantitative assessment of waste generated and released at each plant. Companies that sign on to CERES must publish information on chemical use, waste generation, and resource consumption. The Keidanren Charter requires participating firms to "scientifically" assess the environmental impacts of "all corporate activities."

While ISO 14001's requirement for environmental assessment is narrower than either BS 7750 or EMAS, limiting a firm's environmental inventory to aspects over which it has "control" and failing to emphasize natural resource and ecosystem impacts, its requirement to identify environmental aspects is still perhaps the central feature of the standard. ISO 14001 requires firms to make each employee aware of the environmental impacts of his or her work activities and the environmental benefits of improved performance.[14] In terms of moving firms toward sustainability, this may be the single most significant section of the standard. Workers who are aware of their personal contribution to environmental degradation are likely to look for opportunities for change. Neither Responsible Care, CERES, nor the Keidanren Charter is as specific in its requirement for environmental assessment at the level of the individual worker. Table 30–2 summarizes code requirements in the area of environmental impact assessments.

Developing New Products, Processes, and Technologies

A particular focus of the Keidanren Charter is technology development. Firms are called upon to develop and supply innovative technologies that "allow conservation of energy and other resources together with preservation of the environment." Companies that sign on to Responsible Care must assess the health, safety, and environmental hazards associated with existing products. Further, in designing and developing new products, these hazards—as well as use of natural resources—must be "key considerations."

ISO 14001 addresses the development of new technologies through its discussion of pollution prevention. In the United States, pollution prevention generally is defined as practices that reduce emissions through improved housekeeping, material substitution, recycling, and product and process innovation. Nearly always, it is associated with

T A B L E   30–2

Comparison of Requirement to Assess Environmental Impacts

ISO 14001	BS 7750	EMAS
Company must "establish and maintain a procedure to identify the environmental aspects of . . . activities, products, and services that [the firm] can control and . . . have an influence, in order to determine . . . which [are] significant." Workers must be aware of their personal contribution to environmental degradation and improvement.	Company must develop a system to identify, examine, and evaluate the environmental effects, direct and indirect, of its activities. A record must be kept of the significant effects.	Company must write an environmental statement with an assessment of "all significant environmental issues" and a report on pollution, resource use, and other environmental activities and submit it to the registering body for public distribution.
Responsible Care	**CERES**	**Keidanren Charter**
Several codes require "regular evaluations of . . . risks." Pollution prevention code requires "quantitative inventory at each facility of waste generated and released."	Not addressed in principles, although data on chemical use, waste generation, resource consumption and other areas are required for CERES report.	"All company activities . . . shall be scientifically evaluated for their impact on the environment."

significant cost savings and increased productivity and efficiency. While pollution prevention featured strongly in an early draft of the ISO standard, the final draft approved in June 1995 broadened the definition to include end-of-pipe treatment. ISO 14001 now defines prevention of pollution as "use of processes, practices, materials or products that avoid, reduce or control pollution, which may include recycling, treatment, process changes, control mechanisms, efficient use of resources and material substitution." This definition is exceedingly broad. In contrast, Responsible Care and CERES give preference to prevention of pollution over other options. For example, the Responsible Care pollution prevention code requires "ongoing reduction of wastes and releases, giving preference first to source reduction, second to recycle/reuse, and third to treatment. The CERES principles require companies to pledge to "reduce and where possible eliminate waste through source reduction and recycling." Table 30–3 compares what each of the six codes requires in terms of pollution prevention.

T A B L E   30–3

Requirement for Pollution Prevention

ISO 14001	BS 7750	EMAS
Requires "commitment" to "prevention of pollution," defined to include pollution control.	Suggested in annex to standard as a corporate policy commitment.	Company must take "measures necessary to prevent pollution or eliminate pollution, and where this is not feasible, to reduce pollutant emissions and waste generation. . ., taking into account of possible clean technologies."
Responsible Care	**CERES**	**Keidanren Charter**
Pollution prevention code requires "ongoing reduction of wastes and releases, giving preference first to source reduction, second to recycle/reuse, and third to treatment."	Company must "reduce and where possible eliminate waste through source reduction and recycling."	"Employees must be educated to ensure the prevention of pollution and the conservation of energy and other resources."

Reducing Impacts throughout Product Life Cycles

The six standards and codes differ importantly in the way they require companies to address the life-cycle impacts of their products. The Keidanren Charter recommends that firms take "care" in product research, design, and development to reduce environmental impacts throughout a product's "production, distribution, . . . use, and disposal." The charter also calls on firms to address the environmental performance of purchased products, suggesting that they be "superior" in terms of their conservation of resources and preservation of the environment.

Other codes address life-cycle impacts by requiring firms to oversee the environmental practices of their suppliers, distributors, and customers. The conduct of firms "upstream" and "downstream" in the product life cycle is a major emphasis of Responsible Care's product stewardship and distribution codes. Responsible Care companies must audit the environmental performance of suppliers, distributors, and customers and work with them to correct any problems. They must stop doing business with firms whose problems do not improve. This requirement has been particularly challenging, requiring sales and marketing personnel to learn to conduct audits and make decisions potentially disruptive of business relationships.

TABLE 30-4

Requirement to Consider Environmental Conduct of Suppliers,
Distributors, and Customers

ISO 14001	BS 7750	EMAS
Company must "communicat[e] . . . relevant procedures and requirements to suppliers and contractors."	Company must ensure that suppliers "comply with the organization's policy requirements."	Company's suppliers must abide by its environmental policy.
Responsible Care	**CERES**	**Keidanren Charter**
Product Stewardship Code requires companies to provide environmental information to suppliers, distributors, and customers. Companies must work with them to bring about appropriate life-cycle use and must terminate contracts with businesses with unsafe practices.	Company must "inform . . . customers of the environmental impacts of [its] products or services and try to correct unsafe use."	When obtaining materials, the company must purchase products that are environmentally "superior." It shall "provide users with information on the appropriate use and disposal, including recycling, of their products."

Similarly, EMAS requires that suppliers abide by participating firms' environmental policies. BS 7750 requires registering companies to ensure that suppliers "*comply* with the organization's policy requirements." [emphasis added] ISO 14001 only requires that companies "*communicat[e]* . . . relevant procedures and requirements to suppliers and contractors" [emphasis added]. Thus, ISO 14001 stands alone in its inattention to environmental performance of businesses beyond company "fence lines." Table 30–4 compares how each of the six codes assigns reponsibility for life-cycle impacts.

Training and Motivating Workers

Each of the codes emphasizes training for personnel whose work impacts the environment. ISO 14001, BS 7750, and EMAS call on firms to train workers, as "appropriate," about their roles and responsibilities in implementing the firm's environmental policy. The Keidanren Charter goes well beyond these standards with its requirement that employees be educated to understand the "importance of daily close management" in preventing pollution and conserving resources. Responsible Care's training requirements are not specific, calling on firms to provide training for "affected employees" but not stipulating its content. In practice, Responsible Care training appears generally to focus on managers, not production workers.[15]

None of the standards or codes discussed in this chapter requires firms to institute management systems to measure and reward workers' contributions to environmental performance. ISO 14001, BS 7750, and EMAS all contain similar provisions requiring firms to make employees aware of "the importance of, and their role in" compliance with the standard, and the consequences of departing from the standard. As mentioned previously, ISO 14001's requirement that each worker understand the environmental impact of his or her actions may help to foster environmental consciousness and motivate performance improvements. ISO 14001 does not, however, directly require firms to provide incentives to encourage workers to support code implementation.

While the CERES principles do not require firms to reward exemplary environmental performance, CERES does ask companies to describe outstanding environmental performance in their annual environmental report. The Keidanren Charter calls upon firms to support employees who independently work to improve community environmental quality. Responsible Care does not require firms to recognize employee contributions to environmental improvements. Few Responsible Care companies use adherence to Responsible Care as a factor in employee performance reviews.[16]

Involving Outside Stakeholders

The move toward sustainable development entails integrating the voice of the environment—outside stakeholders such as environmental advocacy and community groups—into corporate decision making. ISO 14001's requirements in this regard are particularly lacking. The only information a firm must disclose is its environmental policy. In contrast, both EMAS and CERES require participating firms to provide specific detailed information on all aspects of their activities.

A related concern is the extent to which firms must respond to public concerns. Responsible Care requires firms to pursue a policy of "openness" with the public. To fulfill this requirement, many chemical firms have now established citizens' advisory groups at major manufacturing facilities. Typically, these groups are comprised of a cross-section of community residents, including critics of the facility. ISO 14001 stipulates that firms have a procedure in place to document and respond to the public. Under ISO 14001, firms may adopt a passive stance toward their communities. Table 30–5 compares the six codes' requirements to disclose information.

CONCLUSION: ISO 14001 AS AN AGENT OF CHANGE

The people who drafted ISO 14001 used BS 7750 as one of their starting points. Comparison of ISO 14001 and BS 7750 suggests that ISO 14001 drafters chose to delete several key features of the British standard as they developed their international protocol: the requirement for continuous improvements in environmental performance, the authority of environmental managers to control a firm's entire operation, and the

T A B L E   30-5

Requirement to Disclose Information

ISO 14001	BS 7750	EMAS
The only information that must be disclosed is a company's environmental policy.	The environmental policy and objectives must be available to the public.	Company must provide "information necessary to understand the environmental impact of the company's activities. [A]n open dialogue with the public should be pursued."
Responsible Care	**CERES**	**Keidanren Charter**
Company must report chemical or environmental hazards to employees, officials, and the public. Community awareness code requires a "policy of openness that provides convenient ways for interested persons to become familiar with the facility, its operations, and products."	Company must "annually complete the CERES Report, [approximately 100 questions dealing with many aspects of corporate environmental performance] which will be made available to the public."	Company must provide information to the public, administrative authorities, international organizations, and other environmental policy-making groups on their environmental activities and protective measures regularly.

imperative to consider natural resource consumption and ecosystem impacts. These deleted features represent missed opportunities to foster environmentally sustainable practices in firms. EMAS, developed at the same time, maintained these features and went further, adding a requirement for public disclosure of firm environmental performance.

The differences between ISO 14001 and the other standards can be attributed in part to the different environmental regulatory contexts in the United States and Europe. Feeling burdened by command and control regulation, U.S. firms helping to develop ISO 14001 sought an international environmental management standard that would impose few additional constraints. Compliance with the law is the only performance requirement included in ISO 14001. Europeans, on the other hand, saw the move toward environmental management standardization as an opportunity to go beyond the weaknesses of the regulatory systems in their countries.

Codes of environmental management practice originating in the United States and Japan go beyond ISO 14001's requirements for developing new technology, taking responsibility for the environmental performance of suppliers, distributors, and customers, and establishing a dialogue with outside stakeholders. ISO 14001's requirement that firms make each employee aware of his or her personal contribution to a firm's environmental impact may raise awareness about how firm practices impede or contribute to sustainability and motivate workers to change their practices. Yet, overall, ISO 14001 appears to push firms in the direction of sustainable practices less directly than the other standards and codes.

BIOGRAPHY

Jennifer Nash, MCP

Jennifer Nash studies corporate environmental management in MIT's Technology, Business, and Environment Program. A focus of her research has been the potential of industry initiatives such as ISO 14000 to push firms in the direction of sustainable development. She is currently investigating changes in practices and values in the U.S. chemical industry brought about by the Responsible Care initiative. Prior to coming to MIT, Nash was Director of the Clean Air Council in Philadelphia, Pennsylvania.

NOTES

1. The author wishes to recognize the contribution of Andria Pomponi in researching and writing this chapter.
2. ISO 14000 is a series of environmental management standards. The standards address the basic environmental management system (ISO 14001), auditing (ISO 14010), performance evaluation (ISO 14031), labeling (ISO 14024), life-cycle assessment (ISO 14040), and product standards (ISO 14060). The standards are of two types: specifications and guidance. ISO 14001 is the only specification standard. The others are guidance standards, meaning that they are descriptive documents, not prescriptive standards.
3. J. Cascio, head of the U.S. delegation to ISO 14000 negotiations, quoted in *Environment Reporter,* The Bureau of National Affairs (Washington, D.C. July 7, 1995), p. 531.
4. The analysis of ISO 14001 in this chapter is based on the draft standard of August 8, 1995, International Organization for Standardization, *Environmental Management Systems— Specifications with Guidance for Use,* Draft International Standard, ISO/DIS 14001, ISO TC 207/SC 1 (Geneva, Switzerland). The analysis of BS 7750 is based on BS 7750; *Specification for Environmental Management Systems,* British Standards Institution (London, England, 1994).
5. Analysis of EMAS is based on Council Regulation (EEC) No. 1836/93 of June 29, 1993, "Allowing Voluntary Participation by Companies in the Industrial Sector in a Community Eco-Management and Audit Scheme," *Official Journal of the European Communities,* No. L (Luxembourg) 168: pp. 1–7.
6. A. Gouldson, "The EC Eco-Management and Audit Scheme: An Overview," *Eco-Management and Auditing,* Vol. 1, Issue 1, (West Yorkshire, United Kingdom, August 1993): pp. 35–41.
7. R. Hunter, "EU Eco-Management and Auditing Regulation," *International Environment Reporter,* The Bureau of National Affairs, Inc., February 9, 1994: pp. 142–149.
8. L. R. Ember, "Responsible Care: Chemical Makers Still Counting on It to Improve Image," *Chemical and Engineering News,* May 29, 1995: pp. 10–18.

9. Responsible Care Guidelines and practices are detailed in Chemical Manufacturers Association, *Responsible Care: A Public Commitment Guiding Principles,* (Washington, D.C., 1991); Chemical Manufacturers Association, *Community Awareness and Emergency Response Code of Management Practices, Distribution Code of Management Practices, Pollution Prevention Code of Management Practices, Process Safety Code of Management Practices, Employee Health and Safety Code of Management Practices, Product Stewardship Code of Management Practices,* (Washington, D.C., undated).

10. CERES principles and reporting requirements are detailed in The Coalition for Environmentally Responsible Economies, *CERES: Guide to the CERES Principles,* (Boston, Mass., 1994); The Coalition for Environmentally Responsible Economies, *1994 CERES Report Standard Form: Annual Environmental Report Form for Companies Endorsing the CERES Principles for 1994 Calendar Year,* (Boston, Mass., 1994).

11. Y. Kume, "Environmental Measures in Global Perspective—Gold of Keidanren Global Environmental Charter," *Keidanren Review on Japanese Economy,* Public Affairs Department, Japan Federation of Economic Organizations, No. 129, (Tokyo, Japan, June 1991): p. 3.

12. Keidanren, "Towards Preservation of the Global Environment, Results of a Follow-up Survey on the Subject of the Keidanren Global Environment Charter," (Tokyo, Japan, May 27, 1992).

13. P. Shrivastava, "Ecocentric Management for a Risk Society," *Academy of Management Review,* Vol. 20, No. 1, January 1995: pp. 118–137; S. Hart, "A Natural-Resource-Based View of the Firm," *Academy of Management Review,* Vol. 20, No. 4, October 1995: pp. 1–29.

14. International Organization for Standardization, *Environmental Management Systems— Specification with Guidance for Use,* Draft International Standard, ISO/DIS 14001, ISO TC 207/SC 1, Section 4.3.2(b) (Geneva, Switzerland).

15. J. Nash and J. Howard, "The U.S. Responsible Care Initiative: The Dynamics of Shaping Firm Practices and Values," (Working Paper, Technology, Business and Environment Program, Massachusetts Institute of Technology, November 1995).

16. Ibid.

CHAPTER 31

ISO 14000 Implications for Companies and Developing Country Trade

Kerstin Pfliegner

INTRODUCTION

In the last few years, an increasing number of national and regional standards in the field of eco-labeling, environmental management, and auditing have been developed. There are now about 20 national eco-labeling schemes worldwide—including those in several developing countries such as Brazil, the Republic of Korea, and India.

The development of environmental management system standards began in 1992 with the British standard BS 7750, which led to the development of similar standards in several other countries. At the regional level, the European Union created a community eco-label in 1992 and in 1993 established the Eco-Management and Audit Scheme (EMAS) as a regulation for all member countries.

The growing international concern with environmental issues and the broad acceptance of the ISO 9000 series of quality management standards encouraged ISO to develop a series of standards for environmental management—ISO 14000. Many of those involved in developing ISO 14000 expect that the standards will be applied worldwide.

Although voluntary, third-party registration might be demanded by the marketplace or governments, thus transforming ISO 14000 into a binding business requirement. The European Committee for Standardization (CEN) will make a decision on the extent to which the final version of ISO 14000 fulfills the requirements of EMAS that apply to environmental management systems. If the standards become a requirement for doing business in developed countries, this will raise questions. What impact will they have on developing countries? Are the standards and the procedures by which they are applied likely to create potential adverse effects on the trade of these countries?

This chapter sets the core requirements of the ISO 14000 series into the wider context of international trade. It discusses some key issues in implementing the ISO

14000 standards and outlines implications of the standards for companies and international trade with a specific focus on potential problems for companies in developing countries. Strategies to support exporters in developing countries and to avoid potential barriers to trade are also discussed.

ENVIRONMENTAL MANAGEMENT SYSTEMS

As yet, there is little experience in implementing the ISO 14001 environmental management system (EMS) standard. An investigation of its implications for companies and developing country trade can only be based on expectations and experience with similar existing standards. The following results are based on the opinions of experts involved in the ISO 14000 standard setting process obtained from questionnaires and personal interviews.[1]

The main impact of ISO 14001 certification is expected to occur in commercial transactions between corporations. Furthermore, certification might be requested by governments as a condition for tenders. Insurance companies and banks may use ISO 14001 certification as a criterion for insurance premiums and credit conditions. In general, certification might be of importance in those industry sectors where environmental risk as well as exposure to environmental legislation is high, such as the chemical and petrochemical, mining, forestry, steel, and electronics industries. In sectors with relatively low environmental impact, it is not likely that the standards will become business practice.

Implications for Companies in General

A company that will implement the ISO 14001 standard has to set up systems covering environmental management, auditing, and performance evaluation. It may also be required to address the use of life-cycle analysis in decision making on new products and processes, which will involve research on these issues. Additionally, a company will have to set up a process for externally communicating its environmental policy. These systems will require integration into many levels and processes of the company and will influence fundamental parameters of management and decision making.

They will require commitment from all employees involved in these processes, in particular from top management. Continual training of personnel will be a significant element of an effective EMS. Implementation and maintenance of the EMS will involve a very complex documentation process. Implementation of ISO 14001 will in general not require different technological equipment since the standard refers to a management system. However, the requirement of "continual improvement" may dictate otherwise later on. If a company is going to continually improve its environmental performance, it is quite likely that it will have to reduce and substitute inputs and keep up with new technological achievements.

As with ISO 9000, companies adopting the standards will be audited by an independent third party (registrar). Although ISO 14001 allows the option for companies to self-declare conformance to ISO 14001, its recognition in business practice remains to be seen. The third-party auditor will be able to check the commitment on each functional level by inspecting the company and speaking to employees. Since the majority of companies have not yet managed environmental aspects within a systems approach, experts believe that the standard will have a significant impact on how companies manage environmental issues in the future.

Costs of Compliance

Compliance with ISO 14001 will be very costly for an individual company. The costs of compliance depend on the time spent for implementation and registration of a company's EMS. A smaller company might, due to a less complex structure and range of products, need less time than a large company and thus incur lower costs.

Experts estimate that a company that has an environmental program and policy in place could reduce the time needed to implement an EMS by about 20 percent, in comparison to a company without an existing environmental program. There is broad consensus among experts that the existence of an ISO 9000 quality management system will facilitate the process of implementing an ISO 14001 EMS. In this case, some of the procedures and necessary expertise already exist. Those companies can comply with the requirements of ISO 14001 by adding to the existing system or modifying it. They might therefore need about 30 percent less time to implement an EMS.[2]

The costs for setting up an EMS will be mainly internal and, as with ISO 9000, measured in employee time. Companies with no environmental or quality system experience, however, will most likely need assistance from external consultants to set up the EMS.

Experience with ISO 9000 has shown that consultancy costs are very high. Some consultancy firms indicate that the costs for ISO 14000 could be even higher than for ISO 9000 since more specialized consultants are needed. Experience with ISO 9000 has shown that third-party registration constitutes about 20 percent of compliance costs. In the event of a combined registration of ISO 9000 and ISO 14000, the fees might be higher than for ISO 9000 alone. The reason for this difference is that the registrar has to send more auditors with greater specialization skills.[3] Companies implementing both systems simultaneously could avoid multiple-registration costs. Once a company is registered, it has to undergo periodic surveillance audits to maintain its certificate. For ISO 9000, the surveillance audit is performed every six months. As calculated elsewhere [UNDP (1996)], the consulting costs for a small-size company without any environmental program or quality management system in place could easily be about $100,000, and registration costs about $20,000, with an additional $10,000 for registration maintenance in periodic intervals. Furthermore, the company would have to calculate internal implementation costs of about 15 months of employee time.

Expected Benefits

ISO 14001 registration can provide commercial value to a company. It is a sign of approval by an independent third-party that trading partners can recognize easily. At the beginning, registered companies will play a pioneer role and therefore achieve a competitive advantage. The certificate will be a means to strengthen their market position.

ISO 14001 registration applies to companies, not products. The influence on consumer behavior and on trading opportunities of a company's products is therefore less obvious than it is in the case of eco-labeling, which is a direct certification of products. However, there might be a public-relations benefit to externally communicating a company's environmental policy. Registration would underscore a commitment to environmental protection. A prerequisite for this benefit is an eco-sensitive consumer market.

Most experts believe that implementation of an ISO 14001 EMS will improve a company's internal efficiency by reducing, for example, energy and raw material inputs. However, there is no consensus as to whether or not savings achieved by this efficiency increase will overcompensate costs, or vice versa. Some experts expect the costs to far outweigh the returns.

Business in industrialized countries is under strong pressure from different stakeholders—the government, general public, and environmental and consumer organizations—to avoid environmental impacts. It is expected that an ISO 14001 certification would diminish this pressure. Some industry representatives involved in the standard-setting process hope that the standard could make room for environmental deregulation. They argue that certification guarantees a company's commitment to regulatory compliance. People involved expect that the majority of companies implementing a system and obtaining certification will show improved environmental performance. However, concerns are raised that ISO 14001, which requires companies to demonstrate that they have procedures to attain and maintain compliance, does not require proof that the companies actually are in compliance with environmental laws.

There is no guarantee that implementation of an EMS will result in improvement of the company's environmental performance. The fact that ISO 14001—in contrast to the European and British scheme—does not set out mandatory environmental performance criteria might have, apart from possible environmental shortcomings, advantages for companies since certification might be easier to achieve.

From an international trade perspective, the standard provides a basis for shared environmental expectations among firms. It might lead to a harmonization of national rules and permit industry and auditors around the world to employ a common language and scale in evaluating EMSs. A single set of environmental standards could help avoid multiple registrations, inspections, certifications, and conflicting requirements of different national standards and would therefore reduce costs of compliance.

It lessens the complication that companies in developing countries have to be assessed for conformity by certification bodies in each importing country. Multinational companies will be provided with a single system to implement everywhere they operate. However, it has to be proven whether or not this single worldwide definition, developed by current industry and standardization leaders, might exclude legitimate environmental concerns and/or erect entry barriers to emerging firms, especially from developing countries.

Impact on Developing Country Trade

Greater pressure on companies in developing countries to fulfill environmental requirements originates from foreign customers or international organizations rather than from local stakeholders. Therefore, ISO 14001 certification is likely to become a means to meet overseas customer demand and to participate in international trade, rather than an element of competitive advantage on the domestic market. Certified exporters might gain faster and wider market access via increased credibility with buyers.

However, according to a survey conducted by the United Nations Industrial Organization (UNIDO), noncompliance with ISO 14001 among industry associations and standardization bodies in developing countries is perceived as a threat to the competitiveness of local companies and is likely to impose barriers to trade. Some TC 207 delegates believe that since the standards are voluntary and do not set performance criteria, they are not likely to create trade barriers.

In contrast, it is argued that as certification spreads from companies in industrialized countries it might impose certain trade restrictions on companies in developing countries, which will need more time to adjust. Though ISO states that the standard should not be used to create trade barriers, some provisions within ISO 14001 have the potential to create such barriers. A company is encouraged to consider the environmental impact of products when defining its environmental objectives and targets. Products not compatible with those goals might be excluded.

Furthermore, the standard foresees that procedures and requirements with respect to environmental aspects identified by the company shall be communicated to suppliers.[4] There is a broad consensus among experts that large companies in industrialized countries will put pressure on suppliers, including those in developing countries, to become third-party certified as a means to improve their own environmental performance and to demonstrate their environmental responsibility. The pressure could go as far as to use certification as a criteria to award preferential trade status, fix supplier quotas, or even to drop suppliers without certification in favor of certified competitors. This has been the experience with ISO 9000 and BS 7750.[5] There are a number of likely obstacles for implementation of ISO 14001 in developing countries; some are listed below.

Lack of Management Commitment

Lack of government incentives, insufficient information, and lack of awareness are possible reasons for insufficient commitment by the management of developing country firms to implement an EMS. Additionally, the Confederation of Indian Industries identifies as likely barriers to management commitment the inability to realize the benefits of an EMS, a perceived complexity of the ISO 14001 standard, confusion about the compatibility of ISO 9000 and ISO 14001, and the impression that implementation of the standard is associated with too much paperwork.[6]

In Mexico, experience with ISO 9000 has shown that limited attention traditionally devoted to procedures, documentation, and records represents an obstacle for ISO

9000 implementation.[7] In Nigerian companies, a preference for individual decision making is often combined with a lack of clearly defined organizational structures and lack of employee training. Because systematic measures might interfere with individual decision making, managers are not committed to implement any management system at all. The required documentation of processes and procedures, for example, could reveal malpractice, corruption, or decision making following priorities such as personal requests from superiors, one's religion, or because of belonging to a certain tribe.[8]

Lack of Resources and Infrastructure

A lack of resources, such as information, capital, technology, training facilities, and qualified consultants and auditors in many developing countries might be a barrier to developing-country participation in ISO 14001. Changes in the structure and operations of an organization required by the provisions of ISO 14001 involve experience and expertise that might not exist in developing countries.

Small companies in particular may find the high costs involved in complying with ISO 14001 prohibitive. A lack of clean technologies is a potential obstacle for developing country producers to comply with environmental legislation and to achieve conformity with ISO 14001. Developing countries describe as insufficient the access to information on the proposed standards.

Most developing countries do not have sufficient financial resources to send delegates regularly to TC 207 meetings. Therefore, it is more difficult for them to articulate their interests and to influence the standard-setting process. This might lead to the perception that the standards are largely a northern issue and may provide a guise for new types of conditionality.

ISO 14001 as a voluntary scheme is based on the existence of national environmental legislation, which a company can use as a basis to formulate its environmental policy and objectives. These requirements are either lacking, are under development, or are badly implemented and enforced in most developing countries. A further problem might be that regulatory bodies do not recognize EMS because of different priorities within the existing legal system. For example, in India, a command and control regulatory framework is encouraging end-of-pipe pollution control, while EMS focuses on preventive strategies.[9]

Experience with ISO 9000 has shown that many developing countries do not have a national accreditation body or certification bodies to assess conformity with the requirements of the standards. Nonavailability of local conformity assessment infrastructure increases the costs of compliance for exporters in these countries. They are forced to seek registration by overseas registrars or such international bodies.

As with ISO 9000, even if certification infrastructure exists in developing countries, certificates issued by a local body might not be accepted by organizations or governments in the target markets because of a lack of confidence. With ISO 9000, importers in industrialized countries often requested certificates from reputable foreign or international bodies.

The credibility of a certification system depends largely on the competence of the auditors who carry out the assessments. In the absence of an international system for qualifying auditors, developing countries have to obtain this expertise by enrolling training courses from organizations abroad. The problem with gaining credibility is that there is a strong reputation effect involved. The credibility of a certification body might be considered differently by various trading partners and is to some extent subjective.

Problems Related to Conformity Assessment

ISO 14001 leaves a lot of room for interpretation by users of the standard. Terms such as *relevant, significant,* or the requirement of *continual improvement* might be difficult to assess and are interpreted differently by users (such as consultants and registrars) in different countries. The influence of standard users on international trade becomes very great. ISO 9000 has already been criticized for being too commercial and open to misuse by consultants. There are different models of national conformity assessment systems among developed countries. The criteria for registrars to certify companies are not internationally harmonized. Auditors are not internationally recognized, and auditor training can vary from country to country. ISO develops international standards, but it does not create an international framework for assessing conformity to the standards. Stakeholders worldwide are understandably concerned that the ISO 14001 specification standard is interpreted consistently, that the registrars (certifiers) are evaluated according to rigorous criteria, that auditors are competent to conduct third-party audits, and that ISO 14001 certificates, once issued, are recognized worldwide.

ENVIRONMENTAL LABELING

The relevance of environmental labeling (EL) for developing countries is directly related to their export of goods. The domestic market for eco-labeled products in those countries is likely to be small. Existing EL schemes are criticized for erecting nontariff trade barriers, especially against producers from developing countries. An example is the European Union (EU) program, which requires companies to observe all applicable EU legislation (which also extends to the production process) to be eligible for the EU eco-label.

The ISO 14000 EL standards aim at avoiding potential trade barriers associated with existing EL schemes. They do not define an internationally uniform labeling scheme but provide guidelines for nondiscriminatory operations within national or regional EL programs. These guidelines can be used by countries either to design future schemes or adjust existing ones. In order to analyze the potential impact of the ISO 14000 EL standards on developing country trade, aspects of existing EL schemes likely to create trade restrictions will be described first. Then, we will look at how the ISO 14000 standards might be able to avoid the creation of barriers to trade. The following elements may be considered critical.

Transparency and Access to Information

The coexistence of different national and regional EL schemes involves a variety of requirements. Exporters in developing countries might find it difficult to get timely and accurate information on those requirements and to adjust to the EL schemes. Investment decisions may be hindered by uncertainty about the contents of the requirements and their period of validity. A lack of information and transparency prevents foreign producers from participating in the development of EL schemes in order to express their interests. Although the access to information on EL schemes depends on many factors, some factors can be influenced by international standards. First, the ISO standards communicate common principles concerning requirements and procedures to be used within all EL programs and therefore provide orientation for producers intending to implement those schemes. Furthermore, the standards call for transparency of EL programs, processes, and methodologies. More transparency will improve the possibility of foreign producers staying informed. This might enable them to participate in the development of criteria and awarding procedures.

Access to the Labeling Program

High costs or fees to enter an EL program might be a barrier for companies in developing countries, especially small firms wishing to apply for a label. The complexity of a program might also hinder access. The ISO 14000 standards call for equal access to a labeling program for all interested parties. This includes avoidance of administrative restrictions that limit access to a program, excessive costs or fees to enter it, and reduction of the overall complexity of the program.

A foreign producer might have no access to a labeling program because his product does not fit into the product categories selected for a label. Experience with existing labeling programs has shown that the proposals for new product categories are made by domestic producers. It is difficult for foreign producers to influence this process for several reasons: lack of access to the selection process, lack of information or limited funds, and lack of research on product categories suitable for eco-labeling. As a consequence, export products from developing countries are more likely to be excluded. The ISO 14000 standards call for the acceptance of products regarded as environmentally friendly in the producing country during the process of defining product categories eligible for an eco-label within a national EL program.

Selection of Compliance Criteria

The determination of criteria for awarding a label within unilateral programs can be more easily influenced by domestic producers. Thresholds related to these criteria are likely to be based on domestic production patterns and to be focused on local conditions and priorities. The criteria can therefore be met more easily by domestic firms. Exporters from developing countries might have problems in complying with criteria because they require the use of inputs, for example specific chemicals or recyclable materials, that are not available in a developing country. A requirement for recycling may even force foreign producers to use materials recyclable in the importing country, though they are less environmentally friendly than the materials traditionally used in the producing country.

Existing eco-labeling schemes are more frequently based on process-related criteria. These criteria require proof of compliance in all production phases, even those that take place outside the control of the company producing the final product. Conformity assessment becomes more complicated and expensive. Process-related criteria might require the use of specific technologies that are difficult to obtain or are expensive. The use of process-related criteria calls for a life-cycle analysis of the products, which requires extensive research and therefore involves high costs. If criteria are set according to local conditions by the country developing the scheme, environmental achievements by developing countries, such as environmentally friendly inputs and/or production and process methods (PPMs), will be ignored. The ISO 14000 standards might lessen these obstacles by promoting the concept of "equivalency." This means that the environmental conditions of the producing country should be taken into account. PPMs regarded as environmentally acceptable in the country of origin should be accepted as equivalent to criteria set by the country awarding the label. Furthermore, requirements for compliance with process-related regulations at the manufacturing site must be flexible and take into account, where possible, the producer country's national environmental requirements. Requirements to meet specific national legislation rather than performance objectives have to be avoided. The determination of criteria should be open to allow foreign producers to influence the process.

At present, scientific knowledge on how to weigh different environmental impacts or on how to evaluate a product's net environmental impact is not available. In consequence many criteria or thresholds chosen within existing schemes to grant a label are not based on scientific knowledge but on value judgments and are therefore not objective. The proposed ISO 14000 standards suggest that criteria should be objective, comprehensive, transparent, and relevant. The selection of criteria should be based on scientific, reproducible methodologies that are periodically reviewed to include new developments. Although the lack of scientific knowledge cannot be solved by the standards, an international mechanism such as the ISO standard-setting process could promote future research activities in this field.

Conformity Assessment

In the field of assessing conformity, producers in developing countries face the same problems with EL as with EMS. A lack of local facilities to assess conformity (e.g., laboratories for product testing) and a lack of credibility are the reasons that most foreign EL schemes require inspections of the exporter's facilities by authorities appointed by them or certification by an internationally recognized certification body.[10] For an exporter applying for the EL in the importing country, an ISO 14001 or ISO 9000 certification could have the following advantage: Those aspects of the inspection of the production site related to environmental quality control could be waived. These certificates might serve as a means to guarantee that a certain product quality is sustained.

The ISO eco-labeling standards provide a basis for mutual recognition. Mutual recognition means that industrialized countries award a product with an eco-label on the basis that it has qualified for the EL scheme in the exporting country. A basis for mutual recognition is the concept of "equivalency" promoted by ISO. Furthermore, the design of national EL programs by developing countries according to ISO guidelines could make these more reliable in the eyes of foreign certification bodies. Additionally, the standards call for testing methods that would follow recognized guidelines. National or industry testing likely to create trade barriers, such as restricted recognition of testing facilities creating an impossible geographic burden, have to be avoided.

Costs of Compliance

The costs of compliance are likely to increase if a foreign producer has to comply with requirements of different eco-labeling schemes in order to stay competitive in all of the markets relevant for his or her exports. Costs of compliance might be influenced by criteria that require the use of inputs, which are expensive or might even have to be bought overseas. In addition, process-related criteria, which tend to be based on environmental and technological conditions in the importing country, can imply high costs for foreign producers. Costs for testing and verification to prove conformity to labeling criteria can be very high, especially if overseas capacities have to be used. The cost of compliance may include costs for training and for restructuring the production process so as to meet the labeling requirements.

MEASURES TO AVOID TRADE BARRIERS FOR DEVELOPING COUNTRIES

The ISO 14000 standards have the potential to avoid some of the negative impacts on developing country trade associated with unilateral EMS standards and EL schemes. However, whether ISO will achieve its goal of abolishing barriers to trade or even create new goals will depend on many other factors that go beyond the standards setting-process. First, it will be necessary that the ISO 14000 international standards will be used as a basis for the design of different national standards on environmental management in order to achieve the intended harmonization. Second, the interpretation and application of the standards must be nondiscriminatory. Third, there is a need for technical and financial assistance to support developing countries in taking advantage of trading opportunities that can arise from the ISO 14000 standards. Furthermore, ISO should allow nonmember countries access to draft standards in order to minimize possible negative trade impacts arising from a time lag in adjusting to standards' requirements.

Acceptance of the Standards and Control over Deviations

Any measures that convince countries to adjust their national or regional standards to international ones and to justify deviations from these could help to avoid new trade barriers. In its Technical Barriers to Trade Agreement (TBT), the World Trade Organization (WTO) encourages its member countries to use relevant international standards as a basis for their national standards. WTO member countries must carefully control their activities on standards setting and conformity assessment with respect to the TBT agreement. All member countries should accept the Code of Good Practice defined in the TBT. This code foresees practices for the preparation, adoption, and application of standards that prevent them from creating unnecessary obstacles to international trade. The mandate of the WTO has to be clarified before deciding whether and by what means WTO could react if unilateral measures in the area of EMS and EL are not justifiable and discriminatory. If environmental management is used as a technical barrier to trade, steps must be undertaken by aggrieved parties to combat offending parties. ISO, supported by its member bodies, could function as an impartial authority and offer experts, data, or other inputs to WTO in the case of disputes.

International guidelines that provide interpretation of ISO 14001 might lead to harmonized and "objective" accreditation and certification procedures. They could lead to conformity-assessment practices that stress effective improvement of environmental performance. The ISO Committee on Conformity Assessment (CASCO) is responsible for questions on how to prove compliance with standards developed by technical committees (TC). During the first joint workshop between the committee on environmental management, TC 207, and CASCO in June 1995, it was proposed that ISO bodies should work out a global system to ensure that registration obtained in one country will be recognized and accepted worldwide.[11]

Mutual Recognition

Mutual-recognition agreements between certification bodies in developed and developing countries for both EMS and EL would allow exporters in developing countries to benefit from their own certification infrastructures and to reduce costs. One prerequisite for mutual recognition is an existent standardization infrastructure in the developing country and confidence in its quality by the importing country.

A precondition for the mutual recognition of EL schemes is that the criteria of the schemes of both countries are equal. However, the criteria might not be completely equivalent in most cases. Therefore experts propose to award the importing country's label if the product- and disposal-related criteria of the importing country are fulfilled. It has to be verified if criteria related to the production process can be accepted, even if they differ from the criteria in the importing country. Another possibility would be to require fulfillment of the importing country's criteria but to recognize and allow certification being undertaken by the exporting country's testing and verification bodies authorized within the local EL program.

Technical and Financial Assistance

Assistance activities should focus on infrastructure development, increased participation of developing countries in the standard-setting process, increased information, awareness raising, and training to build up local capacity.

Exporters in developing countries need to know the standards relevant for their export markets and need to understand the standards' requirements as well as procedures of conformity assessment. Developing countries should obtain information and become actively involved as early as possible to avoid a lag with respect to the implementation timetable. Financial assistance would enable those countries to participate regularly at ISO meetings. Active participation in the standard-setting process allows developing countries to advance their interest and diminish any psychological barriers that may arise from the perception that the standards are imposed by industrialized countries.

Measures to raise awareness of the importance and potential benefits of ISO 14000 contribute to an increased commitment of both government and industry. There is a strong need for training and capacity building related to EMS in developing countries, especially if they have export-led strategies. Training should focus on representatives from government standards bodies, local training and certification bodies, consultants, and business leaders. Assistance could also include teaching material and curriculum development. Training seminars and fellowships for specialized training of individuals are a part of the ISO technical assistance program for developing countries. ISO also provides developing countries with information and contacts for training conducted by ISO member bodies in OECD countries. For the future, ISO, in cooperation with other institutions, should initiate efforts to construct a system by which qualified consultants, trainers, and auditors in environmental management could be accessed by all countries in need of their expertise.

Companies that decide to implement ISO 14001 should receive further assistance and implementation facilitation. Small-scale producers will have the largest need for support. They will need technical and financial assistance in order to obtain adequate technologies.

The problem of limited resources can also be overcome by regional cooperation between developing countries. The Latin American Integration Association (ALADI), for example, promotes the establishment of a cooperation system to strengthen standardization and certification institutions in 11 Latin American countries.[12]

Support within the Private Sector

The private sector itself plays an important role in avoiding potential trade barriers that may arise from ISO 14000. First, certified companies in industrialized countries demanding compliance with specific environmental targets for developing country suppliers should take the economic, social, and environmental conditions and preferences of the supplier country into account. Second, they could provide suppliers in developing countries with sufficient time and advance information to adjust to new environmental requirements. Third, purchasers in industrialized countries can help raise the performance of the suppliers they have significant trade relations with.

Large companies in environmentally sensitive sectors in industrialized countries have experience with environmental issues and are a valuable source of expertise for small companies in developing countries. They should provide consultation and assistance aimed at transfer of clean technologies and know-how, for example, in the form of visiting firm consultants or experience-sharing workshops. Cooperative strategies within the private sector, especially among SMEs, should be promoted and supported. Business associations and networks as well as chambers of commerce are a source to help businesses identify the relevant environmental regulations and ongoing changes.

The Confederation of Indian Industries provides an example for an active business network. Besides awareness-raising on ISO 14001, the CII is organizing training and conducted a recent workshop on EMS in cooperation with the International Chamber of Commerce. These activities are accompanied by a planned project on EMS certification in a cluster of small-scale firms. The purpose of this project is the demonstration of EMS implementation and the active support for selected small firms to achieve certification. The demonstration project will serve the development of an EMS guide for small enterprises, which has not yet been provided by ISO.

CONCLUSION

By creating the ISO 14000 series, the International Organization for Standardization is trying to resolve a difficult balance: It aims to improve the environment while also trying to facilitate trade. Whether or not both objectives can be achieved remains to be seen. The "rigidity" and "ethics" that develop while the standards are applied by companies, consultants, and registrars as well as the level of national environmental legislation a company has to comply with will be crucial for the expected improvement of the global environment. The level of environmental performance attained by ISO 14001 will be tied to regulatory requirements in any given country. Even with ISO 14001 implementation, companies in a country with weak and poorly enforced environmental laws will likely still lag behind companies in countries that have more highly developed regulations. National governments therefore have an important role to play in strengthening their environmental laws. Given that regulations differ from country to country, ISO 14001 certification cannot be used to evaluate a company's environmental performance. It is simply a measure of a company's commitment to meet the requirements of a country where it operates. With regard to transnational corporations, ISO 14000 standards cannot ensure that the highest standards are applied across their operations worldwide.

From a trade perspective, the ISO 14000 standards have the potential to bring benefits for exporters in developing countries. Certification of a company's EMS might improve market access, and the EL standards might lead to nondiscriminatory practices. Exporters in developing countries would also benefit from a harmonization of different unilateral environmental management standards. There is likely to be pressure on companies in developing countries originating from their trading partners in industrialized countries to become ISO 14001-certified, and the certificate will become a tool to achieve a competitive advantage. However, a lack of information, capital, technology, expertise, and local infrastructure in most developing countries can become obstacles to implementation of and adherence to these standards. Therefore, developing countries have to seek cooperation with international organizations, national governments, and standards bodies for technical and financial assistance. Small firms in particular could benefit from cooperative arrangements within the private sector. Direct support to suppliers in developing countries by their trading partners in industrialized countries could also help.

As stressed by the WTO in its TBT-agreement, the ISO has an important role in creating international standards and facilitating international trade. Only if WTO member countries adopt ISO 14000, avoid conflicting requirements, and carefully control their conformity assessment activities can the objective of international standard setting be achieved.

BIOGRAPHY

Kerstin Pfliegner

Kerstin Pfliegner works as a consultant for the Private Sector Development Program of the United Nations Development Program, New York. She studied economics and business management at the Universities of Munich and Hamburg in Germany. After earning her degree in business economics, she followed courses in environmental economics conducted jointly by the University of Witten and the Wuppertal Institute for Climate, Environment, and Energy. Ms. Pfliegner has several years of working experience in private-sector companies and as a researcher and lecturer at universities.

REFERENCES

Abalaka (1995): Statement presented by Prof. J. A. Abalaka, Director General Standards Organization of Nigeria at the UNIDO Expert Group meeting to discuss the potential effects of ISO 9000 and ISO/DIS 14000 on the Industrial Trade of Developing Countries, 23–25 October 1995, Vienna, Austria.

ALADI (1995): *Technical Barriers to Trade within ALADI*, statement presented at the UNIDO Expert Group meeting to discuss the potential effects of ISO 9000 and ISO/DIS 14000 on the Industrial Trade of Developing Countries, 23–25 October 1995, Vienna, Austria.

CII (1995): *Role of EMS -CII*, statement presented at the UNIDO expert Group meeting to discuss the potential effects of ISO 8900 and ISO/DIS 14000 on the Industrial Trade of Developing Countries, 23–25 October 1995, Vienna, Austria.

Hillary (1995): *ISO 14001 and EMAS Comparison*, Center for Environmental Technology, London.

ISO (1995): Environmental Management Systems—General Guidelines on Principles, Systems and Supporting Techniques, Draft International Standard ISO/DIS 14004.

ISO (1995a): Environmental Management Systems—Specification with guidance for use, Draft International Standard ISO/DIS 14001.

UNCTAD (1994): International Cooperation on Eco-Labeling and Eco-Certification Programs, TD/B/WG.6/2.

UNCTAD (1995): Trade, Environment and Development Aspects of Establishing and Operating Eco-Labeling Programs, TD/B/WG.6/5.

UNDP (1996): ISO 14000 Environmental Management Standards and Implications for Exporters to Developed Markets, Private Sector Development Programme, United Nations Development Programme, New York.

UNIDO (1995): Expert Group Meeting on the Potential Effects of ISO 9000 and ISO 14000 Series and Environmental Labeling on the Trade of Developing Countries. Report, Vienna, 23–25 October 1995.

NOTES

1. From 22 mailed questionnaires, we received 15 responses. Six of these responses were from developing countries. Additional information was obtained from some respondents by personal interviews.

2. Estimated by R. Ferrone, consultant, Excel Partnership, Inc., Sandy Hook (USA).

3. As argued by Lloyds, an international registrar.

4. See: ISO (1995): ISO/DIS 14001, subclause 4.1.a and subclause 4.3.6.c.

5. For companies certified against BS 7750, it became a practice to send out questionnaires to suppliers in order to evaluate their performance. In some cases, the questionnaires are very complex, requiring extensive investigations to answer them. For example, the company Design for Distribution (D2D) developed an "accredited vendor program," which requested from suppliers wishing to become accredited vendors that they satisfy a set of entry criteria, including environmental criteria. Depending on their answers to the questionnaire, suppliers are placed in one of four grades. Suppliers that fail to improve their performance are dropped. See: R. Hillary, (1995).

6. See: CII (1995).

7. See: International Environmental Systems Update (1995).

8. See: CII (1995) and Abalaka (1995).

9. See: CII (1995).

10. For example, the French eco-labeling scheme insists that an on-site inspection should be conducted by a certified official of the standard-setting authority AFNOR. See: UNCTAD (1994), p. 15.

11. These bodies are the Quality System Assessment Recognition (QSAR) and CASCO.

12. See: ALADI (1995).

EPA Policy Statement "Incentives for Self-Policing: Discovery, Disclosure, Correction and Prevention of Violations"

[Federal Register: December 22, 1995 (Volume 60, Number 246)] [Notices]
[Pages 66705–66712]
From the Federal Register Online via GPO Access [wais.access.gpo.gov]

Part III
Environmental Protection Agency

Incentives for Self-Policing: Discovery, Disclosure, Correction
and Prevention of Violations; Notice

ENVIRONMENTAL PROTECTION AGENCY

[FRL–5400–1]

Incentives for Self-Policing: Discovery, Disclosure, Correction
and Prevention of Violations

AGENCY: Environmental Protection Agency (EPA).

ACTION: Final Policy Statement.

SUMMARY: The Environmental Protection Agency (EPA) today issues its final policy to enhance protection of human health and the environment by encouraging regulated entities to voluntarily discover, and disclose and correct violations of environmental requirements. Incentives include eliminating or substantially reducing the gravity component of civil penalties and not recommending cases for criminal prosecution where specified conditions are met, to those who voluntarily self-disclose and promptly correct violations. The policy also restates EPA's long-standing practice of not requesting voluntary audit reports to trigger enforcement investigations. This policy was developed in close consultation with the U.S. Department of Justice, states, public interest groups and the regulated community, and will be applied uniformly by the Agency's enforcement programs.

DATES: This policy is effective January 22, 1996.

FOR FURTHER INFORMATION CONTACT: Additional documentation related to the development of this policy is contained in the environmental auditing public docket. Documents from the docket may be obtained by calling (202) 260-7548, requesting an index to docket #C–94–01, and faxing document requests to (202) 260-4400. Hours of operation are 8 A.M. to 5:30 P.M., Monday through Friday, except legal holidays. Additional contacts are Robert Fentress or Brian Riedel, at (202) 564-4187.

SUPPLEMENTARY INFORMATION:

I. Explanation of Policy

A. Introduction

The Environmental Protection Agency today issues its final policy to enhance protection of human health and the environment by encouraging regulated entities to discover voluntarily, disclose, correct and prevent violations of federal environmental law. Effective 30 days from today, where violations are found through voluntary environmental audits or efforts that reflect a regulated entity's due diligence, and are promptly disclosed and expeditiously corrected, EPA will not seek gravity-based (i.e., non-economic benefit) penalties and will generally not recommend criminal prosecution against the regulated entity. EPA will reduce gravity-based penalties by 75% for violations that are voluntarily discovered, and are promptly disclosed and corrected, even if not found through a formal audit or due diligence. Finally, the policy restates EPA's long-held policy and practice to refrain from routine requests for environmental audit reports. The policy includes important safeguards to deter irresponsible behavior and protect the public and environment. For example, in addition to prompt disclosure and expeditious correction, the policy requires companies to act to prevent recurrence of the violation and to remedy any environmental harm which may have occurred. Repeated violations or those which result in actual harm or may present imminent and substantial endangerment are not eligible for relief under this policy, and companies will not be allowed to gain an economic advantage over their competitors by delaying their investment in compliance. Corporations remain criminally liable for violations that result from conscious disregard of their obligations under the law, and individuals are liable for criminal misconduct.

The issuance of this policy concludes EPA's eighteen-month public evaluation of the optimum way to encourage voluntary self-policing while preserving fair and effective enforcement. The incentives, conditions and exceptions announced today reflect thoughtful suggestions from the Department of Justice, state attorneys general and local prosecutors, state environmental agencies, the regulated community, and public interest organizations. EPA believes that it has found a balanced and responsible approach, and will conduct a study within three years to determine the effectiveness of this policy.

B. Public Process

One of the Environmental Protection Agency's most important responsibilities is ensuring compliance with federal laws that protect public health and safeguard the environment. Effective deterrence requires inspecting, bringing penalty actions and securing compliance and remediation of harm. But EPA realizes that achieving compliance also requires the cooperation of thousands of businesses and other regulated entities subject to these requirements. Accordingly, in May of 1994, the Administrator asked the Office of Enforcement and Compliance Assurance (OECA) to determine whether additional incentives were needed to encourage voluntary disclosure and correction of violations uncovered during environmental audits. EPA began its evaluation with a two-day public meeting in July of 1994, in Washington, D.C., followed by a two-day meeting in San Francisco on January 19, 1995 with stakeholders from industry, trade groups, state environmental commissioners and attorneys general, district attorneys, public interest organizations, and professional environmental auditors. The Agency also established and maintained a public docket of testimony presented at those meetings and all comment and correspondence submitted to EPA by outside parties on this issue. In addition to considering opinion and information from stakeholders, the Agency examined other federal and state policies related to self-policing, self-disclosure and correction. The Agency also considered relevant surveys on auditing practices in the private sector. EPA completed the first stage of this effort with the announcement of an interim policy on April 3 of this year, which defined conditions under which EPA would reduce civil penalties and not recommend criminal prosecution for companies that audited, disclosed, and corrected violations.

Interested parties were asked to submit comment on the interim policy by June 30 of this year (60 FR 16875), and EPA received over 300 responses from a wide variety of private and public organizations. (Comments on the interim audit policy are contained in the Auditing Policy Docket, hereinafter, "Docket.") Further, the American Bar Association SONREEL Subcommittee hosted five days of dialogue with representatives from the regulated industry, states and public interest organizations in June and September of this year, which identified options for strengthening the interim policy. The changes to the interim policy announced today reflect insight gained through comments submitted to EPA, the ABA dialogue, and the Agency's practical experience implementing the interim policy.

C. Purpose

This policy is designed to encourage greater compliance with laws and regulations that protect human health and the environment. It promotes a higher standard of self-policing by waiving gravity-based penalties for violations that are promptly disclosed and corrected, and which were discovered through voluntary audits or compliance management systems that demonstrate due diligence. To further promote compliance, the policy reduces gravity-based penalties by 75% for any violation voluntarily discovered and promptly disclosed and corrected, even if not found through an audit or compliance management system. EPA's enforcement program provides a strong incentive for responsible behavior by imposing stiff sanctions for noncompliance. Enforcement has contributed to the dramatic expansion of environmental auditing measured in numerous recent surveys. For example, more than 90% of the corporate respondents to a 1995 Price-Waterhouse survey who conduct audits said that one of the reasons they did so was to find and correct violations before they were found by government inspectors. (A copy of the Price-Waterhouse survey is contained in the Docket as document VIII–A–76.)

At the same time, because government resources are limited, maximum compliance cannot be achieved without active efforts by the regulated community to police themselves. More than half of the respondents to the same 1995 Price-Waterhouse survey said that they would expand environmental auditing in exchange for reduced penalties for violations discovered and corrected. While many companies already audit or have compliance management programs, EPA believes that the incentives offered in this policy will improve the frequency and quality of these self-monitoring efforts.

D. Incentives for Self-Policing

Section C of EPA's policy identifies the major incentives that EPA will provide to encourage self-policing, self-disclosure, and prompt self-correction. These include not seeking gravity-based civil penalties or reducing them by 75%, declining to recommend criminal prosecution for regulated entities that self-police, and refraining from routine requests for audits. (As noted in Section C of the policy, EPA has refrained from making routine requests for audit reports since issuance of its 1986 policy on environmental auditing.)

1. Eliminating Gravity-Based Penalties

Under Section C(1) of the policy, EPA will not seek gravity-based penalties for violations found through auditing that are promptly disclosed and corrected. Gravity-based penalties will also be waived for violations found through any documented procedure for self-policing, where the company can show that it has a compliance management program that meets the criteria for due diligence in Section B of the policy.

Gravity-based penalties (defined in Section B of the policy) generally reflect the seriousness of the violator's behavior. EPA has elected to waive such penalties for violations discovered through due diligence or environmental audits, recognizing that these voluntary efforts play a critical role in protecting human health and the environment by identifying, correcting and ultimately preventing violations. All of the conditions set forth in Section D, which include prompt disclosure and expeditious correction, must be satisfied for gravity-based penalties to be waived.

As in the interim policy, EPA reserves the right to collect any economic benefit that may have been realized as a result of noncompliance, even where companies meet all other conditions of the policy. Economic benefit may be waived, however, where the Agency determines that it is insignificant.

After considering public comment, EPA has decided to retain the discretion to recover economic benefit for two reasons. First, it provides an incentive to comply on time. Taxpayers expect to pay interest or a penalty fee if their tax payments are late; the same principle should apply to corporations that have delayed their investment in compliance. Second, it is fair because it protects responsible companies from being undercut by their noncomplying competitors, thereby preserving a level playing field. The concepts of recovering economic benefit was supported in public comments by many stakeholders, including industry representatives (see, e.g., Docket, II–F–39, II–F–28, and II–F–18).

2. 75% Reduction of Gravity

The policy appropriately limits the complete waiver of gravity-based civil penalties to companies that meet the higher standard of environmental auditing or systematic compliance management. However, to provide additional encouragement for the kind of self-policing that benefits the public, gravity-based penalties will be reduced by 75% for a violation that is voluntarily discovered, promptly disclosed and expeditiously corrected, even if it was not found through an environmental audit and the company cannot document due diligence. EPA expects that this will encourage companies to come forward and work with the Agency to resolve environmental problems and begin to develop an effective compliance management program. Gravity-based penalties will be reduced 75% only where the company meets all conditions in Sections D(2) through D(9). EPA has eliminated language from the interim policy indicating that penalties may be reduced "up to" 75% where "most" conditions are met, because the Agency believes that all of the conditions in D(2) through D(9) are reasonable and essential to achieving compliance. This change also responds to requests for greater clarity and predictability.

3. No Recommendations for Criminal Prosecution

EPA has never recommended criminal prosecution of a regulated entity based on voluntary disclosure of violations discovered through audits and disclosed to the government before an investigation was already under way. Thus, EPA will not recommend criminal prosecution for a regulated entity that uncovers violations through environmental audits or due diligence, promptly discloses and expeditiously corrects those violations, and meets all other conditions of Section D of the policy.

This policy is limited to good actors, and therefore has important limitations. It will not apply, for example, where corporate officials are consciously involved in or willfully blind to violations, or conceal or condone noncompliance. Since the regulated entity must satisfy all of the conditions of Section D of the policy, violations that caused serious harm or which may pose imminent and substantial endangerment to human health or the environment are not covered by this policy. Finally, EPA reserves the right to recommend prosecution for the criminal conduct of any culpable individual. Even where all of the conditions of this policy are not met, however, it is important to remember that EPA may decline to recommend prosecution of a company or individual for many other reasons under other Agency enforcement policies. For example, the Agency may decline to recommend prosecution where there is no significant harm or culpability and the individual or corporate defendant has cooperated fully.

Where a company has met the conditions for avoiding a recommendation for criminal prosecution under this policy, it will not face any civil liability for gravity-based penalties. That is because the same conditions for discovery, disclosure, and correction apply in both cases. This represents a clarification of the interim policy, not a substantive change.

4. No Routine Requests for Audits

EPA is reaffirming its policy, in effect since 1986, to refrain from routine requests for audits. Eighteen months of public testimony and debate have produced no evidence that the Agency has deviated, or should deviate, from this policy.

If the Agency has independent evidence of a violation, it may seek information needed to establish the extent and nature of the problem and the degree of culpability. In general, however, an audit which results in prompt correction clearly will reduce liability, not expand it. Furthermore, a review of the criminal docket did not reveal a single criminal prosecution for violations discovered as a result of an audit self-disclosed to the government.

E. Conditions

Section D describes the nine conditions that a regulated entity must meet in order for the Agency not to seek (or to reduce) gravity-based penalties under the policy. As explained in the Summary above, regulated entities that meet all nine conditions will not face gravity-based civil penalties, and will generally not have to fear criminal prosecution. Where the regulated entity meets all of the conditions except the first (D(1)), EPA will reduce gravity-based penalties by 75%.

1. Discovery of the Violation Through an Environmental Audit or Due Diligence

Under Section D(1), the violation must have been discovered through either (a) an environmental audit that is systematic, objective, and periodic as defined in the 1986 audit policy, or (b) a documented, systematic procedure or practice which reflects the regulated entity's due diligence in preventing, detecting, and correcting violations. The interim policy provided full credit for any violation found through "voluntary self-evaluation," even if the evaluation did not constitute an audit. In order to receive full credit under the final policy, any self-evaluation that is not an audit must be part of a "due diligence" program. Both "environmental audit" and "due diligence" are defined in Section B of the policy. Where the violation is discovered through a "systematic procedure or practice" which is not an audit, the regulated entity will be asked to document how its program reflects the criteria for due diligence as defined in Section B of the policy. These criteria, which are adapted from existing codes of practice such as the 1991 Criminal Sentencing Guidelines, were fully discussed during the ABA dialogue. The criteria are flexible enough to accommodate different types and sizes of businesses. The Agency recognizes that a variety of compliance management programs may develop under the due diligence criteria, and will use its review under this policy to determine whether basic criteria have been met.

Compliance management programs which train and motivate production staff to prevent, detect and correct violations on a daily basis are a valuable complement to periodic auditing. The policy is responsive to recommendations received during public comment and from the ABA dialogue to give compliance management efforts which meet the criteria for due diligence the same penalty reduction offered for environmental audits. (See, e.g., II–F–39, II–E–18, and II–G–18 in the Docket.) EPA may require as a condition of penalty mitigation that a description of the regulated entity's due diligence efforts be made publicly available. The Agency added this provision in response to suggestions from environmental groups, and believes that the availability of such information will allow the public to judge the adequacy of compliance management systems, lead to enhanced compliance, and foster greater public trust in the integrity of compliance management systems.

2. Voluntary Discovery and Prompt Disclosure

Under Section D(2) of the final policy, the violation must have been identified voluntarily, and not through a monitoring, sampling, or auditing procedure that is required by statute, regulation, permit, judicial or administrative order, or consent agreement. Section D(4) requires that disclosure of the violation be prompt and in writing. To avoid confusion and respond to state requests for greater clarity, disclosures under this policy should be made to EPA. The Agency will work closely with states in implementing the policy. The requirement that discovery of the violation be voluntary is consistent with proposed federal and state bills which would reward those discoveries that the regulated entity can legitimately attribute to its own voluntary efforts.

The policy gives three specific examples of discovery that would not be voluntary, and therefore would not be eligible for penalty mitigation: emissions violations detected through a required continuous emissions monitor, violations of NPDES discharge limits found through prescribed monitoring, and violations discovered through a compliance audit required to be performed by the terms of a consent order or settlement agreement.

The final policy generally applies to any violation that is voluntarily discovered, regardless of whether the violation is required to be reported. This definition responds to comments pointing out that reporting requirements are extensive, and that excluding them from the policy's scope would severely limit the incentive for self-policing (see, eg., II–C–48 in the Docket).

The Agency wishes to emphasize that the integrity of federal environmental law depends upon timely and accurate reporting. The public relies on timely and accurate reports from the regulated community, not only to measure compliance but to evaluate health or environmental risk and gauge progress in reducing pollutant loadings. EPA expects the policy to encourage the kind of vigorous self-policing that will serve these objectives, and not to provide an excuse for delayed reporting. Where violations of reporting requirements are voluntarily discovered, they must be promptly reported (as discussed below). Where a failure to report results in imminent and substantial endangerment or serious harm, that violation is not covered under this policy (see Condition D(8)). The policy also requires the regulated entity to prevent recurrence of the violation, to ensure that noncompliance with reporting requirements is not repeated. EPA will closely scrutinize the effect of the policy in furthering the public interest in timely and accurate reports from the regulated community.

Under Section D(4), disclosure of the violation should be made within 10 days of its discovery, and in writing to EPA. Where a statute or regulation requires reporting be made in less than 10 days, disclosure should be made within the time limit established by law. Where reporting within ten days is not practical because the violation is complex and compliance cannot be determined within that period, the Agency may accept later disclosures if the circumstances do not present a serious threat and the regulated entity meets its burden of showing that the additional time was needed to determine compliance status.

This condition recognizes that it is critical for EPA to get timely reporting of violations in order that it might have clear notice of the violations and the opportunity to respond if necessary, as well as an accurate picture of a given facility's compliance record. Prompt disclosure is also evidence of the regulated entity's good faith in wanting to achieve or return to compliance as soon as possible. In the final policy, the Agency has added the words, "or may have occurred," to the sentence, "The regulated entity fully discloses that a specific violation has occurred, or may have occurred * * *."

This change, which was made in response to comments received, clarifies that where an entity has some doubt about the existence of a violation, the recommended course is for it to disclose and allow the regulatory authorities to make a definitive determination. In general, the Freedom of Information Act will govern the Agency's release of disclosures made pursuant to this policy. EPA will, independently of FOIA, make publicly available any compliance agreements reached under the policy (see Section H of the policy), as well as descriptions of due diligence programs submitted under Section D.1 of the Policy. Any material claimed to be Confidential Business Information will be treated in accordance with EPA regulations at 40 C.F.R. Part 2.

3. Discovery and Disclosure Independent of Government or Third Party Plaintiff

Under Section D(3), in order to be "voluntary," the violation must be identified and disclosed by the regulated entity prior to: the commencement of a federal, state or local agency inspection, investigation, or information request; notice of a citizen suit; legal complaint by a third party; the reporting of the violation to EPA by a "whistleblower" employee; and imminent discovery of the violation by a regulatory agency.

This condition means that regulated entities must have taken the initiative to find violations and promptly report them, rather than reacting to knowledge of a pending enforcement action or third-party complaint. This concept was reflected in the interim policy and in federal and state penalty immunity laws and did not prove controversial in the public comment process.

4. Correction and Remediation

Section D(5) ensures that, in order to receive the penalty mitigation benefits available under the policy, the regulated entity not only voluntarily discovers and promptly discloses a violation, but expeditiously corrects it, remedies any harm caused by that violation (including responding to any spill and carrying out any removal or remedial action required by law), and expeditiously certifies in writing to appropriate state, local and EPA authorities that violations have been corrected. It also enables EPA to ensure that the regulated entity will be publicly accountable for its commitments through binding written agreements, order or consent decrees where necessary. The final policy requires the violation to be corrected within 60 days, or that the regulated entity provide written notice where violations may take longer to correct. EPA recognizes that some violations can and should be corrected immediately, while others (e.g., where capital expenditures are involved), may take longer than 60 days to correct. In all cases, the regulated entity will be expected to do its utmost to achieve or return to compliance as expeditiously as possible. Where correction of the violation depends upon issuance of a permit which has been applied for but not issued by federal or state authorities, the Agency will, where appropriate, make reasonable efforts to secure timely review of the permit.

5. Prevent Recurrence

Under Section D(6), the regulated entity must agree to take steps to prevent a recurrence of the violation, including but not limited to improvements to its environmental auditing or due diligence efforts. The final policy makes clear that the preventive steps may include improvements to a regulated entity's environmental auditing or due diligence efforts to prevent recurrence of the violation. In the interim policy, the Agency required that the entity implement appropriate measures to prevent a recurrence of the violation, a requirement that operates prospectively. However, a separate condition in the interim policy also required that the violation not indicate "a failure to take appropriate steps to avoid repeat or recurring violations"—a requirement that operates retrospectively. In the interest of both clarity and fairness, the Agency has decided for purposes of this condition to keep the focus prospective and thus to require only that steps be taken to prevent recurrence of the violation after it has been disclosed.

6. No Repeat Violations

In response to requests from commenters (see, e.g., II–F–39 and II–G–18 in the Docket), EPA has established "bright lines" to determine when previous violations will bar a regulated entity from obtaining relief under this policy. These will help protect the public and responsible companies by ensuring that penalties are not waived for repeat offenders. Under condition D(7), the same or closely-related violation must not have occurred previously within the past three years at the same facility, or be part of a pattern of violations on the regulated entity's part over the past five years. This provides companies with a continuing incentive to prevent violations, without being unfair to regulated entities responsible for managing hundreds of facilities. It would be unreasonable to provide unlimited amnesty for repeated violations of the same requirement. The term "violation" includes any violation subject to a federal or state civil judicial or administrative order, consent agreement, conviction or plea agreement. Recognizing that minor violations are sometimes settled without a formal action in court, the term also covers any act or omission for which the regulated entity has received a penalty reduction in the past. Together, these conditions identify situations in which the regulated community has had clear notice of its noncompliance and an opportunity to correct.

7. Other Violations Excluded

Section D(8) makes clear that penalty reductions are not available under this policy for violations that resulted in serious actual harm or which may have presented an imminent and substantial endangerment to public health or the environment. Such events indicate a serious failure (or absence) of a self-policing program, which should be designed to prevent such risks, and it would seriously undermine deterrence to waive penalties for such violations. These exceptions are responsive to suggestions from public interest organizations, as well as other commenters. (See, e.g., II–F–39 and II–G–18 in the

Docket.) The final policy also excludes penalty reductions for violations of the specific terms of any order, consent agreement, or plea agree. (See, II–E–60 in the Docket.) Once a consent agreement has been negotiated, there is little incentive to comply if there are no sanctions for violating its specific requirements. The exclusion in this section applies to violations of the terms of any response, removal or remedial action covered by a written agreement.

8. Cooperation

Under Section D(9), the regulated entity must cooperate as required by EPA and provide information necessary to determine the applicability of the policy. This condition is largely unchanged from the interim policy. In the final policy, however, the Agency has added that "cooperation" includes assistance in determining the facts of any related violations suggested by the disclosure, as well as of the disclosed violation itself. This was added to allow the agency to obtain information about any violations indicated by the disclosure, even where the violation is not initially identified by the regulated entity.

F. Opposition to Privilege

The Agency remains firmly opposed to the establishment of a statutory evidentiary privilege for environmental audits for the following reasons:

1. Privilege, by definition, invites secrecy, instead of the openness needed to build public trust in industry's ability to self-police. American law reflects the high value that the public places on fair access to the facts. The Supreme Court, for example, has said of privileges that, "[w]hatever their origins, these exceptions to the demand for every man's evidence are not lightly created nor expansively construed, for they are in derogation of the search for truth." United States v. Nixon, 418 U.S. 683 (1974). Federal courts have unanimously refused to recognize a privilege for environmental audits in the context of government investigations. See, e.g., United States v. Dexter, 132 F.R.D. 8, 9–10 (D.Conn. 1990) (application of a privilege "would effectively impede [EPA's] ability to enforce the Clean Water Act, and would be contrary to stated public policy.")

2. Eighteen months have failed to produce any evidence that a privilege is needed. Public testimony on the interim policy confirmed that EPA rarely uses audit reports as evidence. Furthermore, surveys demonstrate that environmental auditing has expanded rapidly over the past decade without the stimulus of a privilege. Most recently, the 1995 Price-Waterhouse survey found that those few large or mid-size companies that do not audit generally do not perceive any need to; concern about confidentiality ranked as one of the least important factors in their decisions.

3. A privilege would invite defendants to claim as "audit" material almost any evidence the government needed to establish a violation or determine

who was responsible. For example, most audit privilege bills under consideration in federal and state legislatures would arguably protect factual information—such as health studies or contaminated sediment data—and not just the conclusions of the auditors. While the government might have access to required monitoring data under the law, as some industry commenters have suggested, a privilege of that nature would cloak underlying facts needed to determine whether such data were accurate.

4. An audit privilege would breed litigation, as both parties struggled to determine what material fell within its scope. The problem is compounded by the lack of any clear national standard for audits. The "in camera" (i.e., non-public) proceedings used to resolve these disputes under some statutory schemes would result in a series of time-consuming, expensive mini-trials.

5. The Agency's policy eliminates the need for any privilege as against the government, by reducing civil penalties and criminal liability for those companies that audit, disclose and correct violations. The 1995 Price-Waterhouse survey indicated that companies would expand their auditing programs in exchange for the kind of incentives that EPA provides in its policy.

6. Finally, audit privileges are strongly opposed by the law enforcement community, including the National District Attorneys Association, as well as by public interest groups. (See, e.g., Docket, II–C–21, II–C–28, II–C–52, IV–G–10, II–C–25, II–C–33, II–C–52, II–C–48, and II–G–13 through II–G–24.)

G. Effect on States

The final policy reflects EPA's desire to develop fair and effective incentives for self-policing that will have practical value to states that share responsibility for enforcing federal environmental laws. To that end, the Agency has consulted closely with state officials in developing this policy, through a series of special meetings and conference calls in addition to the extensive opportunity for public comment. As a result, EPA believes its final policy is grounded in common-sense principles that should prove useful in the development of state programs and policies. As always, states are encouraged to experiment with different approaches that do not jeopardize the fundamental national interest in assuring that violations of federal law do not threaten the public health or the environment, or make it profitable not to comply. The Agency remains opposed to state legislation that does not include these basic protections, and reserves its right to bring independent action against regulated entities for violations of federal law that threaten human health or the environment, reflect criminal conduct or repeated noncompliance, or allow one company to make a substantial profit at the expense of its law-abiding competitors. Where a state has obtained appropriate sanctions needed to deter such misconduct, there is no need for EPA action.

H. Scope of Policy

EPA has developed this document as a policy to guide settlement actions. EPA employees will be expected to follow this policy, and the Agency will take steps to assure national consistency in application. For example, the Agency will make public any compliance agreements reached under this policy, in order to provide the regulated community with fair notice of decisions and greater accountability to affected communities. Many in the regulated community recommended that the Agency convert the policy into a regulation because they felt it might ensure greater consistency and predictability. While EPA is taking steps to ensure consistency and predictability and believes that it will be successful, the Agency will consider this issue and will provide notice if it determines that a rulemaking is appropriate.

II. Statement of Policy: Incentives for Self-Policing

Discovery, Disclosure, Correction and Prevention

A. Purpose

This policy is designed to enhance protection of human health and the environment by encouraging regulated entities to voluntarily discover, disclose, correct and prevent violations of federal environmental requirements.

B. Definitions

For purposes of this policy, the following definitions apply:

"Environmental audit" has the definition given to it in EPA's 1986 audit policy on environmental auditing, i.e., "a systematic, documented, periodic and objective review by regulated entities of facility operations and practices related to meeting environmental requirements."

"Due diligence" encompasses the regulated entity's systematic efforts, appropriate to the size and nature of its business, to prevent, detect and correct violations through all of the following:

(a) Compliance policies, standards and procedures that identify how employees and agents are to meet the requirements of laws, regulations, permits and other sources of authority for environmental requirements;

(b) Assignment of overall responsibility for overseeing compliance with policies, standards, and procedures, and assignment of specific responsibility for assuring compliance at each facility or operation;

(c) Mechanisms for systematically assuring that compliance policies, standards and procedures are being carried out, including monitoring and auditing systems reasonably designed to detect and correct violations, periodic evaluation of the overall performance of the compliance management system, and a means for employees or agents to report violations of environmental requirements without fear of retaliation;

(d) Efforts to communicate effectively the regulated entity's standards and procedures to all employees and other agents;

(e) Appropriate incentives to managers and employees to perform in accordance with the compliance policies, standards and procedures, including consistent enforcement through appropriate disciplinary mechanisms; and

(f) Procedures for the prompt and appropriate correction of any violations, and any necessary modifications to the regulated entity's program to prevent future violations.

"Environmental audit report" means the analysis, conclusions, and recommendations resulting from an environmental audit, but does not include data obtained in, or testimonial evidence concerning, the environmental audit.

"Gravity-based penalties" are that portion of a penalty over and above the economic benefit, i.e., the punitive portion of the penalty, rather than that portion representing a defendant's economic gain from non-compliance. (For further discussion of this concept, see "A Framework for Statute-Specific Approaches to Penalty Assessments," #GM–22, 1980, U.S. EPA General Enforcement Policy Compendium.)

"Regulated entity" means any entity, including a federal, state or municipal agency or facility, regulated under federal environmental laws.

C. Incentives for Self-Policing

1. No Gravity-Based Penalties

Where the regulated entity establishes that it satisfies all of the conditions of Section D of the policy, EPA will not seek gravity-based penalties for violations of federal environmental requirements.

2. Reduction of Gravity-Based Penalties by 75%

EPA will reduce gravity-based penalties for violations of federal environmental requirements by 75% so long as the regulated entity satisfies all of the conditions of Section D(2) through D(9) below.

3. No Criminal Recommendations

(a) EPA will not recommend to the Department of Justice or other prosecuting authority that criminal charges be brought against a regulated entity where EPA determines that all of the conditions in Section D are satisfied, so long as the violation does not demonstrate or involve:

      (i) a prevalent management philosophy or practice that concealed or condoned environmental violations; or

      (ii) high-level corporate officials' or managers' conscious involvement in, or willful blindness to, the violations.

  (b) Whether or not EPA refers the regulated entity for criminal prosecution under this section, the Agency reserves the right to recommend prosecution for the criminal acts of individual managers or employees under existing policies guiding the exercise of enforcement discretion.

4. No Routine Request for Audits

EPA will not request or use an environmental audit report to initiate a civil or criminal investigation of the entity. For example, EPA will not request an environmental audit report in routine inspections. If the Agency has independent reason to believe that a violation has occurred, however, EPA may seek any information relevant to identifying violations or determining liability or extent of harm.

D. Conditions

1. Systematic Discovery

The violation was discovered through:

  (a) an environmental audit; or

  (b) an objective, documented, systematic procedure or practice reflecting the regulated entity's due diligence in preventing detecting, and correcting violations.

The regulated entity must provide accurate and complete documentation to the Agency as to how it exercises due diligence to prevent, detect and correction violations according to the criteria for due diligence outlined in Section B. EPA may require as a condition of penalty mitigation that a description of the regulated entity's due diligence efforts be made publicly available.

2. Voluntary Discovery

The violation was identified voluntarily, and not through a legally mandated monitoring or sampling requirement prescribed by statute, regulation, permit, judicial or administrative order, or consent agreement. For example, the policy does not apply to:

  (a) emissions violations detected through a continuous emissions monitor (or alternative monitor established in a permit) where any such monitoring is required;

(b) violations of National Pollutant Discharge Elimination System (NPDES) discharge limits detected through required sampling or monitoring;

(c) violations discovered through a compliance audit required to be performed by the terms of a consent order or settlement agreement.

3. Prompt Disclosure

The regulated entity fully discloses a specific violation within 10 days (or such shorter period provided by law) after it has discovered that the violation has occurred, or may have occurred, in writing to EPA;

4. Discovery and Disclosure Independent of Government or Third Party Plaintiff

The violation must also be identified and disclosed by the regulated entity prior to:

(a) the commencement of a federal, state or local agency inspection or investigation, or the issuance by such agency of an information request to the regulated entity;

(b) notice of a citizen suit;

(c) the filing of a complaint by a third party;

(d) the reporting of the violation to EPA (or other government agency) by a "whistleblower" employee, rather than by one authorized to speak on behalf of the regulated entity; or

(e) imminent discovery of the violation by a regulatory agency.

5. Correction and Remediation

The regulated entity corrects the violation within 60 days, certifies in writing that violations have been corrected, and takes appropriate measures as determined by EPA to remedy any environmental or human harm due to the violation. If more than 60 days will be needed to correct the violation(s), the regulated entity must so notify EPA in writing before the 60-day period has passed. Where appropriate, EPA may require that to satisfy conditions 5 and 6, a regulated entity enter into a publicly available written agreement, administrative consent order or judicial consent decree, particularly where compliance or remedial measures are complex or a lengthy schedule for attaining and maintaining compliance or remediating harm is required;

6. Prevent Recurrence

The regulated entity agrees in writing to take steps to prevent a recurrence of the violation, which may include improvements to its environmental auditing or due diligence efforts;

7. No Repeat Violations

The specific violation (or closely related violation) has not occurred previously within the past three years at the same facility, or is not part of a pattern of federal, state or local violations by the facility's parent organization (if any), which have occurred within the past five years. For the purposes of this section, a violation is:

(a) any violation of federal, state or local environmental law identified in a judicial or administrative order, consent agreement or order, complaint, or notice of violation, conviction or plea agreement; or

(b) any act or omission for which the regulated entity has previously received penalty mitigation from EPA or a state or local agency.

8. Other Violations Excluded

The violation is not one which (i) resulted in serious actual harm, or may have presented an imminent and substantial endangerment to, human health or the environment, or (ii) violates the specific terms of any judicial or administrative order, or consent agreement.

9. Cooperation

The regulated entity cooperates as requested by EPA and provides such information as is necessary and requested by EPA to determine applicability of this policy. Cooperation includes, at a minimum, providing all requested documents and access to employees and assistance in investigating the violation, any noncompliance problems related to the disclosure, and any environmental consequences related to the violations.

E. Economic Benefit

EPA will retain its full discretion to recover any economic benefit gained as a result of noncompliance to preserve a "level playing field" in which violators do not gain a competitive advantage over regulated entities that do comply. EPA may forgive the entire penalty for violations which meet conditions 1 through 9 in section D and, in the Agency's opinion, do not merit any penalty due to the insignificant amount of any economic benefit.

F. Effect on State Law, Regulation or Policy

EPA will work closely with states to encourage their adoption of policies that reflect the incentives and conditions outlined in this policy. EPA remains firmly opposed to statutory environmental audit privileges that shield evidence of environmental violations and undermine the public's right to know, as well as to blanket immunities for violations that reflect criminal conduct, present serious threats or actual harm to health and the environment, allow noncomplying companies to gain an economic advantage over their competitors, or reflect a repeated failure to comply with federal law. EPA will work with states to address any provisions of state audit privilege or immunity laws that are inconsistent with this policy, and which may prevent a timely and appropriate response to significant environmental violations. The Agency reserves its right to take necessary actions to protect public health or the environment by enforcing against any violations of federal law.

G. Applicability

(1) This policy applies to the assessment of penalties for any violations under all of the federal environmental statutes that EPA administers, and supersedes any inconsistent provisions in media-specific penalty or enforcement policies and EPA's 1986 Environmental Auditing Policy Statement.

(2) To the extent that existing EPA enforcement policies are not inconsistent, they will continue to apply in conjunction with this policy. However, a regulated entity that has received penalty mitigation for satisfying specific conditions under this policy may not receive additional penalty mitigation for satisfying the same or similar conditions under other policies for the same violation(s), nor will this policy apply to violations which have received penalty mitigation under other policies.

(3) This policy sets forth factors for consideration that will guide the Agency in the exercise of its prosecutorial discretion. It states the Agency's views as to the proper allocation of its enforcement resources. The policy is not final agency action, and is intended as guidance. It does not create any rights, duties, obligations, or defenses, implied or otherwise, in any third parties.

(4) This policy should be used whenever applicable in settlement negotiations for both administrative and civil judicial enforcement actions. It is not intended for use in pleading, at hearing or at trial. The policy may be applied at EPA's discretion to the settlement of administrative and judicial enforcement actions instituted prior to, but not yet resolved, as of the effective date of this policy.

H. Public Accountability

(1) Within 3 years of the effective date of this policy, EPA will complete a study of the effectiveness of the policy in encouraging:

(a) changes in compliance behavior within the regulated community, including improved compliance rates;

(b) prompt disclosure and correction of violations, including timely and accurate compliance with reporting requirements;

      (c) corporate compliance programs that are successful in preventing violations, improving environmental performance, and promoting public disclosure;

      (d) consistency among state programs that provide incentives for voluntary compliance.

      EPA will make the study available to the public.

(2) EPA will make publicly available the terms and conditions of any compliance agreement reached under this policy, including the nature of the violation, the remedy, and the schedule for returning to compliance.

I. Effective Date

This policy is effective January 22, 1996.

Dated: December 18, 1995.

Steven A. Herman, Assistant Administrator for Enforcement and Compliance Assurance. [FR Doc. 95–31146 Filed 12-21-95; 8:45 AM] BILLING CODE 6560–50–P

The ICC Business Charter for Sustainable Development

This Charter lays out 16 "principles for environmental management" that translate sustainability principles into operations terms. Over 1,200 corporations, including more than 25 percent of the *Fortune 500,* have endorsed these principles.

1. *Corporate priority.* To recognize environmental management as among the highest corporate priorities and as a key determinant to sustainable development; to establish policies, programmes and practices for conducting operations in an environmentally sound manner.

2. *Integrated management.* To integrate these policies, programmes and practices fully into each business as an essential element of management in all its functions.

3. *Process of improvement.* To continue to improve corporate policies, programmes and environmental performance, taking into account technical development, scientific understanding, consumer needs and community expectations, with legal regulations as a starting point; and to apply the same environmental criteria internationally.

4. *Employee education.* To educate, train and motivate employees to conduct their activities in an environmentally responsible manner.

5. *Prior assessment.* To assess environmental impacts before starting a new activity or project and before decommissioning a facility or leaving a site.

6. *Products and services.* To develop and provide products or services that have no undue environmental impact and are safe in their intended use, that are efficient in their consumption of energy and natural resources, and that can be recycled, reused, or disposed of safely.

7. *Customer advice.* To advise, and where relevant educate customers, distributors and the public in the safe use, transportation, storage and disposal of products provided; and to apply similar considerations to the provision of services.

8. *Facilities and operations.* To develop, design and operate facilities and conduct activities taking into consideration the efficient use of energy and materials, the sustainable use of renewable resources, the minimization of adverse environmental impact and waste generation, and the safe and responsible disposal of residual wastes.

9. *Research.* To conduct or support research on the environmental impacts of raw materials, products, processes, emissions and wastes associated with the enterprise and on the means of minimizing such adverse impacts.

10. *Precautionary approach.* To modify the manufacture, marketing or use of products or services or the conduct of activities, consistent with scientific and technical understanding to prevent serious or irreversible environmental damage.

11. *Contractors and suppliers.* To promote the adoption of these principles by contractors acting on behalf of the enterprise, encourage and, where appropriate, require improvements in their practices to make them consistent with those of the enterprise; and to encourage the wider adoption of these principles by suppliers.

12. *Emergency preparedness.* To develop and maintain, where significant hazards exist, emergency preparedness plans in conjunction with emergency services, relevant authorities and local community, recognizing potential transboundary impacts.

13. *Transfer of technology.* To contribute to the transfer of environmentally sound technology and management methods throughout the industrial and public sectors.

14. *Contributing to the common effort.* To contribute to the development of public policy and to business, governmental and intergovernmental programmes and educational initiatives that will enhance environmental awareness and protection.

15. *Openness to concerns.* To foster openness and dialogue with employees and the public, anticipating and responding to their concerns about the potential hazards and impacts of operations, products, wastes or services, including those of transboundary or global significance.

16. *Compliance and reporting.* To measure environmental performance; to conduct regular environmental audits and assessments of compliance with company requirements, legal requirements and these principles; and periodically to provide appropriate information to the Board of Directors, shareholders, employees, the authorities and the public.

CERES Principles

The Coalition for Environmentally Responsible Economies (CERES) developed the CERES Principles as a voluntary code in which companies pledge to take responsibility for and continually improve their environmental performance.

INTRODUCTION TO THE CERES PRINCIPLES

By adopting these Principles, we publicly affirm our belief that corporations have a responsibility for the environment, and must conduct all aspects of their business as responsible stewards of the environment by operating in a manner that protects the Earth. We believe that corporations must not compromise the ability of future generations to sustain themselves.

We will update our practices constantly in light of advances in technology and new understandings in health and environmental science. In collaboration with CERES, we will promote a dynamic process to ensure that the Principles are interpreted in a way that accommodates changing technologies and environmental realities. We intend to make consistent, measurable progress in implementing these Principles and to apply them to all aspects of our operations throughout the world.

Protection of the Biosphere

We will reduce and make continual progress toward eliminating the release of any substance that may cause environmental damage to the air, water, or the earth or its inhabitants. We will safeguard all habitats affected by our operations and will protect open spaces and wilderness, while preserving biodiversity.

Sustainable Use of Natural Resources

We will make sustainable use of renewable natural resources, such as water, soils and forests. We will conserve nonrenewable natural resources through efficient use and careful planning.

Reduction and Disposal of Wastes

We will reduce and where possible eliminate waste through source reduction and recycling. All waste will be handled and disposed of through safe and responsible methods.

Energy Conservation

We will conserve energy and improve the energy efficiency of our internal operations and of the goods and services we sell. We will make every effort to use environmentally safe and sustainable energy sources.

Risk Reduction

We will strive to minimize the environmental, health and safety risks to our employees and the communities in which we operate through safe technologies, facilities and operating procedures, and by being prepared for emergencies.

Safe Products and Services

We will reduce and where possible eliminate the use, manufacture or sale of products and services that cause environmental damage or health or safety hazards. We will inform our customers of the environmental impacts of our products or services and try to correct unsafe use.

Environmental Restoration

We will promptly and responsibly correct conditions we have caused that endanger health, safety or the environment. To the extent feasible, we will redress injuries we have caused to persons or damage we have caused to the environment and will restore the environment.

Informing the Public

We will inform in a timely manner everyone who may be affected by conditions caused by our company that might endanger health, safety or the environment. We will regularly seek advice and counsel through dialogue with persons in communities near our facilities. We will not take any action against employees for reporting dangerous incidents or conditions to management or to appropriate authorities.

Management Commitment

We will implement these Principles and sustain a process that ensures that the Board of Directors and Chief Executive Officer are fully informed about pertinent environmental issues and are fully responsible for environmental policy. In selecting our Board of Directors, we will consider demonstrated environmental commitment as a factor.

Audits and Reports

We will conduct an annual self-evaluation of our progress in implementing these Principles. We will support the timely creation of generally accepted environmental audit procedures. We will annually complete the CERES Report, which will be made available to the public.

Disclaimer

These Principles established an ethic with criteria by which investors and others can assess the environmental performance of companies. Companies that endorse these Principles pledge to go voluntarily beyond the requirements of the law. The terms *may* and *might* in Principles one and eight are not meant to encompass every imaginable consequence, no matter how remote. Rather, these Principles obligate endorsers to behave as prudent persons who are not governed by conflicting interests and who possess a strong commitment to environmental excellence and to human health and safety. These Principles are not intended to create new legal liabilities, expand existing rights or obligations, waive legal defenses, or otherwise affect the legal position of any endorsing company, and are not intended to be used against an endorser in any legal proceedings for any purpose.

Public Environmental Reporting Initiative Guidelines

The Public Environmental Reporting Initiative (PERI) Guidelines promote voluntary disclosure of corporate environmental performance.

GUIDELINE COMPONENTS

Each reporting organization may decide how, when, and to what extent to present the PERI reporting components listed below. No specific order of presentation is mandatory or encouraged. The recommended content to be included is as follows:

1. Organizational Profile

Provide information about the organization that will allow the environmental data to be interpreted in context:

- Size of the organization (e.g., revenue, employees).
- Number of locations.
- Countries in which the organization operates.
- Major lines of activity.
- The nature of environmental impacts of the organization's operations.

Provide a contact name in the organization for information regarding environmental management.

2. Environmental Policy

Provide information on the organization's environmental policy(ies) (e.g., scope and applicability, content, goals and date of introduction or revision, if relevant).

3. Environmental Management

Summarize the level of organizational accountability for environmental policies and programs and the environmental management structure (e.g., corporate environmental staff and/or organizational relationships). Indicate how policies are implemented throughout the organization and comment on such items as:

- Board involvement and commitment to environmental matters.
- Accountability of other functional units of the organization.
- Environmental management systems in place (if desired, include references or registration under—or consistency with—any relevant national or international standards).
- Total Quality Management (TQM), Continuous Improvement or other organizationwide programs that may embrace environmental performance.
- Identify and quantify the resources committed to environmental activity (e.g., management, compliance, performance, operations, auditing).
- Describe any educational/training programs in place that keep environmental staff and management current on their professions and responsibilities.
- Summarize overall environmental objectives, targets and goals, covering the entire environmental management program.

4. Environmental Releases

Environmental releases are one indicator of an organization's impact on the environment. Provide information that quantifies the amount of emissions, effluents or wastes released to the environment. Information should be based on the global activity of the organization, with detail provided for smaller geographic regions, if desired. Provide the baseline data against which the organization measures itself each year to determine its progress, and quantify, to the extent possible, the following—including historical information (e.g., last three years, where available) to illustrate trends:

- Emissions to the atmosphere, with specific reference to any:
- Chemical-based emissions (include those listed in any national reportable inventories, e.g., TRI in the U.S., NPRI in Canada, SEDESOL's Emissions Inventory in Mexico).
- Use and emissions of ozone-depleting substances.
- Greenhouse gas emissions, e.g., carbon dioxide, methane, nitrous oxide and halocarbons.

- Discharges to water (include those considered to be a priority for your organization).
- Hazardous waste, as defined by national legislation. Indicate the percentage of hazardous waste that was recycled, treated, incinerated, deep-well injected or otherwise handled, either on- or off-site. Comment on how hazardous waste disposal contractors (storers, transporters, recyclers or handlers of waste) are monitored or investigated by the organization.
- Waste discharges to land. Include information on toxic/hazardous wastes, as well as solid waste discharges from facilities, manufacturing processes or operations.
- Objectives, targets and progress made regarding the above-listed items, including any information on other voluntary program activity (e.g., U.S. EPA 33/50 program).
- Identify the extent to which the organization uses recommended practices or voluntary standards developed by other organizations, such as the International Chamber of Commerce, the International Standards Organizations, CMA, API, CEFIC, U.S. EPA, Environment Canada, MITI Guidelines, etc.

5. Resource Conservation

- **Materials conservation**   Describe the organization's commitment to the conservation and recycling of materials and the use and purchase of recycled materials. Include efforts to reduce, minimize, reuse or recycle packaging.
- **Energy conservation**   Describe the organization's activity and approach to energy conservation: commitment made to reduce energy consumption, or to use renewable or more environmentally benign energy sources, energy efficiency program activities, reductions achieved in energy consumption and the resulting reductions achieved in VOCs, NOX, air toxics and greenhouse gas emissions.
- **Water conservation**   Describe the organization's efforts in reducing its use of water or in recycling of water.
- **Forest, land and habitat conservation**   Describe the organization's activities to conserve or reduce/minimize its impact on natural resources such as forest, lands and habitats.

6. Environmental Risk Management

Describe the following:

- Environmental audit programs and their frequency, scope, number completed over the past two years—as well as extent of coverage. Indicate whether the audits are conducted by internal or external personnel or organizations, and to whom and to which management levels the audit findings are reported. Describe follow-up efforts included in the program to ensure improved performance.

- Remediation programs in place or being planned, indicating type and scope of activity.

- Environmental emergency response programs, including the nature of training at local levels, frequency and the extent of the program. Indicate the degree and method of communications extended to local communities and other local organizations regarding mutual aid procedures and evacuation plans in case of an emergency.

- Workplace hazards. Indicate the approach taken to minimize health and safety risks in the organization's operations, and describe any formal policies or management practices to reduce these risks (e.g., employee and contractor safety training and supervision, statistical reporting).

7. Environmental Compliance

Provide information regarding the organization's record of compliance with laws and regulations. Summary history for the last three years should be given. Additional detail should be provided for any significant incidents of noncompliance since the last report, including:

- Significant fines or penalties incurred (define in accordance with local situation, e.g., over $25,000 in the U.S.) and the jurisdiction in which it was applied.

- The nature of the noncompliance issues, (e.g., reportable, uncontrolled releases, including oil and chemical spills at both manufacturing and distribution operations).

- The scope and magnitude of any environmental impact.

- The programs implemented to correct or alleviate the situation.

8. Product Stewardship

This component defines "product" as the outcome of the organization's activity and is applicable whether an organization manufactures, provides services, advocates, governs, etc. In addition, the section is intended to focus on both the organization's activities in producing its products or services not addressed elsewhere in the guidelines and any activities associated with the "end-of-life" of products or services.

Provide information that indicates the degree to which the organization is committed to evaluating the environmental impact of its products, processes and/or services.

Describe any program activity, procedure, methodology or standard that may be in place to support the organization's commitment to reduce the environmental impacts of its products and services. For example:

- Discuss technical research or design: (e.g., new products, services or practices, redesign of existing products or services, practices implemented or discontinued for environmental reasons, design for recyclability or disassembly, or redesign of accounting practices).
- Provide information on waste reduction/pollution prevention programs from the organization's products,processes or services, including conservation and reuse of materials, and the use of recycled materials.
- Describe the organization's efforts to make its products, processes and services more energy efficient.
- Describe post-consumer materials management, or end-of-life programs, such as product take-back.
- Detail customer cooperative or partnership programs and their development; (e.g., used oil collection and energy efficiency services).
- Describe supplier programs and cooperative or partnership activities designed to reduce environmental impacts or add environmental value to the design or redesign of products and services.
- Include information regarding selection criteria for environmentally responsible suppliers and standards to which they must adhere.
- Identify the scope of the supplier certification process (e.g., all suppliers, major suppliers or those in specific sectors).

Other components:

- Specify product stewardship targets and goals, and comment on established procedures to monitor and measure company performance.
- Provide any baseline data against which the organization can measure its progress.

9. Employee Recognition

Include information regarding employee recognition and reward programs that encourage environmental excellence. Comment on other education and information programs that motivate employees to engage in sound environmental practices.

10. Stakeholder Involvement

Describe the organization's efforts to involve other stakeholders in its environmental initiatives.

Indicate any significant work undertaken with research or academic organizations, policy groups, nongovernmental organizations and/or industry associations on environmental issues—including cooperative efforts in environmentally preferable technologies.

Describe how the organization relates to the communities in which it operates, and provide a description of its activities. For example, indicate the degree to which the organization shares pertinent facility-specific environmental information with the communities in which it has facilities.

Where to Obtain ISO 14000 Standards

For more information about TC 207 and the ISO 14000 series, contact ISO at the following address:

International Organization for Standardization (ISO)
1 rue de Varembe
Case postale 50
CH-1211
Geneva 20
Switzerland
41-22-749-0111
Fax: 41-22-733-3430
Internet: http://www.iso.ch

The draft and final standards for EMS and Auditing are available in the United States, Canada, and Mexico from the following sources:

American National Standards Institute (ANSI)
11 West 42nd Street
New York, NY 10036
212-642-4900
Fax: 212-398-0023
Internet: http://www.ansi.org

American Society for Quality Control (ASQC)
611 East Wisconsin Avenue
P.O. Box 3005
Milwaukee, WI 53201
414-272-8575; 800-248-1946
Fax: 414-272-1734
Internet: http://www.asqc.org

American Society for Testing and Materials (ASTM)
100 Barr Harbor Drive
West Conshohocken, PA 19428
610-832-9500; 215-299-5585
Fax: 610-832-8666
Internet: http://www.astm.org

Canadian Standards Association
178 Rexdale Boulevard
Etobicoke, Ontario
Canada M9W-1R3
416-747-4044
Fax: 416-747-2475
Internet: http://www.csa.ca

Dirección General de Normas
Calle Puente de Tecamachalco
#No.6
Lomas de Tecamachalco
Sección Fuentes
Naucalpan de Juárez 53 950
52-5-729-9300
Fax: 52-5-729-9484

NSF International
P.O. Box 130140
Ann Arbor, MI 48113
313-769-8010; 800-673-6275
Fax: 313-769-0109
Internet: http://www.nsf.com

Standards Council of Canada
Suite 1200
45 O'Conner Street
Ottawa, Ontario
Canada K1P-6N7
800-276-8220; 613-238-3222
Fax: 613-995-4564
Internet: info@scc.ca

Environmental Management System Registrars

The following is a selected listing of registrars who offer environmental management system registration services to ISO 14001 and other EMS standards, such as BS 7750, in North America and in other countries. Many of the following bodies are also accredited to provide verification of compliance to the European Eco-Management and Audit Scheme Regulation (EMAS).

North America

ABS Quality Evaluations, Inc.
16855 Northchase Drive
Houston, TX 77060
Phone: 713-873-9400
Fax: 713-874-9564

AFAQ, Inc.
Woodfield Executive Center
1101 Perimeter Drive, Suite 450
Schaumburg, IL 60173
Phone: 847-330-0606
Fax: 847-330-0707

AIB Registration Services
1213 Bakers Way
Manhattan, KS 66502
Phone: 913-537-4750
Fax: 913-537-1493

AIB-Vincotte (AV Qualité)
2900 Wilcrest Suite 300
Houston, TX 77042
Phone: 713-465-2850
Fax: 713-465-1182

American Quality Assessors
1200 Main Street, Suite 107M
Columbia, SC 29201
Phone: 803-779-8150
Fax: 803-779-8109

ASCERT USA, Inc.
1054 31st Street, NW Suite 330
Washington, DC 20007
Phone: 202-337-3214
Fax: 202-337-3709

The American Society of Mechanical Engineers
United Engineering Center
345 E. 47th Street
New York, NY 10017
Phone: 212-705-8590
Fax: 212-705-8599

Associated Offices Quality Certification
650 N. Sam Houston Parkway East, Suite 228
Houston, TX 77060
Phone: 713-591-7882
Fax: 713-448-5602

Bellcore Quality Registration
6 Corporate Place Room 1A230
Piscataway, NJ 08854
Phone: 908-699-3739
Fax: 908-336-2244

British Standards Institution Quality Assurance
British Standards Institution, Inc.
8000 Towers Crescent Drive, Suite 1350
Vienna, VA 22182
Phone: 703-760-7828
Fax: 703-761-2770

Bureau Veritas Quality International (North America), Inc.
509 N. Main Street
Jamestown, NY 14701
Phone: 716-484-9002
Fax: 716-484-9003

BVQI (NA)—West Coast Office
1245 Oakmead Parkway, Suite 105
Sunnyvale, CA 94086
Phone: 408-730-9001 or 800-900-0476
Fax: 408-739-9003

BVQI (NA)—East Coast Office
50 Park Row West
Providence, RI 02903
Phone: 401-273-7810
Fax: 401-273-7812

BVQI (NA)—Western Great Lakes Office
7001 Orchard Lake Road, Suite 210A
West Bloomfield, MI 48322
Phone: 810-539-0667 or 800-883-9002
Fax: 810-539-0668

CGA Approvals—Canadian Operations of International Approval Services
55 Scarsdale Road
Toronto, Ontario
Canada M3B-2R3
Phone: 416-447-6468
Fax: 416-447-7067

The Canadian General Standards Board
222 Queen Street, Suite 1402
Ottawa, Ontario
Canada K1A-1G6
Phone: 613-941-8657
Fax: 613-941-8706

Centerior Registration Services
300 Madison Avenue
Edison Plaza
Toledo, OH 43652
Phone: 419-249-5268
Fax: 419-249-4126

Davy Registrar Services, Inc.
One Oliver Plaza
Pittsburgh, PA 15222-2604
Phone: 412-566-3086
Fax: 412-566-5290

DLS Quality Technology Associates, Inc.
108 Hallmore Drive
Camillus, NY 13031
Phone: 315-468-5811
Fax: 315-468-5811

DNV Industries, Inc.
16340 Park Ten Place, Suite 100
Houston, TX 77084
Phone: 713-579-9003
Fax: 713-579-1360

Electronic Industries Quality Registry
2500 Wilson Boulevard
Arlington, VA 22201-3834
Phone: 703-907-7563 or 800-222-9001
Fax: 703-907-7966

Entela, Inc., Quality System Registration Division
3033 Madison Avenue SE
Grand Rapids, MI 49548
Phone: 616-247-0515, 800-888-3787
Fax: 616-247-7527

Factory Mutual Research Corporation
1151 Boston-Providence Turnpike
PO Box 9102
Norwood, MA 02062
Phone: 617-255-4883
Fax: 617-762-9375

Global Registrars, Inc.
4700 Clairton Boulevard
Pittsburgh, PA 15236
Phone: 412-884-2290
Fax: 412-884-2268

HSB Registration Services
One State Street
PO Box 5024
Hartford, CT 06102-5024
Phone: 800-472-1866 or 860-722-5294
Fax: 860-722-5530

Instituto Mexicano de Normalización A.C. y Certificatión A.C.
Manuel Maria Contreras No. 133, 1 er. Piso
Col. Cuauhtémoc
Mexico
Distrito Federal 06470
Phone: 525-566-4750
Fax: 525-546-4546

Intertek Services Corporation
313 Speen Street, Suite 200
Natick, MA 01760
Phone: 508-647-5147
Fax: 508-647-6714

ISOQAR
One World Trade Center, Suite 7967
New York, NY 10048
Phone: 212-432-5900
Fax: 212-524-0745

KEMA Registered Quality, Inc.
4379 County Line Road
Chalfont, PA 18914
Phone: 215-822-4258
Fax: 215-822-4285

Kemper Registrar Services, Inc.
Plaza One Building, Suite 305
1 State Highway 12
Flemington, NJ 08822-1731
Phone: 908-806-7498 or 800-555-2928
Fax: 908-806-6937

KPMG Quality Registrar
150 John F. Kennedy Parkway
Short Hills, NJ 07078
Phone: 800-716-5595
Fax: 201-912-6050

**Litton Systems Canada
Limited**
Quality System Registrars
25 City View Drive
Etobicoke, Ontario
Canada M9W-5A7
Phone: 800-267-0861
Fax: 416-246-2049

**Lloyd's Registrar Quality
Assurance Limited**
34–41 Newark Street
Hoboken, NJ 07030
Phone: 201-963-1111
Fax: 201-963-3299

National Quality Assurance
4 Post Office Sq. Road
Acton, MA 01702
Phone: 508-635-9256
Fax: 508-263-0785

**National Standards Authority
of Ireland**
Worldwide Certification
Services
5 Medallion Center (Greeley
Street)
Merrimack, NH 03054
Phone: 603-424-7070
Fax: 603-429-1234

NSF International
3475 Plymouth Road
PO Box 130140
Ann Arbor, MI 48113-0140
Phone: 313-332-7330
Fax: 313-669-0196

**OMNEX—Automotive
Quality Systems Registrar**
PO Box 15019
Ann Arbor, MI 48106
Phone: 313-480-9940
Fax: 313-480-9941

Performance Review Institute
161 Thronhill Road
Warrendale, PA 15086-7527
Phone: 412-772-1616 or
800-352-7293
Fax: 412-772-1699

**Perry Johnson Registrars,
Inc.**
3000 Town Center, Suite 630
Southfield, MI 48075
Phone: 800-800-7910
Fax: 810-358-0882

**Professional Environmental &
Caring Services QA Ltd.**
PECS QA North America, Inc.
533 Main Street
Acton, MA 01720
Phone: 508-263-4811
Fax: 508-263-5734

**Quality Certification Bureau,
Inc.**
9650 20th Avenue, Suite 103
Advanced Technology Centre
Edmonton, Alberta
Canada T6N-1G1
Phone: 800-268-7321
Fax: 403-496-2464

Quality Management Institute
90 Burnhamthorpe Road W,
Suite 300
Mississauga, Ontario
Canada L5B-3C3
Phone: 905-272-3920;
800-465-3717
Fax: 905-272-3942

**Quality Systems Assessment
Registrar**
Head Office
7250 W. Credit Avenue
Mississauga, Ontario
Canada L5N-5N1
Phone: 800-461-9001 or
905-542-0547
Fax: 905-542-1318

**Quality Systems Registrars,
Inc.**
13873 Park Center Road, Suite
217
Herndon, VA 22071-3279
Phone: 703-478-0241
Fax: 703-478-0645

**Raytheon Quality Registrar,
Inc.**
2 Wayside Road
Burlington, MA 01803
Phone: 617-238-2900
Fax: 617-238-3200

**Scott Quality Systems
Registrars, Inc.**
8 Grove Street, Suite 200
Wellesley, MA 02181
Phone: 617-239-1110
Fax: 617-239-0433

**SGS International
Certification Services
Canada, Inc.**
90 Gough Road, Unit 4
Markham, Ontario
Canada L3R-5V5
Phone: 905-479-1160;
800-636-0847
Fax: 905-479-9452

**SGS International
Certification Services, Inc.**
Meadows Office Complex
301 Route 17 N.
Rutherford, NJ 07070
Phone: 800-747-9047
Fax: 201-935-4555

**Smithers Quality
Assessments, Inc.**
425 W. Market Street
Akron, OH 44303-2099
Phone: 216-762-4231
Fax: 216-762-7447

Steel Related Industries Quality System Registrar, Inc.
SRI Quality System Registrar
2000 Corporate Drive, Suite 330
Wexford, PA 15090
Phone: 412-934-9000
Fax: 412-935-6825

The Bureau de Normalisation du Quebec—Quality System Registration
70 rue Dalhousie, Bureau 220
Quebec, Quebec
Canada G1K-4B2
Phone: 418-643-5813
Fax: 418-646-3315

TRA Certification, A Division of T.R. Arnold & Associates, Inc.
700 E. Beardsley Avenue
PO Box 1081
Elkhart, IN 46515-1081
Phone: 219-264-0745
Fax: 219-264-0740

TUV America and TUV Product Service
TUV America, Inc., and TUV Product Service, Inc. (headquarters)
5 Cherry Hill Drive
Danvers, MA 01923
Phone: 508-777-7999
Fax: 508-762-8414

TÜV ESSEN
2099 Gateway Place, Suite 200
San Jose, CA 95110
Phone: 408-441-7888
Fax: 408-441-7111

TUV Rheinland of North America, Inc.
TUV Rheinland, North American Headquarters
12 Commerce Road
Newtown, CT 06470
Phone: 203-426-0888
Fax: 203-270-8883

Underwriters Laboratories, Inc.
1285 Walt Whitman Road
Melville, NY 11747-3081
Phone: 516-271-6200
Fax: 516-271-6242

Underwriters Laboratories of Canada
7 Crouse Road
Scarborough, Ontario M1R 3A9
Canada
Phone: 416-757-3611
Fax: 416-757-8915

Vehicle Certification Agency
VCA North America
Colonial House Office Park, Suite 220
42000 W. Six Mile Road
Northville, MI 48167
Phone: 810-344-2190
Fax: 810-344-2191

Warnock Hersey Professional Services Ltd.
8810 Elmslie Street
LaSalle, Quebec
Canada H8R-1V8
Phone: 514-366-3100
Fax: 514-366-5350

Austria

BVQI
A-1030 Wein
Marokkanergasse 22/3, Austria
Phone: 43 1 713 15 68
Fax: 43 1 712 54 35

Belgium

S. A. Bureau Veritas Quality International (Belgium) N.V.
Place Bara 26 Bte 17/19
B-1070 Brussels, Belgium
Phone: 32 2 520 2090
Fax: 32 2 520 2030

France

BVQI France
Immeuble Apollo, 10
Rue Jacques Daguerre
92565 Rueil-Malmaison
Cedex, France
Phone: 33 1 47 14 43 30
Fax: 33 1 47 14 43 25

AFAQ
116 Avenue Aristide Briande
Box DP 40
Bagneux 92224
France
Phone: 33 1 461 13737
Fax: 33 1 461 13710

Ascert International 45/47 Avenue Carnot
Cachan 94230
France
Phone: 33 1 461 57060
Fax: 33 1 461 57069

Det Norske Veritas
10 Rue Lionel Terray
Rueil Malmaison 92508
Fax: 33 1 471 49929
Fax: 33 1 470 84294

Germany

BVQI
Sachsenfeld 4, Haus 5
Hansa Carree, Postfach 100940
Hamburg 1, Germany D20006
Phone: 49 40 23 62 5120
Fax: 49 40 23 62 5100

BVQI
Huyssennallee 5
D-45128 Essen, Germany
Phone: 49 201 810 7614
Fax: 49 201 810 7620

German Association for the Certification of Quality Management Systems
August-Schanz Str. 21
Frankfurt/Main D-60433
Germany
Phone: 49-69-9542-130
Fax: 49-69-9542-1311

The Netherlands

KIWA NV
P.O. Box 70
2280 AB Ryswyk
The Netherlands
Phone: 31 70 395 3535
Fax: 31 70 395 3420

NV KEMA
Department KCS/KKS
PO Box 9035
6800 ET Arnhem
Phone: 31 85 569 111
Fax: 31 85 515606

Sweden

BVQI Sweden
Stora Badhusgatan 20
S-411 21 Gotenborg, Sweden
Phone: 46 31 17 14 15
Fax: 46 31 13 39 73

Switzerland

Schweiz Vereinigung fur Qualitats und Management Systems (SQs)
Industriestrasse 1 CH-3052
 Zollikofen
Switzerland
Phone: 41 31 910 3535
Fax: 41 31 910 3545

SGS International Certification Services AG
Technopark
Pfingstweidstrasse 308005
 Zurich
Switzerland
Phone: 46 1 445 1680
Fax: 46 1 445 1688

United Kingdom

BSI Quality Assurance
PO Box 375
Milton Keynes, MK14 6LL
United Kingdom
Phone: 01908-220908
Fax: 01908-220671

British Approval Service for Electric Cables
Silbury Court
360 Silbury Boulevard
Milton Keynes MK9 2AF
United Kingdom
Phone: 441 908 691 121
Fax: 441 908 692 722

BVQI Ltd.
London Central Office
70 Borough High Street
London SE1 1XF
Phone: 44 171 378 8113
Fax: 44 171 378 8014

BVQI
14 Challenge House
Sherwood Drive, Bletchley
Milton Keynes MK36DP

United Kingdom
Phone: 44 190 836 6724
Fax: 44 190 836 6725

BVQI
Suite G1, Norton Centre,
 Poynernook Road
Aberdeen AB1 2RN
Scotland
Phone: 44 122 421 2838
Fax: 44 122 421 0924

BVQI
223 Wolverhampton Street
Dudley, West Midlands
 DY1 1EF
Phone: 44 384 459 546
Fax: 44 384 238 741

Ceramic Industry Certification Scheme Ltd.
Queens Road, Penkhull
Stoke-On-Trent, ST4 7LQ
United Kingdom
Phone: 44-1782-411-008
Fax: 44-1782-412-331

Electricity Association Quality Assurance Ltd. (EAQA)
30 Millbank
London, England SW1P 4RD
Phone: 441-71-344-5947
Fax: 441-71-828-9237

The Loss Prevention Certification Board Ltd.
Melrose Avenue
Borehamwood, Hertfordshire,
 WD6 2BJ
United Kingdom
Phone: 44-081-207-2345
Fax: 44-081-207-6305

SGS Yarsley International Certification Services Ltd. (SGS ICS)
Portland Road
East Grinstead
W. Sussex RH19 4ET
United Kingdom
Phone: 44 134 241 0088
Fax: 44 134 230 5305

Sira Certification Service/Sira Test and Certification Ltd.
South Hill Chislehurst
Kent, BR7 5EH
United Kingdom
Phone: 44-181-467-2636
Fax: 44-181-295-1990

TRADA Certification Limited
Stocking Lane, Hughenden
 Valley
High Wycombe, Bucks HP14
 4NR
Phone: 44 149 456 5484
Fax: 44 149 456 5487

United Registrar of Systems Ltd.
11A Rossall Road
Thorton-Cleveleys Blackpool,
 FY5 1AP
England
Phone: 125-382-0060
Fax: 125-386-3310

APPENDIX G

Glossary of Acronyms

AFNOR	French Standards Organization
AFPA	American Forest and Paper Association
AIHA	American Industrial Hygiene Association
ANSI	American National Standards Institute
API	American Petroleum Institute
ASQC	American Society for Quality Control
ASME	American Society of Mechanical Engineers
ASTM	American Society for Testing and Materials
BCCA	Board Committee on Conformity Assessment
BSI	British Standards Institute
BVQi	Bureau Veritas Quality International Ltd.
CAA	Clean Air Act
CASCO	ISO Council Committee on Conformity Assessment
CD	Committee Draft
CEN	Comité Européen de Normalisation (European Committee for Standardization)
CENELEC	Comité Européen de Normalisation Électrotechnique
CMA	Chemical Manufacturers Association

CSA	Canadian Standards Association
DIN	Deutsches Institut für Normung (German standards organization)
DIS	Draft International Standard
EA	Environmental Audit
EAC	European Accreditation of Certification
EAF	Environmental Auditing Forum
EAPS	Environmental Aspects in Products Standards
EAR	Environmental Auditing Roundtable
EARA	Environmental Auditors Registration Association
EC	European Commission
EI	Environmental Indicators
ELP	Environmental Leadership Program
EMAS	Eco-Management and Audit Scheme
EMS	Environmental Management System
EPE	Environmental Performance Evaluation
EU	European Union. (Countries belonging to the EU are Austria, Belgium, Denmark, Finland, France, Germany, Greece, Ireland, Italy, Luxembourg, The Netherlands, Portugal, Spain, Sweden, and the United Kingdom.)
EVABAT	Economically Viable Application of Best Available Technology
FDIS	Final Draft International Standard
FTC	Federal Trade Commission
GATT	General Agreement on Tariffs and Trade
GEMI	Global Environmental Management Initiative
IAAR	Independent Association of Accredited Registrars
IAF	International Accreditation Forum
IATCA	International Auditor and Training Certification Association
ICC	International Chamber of Commerce
IEC	International Electrotechnical Commission
ILO	International Labor Organization
INEM	International Network for Environmental Management

IQA	Institute of Quality Assurance
IRCA	International Registrar of Certified Auditors
ISO	International Organization for Standardization
LCA	Life-Cycle Assessment
LRQA	Lloyds Register Quality Assurance Ltd.
MSDS	Material Safety Data Sheets
NAFTA	North American Free Trade Agreement
NGO	Non-Government Organization
OHSMS	Occupational Health and Safety Management Standard
OSHA	Occupational Safety and Health Administration (United States)
RAB	Registrar Accreditation Board
RvA	Raad voor Accreditatie (Dutch Council for Accreditation)
SAGE	Strategic Advisory Group on the Environment
SC	Subcommittee
SIC	Standard Industrial Classification code
SME	Small and Medium-size Enterprises
ST	SubTAG
TAG	Technical Advisory Group
TBT	Agreement on Technical Barriers to Trade
TC	Technical Committee
UKAS	United Kingdom Accreditation Service
UNCTAD	United Nations Council on Trade and Development
UNEP	United Nations Environment Program
VPP	Voluntary Protection Program
WD	Working Draft
WG	Working Group
WTO	World Trade Organization
WWF	World Wildlife Fund

Glossary of Terms

accreditation Procedure by which an authoritative body formally recognizes that a body or person is competent to carry out specific tasks. (ISO/IEC Guide 2)

accreditation body Body that gives formal recognition that a body or person is competent to carry out specific tasks. (ISO/IEC Guide 2)

accreditation criteria Set of requirements that is used by an accreditation body that is fulfilled by a conformity assessment body in order to be accredited.

accreditation system System that has its own rules of procedure and management for carrying out accreditation.

accredited body Body to which accreditation is granted.

assessment A determination of the significance, value or importance of something.

assessment body Third party that assesses products and registers the quality systems of suppliers.

assessment system Procedural and managerial rules for conducting an assessment leading to the issue of a certification document and its maintenance.

audit conclusion Professional judgment or opinion expressed by an auditor about the subject matter of the audit, based on and limited to reasoning that the auditor applied to the audit findings. (ISO 14010 Clause 3.1)

audit criteria Policies, practices, procedures or requirements against which the auditor compares collected evidence about the subject matter. Note: Requirements may include but are not limited to standards, guidelines, specified organizational requirements, and legislative or regulatory requirements. (ISO 14010 Clause 3.2)

audit evidence Verifiable information, records, or statements of fact. Note: Audit evidence, which can be qualitative or quantitative, is used by the auditor to determine whether audit criteria are met. Audit evidence is typically based on interviews, examination of documents, observation of activities and conditions, existing results of measurements and tests, or other means within the scope of the audit. (ISO 14010 Clause 3.3)

audit findings   Results of the evaluation of the collected audit evidence compared against the agreed audit criteria. Note: The audit findings provide the basis for the audit report. (ISO 14010 Clause 3.4)

audit team   Group of auditors, or a single auditor, designated to perform a given audit; the audit team may also include technical experts and auditors-in-training. Note: One of the auditors on the audit team performs the function of lead auditor. (ISO 14010 Clause 3.50)

auditee   Organization to be audited. (ISO 14010 Clause 3.6)

auditor (environmental)   Person qualified to perform environmental audits. Note: Qualification criteria for environmental auditors are given in 14012. (ISO Clause 3.7)

certificate of conformity—Document issued under the rules of a certification system that indicates an adequate confidence is provided that a duly identified product, process, or service is in conformity with a specific standard or other normative document.

certification   Procedure by which a third party gives written assurance that a product, process, or service conforms to specified requirements.

certification body   Body that conducts certification of conformity.

certification system   System that has its own rules of procedure and management for carrying out certification of conformity.

client   Organization commissioning the audit. Note: The client may be the auditee, or any organization which has the regulatory or contractual right to commission an audit. (ISO 14010 Clause 3.8)

comparative assertion   Environmental claim regarding the superiority or equivalence of one product versus a competing product that performs the same function. (ISO/CD 14040.3 Clause 2)

compliance   An affirmative indication or judgment that the supplier of a product or service has met the requirements of the relevant specifications,contract, or regulation.

conformance   An affirmative indication of judgment that a product or service has met the requirements of the relevant specifications, contract, or regulation.

conformity assessment   Includes all activities that are intended to ensure the conformity of products or systems to a set of standards, including testing, inspection, certification, and so on.

continual improvement   Process of enhancing the environmental management system to achieve improvements in overall environmental performance, in line with the organization's environmental policy. Note: The process need not take place in all areas of activity simultaneously. (ISO 14001 Clause 3.1)

contractor   The organization that provides a product to the customer in a contractual situation.

corrective action   An action taken to eliminate the causes of an existing nonconformity, defect, or other undesirable situation in order to prevent recurrence.

customer   The ultimate consumer, user, client, beneficiary, or second party.

design review   A formal, documented, comprehensive, and systematic examination of a design to evaluate the design requirements and the capability of the design to meet these requirements and to identify problems and propose solutions.

EN 45000   A series of standards set up by the EC to regulate and harmonize certification, accreditation, and testing activities.

environment   Surroundings in which an organization operates, including air, water, land, natural resources, flora, fauna, humans, and their interrelation. Note: Surroundings in this context extend from within an organization to the global system. (ISO 14001 Clause 3.2)

environmental aspect   Element of an organization's activities, products, or services that can interact with the environment. Note: A significant environmental aspect is an environmental aspect that has or can have a significant environmental impact. (ISO 14001 Clause 3.3)

environmental audit   Systematic, documented verification process of objectively obtaining and evaluating audit evidence to determine whether specified environmental activities, events, conditions, management systems, or information about these matters conform with audit criteria, and communicating the results of this process to the client. (ISO 14010 Clause 3.9)

environmental claim   Any environmental declaration that describes or implies by whatever means the effects that the raw material extraction, production, distribution, use, or disposal of a product or service has on the environment. This applies to effects that are local, regional, or global and to the environment in which an individual lives, affects, or is affected by. (ISO/CD 14021 Clause 3.1; ISO/WD 14022 Clause 4.2)

environmental impact   Any change to the environment, whether adverse or beneficial, wholly or partially resulting from an organization's activities, products, or services. (ISO 14001 Clause 3.4)

environmental indicator   An expression that is used to provide information about environmental performance or the condition of the environment. Note: The expression can be relative or absolute. (ISO/WD 14031.4 Clause 3.10)

environmental label/declaration   A claim indicating the environmental aspects of a product or service that may take the form of statements, symbols, or graphics on the product or package labels, product literature, technical bulletins, advertising, publicity, etc. (ISO/WD 14020.1 Clause 4.1)

environmental labeling Type 1 program   Voluntary, multiple criteria-based, practitioner programs that award labels claiming overall environmental preference of a product within a particular product category based on life-cycle considerations. (ISO/CD 14024.2 Clause 4.1)

Environmental Management System (EMS)   The part of the overall management system that includes organizational structure, planning activities, responsibilities, practices, procedures, processes, and resources for developing, implementing, achieving, reviewing, and maintaining the environmental policy. (ISO 14001 Clause 3.5)

environmental management system audit   A systematic and documented verification process of objectively obtaining and evaluating evidence to determine whether an organization's environmental management system conforms to the environmental management system audit criteria set by the organization and for communication of the results of this process to management. (ISO 14001 Clause 3.6)

environmental management system audit criteria   Policies, practices, procedures, or requirements that are covered by ISO 14001 and, if applicable, any additional EMS requirements against which the auditor compares collected audit evidence about the organization's environmental management system. (ISO/DIS 14011 Clause 3.3)

environmental objective   Overall environmental goal, arising from the environmental policy, that an organization sets for itself to achieve, and which is quantified where practicable. (ISO 14001 Clause 3.7)

environmental performance   Measurable results of the environmental management system, related to an organization's control of its environmental aspects, based on its environmental policy, objectives, and targets. (ISO 14001 Clause 3.8). Note: In the *Environmental Management Environmental Performance Evaluation Guideline,* environmental performance is defined as results of an organization's management of its environmental aspects. (ISO/WD 14031.4 Clause 3.6)

environmental performance evaluation   Process to measure, analyze, assess, report, and communicate an organization's environmental performance against criteria set by management. (ISO/WD 14031.4 Clause 3.8)

environmental policy   Statement by the organization of its intentions and principles in relation to its overall environmental performance, which provides a framework for action and for the setting of its environmental objectives and targets. (ISO 14001 Clause 3.9)

environmental symbol   Any symbol in the public domain that conveys or implies or is likely to be interpreted as making an environmental claim (ISO/WD 14022 Clause 4.1)

environmental target   A detailed performance requirement, quantified where practicable and applicable to the organization or parts thereof, that arises from the environmental objectives and is set and met in order to achieve those objectives. (ISO 14001 Clause 3.10)

finding   A conclusion of importance based on observation.

follow-up audit   An audit whose purpose and scope are limited to verifying that corrective action has been accomplished as scheduled and to determining that the action effectively prevented recurrence.

gravity-based penalty   The seriousness or punitive portion of a penalty.

inspection   Activities such as measuring, examining, testing, and gauging one or more characteristics of a product or service and comparing these with specified requirements to determine conformity.

interested party   Individual or group concerned with or affected by the environmental performance of an organization. (ISO 14001 Clause 3.11)

lead auditor (environmental)   Person qualified to manage and perform environmental audits. Note: Qualification criteria for lead environmental auditors are given in ISO 14012. (ISO/DIS 14010 Clause 3.10)

licensee   A party authorized by a practitioner to use an environmental label. (ISO/CD 14024.2 Clause 4.9)

life cycle   Consecutive and interlinked stages of a product or service system, from the production and delivery of raw material or generation of natural resources to the final disposal. (ISO/WD 14020.1 Clause 4.3)

Life-Cycle Assessment (LCA) Compilation and evaluation, according to a systematic set of procedures, of the inputs and outputs and the potential environmental impacts of a product system throughout its life cycle. (ISO/CD 14040.3 Clause 2)

life-cycle characterization Element of the life-cycle impact assessment phase in which the potential impacts associated with the inventory data in each of the selected categories are analyzed. (ISO/CD 14040.3 Clause 2)

life-cycle classification Element of the life-cycle impact assessment phase in which the inventory parameters are grouped together and sorted into a number of impact categories. (ISO/CD 14040.3 Clause 2)

life-cycle impact assessment Phase of life-cycle assessment aimed at understanding and evaluating the magnitude and significance of the potential environmental impacts of a product system. (ISO/CD 14040.3 Clause 2)

life-cycle interpretation Phase of life-cycle assessment in which a synthesis is drawn from the findings of either the inventory analysis or the impact assessment, or both, in line with the defined goal and scope. (ISO/CD 14040.3 Clause 2)

life-cycle inventory analysis Phase of life-cycle assessment involving compilation and quantification of inputs and outputs, for a given product system throughout its life cycle. (ISO/CD 14040.3 Clause 2)

mark of conformity Protected mark, applied or issued under the rules of a certification system that indicates confidence that the relevant product, process, or service is in conformity with a specific standard or other normative document.

nonconformity The nonfulfillment of a specified requirement.

organization Company, corporation, firm, enterprise, authority or institution, or part or combination thereof, whether incorporated or not, public or private, that has its own functions and administration. Note: For organizations with more than one operating unit, a single operating unit may be defined as an organization. (ISO 14001 Clause 3.12)

organization structure The responsibilities, authorities, and relationships, arranged in a pattern, through which an organization performs its functions.

package/packaging A material or item that is used to protect or contain a product during transportation, storage, or marketing. A package can also be a material or item that is physically attached to, or included with, a product or its container for the purpose of marketing the product or communicating information about the product. (ISO/CD 14021 Clause 3.4; ISO/WD 14022 Clause 4.5)

practitioner Third-party body that operates an environmental labeling program. (ISO/CD 14024.2 Clause 4.6) May also be used as meaning an individual or group of people that conducts a life-cycle assessment study. (ISO 14040)

prevention of pollution Use of processes, practices, materials, or products that will avoid, reduce, or control pollution, which may include recycling, treatment, process changes, control mechanisms, efficient use of resources, and materials substitution. Note: The potential benefits of prevention of pollution include the reduction of adverse environmental impacts, improved efficiency, and reduced costs. (ISO 14001 Clause 3.13)

procedure A specified way to perform an activity.

process A set of interrelated resources and activities that transforms inputs into outputs.

product Any good or service. (ISO/CD 14024.2 Clause 4.2)

product category Group(s) of products which have equivalent functions. (ISO/CD 14024.2 Clause 4.3)

product function characteristics Attribute(s) and characteristic(s) in the performance and use of a product. (ISO/CD 14024.2 Clause 4.4)

product environment criteria Environmental requirements that the product shall meet to be awarded an environmental label. (ISO/CD 14024.2 Clause 4.5)

purchaser Anyone in a product or service supply chain who buys the product or service from a seller. (ISO/WD 14020.1 Clause 4.2)

qualified environmental claim An environmental claim which is accompanied by an explanatory statement that describes the limits of the claim. (ISO/CD 14021 Clause 3.5)

quality system Organization structure, procedures, processes, and resources needed to implement quality management.

recognition agreement An agreement that is based on the acceptance by one party of results presented by another party, from the implementation of one or more designated functional elements of a conformity assessment system.

registration Procedure by which a body indicates relevant characteristics of a product, process, or service, or particulars of a body or person, in an appropriate, publicly available list.

registration body Body that conducts a certification of conformity.

registration system System having its own rules of procedure and management for carrying out the assessment leading to the issuance of a registration document and its subsequent maintenance.

Responsible Care® Comprehensive guidelines for management systems adopted by the Chemical Manufacturers Association (CMA) in 1988. Membership to CMA requires participation in the Responsible Care Program.

root cause A fundamental deficiency that results in a nonconformance and must be corrected to prevent recurrence of the same or similar nonconformance.

self-declaration environmental claims An environmental claim that is made, without independent third-party certification, by manufacturers, importers, distributors, retailers, or anyone else likely to benefit from such a claim. (ISO/CD 14021 Clause 3.2)

site All land on which the activities under the control of an organization in a given location are carried out, including any connected or associated storage of raw materials, byproducts, intermediate products, end products, and waste material, and any equipment or infrastructure involved in the activities, whether or not fixed. Where applicable, the definition of site shall correspond to definitions specified in legal requirements.

specification The document that prescribes the requirements with which the product or service must conform.

stakeholders Any party affected by an environmental labeling program. (ISO/CD 14024.2 Clause 4.8) The groups or organizations having an interest or stake in an organization's EMS program, including regulators, shareholders, customers, suppliers, special interest groups, residents, competitors, investors, bankers, media, lawyers, insurance companies, trade groups, unions, ecosystems, cultural heritage, and geology.

subcontractor An organization that provides a product to the supplier.

subject matter A specified environmental activity, event, condition, management system, and/or information about these matters. (ISO/DIS 14010 Clause 3.12)

supplier An organization that provides a product to the customer.

system boundary Interface between the product system being studied and its environment or other systems.

technical expert Person who provides specific knowledge or expertise to the audit team, but who does not participate as an auditor. (ISO/DIS 14010 Clause 3.13)

third party Person or body that is recognized as being independent of the parties involved, as concerns the issue in question. Note:

Parties involved are usually supplier ("first party") and purchaser ("second party") interests. (ISO/CD 14024.2 Clause 4.7)

transparency Open and comprehensive presentation of information. (ISO/CD 14040.3 Clause 2)

verification Confirmation made, by a purchaser or a third party, of the adequacy and compliance with relevant regulations of those data and evaluation methods thereof which indicate decreasing environmental burdens of products and services and become the basis of self-declaration environmental claims. (ISO/WD 14023 Clause 4.2) Process of authenticating evidence. (ISO 14010) The act of reviewing, inspecting, testing, checking, auditing, or otherwise establishing and documenting whether items, processes, services, or documents conform to specified requirements.

EPA Pollution Prevention Programs

For more information about the following programs or other pollution prevention initiatives, contact:

> United States Environmental Protection Agency
> 401 M Street SW
> Washington, DC 20460
> Phone: (202) 260-2090

Design for the Environment (DfE): A joint effort between EPA and industry, DfE promotes pollution prevention and industrial ecology through consideration of environmental impacts at the earliest stages of product design, including management accounting, capital budgeting, lending, and risk management.

Common Sense Initiative (CSI): A program that examines pollution on an industry-by-industry approach instead of the pollutant-by-pollutant method. The six pilot industries involved in CSI include electronics and computers, automobile assembly, metal plating and finishing, printing, iron and steel, and oil refining.

Environmental Leadership Program (ELP): The ELP encourages innovative approaches to management, compliance, and pollution prevention. The program is in effect at twelve pilot sites. The sites are testing a variety of concepts, including the following: environmental management systems, multimedia compliance assurance, third-party verification, self-certification, public accountability, community involvement, and mentoring.

Project XL: A project in which a select group of entities tests alternative approaches to reduce costs of environmental management and achieve environmental performance beyond traditional command-and-control regulatory requirements.

INDEX